The Rise and Fall of Political Orders

T0349143

Drawing on political theory, comparative politics, international relations, psychology, and classics, Ned Lebow offers insights into why social and political orders form, how they evolve, and why and how they decline. Following *The Tragic Vision of Politics* and *A Cultural Theory of International Relations*, this book thus completes Lebow's trilogy with an original theory of political order. He identifies long- and short-term threats to political order that are associated respectively with shifts in the relative appeal of principles of justice and lack of self-restraint by elites. Two chapters explore the consequences of late modernity for democracy in the United States, and another chapter, co-authored with Martin Dimitrov, the consequences for authoritarianism in China. *The Rise and Fall of Political Orders* forges new links between political theory and political science via the explicit connection it makes between normative goals and empirical research.

RICHARD NED LEBOW is Professor of International Political Theory in the Department of War Studies, King's College London, Bye-Fellow of Pembroke College, University of Cambridge, and James O. Freedman Presidential Professor (Emeritus) of Government of Dartmouth College. He has authored, co-authored, or edited 34 books and over 250 peer-reviewed articles and chapters. He has made contributions to the fields of international relations, political psychology, history, political theory, philosophy of science, and classics.

The Rise and Fall of Political Orders

Richard Ned Lebow

King's College London

CAMBRIDGE
UNIVERSITY PRESS

CAMBRIDGE
UNIVERSITY PRESS

University Printing House, Cambridge CB2 8BS, United Kingdom

One Liberty Plaza, 20th Floor, New York, NY 10006, USA

477 Williamstown Road, Port Melbourne, VIC 3207, Australia

314–321, 3rd Floor, Plot 3, Splendor Forum, Jasola District Centre,
New Delhi – 110025, India

79 Anson Road, #06-04/06, Singapore 079906

Cambridge University Press is part of the University of Cambridge.

It furthers the University's mission by disseminating knowledge in the pursuit of
education, learning, and research at the highest international levels of excellence.

www.cambridge.org
Information on this title: www.cambridge.org/9781108472869
DOI: 10.1017/9781108578820

© Richard Ned Lebow 2018

This publication is in copyright. Subject to statutory exception
and to the provisions of relevant collective licensing agreements,
no reproduction of any part may take place without the written
permission of Cambridge University Press.

First published 2018

Printed and bound in Great Britain by Clays Ltd, Elcograf S.p.A.

A catalogue record for this publication is available from the British Library.

Library of Congress Cataloging-in-Publication Data
Names: Lebow, Richard Ned, author.
Title: The rise and fall of political orders / Richard Ned Lebow,
King's College London.
Description: Cambridge, United Kingdom; New York, NY, USA:
Cambridge University Press, 2018. |
Includes bibliographical references and index.
Identifiers: LCCN 2018014875 | ISBN 9781108472869 (hardback) |
ISBN 9781108460682 (paperback)
Subjects: LCSH: State, The – History. | Order – History. |
Comparative goverment – History. | Democracy – History.
Classification: LCC JC11.L42 2018 | DDC 320.01–dc23
LC record available at https://lccn.loc.gov/2018014875

ISBN 978-1-108-47286-9 Hardback
ISBN 978-1-108-46068-2 Paperback

Cambridge University Press has no responsibility for the persistence or accuracy
of URLs for external or third-party internet websites referred to in this publication
and does not guarantee that any content on such websites is, or will remain,
accurate or appropriate.

To my many mentors whom I imagine as the audience for this book.

Contents

Figures

Acknowledgments

All of my projects benefitted from bibliographic and other assistance provided by people working on related problems or in related fields. This book is no different, and I thank Richard Bohmer, Peter Griess, Andrew Lawrence, Nick Lawrence, David Lebow, Seán Molloy, Russell Muirhead, Dorothy Noyes, Benoit Pelopidas, Simon Reich, and Jens Steffek for bringing relevant books and articles to my attention. Joseph Bafumi, Felix Berenskoetter, Carol Bohmer, Richard Bohmer, Martin Dimitrov, Toni Erskine, Mervyn Frost, Richard t'Hart, Andrew Lawrence, David Lebow, Amy Lidster, Maryyum Mehmood, Seán Molloy, Dorothy Noyes, Timothy James Potenza, Simon Reich, Nick Rengger, Benjamin Valentino, and Feng Zhang read and commented on chapters or the entire manuscript. Early on in the project I queried colleagues about whether all principles of justice build on fairness and equality and could be reduced to one or both of these principles. Bertrand Badie, Richard Beardsworth, Mervyn Frost, Fritz Kratochwil, Jens Steffek, and Mike Williams were all forthcoming with thoughts and suggestions and we had a lively email exchange.

I am even more indebted to my collaborators. The twelve Dartmouth students in my autumn 2006 seminar on "The Politics of Self-Interest" did the initial coding of presidential speeches, sitcoms, popular songs, and comic strips. Roger Giner-Sorolla, Professor of Psychology at the University of Kent, and Laura Niemmi, postgraduate fellow at Duke University, helped to design and then oversaw the implementation of a set of experiments and survey on the relative appeal of the principles of fairness and equality and how this correlates with voting preferences. Martin Dimitrov, former Dartmouth colleague and now Professor of Political Science at Tulane University, co-authored Chapter 7. It builds on my analysis of Georgian Britain to assess the likelihood that China's regime can endure without fundamental change. Joel Levine, Professor Emeritus of Mathematics at Dartmouth, helped me analyze presidential speeches with his program, "Data Without

Variables." Jami Cotler, Professor of Computer Science at Siena College, made an even bigger contribution to my data analysis and presentation.

Early on, I gave talks on individual chapters at the Universities of Southampton and Frankfurt, and I thank Tracy Strong, Chiara Forlati and their colleagues at the former and Harald Mueller and his colleagues at the latter for their criticism and encouragement. Harald was also kind enough to invite me to an extremely informative ethology conference at the Frankfurt Peace Research Institute (PRIF). Thanks also to Ole Jacob Sendung and his colleagues at the Norwegian Institute of International Affairs (NUPI) for inviting to present a "master class" that included several talks on this book project. This was my first real opportunity to lay out my arguments and I received excellent feedback. When the book was nearing completion, the Dickey Center at Dartmouth College hosted a manuscript review. I benefitted from the feedback of former colleagues Joseph Bafumi, Russell Muirhead, and Benjamin Valentino. Prior to submitting the manuscript, I gave a talk on the book at the University of Kent in Canterbury. I am grateful to Kafui Osuteye, Richard Sakwa and their colleagues for their thoughtful and helpful feedback.

I also wish to thank Palgrave Macmillan for letting me reprint extracts from *The Politics and Business of Self-Interest from Tocqueville to Trump* (2017).

Finally, I would like to thank John Haslam of Cambridge University Press for his steady support and intelligent suggestions. This is the eighth book I have published with John and Cambridge, and all have benefitted from his input and oversight of the reviewing and production.

Introduction

This third volume of my trilogy fulfills the rash promise I made in *The Tragic Vision of Politics* (2003) to produce a theory of order. It seeks to explain, at least in part, how and why orders form, evolve and decay. I attempt to show the utility of my theory in case studies of democracy in the United States and authoritarianism in China. Toward these theoretical and practical ends, I draw on literature in political theory, history, comparative and international politics, ethology, psychology, and literature.

My book builds on the epistemological foundations and substantive arguments of the two previous volumes – *The Tragic Vision of Politics* (2003) and *A Cultural Theory of International Relations* (2008). In *Tragic Vision of Politics*, I adopt Thucydides' strategy of tacking back and forth among orders at the individual, state, and regional levels of society to better understand how they function and influence one another. Ancient Greeks framed the problem in a manner not dissimilar from our notion of fractals; they thought orders revealed the same patterns at different degrees of magnification. For Thucydides, and for Plato, order and disorder, balance and imbalance, and growth and decay are roughly similar for people, poleis, and Hellas.

This symmetry across levels of analysis may have characterized late fifth and early fourth-century Greece. In traditional societies, political, economic, and social orders were largely coterminous, as they still are in some societies in the Amazon Basin and New Guinea. With modernity, these domains have become increasingly distinct, although never insulated from one another. The disciplines of anthropology, economics, sociology, and political science rest on the conceit that they can be studied independently of one another. Nobody today would follow the ancient Greeks in treating social and political spheres as inseparable. It would, however, be a mistake to deny deep connections between individuals and their domestic society, and between order and disorder at the personal, state, regional, and international levels.

A Cultural Theory of International Relations elaborates the Greek understanding of the psyche and demonstrates its relevance to foreign policy and international relations in a series of case studies. Its principal claim is that *thumos* – infelicitously but unavoidably rendered in English as "spirit" – has been neglected by modern social science yet remains an important source of human behavior. It captures the Greek insight that self-esteem is an important human need, and one that often rivals and trumps appetite. For Thucydides, Plato, and Aristotle people achieve self-esteem by excelling in activities valued by their society; we could add family and peer group to the list. They feel good about themselves when they win the approbation of those who matter to them. People often project their needs for self-esteem on to their states and *thumos* accordingly encourages the striving for national status and distinction. It is a major source of national solidarity and international conflict.

A Cultural Theory of International Relations develops a paradigm of politics based on *thumos* and presents it as an ideal type that can be used to understand international relations. I maintain that *thumos*, along with appetite and the emotion of fear, generates distinct logics of conflict, cooperation and risk-taking, and gives rise to different kinds of hierarchies. *Thumos*- and appetite-based hierarchies appeal to different principles of justice: fairness versus equality. In the real world – in contradistinction to the ideal type worlds of my theory – appetite, *thumos*, and fear are always present to some degree and responsible for domestic and foreign policies that sometimes appear contradictory. The relative importance of these three motives is a function of the degree to which reason restrains and educates *thumos* and appetite. Fear rises in importance as reason loses control of either and self-restraint gives way to self-indulgence. At a deeper level, changes in the relative importance of appetite and spirit are due to shifts in values and material conditions within societies. I discuss this evolution in Chapter 3.

My epistemology is further developed and elaborated in *Why Nations Fight* (2010), *Forbidden Fruit: Counterfactual and International Relations* (2010), and *Max Weber and International Relations* (2017). They are components of a broader project that seeks to reframe our approach to international relations, and social science more generally. It embeds the study of political behavior in psychology, history, and philosophy. Psychology offers insights not only into individual and group behavior, but also into human motives beyond appetite. It also problematizes the concept of reason and situates it in a cultural context. History reveals how culture and epoch determine which human drives dominate and how they are channeled. Yoked to psychology, it alerts us to how each culture and epoch confronts different kinds of challenges that have profound implications for political behavior. Political philosophy directs our attention to the big questions of human existence, most notably, how should society be organized and who should rule?

I treat these origins, evolution, and decay of orders at a very abstract level because I believe, *pace* Weber, that micro and macro outcomes in the social world are context dependent. Context is determining because decisions and policies are generally path dependent. Outcomes in turn are often the product of path dependence, confluence, accident, and agency. Even when actors behave rationally – not always the norm – they may be framing their decisions in terms of other problems and goals, making their choices appear less than fully rational. Outcomes and their follow-on effects are the products of complex, often non-linear, interactions among multiple actors. For this reason, actor expectations, even if the result of careful assessments, may be confounded. And understanding why actors behave as they do is only a starting point; we also need to know how their choices and behavior are aggregated.[1] The best analytical strategy is to develop ideal types and use them as starting points for narrative explanations or forecasts that build in context.

My trilogy has normative as well as theoretical goals. I wrote the first volume, *The Tragic Vision of Politics*, at the end of the Cold War. The United States, under President Bill Clinton, was showing an increasing lack of restraint in its dealing with other actors in a world some realists now triumphantly described as "unipolar." I sought to recapture the wisdom of what I called classical realism. Imbued with a tragic understanding of life, its proponents, beginning with Thucydides, warn of the effects of hubris, emphasize the practical value of goals and means consonant with the ethical values of the time, and consider great powers their own worst enemies. The book was published in 2003, the year the United States and Britain invaded Iraq. In conception, planning, and execution this intervention was a textbook case of hubris. Instead of consolidating US authority around the world, as the Bush administration expected, it seriously eroded its standing and influence. The invasions of Afghanistan and Iraq further destabilized the Middle East, promoted the rise of ISIS, and were indirectly responsible for follow-on humanitarian disasters in Iraq, Syria, and Yemen.

This volume is equally timely. It appears in the aftermath of Donald Trump's presidential victory in the United States and the Brexit referendum in Britain. Many Americans believe their constitutional order is at risk, and many Europeans believe their supranational project is threatened. The two crises share some important causes. They also feed on one another in a variety of ways. NATO intervention in Libya and the Syrian civil war prompted a flood of refugees into Europe. Right-wing, anti-EU nationalists have exploited this phenomenon to dramatically increase their share of the vote in some half-dozen countries. They oppose European integration, the European Court, and the free flow of people and ideas. They are supported by an American president who also opposes immigration, and worries other Europeans by tweeting his admiration for President Putin of Russia and doubts about the viability of NATO.

Most studies of the viability of the postwar order understandably address the threats to it; they are interested in their immediate causes, and often, in their shorter-term consequences. I direct my attention more to the causes of these causes, which have developed or unfolded over decades, or even centuries. Maestro Seiji Ozawa recalls that Herbert von Karajan told his assistant conductors that it was their responsibility to create long phrases. "Don't just read individual measures; read longer units," he insisted. Ozawa says that they were accustomed to reading four to eight measure phrases at the time, but that Karajan sought order and purpose in sixteen, even thirty-two measures. Nothing in the score indicated the need to do this, but he believed that it provided deeper insight into the meaning of the music.[2] I attempt something similar by offering a longer read of the underlying causes and mechanisms responsible for the fragility of Western domestic and regional orders and their Chinese authoritarian counterpart.

To the extent that scholars look for underlying causes of disorder they often turn to economics and focus on the growing disparity between the rich and the rest in the developed world. Thomas Piketty, among others, has documented this disturbing phenomenon and helped to raise public consciousness about it.[3] Scholars and pundits have also sounded the tocsin about the negative consequences of globalization. Most of these analyses consider inequality as de facto destabilizing without considering the broader context in which it is understood and evaluated by the people it most affects. This is one focus of my book. I develop a theory of order that posits a set of relationships among values, hierarchies, and principles of justice, and identifies the underlying conditions of resilience and fragility. This includes the subset of conditions in which inequality is most unacceptable. They have to do with the relative importance society puts on appetite versus honor and equality versus fairness, the thickness of the rule packages governing elite behavior, and the extent to which they conform to them.

Such an understanding of political order indicates that wealth and its display assume different meanings – positive and negative – in different social contexts where they may also have divergent consequences for political stability. To fathom these relationships, and others important for order and disorder – and more importantly, for human fulfilment – we must go beyond economics to sociology, political science, philosophy, and history, and beyond theories that attribute outcomes to so-called structural factors, whether they be the market or the balance of power. Attempts to explain the behavior and contentedness of people in terms of their economic interests and relative affluence do not take us very far and blinds us to the more important question of what values and goals people adopt and pursue. This is equally true of politics, where leaders and peoples make different choices. Goals and strategies are culturally and historically specific, not something that is universal and readily specified.

I have a second, parallel agenda that has to do with political theory. I offer my book as an example of how to repair the rift between political science and political philosophy. The latter owes its origins to the fact that no one can make a rule and expect others to follow it without providing some kind of reasoned argument about why it is necessary or advisable. Every argument gives rise to a counter-argument, and every claim a counter-claim. There is no politics without argument, not even war is an alternative because once hostilities cease argument resumes. Arguments, moreover, are more than window dressing for rule by fiat. Good arguments – defined in terms of their appeal – are an important source of influence.

There is no political order without an argument that explains why that order is worthwhile. And no political order is immune from counter-claims by those who want to replace or reform it. A key concern of these arguments is who should rule. In this respect, political theory is political science because arguments about who should rule are part of the explanation for who does rule.

This idea is at the very heart of the book. It is the kind of political theory that is political science, and the kind of political science that is political theory. It harks back to Aristotle whose political science deeply informs my project. It is also apparent in the great works of nineteenth- and twentieth-century political theory and political science, many of which I also draw on. I nevertheless differ from Aristotle and some modern philosophers in an important way. I do not believe that politics is the key to the good life or should be considered a higher form of activity that any other. I follow Michael Oakeshott in believing that politics should aim no higher than "making arrangements for society."[4] Oakeshott doubted we could ever figure out the "right" way to live, even as individuals, let alone as a society. This was because we were multiple selves, "a seething mass of unresolved contradictions."[5] I make a similar argument in *The Politics and Ethics of Identity*.

Yet the deep connection between political theory and political science seems to have been largely severed in the postwar era – with the recent development of international political theory a notable exception. Partly this is because political science overvalues arguments about methods, especially statistical or rationalist ones, often at the expense of talking about or trying to understand politics. And partly it is because political theory has isolated itself. Some political theorists too readily assume that their task is solely to ascertain how things should be, and to communicate this "guidance" to the political world. They believe that if we reason well about politics, we will arrive at the truth about how politics should go, and there is no reason why the real political world cannot be brought into correspondence with the truth. These assumptions are mistaken, even arrogant.

Pre-Kantian political theory was more interpretative and less didactic. It was humble about our ability to ascertain the truth about politics and justice, it saw the partial truth on different sides in arguments about justice. It saw how these arguments serve to persuade and to legitimatize; it recognized the empirical force of ideas, often very flawed ideas. This book returns to that older practice of political theory – a practice that integrated political theory and political science by tending to the real-world force of ideas and arguments. Nothing is more elemental than political order, and nowhere is the force of ideas more apparent and important. The core argument of this book is that there is no political order without an argument about why that order is just – an argument that works, that persuades, at least some. And there is no political order that is invulnerable to counter-arguments, which is why no political order is permanent. In short, ideas and arguments about justice are the fundamental cause of political order and disorder. By bringing this elemental and profound insight back into focus for a new generation of readers, this book gives hope of rejoining political science and political theory.

How should you read this book, as it is neither traditional political science nor political theory? It poses a larger set of questions than most political science research, finds only partial and plausible answers to them, and at a level of analysis that does not lend itself to many testable propositions or policy prescriptions. It asks questions more appropriate to political theory, but not with the intention of arguing the right or just way of doing something. Rather, the book inquires into beliefs people hold about justice and how they affect their behavior. The theoretical "meat" of the book is found in the first instance in the four theoretical chapters that pose a novel way of looking at political orders and evaluating their robustness. They develop a framework for thinking about this problem and how it should be studied. They elaborate multiple, initially divergent but ultimately convergent, pathways to disorder. They identify their triggers and likely consequences. They attempt to make them more comprehensible and vivid through short historical illustrations drawn from different epochs and cultures.

One of Cambridge's readers described *The Rise and Fall of Political Orders* as "a very Lebowish book" that turns to art, literature, music, and philosophy to elaborate foundational concepts. It supplements traditional argument with "playfulness" to construct a "strong statement for political understanding and action." This kind of writing hopes to invoke what the late eighteenth-century German poet Novalis [Georg Philipp Friedrich Freiherr von Hardenberg] called *den Zauberstab der Analogie*, literally "the magic wand of analogy." He envisaged it as an effective vehicle of education, and ultimately of reconciling man and nature. I accept his first claim, and toward this end make connections between art and politics throughout the book. My artistic and philosophical references, and historical examples from the classical world or Middle Ages do more than illustrate my arguments. They enable them in the sense that my engagement with these works of literature and philosophy provided the perspective on life and politics that made this book possible and the two that preceded it in the trilogy. I hope at least some readers will find it an effective and rewarding strategy.

One of my former PhD students, Felix Berenskoetter, now a prominent international scholar in his own right, asked me for whom I was writing. Who did I want to read my book? I had to confess that I had not posed this question, at least explicitly. I thought I was writing for myself. I wanted to know more about why people lived in political orders and why they prospered and declined, sometimes grew stronger and sometimes failed. These were not only the central questions of political science – in the traditional understanding of the term – but were made even more timely by recent events. Upon reflection, I realized that I imagined former mentors as my prime audience, among them Isaiah Berlin, Karl Deutsch, Herman Finer, John Herz, Hans Morgenthau, and Melvin Richter. They shared my interests – more properly, I shared theirs. I learned from them to root my research in big, important questions and not to be afraid to look outside my own field for my insights and answers. Writing what would win their approbation – and might appeal to younger scholars who think like them – is my goal.

Structure of the Book

Chapter 1 attempts to define order and disorder. I suggest that order can be defined as legible, predictable behavior in accord with recognized norms. Robust orders also require a high degree of solidarity among their members. The two conditions are related because it is social cooperation that produces legible and predictable patterns of behavior. Any definition of order must accordingly incorporate the organizing principle of social rank. It is another source of norms and solidarity, but also of conflict. Finally, we must recognize that orders are based on, and draw strength from, their ability to advance fundamental human needs, which include physical and material security, self-esteem, and social contact. We might define order as a hierarchical arrangement, supported by most of its members, that fosters security, self-esteem, and social contact, encourages solidarity, and results in legible, predictable behavior.

I distinguish between top-down and bottom-up orders. Top-down orders – governments, bureaucracies, and military organizations generally qualify – rely on rules and procedures that have originated with central authorities, or are otherwise sanctioned and enforced by them. Bottom-up orders are the product of an iterative and self-correcting process of trial and error with multiple feedback loops and branches in logic. They are on the whole an emergent property. Top-down and bottom-up orders are ideal types as they rarely exist independently of each other and generally penetrate one other to some degree. Most social orders incorporate and rely on both forms. Their coexistence may be necessary for any large social-political unit, but it is never unproblematic. Each kind of order meets particular needs, and problems can arise where the two intersect.[6]

They are ideal types in a second sense: every society has multiple top-down and bottom-up orders, and both may be highly fragmented. Carlos Noreña describes the administration of the Roman Empire in Nero's time as "for the most part cumbersome, sluggish, and sub-divided into many moving (and disconnected) parts, the overall structure of imperial government was largely insulated from the particular impulses of this or that emperor, or the short-term developments that occurred during this or that reign."[7] This account applies equally to many contemporary top-down orders.

I go on to make the case of process theory and a serious recognition of the importance of agency. I counter the principal objection raised to my multi-volume project: that it relies on ancient Greek thinkers who have a parochial and western understanding of the human psyche and the nature of political order. I then explore the relationship between order and freedom, arguing that the latter depends on the former, although it is by its very nature to some degree in conflict with it. Robust orders find ways of channeling and exploiting these tensions so that they serve as powerful, and necessary, sources of change. I conclude by noting the increasing importance of the principle of equality in the modern world and the challenges and opportunities it presents to modern political orders.

Chapter 2 analyzes the nature of order and the similarities and differences between physical and social orders. It argues that equilibrium is inappropriate to the study of social phenomena and that the most stable orders are those that undergo significant, incremental change. Given the open-ended nature of the social world, political orders and their evolution cannot be understood in isolation from their economic, social, and intellectual contexts. For the same reason, universal, falsifiable propositions about order are all but impossible. We can nevertheless identify some general reasons for the construction, evolution, decline, and reconstitution of orders and some of the dynamics associated with these processes. Toward this end, I rely on Weberian ideal-type descriptions of societies. The reasons and dynamics I identify can serve as starting points for narratives that analyze specific societies and take into account relevant features of context.

My analysis rests on four substantive assumptions. First, disorder at the top-down level is the default, and all robust orders at this level are temporary; second, robust orders, top-down or bottom-up, must be justified with reference to accepted principles of justice; third, orders become threatened when those principles are challenged, or the discrepancy between them and practice becomes apparent and unacceptable; and fourth, orders require solidarity to soften the consequences of hierarchy.

Principles of justice are central to my analysis of the rise, evolution, decline, and reconstitution of orders. Justice is a fundamental human concern, but so too is order because of the security, material, and emotional benefits it can provide. If justice is the foundation of order, order is necessary for justice. In an ideal world, they would be mutually reinforcing, but this is never the case. They are always to some degree at odds, and difficult trade-offs must be made between them. Those who advocate reforms on the grounds of justice invariably meet opposition from those who assert that the status quo is essential to order and stability. The difficulty of predicting the consequence of changes and a general preference for the evils we know over those we do not, may help explain why people are often willing to put up with orders they consider unjust.

I contend that by far the two most important principles of justice are fairness and equality. There are other principles, but they are more limited in scope and most can be reduced to fairness or equality. Commutative justice refers to relations between individuals or institutions regarding contracts and the equitable exchange of goods. It is restricted to a specific domain, and the norms and laws governing it rest on the principles of fairness or equality, usually some combination of the two. The same is true of procedural justice that refers to the methods used to settle disputes and allocate resources. Here too, norms, laws, and arguments are invariably justified, or invoke, in the case of arguments, principles of fairness or equality.

Chapter 3 examines the origins of social and political orders. It is possible that hominids of all kinds inherited a propensity to live in social groups because it greatly enhanced their prospect of survival. For apes and other primates, social groups provide security and facilitate hunting. Human communities may have arisen for the same reasons. Social orders among humans and animals require high degrees of cooperation, and appear to rest on behavior we associate with the principles of fairness and equality. Different primate groups and human societies rely on different degrees and combinations of these principles.

Among humans, interest, honor, and fear generate different logics of cooperation, conflict, and risk-taking. They also provide different motives for adherence to rules and norms, which I elaborate. They need to be theorized in tandem because of their interaction effects. Compliance for reasons of fear, interest, or honor can over time make it habitual. This, in turn, can make enforcement easier for either top-down or bottom-up orders. The relative importance of each mechanism for compliance varies within both kinds of order but there is much more variance among top-down orders. Modernity has also affected them in more fundamental ways. Andreas Kalyvas and Ira Katznelson rightly observe that "modernity generates diversity that is always conflictual."[8] To get a handle on this change, I review the expectations of key nineteenth-century sociologists and the theoretical assumptions on which they were based. None of them refer specifically to top-down or bottom-up orders, but implicitly make this distinction. Their expectations about their basis and relative importance vary considerably. Their approaches are useful starting points for mine.

Chapter 4 analyzes the decline and collapse of orders. They are fragile because they are hierarchical. Stratification encourages exploitation. Elites have power and prestige that they can usually translate into material, social, and sexual rewards. Those at the bottom have little to no power or prestige and must labor more and receive less. Why do people, or collective agents, accept, endorse, and offer up their labor, wealth, even their lives, for orders in which others reap most of the benefits?

I believe answers are to be found in the powerful emotional and substantive rewards that orders provide. Most people believe they are more secure, better off and have higher status within orders than they would outside of them, even though they may be worse off relative to many, perhaps most, other members of their society. Social integration confers identity, enhances self-worth and enables social relationships and intimacy. Elites, moreover, are generally astute enough to propagate discourses with the goal of legitimizing the orders from which they benefit. These discourses invoke metaphorical carrots and sticks, the latter by raising the prospect of internal chaos or conquest by some external foe if order is not maintained, and the former by exaggerating the material and psychological benefits of belonging. When these discourses find traction, they reinforce elite-sanctioned practices and may make them habitual. Discourses also attempt to shape expectations of what is reasonable for orders to provide. This is the goal of all golden age narratives, which justify suffering and injustice in the worlds of their readers and accordingly lower their expectations about what their rulers can reasonably be expected to provide.

Most orders survive because they deliver at least in part what they promise, or convince people that they do. When orders consistently fail to meet expectations, people are likely to become disenchanted and more willing to support moderate, even radical, change. Discontent and change are also promoted by shifts in principles of justice. These two underlying causes of decline are often related. Agency is critical to both, but especially to perceptions of a growing gap between the theory and practice of orders – top-down or bottom-up.

I identify and explore pathways to disorder that are novel to the social science literature and derived from my analysis of *thumos*- and appetite-based worlds. Both worlds are sufficiently competitive that actors are tempted to violate the rules by which honor or wealth is attained. When enough actors do so, those who continue to obey the rules are at a serious handicap. There is a strong incentive to defect for all but the most ethically committed actors. This problem is best alleviated by the proliferation of multiple pathways to honor and standing, which allow more people to achieve these goals. Competition may nevertheless be intense in many of these pathways, especially high-status ones.

Competition in appetite-based worlds need not be zero-sum because the total wealth of a society can be increased. Actors nevertheless often frame the acquisition of wealth as a winner-take-all competition even when cooperation would result in larger payoffs. Lack of self-restraint in the form of defection encourages others to follow suit. So too does conspicuous consumption, which is the principal means by which actors in appetite-based worlds seek status.

Rules for achieving honor or wealth can be violated by actors at any level of their respective hierarchies. The most serious problem, I maintain, is defection by those at the top. It reduces the incentive others have for playing by the rules and can set in motion a vicious cycle that significantly weakens the order in question. Here too, I follow Aristotle, who argues that the principal cause of the breakdown of orders is the unrestricted pursuit by actors – individuals, factions, or political units – of their parochial goals. Their behavior leads others to worry about their ability to satisfy their spirit or appetites, and perhaps fear for their well-being or survival. Fearful actors are likely to implement precautions that run the gamut from bolting their doors at night to acquiring allies and more and better arms. Mutually reinforcing changes in behavior and framing often start gradually but accelerate rapidly and bring about a phase transition. When this happens, actors enter fear-based worlds.

Lack of restraint, especially by high-status actors, subverts the principles of justice associated with their hierarchies. Unconstrained indulgence of *thumos* intensifies the competition for honor and gives rise to acute and disruptive conflict within the dominant elite. It has wider consequences for the society because it not infrequently leads to violence and reduces, if not altogether negates, the material and security benefits clientelist hierarchies are expected to provide for non-elite members of society. Unconstrained appetite also undermines an elite's legitimacy and arouses resentment and envy in other actors. It encourages others to emulate elite self-indulgence and disregard the norms restraining the pursuit of wealth at the expense of the less fortunate. In the modern world, both kinds of imbalance are endemic. The two pathways to decline can be synergistic, making decline that much more likely once societies have traveled a certain distance down these pathways.

Chapters 5 through 8 attempt to demonstrate the utility of my theory in diverse national contexts. They address a question of fundamental political importance: the threats late modernity poses for democratic and authoritarian orders and their likelihood of surmounting them. Democracy has been taken for granted as liberal western scholars depict it, and capitalism too, as the only rational responses to the modern age. Many allege their triumph is all but inevitable. Globalization has nevertheless produced a strong populist backlash against liberal capitalism, and not only in developing countries. In Europe, it has given rise to powerful nationalist parties that oppose immigration and are intolerant of minorities and human rights. The United Kingdom voted to leave the EU in a 2016 referendum, and there is significant support for doing this in France, Italy, Spain, and Greece. In the United States, anti-globalist populism helped to elect Donald Trump President in 2016. Plummeting trust in the institutions and practices of advanced liberal democracies has encouraged serious thought for the first time since the 1930s about their potential "deconsolidation."

Stable authoritarianism has been regarded as an oxymoron by liberal western analysts. African coups, the Arab Spring, and turmoil after the death of long-serving dictators, indicate authoritarian regimes are generally not long-lived, not that their collapse leads to democracy. Most have been replaced by other authoritarian leaders or regimes. As this book goes to press, attention is focused on Zimbabwe, where military intervention removed one of the world's longest ruling and oldest dictators. There is much hope for the future, but also fear that dictatorship will be reinstituted.

China and North Korea remain the most enduring challenges to those who believe that democracy is all but inevitable. North Korea can hardly be called a successful state given its enduring economic crisis and isolation. China has experienced striking economic and educational growth and its authoritarian and repressive regime gives every appearance of legitimacy. Most western analysts believe it is only a matter of time before its internal contradictions bring about its demise unless it undertakes serious efforts at liberalization.

Chapters 5 and 6 analyze the United States. For many, the election of Donald Trump, and even more his presidency, constitutes a serious threat to democracy. The election dramatized deep and seemingly unbridgeable cleavages between segments of the electorate. I offer an underlying explanation of these differences, which I attribute to value shifts and related conflicts in American society. The dominance of the principle of fairness has given way to that of equality, but this shift is unevenly reflected in the society, and the resulting division is an underlying cause of the ongoing culture and political wars. There has also been a shift away from self-interest well understood – appetite constrained by reason – to self-interest more narrowly formulated. Both shifts have promoted elite self-indulgence, disregard for norms, and a decline in tolerance, compromise, and comity. This phenomenon intensifies cultural and political conflicts.

I generate multiple streams of data to document these value shifts. To study the decline of communal commitments and the rise of narrow self-interest I use qualitative and computer-coded content analyses of presidential and election speeches, and qualitative analyses of popular sitcoms and songs over a period of sixty years. To study the shift from fairness to equality, and its uneven distribution, I rely on qualitative analyses of recent sitcoms that appeal to different demographics. To demonstrate the connection between different understandings of fairness and equality and voting preferences for Trump or Clinton, I turn to quantitative and qualitative analyses of their campaign speeches and experiments.

Chapters 7 and 8, the latter co-authored with Martin Dimitrov, address the assumption of so many western scholars that the only rational response to the modern world is some form of capitalist democracy. Is this a reasonable assumption or an ideological one? Does it provide the basis for questioning the likely survival of the communist regime in China? Or is it used to justify opposition to it? We pose these questions in a double case study – a counterintuitive one – of Georgian Britain and present-day China.

The differences between the two countries and their epochs are obvious. But there are many striking similarities. They include revolutions, foreign enemies supporting the losers in those revolutions, remarkable economic growth, rise to great power status, one-party governance (de facto in Georgian Britain from 1721 to 1760), self-replicating elites who used their control over government and administrations to enrich themselves and their families, tight controls over judiciary and media to propagate official discourses and limit critical ones, violent suppression of demonstrations and transport or imprisonment of dissidents, and rural areas ruled by local officials largely independent of central control who provoked or struggled to control almost daily popular protests. Both regimes came to power after civil wars, devoted considerable efforts, especially in their first few decades, in suppressing dissidents and rebellious nationalities in outlying provinces. Due to the spread of market relations, and central authority in the case of China, disparate regions became more integrated and economically dependent, but both countries were a patchwork of distinctive regions and communities with distinct traditions and dialects. As the dominant ideologies of divine right and communism lost appeal, elites became more corrupt and made increasing use of nationalism, economic rewards, and fear of instability as props for their respective regimes. Acquisitiveness and venality gained widespread acceptance throughout these societies.

Our pairing of Britain and China is motivated by more than their similarities. Britain is the quintessential democratic success story. Georgian England made the transformation from a divine right monarchy with a tiny political and economic elite to a burgeoning parliamentary system that reformed its institutions to allow a transfer of political power to the "middling" and working classes. How did Georgian Britain develop into its Victorian successor, considered at the time, and in retrospect, among the most stable political systems of its age? Are there lessons about political stability from the Georgian case that might help us better frame our inquiry into China? Our inquiry does not prejudge our answer to the critical question about Chinese stability posed in the opening paragraph. This is because Georgian England offers lessons about how one-party regimes – the Whigs in this instance – endure in eras of dramatic change and challenge, and also how they are transformed.

Our research strategy does not engage in direct cross-case comparisons. Rather, we ask the same questions about each country, derived from the earlier theoretical chapters of what is responsible for political stability and its decline. To what degree can post-1688 Britain and present-day China be considered stable regimes in light of their undemocratic governance and rapid economic and social transformation? What were or are their sources of legitimacy – and the greatest threats to political stability? How would leaders of both countries respond to these questions? To what extent did – or do – their understandings help to buttress or undermine the stability of their political systems? And what about the beliefs in this regard of other relevant actors?

Chapter 9 is the first of two concluding chapters. It revisits the definition of order, and the distinction between top-down and bottom-up orders. I acknowledge tensions in my definition, but contend that they capture an essential feature of order and accordingly encourage a dialectical approach to its study. Order and disorder are not binaries, but closer to being co-constitutive. Disorder is inherent in order. Any kind of reasonably robust order must contain enough disorder to give agents some freedom from constraint and allow, or accept, at least tacitly, violations of its norms. This might be called productive disorder, because it allows, even encourages, challenges that may prove vehicles for its evolution. The cycle of challenge and response is a process critical to order.

Another key tension is that between what we might call the actual robustness of order and the assessment of it by political actors. The degree of robustness very much influences, if not determines, what actors think about it. A widespread belief that order is robust may help make that belief self-fulfilling, just as the belief that it is near collapse can lead to behavior that pushes it over the edge. However, it is also the case that overconfidence or exaggerated fears of instability can hasten an order's demise. It is by no means a stretch of imagination to describe robustness as a state of mind. There are, moreover, no objective yardsticks that can be used independently to assess robustness. At best, we can form rough estimates by public opinion polls, measures of protests and the nature of responses to them, and contemporary and historical comparisons. It is only in retrospect that the robustness of an order becomes apparent. This helps to explain why astute observers were surprised by such events as the French Revolution; the survival of Georgian Britain; the outbreak of war in 1914; the absence of superpower war after the Cold War began; and the collapse of the Soviet Union.

I next turn to free-riding and exploitation as they are only really possible in robust societies. I posit a negative relationship between free-riding and exploitation on the one hand and the robustness of orders on the other. In developed, democratic countries, both activities should decline, become increasingly regarded as deviant, and those who engage in them the objects of shaming or punishment. The perception of what constitutes free-riding and exploitation should also change as the principle of equality becomes increasingly dominant in western societies. A rise in either free-riding or exploitation, and more telling, the emergence of discourses that justify them, are signs of decline and disorder. Drawing on the empirical findings of Chapters 5 and 6, I suggest that these discourses have become more evident in the United States and free-riding and exploitation more acceptable. These changes do not bode well for political order.

The following section addresses deviance, but from the perspective of those in power. I theorize a curve of tolerance. Leaders and supporters of new regimes are likely to be relatively intolerant of deviance and political dissent – I treat dissent as one form of deviance. So are leaders and supporters of declining regimes, although this will depend on their perceived ability to suppress and punish deviance. Leaders and supporters of established regimes who believe they possess some degree of robustness are likely to be more tolerant. Leader assessments of robustness are accordingly a reasonable predictor of responses to dissent. Dissent also tells us something about robustness. It should be the greatest when orders are perceived to be robust or weak and declining, but dissent will differ in character in each of these circumstances.

Chapter 10, the second concluding chapter, steps back from my data to take a von Karajan-like, longer-range perspective on political orders and the problems late modernity poses for them. I argue that the political crisis of the West, and the impending one in China, are products of late modernity. The conflict between the principles of equality and fairness, and *thumos* and appetite are the underlying causes of this crisis. This confluence generates contradictions and stresses that threaten democratic and authoritarian regimes alike. There is no solution to this challenge beyond a set of uneasy and shifting set of compromises that will always be open to criticism of all kind. To succeed in the sense of reducing tensions, these compromises must be open to renegotiation, a political mindset difficult to envisage, let alone implement, when they have become the focus of so much partisan discord and overlap with other key political cleavages.

I conclude with epistemological reflections that draw on Max Weber's approach to knowledge. He believed that the starting point of ethical social science was for researchers to make explicit their substantive and epistemological assumptions. Beliefs and related assumptions about politics and how it should be studied are invariably parochial. They are a function of one's place in society and culture, and that culture's place in history. Weber maintained that these beliefs largely determine what we choose to study, how we approach the subject, what we consider evidence, how we evaluate, and therefore the conclusions we reach. There is no effective way of separating facts from values. Weber struggled – largely unsuccessfully – to come to terms with his priors. I have tried to do the same. I make my normative commitments explicit in Chapter 1 and explain how they led me to research order and justice. I am under no illusion that my research questions, approach to them, and findings, reflect my life experiences, the broader Zeitgeist, and the moment in history when I research and write. I consider some of the consequences of these limitations.

Fitting Parts into a Whole

My epistemology and substantive arguments are sufficiently complex, as is the relationship between them, that it is useful to close with a brief reprise. My most overriding concern is with balancing freedom and authority in a way that permits human beings to develop their potential and seek personal fulfilment and happiness in a secure and nurturing but not oppressive or controlling environment. Such a goal is admittedly utopian, but utopias are useful templates for assessing existing orders and establishing goals toward which to strive.

I believe that liberal democracy is the political order most conducive to human fulfilment and happiness. I understand that such systems are imperfect, and that many deny the possibility of fulfilment and happiness to significant percentages of their populations. I also recognize that liberal democracy is not universally applicable in current circumstances, and that efforts to export it are just as likely to backfire, as they have in Libya, Afghanistan, and Iraq. I reject as ideology the claim that laissez-faire, democratic orders are the only rational response to modernity. Corporate, authoritarian regimes may be just as economically efficient and, in some circumstances – notably, in the aftermath of near-anarchy – they may contribute more to order and happiness, certainly in the short term.

Given my focus, I concentrate my analysis on the more developed countries, notably the western democracies and China. I examine order primarily at the domestic level and here, as noted, I focus on the interaction of top-down and bottom-up orders. However, my primary interest is in top-down orders and the challenges they currently confront. I have a few words to say about international relations, but surprisingly few perhaps, given my long-standing interest in the subject. I intend to address the problem of international order in a follow-on study that will draw on the theory and findings of this book.

My normative commitments generate a series of empirical questions. The principal one concerns the vulnerabilities of democratic and authoritarian orders. What are the conditions and pathways that threaten their decline and possible transformation? Can a general understanding of this kind offer insights into the political futures of the United States and China? I believe it will and, drawing on Thucydides, Plato, and Aristotle, identify pathways of decline associated with *thumos*- and appetite-based worlds. Both start with elite abuse of their rule packages and through different processes end up in fear-based worlds in which political actors are prone to preemption and violence. These worlds are, of course, ideal types; in historical worlds both motives are at work. The pathways I describe in ideal-type worlds can be observed in real worlds, but often interact in synergistic and unpredictable ways. How far either of them progress toward disorder and how they interact are situation dependent. My propositions about decline are accordingly starting points for explanatory narratives or forecasts that build in features of context. Martin Dimitrov and I do this in Chapter 7.

Elite abuse of rule packages is not random but associated with triggering causes. They differ in *thumos*- and appetite-based worlds, and Chapter 4 elaborates some of these different causes. Elite abuse in both worlds also has some important underlying causes in common. Most important here are shifts in the appeal of principles of justice, loss of legitimacy of discourses that account for gaps between the principles in theory and practice, and the absence of checks and balances that constrain elites. Shifts in the principles of justice are a product of modernity, as is the shift in understandings of self-interest. There are accordingly links that can be documented between underlying and immediate causes, but the latter are still to a considerable degree independent of the former. We cannot predict order or disorder on the basis of the underlying causes. Once again, they are starting points of explanatory or forward-looking narratives that address single cases and do so by folding in path dependence, confluence, and agency.

Notes

1 Lebow, *Constructing Cause in International Relations*, for an elaboration of this argument.
2 Murakami, *Absolutely on Music*, p. 93.
3 Piketty, *Capital in the Twenty-First Century* and *Economics of Inequality*; Atkinson, *Inequality*. Also, Frank, *Falling Behind*; Bertrand, and Morse, "Trickle Down Consumption."
4 Oakeshott, *Rationalism in Politics and Other Essays*, p. 45.
5 Oakeshott, *Notebooks*, p. 196.
6 Here too, I draw on the Greeks. Aristotle, one of the earliest and most sophisticated theorists of politics, conceptualizes three levels of order: natural

order (*kosmos*), by which he means the natural powers and dispositions of humankind; customary order (*ethē* or *agraphoi nomoi*), characterized by habitual practices; and laws (*nomos* and *taxis*), which describe stipulated practices. Customary order cannot directly be equated with bottom-up orders, but can with their associated values and norms. Laws are the product of top-down orders.

7 Noreña, "Nero's Imperial Administration."
8 Kalyvas and Katznelson, "Adam Ferguson Returns."

1   Political Order

The heavens themselves, the planets
and this centre
Observe degree, priority and pace,
Insisture, course, proportion, season,
form,
Office and custom, in all line of order;
... but when the planets
In evil mixture to disorder wander,
What plagues and what portents!
what mutiny!
What raging of the sea! shaking of the earth!
Commotion in the winds!

Shakespeare[1]

In these lines from *Troilus and Cressida* Shakespeare conceives of order as the regular and proportional movement of the component parts of a whole. He is describing the heavens, but presumably has the human world in mind as well. In his time, the reigning understanding of order was hierarchical, with everything above being superior and more perfect to everything beneath. The cosmos and its order was accordingly a model for humans to emulate.

I follow Shakespeare and others in believing that social order can be defined as legible, predictable behavior in accord with recognized norms.[2] Behavior of this kind has the potential to build solidarity and cooperation, both of which encourage common identities. They, in turn, help to build and sustain order. The absence of solidarity, meaningful norms and predictable behavior are the marks of disorder.

Predictable behavior is possible without solidarity, as in the *favelas* of Rio de Janeiro or the streets of Mogadishu, but it is likely to involve a significant degree of force and predation.[3] In the *favelas*, drug gangs have a near monopoly of force – aside from periods of army intervention – and use it to impose their will. Violators are generally punished, unless they are respected and well-connected, and residents derive a false sense of security.[4] In 2017, there was a 40 percent reported rise in violent attacks on residents, attributed to evangelical Christian drug gangs. These *bandidos evangélicos* want to suppress and drive out priests and followers of Umbanda and Candomblé, blends of African traditions and Christianity. The attackers are connected with powerful outside political forces and are likely to have their backing.[5] Self-policing and governing in Michoacán, Mexico has had a similar outcome. Local proprietors of avocado farms underwrite what has become, in effect, a self-governing mini-state, but at great cost to inhabitants. Drug use, suicide, and violence are soaring – the very problems that are products of a weak state, regenerated as well by a strong one.[6]

Many of Shakespeare's contemporaries imagined that the heavenly bodies were created and set in motion by God and that their motions enacted divine will. It is the ultimate example of what I call a top-down order. A modern-day secular equivalent is vehicular traffic, which is frequently cited as the quintessential example of order. For traffic to flow rapidly and safely, drivers must stay on the side of the road when moving in the same direction, halt at stop signs and red lights, and adhere to other important "rules of the road" (e.g. signal for turns, pass in the outside lane, refrain from blocking intersections). The rules are set by authorities, but people for the most part obey because they recognize that they are in their interest.[7]

Top-down order relies on a combination of enforcement and voluntary compliance – more about this in Chapter 3. It rests on the Hobbesian assumptions that government – or a hegemon in international affairs – is necessary to coordinate mutually beneficial cooperation and punish those who do not conform. And further, that most actors conform because they see the utility of this arrangement.

Traffic in some other parts of the world functions differently. First-time visitors to India are struck by the seeming chaos of the streets; humans and animals, the former on foot, mopeds, three-wheeled rickshaws, cars, and track moving in all directions and swerving to and fro to avoid one another. There is nevertheless order in this seeming disorder, and accidents are no more frequent than in western cities. Indian and Chinese traffic patterns of this kind are best described as bottom-up order. It is the product of multiple agents following a few simple rules in their interactions with others in their immediate vicinity.

Top-down orders rely on rules and procedures that have originated with central authorities, or are otherwise sanctioned and enforced by them. Bottom-up orders are the product of an iterative and self-correcting process of trial and error with multiple feedback loops and branches in logic. In the case of Indian traffic, independent agents – some in vehicles, some on foot, and some with animals – follow a few simple rules in their relationships with one another, giving rise to order as an emergent property. For a book about order, the most important point here is that governance includes more than government.[8]

Urban traffic in New York or London can come to a complete halt due to gridlock or other kinds of blockages. Drivers can do little in these circumstances, although cyclists have the option of shifting to sidewalks or pavements. Indian traffic rarely encounters such problems because of the nature of its flow, the initiatives individual drivers must make to negotiate it, and the greater opportunities for them to do so. China offers another interesting comparison. The author has observed how traffic moves slowly but steadily in those parts of provincial cities, usually the peripheries, where streets are still unpaved and there are no seeming rules of the road. In urban centers, where streets are paved, lanes divided, and there are traffic lights, traffic is not necessarily any heavier, but stoppages are more common. Paradoxically, the most successful orders may be those closest to the edge of chaos, like Indian and Chinese vehicular traffic.

This observation about traffic can be extended to organizations and governments, which are forms of top-down order. The most extreme and common version of a top-down order may be military organizations. Armies are notoriously poor governors. They are rigidly hierarchical, and units in contact with the population of their own or an occupied country, must implement rules and procedures that have often been framed without any understanding of local conditions. They must be worded in ways to make them legible to those charged with their enforcement, often at the expense of effectiveness. Lower ranks almost invariably lack the independence to bend or ignore orders to respond in ways that they think more appropriate to their mission.[9] Rules and procedures are most likely to reflect what the military is capable of executing, not what might be most responsive to its mission. Generals do not infrequently try to persuade their political superiors – when they have them – to redefine their missions to make them compatible with their organizational routines and what they believe they are capable of performing.

Bureaucracies can be likened to armies without weapons. They respond to similar problems in similar ways. I served as a scholar-in-residence in the Central Intelligence Agency toward the end of the Carter administration and beginning of the Reagan one. Solidarity emerged as a powerful force in Poland and in the winter of 1980–1 and the White House worried that the Soviet Union might invade. The Soviets did consider military action, but in the end forced the Polish United Workers' Party to replace Stanisław Kania with Wojciech Jaruzelski and impose martial law. The White House wanted to know when and if the Soviet Union would invade Poland, and the intelligence community unsuccessfully sought to limit its brief to what it felt competent to do: advising the President if the Soviets were *prepared* to invade.[10]

Bureaucracies are as arbitrary and heavy-handed as armies, and for much the same reason. Both frequently flout the very rules that govern them. Instructed to restrict immigration by Labour and Conservative governments, the British Home Office was supposed to be guided by legislation and rules and procedures it promulgated. In pursuit of its goal it consistently violates this legislation and its own rules. In August 2017, Conservative Home Secretary Amber Rudd was condemned by the High Court for refusing to obey repeated court orders to release from detention a torture victim from Chad who had applied for political asylum.[11] In September, she ignored court orders not to deport a twenty-three-year-old Afghani asylum seeker. She ignored a subsequent court order to repatriate him even though he was in hiding from the Taliban in his hotel room in Kabul after they threatened to behead him.[12]

Such behavior appears irrational. It might make sense if Rudd and her colleagues believe, as they appear to, that their defiance of the law and the publicity it inevitably receives will intimidate others from seeking asylum in Britain. There is, of course, no evidence for this belief.

When bureaucracies follow their own rules they can behave equally irrationally. In 2010, the Home Office destroyed the landing cards of Caribbean immigrants from the 1950s and 1960s despite pleas from case officers that it would make it correspondingly more difficult, if not impossible, to document the status of these immigrants. A Home Office spokesman claimed that the slips were destroyed "on data protection grounds"! Case officers and others had some leeway before Theresa May became Secretary of State for the Home Department, but after 2013, those who complained were told "These are the rules, stick to them."[13] In his 1926 novel, *The Castle*, Franz Kafka depicts bureaucracy as dystopian and increasingly ineffective and arbitrary because of the widely shared belief among its officials that it could never err. Kafka's account strikes me as closer to the truth than Weber's.[14]

Shakespeare wrote *Troilus and Cressida* at a time when thinkers who broke free of traditional Christianity were beginning to think about order in a different way. Machiavelli, for one, believed that change was constant and instability the norm. He emphasizes how the Roman Republic was healthy because it was characterized by social friction and conflict. The evolving relationship between competing forces produced change in the form of creative stability.[15] "Those who condemn the disturbances between the nobles and the plebians," he wrote, "condemn those very things that were the causes of Roman liberty."[16] Machiavelli admired leaders who displayed flexibility and constantly adjusted their goals and the means by which they were pursued in response to changing circumstances and opportunities. For Machiavelli, decline and collapse were the default due to changes in the distribution of power, and political leaders who could not adjust to new conditions. Political orders survived through a combination of political skill and good fortune, but also because they "renew themselves through their own institutions."[17]

Shakespeare may well have subscribed to a similar view. His seeming affirmation of the Great Chain of Being and its rigid order and hierarchy in Act 1, scene 2 of *Troilus and Cressida* is undercut by what follows.[18] The play violates order by mixing genres in a confusing way, oscillating between bawdy comedy and dark tragedy. Its characters are hard to read and evoke varying responses from theater-goers and critics. Their behavior and dialogue problematize hierarchy, honor, and love, and encourage us to reflect upon the earlier reference to the ordered cosmos as ironic in intent. Shakespeare may also be suggesting that disorder is inevitable once belief in natural hierarchy disappears. In act 1, scene 3, he has Ulysses say as much: "Take but degree away, untune that string, And hark what discord follows."[19]

In contrast to equilibrium theorists and rationalist modelers, some modern political scientists root themselves in the Machiavellian tradition.[20] They see order as fluid, in response to changing conditions and requirements, and stress the need of governments and leaders to development responsiveness. Machiavelli compares politics to medicine: "doctors tell us about tuberculosis: in its early stages it's easy to cure and hard to diagnose, but if you don't spot it and treat it, as time goes by it gets easy to diagnose and hard to cure."[21]

Karl Deutsch emphasized that successful government administration – top-down order – requires responsiveness as well as capabilities.[22] Capabilities derive from structure, hierarchy, and resources, but responsiveness demands policies tailored to circumstance and the needs of the population, subject to rapid reformulation, and leeway for junior officials to interpret and apply these policies as they see fit. This leeway might give rise to a circumscribed form of bottom-up order. However, giving such latitude to subordinates is almost certain to be resisted as it is threatening to the principle of top-down orders and the authority of those who run them. Nor is it always beneficial as junior officials, in the absence of sufficient oversight, might act in ways at odds with the values and legitimacy of the organization. Taizo Nishimoro ran three of Japan's largest corporations. At Toshiba he was famous – and infamous – for devolving responsibility to make the company more responsive to customer needs. Lax control also allowed a profit-padding scandal to develop that humiliated the company when it became public in 2015.[23] Responsiveness depends upon learning, and this is particularly difficult for top-down orders. Learning demands open minds and perspectives, qualities not prominent in organizations. Their leaders are more likely to learn superficial and misleading lessons and confirm their expectations tautologically.[24]

For all these reasons, top-down political orders often appear more robust than is warranted. They may function well in a limited range of circumstances – those in which they can minimize or control uncertainties – but even here their seeming authority may be misleading. Charles Perrow describes how tightly coupled complex systems (e.g. nuclear power plants, electrical grids, air traffic control, major hospitals) only function effectively when operators make informal arrangements among themselves to circumvent many of the rules and replace them with simplified, informal procedures.[25] Bottom-up order may be more essential in a society with highly regimented top-down orders. They are also less tolerated by such orders, as the communist experience in the Soviet Union and communist countries of Eastern Europe testify.[26]

Top-down systems can suffer catastrophic failures when confronted with unanticipated developments. This is because efforts to respond, based on existing repertoires or informal procedures, may not be at all appropriate to the challenge. They can also have the unintended and counterintuitive effect of exaggerating the problem, as they did at the Three Mile Island and Chernobyl nuclear plants.[27] A nice political example is provided by efforts of the Polish Communist Party in the 1950s to control dissent at their new steel city of Nowa Huta. Their heavy-handed efforts at repression provoked more resistance and compelled them to negotiate with the workers and ultimately gave rise to the Solidarity movement.[28]

During the Cold War, I warned of the potential for catastrophe in US nuclear command and control; efforts to prevent accidental or unauthorized launch of nuclear weapons might make such an event more likely in a crisis situation because of the interactions between a complex mechanical system and emotionally aroused human operators.[29] Highly structured top-down orders entail another kind of risk: they socialize actors in ways that minimize their ability or willingness to act independently. As a first-year student at the University of Chicago in the late 1950s, I was in awe of my classmates, most of whom had been higher achievers in secondary school, and at least a score of them valedictorians. I soon discovered that some of these students were not performing well. Living away from home for the first time, free to indulge in previously proscribed pleasures, not forced to study by parents, and attending a university that all but refused to act *in loco parentis*, they lacked the commitment or knowhow to discipline themselves.

In 1979, I went to Moscow to attend a meeting of the International Political Science Association where I encountered a more extreme and tragic manifestation of this phenomenon. The Soviets were keen to host the meeting and agreed to allow scholars from all countries to attend, including those from Taiwan and Israel, with whom they had no official relations. The Israeli delegation let it be known that on Saturday morning they would gather in front of the one functioning synagogue in central Moscow. Janice Gross Stein and I accompanied them and met with Jewish Muscovites. Many of those to whom we spoke were interested in migrating to Israel or America and asked more or less the same set of questions. Once they arrived, who would tell them where to live and work? We explained that after some help with initial settlement, these decisions, and all others, were theirs to make. They found this puzzling and even frightening. Having grown up in a system where others made the most fundamental choices for them, they were unprepared and even threatened by the prospect of looking after themselves.[30]

Bottom-up orders reveal different kinds of vulnerabilities. They can be more rapid in response to local challenges, even extreme ones, but may find it difficult to respond to those that require considerable outside resources. Disasters like floods and fires illustrate the strengths and weaknesses of bottom-up orders. Local communities quickly organize, often without reliance on officials, to fill sandbags or provide quarters, clothes, and food for people who have been evacuated. If there is much destruction, they in turn become dependent on others for supplies and funds for rebuilding.[31] Bottom-up orders are also at a serious disadvantage in conflicts with top-down orders because of the respective power balance. When boundaries between bottom-up and top-down orders are ill-defined or poorly recognized in practice, there is a risk of conflict and disorder where they come into contact. In our Indian traffic example, disorder is highest at the transition points between traditional and modern traffic patterns.

Top-down and bottom-up orders rarely exist independently of each other and generally penetrate one other to some degree. Most societies incorporate and rely on both forms. Their coexistence may be necessary for any large social-political unit, but it is never unproblematic. Each kind of order meets particular needs, and problems arise, as noted, where the two intersect. In a fascinating book about recess in American schools, Anna Beresin found that pupils allowed free time in the schoolyard organized their own rules about space, games, and comportment.[32] Recess order is bottom-up and emergent, in contrast to classroom order, clearly imposed from above. Jostling, name-calling, and fights arose in the liminal space between the orders, when students spilled out of the classroom or were forced back into school following recess. This phenomenon is widespread. In healthcare, a substantial proportion of medical errors occur during handovers from one department or professional to another. This is because the so-called "systems" for patient care "are a patchwork of poorly connected – or entirely unconnected – constituent parts that don't work well together."[33] These problems are likely to be most pronounced when bottom-up orders hand off to top-down ones, or vice versa.[34]

Robust orders of scale require synergy between their top-down and bottom-up components. Like Yin and Yang, these seemingly opposing forms can be made to some degree complementary, interconnected, and interdependent.[35] They may even give rise to each other, as top-down orders do with bottom-up ones in the tightly coupled systems that Perrow describes.[36] There is also good reason to suppose that societies came before governments, and that top-down orders were based on and outgrowths of bottom-up ones.[37]

Bottom-up orders can also impede the development of top-down ones. In Italy, the family is the most fundamental social institution. Luigi Barzini describes it as "the only fundamental institution in the country, a spontaneous creation of the national genius, adapted through the centuries to changing conditions, the real foundation of whichever social order prevails. In fact, the law, the State, and society function only if they do not directly interfere with the family's supreme interests."[38] The family became so strong in Italy because for so long the state – really multiple political units – was weak and abusive and government and law resented as unjust. But the family, once strong, is a barrier to the development of strong institutions. This phenomenon is by no means limited to Italy.

The most robust top-down orders may be those that build on and copy bottom-up rules and practices. What works on the street, in everyday life or in face-to-face encounters in different professional domains, is often the product of trial and error, implicit and explicit communication among actors, and common attempts to maximize certain shared values or goals. To the extent that these values and goals are widely shared, their adoption by top-down orders and efforts to regularize and enforce them can win popular approval and enhance efficiency.

Consider again the problem of healthcare. It is by definition an experimental practice. Each patient interaction is a test of evaluative or therapeutic strategies, and clinical day-to-day practice that generates as much useful medical knowledge as laboratory research and experiments.[39] Many of the benefits of this bottom-up source of knowledge are lost in the absence of deliberate efforts to capture and utilize them. Tucker and Edmonson found that 93 percent of all problems discovered and solved by nurses were not elevated to a higher level where more general solutions could be found and implemented.[40]

The growing use by doctors of WhatsApp offers a concrete illustration of this problem. WhatsApp is now ubiquitous in National Health Service (NHS) hospitals. It allows doctors to rapidly exchange clinical information, in contrast to authorized but slow or uncertain means like hospital pagers and fax machines. According to one physician: "Instant messaging is a more efficient way for us to communicate, but we need a system that doesn't put patient confidentiality on the line." *The Guardian* found that use of these apps breaks down traditional hierarchies and allows doctors to communicate more freely with their immediate clinical team. Another physician noted: "From the most junior doctor to the most senior (though in practice often excluding the consultant), these groups allow all of us to work together more effectively, and enable shyer or less experienced team members to seek help when they need it. They inspire camaraderie." The NHS in England nevertheless forbids the use of WhatsApp, fearful of a breach of patient confidentiality. Doctors insist that "this is not a problem."[41]

Modern healthcare organizations, according to Bohmer, need to combine the benefits of bottom-up and top-down orders in creative but systematic ways to produce self-correcting healthcare organizations.[42] Bohmer is aware that what works at the local level may not be scalable. In the first instance this is often due to the shift from face-to-face to impersonal means of interaction and transmission. Clinical knowledge may also be resisted when it is perceived to threaten the prerogatives of leadership, profits, or institutional independence. For these reasons, doctors have consistently opposed the greater empowerment of nurses despite its demonstrable benefits to patients. Conversely, what appears to be logical, orderly, and effective at the system level may be unacceptable or unworkable at the local level. This is most likely when the values those at the top attempt to maximize are not the same as those lower down the organizational or social ladder.

A case in point is the destruction of mature, healthy trees, beloved by residents, by councils in Sheffield and London intent on saving money. They engaged in sham consultations by arranging drive-by presentations and soliciting written opinions that were not read or ignored if they were.[43] In Tooting Bec Common, the Wandsworth Council falsely insisted that the trees they removed were diseased, and that they had the support of residents – more than 6,500 of whom had taken the time and trouble to formally object when the project was first broached.[44] The councils were under pressure to save money because the Conservative government had reduced their budgets. The central government was passing the buck and requiring units lower down to make the hard choices and catch the flak for them. The councils, which could be described as meeting points of top-down and bottom-up orders, did their bidding and became the source of contention between the two orders.

At the outset of this chapter, I defined order as legible, predictable behavior in accord with recognized norms. I claimed that robust orders require a high degree of solidarity among their members. The two conditions are related because social interaction and cooperation is the source of most norms and predictable patterns of behavior. In Chapter 3 I stress that all but the smallest of orders (e.g. hunter-gatherers, kibbutzim) are to varying degrees hierarchical. Any definition of order must accordingly incorporate the organizing principle of social rank. It is another source of norms and solidarity, but also of conflict. Finally, we must recognize that orders are based on, and draw strength from, their ability to advance fundamental human needs, which include physical and material security, self-esteem, and social contact. We might refine our definition of order and describe it as a hierarchical arrangement, supported by most of its members, that fosters security, self-esteem, and social contact, encourages solidarity, and results in legible, predictable behavior.

One further caveat must be entered. I have distinguished top-down from bottom-up orders, and now want to make an equal distinction between government and society. Society precedes government, although government can transform society. Consider how different the societies of Langue d'Oc were from Île-de-France before they were conquered and incorporated into the French state, or Scottish society from English prior to the Act of Union in 1707. Hundreds of years of unification made these societies more like French and English ones, and all the more so in France with its centralizing and intrusive government. So-called totalitarian regimes like the Soviet Union, China, and North Korea constitute even stronger cases for top-down social transformations.

The society–state difference is important to keep in mind when analyzing the origins of states and their decline. As noted, societies precede states and generally survive them. One of the most important political facts of the last 100 years is how long-lived societies are in comparison with states, and how much more so with respect to regimes, many of which have a short life. Societies too can decline, but it is usually a much slower process. My analysis of decline focuses largely on political orders, namely states and their regimes. But I implicate societies in this process because social change can be, and often is, the principal underlying cause of regime or state decline.

Top-down and bottom-up orders roughly – but only roughly – coincide with state and society. Governments and most of their associated bureaucracies are unambiguously top-down orders and most, but by no means all of civil society, can be characterized as bottom-up order. The distinction is not a binary but a continuum with a fair number of institutions – depending on the society, of course – found in the middle. Take the English councils in my earlier example. They behaved in a way to make them part of the top-down order, and appear to the community as such. Had they behaved differently they might have been regarded as more reflective of community values and preferences, and thus an expression of bottom-up order. As scholars reading this book will recognize from personal experience, heads of department make similar choices. They can act – or be perceived to act – as the hired guns of the university administration or as spokespersons for their colleagues.

Reason and Emotion

Political Order highlights a different feature of the Greek understanding of the psyche: the role reason plays in discovering what makes for a happy life. To achieve this much-desired state, Plato maintains that reason must constrain and educate appetite and *thumos* alike. This is true, he insists, for cities as well as for people. I believe he is right in seeing a close connection between people and their *poleis*. Social psychologists concur, mustering considerable evidence that people's values and practices are very much shaped by their societies.[45] The happy life and the balanced psyche therefore depend very much on the nature of the political order and the kind of education and role models it provides.

But what kind of education is best, and who has the knowledge to decide? For Plato, it was a philosopher king. Karl Popper was wrong in accusing him of being the father of totalitarianism, but there can be little doubt that Plato's Republic is an authoritarian society with minimal free choice for its citizens.[46] Liberal-democratic philosophy has a very different take on education. It can empower people to make their own choices and expects self-interest and economic opportunity to lead many, if not most, to a happier life. It relies on a combination of substantive and instrumental interest, the former to guide people toward appropriate goals, and the latter to aid in achieving them. The liberal vision is open to different objections: most notably, its assumption that people left to their own devices will make intelligent choices. The Marxist approach is, if anything, more problematic. More fundamentally, as Immanuel Kant recognized, there is a paradox between human reason and the frightening and violent social world it has helped to bring about. He also thought it unlikely that the people who benefit from this state of affairs would somehow use their reason to change it.[47] *Pace* Kant, I believe that there is no obvious pathway to order and happiness.

Plato is on firmer ground in thinking that disorder at all levels is the result of reason's loss of control to either appetite or *thumos*. But why does this happen? Plato and Aristotle thought that most people were never constrained by reason to begin with, which is one reason they opposed democracy. They believed the *dēmos* would use its power to expropriate the wealth of the elite. There is about as much evidence in support of this fear as there is for illegal voting in the United States. Thucydides' account of the Peloponnesian War suggests that the rich and powerful are more often the source of discontent and disorder. I build my theoretical account of decline on his insight. In appetite- and *thumos*-based worlds alike, elite failure to exercise self-restraint is the key source of disorder. In both worlds, there are different kinds of rule packages – the norms proscribing appropriate behavior for a given status. They unravel in different ways, but ultimately make the transition to similar fear-based worlds. I will explore these pathways and their associated mechanisms in some detail.

Jean-Jacques Rousseau famously claimed that the Enlightenment was throwing "garlands of flowers over the chains of reason which weigh us down."[48] The *philosophes* and their fellow-travelers undoubtedly overvalued reason, and so does modern social science. However, rejecting it in favor of the passions is just as misguided. A middle way makes more sense, and especially one that emphasizes the positive and negative interactions of reason and emotions. Once again, Aristotle is my guide. He insists that emotions are essential to good decision-making, learning, and wisdom more generally. David Hume makes a similar argument.[49] Research in neuroscience offers strong support for these claims.[50] It demonstrates that affect and reason are equally essential to the good performance of complex cognitive tasks. Together, they determine the kind of sensory inputs to which we respond, how we evaluate this information, and how we respond to it.

Plato and Aristotle conceive of the rise and fall of orders, and life more generally, as a natural and cyclical process. They consider disorder the default because order is achieved and maintained only with great difficulty. Machiavelli made a similar claim, as does Shakespeare in *Coriolanus*.[51] I build on this tradition, but disassociate myself from organic analogies. People mature, age and die for quite different reasons than political orders. The more relevant analogy is between individual and social order, and here, I have noted, the Greeks are on firmer ground in thinking that some of the same processes are common to both. We must nevertheless exercise caution because there are important differences between people and political units.

Disorder is as slippery a concept as order. For Thucydides, it meant *stasis* (civil war or breakdown), and his accounts of Corcyra and the plague in Athens provide graphic examples. Realist theorists of international relations believe they follow Thucydides by invoking the concept of anarchy to describe what they call the international "system." This is a misunderstanding of Thucydides – and more importantly, of political reality. *Stasis* is a rare, or at least, unusual state, and hardly the norm. For Thucydides, and for Aristotle too, the default, and common condition of most *poleis*, was non-violent civil conflict in which competing people and factions advanced, or tried to impose, different conceptions of order. The degree of consensus varied widely from polis to polis, and highly consensual ones were uncommon to rare.

I am not alone in arguing that this Thucydidean understanding applies to international relations. True anarchy is a rare event. World War II on the Eastern Front may qualify, but it was an extraordinary and short-lived situation. International relations constitute a society, not a system, and is for the most part rules-based.[52] Not all actors will follow the rules in all situations, and neither will rules necessarily cover all situations, so there will almost certainly be a degree of disorder. The same is true of regional societies, with Europe being the most robust. War is considered out of the question among European Union (EU) members, but there is localized disorder. Some of it is the result of refugees who resist settlement in camps and are sometimes the focus of violence. At the interstate level, Brexit provides an example. There are no real rules governing what happens after a state invokes Article 50 of the Treaty of the EU as it had never been done before.[53] As this book goes to press, British and European leaders are negotiating the terms of Brexit, and are nowhere close to agreement on procedures, let alone the substance of Britain's future relationship with the EU.[54]

Domestic societies are considerably more rules-based, although for similar reasons disorder can also appear. In the United States, since 1976 there have been eighteen gaps in government funding due to disputes between the Congress and the President. Seven of them led to government employees being furloughed. The longest, in the Clinton administration, 1995–96, lasted twenty-seven days and caused major disruption.[55] The closest domestic societies come to disorder is in so-called failed states. In Somalia, for example, there may be something approaching anarchy at the macro-level, but at the micro-level, as in Brazil's favelas and Cairo's slums, people have developed norms to regulate their social and economic relationships. In the absence of top-down order, bottom-up order often expands to take over many of its functions.

It is more accurate to say that the default failure of political orders is the breakdown of top-down orders. I hazard a guess that in the twentieth century, the average life expectancy of a regime is perhaps two generations. Transitions between regimes are likely to be high points of disorder, but relatively few of them are the result of, or causes of, civil wars. International, regional, or domestic breakdown is relatively uncommon. More frequent is temporary disruption associated with changes of regimes that mark the transition from one period of relatively stability to another. More common still may be partial or local disruptions of order. Here too, bottom-up orders may expand to provide services, security, or whatever else threatens more acute disorder.

Only the most extreme forms of disorder resemble Thucydidean *stasis* or Hobbes' state of nature where almost everyone's life and property is at risk. Disorder is unquestionably the opposite of order, but both are best understood as Weberian ideal types. In practice, order is never fully achieved, and neither is total disorder. Almost all societies are found along a continuum between these polar opposites. Shifts in position in both directions are common, but rarely push societies toward either extreme.

Process vs. Structure

Change is a feature of the world and stability in the social world is always a fiction, although a useful, perhaps essential, one for everyday life. Stability promotes emotional well-being as change is often regarded as frightening. It facilitates social relations by making behavior more predictable. The concern for stability may be greatest with regard to the self. For many reasons, we delude ourselves into believing that we are unitary and consistent selves despite all the evidence to the contrary.[56] We are, of course, surprised, sometimes shocked, and exaggerate the extent of change when we confront it – and all the more so when we have previously denied it or its possibility. In the aftermath of 9/11 many talking heads insisted that we were living in a new world.

Social science must free itself of the stability bias and become more engaged with the problem of change. Theories of process are an important step in this direction because they are founded on the expectation of change and seek to describe the mechanisms and processes that make it possible. In the hard sciences, evolution is the quintessential example of such a theory. In *A Cultural Theory of International Relations*, I offer a two-fold justification for the superiority of this approach.[57] Systemic theories do not allow their structures to vary because they would lose their alleged explanatory value. However, by holding them constant they make it difficult, if not impossible, to study change. At best, they recognize multiple equilibria (e.g. unipolar, bipolar, multipolar) and the possibility of phase transitions between these states.

The second justification is the importance of context. Systemic theories employ a few variables at most and, of necessity, downplay or ignore learning, confluence, agency, and accident. They aim to make predictions. Process theories are at best starting points for explanatory narratives or future-oriented forecasts. They rest on the assumption that the world is complex, open-ended, and non-linear, and that most important outcomes are context dependent. Consider the balance of power in international relations. Balances sometimes form in timely ways against aggressive states. But balancing is not infrequently directed against states whose leaders harbor no threatening intentions. Balancing can preserve the peace, but can be a cause of war, as it was in 1914, or a source of tension, as it was during the Cold War.[58] Whether balances form and what effects they have can only be understood in context.

In contrast to structural theories, those that emphasize process leave room for and indeed foreground the importance of agency. The importance scholars place on it, I argue below, also varies as a function of their understanding of order as natural or artifice.

Agency

I follow Aristotle in believing that order is natural in the sense that human beings require it to lead secure, productive, and happy lives. But all orders are artifacts because they are human creations. This is why they vary so enormously in almost any dimension we choose for purposes of comparison. Across the ages, philosophers have nevertheless sought to naturalize orders.[59] In his *Timaeus*, Plato describes order as the product of a demiurge who arranges pre-existing matter in accord with eternal and unchanging forms.[60] In his *Republic*, he constructs what he believes to be a just kind of order, one that takes advantage of the differing capabilities of people. The Christians followed Plato's approach. Augustine described order as a God-given pattern that arranged discrepant parts to promote a desired result; "the disposition of equal and unequal things" was arranged "in such a way as to give each its proper place."[61] Order for Augustine is hierarchical and based on the differences between animals and people and differing capabilities among people. Order is not natural for human beings since their fall from grace, and must be imposed and maintained by secular and religious authorities.

In the thirteenth and fourteenth century nominalist philosophers criticized the Augustinian synthesis of Greek and Jewish thought on the grounds that it imposed limits on God's freedom and omnipotence. William of Ockham rejected the relational pattern of order in favor of a contingent one. He insisted that all created things are singular, existing

apart from other things and knowledge about them is acquired by observation of their external relationships, not by deductive inference.[62]
Ockham initiated a shift away from the conception of order as imposed
to one in which it was, if not arbitrary, at least indeterminate, and outside
of any general rules or laws.[63]

These differing perspectives are reflected in the Hobbesian and
Grotian approaches to order, which are foundational to contemporary
understandings.[64] Hobbes follows Ockham and believes human beings
create their own orders; government is therefore an "artificial animal."
Being man-made and thus imperfect, orders are by definition precarious.[65] Grotius believes in God's rational nature and omnipotence. The
natural and social worlds are not the product of chance, but of necessity, and God is the first, efficient, and final cause of everything. Grotius
describes political orders as part of a greater whole; hierarchy is rational
and purposeful, and reveals the law of unity, which we call God. It has
the potential to be enduring.[66] For Hobbes, order is constructed; for
Grotius, it is discovered.

These conceptions embed different conceptions of agency. For
Christians and Grotius, agency must be informed by higher purpose, but
also constrained and channeled by authority and hierarchy. For Hobbes,
human agency answers to no higher law or purpose and is the source of
all hierarchies and orders. It needs to be controlled and limited because
people are notoriously incapable of disciplining themselves. Hobbes
turns to the Leviathan and force to maintain order, as do the realists who
claim to be his intellectual descendants. Locke and liberals rely more on
institutions and the positive incentives they provide for conforming to
norms. Realists and liberals alike emphasize agency and attribute order
and disorder to it. Despite these philosophical origins, modern social
science is deeply troubled by agency and, I contend, has done its best to
define it away. In doing so, it has also come close to re-naturalizing order.

Agency means the independence of actors, but within the confines
of social and psychological constraints.[67] Social scientists give the
appearance of valuing agency because they locate so many of their theories and models at the individual level of analysis. Most, however,
deny any real agency to actors. They are treated as interchangeable, and
moved, not by their goals and subjective understandings of their environments, but by assumed goals and so-called objective constraints and
opportunities that their environment generates. They are conceived of as
instrumentally rational, and therefore capable, given adequate information, of judging environmental incentives accurately – i.e. the same way
the analysts do. They are less like people and more like non-reflexive
and interchangeable electrons that transmit electrical charges. To give

actors agency would make parsimonious theories and models impossible because of the variation this would, of necessity, introduce.

Social scientists characterize orders as structures. This framing enables their naturalization without this transformation ever being acknowledged. These so-called structures are often assumed to have equilibria to which they will return unless deviations from it are dramatic enough to produce new equilibria. In Chapter 2 I acknowledge that equilibrium is a feature of many physical and biological systems, but insist that it is not a property of social orders. In social and political worlds, equilibria are products of theory and find little empirical support. Many theorists nevertheless treat structures as semi-natural, as do realists with the balance of power, and economists and philosophical realists with markets. Friedrich Hayek coined a now-famous distinction between the "command economy" (socialism) and the "market economy" (capitalism). The former, he asserted, was based on *taxis*, an artificial, man-made, discretionary, and coercive order. The latter was an example of *kosmos*, or "natural" order, as the market emerges as an evolutionary outcome from forces beyond human design or control and about which our understanding is, by definition, limited.[68] This alleged distinction is ideology, not science. Hayek, his numerous acolytes, and social scientists more generally, ignore the extent to which any of the so-called structures that they study are demonstrably artifice; they function differently, or not at all, in different cultures or epochs.

Orders are naturalized by the claim that the structures in question are the only "rational" responses to systemic conditions. This is another questionable move. When a degree of convergence is observable – which it is decidedly not in the case of balancing – structural theorists almost invariably misattribute its causes. Liberal capitalism is arguably attributable as much to external political pressure on occupied and developing countries and imitation as it is to so-called system pressures. Indeed, there is much economic behavior seemingly at odds with market imperatives that is rewarded rather than punished because of institutional structures, political influence, and beliefs.

Consider laissez-faire capitalism. In *Forbidden Fruit* I use a counterfactual to demonstrate that the allied victory in World War I was highly contingent. Had the United States not intervened, and the Central Powers won, much of Europe, and Japan as well, would have had authoritarian, corporatist variants of capitalism, and there is no reason to regard them as any less efficient or open to innovation. Had World War I been averted – an equally compelling counterfactual in my view – and Europe developed peacefully somewhat along the lines it did in the post-World War II era, we would have developed a different set of ideas about the kinds of domestic and international structures that were the most rational, that is best suited to our world.[69] Dominant institutions and practices are the products of highly contingent developments and we must resist the temptation to see them as all but inevitable and thereby to naturalize them.

My approach is nevertheless Hobbesian in its emphasis on artifice and imperfection. I take agency seriously and address it in a meaningful way. As a general rule, elites that exercise self-restraint are likely to forestall decline, and may even strengthen their orders under trying circumstances. In Europe, the Great Depression destroyed democratic governments in Austria and Germany, and severely weakened democracy in France. Britain muddled through, and democracy emerged stronger in the United States.[70] Agency was decisive in Germany, Austria, and the United States. In Germany, appallingly bad decisions by Hindenburg, business leaders, bureaucrats, the communist party, and the Prussian police allowed Hitler to become chancellor and illegally consolidate power.[71] In the United States, Roosevelt's radio appeals to voters, successful coalition building, and a comprehensive legislative program sustained hope and faith in the political system.[72] Agency is equally important at the micro-level. Scott Straus documents the great variation in violence against Tutsis across locales in Rwanda. He attributes it to the intervention or passivity of local leaders. When leaders intervened early to forestall or stop violence, Tutsis survived, although some towns were later overrun by more powerful outside forces intent on genocide.[73] Chapter 6 makes the case for agency at both levels being decisive in the survival and evolution of regimes more generally.

Successful orders depend on the *phronēsis* (practical wisdom) of key political actors, and in democracies, of the *dēmos* as well. Aristotle defines *phronēsis* as a sophisticated understanding of what goals are beneficial and realistic and what means are appropriate to achieving them. Reason helps to build *phronēsis*, but not when it generates simplistic epistemologies and framings of the world (e.g. autonomous, rational actors, *homo economicus*), and overvaluation of so-called structures (e.g. the balance of power, the market, equilibrium) for understanding and addressing complex social problems. Instrumental reason, uneducated and unchecked by appropriate role models and norms leads people to selfish, short-term formulations of interest. Discourses can legitimize and facilitate this phenomenon. James Kwak shows how the hold over policymakers of "primitive notions" of economics is the product of decades- long campaigns by business leaders and think tanks to convert politicians to simplistic, libertarian views of the economy.[74]

My assumption of disorder at the top-down level as the default condition of humanity is a pessimistic one. I believe this attitude is warranted, especially in the modern era. Regime turnover and collapse has been high in the modern era, often accompanied by considerable violence. Political theorists and political scientists since Hobbes and Machiavelli have recognized that the creation and maintenance of order is more difficult than in the past, and that its breakdown may be more disruptive and have a higher cost in lives.[75] Max Weber, for one, thought order more difficult to maintain at top-down and bottom-up levels because the gods had gone over the horizon. The *Entzauberung* (demystification) of the world undercut the legitimacy of any ordering principle and the bureaucratization of society was confining humans in a steel-hardened cage. People were more discontent and less able to agree about alternatives.[76]

John Mueller, Joshua Goldstein, and Steven Pinker are among those who make the opposite case; they insist that war, or violence more generally, has declined in the modern era.[77] The modern state's monopoly of force has led, in some contexts, to declining rates of violent death and the number, although not the casualties, of interstate wars have declined over the last four centuries. Political risks also vary across levels of complexity. The claim that the level of violence has decreased in the modern world has become conventional wisdom, but there are many reasons for responding with caution.

Steven Pinker, the most prominent spokesperson for the decline of violence school, relies on statistics that ignore deaths from war-related disease, malnutrition, and migration, and discounts as irrational the possibility that an event like the Cuban missile crisis could lead to a catastrophic nuclear war.[78] We must also consider – which Pinker does not – the many more millions of lives that were shortened and made painful to unbearable by state terror. The long-term decline in violence, to the extent there is one, is largely due to the rise of the territorial state and its near monopoly of the means of violence over its territory. While reducing interpersonal and group violence, it has enabled organized violence on a new scale, as witnessed by Leopold II's colonization of the Congo; Stalin's collectivization and purges; Hitler's genocide; Mao Zedong's Great Leap Forward and the resulting famine; and Pol Pot's genocide. Stalin, Hitler, and Mao alone are estimated to have been responsible for the deaths of some 100 million people.[79] Like claims of a Democratic Peace, those for a decline in violence rest on self-serving assumptions and selective use of data.

Pessimism does not mean that we should abandon hope and adopt a Stoic attitude to life. In John le Carré's *A Small Town in Germany*, a British diplomat describes his lifetime mission as forestalling chaos. "Every night, as I go to sleep, I say to myself: another day achieved, another day added to the unnatural life of a world on its deathbed. And if I never relax, if I never lift my eye, we may run on for another hundred years."[80] We should all have similar aims. Pessimistic optimism of this kind seeks to maintain what benefits society offers and make incremental improvements in it whenever possible. I firmly believe that such minimalism is likely to be more effective in the long run than efforts to introduce or impose far-reaching reforms based on abstract formulations and what is often unwarranted optimism. Albert Hirschman makes a similar point. He contends that structural views of progress encourage pessimism and discount anything but comprehensive and integrated solutions to problems.[81] Minimalist strategies, by contrast, are likely to be more effective than efforts to introduce or impose far-reaching reforms based on what is often unwarranted optimism.

Objections

The most frequently voiced criticism of my multi-volume project is not epistemological or empirical but cultural. Some critics fault me for making universal claims based on an entirely western conception. I acknowledge this cultural provenance but do not see it as limiting for two reasons. The Greek understanding of human nature, like many modern concepts (e.g. kinship, anxiety, markets) has universal applications. How human needs, drives, and emotions find expression are, of course, a function of cultural and temporal contexts. The Greek formulation is only a starting point for analyses that must go on to assess the relative importance societies place on appetite and *thumos* and how they attempt to channel and restrain them. Comparative analysis of this kind is not only feasible but also productive.

The understandings Thucydides, Plato and Aristotle have of order are not unique to the Greeks. My *Tragic Vision of Politics* describes striking similarities across cultures. Greek, Jewish, Confucian, and Muslim philosophers consider empathy and friendship foundational to order at every level of social aggregation.[82] Recent work on classical Chinese thought and Ming Dynasty China finds similarities with ancient Greeks. Confucians, like classical Greek thinkers, thought human nature only took on character in context and that the cultural order precedes the political one. Confucians also believed that people outside society, or those who conceived of themselves as autonomous actors, were more like animals than human beings, and a danger to themselves and everyone around them. Echoing Aristotle, Confucians recognized the importance of instrumental reason, but believed that successful behavior and policies also "involve commitment, empathy, affection, mutual support, and human obligations."[83]

Feng Zhang tells us that Ming emperors deployed an instrumentalist strategy of hegemony to achieve desired ends. Less frequently, they practiced what he calls "expressive hegemony." It rested on Confucian principles of propriety, and sought to establish ethical relationships from which all parties benefitted. Such strategies were more likely to be adopted under conditions of relational amity. When it prevailed, China was honored by its neighbors and provided practical benefits (i.e. trade and security) to them in return.[84] This kind of clientelist relationship is a direct parallel to the Greek ideal of *hēgemonia*.[85] Shogo Suzuki contends that something similar featured in Japanese political thought and practice.[86]

David Kang maintains that Confucian clientelist practices account for the glaring discrepancy in the frequency of war between the European and East Asian regional systems. From 1368 to 1841 – from the onset of the tributary system to the Sino-British Opium War – there were only two wars involving China, Korea, and Japan. The three countries on the whole maintained peaceful and friendly relations that ensured regional stability in the face of significant power shifts. The key to peace was the unquestioned cultural dominance of China and its reluctance to expand territorially at the expense of its "civilized" neighbors. Other political units accepted China's primacy and sought to benefit from it culturally and economically. Korean, Vietnamese, and Japanese elites copied Chinese institutional, linguistic, and cultural practices, which in turn facilitated closer and more productive relations with China.[87] In this volume, I engage Asia directly with a case study of China, co-authored with China and comparative politics scholar Martin Dimitrov. We make the case for the universal applicability of core concepts of my theory of political order, so long as they are applied with appropriate sensitivity to context.

Equality

Let us return to stability of orders and their hierarchies. I want to flag the destabilizing consequences of the dramatic increase of inequality in an era of equality. Beginning in the eighteenth century, equality began to challenge fairness as the appropriate principle of distributive justice. It found expression in the political arena with demands for political representation and universal franchise. In England, it also focused on the dissolution of "rotten boroughs," districts where a handful of electors, bound to the local lord, returned members of Parliament. Dreams of primitive socialism stretch far back in history, but Adam Smith was the first modern philosopher to evaluate property rights in terms of distributive justice. He thought it immoral that some people should live in luxury and others in poverty. There is nothing "natural," he insisted, about the uneven distribution of goods of all kinds because the difference in talents among men is much less than commonly supposed. He made the condition of the least wealthy the benchmark for assessing the success of any society.[88]

Concern for equality, in either the distribution of wealth or equal access to opportunities that lead to it, dominates contemporary philosophy.[89] Newspaper and TV commentary in America and Europe is filled with discussions of growing inequality and its likely political consequences. These are, of course, liberal-humanitarian voices. There is a counter-discourse that maintains that inequality is inescapable and that we should not be dismayed by the existence of a Gini coefficient – the accepted measure of inequality among values of a frequency distribution. It is almost entirely driven by how rich the wealthy are; if everyone's income doubled, the gap between the rich and poor would increase considerably. For this reason, Deidre McCloskey is upbeat about the future in a well-received book.[90] Rather than making comparisons between rich and poor, she argues, we should ask if those at the bottom are better off than they were fifty and 100 years ago. McCloskey argues that what counts is absolute, not relative, wealth. This is typical of an economist, but curiously out of place in a book that stresses the importance of what people believe.

There is abundant evidence that both kinds of wealth matter, and that relative wealth more so when people leave poverty behind. Air rage provides a compelling example. It is four times higher in the coach section of an aircraft with a first-class cabin than in a plane without one. It is twice as likely if economy passengers board at the front and have to walk through the first-class section to their smaller, cramped seats. First-class passengers in turn are several times more likely to succumb to air rage if they have to mix with economy passengers before or during the boarding process.[91] Wealth confers status and both are relative in the minds of most people.

I muster survey and experimental evidence in Chapter 6 to show that Europeans and Americans are drawn to both fairness and equality. They believe that people should be rewarded proportionately to their contribution to society, but that the current distribution of rewards is unfair and should be made more equal. Equality has undeniably become the dominant principle of justice in the western world, prompting a greater concern – contrary to the argument of McCloskey – on relative versus absolute wealth. Public opinion polls indicate that in countries where disease and religious and ethnic violence are not immediate concerns, people feel most threatened by inequality.[92] People become positively enraged by what they consider to be gross and undeserved inequalities in income. A recent defining moment in Britain was the discovery in 2017 that Bath University's vice-chancellor was paid over £468,000 plus benefits, and received a substantial increase when staff salaries were frozen or even reduced. The head of Bath's Unite union complained: "There are porters at this university who get paid less in a year than she got in her last pay rise." Student and staff protests forced her resignation.[93]

Adam Smith would be dismayed by recent developments in the United States. Inequality was high between the World Wars and fell to all-time lows after 1945. It began growing again in about 1980. Today, the percentage of income going to the richest 1 percent of the population has increased almost tenfold in the United States since 1945.[94] In 2012, the net worth of the 400 wealthiest Americans exceeded that of the bottom half of all Americans.[95] Research indicates that economic gains for the rich have resulted in losses for the middle class and that the latter spends beyond its means to imitate the lifestyle of the wealthy.[96] Studies find that rich Americans live fifteen years longer on average than poorer peers in their age cohort.[97] Differences in wealth and health are becoming self-perpetuating as upward mobility declines. In recent years, public colleges have lost most of the funding from states, and with it the ability to offer financial aid to students from poorer backgrounds. These institutions of higher learning are no longer a vehicle of upward mobility for the underprivileged. The percentage of students receiving Pell Grants – which typically go to those in the bottom half of the income distribution – fell from 24.3 to 21.8 percent in 2011–12. At top private universities and colleges it has held constant at 16 percent, but these institutions educate a relatively smaller percentage of students.[98]

The country is not only divided between rich and poor, but between educated and uneducated, healthy and obese, secular and religious, liberals and conservatives, immigrant and anti-immigrant, and gun-toting and gun-opposing lobbies. Many, if not most, of these cleavages are reinforcing. Two distinct cultures are emerging, characterized by different, and arguably incompatible, beliefs, values, and expectations. This division is an underlying cause of the striking polarization of American politics that became pronounced in the 1980s and more so during and after the 2016 presidential election.[99]

The building strength of partisan antipathy – "negative partisanship" – has radically altered politics. As partisan affect has intensified, it is also more structured; in-group favoritism is increasingly associated with out-group animus. Hostility toward the opposing party has eclipsed positive affect for one's own party as a motive for political participation.[100] Anger has become the primary tool for motivating voters. Ticket splitting is dying out. But perhaps the most important consequence of the current power of political anger is that there has been a marked decline in the accountability of public officials to the electorate.[101]

This phenomenon is not unique to the United States. In Britain the gap between rich and poor has also widened. The financial, governmental, and business elite is still dominated by "old boys," but now also "old girls," of affluent backgrounds who attended the right schools and universities.[102] In 2008 the wealth of the 100 richest families in the UK increased disproportionately to the rest and is now equal to 30 percent of the country's households.[103] As in the United States, greater wealth confers many advantages, including longevity.[104] There are striking differences across postal codes, with people in the richest neighborhoods having the longest lifespans.[105] In Europe, the 10 percent paid the highest salaries earn as much as the bottom 50 percent.[106] More extreme stratification exists throughout much of the developing world.[107] In 2015 half the wealth of the globe was held by only 1 percent of its population, and the 80 richest people on the planet owned as much as the poorest 3.5 billion.[108] The gap in average lifespan between Japan and Sierra Leone is forty years, the same as that between Victorian and contemporary London.[109]

Unequal distribution of wealth is not in itself a strong enough cause of resentment to challenge orders and their legitimacy. Ever since settled agricultural societies emerged there has been a striking gap between rich and poor, and in some eras, including the first century of the industrial revolution, the gap increased noticeably.[110] The discrepancy between wealthy and poor is less important than what those who are disadvantaged think about it. This is affected in the first instance, I theorize, by the dominant principle of justice in the society. Fairness – more about this later – justifies hierarchies of status and wealth. Equality denies these hierarchies of legitimacy, or insists that they be made much flatter, and has unquestionably become the dominant principle of justice in the modern era. To legitimize hierarchies in an era of equality, elites must convince others that their privileges are based on achievement and well deserved or, as John Rawls proposes, benefit society as a whole.[111]

Also important are the ways in which status and wealth are claimed and displayed. Some forms of display are acceptable and reinforce hierarchies without alienating those on the lower rungs. They may include and reinforce the sense of community to which people of differing status belong. Chapter 7 argues that local and national festivals in Georgian England often had this effect. In many European and American cities during the nineteenth and first half of the twentieth centuries, attendance at the opera, sitting in the stalls or box seats, and bedecked in appropriate finery was a means of asserting standing but also of building community through a shared activity among diverse sections of the commercial classes. Those in the upper tiers understood and reinforced the hierarchy by their attendance and deference to the wealthy.[112] Gazes went up as well as down. In Barcelona, mistresses of the wealthy bourgeoisie seated in the balcony of the Teatre del Liceu opera were an object of interest to other attendees. The wife of one of the local grandees in a family box below is reported to have put her opera glass down and turned to her friend to report with satisfaction that her husband's mistress was more attractive than their neighbor's mistress.[113]

"In your face" exercises of power or displays of wealth that violate conventional norms are more likely to arouse ire. In what was widely read as an abuse of their wealth, David Geffen, Larry Ellison, and other California billionaires sought in the first decade of this century to close Carbon Beach in Malibu. The public was enraged and a lengthy legal and political quarrel ensued. In the end, Geffen, Ellison, and others were fined and compelled to remove the wall and other obstacles they had erected. Some of this money was used to provide a new wheelchair accessible path for the public to reach the beach.[114] In 2017 investor Martin Shkreli became the "most hated man" in America in the eyes of many. He purchased Turing Pharmaceuticals and immediately raised the price of Daraprim, a drug used to treat toxoplasmosis and HIV, from $13.50 to $750 per pill. He was subsequently arrested for an unrelated securities fraud, and lawyers found it difficult to swear in a jury because so many of the prospective jurors interviewed confessed that he was already guilty in their minds because of his outrageous attempt to exploit HIV patients.[115] This phenomenon is not restricted to the United States. In November 2016 the Chinese government faced a bitter public outcry after executing a villager who murdered an official who had illegally demolished his home on the eve of his wedding. He had become a poster child victim of abuse by unconstrained officials and courts.[116]

People can react differently to the same "provocation." In the 2016 American presidential election, Donald Trump, a billionaire real estate tycoon, made a pitch to working people whose income and status had sharply declined in the previous decade. Media revelations of his avoidance of federal taxes for perhaps two decades – by exploiting a loophole that he and the real estate industry persuaded congress to create –was only marginally damaging among these voters, while others took it as proof of his skill.[117] The same was true of his misogyny and release of a video in which he talks about groping women's genitals.[118] Trump's whitewashing of neo-Nazis and the Ku Klux Klan at the August 2017 protests in Charlottesville, by equating them with those protesting racism, provoked much wider condemnation.[119] Responses to blatant self-aggrandizement by the wealthy and powerful are culturally and contextually specific.

Generalizations about public reactions to inappropriate displays of wealth or power may have more explanatory power when linked to the mechanisms by which legitimacy is sustained or undermined. I identify two such mechanisms.

In appetite-based societies, when elites routinely violate norms and laws (e.g. cheating on their taxes), and knowledge of their behavior becomes widespread, others are tempted to emulate them. When they do, norms that sustain order are quickly eroded. One sign that this process is under way is respect for, rather than anger at, those who "cheat" big and get away with it. In honor-based societies, the competition for honor and standing within elites is intense. It encourages shortcuts and cheating. This sometimes takes the form of looking for support outside the elite, and making promises to clients that expand the arena of conflict and threaten the survival of order. In later chapters, I explore these mechanisms and the conditions that enable, amplify, or retard them. I also show how they are mediated by language, and how discourses evolve to legitimize behavior that was once unacceptable.

For the moment, I want to flag the possibility of a historic change in western societies. Wealth is opening up new realms of self-indulgence. It buys cosmetic surgery, joint replacements, organ transplants and, sometimes, queue jumping to get them sooner. Modern medicine may soon permit greatly extended longevity with bodies that age more slowly and allow longer, healthier, and more active lives. Immortality will in all probability remain an unrealized dream, but the prospect of living say to the age of 120 may well become feasible.[120] Such longevity will, in all likelihood, be available only to the rich as it will be costly every step of the way. It will be responsible for a far greater psychological divide between rich and poor than has existed until now. Those who lack the money to pay for these biological benefits will also differ from previous underclasses because they will be living in an age in which equality is the foundational principle of justice. This has already given rise to correspondingly greater resentment of inequalities, and nothing is quite so unequal as diverging lifespans between haves and have-nots. Resentment is likely to find political expression and threaten the functioning, if not the survival, of political orders including democratic ones.

For all of these reasons, it is important to develop a better understanding of the nature of order, the conditions under which it forms, and most importantly how and why it unravels and what might be done to retard or forestall stasis. Such knowledge can provide impetus and compelling justifications for political action. Any answers we find are certain to highlight the importance of principles of justice. How societies theorize justice and how actors perceive the gap between theory and practice has major implications for the legitimacy of orders and pressures for reforms or more radical changes. I took a first step in examining the relationship between justice and order in the conclusion to *National Identities and International Relations*.[121] In this book I theorize this relationship more extensively, examine its implications for domestic, regional, and international orders, and explore the ways in which changes in either justice or order can affect the other.

The robustness of orders has long been an important question in political science. Max Weber invoked the concept of legitimacy as an ideal type description of robustness. He considered some degree of legitimacy a defining condition of the modern state.[122] Bernard Crick calls it "the master variable of political science."[123] Legitimacy is commonly equated with regime support and empirically established on the basis of voting behavior or public opinion polls.[124] Like order, it nevertheless remains an "essentially contested concept," whose meaning and utility are vigorously debated.[125] The difficulty of measuring legitimacy has encouraged social scientists to rely on ex post facto determinations of legitimacy or robustness. This is a western version of the Chinese concept of the Mandate of Heaven, where the collapse of a dynasty was evidence that it had lost divine sanction. Thus nobody predicted the collapse of the German Democratic Republic or Soviet Union, but in the aftermath the consensus quickly developed that they were political systems on the edge of chaos waiting for the right catalyst to tip them over the edge.[126] Conversely, Edmund Burke feared that the British constitutional monarchy stood "on a nice equipoise" with "steep precipices, and deep waters on all sides," and too much of a tilt in any direction in pursuit of balance risked "oversetting."[127]

Why Order?

Raymond Aron wisely observed that order is both a normative and explanatory concept and is frequently used in both ways, and confusingly so.[128] To this point I have approached order from an analytical perspective and tried to define what it is and what maintains or undermines it. My analysis is nevertheless motivated by normative concerns. For most people, happiness and fulfillment – and the two are very much related – can only be achieved in society. Any society of scale – and today, they all are – must include top-down as well as multiple bottom-up orders. They function in different ways and, depending on how they function, enable or impede human fulfillment.

Naming something enables its study, and studying it not only changes how we think about it but sometimes what is does, how it performs, or in this case how it is achieved and maintained. Particularly important in this respect is the extent to which we envisage what we are naming and studying as a product of a particular context or configuration or something independent, but capable of influencing them. According to Jens Bartelson, many early modern and Enlightenment historians regarded war as a productive force and essential part of political life. It was "capable of producing substances only because it lacked a substance of its own."[129] It was accordingly always analyzed in context. This changed in the nineteenth century when, most notably through the writings of Carl von Clausewitz, war became the subject of philosophical, not just politico-historical analysis.

Something similar has happened to order. Isaiah Berlin thought western philosophy was dominated from its beginning by three questions: what is the right life, how is it discovered, and how is it achieved? Political theorists assumed that reason could answer these questions, that each had only one right answer, and that it could only be attained in an appropriately designed social-political order. Order was a goal and instrumentality, but not something, so to speak, that had an independent existence. It was not until the late nineteenth century that order was conceived of as something in its own right, with properties independent of the society in which it operated. I address both kinds of order, and tack back and forth between the two. Theorizing about order in the abstract helps to frame any inquiry of how specific orders advance or retard human goals, and more broadly about the ways in which they, and changes in them, affect their societies.

Plato and Enlightenment thinkers, Marxists, and more recent utopians like B. F. Skinner, designed political orders on the assumption that society was necessary not only to educate and discipline people but to enable them to realize their potential.[130] Greek stoics and German Romantics developed an alternative vision; they considered people ends in themselves and regarded society as a barrier to human fulfillment.[131] Romantics are in this tradition and insist we must escape social conditioning and constraints and discover ourselves by looking inwards or communing with nature.

Philosophers, political leaders, and technocrats have no privileged access to truth. Many philosophers delude themselves into believing that they can construct logically consistent and universally applicable systems of ethics. It is equally absurd, if not downright arrogant, to believe, as David Miller among others does, that philosophers can adjudicate value conflicts.[132] The same kind of arrogance characterizes social scientists, city planners, and ideologues whose efforts at large-scale social engineering ride roughshod over conflicting values and the diverse goals of the people they are trying to "improve."

More cautious and limited efforts to improve society still risk the "Oedipus effect"; they can lead to outcomes diametrically opposed to those intended. An amusing early example is a decree of Frederick II of Prussia in the 1770s aimed at improving the roads around Berlin. He ordered every peasant traveling to the capital to deposit two paving stones at a city gate. The stones were heavy to carry, so peasants waited until they were just outside Berlin and picked up previously laid stones and carried them a short distance to the gate.[133] A recent and tragic example concerns efforts to rescue Libyans fleeing their war-torn country. Rescuing migrants aboard unseaworthy craft closer to the Libyan coast saved hundreds of lives. But it produced a deadly incentive for more migrants to risk the journey and for smugglers to launch more boats. "Migrants and refugees – encouraged by the stories of those who had successfully made it in the past – attempt the dangerous crossing since they are aware of and rely on humanitarian assistance to reach the EU."[134] A 2017 House of Lords study found that naval efforts to destroy smugglers' boats encouraged them to send people to sea in even less seaworthy vessels.[135]

The Romantic project is equally illusory. People cannot find their true selves and moral compasses by looking inwards or communing with nature. Thomas Hobbes constructed his state of nature as a thought experiment to demonstrate that people removed from their roles and constraints of society are deprived of their humanity and reduced to a bundle of raw appetites guided by short-term instrumental reason.[136] Mozart and Da Ponte dramatize this social truth in their opera *Don Giovanni*. They offer the eponymous Don as the inevitable outcome of the Enlightenment project: a man liberated from external and internal restraints and, as a result, a danger to himself and everyone around him. Don Giovanni challenged the idealistic and naïve expectation that human beings will use freedom and reason to make themselves into more ethical beings. Mozart and Da Ponte suggest that reason is more likely to be directed outwards, with the goal of satisfying unconstrained and therefore more urgent appetites. It will not produce a more harmonious society, but one in which a minority effectively assert their will and exploit the majority. The winners in this struggle will not be any happier, only more driven.[137] Robert Musil offers a similar take in his *Man Without Qualities*.

The quest for inner and integrated selves is futile. Many contemporary psychologists and philosophers deny identity any ontological status. They follow David Hume in suggesting that, at best, we are "minimal" selves; we have a stream of reflections and dreams that suggest the illusion of identity.[138] In *The Politics and Ethics of Identity*, I argue that so-called identities actually consist of a large number of self-identifications that are based largely on affiliations, roles and relationship to our bodies. These self-identifications are labile, not infrequently in conflict, and rise and fall in importance as a function of context and priming.[139] The origins, character, and relative importance of self-identification are largely social. Society also defines affiliations and roles and legitimizes our performance of them. Self-fashioning is not altogether illusory, as key critical theorists and poststructuralists contend, but is severely constrained.

If order is necessary, top-down order, imposed and maintained by coercion, is not. Order of this kind has been the goal of tyrants from time immemorial. In the Middle Ages, the Catholic Church and political leaders vied for power but both envisaged it as absolute. In the 1920s and 1930s, stability was the catchword of European dictators from Portugal to Poland, keen to gain popular backing by promising that their corporatist forms of government and rule by "strongmen" would avoid the chaos of parliamentary democracy.[140] Contemporary dictators sill invoke this formula.

We cannot sacrifice order or freedom. We must find some accommodation between these two reinforcing but sometimes contradictory goals. In violation of the ground rules of philosophy, any solution must be flexible, untidy, and unstable, allow protest and negotiated change and, by definition, be logically indefensible. Society must provide enough order to protect life and property and create offices that honor achievements of all kinds. Only then can people develop the affiliations, roles, and aspirations that provide psychological stability and meaning, and make behavior to a large degree predictable. There must be sufficient freedom to allow the emergence of diverse niches that enable individual choice and some degree of self-fashioning as well as tolerance for these different choices. Johann Georg Hamann, the leading philosopher of the early nineteenth-century *Sturm und Drang* movement, proclaimed that rules were made to be broken.[141] Societies that are too ordered leave little space for autonomy and self-fashioning. With Prussia in mind, Nietzsche worried that all-controlling states do not produce rebels but conformists and a "herd mentality."[142]

Order and freedom must not be framed as binaries. Order is necessary for freedom and creativity. In the words of Emile Durkheim, freedom "is the fruit of regulation."[143] Freedom in turn can sustain or undermine order. Eighteenth- and nineteenth-century classical music provides a cogent illustration of both their interdependence and inescapable tensions.

Royals and aristocrats supported *opera seria* to assert individual standing, and more generally to legitimize their class and its right to rule. *Opera seria* celebrated the wisdom and virtues of ancient royalty and aristocrats, which it portrayed as idealized mirror images of their modern-day counterparts.[144]

The music performed for aristocratic audiences was highly structured, as were the orchestras that performed them. The circle of fifths emerged as a set of stipulated relationships among the twelve tones of the chromatic scale and their corresponding major and minor key signatures.

Franz Joseph Haydn elaborated "rules" of composition based on this system. Normality is boring because it is so predictable. Composers were accordingly encouraged to violate harmonic order in proscribed ways; they could introduce minor dissonances but had to resolve them in a finale that restored order. Haydn and his contemporaries adhered to these rules to make their music intelligible, acceptable but also enjoyable to listeners. Conventions invite violations, but the frisson of excitement they generate depends on these violations being understood as such and ultimately overcome. The eighteenth-century English music critic Charles Burney noted: "Suspension and anticipation of some sound" – presumably resolution of dissonance – provides the musical "sauce" on the "palate."[145] Philosophers, among them Burke and Rousseau, applied musical concepts like harmony and dissonance to political orders.

Mozart pushed the limits of musical conventions, but never jettisoned them because he wanted his music to be appreciated – and supported financially.[146] Most artistic genres, and many social practices, invite, even encourage, violations.

Beethoven took rebellion a giant step further and spurned most musical rules. E. T. A. Hoffmann, a contemporary composer and critic, wrote that Beethoven rejected Aristotle's notion of art as *mimesis*, or the copying nature. His review of the Ninth Symphony described it as not of this world, but an expression of genius, in the sense understood by Kant, because it made its own rules.[147] French listeners in the early 1800s were not alone in finding Beethoven unapproachable. To their ears his symphonies were filled with barbaric chords, and had no meaning because they were outside existing aesthetic categories.[148] Austrian and German audiences struggled even more with Beethoven's late quartets.[149] Ironically, Beethoven, the Enlightenment freethinker and rebel, was posthumously made into a German nationalist and his music lauded as a triumph of German culture.[150] His creative rebellion was "normalized," and other Romantics emulated him. Those who succeeded, like Brahms, became respected establishment figures, a status with which he was never fully comfortable.

Classical music was transformed in the process. Performances of *opera seria* were social events, and the elite came to see and be seen. They ate and talked through the performance. The largely aristocratic audience was more important than the common folk who wrote and performed the music. Nineteenth-century music was more the preserve of the bourgeoisie, who, like aristocrats before them, went to concert halls to be seen, but also to listen – to music, not to one another. Attendance at concerts and theater helped to strengthen class and cultural identities. In France, the public – those who attended events of this kind – became regarded as the "nation," a social construct intended to challenge the power and authority of the king.[151]

The bourgeoisie considered silence a sign of politeness and noise a mark of social inferiority.[152] Concert halls became secular temples where creative genius could be worshipped and the *Bildungsbürgertum* (middle-class intellectuals) claim status through participation in this ritual. The first public opera house, built by Frederick the II in 1741–42, in Palladian style, evokes a classical temple. This style of architecture, widely copied elsewhere for opera houses and concert halls, became increasingly para-doxical as the music performed there became Romantic and, a century later, atonal and modern. The readily understood order of these buildings and their message of hierarchy and social unity were increasingly at odds with the individual expression and the profound subjectivity of the music being performed within.[153] So-called classical music, which began as a prop of the political and social order, had evolved to challenge it. Not surprisingly, some modern composers (e.g. Mahler, Berg, Stravinsky, Schoenberg, Prokofiev, Shostakovich) met fierce resistance from bour-geois audiences and communist critics and governments. Supporters of atonal music, like Theodor Adorno, welcomed this disintegration and hoped it would hasten the process in the wider society.[154] In retrospect, it is apparent that both sides greatly exaggerated the political significance of modern classical music.

Art can speak to us directly, that is unmediated by words.[155] Nietzsche thought music superior to literature for this reason.[156] However, music, like any art form or social practice, is better understood – sometimes, only understood – with reference to well-known conventions. They leave considerable leeway for interpretation. Joseph II, Emperor of Austria, personally directed Vienna's Burgtheater, where Mozart and Da Ponte's *Marriage of Figaro* premiered. He had no objection to its contents, only to its length. By contrast, when Napoleon heard the opera in Paris, he was thunderstruck and is alleged to have exclaimed: *"C'est déja la révolution en action* (It's already the Revolution in practice)."[157] These different readings indicate the extent to which order *and* its violation are in the eyes of the beholder, and even in circumstances where the genre and its conventions are well understood.[158]

In *Politics and Ethics of Identity* I argue that one of the most important and hard-won forms of freedom is self-fashioning and the reflection and role playing it entails. I further maintain that much role playing is directly associated with or inspired by the arts.[159] Remaking ourselves, or merely experimenting with other possible political, economic, religious, intellectual, social, and sexual selves, is a powerful source of insight, self-validation and fulfillment in the modern world. There can be little doubt that the composers who discovered or asserted themselves by violating or rejecting musical conventions were engaging in productive self-fashioning. In the early nineteenth century, Romantic writers and philosophers, often taking their cue from Rousseau and Beethoven, argued that self-fashioning was both feasible and everyone's responsibility.

Self-fashioning brings us full circle to Plato and the analogy he draws between personal and social orders. He insists that they are not only subject to the same typology and dynamics, but deeply influence one another.[160] Order or disorder at the individual or social level has important consequences for order at the other level, and for regional and international societies as well.[161] In the modern era, individual order was initially conceived along roughly similar lines: in terms of self-restraint and self-control, and gaining respect and self-confidence by conforming to the social code. This understanding is evident in Jane Austen novels, which depict individuals who find themselves enmeshed in society but unlike their ancient Greek counterparts alienated from it.[162]

In *Politics and Ethics of Identity* I argue that the strengthening of interiority and the proliferation of rules intensified alienation and prompted a new and increasingly important concern with identity.[163] Identity was the vehicle to make the self whole again, and in some formulations provides ethical and social guidance. I identify four generic identity projects, two of them anti-modern in the sense that they attempt to do away as far as possible with interiority and reflexivity, or make it mirror the social self. In Mead's language, they attempt to prevent an "I" from emerging, or make it a mirror image of the "Me." Both strategies condemn self-fashioning. The two modern strategies vaunt interiority and reflexivity and encourage people to become themselves through self-fashioning. The Anglo-American liberal strategy believes that society stimulates self-fashioning by making diverse role models available. People can emulate or mix and match and in turn become role models for others. The Romantic, continental strategy condemns society as autocratic and inimical to individuality and encourages people to discover themselves by going outside of it and looking within or communing with nature.[164] To the degree it is associated with a political project it is anarchism.

These four identity strategies can also be characterized with respect to their take on freedom and authority. The two traditional approaches attempt to limit or prevent individual freedom by limiting the inner self or making its contents uniform across people and supportive as far as possible of the externally imposed social self. The two modern approaches value freedom over authority. The liberal strategy assumes they are to some degree compatible, and that authority and the order it creates enable freedom. The Romantic strategy, like its anti-modern counterparts, regards freedom and authority as unalterably opposed.

The four strategies of identity construction all find adherents in the modern world, but all are deeply problematic. Religious fundamentalism of all kinds attempts to restrict interiority and self-fashioning and impose a rigid set of beliefs and practices on adherents. Fundamentalists have created tight-knit communities in which members are told what to think, how to dress and behave and encouraged to commit their lives and resources to movement goals. They have grown in scope and influence because of their promise of escape from anomie. But they are the ultimate expression of what Nietzsche called the "herd mentality," and are limited in their appeal to certain situations and personality types.

Totalitarianism and fundamentalism are parallel projects, and by their nature intolerant of dissent. They appeal to people anxious to forego their autonomy for whatever reason and often pressure others to accept their values and practices. Orthodox Marxist efforts to substitute collective for individual identities have largely failed. The Soviet Union collapsed, and Communist China and Vietnam have evolved into different kinds of political units. North Korea is the only regime still committed to a totalitarian form of identity construction and it is widely regarded as unstable. In few other countries could a high-ranking official be executed by anti-aircraft fire for falling asleep during a talk by the leader.[165]

Identity strategy three, the liberal strategy, is in my view the most realistic one because it alone does not aim to overcome the tension between reflexive and social selves, only to reduce it. However, it unreasonably assumes that society will become open and accessible to all, that positive role models will proliferate and be recognized as such, and that people will have the desire, psychological resources and external freedom to exploit these role models and mix and match from them to create their own identities. Marxists and postmodernists have a ready rejoinder: people emulate role models for the wrong reasons, largely in response to advertising, peer group pressure and other powerful social cues. Contrary to liberal expectations, western societies offer narrower rather than expanded role models, and as Marx and Georg Lukács warned, they are increasingly constructed around commodities.[166]

French Marxist Louis Althusser argues that the modern state recognizes the individual as the source of initiatives and responsibility. Society nevertheless maintains order and coherence by positioning individuals within political, social and economic categories, and by policing these statuses. The modern state accordingly encourages autonomy while imposing subjection.[167] The contemporary literature in philosophy and psychology also emphasizes the social side of the equation.[168] Typical is the claim of Kenneth Gergen that free will and self-fashioning are highly constrained by linguistic and social practices. They socialize individuals to acceptable conceptions of self.[169]

All four strategies create novel opportunities and challenges for political orders. The two anti-modern strategies, with their emphasis on doing away with, or minimizing, interiority, encourage totalitarian orders.

Political systems of this orientation are likely to fail because they alienate people who opt for modern identity strategies and, more importantly, because top-down, bureaucratic management of the economy, education, and other domains is grossly inefficient. Anti-modern strategies work best in small groups that are alienated from the broader society, as the Separating Puritans were in the seventeenth century and many millennial Christian sects are today. Prior to the English Revolutions, Puritans had to emigrate to find the political space to practice and impose their orthodoxy, and did not survive for long because of internal dissent and rebellion. Modern-day sects build solidarity on their differences from the rest of society and their knowledge that the world as we know it is soon going to end.[170]

The two modern strategies are the products of the Enlightenment and Counter-Enlightenment. Strategy three requires a liberal democratic political system with a robust civil society. That society must offer diverse role models, encourage self-fashioning, social experimentation, and welcome the diverse identities that result. This puts a premium on diversity and tolerance, which is difficult to achieve and maintain. Even when it exists, Marxists and postmodernists rightly note that most people emulate role models for the wrong reasons: largely in response to advertising, peer group pressure, and other social cues.[171] Cable and satellite TV have allowed hundreds of channels to proliferate, but in the United States especially there is a restricted range of programming as most channels carry the same content. The role models society offers may have narrowed rather than expanding. If so, socialization and commercialization make a mockery of autonomy, leaving meaningful freedom available only to a relatively small, well-educated and resource-rich elite – and there is little evidence that such people are any less entrapped by consumer tastes than their less affluent peers.

Strategy four, the Romantic-anarchic project, identifies society as the enemy, and encourages alienation and resistance, which is hardly a recipe for legitimacy and solidarity. This strategy also encourages the proliferation of counter-cultures held together by members' disdain for the dominant culture and what it considers the self-delusion of more contented citizens. If anything it is more of a threat to any political order than the liberal strategy. Due to the modern concern – some might say, fixation – on identity, contemporary political orders face challenges that their predecessors did not. In addition to providing some degree of security necessary for people to get on with their ordinary lives, they must cater to an additional, and powerful, set of psychological needs. And for three of the four identity strategies – the two anti-modern and the Romantic – these needs can only be fulfilled at the expense of the broader society and order. I return to these four strategies in the conclusion, where I explore the implications of the value shifts I document for them and political order more generally.

Notes

1 Shakespeare, *Troilus and Cressida*, Act 1.84–100.
2 See also Elster, *Cement of Society*; McKinlay and Little, *Global Problems and World Order*; Falk, *End of World Order*; Kratochwil, *International Order and Foreign Policy*.
3 Pengalese, "Bastard Child of the Dictatorship"; Arias and Rodrigues, "Myth of Personal Security"; Hechter and Kabiri, "Attaining Social Order in Iraq."
4 Pengalese, "Bastard Child of the Dictatorship"; Arias and Rodrigues, "Myth of Personal Security."
5 Andres Schipani and Joe Leahy, "Rio's born-again bandits prey on rivals," *Financial Times*, October 28 2017, p. 7.
6 Max Fisher Amanda Taub, and Dalia Martínez, "Losing Faith in the State, Some Mexican Towns Quietly Break Away," *New York Times*, January 7 2018, www.nytimes.com/2018/01/07/world/americas/mexico-state-corruption .html (accessed March 3 2018).
7 Lewis, *Convention*, for this now-famous example.
8 Rosenau, "Governance, Order, and Change in World Politics."
9 One of the reasons the German army was so effective in both world wars in comparison to its adversaries was its pioneering use of novel strategies and tactics and the greater degree of freedom given to non-commissioned officers. Herwig, "Dynamics of Necessity"; Samuels, *Command or Control?*; Bull, *German Assault Troops of the First World War*; Audoin-Ruzeau, "Combat and Tactics."
10 Personal experience of the author; Douglas J. MacEachin, "US Intelligence and the Polish Crisis," Central Intelligence Agency, 2007, www.cia.gov/ library/center-for-the-study-of-intelligence/csi-publications/books-and-monographs/us-intelligence-and-the-polish-crisis-1980–1981/index.htm (March 27 2018); Mastny, "Soviet Non-Invasion of Poland in 1980/81 and the End of the Cold War."

11 Diane Taylor, "Judge condemns Amber Rudd for ignoring orders to release torture victim," *Guardian*, August 23 2017, www.theguardian.com/uk-news/2017/aug/23/judge-amber-rudd-orders-torture-victim-asylum-seeker-detention (accessed October 21 2017).

12 Charles Falconer, "If Amber Rudd can't explain why she defied the courts, she should go," *Guardian*, September 19 2017, www.theguardian.com/commentisfree/2017/sep/19/home-secretary-courts-amber-rudd-deport-samim-bigzad (accessed October 21 2017).

13 Amelia Gentleman, Whistleblowers contradict No 10 over destroyed Windrush landing cards," *Guardian*, 17 April 2018, www.theguardian.com/uk-news/2018/apr/18/whistleblowers-contradict-no-10-over-destroyed-windrush-landing-cards, and "Home Office destroyed Windrush landing cards, says ex-staffer," *Guardian*, 17 April 2018, www.theguardian.com/uk-news/2018/apr/17/home-office-destroyed-windrush-landing-cards-says-ex-staffer (both accessed 18 April 2018).

14 Kafka, *Castle*. Also, Wilson, *Bureaucracy*, who argues that bureaucracies are inefficient because of their rules and procedures, constraints, incentives, culture, and values.

15 Machiavelli, *Discourses on Livy*, book 1, ch. 2.

16 Ibid., book 1, ch. 4.

17 Ibid., book 3, ch. 1.

18 The opening lines of my Shakespeare quote at the outset of this chapter have a strong resemblance to the Elizabethan homily "On Order and Obedience." It is part of the 1547 *Book of Homilies*, which was required reading in Anglican churches. Some of the parallel lines from the homily include: "Almighty God hath created and appointed all things, in heaven, earth and waters, in a most excellent and perfect order ... And man himself also hath all his parts both within and without ... in a profitable, necessary and pleasant order. Every degree of people, in their vocation, calling and office, hath appointed to them their duty and order." Shakespeare was undeniably familiar with the homily, and it may have been in his mind when writing *Troilus and Cressida*.

19 Shakespeare, *Troilus and Cressida*, I, iii, II.113–14.

20 Montesquieu, while modern in other ways, represents a continuation of the stability tradition. He argued that change and variability in the law was more dangerous than lack of reform.

21 Machiavelli, *Discourses on Livy*, book 1, ch. 3.

22 Deutsch, *Nerves of Government*, chs. 11–13.

23 "Business titan who shook the corporate pillars of Japan," *Financial Times*, October 27 2017, p. 8.

24 Lebow, *Avoiding War, Making Peace*, chs. 2–5 for examples.

25 Perrow, *Normal Accidents*.

26 Lebow, *Unfinished Utopia*, for how this worked in Stalinist Poland.

27 Perrow, *Normal Accidents*, pp. 15–31; Clements, "Three Mile Island Unit 2"; OECD, Nuclear Regulatory Agency, "Chernobyl: Executive Summary," 2008, www.oecd-nea.org/rp/chernobyl/c0e.html (accessed October 23 2017).

28 Perrow, *Normal Accidents*, pp. 15–31.

29 Lebow, *Nuclear Crisis Management*.

30 *Numbers*, 32:13.

31 Aitlin Dickerson and Louis Ferré-Sadurní, "'Like Going Back in Time':
   Puerto Ricans Put Survival Skills to Use," *New York Times*, October 24
   2017, www.nytimes.com/2017/10/24/us/hurricane-maria-puerto-rico-coping
   .html?hp&action=click&pgtype=Homepage&clickSource=story-heading
   &module=photo-spot-region&region=top-news&WT.nav=top-news&_r=0
   (accessed October 24 2017).
32 Beresin, *Recess Battles.*
33 Bohmer, *Designing Care*, p. 4.
34 Interview with Richard Bohmer, August 24 2017.
35 Robin Wang, "Yinyang (Yin-yang)," *Internet Encyclopedia of Philosophy*, www
   .iep.utm.edu/yinyang/ (accessed August 30 2017).
36 Perrow, *Normal Accidents.*
37 Scott, *Against the Grain*, pp. 116–49.
38 Barzini, *Italians*, pp. 190–91.
39 Bohmer, *Designing Care*, p. 151.
40 Tucker and Edmonson, "Why Hospitals Don't Learn from Their Failures."
41 Georgina Gould, "Should doctors use WhatsApp to bypass archaic NHS
   tech?" *Guardian*, June 5 2017, www.theguardian.com/healthcare-network/
   views-from-the-nhs-frontline/2017/jun/05/should-doctors-use-whatsapp-to-
   bypass-archaic-nhs-tech (accessed January 5 2018).
42 Bohmer, *Designing Care*, pp. 151–76.
43 Alison Teal, "I'm defying the council I serve on to stop it felling trees,"
   Guardian, June 29 2017, www.theguardian.com/commentisfree/2017/jun/
   29/sheffield-council-threat-not-deter-anti-tree-felling-campaign (accessed
   October 24 2017); Matt Watts, "Council blasted over £78,000 deal to destroy protected trees," *Evening Standard*, September 2 2014, www.standard
   .co.uk/news/london/council-blasted-over-78000-deal-to-destroy-protected-
   trees-9705902.html (accessed October 24 2017); Victoria Allen, "Tooting
   chainsaw massacre: Stretch of 51 horse chestnuts that stood for 140 years
   are felled after council decided trees were a 'public threat,'" *Daily Mail*,
   www.dailymail.co.uk/news/article-4927214/Wandsworth-Council-cuts-
   51-horse-chestnut-trees.html (accessed October 24 2017); Helen Pidd,
   "Artists plan painting protest to save 'living memorial,'" *Guardian*, October
   30 2017, p. 11.
44 John Crace, "No end in sight to my search for the perfect chocolate crois-
   sant," *Guardian*, October 28 2017, p. 15.
45 Lebow, *Politics and Ethics of Identity*, chs. 1–2 for this literature and controversies surrounding it.
46 Popper, *Open Society and Its Enemies.*
47 Molloy, *Kant's International Relations*, for a persuasive reading of this tension
   in Kant and his invocation of God and providence as a possible solution.
48 Rousseau, "Discourse on the Science and Arts."
49 Hume, *Treatise on Human Nature*, 3.2.5 and 3.3.
50 Lebow, "Greeks, Neuroscience and International Relations" reviews the relevant literature.
51 Machiavelli, *Prince* and *Discourses*; Shakespeare, *Coriolanus*, 1.1.
52 Bull, "Order vs. Justice in International Society"; Lebow, *National
   Identifications and International Relations*, 13–21, for elaboration of this claim.

53 Wikipedia, "Article 50 of the European Union," August 8 2017, https://en.wikipedia.org/wiki/Article_50_of_the_Treaty_on_European_Union (accessed August 25 2017).

54 Armstrong, *Brexit Time*; Shipman, *All Out War*.

55 Brass, "Shutdown of the Federal Government."

56 Lebow, *Politics and Ethics of Identity*, ch. 1 for document and analysis of this illusion.

57 Lebow, *Cultural Theory of International Relations*, ch. 2. See also "Weber and Knowledge."

58 Lebow and Stein, *We All Lost the Cold War*, chs. 2, 13–14; Lebow, *Conflict Management and Resolution*, chs. 3–5, 7.

59 Rengger, *International Relations*, pp. 3–11, for a short account of the "evolution of the problem of order."

60 Plato, *Timaeus*.

61 Augustine, *City of God*, p. 980.

62 Oakley, *Natural Law*, p. 29

63 Ibid., pp. 27–33; Oakley, *Crucial Centuries*, pp. 165–68.

64 Bain, "*Anarchical Society* as Christian Political Theology."

65 Hobbes, *Leviathan*, pp. 16, 242; Oakeshott, "Introduction to the Leviathan," p. 60.

66 Grotius, *Commentary on the Law of Prize and Booty*, pp. 20–21, and *Truth of the Christian Religion*, pp. 37–38.

67 Lebow, *Politics and Ethics of Identity*, pp. 284–86.

68 Hayek, *Law, Legislation, and Liberty*, pp. 35–54.

69 Lebow, *Forbidden Fruit*, ch. 1.

70 Leuchtenberg, *Franklin Roosevelt and the New Deal*; Katznelson, *Fear Itself*.

71 Eyck, *History of the Weimar Republic*, vol. II; Dorpalen, *Hindenburg and the Weimar Republic*; Broszat, *Hitler and the Collapse of Weimar Germany*; Mommsen, *Rise and Fall of Weimar Democracy*; Evans, *Coming of the Third Reich*.

72 Leuchtenberg, *Franklin Roosevelt and the New Deal*; Katznelson, *Fear Itself*.

73 Straus, "Order in Disorder."

74 Kwak, *Economism*.

75 Rengger, *International Relations*, pp. 6–10, for discussion.

76 Weber, "Science as a Vocation," and Protestant Ethic and the Spirit of Capitalism, p. 178, quoting Friedrich Nietzsche, *Ecce Homo*. Lebow, *Max Weber and International Relations*, chs. 1–2 for discussion.

77 Mueller, *Retreat from Doomsday*; Goldstein, *Winning the War on War*; Pinker, *Better Angels of Our Nature*; Singer, *Most Good You Can Do*.

78 For critiques of Pinker's arguments and statistics, see Pasquale Cirillo and Nassim Nicholas Taleb, "What are the chances of a third world war?," Real World Risk Institute Working Paper, no date, www.google.it/search?q=Taleb%2C+%E2%80%9CWhat+are+the+chances+of+a+third+world+war%3F%E2%80%9D+&ie=utf-8&oe=utf-8&client=firefox-b&gfe_rd=cr&dcr=0&ei=8uq5Wty3Ca qaX7rrmOgJ (accessed March 27 2018); John Gray, "Steven Pinker is wrong about violence and war," *Guardian*, March 13 2015, www.theguardian.com/books/2015/mar/13/john-gray-steven-pinker-wrong-violence-war-declining

(accessed August 3 2017); energyskptic, 13 fallacies of Steven Pinker's "The Better Angels of Our Nature: Why Violence Has Declined," November 29 2015, http://energyskeptic.com/2015/13-fallacies-of-steven-pinkers-the-better-angels-of-our-nature-why-violence-has-declined-and-slate-the-world-is-not-falling-apart (accessed August 3 2017). For a broader critique of the decline of violence thesis, see Lebow, *Why Nations Fight*, ch. 1.

79 Pinker, *Better Angels of Our Nature*; Timothy Snyder, "Hitler vs. Stalin: Who Killed More?," *New York Review of Books*, March 10 2011, www.nybooks.com/articles/archives/2011/mar/10/hitler-vs-stalin-who-killed-more/ (accessed March 10 2015); Arifa Skbar, "Mao's Great Leap Forward 'killed 45 million in four years,'" *Independent*, March 10 2015, www.independent.co.uk/arts-entertainment/books/news/maos-great-leap-forward-killed-45-million-in-four-years-2081630.html (accessed March 10 2015); Jones, *Genocide*; MacFarquhar and Schoenhals, *Mao's Last Revolution*; Mann, *Dark Side of Democracy*; Valentino, *Final Solutions*; Midlarsky, *Killing Trap*.

80 Le Carré, *A Small Town in Germany*, p. 255.

81 Hirschman, *Journeys Toward Progress* (Garden City, NY: Doubleday, 1965), ch. 4.

82 Lebow, *Tragic Vision of Politics*, ch. 7.

83 Zhang, *Chinese Hegemony*, pp. 3–24, 27, 182.

84 Ibid., pp. 7, 21–22.

85 Lebow, *Tragic Vision of Politics*, chs. 2 and 3.

86 Suzuki, "Europe at the Periphery of the Japanese World Order."

87 Kang, *China Rising* and *East Asia Before the West*, pp. 82–106; Cohen, "China's Rise in Historical Perspective"; Nathan and Scobell, *China's Search for Security*; Scobell, *China's Use of Military Force*; Kelly, "A 'Confucian Long Peace' in Pre-Western East Asia?"; Chanda, "When Asia Was One."

88 Smith, *Wealth of Nations*; Fleischacker, *A Short History of Distributive Justice*, pp. 32–40.

89 Rawls, *Theory of Justice*; Dworkin, "Equality of Welfare" and "Equality of Resources"; Sen, "Equality of What?"; Cohen, "Equality of What?"

90 McCluskey, *Bourgeois Inequality*, pp. 46–47.

91 DeCelles and Norton, "Physical and Situational Inequality on Airplanes Predicts Air Rage."

92 Jacob Poushter, "What is the greatest threat in the world? Depends on where you live," *Pew Research Center*, Spring 2014 world survey, www.pewresearch.org/fact-tank/2014/10/16/what-is-the-greatest-threat-to-the-world-depends-on-where-you-live/ (accessed May 6 2017).

93 Richard Adams, "Bath University vice-chancellor quits after outcry over £468k pay," *Guardian*, November 28 2017, www.theguardian.com/education/2017/nov/28/bath-university-vice-chancellor-quits-after-outcry-over-468k-pay (accessed December 13 2017).

94 Atkinson, *Inequality*. Also, Frank, *Falling Behind*; Bertrand and Morse, "Trickle Down Consumption"; Piketty, *Capital in the Twenty-First Century*; Scheidel, *Great Leveler*, pp. 1–23.

95 Bricker et al., "Changes in US Family Finances from 2007 to 2010."

96 Frank, *Falling Behind*; Bertrand and Morse, "Trickle Down Consumption."
97 Jessica Glenza, "Rich Americans live up to 15 years longer than poor peers: Studies find," *Guardian*, April 7 2017, www.theguardian.com/us-news/2017/apr/06/us-healthcare (accessed April 7 2017).
98 David Leonhardt, "The Assault on Colleges – and the American Dream," *New York Times*, May 25 2017, www.nytimes.com/2017/05/25/opinion/sunday/the-assault-on-colleges-and-the-american-dream.html?action=click&pgtype=Homepage&clickSource=story-heading&module=opinion-c-col-left-region&region=opinion-c-col-left-region&WT.nav=opinion-c-col-left-region&_r=0 (accessed May 25 2017).
99 Scheidel, *Great Leveler*, p. 38, for economic data. Stanley Feldman and Jeanne Zaino, "Election confirms deep ideological divide," *CBS News*, November 7 2010, www.cbsnews.com/news/election-confirms-deep-ideological-divide/ (accessed October 11 2014). For different perspectives, see Morris Fiorina, "America's Missing Moderates: Hiding in Plain Sight," *American Interest*, February 12 2013, www.the-american-interest.com/articles/2013/2/12/americas-missing-moderates-hiding-in-plain-sight/ (accessed October 11 2014); Alan I. Abromowitz, "America's Polarized Public: A Reply to Morris Fiorina," *American Interest*, March 11 2013, www.the-american-interest.com/articles/2013/03/11/polarizeowd-or-sorted-just-whats-wrong-with-our-politics-anyway/ (accessed October 11 2014); Marmot, *Health Gap*: Reich, *Saving Capitalism*; Piketty, *Economics of Inequality*. For a different view about the importance of equality, see Frankfurt, *On Inequality*.
100 Iyengar and Krupenkin, "Strengthening of Partisan Affect."
101 Abramowitz and Webster, "All Politics is National"; Iyengar and Krupenkin, "Strengthening of Partisan Affect"; Andersen and Sun, "Enemy Construction and the Press"; Thomas B. Edsall, "What Motivates Voters More Than Loyalty? Loathing," *New York Times*, March 1 2018, www.nytimes.com/2018/03/01/opinion/negative-partisanship-democrats-republicans.html (accessed March 4 2018).
102 Goldthorpe, *Social Mobility and Class Structure in Modern Britain*; on-going publications since 2012 of the UK government's "The Social Mobility and Child Poverty Commission."
103 Larry Elliot and Ed Pilkinton, "Half global wealth held by the 1%," *Guardian*, January 19 2015, pp. 1 and 6.
104 Larry Elliott, "Revealed: how the wealth gap holds back UK," *Guardian*, December 9 2014, pp. 1, 5; Sabrina Tavernise, "Disparity in the Life Spans of the Rich and Poor is Growing," citing a study by the Brookings Institution, *New York Times*, February 13 2016, www.nytimes.com/2016/02/13/health/disparity-in-life-spans-of-the-rich-and-the-poor-is-growing.html?hpw&rref=health&action=click&pgtype=Homepage&module=well-region&region=bottom-well&WT.nav=bottom-well (accessed February 13 2016).
105 Simon Rogers, "London by numbers," *Guardian*, July 13 2009, www.theguardian.com/news/datablog/2009/jul/13/london-population-demographics-crime (accessed February 13 2014); Press Association, "Healthy

life expectancy survey puts Richmond Upon Thames on top," *Guardian*, September 18 2013, www.theguardian.com/society/2013/sep/18/healthy-life-expectancy-survey-kingston-upon-thames (accessed February 13 2014).

106 Katie Allen, "Top 10% highest earners in Europe paid as much as bottom 50%, report finds," *Guardian*, December 15 2016, www.theguardian.com/money/2016/dec/15/top-10-highest-earners-in-europe-paid-as-much-as-bottom-50-report-finds (accessed December 16 2016).

107 "New Zealand and Mexico the OECD economies most affected by inequality," *Guardian*, DATABLOG, December 11 2014, www.theguardian.com/news/datablog/2014/dec/09/new-zealand-mexico-oecd-economies-most-affected-inequality (accessed December 11 2014).

108 Elliot and Pilkinton, "Half global wealth held by the 1%"; Jill Trainor, "Half the world's wealth now in hands of 1% of population," *Guardian*, October 13 2015, p. 12. The first article cites Oxfam's research and the second that of Credit Suisse.

109 Marmot, *Health Gap*, ch. 1.

110 Scheidel, *Great Leveler*, for a controversial explanation.

111 Rawls, *Theory of Justice*.

112 Johnson, *Listening in Paris*, ch. 1.

113 Private communication from Dorothy Noyes, October 10 2016. McDonogh, "Night at the Opera" and *Good Families of Barcelona*, on the social context of nineteenth-century opera in Spain.

114 Linda S. Zhang, Associated Press, "Malibu's exclusive 'Billionaire's Beach' is now open to the public after a decade-long legal fight," *Business Insider*, July 7 2015.

115 Andrew Pollack, "Drug Goes From $13.50 a Tablet to $750, Overnight," *New York Times*, September 20 2015, www.nytimes.com/2015/09/21/business/a-huge-overnight-increase-in-a-drugs-price-raises-protests (accessed July 1 2017); Stephanie Clifford, "Shkreli's Lawyer Calls Him 'Strange' but Berates Fraud Case Against Him," *New York Times*, June 28 2017, www.nytimes.com/2017/06/28/business/dealbook/martin-shkreli-fraud-trial-opens.html (accessed July 1 2017). Associated Press, "Potential Martin Shkreli jurors: We can't be impartial over 'most hated man' in US," *Guardian*, June 26 2017, www.theguardian.com/business/2017/jun/26/martin-shkreli-trial-jury-selection-pharma-bro-daraprim (accessed July 30 2017); Dominic Rushe, "'I hate him': Martin Shkreli court transcript reveals struggle for impartial jurors," *Guardian*, August 18 2017, www.theguardian.com/us-news/2017/aug/17/martin-shkreli-trial-jurors-wu-tang-clan (accessed August 18 2017).

116 Tom Phillips, "Outcry as China executes symbol of injustice Jia Jinglong," *Guardian*, November 15 2016, www.theguardian.com/world/2016/nov/15/outcry-as-china-executes-symbol-of-injustice-jia-jinglong (accessed March 27 2018); Javier C. Hernández, "Villager's expectations ignites uproar over judicial inequality in China," *International New York Times*, November 22 2016, p. 4.

117 David Barstow, Susanne Craig Russ Buettner, and Megan Twohey, "Donald Trump Records Show He Could Have Avoided Taxes for Nearly Two

Decades," *New York Times*, October 1 2016, www.nytimes.com/2016/10/02/us/politics/donald-trump-taxes.html (accessed October 9 2015); "Latest Election Polls 2016," *New York Times*, October 9 2016, www.nytimes.com/interactive/2016/us/elections/polls.html (accessed October 9 2016).

118 Alexander Burns, Maggie Haberman, and Jonathan Martin, "Donald Trump Apology Caps Day of Outrage Over Lewd Tape," *New York Times*, October 7 2016, www.nytimes.com/2016/10/08/us/politics/donald-trump-women (accessed October 11 2106).

119 Glenn Thrush and Maggie Haberman, "Trump Is Criticized for Not Calling Out White Supremacists," *New York Times*, August 12 2017, www.nytimes.com/2017/08/12/us/trump-charlottesville-protest-nationalist-riot.html?mcubz=1 (accessed August 29 2017); Glenn Thrush, "New Outcry as Trump Rebukes Charlottesville Racists 2 Days Later," *New York Times*, August 14 2017, www.nytimes.com/2017/08/14/us/politics/trump-charlottesville-protest.html?mcubz=1 (accessed August 29 2017).

120 Hannah Devlin, "Is it really possible to live until you're 146? The science of ageing," *Guardian*, May 2 2017, www.theguardian.com/science/2017/may/02/is-it-really-possible-to-live-until-youre-146-the-science-of-ageing (accessed July 7 2017).

121 Lebow, *National Identities and International Relations*, ch. 7.

122 Weber, *Economy and Society*, II, pp. 905–7, and "Profession and Vocation of Politics."

123 Crick, *American Science of Politics*, p. 150.

124 Marquez, "Irrelevance of Legitimacy."

125 Hurrelmann, Schneider and Steffek, "Conclusion." Marquez, "Irrelevance of Legitimacy" contends that legitimacy is usually a residual concept that bundles together many others and diverse mechanisms. He suggests reserving the term for those instances where particular relations of domination are internalized. Beetham, *Legitimation of Power*, also makes this point.

126 Hermann and Lebow, *Ending the Cold War*, for a discussion of this ex post facto determinism.

127 Burke, *Burke's Speech on Conciliation with America*, p. 134.

128 Aron at a 1965 conference as reported by Hoffmann, *Conditions of World Order*, pp. 1–2; Pelopidas, "Nuclear Weapons Scholarship." Rengger, *International Relations*, pp. 17–18.

129 Bartelson, *War in International Thought*. Barkawi, *Soldiers of Empire* for a recent account that theorizes from war in the abstract to war in practice.

130 Berlin, "Political Ideas in the Twentieth Century" and "Birth of Greek Individualism."

131 Lebow, *Politics and Ethics of Identity*, chs. 5 and 9 for the new kind of identity project that emerged with Rousseau and the Romantics.

132 Miller, *Principles of Social Justice*, pp. 38–39.

133 Blanning, *Frederick the Great*, pp. 408–17.

134 Stuart A. Thompson and Anjali Singhvi, "Efforts to Rescue Migrants Caused Deadly, Unexpected Consequences," *New York Times*, June 14 2017, www.nytimes.com/interactive/2017/06/14/world/europe/migrant-rescue-efforts-deadly.html (accessed June 14 2017).

135 Alan Travis, "EU-UK naval mission on people smuggling led to more deaths, report says," *Guardian*, July 12 2017, www.theguardian.com/world/2017/jul/11/eu-naval-tactics-operation-sophia-stop-people-smuggling-cause-more-deaths-report-says (accessed July 12 2017).

136 Hobbes, *Leviathan*, chs. 13–14.

137 Lebow, *Politics and Ethics of Identity*, ch. 4.

138 Strawson, "The Minimal Self" and *Selves*; Zahavi, "Unity of Consciousness and the Problem of Self."

139 Lebow, *Politics and Ethics of Identity*, ch. 4 for a review of this literature and a critique of the concept of identity.

140 Pinto, *Salazar's Dictatorship*; Hanebrink, *In Defense of Christian Hungary*, p. 165; Berend, *Decades of Crisis*, p. 305; Müller, *Contesting Democracy*, pp. 108–10.

141 Berlin, "Counter-Enlightenment."

142 Nietzsche, *Human, All-Too-Human*, p. 235.

143 Durkheim, *Moral Education*, p. 54.

144 Zaslaw, *Classical Era*; Taruskin, *Music in the Seventeenth and Eighteenth Centuries*, pp. 171–76.

145 Burney, *General History of Music*, I, p. xvii.

146 Lebow, Politics and Ethics of Identity, ch. 4.

147 Taruskin, *Music in the Seventeenth and Eighteenth Centuries*, p. 643.

148 Johnson, *Listening in Paris*, p. 376.

149 Dusinberre, *Beethoven For A Later Age*.

150 Buch, *Beethoven's Ninth*, chs. 6–10; Bokina, *Opera and Politics*, pp. 65–85.

151 Bokina, *Opera and Politics*, pp. 92–93; Baker, "Public Opinion as Political Invention"; Ozouf, "Public Opinion at the End of the Old Regime." On the emergence of the public sphere, see Habermas, *Structural Transformation of the Culture Sphere*; Blanning, *Culture of Power and the Power of Culture*, Part II.

152 Johnson, *Listening in Paris*, p. 232.

153 Blanning, *Romantic Revolution*, pp. 36–42 and *Frederick the Great*, pp. 42, 141–42.

154 Adorno, "On the Social Situation of Music."

155 Cited in Murakami, *Absolutely Music*, pp. 70–71.

156 Nietzsche, *Birth of Tragedy*, Sections 1 and 3.

157 Quoted in Dolar, "If Music Be the Food of Love."

158 Another nice example concerns Bach. The many analogies of orchestras to social and military organizations have prompted some recent historians to speculate – unreasonably, in my view – that his musical transgressions of harmonic order were intended to communicate subversive views. Taruskin, *Music in the Seventeenth and Eighteenth Centuries*, pp. 185–92; McClary, "Blasphemy of Talking Politics during Bach Year."

159 Lebow, *Politics and Ethics of Identity*.

160 Plato, *Republic*, Book 1.

161 Thucydides, *History of the Peloponnesian War*, tells a similar tale of the decline of individual and social order in Athens. See Lebow, *Tragic Vision of Politics*, ch. 3.

162 Austen, *Sense and Sensibility, Pride and Prejudice, Emma*; Lynch, *Economy of Character*, pp. 107–51; Armstrong, *How Novels Think*, pp. 7, 16–18, 43–59, 79–80.

163 Lebow, *Politics and Ethics of Identity*, ch. 1

164 Ibid.

165 Justin McCurry, "North Korea executes official with anti-aircraft gun in new purge – report," *Guardian*, August 30 2016, www.theguardian.com/world/2016/aug/30/north-korea-reportedly-executes-officials-anti-aircraft-gun-purge (accessed August 30 2016).

166 Lukács, *History and Class Consciousness*; Adorno and Horkheimer, *Dialectic of Enlightenment.*

167 Althusser, "Ideology and Ideological State Apparatuses."

168 Lebow, *Politics and Ethics of Identity*, ch. 1.

169 Gergen, *Saturated Self* and "Social Construction of Self."

170 Lebow, *Politics and Ethics of Identity*, ch. 6.

171 Horkheimer and Adorno, *Dialectic of Enlightenment*; Bauman, "Self in Consumer Society."

2   Justice, Solidarity, and Order

> When Adam dalf, and Eve span, who was thanne a gentilman?
>
> John Ball[1]

This chapter develops a framework for the study of political order. I open with a discussion of the similarities and differences between order in the physical and social worlds. I argue that equilibrium, a commonly observed phenomenon in the physical world, is rarely found in the social world. It is also inappropriate because the most stable social and political orders are those that undergo significant change, but incrementally. For this reason, it is important to uncouple change from stability. They refer to different things, and relate in complex ways. As a general rule, little or no change is detrimental to stability, as is too rapid or dramatic change. The Goldilocks position lies somewhere between these extremes, but just where will be determined by context.

The open-ended and non-linear nature of the social world makes it highly context dependent and all but impossible to offer universal, falsifiable propositions about order, or much of anything else for that matter. Recognizing this problem Max Weber anchored his approach to knowledge in the study of singular events. He did not restrict singular to the individual, but included the behavior of groups, institutions, nations, and developments such as the emergence of the territorial state and capitalism.[2] Weber's approach conforms to what philosophers of science call "singular causation." It refers to events that are causal but non-repetitive and in which ex post facto causal understandings cannot be used to predict future events.[3]

We can nevertheless construct causal accounts of the origin, evolution, decline, and reconstitution of bottom-up and top-down orders. We can also identify some of the processes and pathways that move orders from one state to another. Toward this end, I follow Weber again in turning to ideal types: of *thumos*- and appetite-based societies. I offer analyses of their formation, evolution, and decline, and use them as the conceptual foundations for my empirical analysis. I am particularly interested in the ways in which both kinds of societies are affected by shifts in the principles of justice that sustain them.

These principles are ideal types, and in a double sense. They can never be defined in ways to satisfy everyone; attempts to do so invariably meet logical, empirical, and normative objections. They are never fully instantiated in practice, and at times hardly at all.

Philosophers have debated from time immemorial the meaning of justice and its expression in such concepts as equality and fairness. There is little to nothing I can or want to add to this debate. I am engaging in an empirical, not a normative inquiry. I am not interested in ideal formulations of how people should behave, but rather the ways in which justice is essential to order. I invoked justice in a similar sense in *Tragic Vision of Politics*, where my interest in ethics was also empirical. I argued that foreign policies that conformed to existing ethical standards were more likely to succeed.

In this book, I turn to justice as an ordering principle of society. It serves a double purpose: a guide for structuring relations among members of a society and distributing rewards, and legitimation for this ordering and distribution. This helps to explain why justice – in theory and practice – is foundational to order, and how this dependence has the potential to make orders robust, but also to undermine them.

My analysis of order rests on four substantive assumptions. First, disorder is the default of all top-down orders; they are more fragile and shorter-lived than bottom-up orders. Second, to achieve any degree of stability, top-down and bottom-up orders alike must justify themselves to relevant actors with reference to accepted principles of justice. Third, the stability of orders is threatened when their principles of justice are challenged and the discrepancy between them and practice becomes unacceptable. Fourth, all top-down orders – and many bottom-up orders – are hierarchical and require some degree of solidarity to soften the unequal distribution of honor and wealth.[4]

Justice is a fundamental human concern, but it is not the only one. People crave security, intimacy, and material well-being. If justice is the foundation of order, it is a prerequisite for these other goals. In an ideal world, order and justice would be mutually reinforcing, but this is rarely, if ever, the case. In the late 1960s and early 1970s, Ali Mazrui and Hedley Bull noted a sharp discrepancy in this regard between the western and non-western powers; the former stressed order and the latter justice.[5] More recently, Bertrand Badie has written with passion about the catastrophic consequences for both the West and the rest of pursuing order at the expense of justice.[6] Order and justice are invariably to some degree at odds, and often very much so. For this reason, advocates of reforms on the grounds of justice invariably meet opposition from those who support existing practices on the basis of alternate principles of justice or who contend that the status quo is essential to order and stability. The difficulty of predicting the consequence of changes, and a general preference for the evil we know over the one we do not, may offer one explanation for why people are often willing to put up with orders they consider unjust.

People think about justice and sometimes act in accord with their understandings of its requirements. More often than not, they look for ways of avoiding these obligations when they are seen as costly or in some other way disadvantageous. The tension between values and practice is more acute for most organizations, including governments. They invoke principles of justice, but rarely instantiate them. For this reason, they must rely on other incentives to get people to conform to their laws, rules, and norms. I theorize four mechanisms of compliance: fear, interest, *thumos*, and habit. The first three appeal to human needs: survival, material well-being, and self-esteem. Habit is the product of long-term conformity to laws, rules, and norms, to or near the point where it becomes almost a reflex reaction. For most of us, stopping at a red light is a good example. Robust orders rely on habitual compliance and are in trouble when it ceases. To stay with the driving example, an increase in running red lights, failing to signal for turns, and parking in spaces reserved for others, including the handicapped, are early signs of disorder.[7]

Orders also require some degree of solidarity among their members. All orders need boundaries, and solidarity helps to define who belongs and who does not. Belonging is also a precondition of solidarity, but not a sufficient condition. Solidarity became a pressing concern for nineteenth-century sociologists – discussed later in this chapter – because they recognized its importance. They disagreed among themselves about whether modernity would create a new basis for solidarity or undermine the sense of community on which existing social and political orders rested, leaving alienation and anomie in its place. Most nineteenth-century thinkers, while not blind to nationalism, did not grasp the extent to which it would provide the most important social glue for states, but also become the principal source of domestic and international conflict and violence. More recent students of nationalism are acutely aware of its Janus-faced nature. They describe solidarity as both the basis of nationality and its consequence.[8]

Equilibrium is Not Stability

In the physical and social sciences order and stability are commonly associated with patterns or structures that are outcomes of random processes.[9] Top-down orders are less random, and some reflect conscious designs. Bottom-up orders are more likely to be emergent properties, but they are by no means random as they too are the product of human reflection and behavior. Design in both kinds of order is intended in large part to regulate behavior and make it, as far as possible, legible, routine, and predictable.

Existing studies of social orders of all kinds focus more on stability than they do on change, and often explain the former with reference to equilibrium. Equilibrium is a feature of some physical and biological systems, but not of the social world, where it is a theoretical fiction. The most stable orders are those that evolve through a process of gradual change. By contrast, those that appear to maintain their equilibria are among the most vulnerable to major upheavals. Focus on equilibrium, moreover, makes it more difficult to explain change, reducing scholarly interest in the phenomenon.

Social scientists who do address change routinely explain it with reference to system constraints and opportunities at either the domestic or international level. Most are more interested in convergence than divergence across societies. They generally attribute convergence in institutions and practices to external pressures or material developments, as liberals do with second image reverse arguments and globalization, and realists do with anarchy and nuclear weapons. For mechanisms of change, liberals and realists rely on selection or rational adaptation. They generally fail to distinguish between these quite different mechanisms, and ignore imitation, which I contend is a major source of convergence.[10]

I maintain that the principal sources of change and convergence – not that the former necessarily implies the latter – are as much ideational as they are material. So-called system pressures, whether in the form of constraints or opportunities, are more often than not in the imagination of scholars and products of their theories, not features of the real world. And changes in institutions and practices have more diverse and important causes than selection or adaptation. Their direction of change cannot be predicted on the basis of real or imagined structural constraints and pressures. This is also true in evolution, where there is a long-standing debate about the relative strengths and causes of divergence and convergence. The latest evidence suggests that when populations are identical initially they generally respond to natural selection in the same way. When there are significant genetic and phenotypic differences among them evolutionary responses can be quite divergent.[11] The same may be true of social orders and political systems. Their internal structure, values, and history are likely to determine their response to constraints and opportunities of all kinds, and can lead to divergence or convergence.

There is rarely a consensus about the constraints and pressures and other critical conditions affecting a government or political elite, or about the most effective ways of responding to them. These understandings and policy preferences are often influenced, if not shaped, by actor goals and other perceived pressures and, in addition, are highly subjective. Political outcomes are almost invariably the result of interactions among numerous actors, and correspondingly difficult to predict. Policies frequently have unintended consequences. Convergence, like order, is more often an emergent property than the product of design.

The social science literature makes a further error in equating order with stability. Many studies deploy the concept of equilibrium as the mechanism responsible for stability, and hence for order, as do balance-of-power theorists.[12] Equilibrium is almost without exception an unwarranted assumption in the social world. Hyman Minsky demonstrated in his now-famous "financial-instability hypothesis" how long stretches of prosperity sow the seeds of the next economic crisis. In certain circumstances, markets are notably inefficient and tend to disequilibrium.[13]

The same phenomenon is evident in international relations, where balancing is sometimes claimed to be a structural feature of the so-called international "system." In a comprehensive study of the balance of power, Kaufman, Little, and Wohlforth draw on evidence across cultures and epochs and find balanced and unbalanced distributions of power about equal in frequency. Military expansion is "well-nigh universal behavior," they conclude, but aggrandizement is often tolerated by "myopic advantage-seeking" actors who pursue narrow short-term interests in preference to system maintenance.[14] As Hans Morgenthau understood, the formation and consequences of the balance of power depend on how actors conceive of and employ it, and above all, on a shared commitment to preserve a regional society and the independence of its members.[15] The balance of power failed to prevent two world wars in the twentieth century and is historically alien to the international relations of East Asia.[16] It is a cultural artifact whose importance and consequences and norms vary across regions and epochs. Max Weber made the same argument about markets.[17]

The concept of equilibrium has additional drawbacks. It assumes that social orders are "systems" and are likely to return to their initial states, or something close to it, following shock and dislocation.[18] Research into chaos and complexity has taught us that even systems with a demonstrated tendency to equilibrium can undergo phase transitions as the result of non-linear interactions; they lose their equilibria or shift to new ones. This phenomenon is well documented in the case of climate.[19] A focus on equilibrium all but forecloses change and transformation unless we consider the circumstances likely to move systems out of their ground states.[20]

There is an even more powerful objection to equilibria in the social world. Changes, even when minor, generate new pressures and accommodations. Collectively, they can transform institutions and practices over time. The sign of success of this process is the recognition we have of transformation but the corresponding difficulty of determining when it occurred or where we should divide the previous order from the present one. All categorizations of this kind strike us as subjective or even arbitrary. I return to this problem in Chapter 7 in discussing when and how Georgian Britain morphed into its Victorian successor. For now, let me say that the use of monarchs or ruling families as historical markers indicates just how difficult it is to find meaningful, conceptual ones.

To further muddy the waters, seeming efforts to uphold existing law and practices often serve as a vehicle for their change, even transform-ation. In the Victorian era, Benthamites made a big push to replace common law with a Napoleonic-style legal code in the expectation that it would make the law more scientific and deprive judges of much of their discretion. They were opposed by Henry Maine, the greatest legal scholar of his generation. He argued that, along with equity and legisla-tion, case law and the judicial discretion it enabled were the means by which "Law is brought into harmony with society." The legal fiction of precedent encourages and conceals gradual change, keeping the letter of the law the same, but allowing its operation to be modified over time and used to sustain a different set of practices or values.[21] Victorian jurist and legal theorist A. V. Dicey argued that evolving judicial interpret-ation of equity secured for all married women the rights that the Court of Chancery had recognized initially for the daughters of the rich with property settlements.[22]

Evolution of this kind renders the concept of stability an oxymoron. Some of the most "stable" political systems – measured in terms of their longevity and absence of major violence – are those that have changed the most over the years, so that comparisons between them at time T and T plus 100 years reveal radically different orders. Compare Georgian England to late Victorian Britain or Victorian Britain to today's United Kingdom. The institutions governing the country today are more or less the same – the supreme court aside – but the political culture, expectations about government, the distribution of power across classes, the demog-raphy of the country and many of its key social and political values would be unrecognizable to Georgians and Victorians. The same institutions (e.g. justices of the peace, parliament, the bureaucracy) no longer function the same way, and in some cases perform different functions.

The Soviet Union and the German Democratic Republic (GDR) no longer exist; they were unable to adjust to evolving economic and political conditions. In June 1989, German Chancellor Helmut Kohl praised Soviet President Mikhail Gorbachev for his reforms and told him that "[Erich] Honecker [General Secretary of the East German Communist Party] is not trying any reforms, and because of this, he is destabilizing the situation."[23] Within a year East Germany was gone. Reforms, however, did not save the Soviet Union; they were sabotaged by opponents, damaging to the economy, and stimulated anti-Soviet nationalism.[24] By 1989 communist rule may have been sufficiently fragile that there was no realistic strategy that could have saved these regimes and countries.

Not all change is gradual. The collapse of the Warsaw Pact and Soviet Union were rapid and dramatic, as were the events and aftermath of the so-called "Arab Spring." Both upheavals began with internal changes in one country that affected others in a kind of amplifying ripple effect. We can borrow the concept of phase transition from physics and chemistry and use it metaphorically to describe these kinds of transformations in domestic politics and international relations. In the case of the GDR, groups of East Germans on holiday in Hungary in July and August of 1989 were the precipitants. Thousands of them wanted to flee to the West and the Hungarian government considered letting them pass through its border with Austria. On October 6, Gorbachev came to Berlin to attend the fortieth anniversary celebrations of the East German regime and was welcomed as a liberator by huge crowds in East Berlin. Shortly afterwards, the GDR Politburo forced Erich Honecker to step down as general secretary and replaced him with Egon Krenz. Demonstrations spread and more East Germans fled to the West via Czechoslovakia, which opened its borders. East Germans gathered at the Berlin Wall and demanded the right to leave without prior permission. Events escalated with new demonstrations in Leipzig and elsewhere, the Wall was breached, and the rest is history.[25]

Non-linearity offers a model of far-reaching change. Bak and Chen performed a series of famous and illustrative experiments. They dropped sand grains, one at a time, to build up mounds until the addition of one more brought about a collapse. Despite large numbers of runs, it was impossible to predict in advance when this would happen, how much of the mound would collapse, and in what direction it would be deformed.[26] Dramatic change in the social, economic, and political world is often the result of accretions of this kind; at a certain point, an additional increment or outside stress has the potential to produce dramatic change – but it is never apparent beforehand when this will happen. The Notting Hill race riots of 1958 offer a nice example. Violence against Black immigrants was routine in this London neighborhood but had never seriously escalated. At the height of August, ten young white Teddy Boys committed a series of minor offenses, and nine were arrested. The next day a Swedish sex worker got into an argument with her Jamaican husband. Teddy Boys intervened, and a small fight broke out. The day after that, the woman was abused by more white youths, who had witnessed the previous fight. They threw a milk bottle at her and shouted "black man's whore." Their name-calling sparked fighting between white and Jamaican youths, which escalated into almost a week of rioting and the arrest of 140 people.[27]

Confluence is another cause of non-linear change. In a previous book I explained the origins of World War I, the American social revolution of the 1960s and 1970s, and the end of the Cold War as the product of the confluence of multiple, independent developments that produced dramatic and reinforcing shifts in beliefs and behavior.[28] Nick Onuf suggests that a confluence of multiple causal chains is necessary also for evolution and climate change, and that these confluences in turn could be the product of many small changes – what he calls "epochal change" – at a deeper level of analysis.[29] I make a similar argument about the territorial state in *Causation and International Relations*. It emerged as a concept and desirable goal as a result of a confluence of linear perspective, changes in mapping, and portraiture. These developments in turn were made possible or accelerated by the philosophical project of individual autonomy.[30]

Peace is equally problematic as a defining characteristic of political order. Kenneth Waltz makes the mistake of equating order and peace, and in doing so builds on a deep-rooted assumption in western philosophy, social science, and religion that the most structured systems are the most peaceful and predictable.[31] Warrior-based societies were highly ordered but extremely violent, as were the Vikings, Maori, Aztecs, and Plains Indians. So too were the aristocratic regimes of eighteenth-century Europe, imperialist empires of the nineteenth and twentieth centuries, and more recently both superpowers during the Cold War. Modern states display varying degrees of internal peace, and Max Weber's definition of the state as a unit with a monopoly of force in a given territory is best regarded as an ideal type. Moreover, in some states, like the United States, much violence originates with police forces charged with maintaining order. They routinely engage in systematic racism, kill African-Americans without warrant and, if brought to justice, are regularly found innocent by juries.[32] The converse proposition is more warranted as the breakdown or collapse of regional or domestic orders often leads to war or lawlessness.

In lieu of peace or equilibrium as an ontological starting point and normative goal of order we must focus on change, incremental and transformative. We can conceive of societies as arrayed along a continuum between the poles of order and chaos. Chaos is the opposite of order; it is characterized by the absence of rules-based behavior, functioning institutions, lawlessness and, often, unpredictability. True chaos would require the collapse of both top-down and bottom-up orders and this rarely happens. When top-down orders collapse, bottom-up orders generally expand their functions. Sometimes, new bottom-up order quickly forms, often in the form of gangs. As noted in Chapter 1, order and predictability do not necessarily co-vary. Hobbes' state of nature is lawless and violent but all too predictable. So too are Brazilian favelas and the streets of Mogadishu.

To avoid chaos, top-down and bottom-up orders must make multiple accommodations. They are often individually negotiated or simply emerge in practice. They accumulate over the course of time like levels of ruins in ancient cities. New accommodations are partially path dependent in that they must take into account the practices and expectations created by previous accommodations. Accommodations in bottom-up orders are rarely, if ever, the product of design. In top-down orders they are the products of compromise and horse-trading, and often incremental changes from existing laws or practices. Accommodations that buttress orders of either kind are often fragile and short-lived.[33] They are likely to be ad hoc, logically indefensible, never more than partially legitimate, and constantly challenged. As Whitehead, Bergson, Simmel, Schütz, and Lévinas all argue, the possibility of change is an important – if not the most important – source of social stability.[34]

So how should we think of order and stability? The previous discussion suggests that there is no simple or elegant solution to this problem. For my purpose, the most reasonable approach may be to define the stability of top-down orders in terms of the longevity of a political order. How long has an order survived without a revolution, serious threat of revolution, or high levels of civil violence? Many systems have rules governing change, and the most stable systems undergo change by mechanisms and processes stipulated, or at least recognized as legitimate, by these rules. Occasionally, orders benefit from illegal activity intended to change the rules about changing the rules, which will be discussed in more detail later. Successful orders accommodate changes in these rules as well as their practices, and by doing so facilitate peaceful change. This does not guarantee survival, but survival without it is more difficult, if not unlikely.

Bottom-up orders change in two principal ways. Old practices decline and new ones emerge as the result of the more or less uncoordinated behavior of actors. Change may be rapid or gradual, marked by repeated confrontations between defenders of old practices and proponents of new or different ones, or stealthy in that it is characterized by quiet, reinforcing cycles of observance (or non-observance) and expectations (or non-expectations) of observance (e.g. the doffing of hats as a sign of respect for women). When conflict over these practices is acute, opponents or proponents of change may attempt to promote or prevent it through the top-down order. Efforts by American supporters of gay marriage to legalize it at the state level, and by their opponents to ban it at the national level, is a case in point.

Gay marriage, equal rights for women and racial integration before it, made their initial progress in society but were then strengthened in the United States by legislation and court decisions. They were to some degree forced from above on society and its bottom-up orders. Bottom-up orders generally resist such change when they have not been its source, but can be sufficiently coerced or rewarded to change their practices over time. Changing practices influence values and what was initially resisted can become accepted and internalized, although, as the following example indicates, it can be a slow and ongoing process. At Dartmouth, in the early years of this century, I was invited to dinner by a fraternity. My host, an African-American student, explained that the fraternity had left its national organization and gone independent in the early 1960s, disgusted by its refusal to admit Jews or African-Americans as members. He recounted how he and several of his "brothers" were sitting in the house one day when the doorbell rang and the visitor turned out to be a representative from the national fraternity. They invited him in and he explained that all had changed. The national now welcomed members regardless of race, ethnicity, or place of national origin, and even had scholarships for underprivileged minority students. He urged them to rejoin. They said he would have to speak to their president and one of the young men volunteered to go upstairs and see if she was in her room. "She?" the national representative exclaimed in a shocked tone of voice.

Bottom-up orders also influence their top-down counterparts, and this interpenetration on the whole facilitates stability by keeping society and government from diverging too far from one another in values and practices. The greater ability of society to influence government may be an important stability for democratic regimes. It is nevertheless a double-edged sword. Changing values and practices at the social level can also have negative consequences for the legitimacy and stability of democratic orders, as Chapters 5 and 6 demonstrate.

Justice and Order

In context-free settings we can readily establish the importance of justice. The dollar ultimatum game demonstrates a universal concern for distributional justice. Two people are given the task of dividing a unit of currency between them. "A" can offer "B" any percentage of the unit of currency in question, and "B" can accept or reject it. No bargaining is allowed, and the players only divide the money between them if "B" accepts "A"'s offer. Across cultures the curve of rejection rises sharply when "A" attempts to keep 65 percent or more of the money in question. The principles of both fairness and equality come into play. Framing the game with reference to either principle encourages the expectation of a 50-50 split. Justice is closely connected to self-esteem. For both reasons people do not want to reward those who are greedy or accept less and be taken for chumps.[35]

The reasons that prompt "B"'s to spurn unfavorable offers could reasonably be expected to have led American workers to reject Mitt Romney and Donald Trump, the Republican Party nominees in the 2012 and 2016 presidential elections. They proposed changes in income and inheritance tax, Medicare, Social Security, and welfare that would penalize the poor and middle class and reward the rich. Yet 44 percent of Americans who voted cast their ballots for Romney and the Republicans, and four years later, 46 percent did so for Trump. Other factors were clearly at work. Public opinion polls indicate that many Republican voters opposed social change, disliked big government, feared immigrants, were hostile to President Obama and Hillary Clinton, and wanted to make America stronger and more respected abroad.[36]

Voting, unlike the dollar ultimatum game, takes places in a historical, political, social, and highly charged setting. Voters appear to be influenced as much – perhaps more – by personalities than issues. Many do not understand that they are playing a distribution game. Those who do, do not always agree about what is being distributed. Voter preferences are frequently emotional, intransitive, influenced by campaign advertising and slogans, and last-minute developments. Many people eligible to vote do not, and not necessarily because they have concluded that their vote will not influence the outcome. Some do not go to the polls because they are too lazy or fail to see what is at stake, and others because they believe – rightly or wrongly – that nothing is at stake; that the outcome of the election will change little.

Elections indicate that we must be careful about generalizing from simple games, rational models, or experiments to the more complex, emotionally charged, and open-ended world. Economists, and their fellow travelers in political science, nevertheless look for ways of simplifying the world, and their treatment of justice offers a striking and disturbing example. Drawing on self-serving interpretations of John Nash and Kenneth Arrow, they define justice as nothing more than rational prudence in contexts where we need to cooperate with other people to get what we want.[37] David Gauthier alleges that the concept of "justice as mutual advantage" harks back to Hobbes and Hume, but this is a shallow reading of these philosophers.[38] By this sleight of hand, justice is reduced to a mathematical problem, and the concept of "should" is no longer what is ethically required, but what is "rational."[39]

If economists mistakenly treat people as populations whose choices can be captured by utility functions, and reduce justice to questions of mutual advantage, philosophers also err by thinking that justice, which most treat as a normative concept, can be defined. Like economists, many believe that the good definitions should have practical value in resolving political differences and controversies. Liberal American political philosophers also mimic economists by limiting justice to problems of distribution.

Justice is a notoriously difficult concept to define, and more so than most concepts because of its normative nature. Plato grapples with this problem in his *Republic*. Cephalus, representative of the commercial class, confidently asserts that justice is speaking the truth and paying one's debts.[40] Polemarchus offers a more traditional understanding: justice is "giving what is proper," or "doing good to friends and harm to enemies."[41] Thrasymachus, speaking as a radical Sophist, insists that justice is nothing more than "the interest of the stronger."[42] Plato's Socrates challenges these definitions, and the jaundiced claim of Glaucon that people only act justly for instrumental reasons. Socrates tries to persuade his interlocutors that justice is a quality of soul that leads people to act justly because it promotes their happiness. It encourages self-mastery over appetite and *thumos*, prompting people to behave in ways that benefit, not only themselves, but the community at large. His conception of justice rests on the principle of fairness which, he believes, enables the harmonious functioning of the polis. An ideal society has three classes of people: producers (craftsmen, farmers, artisans, etc.); auxiliaries (warriors); and guardians (rulers). Justice consists of ordered relations among three classes, which requires each group to perform its proper function.[43] The several definitions of justice that Socrates interrogates find contemporary resonance, as does his own account.[44]

Moral philosophers are committed to discovering principles of justice most appropriate to their societies. Of necessity, the assumptions and criteria they use to make these determinations are highly subjective. They reflect the values of their societies – or reactions against them – and both responses are conditioned by history and culture and are therefore local and parochial. Given the importance of equality in the contemporary West, it should come as no surprise that almost every western account of justice rests on the foundation of equality. This near-consensus does not lead to any broader agreement because philosophers do not agree among themselves about equality, how it might be achieved, or how it ought to be applied.[45]

Many moral philosophers believe – wrongly again, in my opinion – that they can help resolve value conflicts.[46] In a highly acclaimed work, David Miller attempts to adjudicate between solidaristic and instrumental relationships. He asserts that we give too much attention to individual choices and not enough "to demands stemming from citizenship." He criticizes Rawls and Dworkin for developing theories of justice based solely on citizenship and seeks "to correct distortions in everyday thinking about fairness."[47] These judgments, no matter how well presented and defended, are purely personal. There can be no objective grounds for preferring any one of these philosophers to the others.

Justice is foundational to my theory of political order. My interest in the first instance is empirical, not normative. My approach harks back to classical philosophy and its concern for order and what holds it together. In contrast to post-Kantian, rationalist philosophy, I make no effort to define justice or to derive principles of behavior from this definition. I want to know more about the ordering principles of successful societies. I draw attention to two such principles – fairness and equality – because they appear to be close to universal and central to social orders. They are also evident among primates, although, of course, not theorized by them. Fairness and equality can be formulated and applied in different ways, and can be reinforcing and cross-cutting depending on the circumstances. Their formulation and relative importance varies across societies and epochs. This variation can help us define the envelope in which robust orders are found.

Equality and fairness – the latter often referred to as "equity" by psychologists – are commonly framed as principles of distributive justice, and much of politics is a struggle over the possession or control of whatever is desired and limited in availability. In the words of Harold Lasswell, politics is about "Who gets what when and how?"[48] In ordered societies, distribution is rule governed, so procedural justice enters the picture.[49] Order and politics encompass more than distribution. There are constitute and commutative forms of justice that describe how actors are constituted and how they ought to behave in commercial transactions, and retributive justice, that concerns the punishment of those who fail to honor norms and laws. Most, if not all, of these principles of justice, I will argue, find expression in some combination of fairness and equality. Each principle in turn has two distinct formulations.

Equality may be the older of the two principles, and it is central to surviving hunter-gather groups.[50] In pre-classical Greece, *nomos* was associated with leaders who distributed meat among their followers. Homer seems to have envisaged fair food distribution as a core constituent of the political order. In classical Greece, *nomos* expanded to encompass laws, rules, procedures, and customs. It still retained a connotation of equality in the word *isonomia*, which was later gradually extended in scope to embrace political rights. Equality remained alive as a concept in Europe and not infrequently surfaced as a demand or practice of breakaway religious sects or peasant rebellions. In 1381, the radical Hertfordshire priest John Ball took an active role in a peasants' revolt.[51] He coined his now-famous line about Adam and Eve, quoted in the frontispiece of this chapter. His intention was to suggest the inherent equality of all human beings and that servitude was accordingly against the will of God.[52]

Equality demands a more or less even distribution of whatever it is that people value. Equality can also be applied to non-distributive questions. According to Aristotle, it requires the victims of wrongdoings to be compensated equally regardless of their wealth or status.[53] Equality before the law has become a central tenet and test of democracy. In the late eighteenth century, Hume and Smith extended the principle of equality to property; they considered it immoral – and against the interests of society – that the poor should suffer to provide luxuries for the rich and that the latter should own considerable property and the former little to none.[54] Many socialists would go a step further and call for the abolition of private property. Equality also pertains to the law; people should have equal access to legal remedies and be treated equally regardless of other differences. In the modern era the scope of law has been widely extended. In some cases – education, for example – the goal of legal intervention was to facilitate equality.[55]

In liberal theory, equality has assumed a second meaning: equality of opportunity.[56] This framing of equality is particularly pronounced in American political theory, where John Roemer argues that it finds expression in two distinct formulations.[57] The first maintains that competition for wealth and status should be judged only with respect to the performance of the duties in question. "Extraneous" attributes like race, gender, and family background and the advantages they provide should not be taken into account. The second insists that society should attempt to level the playing field, especially in the critical formative years of life.

Either formulation is consistent with hierarchy and can be considered an effort to justify it. If everyone is equal at the onset of a competition the

outcome reflects the skill, virtue, commitment – and, admittedly, sometimes the good luck – of the contestants. Liberal equality thus reintroduces
the principle of fairness through the back door, and indeed was initially
propagated by representatives of the commercial classes who opposed the
virtues of appetite over that of *thumos* to justify their claim to power.[58] For
contemporary neoliberals, it is a justification for the growing disparity of
wealth in the western world. I return to this question in Chapter 6.

The principle of fairness goes by many names. They include "virtue,"
"merit," "worthiness," and "deservingness." It is an ancient concept,
but one associated with societies having a division of labor and hierarchy based on birth or achievement. It makes its earliest appearance
in warrior-based honor societies that were first theorized in the ancient
world. We have evidence of fairness in the *lex talonis* law systems that date
back to ancient Babylonia. The codes of Hammurabi and Hebrew law
stress fairness, but only in the context of compensation for loss. By the
fifth century, the discourse of virtue provided secular justifications for
Greek aristocratic and oligarchic hierarchies. Plato and Aristotle develop
different versions of it in their writings. They sought to downgrade the
principle of equality because it was mobilized in support of democracy.[59]

Until quite recently, fairness was also the dominant principle of regional
and international orders. In Europe, and subsequently worldwide, states
gained honor and often territory and wealth by displaying their military prowess. The resulting hierarchy of great and lesser powers was
justified on the basis of the responsibility the former allegedly assumed
for the maintenance of order and survival of the system. This informal
understanding was given official status by the Congress of Vienna.[60]

Fairness offers "merit" as a countervailing principle to equality. It
insists that some people are more deserving of wealth or status than
others. It justifies the resulting hierarchies on the grounds that those
who occupy higher rungs deserve more because of their greater contribution to the general welfare. Plato and Aristotle invoke the principle to
justify the political authority of elites.[61] For Aristotle, an aristocrat and
defender of aristocracy, well-born people alone had leisure and with it
the possibility of attaining virtue and of providing good government for
the polis. Politics in ancient Greece and Rome was framed in terms of
virtue. Individuals and groups vying for power claimed to possess qualities that made them more qualified to rule. In the eighteenth and nineteenth centuries, liberal thinkers contested the claim that some people
possessed more moral worth than others because of their "noble birth."
They affirmed the natural equality of human beings.

A second and modern formulation of fairness stipulates that whatever is available should go to those who need it the most. Its most famous

expression is found in Marx's dictum: "From each according to his abilities, to each according to his need."[62] It is evident today in such practices as handicapped parking spaces, special education programs, scholarships based on need, and tax deductions for medical expenses. Although this was certainly not Marx's intention, fairness framed this way can be used to justify hierarchies, or at least make them more acceptable. It softens their consequences by looking after those who have lost out or are unable to compete.

There are other principles of justice, and they are more limited in scope. Commutative justice refers to relations between individuals or institutions regarding contracts and the equitable exchange of goods. The laws and norms governing it rest on the principles of fairness or equality, and usually some combination of the two. The same is true of procedural justice, expected to govern the methods used to settle disputes and allocate resources.[63] Here too the arguments in support of procedural justice invariably rely on the principles of fairness or equality. William Barbieri has made the case for "constitutive justice," on the grounds that membership in a community is logically prior to distribution and subject to its own form of justice.[64] It is another principle that can be reduced to fairness and equality. This applies also to organizational justice, which refers to how employees judge its productivity, their contribution to it, and their relationship to the organization.[65]

Justice can be framed in terms of rights. Robert Nozick, arguably the most extreme proponent of this approach, rejects equality as a principle. This move, he claims, "is justified by a fundamental moral insight." A just outcome is one in which no rights were abused in the trail of transactions leading up to it. His theory of justice is not what he calls a "patterned" one. A just outcome might be grossly unequal, but nevertheless be just because it is based on a trail of proper transactions between or among rights holders. What does matter is that the initial set of holdings is just. Here at the beginning of trading – when the market opens, as it were – fairness and equality find traction. Equality is present in another way for Nozick and liberal rights theorists who consider just outcomes that many others would consider unequal and therefore unjust. It resides in the equal sets of rights individuals are taken to possess.[66] In effect, Nozick is defending the status quo, and doing so by rejecting equality and fairness as principles. He never asks how these rights came into being and if they were the result of coercion and oppression. This may help to explain why it has found so little traction.

Michael Walzer categorizes types of benefits and burdens and looks for principles relevant to each. His theory of justice maintains that different principles should govern different spheres of activity.[67] The rules of friendship are accordingly different from those of market competition. Drawing on Aristotle's conceptualization of friendship, Walzer argues that friends do things for one another because they are friends – but they become close friends in part because they treat each other as equals and with fairness. In market transactions, equality is central; buyers and sellers should be treated the same way and have access to the same market mechanisms. Similar arguments are made by Jon Elster and H. P. Young, both of whom maintain that different principles of justice should apply in different spheres of life.[68]

In his influential theory of justice, John Rawls argues that it is achieved through a proper balance of liberty and equality. He assumes a society of moderate scarcity populated by actors who are not entirely selfish, prefer cooperation to conflict, and are accordingly willing to advance their interests through compromises. He contends that people placed behind a "veil of ignorance" – deprived of their existing possessions and status in society – would find the two principles of justice he proposes the most acceptable. They would agree that everyone should "have an equal right to the most extensive basic liberty compatible with a similar liberty for others."[69] He enumerates a list of essential liberties, almost all drawn from the US Constitution's Bill of Rights. People would also insist on equal opportunity to acquire wealth and offices, but under conditions of "fair equality of opportunity" that are of the greatest benefit to the least advantaged members of society.[70] This requires offices and positions to be distributed on the basis of merit, but that everyone has a reasonable opportunity to acquire the skills necessary to compete for them.

Rawls' liberal world attempts to blend the principles of fairness and equality, and to find a justification for making trade-offs between them. His principle of liberty is a constitutive one, as it describes a set of conditions (e.g. freedom of speech, assembly, religion) that enable a liberal political order and independent civil society. These conditions require or enable fairness or equality, but, he insists, cannot be reduced to them because they concern distribution only indirectly. Rawls' principle of liberty fails to meet the test of universality. It would be incomprehensible to anyone in ancient Europe and much of the contemporary world. It is liberal ideology masquerading as moral philosophy.

Rawls supposes universal, innate understandings of justice. To test his claim, we would have to conduct an experiment by putting people in the original condition – stripping them of their roles, possessions, and personae and intellectual commitments – and have them construct what they considered to be an ideal society, or evaluate constitutive, procedural, and distributive principles that are presented to them. We might reasonably expect that people from different cultures and epochs would respond differently. In former times – and in the present day – where fairness is the dominant principle, people might not be troubled at all by hierarchies and consider differentiation in wealth and status as critical to order and a good life.

More problematic for Rawls is the impossibility of conducting such an experiment. Rawls, Walzer, and Nozick are representatives of the liberal tradition and assume that the appropriate starting place for any understanding of justice is the autonomous individual. Ronald Dworkin and Amartya Sen, at least implicitly, require these individuals to transform their attributes and advantages into a successful life.[71] Such a person is pure fiction. The ancient Greeks and Hobbes understood that people removed from their affiliations, roles, and the constraints of society are largely deprived of their humanity and reduced to a bundle of raw appetites guided by short-term instrumental reason.[72] They would be like mythical wolf-children, or the odd historical feral child: without language, empathy, social skills, or cognitive capacity to grasp the meaning of justice. Two centuries before Rawls, David Hume conducted an amusing but compelling thought experiment to demonstrate the impossibility of explaining the concept of justice to Adam and Eve. Justice must be internalized to work, a process beyond the ken of the inhabitants of the Garden of Eden, Hume believed, or of any small group of hunter-gatherers.[73] Rawls commits an error common to Romantics and many contemporary philosophers who assume that people have identities independent of their affiliations, roles, relationship to their bodies, and histories.[74] He is another example of someone pushing an ideology in the guise of objective inquiry.

There are social, as opposed to individual, understandings of justice. One of the oldest and most universal may be what the ancient Greek called *xenia* (guest friendship). It required travelers to offer food and shelter to needy travelers. They in turn were expected to honor their hosts and not overstay their welcome.[75] All forms of solidarity, of which guest friendship is only one, rest on "special obligations" or duties. These duties may be to one's family fellow citizens, nation, to humanity or the planet. They too are ultimately based on principles of fairness or equality. To varying degrees, they underlie the norms of family life in all cultures. They also justify civic duties such as paying taxes and military service. For evidence, we need look no further than the arguments of those who oppose particular arrangements; they invariably invoke the principles of fairness or equality (e.g. it is unfair for the rich to pay less tax than the poor; that military service, like all obligations, should be borne equally and not levied disproportionately on the poor or less educated). These examples suggest that governments also have obligations to their citizens. Most of these also rest on principles of fairness or equality (e.g. the right of habeas corpus, healthcare, pensions).

Analyses of distribution frequently fail to distinguish between fairness and equality. In an otherwise excellent policy text, Deborah Stone writes: "Keep in mind that in a distributive conflict, *all* sides seek equality; the conflict comes over how the sides envisage a fair distribution of whatever is at stake."[76] Fairness and equality are different principles and identify different criteria for distribution. In the pages that follow Stone does a thorough job of identifying nine criteria: membership, merit, rank, group-based, need, value, competitions, lotteries, and elections.[77] She describes them all as principles of equality, but only membership and competition might qualify, depending on what percentage of the population is included. Merit, rank, need, and value are forms of fairness. Lotteries and elections are forms of commutative justice, and can be reduced to equality or fairness.

The elision of fairness and equality is not a sign of intellectual sloppiness but rather of efforts in the modern era to combine these principles. Consider the institution of the Electoral College and the American practice – continually challenged in the courts – of affirmative action. They are highly contentious, in large part because of how they try to combine fairness and equality. The Electoral College was set up to strike a balance between the more populous urbanized states and less populous rural ones, privileging fairness over equality, but also recognizing equality by awarding more electoral votes to populous states. Democrats especially resent the advantage this gives to Republican states and the presidential victory it provided to Donald Trump, who trailed Hillary Clinton by three million popular votes. In theory, a candidate could win the Electoral College with no more than 20 percent of the popular vote.

Affirmative action was based on fairness – giving special privileges to African-Americans, many of whom were otherwise disadvantaged in the university admission process – in the hoping of achieving the longer-term goal of racial equality. Proponents argued that it was redressing de facto affirmative action for well-to-do whites, many of whom attended better-funded and higher-quality primary and secondary schools. Some gained admission to private universities on the basis of being "legacies," that is sons or daughters of graduates. Those opposed to affirmative action argued that it was unfair because the same admission criteria were not applied across the board.

The controversy of affirmative action also involves different understandings of fairness and equality. Those in favor define fairness in terms of giving more to those who need it more, and equality in terms of equal distribution (their longer-term goal being equalization of black and white incomes by means of education and the better career opportunities this provides). Those opposed define fairness as giving more to those who deserve more by virtue of their relative excellence, and equality in the liberal sense of an equal opportunity to compete. Beginning in the 1950s many conservatives argued that African-Americans had no claim to equal school funding because they did not produce enough tax revenue to support it.[78] As this example illustrates, framings can be selective and self-serving, but the ability of the two sides to appeal to what to them were obvious principles of justice made them more unyielding and their conflict more acute.

When two principles of justice are combined, as they are in the Electoral College and affirmative action, it becomes difficult to keep them distinct. This has been taken another step in contemporary western discourses where fairness and equality are increasingly used interchangeably in everyday discourse. Equality is described as fairness, and fairness as equality.[79] This is promising in one respect because all best worlds combine the two principles in some form, as utopia builders from Plato to Rawls sought to do. But it is confusing and leads to misunderstandings and people talking at cross-purposes. It also finesses hard choices. There are good normative and analytical reasons to differentiate the two principles.

David Hume was among the first modern thinkers to offer an account of justice and government that is historical and dispenses with the fictions of the state of nature and the social contract.[80] Early human societies, he contends, were little more than extended family groups – bottom-up orders in my language. They functioned on the basis of what he calls "natural justice," something that derives from love of oneself and one's friends. People come to know and experience the feelings of others and develop sympathy for them.[81] Such sympathy grows fainter with physical and social distance.[82] "Artificial justice" then developed and consists of conventions intended to reduce conflict in conditions of scarcity. Hume theorizes that it is a response to problems people encounter as their societies become larger and more complex.[83]

As the size of communities increases, so do disputes over all kinds of possessions. People are motivated to reduce conflict and develop mechanisms to do this by trial and error. Their experiments take the form of interpersonal agreements that, if successful, prompt imitation. By this means certain conventions and practices become more general.[84] When society reaches a certain size some people can ignore or flout conventions and get away without being observed or punished.[85] The attractiveness of free-riding creates the need for some enforcement mechanism and, ultimately, for government.[86] People will only restrain themselves when they believe that others will do so as well. The expectation of reciprocity in self-restraint accordingly demands some authority that enforces rules.[87]

Hume was probably right in reasoning that equality was the dominant principle of justice among hunter-gathers and early agriculturalists. Anthropologists tell us that it is true today – or was until quite recently – among isolated hunter-gatherer societies. Groups like the Dobe Ju/ 'hoansi (formerly described as the !Kung) in southern Africa, and the BaMbuti of the Ituri Forest in Zaire (formerly called Pygmies) had no government or even informal leadership. They created solidarity on the basis of kinship, friendship, and equality. They learned the principle of fairness from outsiders and used it to govern their relations with them, but not among themselves.[88]

Elsewhere in the world, sedentary agriculture and economic development led to larger societies and more formal kinds of hierarchies. They often employ principles of fairness and equality, and struggle to reconcile them. This is certainly the case in many, if not most, present-day states. Generally, everyone is liable to pay income tax, but many governments levy no tax on those they deem poor and impose proportionately higher rates on those with higher incomes. In the US Congress, representation in the Senate is based on equality and in the House of Representatives on proportionality, the latter a form of fairness.[89] The United Nations does something similar with the Security Council and General Assembly. Utopias almost invariably incorporate both principles of justice. John Rawls, for one, prioritizes equality in wealth, but is willing to allow some actors to receive additional compensation if they demonstrably increase the overall wealth or well-being of the society.[90]

Discourses about justice are unique to human beings. However, many primate societies appear to function on the basis of fairness and equality. Noted ethologist Frans de Waal reports that young chimpanzees learn rules of comportment and subsequently trust only those who follow them. One of the most important rules is to share food if, for whatever reason, you have more than others. Alpha males, who are generally allowed to eat first on what we would call the principle of fairness, nevertheless uphold the principle of equality by distributing most of what they are given to others. Reciprocal performance of these principles of justice behavior builds trust and solidarity and reduces social conflict.[91] Christopher Boehm reports that human foragers deal the same way with the meat problem. "They invariably treat a sizable carcass as being community rather than individual property, and they put its distribution in the hands of a neutral party who will not try to politicize the meat distribution and come out ahead."[92]

Plato was among the first philosophers to assert that orders depend on principles of justice. His Protagoras recounts a founding myth of Greek society.[93] At the outset, humans fed, housed, and clothed themselves by relying on instinct. They lived isolated lives and were prey to wild animals. They banded together for self-protection, but treated one another so badly that they soon sought refuge again in their individual caves. Zeus took pity on them and sent Hermes to give them *aidōs* (respect, reverence) and *dikē* (justice) so that they could live together harmoniously. *Dikē* is an ordering principle that requires people to treat others as equals, attempt to see things from their point of view, and to empathize with them.

Justice in this understanding is closely related to trust. Trust is the expectation that others will honor their promises and conform to their rule packages. Political orders, like their economic and social counterparts, rely on a high degree of trust, as many critical actions are sequential rather than simultaneous. Actors are unlikely to commit themselves to any venture involving significant upfront costs if they do not believe that others live up to their part of the bargain.[94] Reciprocity, the principal mechanism of trust, builds on the principles of fairness and equality: tit-for-tat in obligations, and equal standing of actors in any bargain regardless of other inequalities between them.

Legitimate orders are those supported by most of their population. Legitimacy is a daily referendum in which people decide to follow or defy norms and laws.[95] All legitimate orders rest on principles of justice, but no order fully lives up to them. As noted, elites are universally more privileged in practice than are warranted by the principles of justice on which their advantages are justified.

Elites invariably sponsor or support discourses to justify the inequalities from which they benefit and to explain away differences between what justice would demand and the realities of their society. Early efforts of this kind generally appealed to gods rather than principles of justice. In western culture, theodicies often took the form of golden ages. The two best known are Hesiod's *Works and Days* and the Garden of Eden story in the Book of Genesis. The former describes the successive degeneration of people from a "golden race" to the present, and from a society governed by justice to one ruled by force.[96] The Garden of Eden is a paradise from which people are expelled because of their violation of God's command not to eat from the tree of knowledge. In *Works and Days* gods, not rulers, are responsible for the current state of affairs, and nothing can be done to improve it. In Genesis, people are responsible, and hunger, death, pain in childbirth and injustice – in Roman Catholic readings – are the price we must pay for Adam and Eve's transgression.[97]

In European culture, cosmic justifications of order were dominant in the Middle Ages and the basis for the divine right of kings. In China, the equivalent was the Mandate of Heaven, and other indigenous forms developed in South and Southeast Asia. Engels and Gramsci made us more sensitive to the extent to which elite-sponsored discourses can create "false consciousness" that reconciles people to orders in which they are exploited.[98]

Discourses of this kind have enabled a wide range of societies to establish more legitimacy than they might otherwise have. Engels and Gramsci lament that one of the distinguishing features of their success is the degree to which respect for authority and the ideology on which it rests are internalized by the very people these orders disadvantage. Marxists and some postmodernists largely ignore the potential of counter-discourses, even though they are active in creating them. These may be successful in arousing opposition to orders, or become more attractive and even popular when disaffection with orders mounts.

A monopoly over discourses and communication channels enhances governmental authority. It stifles imagination and dissent, the former being the prerequisite of dissent. Combined with some kind of intrusive police apparatus – as control over discourses so often is – it can make it difficult for any opposition that does develop. Many traditional orders benefitted from near total elite control over discourses. In Medieval Europe, the Catholic Church prohibited translations of the Latin bible into vulgate because churchmen correctly understood that they would lose control over the text that sustained their authority. The first English translation, by William Tyndale in 1525, was banned in England and English clerics visiting the continent were instructed to buy and burn as many copies as they could.[99] Access to the bible in English enabled the rise of the Puritans and other dissenting sects and their rejection of religious and civil authority was an underlying cause of the English Civil War.

Monopolizing discourses is more difficult for modern governments, but not impossible. Czarist Russia tried and failed to do this. Stalin's Soviet Union was reasonably effective, and his successors attempted, with less success, to follow suit. Contemporary dictatorships struggle to control discourses and communication channels, and North Korea is arguably the most successful. In *1984* George Orwell explored the mechanisms that can be mobilized toward this end. They include control of the media, relentless propaganda, transformation and dumbing down of language to prevent independent thought, and a police apparatus that prevents the formation of civil society.

Monopolization of discourses may be threatening to orders in the longer term. China aspires to this level of control, and its recent tightening of censorship is described in Chapter 8. The regime regards control of information as a source of stability. The fragmentation of society it encourages and the stifling or suppression of dissent discourage or impede creativity and productivity, making such societies less competitive. So too does the central control over political, economic, and cultural life that monopolization requires. Liberals describe these features of the Soviet Union as the most important underlying cause of its collapse. North Korea went from a rapidly developing economy to a basket case, with a population haunted by the prospect of famine, and now, with some encouragement of the market, is once again a developing economy.[100] Chapter 8 explores this problem and asks, using a case study of China, if authoritarian regimes can develop long-term stability.

In 1932, in a speech to the British House of Commons, Prime Minister Stanley Baldwin warned that in a future war "the bomber will always get through" and that Britain's cities would be destroyed.[101] He was, of course, wrong. Discourses, by contrast, are much more likely to get through, as they did in the eras of Christian and Muslim proselytizing. Enlightenment assaults on the cosmic order, and especially the divine right of kings, and propagation of the belief that people had the capability to understand and reshape their physical and social environments had wide appeal. According to Tocqueville, pre-revolutionary France was made ripe for revolution by the influence elite anti-establishment narratives of this kind had on the masses.[102] *Ancien régimes* sought to suppress books that might lead people to question the authority of church or state, but this notoriety made such books more popular, and greater demand for them made them more available.[103]

Discourses are double-edged swords. They help sustain the *nomos* essential to any society. By *nomos*, I mean the norms, rules, laws and accepted practices that make behavior legible and more predictable by directing it down some channels and away from others. *Nomos* facilitates the legitimization of hierarchies, but unlike golden age narratives also encourages people to hope, even expect, that their societies will live up to their ethical justifications and abide by their sanctioned practices. The more societies propagate and publicize discourses intended to justify them, the more they are compelled to honor them. As Donald Davidson suggests, "justifications of actions can also be their causes."[104] Elites and their orders also become vulnerable to immanent critiques that expose the gap between theory and practice. Modern history especially is replete with critical discourses of this kind and political movements that sponsor or build on them to promote change. Political elites can often suppress these discourses and those who produce and distribute them, but help to validate them by these efforts.

The ability of critics to produce and publicize counter-discourses, the ease with which authorities can suppress or counter them, and the relative

appeal of discourses and counter-discourses is always context dependent
and thus outside of any general theory.[105] Some generalizations are
nevertheless possible. Theodicies do not depend on appropriate elite
behavior. Indeed, elite exploitation and mass suffering are perfectly
consistent with them. Widespread suffering might even be offered as
confirmation of the claims of such works as Hesiod's *Works and Days*
and the Garden of Eden story in *Genesis*. By contrast, discourses that
defend elite status privileges, on the basis of the benefits that elites
provide to the society, are open to challenge when elites fail to live up
to their self-proclaimed rule packages. All modern governments and
political orders rest on such claims, which can build legitimacy – or
make them vulnerable – depending on public attitudes. This explains
why political protest is more prevalent and more successful in the
modern era.

Discourses intended to sustain orders invariably invite immanent
and empirical critiques. The Book of Genesis and its Garden of Eden
story provide a nice example. Augustine sought to strengthen this discourse by portraying Adam, Eve, and the serpent as real beings, not as
allegory, as Jews and some early Christians like Origen maintained. He
was successful in imposing this view on Catholicism, and convinced that
it would help propagate the religion. By the Renaissance it had become a
source of doubt and stimulus for disbelief. It brought into sharper focus
the ethical dilemmas associated with the story, especially the inexplicable
transformation from innocence to wickedness. It also encouraged people
to look for the real Garden of Eden, to compute how many generations
had elapsed since creation, and to ponder where and how Cain would
have found a wife once expelled from his family if his parents, Adam
and Eve, were the first humans. The discovery of the New World and
its peoples who felt no shame in nudity was the first of many empirical
conundrums for true believers.[106] Geology's discovery of the age of the
earth, and biology's of evolution, would only heighten these tensions and
convince many to dismiss Genesis as a fable.[107]

Critics of Marxism and neoliberalism have highlighted internal
contradictions in their internal logic as well as critiquing them on empirical grounds. The stronger and more vivid the claims of a discourse,
the more likely the possibility of an immanent critique, and the more
powerful the discourse, the more effective the critique – in the absence
of its suppression. But, I have argued, suppression may only shift the
grounds of the contest, and in the longer term in a way unfavorable to
those attempting to uphold the discourse in question.

Discourses and legitimacy can also be undercut by actions sharply
at odds with the proclaimed values and goals of the top-down order.

The Stalin-Hitler Pact prompted great disillusionment among both Nazi and Communist true believers. It provoked the wry observation of a British diplomat that, "All the isms are now wasms."[108]

Counter-elites can also do their best to expose discrepancies between theory and practice. Gandhi's policy of Satyagraha was intended to arouse and intensify dissonance among British colonial officials and the British people more generally about the gulf between their claims and practice.[109] Mervyn Frost and the author have explored a foreign policy version in which weaker political movements or states provoke more powerful states into behaving in ways at odds with their proclaimed values and goals. By doing so, the weaker party can build support or undermine that of the stronger power. We document four historical examples of successful ethical trapping: in the American colonies, Spain, Northern Ireland, and the Gaza Strip.[110]

Discourses can generate misplaced trust in and respect for elites. The more the *dēmos* trust the elite, the more the elite can exploit them. This results in orders that deviate further from their proclaimed principles of justice. The less faith the *dēmos* have in elites, the more likely they are to hold them accountable to relevant principles of justice. Too much trust threatens justice and order, as does too much distrust. In practice, order and justice need to be balanced, and this requires a degree of distrust, but not so much to cause high levels of alienation and violation of norms.[111] Order also requires some degree of tension between discourses and behavior that support existing values and practices and those that oppose them. I explore these tensions and their implications for order in the chapters that follow.

Notes

1 Walsingham, *Historia Anglicana*, II, p. 375. Friedman, "'When Adam Delved …'" for a slightly different version.

2 Weber, "Conceptual Exposition"; Lebow, "Weber and Knowledge."

3 Scriven, "Explanations, Predictions and Laws"; Lebow, *Causation in International Relations*, chs. 1–3.

4 On hierarchy, Weber, *Political Writings*, p. 311; Fiske, "Interpersonal Stratification: Status, Power, and Subordination." On solidarity, Rousseau, *Discourse on Political Economy*, *Social Contract*, and *Government of Poland*; Durkheim, *Division of Labor in Society*, pp. 229–30.

5 Mazrui, *Towards and Pax Africana*; Bull, "Order vs. Justice in International Society."

6 Badie, *Les temps humilés*.

7 Lebow, *Self-Interest from Tocqueville to Trump*, ch. 1. for running red lights and its broader political and social implications.

8 Kohn, *Idea of Nationalism*; Deutsch, *Nationalism and Social Communication*; Anderson, *Imagined Communities*.

9 Linneweaver, Davies, and Ruse, "What is Complexity?"

10 Lebow, "Darwin and International Relations."

11 Losos, *Impossible Destinies*, pp. 276–77.

12 Braumoeller, *Great Powers and the International System*, for the most recent attempt in international relations.

13 Minsky, "Financial Instability Hypothesis"; *Economist*, "Minsky's Moment," July 30 2016, www.economist.com/news/economics-brief/21702740-second-article-our-series-seminal-economic-ideas-looks-hyman-minskys (accessed August 15 2017).

14 Kaufman, Little, and Wohlforth, *Balance of Power in World History*, pp. 229–30.

15 Morgenthau, *Politics Among Nations*, pp. 21, 159–66, 270–84, and *In Defense of the National Interest*, p. 60.

16 Kang, "Hierarchy and legitimacy in International Systems" and *East Asia Before the West.*

17 Weber, "Die Objectivitätsozialwissenschaftlicher und sozialpolitischer Erkenntnis," (The "Objectivity" of Knowledge in the Social Sciences), pp. 175–78. For a recent recognition and application of the social truth, see Nelson, and Katzenstein, "Uncertainty, Risk, and the Financial Crisis of 2008."

18 Lebow, *National Identifications and International Relations*, ch. 1, for a critique of the concept of system applied to social and political orders.

19 Gleick, *Chaos*, pp. 12–19; Goldstein, "Emergence as a Construct: History and Issues"; Goodwin, *How the Leopard Changed Its Spots.*

20 Lebow, *Cultural Theory of International Relations*, ch. 1 on this point.

21 Maine, *Ancient Law*, p. 20.

22 Dicey, *Lectures on the Relation between Law and Public Opinion during the Nineteenth Century*, p. 377.

23 Mikhail Gorbachev and the German Question, p. 161, document published in Russian. Quoted in Sarottte, *Collapse*, p. 22.

24 Brown, *Rise and Fall of Communism*, pp. 481–502.

25 Lévesque, *Enigma of 1989*, pp. 149–64; Sarotte, *Collapse*, chs. 6–7.

26 Bak and Chen, "Self-Organized Criticality."

27 Mark Olden, "White riot: The week Notting Hill exploded," *Independent*, August 29 2008, www.independent.co.uk/news/uk/home-news/white-riot-the-week-notting-hill-exploded-912105.html (accessed March 20 2014).

28 Lebow, *Forbidden Fruit*, chs. 1 and 3.

29 Onuf, "Recognition and the Constitution of Epochal Change."

30 Lebow, *Constructing Cause in International Relations*, ch. 4.

31 Waltz, *Theory of International Politics.*

32 Mapping Police Violence.org, "Mapping Police Violence," October 17 2017, https://mappingpoliceviolence.org/ (accessed March 27 2018); Jelani Cobb, "The Matter of Black Lives," *New Yorker*, March 14 2016, www.newyorker.com/magazine/2016/03/14/where-is-black-lives-matter-headed (accessed October 27 2017).

33 Lebow, *Cultural Theory of International Relations*, chs. 2 and 3; Behr, *Politics of Difference*, p. 33.

34 Behr, *Politics of Difference*, for a discussion of some of these authors.

35 Wikipedia, "Ultimatum Game," http://en.wikipedia.org/wiki/Ultimatum_game (accessed October 13 2014); *International Security* 20, no. 1 (1995),

pp. 39–52. Knoch, Pascual-Leone, Meyer, Treyer and Fehr, "Diminishing Reciprocal Fairness by Disrupting the Right Prefrontal Cortex," make the case for humans being hardwired to favor equality.

36 Abramowitz, "Partisan Polarization and the Rise of the Tea Party Movement"; Bafumi and Herron, "Prejudice, Black Threat, and the Racist Voter in the 2008 Election"; Emily Ekins, "Five Kinds of Trump Voters: Who Are They and What They Believe," *Voter Study Group*, June 2017, www.voterstudygroup .org/reports/2016-elections/the-five-types-trump-voters (accessed August 5 2017).

37 Barry, *Theories of Justice*, I, p. 6.

38 Gauthier, *Morals by Agreement*.

39 Ibid., pp. 51–53.

40 Plato, *Republic*, 328e–331d.

41 Ibid., 332c.

42 Ibid., 338c.

43 Ibid., Books II–IV.

44 Miller, *Principles of Social Justice*, p. 21, characterizes justice as a social virtue that tells us how to order our relationships, what we must rightly do for one another; Stuart Hampshire, *Innocence and Experience*, p. 63, writes that "from the earliest time to today, justice refers to an ordered and reasonable procedure of weighing claims." Rawls, *Theory of Justice*, equates it with fairness, which he describes as a society of free citizens holding equal basic rights and cooperating within an egalitarian economic system. MacIntyre, *Whose Justice?*, p. 39, says "Justice is a disposition to give to each person, including oneself, what that person deserves and to treat no one in a way incompatible with their deserts."

45 Roemer, *Equality of Opportunity*, for an overview.

46 Miller, *Principles of Social Justice*.

47 Ibid., pp. 39–40.

48 Lasswell, *Who Gets What, When, and How?* Lasswell also offers broader definitions of politics in this book: as the conditions and justification of influence and control, and as deliberation and action toward the common good.

49 Deutsch, *Distributive Justice*, p. 1. Homans, *Social Behavior*, for the pioneering study of distributive justice.

50 See Chapter 3 for discussion.

51 Dobson, *Peasants Revolt*; Justice, *Writing and Rebellion*.

52 Walsingham, *Historia Anglicana*, II, p. 375.

53 Aristotle, *Nicomachean Ethics*, 1132a4–a5.

54 Smith, *Wealth of Nations*, I.viii.36; Hume, *Enquiry Concerning the Principles of Morals*, 3.9–12.

55 Hjorth, *Equality in International Society*, p. 6; Crosland, *Future of Socialism*, for an attack on public schools, inherited wealthy, and other privileges that sustain the British elite.

56 Rawls, *Theory of Justice* for a justification of an unequal distribution if it was arrived at fairly and benefits the society as a whole.

57 Roemer, *Equality of Opportunity*, for a review and critique of the relevant literature.

58 Hirschman, *Passions and the Interests*; Hont, *Jealousy of Trade*; Lebow, *Cultural Theory of International Relations*, ch. 3.
59 Plato, *Republic*, 560e5, 561a6–562a2, 561c6–d5 and 572-b10–573b4.
60 Lebow, *National Identities and International Relations*, ch. 4.
61 Aristotle, *Nicomachean* Ethics,1131b29–1131b30. Lebow, *Cultural Theory of International Relations*, chs. 3 and 4 for a discussion.
62 Marx, *Critique of the Gotha Program*.
63 For psychological studies on procedural justice, Thibaut and Walker, *Procedural Justice*; Leventhal, "Fairness in Social Relationships"; Lind, Kanfer, and Earley, "Voice Control and Procedural Justice"; Lind and Tyler, *Social Psychology of Procedural Justice*; Brockner and Wiesenfeld, "Integrative Framework for Explaining Reactions to Decisions."
64 Barbieri, *Constitutive Justice*, pp. 2–3.
65 Colquitt, Greenberg and Scott, "Organizational Justice"; Colquitt, Greenberg and Zapata-Phelan, "What is Organizational Justice?" Crawshaw, Cropanzano, Bell, and Nadisic, "Organizational Justice."
66 Nozick, *Anarchy, State, and Utopia*.
67 Walzer, *Spheres of Justice*.
68 Elster, *Local Justice*; Young, *Equity*.
69 Rawls, *Theory of Justice*, p. 52.
70 Ibid.
71 Dworkin, "What is Equality? Parts I and II; Sen, *Commodities and Capabilities*.
72 Hobbes, *Leviathan*, chs. 13–14.
73 Hume, *Treatise of Human Nature*, 3.2.2.10.
74 Lebow, *Politics and Ethics of Identity*, ch. 1.
75 Finley, *World of Odysseus*, pp. 99–101, on guest friendship in the Homeric age.
76 Stone, *Policy Paradox*, p. 39.
77 Ibid., pp. 39–60.
78 MacLean, *Democracy in Chains*.
79 Scott, *Heart of Midlothian* is based on this premise.
80 Hume, *Treatise of Human Nature*, 3.2.2.15, on the state of nature.
81 Ibid., 2.3.6.8 and *Enquiry Concerning the Principles of Morals*, section 3, appendix 3.
82 Hume, *Enquiry Concerning the Principles of Morals*, 5.2.42.
83 Hume, *Treatise of Human Nature*, 3.2.2.4.
84 Ibid., 3.2.2.1–22.
85 Ibid., 3.3.1.10; *Enquiry Concerning the Principles of Morals*, section 4.
86 Hume, *Treatise of Human Nature*, 3.2.7.
87 Ibid., 3.2.2.10.
88 Turnbull, *Forest People*, pp. 110–14; Lee, Dobe Ju/'hoansi, pp. 109–24; Biesele and Hitchcock, Ju/'hoan San of Nyae Nyae and Namibian Independence, pp. 65–90.
89 Madison, "Federalist 62."
90 Rawls, *Theory of Justice*.
91 De Waal, "Natural Normativity."
92 Boehm, *Moral Origins*.
93 Plato, *Protagoras*, 322c8–323.

94 Warren, *Democracy and Trust*, on the debate over trust and democracy.

95 Linz, *Breakdown of Democratic Regimes*, pp. 15–17.

96 The nineteenth-century British classicist George Grote observed that Hesiod's story of the five ages represents a fusion of two distinct and incompatible myths. The first, which predates Hesiod, is the myth of the Four Ages, all bearing names of metals, and succeeding each other in declining order of value. The second is the age of heroes, which Hesiod or a precursor inserted between the third and fourth age. Berlin, *Crooked Timber of Humanity*, p. 25.

97 Lebow, *Politics and Ethics of Identity*, ch. 2, for an analysis and comparison of these texts.

98 Marx and Engels, *German Ideology*; Gramsci, *Letters From Prison*.

99 Greenblatt, *Renaissance Self-Fashioning*.

100 Eberstadt, *North Korean Economy*; Cha, *North Korea*.

101 Stanley Baldwin, "Fear of the Future," November 10 1932, House of Commons Debate, International Affairs, *Hansard*, 270, pp. 631–35, http://hansard.millbanksystems.com/commons/1932/nov/10/international-affairs#S5CV0270P0_19321110_HOC_284 (accessed February 21 2016).

102 Tocqueville, *Old Regime*, pp. 142–44; Israel, *Revolutionary Ideas*, pp. 30–53.

103 Blanning, *Joseph II and Enlightened Despotism*, pp. 136–44

104 Davidson, "Actions, Reasons, and Causes."

105 Skocpol, *State and Social Revolutions*; Goldstone, *Revolutions in Early Modern Europe*; Goldstone, Gurr, and Moshiri, *Revolutions in the Late Twentieth Century*.

106 Greenblatt, *Rise and Fall of Adam and Eve*, pp. 241–61.

107 Maddox, *Reading the Rocks*.

108 Kotkin, *Stalin*, p. 673, citing a memorandum in the Chamberlain Papers.

109 Erikson, *Gandhi's Truth*.

110 Frost and Lebow, "Ethical Traps."

111 Lebow, "Trust in International Relations."

3 Why Do Orders Form?

> Hence it is evident that the state is a creation of nature, and that man is by nature a political animal. And he who by nature and not by mere accident is without a state, is either above humanity, or below it; he is the 'Tribeless, lawless, heartless one,' whom Homer denounces – the outcast who is a lover of war; he may be compared to a bird which flies alone.
>
> Aristotle[1]

This chapter addresses the origins of social and political orders. I begin by noting how bottom-up orders are necessary to satisfy human needs. Top-down orders also become essential in a conflictual world, and one in which societies grow in size. I suggest that we can learn something about the origins of human society by looking at primate societies. This comparison also tells us something about how they are organized. Human and animal societies require high degrees of cooperation, and this appears to be sustained through the principles of fairness and equality. Primate and human societies rely on different combinations of these principles.

Humans rely on multiple mechanisms of cooperation, chief among them fear, interest, and honor. They rest on different principles of justice and collectively have the potential to make compliance habitual. This makes enforcement easier for either top-down or bottom-up orders, which usually, although not always, enhances the likelihood of compliance. The relative importance of each mechanism for compliance varies within both kinds of order but there is much more variance among top-down orders. Modernity has affected all of them in fundamental ways. To get a handle on the nature of this change, I review the expectations of key nineteenth-century sociologists and the theoretical assumptions on which they were based. None of them refer specifically to top-down or bottom-up orders, but implicitly make this distinction. Their expectations about their basis and relative importance vary considerably. Their approaches are useful starting points for mine.

Origins

Aristotle describes human beings as *zoon politkon*, by which he means political animals.[2] He considers the polis "natural," as people, unlike many animals, are not self-sufficient.[3] Hermits, outcasts, and other loners aside, humans live in social and political orders. Contemporary westerners become seriously depressed in the absence of social contact. Lonely people are 50 percent more likely to die prematurely.[4] Elderly people with spouses have a 90 percent chance of living beyond the age of sixty-five, but this falls to 65 percent for the un-partnered. Solitary confinement, David Hume thought, "is perhaps the greatest punishment we can suffer."[5] It is almost universally considered a form of punishment bordering on torture.[6]

Archaeological evidence supports Aristotle's claim. Neanderthals and some other early hominids prepared their food, but ate alone or as a nuclear family. Neanderthal families appear to have huddled around separate fires, located close to other families, but far enough apart to reduce the likelihood that someone would steal their food. Prehistoric humans ate together in larger groups. Homo sapiens is also unique for its willingness to eat with strangers. Martin Jones reports that archeologists "know of no other species that will gather to share food with a complete stranger."[7]

People everywhere develop uplifting origin stories and myths about their pasts.[8] In his *Aeneid* Virgil portrays the Trojans as the founders of Rome, a lineage that would later be claimed by a score of European societies.[9] These stories bear little relationship to historical truth, but tell us a lot about the needs of people to glorify their communities as a means of building individual self-esteem and collective solidarity.[10] Ancient historians have had a field day debunking the myths of Troy and Romulus and Remus.[11] For much the same reason, people invent negative stories about their neighbors. Johann Magnus, a seventeenth-century historian of Sweden, wrote that Denmark was populated when King Erik "sent [there] all the useless and dissolute sort of People."[12]

We have few historical records about the founding of orders, and they invariably describe relatively recent attempts to found offshoot communities by settlers from older societies.[13] Recent research on the first cities in the ancient world stresses the foundational role of powerful individuals and groups, but also of local resources and contingency.[14] It further suggests that societies and small settlements arose thousands of years before what might be called "statelets" made their first appearance. Bottom-up orders preceded top-down ones and their members may well have resisted incorporation into larger units. States require surplus and their formation promotes its creation through extraction. A peasantry will not otherwise produce a surplus.[15] Warfare and slavery follow upon the creation of states, or at least become more acute in their aftermath. Owen Lattimore observed that city walls were built as much to keep residents in as to keep others out.[16]

Early states had trouble holding their populations and were prone to collapse and fragmentation. Collapse was often a product of their success. It brought larger numbers of people together in close quarters and made them increasingly dependent on monoculture and more vulnerable to parasites and other pathogens that affected crops, livestock, and humans. Dense settlements also undermined themselves through salinization and deforestation. Collapse might nevertheless mean nothing more than fragmentation into smaller settlements, some of them preexisting. Episodes of collapse and reintegration were repetitive and commonplace.[17] Collapse of top-down orders did not necessarily bring about a decline in physical well-being because bottom-up orders probably remained robust. Larger and more complex societies developed gradually, and seemingly in response to a division of labor and the greater agricultural surplus it provided.[18] It supported a warrior class, better weapons, more time for military training, all of which allowed the conquest of neighbors. At a much later date, empires emerged. The period 3200 to 2800 BCE is generally described as the era of "high civilization" in the Near East, during which Babylonia produced complex political, economic, and social orders.[19]

States required writing because once a settlement has more than a few thousand people, clerks can no longer keep records in their heads. Most early writing takes the form of tax records and commercial transactions. Law developed in response, and it too was written down.[20] Studies of ancient law lack reliable, if any, sources, because law came into effect long before it was committed to writing.[21] We do have records of more recent settlements, among them the English in Bermuda, Virginia, Massachusetts, Maine, and Newfoundland. They indicate formal arrangements for bottom-up orders in the form of compacts that settlers signed prior to departure. They invariably broke down not long after their arrival.[22]

Enlightenment philosophers developed contract theory to explain and justify political orders. For most of these theorists, contracts were thought experiments; they did not believe that historical orders – recent settlement aside – had begun this way. We know next to nothing about the circumstances in which any of these communities formed or what led them to organize and develop their diverse practices and beliefs. The most we can do is assume they were considered responses to the situations people faced. In his pamphlet opposing the proposed American constitution, "Brutus" infers: "The mutual wants of men, at first dictated the propriety of founding societies; and when they were established, protection and defense pointed out the necessity of instituting government."[23] Max Weber tells a similar tale.[24] Whiggish accounts of this kind portray cities and states as positive developments and steps up the imagined ladder of civilization. This view has come under attack recently by those who contend that cities and empires were more oppressive and injurious to health and longevity than hunting and gathering.[25]

It is difficult to make the case that cities, empires, and nation-states better serve human needs. They may promote greater security, but at significant cost. Archaeological evidence suggests that early hunter-gatherers were healthier and taller than modern farmers and city dwellers until the twentieth century.[26] Contemporary humans live longer on average and have a higher standard of living in some cities, but this is also a recent development. This was true well into modern times. For centuries Londoners died off at a much faster rate than the rural population and only survived as a city because its population was constantly replenished from the hinterland.[27]

Critics of the modern age contend that people were better off when they led simpler lives, but this assertion too is open to serious challenge.[28] It reflects nostalgic yearning for the pre-industrial life, just as, in an earlier stage of development, there was nostalgia for the pre-agricultural life.[29] Any comparison of the modern world with its pre-industrial predecessor, of empires with simpler agricultural communities, or of these settlements with hunter-gatherer bands, depends on the criteria we use, and they are thoroughly subjective.

Evolutionary psychology also makes opposing claims. Some of its practitioners assume that the present world is the best of all worlds in the sense of species fitness. Evolutionary psychologists reject out of hand the idea that the social and political worlds are path dependent and the contingent product of multiple causes, agency and chance, interacting in non-linear ways. Some contend that our world is a product of human evolutionary adaption to the Pliocene and that many traits conducive to survival in that epoch (e.g. addiction to fat, warfare) no longer are functional.[30]

Those on either side of this controversy believe that complex social patterns can be accounted for on the basis of a few simple assumptions and rules. They begin by asking what physiological features favor existing – or earlier – human circumstances and what evolutionary processes could have brought them about. Critics rightly object that their procedure involves circular reasoning because it works from the present backwards to construct an evolutionary narrative to account for the present – and a present, moreover, that is invariably characterized in a way that invites criticism on empirical and normative grounds.[31]

It is possible that hominids of all kinds inherited a propensity to live in social orders because it greatly enhanced the prospect of survival.[32] For apes and other primates, social groups provide security and facilitate hunting. Human communities may have arisen for the same reasons. Archaeological and other evidence indicates that for most of their existence human beings lived in bands, like many other primates, and only very recently in villages and cities. For our purposes, it is irrelevant whether the similarities between human and primate communities are the result of evolution, conscious adaptation, or imitation.[33] What matters is that cooperation develops, is essential to all orders, and is facilitated and sustained by principles of justice. This is an empirical truth, about whose origins we can only speculate.

Social orders among humans and animals require high degrees of cooperation. We find evidence of such cooperation among species as diverse as orcas, elephants, and parrots.[34] Among primates, alpha males routinely intervene to stop fights among other members of their group. They prefer grooming and sex with particular partners, but in stopping fights generally act impartially and independently of their social bonds.[35] Competition among males, and females, in primates and humans also suggests that members of these species may need social groups, but also have difficulty in living with one another. Immanuel Kant characterized this tension as the "unsocial sociality" of humankind.[36] For Freud, it was attributable to irreconcilable but fundamental human drives.[37] Kant and Freud both believed that humans could not survive for long or fulfill their needs in the absence of society.

A wide range of species enforces what can be characterized as the principle of fairness. Coyotes expel individuals from their pack who are selfish when it comes to hunting or food sharing. Cleaning fish do the same.[38] Reciprocity in the form of giving and receiving is a central feature of social life among chimpanzees and bonobos. There is little evidence of food stealing among these primates; they respect possession and will punish and chase off thieves and freeloaders. Alpha males will not take food from others, but beg for it. Those who grab food lose support and encourage younger challengers to step forward. Sharing is nevertheless more frequent with grooming partners, which offers more evidence for reciprocity, and also for memory and gratitude.[39]

Many animals appear to possess a commitment to equality. Capuchin monkeys are particularly sensitive to what they and others receive. Frans de Waal and his students conducted experiments in which Capuchins were given two foods valued differently, like cucumbers and grapes.

Offering one animal the preferred food and the other the less valued one prompts anger at the experimenter.[40] Additional evidence of the importance of equality among Capuchins is their refusal to work when they observe others who do not but still get food rewards. Experiments with dogs indicate that they can easily be taught to put their paw out for food but will do so less often if they observe other dogs who receive food without having to put out their paws. Among cooperative mammals, individuals look to see what others get and become angry if they receive less.[41]

Do chimps share out of a sense of reciprocity or do they simply feel good in the presence of those who have groomed them? Are Capuchins influenced by fairness or just holding out for grapes? Answers to these questions hinge on the intentionality of animals, and this can rarely, if ever, be determined from observation. The biological world is full of non-intentional behavior: plants reach out to the sun, fish rise to the surface when there is a disturbance that suggests the presence of food, and many animals will flee or fight depending on the distance between them and aggressors. We must be very careful about making inferences from behavior to intention. And all the more so when making connections between animal behavior and human principles of justice.[42]

There is evidence that some animals are proactive in striving for equal division of rewards. Ethologists who study these species suggest that their subjects imagine or foresee the possibility of another animal receiving more than they do, and possibly the negative consequences for themselves of having more than others. Bonobos seem to recognize the need for sharing. In one experiment, a male bonobo was repeatedly given chocolate. At a certain point the animal in question insisted that the chocolate be shared with others. Was he worried about being punished when he later rejoined his peers?[43]

In summary, both the principles of fairness and equality appear to characterize animal behavior and appear to be foundational to their communities. Hierarchies led by alpha males are based on the principle of fairness; the alpha male and other high-ranked males get first access to food and mates in return for the leadership and protection they provide. However, they share or distribute most of what they receive to other members of the group. The expulsion of free riders and cheaters is consistent with the principles of fairness and equality; each member of the group is expected to contribute in return for the benefits group membership provides. In monkeys and apes, social behavior tends to be phylogenetically fixed within species, although with some flexibility. Members work together to hunt, share the spoils, and engage in mutual grooming. Every chimpanzee group has a unique combination of tools and techniques. There is no evidence that groups learn from others, so reinvention is the most likely explanation for what duplication is observed.[44]

It is certainly possible that we inherited behavioral orientations that confer survival advantages, and concern for justice may be one of them. Courage and fright are also universal, and it is easy to deduce the advantages they conferred to ancestors who lived in the wild. The young of related mammalian species elicit a favorable response from most people, and this too presumably facilitates their survival. Adam Smith thought sympathy of this kind one of the most universal human traits.[45] Darwin reasoned that social instincts "which no doubt were acquired by man, as by the lower animals, for the good of the community, will from the first have given him some wish to aid his fellows, and some feeling of sympathy."[46]

Darwin reasoned that any animal endowed with well-marked social instincts would acquire a moral sense or conscience if and when it developed sufficient intellectual powers. Kitcher and Korsgaard are among the many philosophers who distinguish humans from other primates because of their seemingly unique ability to reflect on their behavior. They describe other animals as "wantons," a term developed by fellow philosopher Harry Frankfurter. Guided by emotions, not by reason, animals cannot meet the Kantian criterion of morality: a judgment of whether the act in question is proper. Only humans, these philosophers insist, can develop the abstract ideals essential to morality – although there is speculation that robots might acquire this potential.[47] In the late eighteenth century, David Hume dismissed such "image of God" distinctions between humans and animals as overdrawn, arguing that both reach conclusions in a similar manner: by emotions and association. By contrast, "the systems philosophers have employ'd to account for the actions of the mind ... suppose such a subtility and refinement of thought, as not only exceeds the capacity of mere animals, but even of children and the common people in our own species."[48]

These philosophical differences are unresolvable and beside the point. For my argument, all that matters is that successful groups across species reward behavior consistent with the principles of fairness and equality and punish behavior at odds with them. Humans are demonstrably different from other animals in that so much of their behavior is determined by culture rather than instinct. Inherited drives, capabilities, and emotions create the envelope in which humanity acts but tell us little about human social, political, or economic practices because they are the product of culture and agency. This is even true of a primal emotion like fear, which is often inaccurately described as a neurological response to danger. Aristotle rightly distinguishes fear from fright. The latter is an instinctive reaction that mediates a fight-or-flight response in the face of imminent danger. Fear is "a pain or disturbance due to imagining some destructive or painful evil in the future." It is aroused by our imagination and the expectation, rather than the reality, of some future eventuality, which may or may not come to pass. Fear is a deliberative and culturally influenced emotion.[49] Human beings appear to be the only animal aware of their mortality, a recognition that has profound consequences for our behavior – but here too, our response is mediated by culture and personality.

Interest, honor, and fear generate different logics of cooperation, conflict, and risk-taking.[50] They prompt different responses in otherwise similar situations. Prediction is made more difficult by the likelihood that all three motives are in play at the same time, making responses sensitive to priming and context. My theory of politics stands in sharp contrast to reductionist approaches like realism or evolutionary psychology that attempt to explain foreign policy, or human behavior, in the case of the latter, with reference to a single motive or adaptation. Proponents of these approaches are compelled to import all kinds of *deus ex machinae* to account for behavior seemingly at odds with their mono-causal accounts, as in the case of altruism for the "selfish gene" hypothesis.[51]

Consider the transition from hunter-gatherer to settled agricultural societies, and later the emergence of urban settlements. These developments have generally been explained with reference to the superiority of settled agriculture in producing surplus food, and with it a warrior caste that could maintain control of a perhaps restive and exploited population and carry out a program of foreign conquest. A food surplus and division of labor also made possible the production of all kinds of goods, and with them more extensive trade. Societies grew in size and complexity and the first empires emerged. Not surprisingly, these empires were located along major river systems – the Nile, Tigris and Euphrates, Indus, Yellow, and Yangtze – where more concentrated and productive agriculture was possible. This quasi-structural explanation tells us nothing about the relative strength of these empires, why and how one succeeded the other, their varying cultures, or why they survived, collapsed, or were transformed. These attributes and pathways are products of local conditions, culture, and agency.[52] Kant, Smith, and Durkheim offer theories of historical development to which this complexity is central and responsible for the progression of society from subsistence, through agricultural to commercial or industrial societies.[53] There are no reasons for preferring one of these accounts over the other, but all three seem to provide plausible accounts of the interplay of biology, geography, culture, and agency.

An alternative approach to order is to treat it as an emergent property. In Chapter 1 I argued that bottom-up orders are for the most part emergent. It is worth considering that top-down orders are too. John Holland defines emergent outcomes as those that arise in the absence of direction by a central executive. Living things and their evolution are products of emergence, and so too may be large-scale social orders. Evolutionary biologist Conway Morris suggests: "First there were bacteria, now there is New York."[54] To the extent that emergent orders – biological or social – have causes they are associated with the agents, rules, and interactions that define physical systems or social orders. The greater the number of component mechanisms and the more they interact without central control, the more flexible systems will be, and more likely to be characterized by emergent properties.[55]

Emergence is often associated with complexity, as it is in Conway Morris' amusing one-liner. And complexity can arise from the interactions of a relatively small number of components. Living things require many genes, and fifty years ago the estimate of human genes was in the millions. Today, it is down to 20,000 and dropping fast.[56] There is a consensus among scientists that complexity in the physical universe is increasing over time, but so is entropy. In the biological world, complexity took a long time coming but then picked up markedly, perhaps exponentially.[57] Morris believes that biological systems are pushing the limits of complexity and hastens to point out that evolution is not a linear story. Greater complexity led to extinction of many species while simplification for some has resulted in success, measured in terms of range and survival. Complexity theorists acknowledge that survival of the fittest is not necessarily "survival of the most complex."[58]

What about the social world? Friedrich Hayek defined order as the opposite of entropy.[59] It is nevertheless a problematic binary. Over the course of history orders have undeniably grown larger and more complex. They are more differentiated with many more roles, institutions, and levels of governance. Pundits differ about their robustness and chances for survival. Economic, administrative, and scientific developments have made it possible to banish famine and eradicate, or limit, the effects of many infectious diseases, and have led to greater human longevity. The same developments also put societies at risk by making them more susceptible to the spread of pathogens whose reach would have been more limited in pre-modern times. Nuclear weapons and global warming constitute serious threats to human survival, and a nuclear war might be destructive to the environment. As we become more dependent on information technology we become more vulnerable to the consequences of its disruption. Hacking of defense, corporate, and political organizations, and interference with nuclear weapons programs and elections by foreign government, and the shutdown of commercial, transport and healthcare services by non-governmental extortionists, are indications of this growing vulnerability.[60] Some contend that the greatest threats to developed societies are the very processes that make them developed.[61]

A more useful way of framing the problem of order and disorder is to recognize that each level of greater complexity makes orders more resilient *and* more vulnerable. The nature of threats also changes with complexity. Simple, small, and relatively isolated societies are particularly vulnerable to food shortages due to bad harvests, natural disasters, environmental damage, attacks from outside, and climate change. More developed and densely settled societies are less at risk from food shortages, but more to pathogens that spread from animals to humans. Given their greater wealth, they are also more likely to be targets of conquest by neighboring societies or nomads. Modern societies, as noted, are vulnerable due to their very complexity, and also to the degree they become dependent on particular technologies. We should nevertheless remember that most threats to disorder come from within and result from the decisions, policies, and self-aggrandizement of political and economic elites. In *Tragic Vision of Politics* I make the case that great powers are their own worst enemies. In *Why Nations Fight* I offer statistical support of this claim from a data set of great power wars from 1648 to the present.

How Do Orders Evolve?

In *A Cultural Theory of International Relations* I describe a historical progression in which appetite and *thumos* alternate as dominant principles. They find somewhat different expression in each iteration. The two drives are associated with different principles of justice and generate different kinds of hierarchies.[62]

The first iteration of appetite-driven worlds is a response to the problem of hunger; hunter-gatherers and early agricultural settlements must often struggle to feed themselves. Appetite becomes dominant again in modern, affluent societies, where it is possible for the wealthy, and many less well-off people, to develop and indulge a range of appetites, especially for consumer goods. This transformation, and the in-between shift to a spirit-based world, is made possible by increasing complexity in the division of labor. In contrast to Marx, my theory is not deterministic because these material conditions are not inevitable and depend in large part on the equally contingent emergence of appropriate values and discourses.

Adam Smith speculates that the first social orders were egalitarian because everyone was poor.[63] This may well be true about bottom-up orders in general. Some societies nevertheless prospered and accumulated enough surplus to sustain a more complex social order, and with it offices unrelated to acquiring, producing, processing, or distributing the means of sustenance. This distance was made a virtue, and high status generally requires people to distance themselves from such primary activities; aristocracies in Europe, Mesoamerica, China, and Japan considered work of any kind degrading. *Thumos* is given more leeway for expression, and is not infrequently directed by society into the display of bravery and military skill with external foes or duels with domestic ones. Such a need was pronounced in many societies where warfare was endemic and the cost of defeat could be catastrophic.[64]

The increasing frequency of war is itself a function of the success of small societies in rising above subsistence levels. Surplus allows population growth, greater propinquity of settlements and greater competition for territory and other scarce resources. As external competition becomes more acute, or its material benefits more obvious, warriors increase their standing and authority in the society. Some of these societies become warrior societies and expand at the expense of their neighbors. Discourses emerge to praise the spirit, denigrate appetite, and justify the resulting hierarchies. Homer's *Iliad* is the quintessential example and this is one of the reasons it became a foundational document of Greek and western civilization.

This process helps to explain the emergence of the great ancient empires like Egypt, Assyria, Persia, Athens, and Rome. Successful empires do more than expand their territorial reach. They foster internal peace and the conditions for economic development. Development gives rise to new classes, including wealthy farmers, who control large tracts of land; producers or finishers of goods, like potters and tanners; merchants who sell or export this produce and products; and scribes who keep official and commercial records. When permitted, members of the new classes adopt the language, dress, and values of the dominant elite, seek acceptance by it, and entry into higher political and social circles. Failure to incorporate into the elite at least some members of the commercial or professional classes impedes unity and ultimately weakens the political unit vis à vis more progressive competitors. The political and social exclusion of new classes, whose claim to status is based on wealth, but also increasingly on public service, encourages them to develop discourses that assert their value, if not superiority. These discourses tend to denigrate spirit-based activities like war and praise appetite-based ones like commerce. The affluence and visibility of these classes, even when they are not integrated into the dominant elite, is usually enough to set in motion the transition from spirit to interest-based worlds. Such a process takes place in roughly the same way in pre-industrial and industrial worlds. Political, social, and intellectual developments in fifth-century Greece and eighteenth-century Europe reveal striking parallels.[65]

Transformations from appetite- to spirit- to interest-based worlds are sequential but never linear. They are not infrequently interrupted by breakdowns in order, and the decay, even disappearance, of key political units, as well as retrogression toward fear-based worlds. These ruptures can and do occur at any stage of historical development. They may be repeated more than once in a unit or system before it transitions to the next stage of development. Ancient Greece and China had multiple breakdowns of order at the unit and regional level. The Peloponnesian War, as portrayed by Thucydides, was the result of reason's loss of control over appetite and thumos in small powers like Corcyra, middle powers like Corinth, and between the two most powerful units in the regional Greek political system: Athens and Sparta. Their imbalance became more acute as the war progressed, spread the conflict to previously uninvolved third parties, and destroyed order throughout most of the Greek world.

At a deeper level, breakdown of order at the unit and regional level in Greece was due to social, intellectual, and economic changes. In *Tragic Vision of Politics* I argue that fifth-century Greece underwent a process akin to modernization that began to transform Athens from a spirit-based to an interest-based society. This transformation was a fundamental cause of imbalance within Athens, and between the Athenian and Spartan alliance systems. Similar changes took place in early modern and modern Europe and in Japan, where they also helped to bring about imbalance, breakdown of order, and destructive wars. It is not accidental that the Peloponnesian War and World Wars I and II occurred when those transitions were only partially completed. Transitions are dangerous periods because they lead to loss of control of reason over *thumos* without offsetting this by more effective control over the appetite. Modern transitions from spirit- to appetite-based societies in Europe were accompanied by three devastating wars (Napoleonic, World Wars I and II).

A deeper level of change involves a transformation in the ordering principles of the society and the ways in which appetite and spirit find expression. Aristotle rightly observes that appetites are often learned; we come to enjoy things that are at first unpleasant.[66] Food is the obvious example. Many hunter-gather societies have monotonous diets; their meals are prepared simply and served without much in the way of garnishes. With the emergence of a division of labor, a more varied and sophisticated diet becomes possible, at least for the elite. It includes high price tag items in short supply – eels and imported wines for ancient

Athenians – that are consumed and served to others as both a matter of taste and a demonstration of wealth.[67] Imperial cuisines may subsequently develop that are more complex and always labor intensive. The wealthy move from gourmand to gourmet, from stuffing one's belly to filling it well, and with food presented in a pleasing manner, on expensive pottery or plate, and in an increasingly elaborate social setting. At a somewhat later stage, there is a shift in drinking habits, from consuming as much alcohol as possible to drinking high-quality spirits, wine or micro-brews in moderation. Staple foods of earlier times (e.g. polenta, oysters, herring) are shunned, but may re-enter the diet later in sophisticated variants or as complements to what are understood to be elegant and refined dishes (as polenta is now served with *fungi porcini*, or seaweed as a wrapper for sushi). Preferred body shapes also change; robust and fat – good predictor of successful childbirth – give way to svelte as more desirable and sexually attractive, along with a preference for clothes that show off such figures. These developments indicate how change in one appetite can serve as a catalyst for changes in others.

Thumos undergoes an even more dramatic transformation. In their first iterations, most spirit-based worlds are warrior societies. Status is achieved through military and athletic prowess. High status is often restricted to an inherited elite, making ascribed status a precondition of its achieved counterpart. As *thumos*-based societies evolve, or return in subsequent iterations, more pathways for winning honor open up, and more members of societies are allowed to compete for honor. In classical Athens, skill in rhetoric and poetry became additional routes to honor. In the course of the last two centuries, numerous honor hierarchies have emerged; status can be gained through almost any kind of skill and accomplishment – even scholarship. Modern, developed societies are no longer warrior societies, although the institution of war exists and warriors continue to have high status. Other means of competition have supplemented war and are seen as less disruptive to order and other social goals. The Olympics, Nobel Prizes, and Eurovision song contests are cases in point.

When equality became the dominant principle of justice hierarchies became increasingly open. In theory it should be possible, at least in the western world, for any individual with commitment and some skills to find a route to winning honor. As the Special Olympics illustrate, we now have high-status competitions for the physically handicapped that attract big audiences. We are witnessing a similar development in international relations where recognition as a great power was once closed to non-Caucasian political units and where non-whites and professionals were frequently excluded from international sports competitions. It would have been unthinkable a century ago for any kind of international congress or organization to be chaired by a leader not from a great power. Recent Secretary Generals of the United Nations have come from less powerful, non-Caucasian countries (e.g. Ban Ki-moon, Kofi Annan).[68]

Change at all three levels has profound implications for the principles of order and their associated hierarchies. Hierarchies emerge with the division of labor that transforms subsistence level, appetite-based societies into spirit-based worlds. These hierarchies are often hereditary, allow little mobility, and divide actors into a small elite who are able to compete for honor, and a large majority who are not. Those at the top feel superior and have their status confirmed by high office and the deference of the masses. They in turn are expected to assume responsibilities toward those who honor them. They justify themselves with reference to the principle of fairness. Second iteration appetite-worlds invariably inherit hierarchies of this kind, and their actors struggle to free themselves of the vertical pattern of relations and to replace it with horizontal ones based on the principle of ontological equality.

Such a process was evident in early Modern Europe and accelerated during the Enlightenment where the concepts of the state of nature and contracts were mobilized to justify orders based on the original equality of actors. It was by no means a smooth transition because many people regarded liberalism and the principle of equality central to it as threatening to long-standing and treasured rights. For aristocrats, privileges were at stake that conferred status and a certain freedom from the law. For the less well-off these rights appeared to offer some safeguards against capitalist exploitation.[69]

Mature appetite-based worlds – those with a more advanced division of labor and fewer restraints on individual actors – reflect more fully the principle of equality. For Adam Smith, its truly liberating feature was its ability to end hierarchies based on personal dependency that entitled and justified the domination of one man by another. To the extent that everyone became a merchant or free laborer, rather than a lord, retainer, serf or peasant, horizontal ties would proliferate and free people from direct, personal, even inherited forms of dependency.[70]

Hierarchies develop in such worlds and they are based on wealth and its display. Display is central because, as Smith observes, people generally seek wealth not only for the material advantages it confers but for the status it brings.[71] The hierarchies that result are informal in the sense that they are not institutionally defined, associated with offices or entitle actors to particular privileges. Nor do they carry associated rule packages, allowing, if unconstrained by law and custom, the practice of an undiluted selfishness far more difficult to indulge in traditional hierarchies.[72] Tensions arise when practice betrays principle as it does when some actors, or group of actors, are excluded from using their physical and mental resources to better themselves, or unfair obstacles are put in their way, or when actors who are rich and powerful use their influence in public institutions to lock-in their advantages and pass them on to their descendants.

Levels two and three of historical change involve a multiplication and blurring of hierarchies. New and more sophisticated appetites develop, new domains open up, or are recognized as arenas where actors can compete for honor and standing, hierarchies become less exclusive, and the expressions of appetite and spirit become increasingly intertwined and difficult to distinguish from one another. Social hierarchies begin to blend features of honor and appetite worlds. Already in the eighteenth century, this was evident in international standing. Recognition as a great power, while based primarily on military power, acquired other markers. Leaders of great powers were expected to conform to and uphold certain principles, and to engage in impressive building programs and support the arts and sciences.[73] After Russia's victory over Sweden at Poltava in 1712, it became a de facto great power but Peter the Great was commonly described as a dangerous barbarian; Leibniz referred to him as "the Turk of the north."[74] Frederick William I, who transformed Prussia into a great power, was considered a despot for imprisoning his son and executing his son's lover.[75]

Domestic hierarchies were also increasingly multiple, and initially based on fairness and equality. Over time they became to varying degrees interpenetrated. Anthony Trollope's novels depict how honor and appetite in Victorian Britain become entangled, but in many ways remained distinct. In Trollope's Palliser novels, the old Duke of Omium lives up to his exalted status by doing nothing beyond ceremonial appearances and entertaining. Toward this end he owns one of the largest palaces in Britain, suitably named Gatherum. His son and successor to the dukedom, Plantagenet Palliser, moves away from this model and feels the need to make a positive contribution to his country. He enters politics, serves a chancellor of the exchequer, and as he eschews personal ambition must be dragged into serving as prime minister. He despises Gatherum and spends his time attempting, unsuccessfully, to perfect and convince others of the value of adopting a decimal system for pennies that involves making a shilling based on ten pence instead of twelve.[76] Trollope's portrayal of both dukes suggests the irrelevancy of the aristocracy in both its traditional and modern guise.

In nineteenth-century America, a country without an aristocracy of birth, affluence became the means of achieving standing. As Tocqueville noted, it replaced high birth, military prowess, education and public service.[77] Affluence could not merely be achieved, it had to be demonstrated through conspicuous consumption. This took the form of urban mansions, country estates, yachts, art collections, and parties to which other members of the elite were invited to experience the owner's generosity and admire his or her possessions. Thorstein Veblen noted that it also involved engaging in totally unproductive pastimes like studying the classics, sailing, tennis, and gardening.[78] By the end of the century the urban rich had established a social register that listed acceptable families based on self-serving criteria that differentiated the inner circle from everyone else.[79] However, wealthy members of minorities, most notably Catholics and Jews, excluded by the Protestant Establishment, nevertheless emulated their lifestyle.[80] Conspicuous consumption offered a sharp contrast to Tocqueville's description of America earlier in the nineteenth century. The post-revolutionary elite were men, many of them recently poor themselves, who had acquired wealth through manufacture, trade, or the professions. They shunned ostentation and were careful to treat their less well-off brethren as their equals.[81]

More traditional expressions of the spirit nevertheless survived and make their way back into appetite-based worlds. Wealth became a necessary but not sufficient condition for entry into the elite. Upwardly mobile people had to learn proper manners, dress appropriately, educate their children at high-status institutions, support cultural and charitable institutions, and demonstrate public service in politics, civic, and religious life. In this sense, domestic society mimicked its international counterpart. However, it is still possible for rich people to gain status merely from conspicuous consumption. This is evident in the acquisition of football teams and supersized yachts by the nouveau super-rich, and the willingness of the public to envy them.[82] Even so, some Russian billionaires are now finding new forms of consumption to distinguish themselves and gain status superior to superyacht owners. They do so by displaying wealth in ways that are more socially acceptable to the non-Russian elite, like supporting museums and charitable institutions.[83]

To recapitulate, three features of the modern world stand out with respect to order: the shift from fairness to equality as the preferred principle of justice; the proliferation of pathways by which one can gain wealth or honor; and the blending of *thumos* and appetite and their respective hierarchies. Individually and collectively they have profound implications for the stability of social and political orders.

Let me turn again to Tocqueville, who argues that when hierarchy is the ordering principle of society people are generally oblivious to the strongest inequalities. When equality becomes enshrined as a goal, and when it is in part achieved in practice, people become more resentful of even the smallest inequality. Paradoxically, Tocqueville wrote, the "desire for equality always becomes more insatiable as equality is greater." People "constantly believe they are going to seize it, and it constantly escapes their grasp. They see it from near enough to know its charms, they do not approach it close enough to enjoy it, and they die before having fully savored its sweetness."[84] Equality can promote contentment and legitimacy or resentment and alienation. These divergent outcomes are not the result of relative gain and deprivation, but reflect how wealth is understood. These differences are expressions of culture, not material conditions.

Multiple pathways to gaining honor and wealth reflect not only the division of labor and diverse needs of developed economies, but the shift toward equality as a dominant principle of justice. With it comes greater propensity to open previously restricted hierarchies to anybody with qualifications. As Georg Simmel observed, this allows us to gravitate toward realms of activity in which we can excel.[85] We in turn gain the approbation of others and feel good about ourselves. We might even make money in the process. In this connection, it is interesting to see how activities, once the preserve of aristocrats, or at least of the rich, were unpaid "gentlemanly" pastimes, in part as a means of excluding others from participation. These activities are now increasingly professionalized, recruit on the basis of talent not class, and have become remunerative. In some sports (e.g. football, soccer, baseball, rugby, and tennis).

The shift to equality that penetrated western society resonates throughout the society. It has opened once-closed hierarchies to non-elite actors. Universities, clubs, amateur and professional sports, professions and corporations, and government are far more likely than in the past to hire and promote people on the basis of their qualifications and performance. In the United States, the State Department was once almost entirely staffed by White Anglo-Saxon Protestant graduates of elite universities. Recent secretaries of state have included women, Jews, Catholics, and an African-American. In Britain, the class barrier is still evident – half of David Cameron's cabinet went to private schools and then to Oxbridge, but it is still more diverse and less titled than Tory cabinets of the twentieth century.[86] With equality, people no longer regard aristocrats and the wealthy as their "betters." Equality raises expectations for equal treatment and upward mobility. To the extent that these goals are met, orders become more robust, and vice versa. An order's legitimacy may be most threatened when there has been considerable progress toward equal treatment and mobility, but then stagnation for whatever reason. Expectations are raised and then dashed. This may explain, in part, why inequality has become an increasingly important political issue in present-day Britain and the United States.

The intermixing of appetite and spirit also has divergent implications for order. Tocqueville was intimately familiar with clientelist hierarchies in France. He thought they were confining but also enabling. Those at the top were required by their rule packages to provide support to those beneath them when they were in need. Appetite-based hierarchies have no such requirement. The wealthy owed nothing to the poor; they had to depend on their own, often meager, resources. For this reason, Tocqueville thought, equality-based societies had the potential to become crueler than any society of the past.[87] Tocqueville witnessed pre-industrial America, where poverty was not so widespread. Later in the century, the growing class of poor had to rely on private charity. Much of it was provided by people only marginally better off, whose religion or sympathy for others led them to share.[88] Increasingly, the emerging upper class also took up charity, and largely because charitable giving became a key marker of status.

Fear was also an important motive for charity by the late nineteenth century. It was a strategy of robber barons like John D. Rockefeller, Andrew Carnegie, and Cornelius Vanderbilt to retain a sense of trust with the public.[89] Wealthy American Jews gave even more proportionately as they felt their status and privileges threatened by the influx of Eastern European Jews.[90] The rich and glitterati who attend the World Economic Forum at Davos also appear fearful. At its 2017 conclave, the Forum proclaimed that "the growing gap between rich and poor" could lead to "a tipping point "that would trigger a period of deglobalisation." In lieu of philanthropy they organized six sessions for their "strategic partners" – a status with a price tag of 600,000 Swiss Francs – to discuss inequality. A further irony involved the extra staff that had to be brought in by big hotels and restaurants to cater for those attending the World Economic Forum. Staff slept up to five in a room while the likes of Jacob Zuma, Theresa May, and Xi Jinping stayed in luxurious, multi-room suites.[91]

The wave of protests and protest votes against western liberal establishments – G20 meetings have become invitations for anarchist riots – suggests that demands for equality have outstripped its achievement.[92] Neo-liberal discourses that attempt to paper over the gap between promise and practice have lost their legitimacy among those who do not share in the benefits of largely deregulated free market economies and free trade agreements. I will explore this phenomenon and its consequences in general terms in the next chapter and more specifically in Chapter 6.

Finally, the principles of fairness and equality have lost their distinction and to a large extent have merged in the popular mind, and also among intellectuals. In Chapter 2 I noted that equality is increasingly defined in terms of fairness, and vice versa. This phenomenon reflects in part the non-recognition of *thumos* in the modern world, the suppression of *thumos*-based discourses, and the increasing reluctance of people to recognize hierarchies that cannot be somehow based on hierarchy. Fairness has accordingly been disassociated from its original meaning – those who contribute the most should receive the most – and increasingly coupled with equality. What are the implications for order of the intertwining of these two motives and principles of justice?

Equality and fairness generate different hierarchies, and traditionally hierarchies based on different principles compete for primacy and generate conflict. Examples include conflicts in the Middle Ages between church and state and those in the modern era between aristocrats and bourgeoisie. In *A Cultural Theory of International Relations* I argue that the intensity of the latter conflict depended on the response of aristocrats to the rising commercial classes. Where accommodation occurred, as in Britain, it took the form of power sharing, intermarriage, and a gradual blurring of the sources of status and wealth. Aristocrats invested in commercial enterprises, and successful businesspeople in property. In Central Europe, where the conflict was most acute, very little accommodation occurred, and aristocrats found new ways of distinguishing themselves from the industrial and commercial classes. Conflict was only muted by the quasi-feudalization of the rising classes, an accommodation that was fragile and a source of aggressive foreign policies in Germany and Austria.[93]

Multiple hierarchies are a source of conflict when they compete for primacy. In early societies, this was most often apparent in struggles between hierarchies based on ascribed versus achieved status. Ascribed status is inherited, as are most kingships. Achieved status described honors and offices awarded on the basis of performance.[94] Both kinds of status are found in many traditional societies. When they are reinforcing – when, for example, the chief is also the most successful hunter or warrior – order and hierarchy are upheld and reinforced. When they are at odds, both are threatened. Homer constructs the *Iliad* around such conflict. Agamemnon, King of Mycenae and commander of the Greek armies in the Trojan War, is at the top of the ascribed hierarchy. He is self-centered, lacking interpersonal skills, and a brave but undistinguished fighter. Achilles, repeatedly described by Homer as "the best of the Achaeans," is at the apex of the achieved hierarchy. Agamemnon expropriates a girl captured in a raid that has been presented to him by other warriors as a prize for his bravery. Agamemnon humiliates Achilles, who is furious and – unwilling to accept inferior standing – withdraws from the fight against Troy. The conflict between the two men closely parallels, and in important ways, supersedes that between Greeks and Trojans.[95] Numerous contemporary analogs spring to mind.

This kind of conflict can occasionally be harnessed for positive ends. The concept of separation of powers embedded in the US constitution is more accurately described as the overlapping of powers. Each branch has certain powers over the other. The president, for example, nominates supreme court justices, but the Senate must approve them. Powerful officials and their branch of government can only expand their power at the expense of others, and will accordingly arouse their opposition. By this means, the founding fathers hoped to transform private vice into public virtue.

Conflicts within and between hierarchies are most likely when new hierarchies emerge and there is as yet no accepted understanding of their relative authority and status. Conflicts in medieval Europe between kings and the Roman Catholic Church, kings and nobles, and kings and universities are cases in point. Contemporary examples include conflicts between branches of government, federal and state authorities or provinces. They are more intense if there are no rules to adjudicate them or prior experience about how to develop them.

There are rarely procedures in place for provinces leaving states because those who set up or run states do not want to recognize, let along legitimize this possibility. For this reason, efforts at separation are rarely achieved by quiet diplomacy; the Norway–Sweden and Czech–Slovak splits are notable exceptions. More often, they provoke violent responses (e.g. Israel, Biafra, Kurdistan, and the Basque region) or political standoffs (e.g. Catalonia and Scotland). Rules develop only when important political actors are willing to consider the possibility of another hierarchy, and this is not easy for those at the top of the existing one, because it invariably involves some loss of power, status, or wealth.

Dominant hierarchies become problematic when conditions change in ways that deprive elites of their justification. If external threats recede, warrior classes have an interest in generating new conflicts to sustain their authority and avoid destructive, inward deflection of competition and aggression. Warrior societies accordingly have incentives to wage frequent wars, but to limit and regulate these conflicts so that they do not disrupt society or demand extraordinary resources. Warriors may start destructive wars largely with the goal of preserving their hold on power at home. Joseph Schumpeter attributed World War I to this motive.[96] Variants of this story can be told about almost any political, economic, intellectual, social, or religious elite. They resort to a common set of strategies to maintain their status. These include appeals to tradition, strengthening their control over the means of entry into the elite, justifying themselves on a new basis, and use of force or governmental institutions to suppress challengers.

Dominant hierarchies sometimes recognize the benefits of sharing power. This is most attractive when leaders are convinced that they can preserve the core of their power and status by this means. The British aristocracy's accommodation with the commercial classes has already been noted in this regard. A more tenuous relationship was the so-called alliance between "iron and grain" in Wilhelminian Germany. Bismarck masterfully crafted a settlement to the German constitutional crisis of the 1860s whereby the Prussian Junkers made peace with the industrialists. The former retained their control over foreign and military policy, and the latter gained control over tariffs within a unified Reich. This uneasy alliance was incapable of making room for a third contender for power: the rising working class organized by the Social Democratic Party. The growing tensions between it and the military-industrial establishment are considered by some to have been an underlying cause of an increasingly aggressive German foreign policy.[97]

Until now my discussion has focused on domestic societies. However, many of these developments are also found in international society. International relations scholars disagree over the extent to which changes in domestic values and practices influence those at the international level, or whether changes in international values and practices penetrate domestic orders.[98] In *National Identifications and International Relations* I document both kinds of change, and how the principle of equality has been mutually reinforcing in domestic and international societies.[99] International society nevertheless differs from its domestic counterparts in important respects. There is much less of a consensus about fundamental values and practices.[100] Secular vs. religious values are in conflict in addition to fairness and equality, all of which promote different practices and bases for status.

International society has nevertheless been affected by changes in many of its more developed and powerful units, but lags behind them. Until very recently, standing was achieved primarily on the basis of military might, and secondarily, on the basis of cultural, scientific and other achievements. In the postwar era, wealth became increasingly important in its own right, and Scandinavia, Canada, the Netherlands, and South Korea, among others, claim standing on the basis of the wealth and the percentage they share with less affluent members of the international community. The two principles of justice have not merged the way they have in many western societies. International society still has a dominant hierarchy with the great powers, or a single superpower, at the apex. Regional systems, some of them based on different principles, have nevertheless developed. This hierarchy, and its fairness-based principle of order, constitutes something of an atavism in today's world, and is increasingly challenged. Practices based on equality (e.g. one state one vote in many international fora) are widespread and often in sharp conflict with the hierarchy that places great powers at its apex. In effect, two principles of order are in conflict, and many different outcomes are possible.[101]

Mechanisms of Compliance

Given the inequalities that pervade all societies, and the exclusion, restrictions, and compulsions associated with their hierarchies, it is nothing short of remarkable that most people in most societies adhere to their stipulated practices and rules. Since Aristotle, philosophers have thought about this problem, and modern sociology has made stratification a central theme. Not surprisingly, nineteenth- and twentieth-century utopias invariably invent worlds in which hierarchies are absent. This is surely a sign that they are recognized and resented, which makes the legitimacy of so many orders that much more puzzling.

Philosophers have come up with four generic explanations for compliance with social and political orders and their hierarchies: fear, interest, honor, and habit.[102] Their importance varies across societies and epochs. Depending on the circumstances, the four sources of compliance can be cross-cutting or reinforcing.

The power of fear has been self-evident from the beginning of civilization. Sophocles has King Menelaus proclaim: "Fear is the cornerstone of all order, I say."[103] Tyrannies are the regimes most dependent on it. Machiavelli thought that a new prince might find it useful to be cruel to impose his will, as Cesare Borgia did successfully in the Romagna.[104] Hobbes stressed the importance of fear in the early-modern world, where people no longer accepted the authority of king and church as God-given. Hierarchy's loss of legitimacy made men feel the equal of all others, as indeed they were, Hobbes argued, in the state of nature where anybody is strong enough to kill anyone else. Order, for Hobbes, is based on convention, and enforced in the first and last resort by fear. Jean Bodin shared his fear of disorder and the need for fear-based rule. The French, he insisted, were "variable as the winds," and "without any sense of judgment. Only terror could control such a restless people."[105]

Thucydides, Plato and Aristotle maintain that fear-based orders will be short-lived if they are not ultimately based on some principle of justice that allows them to rely primarily on voluntary compliance.[106] Recent work on postwar communist regimes in Eastern Europe indicates that even at the height of Stalinism national leaders were unable to impose their preferences by fiat. Katherine Lebow found that policy implementation required considerable negotiation with relevant segments of society and sometimes met notable resistance, including violent opposition and sabotage. Not infrequently, negotiations led to outcomes at variance with those leaders initially tried to impose.[107] Force can intimidate effectively when the leader or governing elite is widely known to be brutal and unrestrained in the use of violence, even torture. Leaders can also pretend to be kind and understanding, while employing others to do their dirty work. Elizabeth I used both approaches. She had cavalry patrolling London's streets at night, dragging suspicious characters before magistrates. She also made secret use of the psychopath Richard Topliffe to torture Catholics and dissenters to get information about purported plots.[108] Stalin pursued this strategy on a massive scale.[109]

Like any mechanism, fear can have unintended effects, and efforts to arouse it can backfire. In the Soviet Union in the 1930s,

More than one third of all industrial workers were classified as 'Stakhanovites,' but worker go-slows, also known as Italian strikes, and the constant queuing for food and basic goods continued to depress productivity. So did quitting in search of lower norms and better pay. Back on June 26, 1940, Stalin had had the criminal penalties for absenteeism and unauthorized job changing augmented; additionally, lateness of just twenty minutes was now criminalized. Violations were punishable by 'corrective labor,' mostly in the form of reduced pay at one's place of employment, but sometimes with several months in a camp . . . And yet, the number of such infractions was likely higher. Some people stole goods from work or otherwise violated discipline deliberately to get fired, so that they could leave undesirable jobs. But managers did not investigate many instances of lateness or refrained from sending cases to the procuracy, instead imposing 'fines' that were not collected. Stalin's orders to mete out punishments for even minor infractions clashed with his directives to meet production targets at all costs.[110]

Fear is aroused by expectation of punishment of oneself or loved ones. Orders with a high degree of popular support rely less on fear than tyrannies do and tend to use it selectively. Punishment nevertheless remains a common mechanism at every level of social aggregation. It encompasses fines, incarceration, denial of privileges, and public shaming. In colonial New England, minor offenders were put on display in stocks. Australian provinces and the Durham Regional Police in greater Toronto found the most effective way of reducing drunken driving was to publish the names of offenders in local newspapers. Bangalore and other locales have followed suit.[111]

Threats of punishment, and law more generally, are embedded in *nomos*.[112] Narratives about *nomos* and its enforcement give it meaning and legitimacy and make it more effective. Durkheim astutely observes that threats and punishment arising from law and more informal *nomos* are directed at a wider audience. They are a social-psychological "reaction against those acts which offend strong and defined common sentiments."[113] They seek to uphold and reinforce these sentiments among compliant members of the population and thereby reinforce solidarity. In practice, Durkheim suggests, threats of punishment and their implementation are "intended above all to act upon honest persons" and "heal the wounds done to collective sentiments" by violations.[114] Robert Cover, by contrast, emphasizes the pain and suffering they cause to those against whom they are directed.[115]

Liberal-institutionalists emphasize the ability of a hegemon and institutions to facilitate cooperation by enforcing rules impartially – especially contracts – and to punishing those who violate them.[116] The criminology literature characterizes the state as a powerful, threatening, but clumsy enforcer. Governmental authorities are not very good at catching perpetrators or in devising punishments that will deter the acts they commit. Some economists insist that local authorities are more effective.[117] But this success comes at a price; local authorities, like unofficial vigilantes and lynch mobs, are more likely to ignore legal restraints and safeguards. In 2016, the *New York Times* carried a story about a small Indiana county that sent more people to prison than San Francisco and Durham, NC combined.[118] Punishment may be most effective in families and small groups, assuming that it is seen as proportional to the offense and used sparingly. Governments and punishments are nevertheless significant as disorder and violence tend to become more pronounced in the absence of central authority. This is tragically evident in so-called failed states.[119]

The interest explanation is also associated with Hobbes and is central to modern social science. It assumes that people are willing to accept lower status and relatively less in return for the greater absolute rewards they receive from societies in which their physical security and material possessions are protected.[120] The rewards Hobbes has in mind are status and wealth. Morris Janowitz makes a similar argument. Order is not a function of repression or forced conformity, but rather self-willed efforts on the part of a community to organize itself to carry out desired ends. This commitment to cooperate to advance common interest arises from friendship, kinship, and other networks and associational ties rooted in family and organizational life.[121]

The wealth assumption of modern economics and much of social science is so entrenched that many scholars are baffled when people appear to be motivated by other goals. At least since the time of Joseph Schumpeter there is a pronounced tendency to assume that people prefer material rewards to such "irrational" things as rectitude, honor, and revenge.[122] Schumpeter was nevertheless clear that entrepreneurs were motivated as much by the quest for status as they were by wealth.[123] Liberals, beginning with John Locke, accordingly see interest as the glue of modern political orders and largely replacing fear as a means of compliance. This transformation rests on the assumption that democratic governments are responsive to citizen preferences.

The honor explanation is an expression of *thumos* as opposed to appetite. In Chapter 1 I noted that ancient Greeks considered it a co-equal, if not more important drive. Its goal is high self-esteem, achieved by excelling in activities valued by one's peers or society and winning their approbation. Homer is the first theorist of honor. His *Iliad* creates an ideal-type honor society and is unrivaled in its description of the beneficial and destructive consequences of the quest for honor and its correlate, revenge. In modern times, Hobbes and Smith described honor as "vanity," and Rousseau as a component of *amour propre*.[124] In *A Cultural Theory of International Relations* I theorize the conditions under which *thumos* serves as a source of cooperation and civic solidarity, or of envy, hatred, and conflict.[125]

Honor relies on different mechanisms than fear or interest. People want to be respected and admired by their peers, and perhaps by posterity. This provides a strong incentive to act in ways that win the respect of relevant audiences and to eschew practices that undermine it. Pursuit of honor encourages self-restraint, adherence to rule packages, and sacrifice for the sake of the community, whether it is a platoon or a nation. In clientelist hierarchies, actors at the top receive honor in return for providing practical benefits for less powerful actors. When effective, honor serves to restrain the powerful by making it conditional on self-restraint and other components of their rule packages.[126]

Honor can provide the social cement that holds orders together in circumstances where central authorities lack the means of physical compulsion. In the Holy Roman Empire, an honor-based order, corporate rights, and identities were local. The Emperor had few, if any, powers of enforcement, so order had to be maintained by consensus. The Empire's hierarchy "was not a chain of command, but a multilayered structure, allowing individuals and groups to disobey one authority whilst professing loyalty to another."[127] Conflict resolution among relevant actors was accomplished more by compromise through brokerage in lieu of imposition or definitive judgments of right or wrong. Almost all important actors had an overriding interest in preserving the empire and the honor and status it provided them, and were accordingly willing to accept negotiated, compromise solutions to their frequent disputes over territory and leadership succession.[128]

In practice, each of these four mechanisms overlaps and can become entwined and reinforcing. In his biography of Stalin, Stephen Kotkin describes how in the 1930s the Soviet dictator sought to use honor to encourage compliance, and how it was framed by those who sought honors as also enhancing their prospects for material reward. They in turn supported, even initiated, the punishment of competitors.

Many writers who disagreed vehemently about aesthetics agreed on the need for top-down imposition of a single approach for everyone. They were also zealous about getting state recognition, as opposed to public favour, and not a few lobbied for or welcomed repressive measures against rivals. Socialist realism served as an administrative system as much as an aesthetic: party directives, censorship, prizes, apartments, dachas, travel – or their denial – as well as myriad personnel employed as cultural apparatchiks, editors, censors, what Bulgakov called 'people with ideological eyes.'[129]

In the ancient and medieval worlds, honor and interest mechanisms of enforcements relied primarily on oral communications. Messages assumed importance and meaning according to the status of the actors who delivered them. They were as much about signaling the sender's superiority over the recipient as they were about conveying messages. Because communications were private, it was easier to tailor them to specific audiences, and to send different, even contradictory messages, to different people. Face-to-face interactions, especially in the context of visits and meals, also encouraged consensus seeking.[130]

Written communications – and now, posts and tweets – are more likely to expose differences, make consensus more difficult, and intensify differences regarding rights, privileges, and responsibilities in the status hierarchy. Paper and electronic trails made it difficult for sender or recipient to deny knowledge of a message or offer a different interpretation. In the Byzantine Empire, where written communications were introduced at an early date, they made doctrinal differences more pronounced than they were in the West and helped to bring about the official divide between Orthodoxy and Roman Catholicism. The use of the written word also encouraged a more elaborate and rigid hierarchy once rights and statuses were fixed in documents. When written communications became the norm in the Holy Roman Empire, they made it more difficult to resolve conflicts and, paradoxically, to maintain a hierarchy.[131] It is possible that information technology will further constrain diplomacy. It has already done so in domestic politics, where statements and positions made or taken in the past are readily accessible and increasingly used to embarrass their authors or keep them from shifting ground.

Aristotle is the first to note the importance of habits as a source of compliance. He observes that children mimic adult behavior and are taught how to behave and toward what ends by their mentors. They are encouraged to internalize what is regarded as good behavior, and when it becomes routine may no longer reflect on it, if they ever did.[132] Habit can be a product of any of the other three explanations for order. Children emulate adults because they fear the consequences of not doing so or expect to gain affection, approval, or material rewards. Habits are also induced by informal regimes that generate rules and often rely on honor for their enforcement. Montesquieu and Durkheim, and more recently Erving Goffman, emphasize the importance of habits as informal mechanisms of social control.[133] Durkheim defines habits as "definite ways of acting that repeat themselves."[134] He describes them as forces interior to the individual that reflect the internalization of the moral codes and practices of society.[135]

Kant offers a more jaundiced take, attributing habits to laziness and cowardice. They "are why such a large portion of men ... gladly remain immature for life, long after nature has freed them from external guidance. For the same reasons, it is all too easy for others to set themselves up as guardians. It is so convenient to be immature!"[136] Hume made a similar argument.[137] Kant, however, also offers a more positive take on habit, which he connects to interest and honor and offers as an explanation for why the "crooked timber" of humanity can nevertheless sustain social order. People want to be respected by others and gain rewards. To do so they give the illusion of acting ethically and display modesty, affection, respect for others, even selflessness. Almost everybody understands the duplicity of this behavior, in large part because they are acting the same way for the same reasons.[138] "When human beings perform these roles, eventually the virtues, whose illusion they have merely affected for a considerable length of time, will gradually really be aroused and merge into the disposition."[139] Virtuous habits can become so deeply entrenched that people act in accord with them in situations where you would least expect it. Nice evidence is provided by CCTV footage of the 2011 riots in London that reveal looters politely queueing outside smashed shop windows to wait their turn to go in and steal goods.[140]

As Durkheim and Weber understood, orders at different stages of development emphasize different strategies of maintaining order. They also use these four mechanisms in different ways. Information about the relative emphasis of fear, interest, honor, and habit within bottom-up and top-down orders, and across societies and epochs, can provide useful insights into the nature of successful orders. Similarly, changes in this distribution are likely to tell us something about their robustness and vulnerability. So too does what we think about these mechanisms and the discourses we propagate about them. Western liberals are convinced that appetite is the cement of society. They ignore honor, and dismiss it as a dangerous distraction when it rears its ugly head.[141] Liberal thinkers all but expunged the concept from the philosophical lexicon.[142] In Chapter 5 I explore the political consequences for liberals and democracy of this narrow focus on appetite.

Liberals focus on appetite because early liberal thinkers were convinced that honor-based societies were more violent and war prone. There is much evidence to support this conclusion, and also that the focus on appetite can reduce violence and build toleration, if not solidarity, among formerly warring classes and states.[143] Appeals to both appetite and honor are more balanced in many societies but – as Chapter 7 on Georgian Britain and Chapter 8 on China suggest – they also create different kinds of problems. Leaders facing economic crises may be tempted to fall back on honor for support and compliance. In doing so, they risk becoming constrained, if not prisoners of the nationalist passions they have aroused.

Solidarity

It would be a double mistake to frame the problem of order from an individual perspective *and* to treat people as autonomous, egoistic actors. This most entrenched conceit of liberalism and social science is an empirical fiction and analytical dead end. People are products of their societies. They are socialized to want certain things, respond to others in proscribed ways, and to adopt particular views of themselves, their interests, society, and the world. Interest and honor may be universal drives, but societies value them differently and may channel them down different pathways. The focus on the autonomous individual ignores the importance of solidarity for political order and also makes it more difficult to achieve. Robust orders require more than the recognition by people that society makes it possible for them to satisfy their needs and desires. People must identify with their society and feel a degree of affiliation and affection with and toward its other members. Lynn Hunt rightly observes that the shift from princely rule to popular sovereignty requires a significant increase in social cohesion.[144]

In traditional societies, rituals are the primary vehicle for negotiating conflicts between the principles of fairness and equality and also of building solidarity. They associate solidarity with conflict resolution. The Athenian Dionysia is a well-documented example.[145] Rituals remain important in many modern societies. The Patum in Catalonia and the Giglio Festival in Nola, Italy have been used to update understandings of justice and community.[146] Rituals are most likely to negotiate conflicts when they are regular, respected, inclusive, and build communal solidarity. In most modern societies, and certainly in democracies, there are other institutional mechanisms (e.g. legislative assemblies, courts, armed forces) that are more likely to serve these ends. Ceremonies and rituals in these societies nevertheless have the potential to build solidarity.

Not all rituals build solidarity. On March 12 each year, Protestants in Northern Ireland celebrate the 1690 victory over Catholics at the Battle of Boyne, which helped to guarantee the Protestant Ascendancy. Marchers traditionally paraded through Catholic neighborhoods in Londonderry, rubbing salt into wounds and provoking violent reprisals.[147] Rituals unite or divide populations, and those that do the former seek to build solidarity within a sub-community at the expense of other sub-communities or the larger community as a whole. Governments that adopt a divide-and-rule strategy are likely to encourage or even introduce rituals that intensify the internal solidary of participants and the hostility of those excluded or targets of these rituals. Divided societies will be less stable in the longer term. Northern Ireland is a case in point.

Solidarity can develop spontaneously when people respond in common ways to dramatic events like floods and fires. The terrorist attacks of 9/11 are an interesting example because they helped to rebuild some of the solidarity in the US Black-White relations. It had declined noticeably as a result of strikingly different Black-White responses to the jury's verdict of innocence in the 1995 O. J. Simpson double murder trial. Following events on television, Americans saw Black and Caucasian firemen rushing into the burning World Trade Center to rescue people and struggling outside to help people of any color escape from the immediate vicinity. However, relations with American Muslims deteriorated as many Americans saw them as outside their community and made them objects of hostility. Majority opinion nevertheless remained "warm" to Muslims and rejected the idea that a majority of adherents to this faith favored terrorism.[148]

Nothing so illustrates the power of society as its ability to shape how we think about death. Fear of death is instinctive, but is not, as Hobbes claims, our prime urge. Its strength varies from society to society. In many, people are willing to sacrifice themselves in the name of honor or for those they love. Socrates drank hemlock and committed suicide rather than leave Athens.[149] In the Roman legion, skirmishers (*velites*) were positioned out in front of legions, composed of the youngest soldiers, to seek out individual combats prior to the engagement of the main forces.[150] Writing about his campaign in Gaul in 52 BCE, Caesar describes the foolhardy bravery of his centurions – successors to *velites* – whose death rate was many times that of his other soldiers. During the siege of Gergovia, centurions ignored the efforts of tribunes and legates to restrain them and forced Caesar into a costly engagement he had wanted to avoid.[151]

This phenomenon is also evident in the Middle Ages and modern world. At the Battle of Mauron in Brittany in 1352, eighty French knights, all members of the Company of the Star, died rather than withdraw because of an oath they had sworn never to retreat.[152] In 1918, the heads of the German navy and army, Alfred von Tirpitz and Erich von Ludendorff demanded a "last battle," which they had no expectation of winning, to be fought on German soil to uphold military honor. Without such a costly engagement, they insisted, the nation would be "ruined."[153] Today, many of us find it difficult to empathize with these actions – as indeed Socrates' contemporaries did with his refusal to flee Athens.

Socrates' sacrifice was an extreme act of solidarity with his society. The other examples of derring-do, actual and intended, were regarded by many contemporaries as sharply at odds with the interests of their societies. These examples raise several interesting questions. Is a high degree of solidarity a prerequisite for robust societies? How is it possible to create such a strong sense of solidarity that people will sacrifice themselves and others for what they perceive to be the broader social good? And why do societies socialize their members into behaving in ways – here I am thinking of Tirpitz and Ludendorff – that may be contrary to some of their most important interests, e.g. survival?

On the first question, the evidence is mixed. There can be no doubt that societies benefit from solidarity, but there is compelling evidence from sociology and economics that suggests it may not be necessary to create and sustain cooperation. Morris Janowitz takes violence as a sign of social disorder in neighborhoods. His research indicates that low levels of violence are due to efforts by individuals to mobilize others to work together to advance common interests. Ruth Kornhauser finds high levels of violence in the absence of such cooperation.[154] Sounding much like Plato, Janowitz argues that cooperation and solidarity arise from friendship, kinship, and other networks and associational ties rooted in family and civic life.[155] Sampson and Wikström replicate their findings in studies of violence in Chicago and Stockholm neighborhoods. They attribute variation in violence to what they call "collective efficacy." This is the extent to which neighbors collaborate to end violence and other forms of social behavior. They further contend that neighbors do not have to be friends for this capacity to develop.[156] Mark Granovetter makes the case for national and international networks based on equally weak ties. They arise from occasional interactions, but may prove critical social resources for jobs, trade, and the like, because they bring together people from different social groups.[157]

Evolutionary psychologists claim to have answered the second question. There is a consensus among them that the puzzle of altruism was resolved in the 1960s by W. D. Hamilton in the course of his research on ants and bees. He maintains, *ceteris paribus*, that a gene for altruism will evolve to stability whenever the benefits to the recipient – measured in terms of the number of future offspring born – exceed the cost, defined in terms of offspring lost. R. L. Trivers extended this formulation to include reciprocal altruism by non-kin.[158] More recent accounts rely on kin selection theory. Anthropologist Christopher Boehm argues that altruism can be explained by the benefits it offers one's offspring.[159] Critics have raised numerous – in my view, telling – objections to these claims.[160]

Evolutionary arguments take for granted that altruistic behavior is self-evident. Like all categorizations of human behavior, altruism is subjective, culturally determined, and context dependent. Even within cultures, there is often no consensus about what constitutes altruism. Consider the bravery of Caesar's centurions. Were they being altruistic or merely foolhardy? They thought the former and Caesar the latter. Tirpitz and Ludendorff considered their plea for Armageddon altruistic; it would save Germany's honor and inspire its postwar recovery. The soldiers being asked to sacrifice their lives thought the generals self-indulgent and destructive of their nation. Variation in so-called altruistic behavior is so great within and across societies that evolution cannot possibly account for it. Altruism is not a scientific term but a social construction. People from the same societies are likely to define it differently depending on their respective political views and social positions. And the extent to which it serves the family, kin-group, or nation may not be at all evident at the time, or afterwards for that matter. There are also fundamental scientific reasons for questioning the evolutionary explanation of altruism.[161]

We need to look for social explanations for willingness to sacrifice one's blood or treasure. A useful starting point is Emile Durkheim's analysis of social solidarity, a topic of lifelong interest to him. Like many thinkers of his era, he observed a striking decline in traditional ways of life in conjunction with industrialization, urbanization, and secularism. Traditional sources of authority were losing legitimacy, and pessimists insisted that Europe was heading toward decadence and even anarchy. Durkheim's account, offered initially in *The Division of Labor*, and subsequently in his study of tribal societies, explored the role of what he called the *conscience commune* (collective consciousness) in traditional and modern societies.[162]

Durkheim was not alone in addressing this problem. Three other roughly contemporary accounts gained prominence, and together with his defined the terms of a continuing debate about the importance and nature of solidarity and the role of society in shaping its members. Earlier in the nineteenth century, Auguste Comte offered a positivist and authoritarian explanation. He saw the division of labor as the distinguishing feature of modern society and a threat to the common sentiments and interactions that had been the social cement of smaller, less economically developed societies. Individuals were "drawn away from the society by the nature of their special activity" and only "very dimly" perceive themselves "related to the public."[163] The very process that enabled society to grow and prosper also threatened to destroy it. Comte's solution was a strong state that would intervene to foster and regulate economic, social, and cultural life.[164]

Herbert Spencer articulated a liberal, laissez-faire rejoinder. As societies had advanced from those dominated by warriors and their quest for honor to commercial ones where interest was dominant, central control and regulation had declined. This did not constitute a threat to society because the division of labor was fostering an increasing harmony of interests among people. In the future, the dominant kind of relationship would be economic and regulated by free individuals acting on the basis of their interests. Society would be thin but sufficient for the purpose of the "bringing together of individuals who exchange the products of their labour, without any genuinely social influence coming to regulate that exchange."[165]

Ferdinand Tönnies agreed with Spencer that modernity was characterized by industrialism and that individuals increasingly competed openly to advance their interests. Traditional beliefs and the orthodoxy associated with them had given way to pluralism, individuality, freedom of thought, and self-expression. Behavior that "manifest the will and spirit" of the society had become increasingly rare. Everyone is "by himself and isolated" and "nobody wants to grant and produce anything for another individual." In contrast to Spencer, Tönnies, influenced by Marx and LaSalle, considered capitalism to have the potential to usher in a new age of serfdom. Only a strong state could forestall this possibility by enforcing contracts and restraining all "the particular wills" inspired by "unchained greed." Even so, Tönnies feared that, "The state of war that society conceals in its bosom must someday come to a head ... breaking all social bonds" and bringing about "the decomposition of the social body."[166]

Durkheim's critique of these thinkers is revealing and largely on point. Comte in his view was too narrowly focused on economic relations. He ignored "the spontaneous consensus of the parts" of traditional societies that was essential to their functioning. This moral-religious consensus produced "reverential respect" for certain beliefs and practices.[167] Comte thought the state could construct a new consensus, as indeed fascist and communist regimes would attempt in the twentieth century. Durkheim presciently observed that uniformity in belief and values "cannot be maintained by force and against the nature of things."[168] The division of labor inevitably promotes diversity in beliefs and values. Collective sentiments grow weaker in the face of centrifugal forces.[169]

Durkheim's critique of Spencer extended this argument. Diverse economic interests would not create solidarity but instability, "for interest only relates men momentarily and externally" and in the most superficial ways. The harmony of interests that Spencer expects laissez-faire capitalism to promote would at best temporarily conceal deeper underlying conflicts. As "there is nothing to curb men's egoism, each individual finds himself on a footing of war with every other, and any truce in this eternal antagonism could not last long."[170] Durkheim criticized Spencer's enthusiasm for contracts, and failure to grasp – in contrast to Comte – that they were a product of society and their operation rested on non-contractual understandings and practices.[171]

Durkheim was highly skeptical of Tönnies' desire to mobilize the state to foster solidarity. At best, this would create a mere "mechanical aggregate," not a society that cohered because of thick relations and shared beliefs among its members. Durkheim insisted that to function effectively any meaningful "life of great social aggregations" had to be "just as natural as that of small aggregates." It should be "neither less organic nor less internal."[172]

Durkheim offered his vision in *The Division of Labor*. He follows Comte in believing that the division of labor, by which he means occupational specialization, has the potential to fill the role formerly occupied by the *conscience collective*. He nevertheless insists that it cannot rest on a purely economic base but requires a moral one. Appetites, especially greed, need to be limited, and this requires some kind of solidarity that subordinates them "to some end that surpasses them."[173] In this connection, Durkheim distinguishes between mechanical and organic solidarity, somewhat counterintuitive terms because the former refers to traditional and the latter to industrial societies.

Mechanical solidarity is the product of a shared consciousness unique to a particular society. It is characterized by robust connections among individuals and between them and their society because of the strength of the *conscience collective*.[174] At its core are religious beliefs and practices that penetrate and pervade all spheres of activity.[175] There is also a personal consciousness that makes people different from others and provides them with a personality. It is not highly developed because there is little role differentiation. People are "homogenous segments" that fit together into a greater whole. "The solidarity that derives from resemblances is at its *maximum* when the *conscience collective* is exactly co-extensive with [the individual's] entire *conscience* and coincides at all points with it; but at this moment his individuality is non-existent."[176] Such a society is, of course, an ideal type, and most closely approximated by clans.[177]

For Durkheim, organic solidarity is a response to the increasing segmentation of social structures and functions that are only loosely connected to one another. People have their own spheres, often quite different and with little overlap or interaction with those of others.[178] People's natural environment is no longer where they were born and grew up but where they work.[179] Functional diversity produces moral diversity. The collective consciousness is still present but has a different character; it is increasingly secular, rational, polyvalent in values, and abstract rather than connected to a particular place.[180] It is also weaker because it "must leave free a part of the individual *conscience*, so that special functions may be established there which it cannot control." Accordingly, the "activity of each is more personal as it becomes more specialized." It is "never entirely original" because "even in our occupational activity we conform to practices and ways of acting that we share with our whole corporation." It nevertheless "leaves much more room for the free play of our initiative."[181] People relate to one another more by law than custom, and a measure of organic solidarity is the development and widespread application of civil, commercial, procedural, administrative and constitutional law.[182]

Durkheim had high hopes for organic solidarity on the grounds that the *conscience collective* would ultimately be based on a highly developed work ethic that would incorporate core liberal values of dignity and independence of the individual, equal opportunity for all, and a commitment to social justice.[183] Bottom-up orders would become more distinct and robust, but collectively supportive of top-down order. Durkheim naively expected these values to become something approaching a universal secular religion and for habit to replace coercion as the principal mechanism of compliance.[184]

Durkheim's account is open to other criticisms. He wrote in an era when anthropology was just getting under way and still empirically impoverished. His picture of pre-industrial societies as homogenous and unarticulated was simply wrong. So too was his description of law in these societies as largely repressive in its function.[185] He held unreasonable expectations about the positive social, intellectual, and political consequences of the division of labor. He thought it would bring about a "spontaneous consensus" of the diverse parts of society. This required a moral transformation that he expected to be brought about by better civic education and expert regulation of economic competition. People would learn about their rights, but also how to perform their duties.

Durkheim was right in thinking that professional roles were increasingly important in the modern world. He was also astute in recognizing that the division of labor could diverge from its "natural course" and fail to produce organic solidarity. Capitalism could result in "anomie" instead. Durkheim developed this concept initially in the context of industrial relations, where he considered it a temporary product of uneven development.[186] In his subsequent work on suicide, he uses it to describe the breakdown of social bonds between individuals and their community that leads to a fragmentation of social identities and rejection of values that enabled self-regulation.[187]

Comte and Tönnies believed that social anarchy could only be averted by state intervention. The nineteenth and twentieth centuries give evidence for the partial success of this strategy. Next to the family, nationalism is arguably the dominant form of social identification in the modern world. It is sponsored by most states – and by dissident nationalities within these states – and has had notable success in building national and group solidarity. When internalized, national identification unites people and justifies, even encourages, sacrifice. It also divides people within states depending on how the nationality is defined. State-sponsored nationalism has been a powerful source of cohesion, solidarity, and civic peace, but also a primary source of domestic and international division and conflict.

Spencer and Durkheim were more optimistic. Spencer expected economic development to overcome traditional sources of social division by creating a harmony of interests. Less government would be needed because people, being free agents, would manage their own lives. They would only enter into accords from which they benefitted. The role of government would shift from punishment to contract enforcement. Durkheim also considered economic development a liberating force, but for largely non-economic reasons. It would encourage education, individualism, secularism, liberalism, and professional diversity. The workplace would become the dominant source of identification and the most significant unit of society. The role of the state would shift from punishment to coordination under some form of socialism in which syndicate leadership would provide the necessary expert advice.

Spencer's liberal idealism has been exposed as an illusion. As Durkheim predicted, freedom from restraint encourages narrow self-interest and conflict. This is true even in constitutional democracies, and is arguably more prevalent in such societies. Solidarity, to the extent that it develops, is with interest or other affinity groups. Contrary to Durkheim's expectations, solidarity in such societies is often high but also highly fragmented.

Scandinavian democracy in its heyday might come the closest to the kind of society Durkheim envisaged. The *conscience collective* also appears high in a country like Japan, but is based on cultural and so-called racial exclusivity – hardly what Durkheim wanted or expected.

By all accounts the *conscience collective* has weakened in Scandinavia and other developed countries that have traditionally stressed collectivism and solidarity.[188] Durkheim's abnormal pathways of capitalist development appear to have become more the norm than the exception. Anomie may be at an all-time high in the developed world, and more prevalent still in those parts of the world where economic development is retarded, wealth more unevenly distributed, and government more authoritarian and repressive. This helps to explain why religious fundamentalism and nationalism are almost everywhere on the rise; they provide order, meaning, social integration, and with them self-respect.

Modern states do not live up to the expectations of Spencer or Durkheim, but most have avoided the anarchy feared by Comte and Tönnies. Western-style democracies have less of a *conscience collective* than Durkheim hoped, and greed and other forms of appetite are accordingly expressed in ways that are harmful to the society as a whole. They are responsible for the growing disparity between the rich and everyone else, and arguably for the more marked conspicuous consumption by the former and greater spending and indebtedness by the latter. Principles of justice are everywhere explicit, with equality in ascendance. But everywhere the gap between theory and practice is more apparent and resented.

This growing gap explains in part the electoral appeal in Europe and the United States of candidates who promise radical change based on nationalism, anti-immigration, and anti-globalization. Elections and referenda in Greece, France, Italy, Britain, and the United States show that the legitimacy of western governments and their governing classes is, at least for the moment, in decline. This situation speaks to the dilemma posed by this chapter: why those most disadvantaged by social and political orders are often their strongest supporters. The upheavals of the 1930s and today indicate that they can also become its most vocal opponents. And they are not alone, as many affluent and better-educated people also spurn their governments. Contrary to liberal expectations, relative affluence and security have not solved the crisis of modernity.

Conclusion

Cooperation is a key focus of social science research. Beginning with Cesare Beccaria in the late eighteenth century, social scientists turned to the study of institutions, and more recently to game theory and rationalist models to find the conditions in which individuals and states will cooperate and develop trust.[189] Similar attention has been directed at leaders. Drawing on Olson's description of politics as "banditry," Robert Bates argues that those who control a territory – those he calls "specialists in violence" – will defend rather than prey on their inhabitants when they believe they will get more from taxation than expropriation.[190] Carles Boix defines order in equally narrow economic terms. He contends that political actors will resort to violence and try to overthrow orders when they think they will be better off this way.[191] Both authors assume that everyone is motivated primarily, or even entirely, by economic gain – a view of life and politics that makes for simple models, but blatantly disregards reality.[192] In Colombia, Sanín Gutiérrez shows how political gains for guerillas led to economic losses, forcing them to choose between these goals.[193] Stuart Kaufman makes a more general and persuasive argument against purely rationalist accounts of ethnic violence. They are, he suggests, something of an oxymoron as highly emotionally charged situations are ones in which actors are least likely to calmly calculate risk and loss. The idea that ethnic violence could be motivated purely by opportunity is an unjustified rational conceit.[194] Northern Ireland can be cited as a particularly compelling counter-example.[195]

Rationalist approaches to cooperation focus on individuals and their autonomous relationship to the state, and understand this relationship in purely cognitive terms. They ignore relationships among individuals, the multiple ways in which people are influenced by the behavior of others, and the role of emotions in creating social bonds and building cooperation. Rationalist models appeal to social scientists because of their parsimony and seeming elegance, but as Nietzsche observed, "a profound thought can nevertheless be very distant from the truth."[196] And it is by no means self-evident that rationalist theories qualify as profound.

Research programs that address cooperation generally limit themselves to discovering its instrumental or enabling causes. The liberal institutionalist, social capital and "thin" constructivist approaches posit the egoistic but rational actor as their analytical unit. They take for granted that people, institutions, and states want to cooperate and would do so if environmental and other constraints could be overcome. Toward this end they invoke social capital, institutions, and regimes, or a hegemon, any or all of which can facilitate coordination and increase the benefits of cooperation and the costs of defection.[197] Other theorists describe cooperation as the unintentional outcome of cumulative self-interested behavior.[198]

When there is predisposition to cooperate, the kinds of mechanisms theorized by rationalists and liberal institutionalists can undoubtedly facilitate it. The more important and prior question is explaining the predisposition to cooperate. The same is true of conflict. Many realists invoke the balance of power and polarity to explain war, but it is an enabling cause at best. Rationalists assume a prior propensity for conflict, just as they do for cooperation, and theorize triggering conditions – without telling us the conditions in which one or the other disposition will prevail. Weber and Morgenthau, to their credit, attempt more fundamental explanations by turning to human nature, but make leaps from individuals to nations without fully elaborating the mechanisms allegedly involved.[199]

I address the underlying rather than enabling causes of cooperation and conflict within the broader framework of a theory of political order. I argue that human beings require social orders to survive as a species and fulfill their desires and potential as individuals. Cooperation is the basis of all social orders and they in turn facilitate and structure it. The key to order among primates is a set of practices that conform to what human philosophers describe as principles of justice. Human orders rely on the same practices. They can be explained with respect to two fundamental principles of justice: fairness and equality. The greater cognitive abilities of humans allow them to reflect on and theorize about their needs and their societies. They have developed discourses about justice and how it might be brought about, but also about why it is acceptable to have societies from which it is largely absent, or where there are glaring discrepancies between principles and practices. Cooperation within existing orders is another matter, and will depend on the extent to which actors value and seek to preserve these orders and their norms through cooperation, even when it is not necessarily in their short-term interest. Order and disorder are a function of values and agency, not so-called structures or abstract rationalist calculations.

Human orders differ in scale. For much of our species' history, people lived in family or extended family groupings, not unlike many other primate species. Larger societies emerged 4–5,000 years ago, and more recently in some parts of the world. Social and political orders gradually became distinct in response to this increase in scale, greatly complicating the problem of order. Political orders are an extension of social orders – ancient Greeks were absolutely explicit about this relationship – and governed more or less by the same dynamics. To endure they must rest on some principle of justice, although discourses may go a long way to reconciling people to political orders where justice is honored more in the breach than in practice.

Orders are hierarchical and people are reconciled to occupying the lower rungs of these hierarchies for four generic reasons: fear, appetite, *thumos*, and habit. Fear has multiple meanings: people can be afraid of living outside society, of the consequences of its decline or collapse, or of punishments meted out and sanctioned by their society. Family-based orders and small societies rely more on shaming than punishment. The latter is more necessary in larger units where social bonds are looser and shaming has less effect. Shame and punishment work when actors conclude that their security, appetite, or standing will suffer as a result.

The relationship between human needs and orders offers the most fundamental explanation of cooperation and conflict. As Aristotle assumes, human needs prompt cooperation and predictable behavior and in turn offer additional incentive for cooperation. They do the same for conflict. To satisfy material, sexual, and other appetites, gain honor or standing, or enhance security, people are sorely tempted to violate the rules of their society, to cheat at the expense of others. According to the Romans: *Homo homini lupus* (man is a wolf to man) in the pursuit of honor. Nobel economists Akerlof and Shiller make a similar argument about the pressures to cheat in pursuit of wealth – although later I will dispute their explanation that this is an inevitable product of the market.[200] When people act this way, they diminish the ability of others to satisfy their needs and desires. Such behavior, not the scarcity of resources, is the principal source of conflict among people and states. It is most acute when honor and standing are at issue, as they are relative rather than absolute, and more likely to promote envy, anger, and desire for revenge. Wealth is absolute, but as Rousseau and Smith noted, it has become a marker of standing in the modern world. It is a relative gain for those who frame it this way.

My hypotheses about disorder are based on ideal-type honor and appetite worlds. I show how they unravel for different reasons and by somewhat different mechanisms. Real worlds, especially modern ones, emphasize both appetite and *thumos*, and generally are also characterized by security concerns. They evolve and dissolve in more complex ways – ways moreover that are always highly context dependent. My ideal types nevertheless constitute an appropriate starting point for studying this process. They also drive home the fundamental truth of all social and political orders: the very features that make them congeal also make them conflict-prone and fragile. Utopias are unattainable in the real world. Even the most successful orders, as Plato recognized in the *Republic*, of necessity encode tensions that produce conflict, change, and instability.

Notes

1 Aristotle, *Politics*, 1253a3–4.
2 Ibid.
3 Ibid., 1253a26–28; Riesbeck, *Aristotle on Political Community*.

4 Denis Campbell, "Loneliness as harmful as diabetes, says top GP," *Guardian*, October 12 2017, p. 4.

5 Hume, *Treatise on Human Nature*, III.ii.v. See also, Fromm, *Escape From Freedom*, pp. 17–18, citing Balzac and Freud in support.

6 Atul Gewande, "Hellhole: The United States holds tens of thousands of inmates in long-term solitary confinement. Is this torture?" *New Yorker*, March   30   2009,   www.newyorker.com/magazine/2009/03/30/hellhole (accessed March 9 2015).

7 Jones, *Why Humans Share Food*, pp. 31, 77–78.

8 Greenblatt, *Rise and Fall of Adam and Eve*, pp. 213–20, for a sample account from different cultures.

9 Virgil, *Aeneid.*

10 Luhtanen and Crocker, "A Collective Self-Esteem Scale."

11 Wiseman, *Remus*; Erskine, *Troy Between Greece and Rome*; Dench, *Romulus' Asylum*; Beard, *SPQR*, pp. 71–74.

12 Related by Pufendorf, "Compleat History of Sweden from its Origin to This Time," and cited by Bartelson, *War in International Thought*, p. 52.

13 Fukuyama, *Origins of Political Order*, pp. 49–59, for a review of the relevant anthropological literature and speculation.

14 Zuiderhoek, *Ancient City*, pp. 20–36.

15 Scott, *Against the Grain*, pp. 151–52.

16 Lattimore, "Frontier in History," p. 138.

17 Scott, *Against the Grain*, pp. 32, 122, 187, 209.

18 Buzan and Lawson, *Global Transformation*, p. 23, on the global transformation associated with modernity as the most recent iteration of this process of relative advantage.

19 Nissen, *Early History of the Ancient Near East*, p. 127.

20 Ibid., 140–41; Nissen, "Emergence of Writing in the Ancient Near East."

21 Gagarin, "Early Greek Law."

22 Gaskill, *Between Two Worlds*, chs. 1–8.

23 Brutus, Letter II, in Madison, Hamilton, and Jay, *Federalist Papers*, p. 448.

24 Weber, *Economy and Society*, II, pp. 904–9.

25 Scott, *Against the Grain*, for the strongest and most recent statement.

26 Jared Diamond, "The Worst Mistake in the History of the Human Race," *Discover*, May 1 1999, http://discovermagazine.com/1987/may/02-the-worst-mistake-in-the-history-of-the-human-race (accessed January 13 2017).

27 Wrigley, "A Simple Model of London's Importance in Changing English Society and Economy," and *Continuity, Chance, and Change*; Inwood, *History of London*, pp. 269–72; Zuiderhoek, *Ancient City*, pp. 73–77, for the urban graveyard thesis and critics.

28 Scott, *Against the Grain*, for the most recent argument of this kind.

29 Lovejoy and Boas, *Primitivism and Related Ideas in Antiquity*, pp. 1–7; Frye, "Varieties of Literary Utopias"; Finley, *"Utopias Ancient and Modern"*; Lebow, *Politics and Ethics of Identity*, ch. 2.

30 Tooby, "Conceptual Foundations of Evolutionary Psychology"; Tooby, "Evolutionary Psychology of the Emotions and their Relationship to Internal Regulatory Variables"; Tooby and Cosmides, "Past Explains the Present";

Gat, "Causes and Origins of 'Primitive' Warfare"; Gorelik, Shackelford, and Weekes-Shackelford, "Resource, Acquisition, Violence, and Evolutionary Consciousness"; Rosen, *War and Human Nature*.

31 Bell, "Beware of False Prophets: Biology"; Lebow, "You Can't Keep a Bad Idea Down" and "Darwin and International Relations."

32 Harcourt and De Waal, *Coalitions in Humans and Other Animals*; De Waal and Tyack, *Animal Social Complexity*; De Waal, *Bonobo*; Boehm, *Hierarchy in the Forest*.

33 Lebow, "Darwin and International Relations" for the difference between these mechanisms and imitation.

34 For visual evidence, "Orca Seal Hunting," Animal Planet, http://animal .discovery.com/tv-shows/weird-true-and-freaky/videos/orca-seal-hunting .htm (accessed January 20 2014); Frozen Planet, "Killer Whales 'Wave Wash' Seal," http://dsc.discovery.com/tv-shows/frozen-planet/videos/killer-whales-wave-wash-seal.htm (accessed January 20 2014).

35 Frans B. M. De Waal, "Natural Normativity," and Lecture, Hessische Friedens-und Konflikt Forschung, Frankfurt-am-Main, October 24 2013.

36 Kant, "Idea for a Universal History."

37 Freud, *Civilization and its Discontents*; Fromm, *Escape from Freedom*, pp. 7–11.

38 De Waal Lecture.

39 De Waal and Tyack, *Animal Social Complexity*; De Waal, *Bonobo* and Lecture.

40 Frans B. M. De Waal, "Monkey Cucumber Grape Experiment," *YouTube*, July 9 2012, www.youtube.com/watch?v=OwR5l8wfXlU (accessed January 20 2014).

41 De Waal and Tyack, *Animal Social Complexity*.

42 For a thoughtful but sympathetic critique, Rowlands, *Can Animals Be Moral*.

43 De Waal Lecture.

44 See the essays in Wrangham, McGrew, de Waal, and Heltne, *Chimpanzee Cultures*.

45 Smith, *Theory of Moral Sentiments*, 1.1.

46 Darwin, *Descent of Man*, chs. 4–5.

47 Kitcher, "Ethics and Evolution"; Korsgaard, "Morality and the Distinctiveness of Human Action"; Alex Hern, "Give robots 'personhood,' says EU Committee," *Guardian*, January 13 2017, p. 4.

48 Hume, *Treatise of Human Nature*, 1.3.16.3. 2.3.16, and *Enquiry Concerning Human Understanding*, 9.2–3.

49 Aristotle, *Rhetoric*, 1382a21–33, 1382b28–35. Konstan, *Emotions of the Ancient Greeks*, pp. 129–55, for a discussion.

50 Lebow, *Cultural Theory of International Relations*.

51 Harman, "History of the Altruism-Morality Debate in Biology"; Lebow, "Darwin and International Relations."

52 Lebow, "Darwin and International Relations," for the differences among evolution as a process, evolution as a metaphor, and conscious adaptation.

53 Smith, *Inquiry into the Nature and Causes of the Wealth of Nations*, I, ch. 1, *Wealth of Nations*, I.iv, and *Lectures on Jurisprudence*, "Report of 1762–63"; Kant, "Conjectures on the Beginning of Human History," pp. 221–34; Durkheim, *The Division of Labor in Society*, pp. 400–1.

54 Quoted in Lineweaver, Davies and Rose, "What is Complexity?"

55 Holland, *Emergence*, pp. 6–7; Goldstein, "Emergence as a Construct: History and Issues"; Goodwin, *How the Leopard Changed Its Spots*.

56 Sean Nee, "How many genes does it take to make a person?" *The Conversation*, October 19 2016, https://theconversation.com/how-many-genes-does-it-take-to-make-a-person-64284?utm_medium=email&utm_campaign=Get%20ready%20for%20Trump%20vs%20Clinton%20round%203&utm_content=Get%20ready%20for%20Trump%20vs%20Clinton%20round%203+Version+A+CID_5183cbdb79ceb5d7b5966df5a43d144c&utm_source=campaign_monitor_us&utm_term=How%20many%20genes%20does%20it%20take%20to%20make%20a%20person (accessed October 24 2016).

57 Morris, "Life."

58 Linneweaver, Davies, and Ruse, "What is Complexity?," p. 3.

59 Hayek, *Rules and Order*, p. 36.

60 Marc Goodman, "The internet of things will turn our machines against us," Wired, January 15 2016, www.wired.co.uk/article/internet-of-hackable-things (accessed July 9 2017); Fred Kaplan, "Vulnerability Is the Internet's Original Sin," *Slate*, October 25 2016, www.slate.com/articles/news_and_politics/war (accessed July 9 2017); Fred Kaplan, *Dark History: The Secret History of the Cyber War* (New York: Simon and Schuster, 2016).

61 Tainter, *Collapse of Complex Societies*; Diamond, *Collapse*; Turchin and Nefedov, *Secular Cycles*; Mitchell, *Carbon Democracy*.

62 Lebow, *Cultural Theory of International Relations*, ch. 3.

63 Smith, *Wealth of Nations*, I.4.

64 Keeley, *War Before Civilization*.

65 Smith, *Wealth of Nations*, I.iv, and *Lectures on Jurisprudence* offer a similar four-stage model of historical development.

66 Aristotle, *Rhetoric*, 1369b16–19.

67 Appalled by this display, Plato, *Republic*, 373a–b, distinguishes between necessary and unnecessary appetites.

68 Lebow, *National Identifications and International Relations*, ch. 4 for elaboration.

69 Ibid., ch. 7.

70 Smith, *Theory of Moral Sentiments*, I.iii.3.5–6.

71 Ibid., I.iii.2.1 and 3.1.

72 Tocqueville, *Democracy in America*, II.4.6., p. 662, on "individualism" and its consequences.

73 Lebow, *Cultural Theory of International Relations*, ch. 6, and *National Identifications and International Relations*, h. 4.

74 Hughes, *Peter the Great*, p. 86.

75 Blanning, *Frederick the Great*, pp. 25–46.

76 Trollope, *Phineas Finn, Phineas Redux, The Duke's Children*, and *Can You Forgive Her?*

77 Tocqueville, *Democracy in America*, I, pp. 3–19.

78 Veblen, *Theory of the Leisure Class*.

79 Baltzell, *Philadelphia Gentlemen* and *Protestant Establishment*.

80 Birmingham, *Our Crowd*.

81 Tocqueville, *Democracy in America*, 2.ii. 20.

82 Simon Greaves, "Wealthy Britons own second-biggest share of superyachts," *Financial Times*, April 18 2016, www.ft.com/content/b53f015a-02fc-11e6-99cb-83242733f755 (accessed January 15 2017).

83 Andrew Jack, "Igor Tsukanov: The Russian banker who wants a museum, not a yacht," *Financial Times*, November 30 2016, www.ft.com/content/b6254ee0-b327-11e6-a37c-f4a01f1b0fa1 (accessed January 15 2017).

84 Ibid., II.2.14, pp. 513–14.

85 Simmel, *Philosophy of Money*, pp. 468–70.

86 Josie Gurney-Read, "Half of the new Cabinet 'went to Oxbridge,'" *Daily Telegraph*, May 11 2015, www.telegraph.co.uk/education/educationnews/11598097/Half-of-the-new-Cabinet-went-to-Oxbridge.html (accessed July 9 2017); Saunders, *Unequal but Fair?*

87 Tocqueville, *Democracy in America*, II.2.20, pp. 530–32 and II.4.6, p. 663.

88 Gross, "Giving in America"; Barker-Benfield, "Origins of Anglo-American Sensibility."

89 McNeese, *Robber Barons and the Sherman Antitrust Act*.

90 Finkelstein, *American Jewish History*, pp. 97–98.

91 Rupert Neate, "The two sides of Davos: luxury for the guests, five beds to a room for the staff," *Guardian*, January 14 2007, p. 9; Andrew Ross Sorkin, "What to Make of the 'Davos Class' in the Trump Era," *New York Times*, January 16 2017, www.nytimes.com/2017/01/16/business/dealbook/world-economic-forum-davos-trump.html?hp&action=click&pgtype=Homepage&clickSource=story-heading&module=second-column-region&region=top-news&WT.nav=top-news (accessed January 16 2017).

92 "Karsten Polke-Majewski," Kurz mal Hölle, *Zeit Online*, July 7 2017, www.zeit.de/gesellschaft/zeitgeschehen/2017-07/g20-protest-welcome-to-hell-hamburg-polizei (accessed July 9 2017); MrCaseyoliver, "Hamburg Riots | G20 protests," *YouTube*, 7 July 2017, www.youtube.com/watch?v=FX6QwEohyRk (accessed July 9 2017).

93 Lebow, *Cultural Theory of International Relations*, ch. 7.

94 Linton, Ralph, *The Study of Man*, p. 115.

95 Homer, *Iliad*, Book 1.

96 Schumpeter, *Imperialism and Social Classes*.

97 Pflanze, *Bismarck and the Development of Germany*, vols. 2–3; Rosenberg, *Imperial Germany*, pp. 33–72; Kehr, *Primat der Innenpolitik*; Lebow, *Cultural Theory of International Relations*, ch. 7 for discussion.

98 Bull, *Anarchical Society*: Bull and Watson, *Expansion of Civil Society*; Vincent, *Human Rights and International Relations*; Linklater and Suganami, *English School of International Relations*; Wight, *Systems of States* make the case for domestic orders shaping international ones. Bartelson, "Short Circuits" and "Towards a Genealogy of 'Society' in International Relations" for the reverse, and Keal, *European Conquest and the Rights of Indigenous Peoples*; Pagden, *Lord of All the World*, for the importance of colonies.

99 Lebow, *National Identifications and International Relations* for elaboration.

100 Frost, "Tragedy, Ethics, and International Relations" and Mayall, "Tragedy, Progress, and International Order," for a debate on the extent of these differences.

101 Lebow, *National Identifications and International Relations*, ch. 7.
102 Lebow, *Cultural Theory of International Relations*, ch. 1 for a discussion.
103 Sophocles, *Ajax*, pp. 1209–10.
104 Machiavelli, *Prince*, XXVII.
105 Bodin, *Six livres*, 2:73.
106 Plato, *Republic*, 571c8–9 and 579d9–10; Aristotle, *Politics*, 1315b11; Thucydides, *Peloponnesian War, passim*, but especially the Melian Dialogue.
107 Lebow, *Unfinished Utopia*.
108 Guy, *Elizabeth*, pp. 170–76, 204–5.
109 Tucker, *Stalin in Power*; Volkogonov, *Stalin*; Kotkin, *Stalin*.
110 Kotkin, *Stalin*, II, p. 782.
111 Kevin Connor, "Naming and shaming those accused of drunken driving," *Toronto Sun*, January 8 2017, www.torontosun.com/2017/01/08/naming-and-shaming-those-accused-of-drunk-driving (accessed June 13 2017); Jagadish Angadi, "City Cops to name, shame drunk drivers on website," *Deccan Herald*, June 13 2017, www.deccanherald.com/content/392566/city-cops-name-shame-drunk.html (accessed June 13 2017); Lucy Osborne, "Trial by Twitter: Fury at police who are naming and shame [sic] drunk drivers on the Internet BEFORE they are convicted," *Daily Mail*, January 1 2014, www.dailymail.co.uk/news/article-2532236/Outrage-hundreds-drink-drivers-named-shamed-Twitter-BEFORE-theyve-chance-fair-trial.html (accessed June 13 2017).
112 Cover, "Supreme Court, 1982 Term."
113 Durkheim, *Division of Labor*, pp. 24–28.
114 Ibid., pp. 62–63.
115 Cover, "Violence and the World."
116 Dahl, "Concept of Power"; North and Weingast, "Constitutions and Commitment."
117 Morrill, *Executive Way*, pp. 72–74; Ostrom, "Revisiting the Commons."
118 Josh Keller and Adam Pearce, "The Small Indiana County Sends More People to Prison than San Francisco and Durham, N.C. Combined. Why?" *New York Times*, September 2 2006, www.nytimes.com/2016/09/02/upshot/new-geography-of-prisons.html (accessed September 2 2016).
119 Schiefflin, "Early Contact as Drama and Misrepresentation in the Southern Highlands of Papua New Guinea"; Migdal, *Strong Societies and Weak States*; Rotberg, *When States Fail*. Woodward, *Ideology of Failed States*, for a critique of the concept. Badie, *Les temps humilés*, for a thoughtful analysis of the political-psychological dynamics of western-non-western interactions that promote failed states.
120 Hobbes, *Leviathan*, I.11.9. Although fear is central to Hobbes, it is a secondary means of control. He recognizes that sovereigns must govern by legitimacy if coercion is to be effective against any minority that resists. His sovereign encourages citizens to concentrate on their material interests, as appetite combined with reason is likely to make them more compliant. Williams, "The Hobbesian Theory of International Relations."
121 Janowitz, "Sociological Theory and Social Control"; Kasarda and Janowitz, "Community Attachment in Mass Society."

122 Schumpeter, *Imperialism and Social Classes*, for an early example, and Lasswell, *Politics* as an important exception. Lebow, *Cultural Theory of International Relations*, ch. 3, for discussion.

123 Schumpeter, *Capitalism, Socialism, and Democracy*, pp. 131–33.

124 Machiavelli, *Prince* and *Discourses*; Hobbes, *Leviathan*; Rousseau, "Fragments on War" and *Discourse on the Origins of Inequality*; Smith, *Theory of Moral Sentiments*.

125 Lebow, *Cultural Theory of International Relations*.

126 Ibid., ch. 3.

127 Wilson, *Holy Roman Empire*, p. 12.

128 Ibid., pp. 45–46.

129 Kotkin, *Stalin*, II, p. 184.

130 Thucydides, 1.119–125, in his account of the Peloponnesian War shows how the airing of grievances publicly contributed to the escalation of conflict and the outbreak of war.

131 Wilson, *Holy Roman Empire*, pp. 13–14, 22, 42, 54.

132 Aristotle, *Politics*, 1252a1–7, 1155a22–613, 162b5–21, 1328b7–9, 1335b38–1336a2, 1336b8–12.

133 Montesquieu, *Spirit of the Laws*; Durkheim, *Division of Labor in Society and Elementary Forms of the Religious Life*; Goffman, *Presentation of Self in Everyday Life*.

134 Durkheim, *Moral Education*, p. 28.

135 Ibid.; Durkheim, "Field of Sociology."

136 Kant, "An Answer to the Question," p. 53.

137 Hume, "Of Civil Liberty."

138 Kant, *Toward Perpetual Peace*, and *Anthropology from a Pragmatic Point of View*; Schneewind, "Good out of Evil"; Molloy, *Kant's International Relations*, pp. 94–96, 100–11.

139 Kant, *Anthropology from a Pragmatic Point of View*, p. 32.

140 Peter Bradshaw, "Notebook," *Guardian*, October 9 2014, p. 37.

141 Schumpeter, *Imperialism and Social Classes*, for an example.

142 Lebow, *Cultural Theory of International Relations*, ch. 3.

143 Lebow, *Why Nations Fight*, ch. 4.

144 Hunt, "French Revolution in Global Context."

145 Goldhill, "Great Dionysia and Civic Ideology."

146 Noyes, *Fire in the Placa*, on how the Patum de Berga festival helped Catalonians negotiate Fascism, post-Fascism, Catalonian nationalism, and now globalization.

147 Bryan, *Orange Parades*.

148 Steven Kull and Shibley Telhami, "The American Public on the 9/11 Decade: A Study of American Public Opinion," Brookings Institution, September 8 2011, www.brookings.edu/research/reports/2011/09/08-opinion-poll-telhami (accessed February 20 2016).

149 Socrates, "Apology."

150 Polybius, *Rise of the Roman Empire*, 1.16; Goldsworthy, *Roman Army at War*, pp. 12–36; Potter, "Roman Army and Navy."

151 Caesar, *Conquest of Gaul*, 7.46–51.

152 Boulton, *Knights of the Crown*, p. 36.
153 Ludendorff, note of October 31 1918, in Hull, *Absolute Destruction*, p. 318; Tirpitz to Prince Max of Baden, October 17 1918, Tirpitz, *Deutsche Ohnmachtspolitik im Weltkriege*, pp. 617–18.
154 Janowitz, "Sociological Theory and Social Control"; Kasarda and Janowitz, "Community Attachment in Mass Society"; Kornhauser, *Social Sources of Delinquency.*
155 Janowitz, "Sociological Theory and Social Control."
156 Sampson and Wikström, "The Social Order of Violence in Chicago and Stockholm"; Bursik, "Social Disorganization and Theories of Crime and Delinquency." Bellair, "Social Interaction and Community Crime," also makes the case for weak ties.
157 Granovetter, "Strength of Weak Ties."
158 Hamilton, "Genetical Evolution of Social Behavior"; Trivers, "Evolution of Reciprocal Altruism"; Alexander, *Biology of Moral Systems*; Dunbar; Van Vugt, Roberts, and Hardy, "Competitive Altruism"; Gintis, Bowles, Boyd, and Fehr, "Explaining Altruistic Behaviour in Humans."
159 Boehm, *Hierarchy in the Forest* and *Moral Origins.*
160 For an overview of this controversy, Wilson, "Group-Level Evolutionary Processes." Lebow, "Darwin and International Relations," for a critique of evolutionary psychology.
161 Ibid. for a review of the relevant literature.
162 Durkheim, *Division of Labor* and *Elementary Forms of the Religious Life.*
163 Comte, *Cours de la philosophie positive*, IV, pp. 357–58, 428–29.
164 Lukes, *Emile Durkheim*, pp. 142–47 on Comte, Spencer, and Tönnies in comparison to Durkheim.
165 Spencer, *Principles of Sociology*, III, p. 180.
166 Tönnies, *Gemeinschaft and Gesellschaft*, pp. 46–47, 420–21.
167 Durkheim, *Division of Labor*, pp. 360–61.
168 Ibid.
169 Ibid., p. 203.
170 Ibid.
171 Ibid.
172 Ibid., p. 421.
173 Ibid., pp. 197–99.
174 Ibid., pp. 106–9.
175 Ibid., p. 169.
176 Ibid., pp. 152, 169, 185–90, 194–95, 226–28, 287, 380.
177 Ibid., p. 177.
178 Ibid., 129–31, 190, 223, 227, 287–89, 367, 400.
179 Ibid., p. 182.
180 Ibid., pp. 169–72.
181 Ibid., p. 131.
182 Ibid., p. 69.
183 Ibid., p. 407.
184 Ibid., p. 172.
185 Lukes, *Emile Durkheim*, pp. 159–73, on Durkheim's discredited assumptions about traditional societies.

186 Ibid., pp. 353, 370.
187 Durkheim, *Suicide*.
188 Einhorn, *Modern Welfare States*.
189 Beccaria, *On Crimes and Punishments*; Becker, *Economic Approach to Human Behavior*; Posner, *Economics of Justice*; Zucker, "Production of Trust."
190 Bates, "Probing the Sources of Political Order."
191 Boix, "Civil Wars and Guerrilla Warfare in the Contemporary World."
192 Cederman, "Articulating the Geo-Cultural Logic of Nationalist Insurgency," for a critique of Boix; Lebow, *Cultural Theory of International Relations* and *Why Nations Fight* for a broader critique of rationalist models.
193 Gutiérrez, "Clausewitz Vindicated."
194 Kaufman, *Nationalist Passions*.
195 Gallagher, *After the Peace*.
196 Nietzsche, *Human, All-Too-Human*, p. 15.
197 Keohane, *International Institutions*; Stein, *Why Nations Cooperate*; Shanks, Jacobson, and Kaplan, "Inertia and Change in the Constellation of International Governmental Organizations; Hajnal, *The G7/G8 System*; Ikenberry, *After Victory*, pp. 248, 257–73.
198 Olson, *Logic of Collective Action*; Stigler and Becker, "De Gustibus Non Est. Disputandum"; Gammon, "Social Psychology of Collective Action"; Axelrod, *Evolution of Cooperation*.
199 Lebow, *Why Nations Fight*, ch. 2 for a critique of these several approaches.
200 Akerlof and Shiller, *Phishing for Phools*, pp. xi–xii.

4   Why Do Orders Break Down?

The beautiful thing that makes a true leader is
Inner strength to keep his hands clean.
                                                                Plutarch[1]

All orders are hierarchical. Even the most democratic and egalitarian
societies are accordingly unequal in their distribution of power, wealth
and status. The Latin word for order – *ordo* – also means social rank.[2]
Stratification of any kind encourages exploitation because those at the
apex have power and prestige that can be usually translated into material,
social, and sexual rewards.[3] Those at the bottom have little to no power
or prestige and must labor more for fewer rewards, yet, paradoxically,
are often the fiercest defenders of their order.[4] Given the hierarchal and
exploitative nature of social orders, the most fundamental puzzle of politics is how they last as long as they do? Why do people, or social units,
accept, endorse, and offer up their labor, wealth, even their lives, for
orders in which others reap most of the benefits?

I believe that part of the answer is the powerful emotional and substantive rewards that orders provide. Even though people may be worse
off relative to other members of their society, most believe they are more
secure, better off, and have more than they would have outside their
society. Social integration confers identity, enhances self-worth, and
enables social relationships and intimacy. Elites, moreover, are generally
astute enough to propagate discourses to make people aware and appre-
ciative of the advantages their order allegedly provides. These discourses
invoke metaphorical carrots and sticks; they exaggerate the material
and psychological benefits of belonging and the degree of chaos likely
to result from any radical change. When such discourses find traction
they reinforce sanctioned practices, making many of them habitual.
Discourses also attempt to shape expectations of what is reasonable for
orders to provide. This process began with golden age narratives like the
Garden of Eden story in the Book of Genesis and Hesiod's *Works and
Days*. They attempt to justify suffering and injustice in the worlds of their

142

readers and lower their expectations about what rulers can reasonably be expected to provide.[5]

In today's world, elite-sponsored discourses encourage people to develop unrealistic hopes about rising up the economic and status ladders. Before the 2008 economic crisis, 81 percent of American college students expected to become richer than their parents, and 59 percent of business students were convinced they would be millionaires before the age of forty.[6] The successful anti-establishment appeals of Donald Trump and Bernie Sanders in the 2016 election can be read as evidence that these discourses are losing traction.

Successful discourses permit a wider gap between theory and practice. Before the modern era, such a discrepancy was not as threatening as it is today. In the Holy Roman Empire, according to Peter Wilson, the gap between theory and practice "was not too troubling because it was almost universally understood as an expression of the imperfection of human, earthly existence. The ruler was expected to embody harmony [*Concordia*], and to manifest it through symbolic-laden actions."[7] Those in authority developed lengthy justification for their elevated status based on the principle of fairness. The order they defended emphasized asymmetrical reciprocity with duties unevenly distributed in Empire. Its hierarchy was neither absolute nor clear, but based on the almost universally accepted principle of interlocking sets of relationships in which all knew their assigned place. "The reality was messier and less consensual. Status was neither exclusively self-determined nor simply imposed from above according to a rational blueprint."[8] Acceptance of hierarchy declined in the late eighteenth century when Europeans began to embrace the ideas of progress and equality. Even then, the Holy Roman Empire retained the loyalty of a surprising percentage of its inhabitants because the corporate identities it sustained provided the collective basis – unsuccessful in the long run – for opposing territorial states and industrialization.

In our world, rhetorical sleights of hand are more difficult to pull off. Nevertheless, some oppressive regimes have been able to convince sizeable percentages of their citizens that they are fortunate to live in their country and that what problems they face are due to the machinations of evil foreign forces and powers. The Pew Research Center found in 2017 that 87 percent of Russians trust Vladimir Putin to do the right thing in foreign affairs.[9] In countries with freedom of the press, leaders are certain to be challenged by counter-discourses that publicize injustices and may even attempt to delegitimize existing orders. Public contestation makes it more likely that when leaders or regimes consistently fail to meet public expectations citizens will become disenchanted and more receptive to moderate, even radical, change. There is enormous variation in the growth and expression of dissatisfaction and the kind of events that undermine discourses and trigger dissent and protest. As this book goes to press, Donald Trump retains 38 percent support among Americans.[10] Research on revolution and ethnic conflict suggest it is a function of perceived threat, opportunity, framing, leadership, and mobilization, with none of these in itself decisive, and all of them acting in concert in non-linear ways.[11] I will return to this question in the concluding chapter.

Most orders – bottom-up and top-down – survive because they deliver at least in part what they promise – or convince people that they do. Orders also benefit from fear of uncertainty and change. "Better the devil we know than the one we do not" is a time-honored and widely shared sentiment that captures the inherent conservatism of much of the human race. Francesco Guicciardini warned that: "Few revolutions succeed, and, when they do, you often discover they did not gain you what you hoped for, and you condemn yourself to perpetual fear, as the parties you defeated may always regain power and work for your ruin."[12] His contemporary Machiavelli said something similar. Only certain, immediate necessity can convince them to accept risk. This is one reason why republics degenerate and are ruined.[13] In effect, "men are quick to change ruler when they imagine they can improve their lot . . . then later discover they were wrong and that things have got worse rather than better."[14]

People derive satisfaction from feeling superior to others, a belief bottom-up and top-down orders have always encouraged. Bottom-up orders are almost always more robust and longer-lived than their top-down counterparts. Governments and regimes come and go but society generally remains, even if it evolves over the course of time. Societies can fragment when their values and practices are not accepted by a significant percentage of the population. This is arguably the case in today's US, where there are sharp divisions over recent social changes, many of which now have top-down legal support. As in all societies, there are multiple bottom-up orders, but fewer of them overlapping in membership in divided or fragmented societies. I return to this question, to US society, and the relationship between bottom-up and top-down orders in chapters 5 and 6.

Bottom-up orders and local identifications have been dominant for most people for much of history. In large empires and pre-modern states, top-down orders were distant and resented by people for intrusions into their lives, especially as it most often took the form of corvée labor, tax collection and military conscription. Even these tasks were often farmed out to local authorities or agents. In the modern world, in an era of nationalism, the relative balance of power between these bottom-up and top-down orders has to some degree shifted in favor of the latter. In the first instance, this is attributable to their greater powers and importance for the ordinary lives of most people. It is also the result of a certain degree of psychological transference that began to become pronounced in Europe in the late eighteenth century. Individual self-esteem for many people is connected with the successes and failures of their state. As Carl von Clausewitz presciently observed in the aftermath of the Napoleonic Wars, conflicts and wars were no longer between princes, but between peoples.[15] My analysis in this chapter is directed at top-down orders, although to be sure, societies cannot be analyzed in isolation from their bottom-up counterparts.

Top-down and bottom-up orders exist beyond the state, in regional and international societies and their institutions. Liberals and constructivists have more to say about how regional and international orders form and solidify than they do about how they decline and collapse. Liberals, and many realists, stress the role of a hegemon in creating and maintaining order. Liberals attribute disorder to the absence or decline of a hegemon and its ability to sustain and enforce institutions and practices it has established.[16] There is little empirical support for these claims. There has never been a hegemon in the modern era, and the orders established in the aftermath of major wars – 1648, 1713, 1815, 1919, and 1945 – were not imposed by a dominant power but the product of negotiation and compromise among multiple parties.[17] I return to this question later in the chapter.

Realists explain war – which they associate with the breakdown of order – in terms of two underlying causes; the human drive for power and the anarchy of international society. They attribute order with reference to a robust balance of power, and disorder and war to its failure to form, breakdown, or insufficient power or credibility on the part of status quo powers attempting to defend the territorial status quo.[18] The balance of power has not been noticeably successful in preventing war, although it has fared better in preventing political units from achieving hegemony.[19] Realism purports to tell us when successful balances of power do or do not form, but there are so many exceptions to the rules proposed by different realists that they are useless for purposes of prediction or explanation. For answers, we must look to domestic politics, ideas, and agency.[20]

The current crisis of the Western order has nothing to do with the balance of power. It is bottom-up in origins, although directed at top-down orders. It is political, economic, and social, not military, in nature. It does not resemble the 1930s, when revisionist states were intent on overturning the existing order by force. In Europe, institutions of the EU are threatened by governments and political movements that have successfully mobilized public opinion against the postwar liberal consensus. In the US, trouble also arises from within and below. Here too, large numbers of people are alienated from their government – and many from their society – for economic, social, and ideological reasons. Neither realism nor liberalism addresses the causes for this discontent, and liberalism, with its emphasis on autonomous actors, self-interest, and appetite, and support for globalization and deregulation, may be a contributing cause of crisis.

In contrast to theories within these realist and liberal paradigms, I contend that the most important causes of disorder in national, regional, and international societies are more psychological and ideational, and less material in nature. In this connection, I emphasize principles of justice. There has been a long-term shift away from fairness and toward equality as the preferred principle of justice. It has been a primary cause of domestic and international unrest since the eighteenth century. As early as the first half of the nineteenth century perceptive aristocrats like Metternich, Talleyrand and Tocqueville recognized that regimes would henceforth have to be justified in terms of equality.[21] The transition to equality is still under way and a major cause of political conflict on almost every continent. Historically, changes in international society lag behind those in many member states, so the international order has only become subject to growing demands for changes on the basis of equality in the postwar era.[22] This transformation is not linear in nature. Not everyone prefers equality to fairness; many people think both appropriate in different, or even the same, circumstances, and in the US and UK fairness is undergoing a revival. These differences, often pronounced within societies, greatly exacerbate conflict.

The shift from fairness to equality is neither the end of history, nor inevitable. Many Westerners oppose it, and there is greater opposition to it elsewhere in the world. In 2016, equality received a major setback in the US with the electoral victory of Donald Trump over Hillary Clinton. From the very outset, Secretary Clinton's campaign speeches stressed equality – of race, gender, and sexual preference – and equality of opportunity.[23] Trump, by contrast, made successful appeals to white men who feel threatened by gender and racial equality and equal treatment of immigrants. Many of these men believe they are disadvantaged with regard to women, minorities, and immigrants, and that this is unfair.[24] Chapter 6 explores these differences and some of their implications for democratic politics.

Pathways to Break Down

Shifts in the relative appeal of principles of justice are perhaps the deepest underlying cause for the fragility of political orders. Then comes the failure of elites to conform to stipulated principles of justice, or of discourses to explain away this discrepancy. These last two causes are related and very much influenced by agency. I now accordingly turn to the conditions that contribute to self-restraint and the honoring of *nomos* by all members of society, but especially elites.

Orders restrain actors, especially powerful ones, by some combination of reason, interest, fear, and habit. Successful orders rely more on self-restraint than constraint, which requires the internalization of a set of norms. Self-restraint is difficult to foster, and increasingly out of fashion in the modern world. In his Presidential inaugural speech, John F. Kennedy drew considerable praise for his plea to fellow Americans to "ask not what your country can do for you, but what you can do for your country."[25] Survey evidence indicates that about one-third of Americans now put their personal material interests above the common when there are no constraints on their behavior beyond conscience.[26] Unrestrained self-interest is most evident on the high seas where there are laws but hardly any enforcement. Kidnapping, murder, poaching, and pollution are rife.[27] It takes high levels of voluntary compliance *and* effective enforcement to restrain illegal forms of self-aggrandizement.[28]

Thumos- and appetite-based worlds are inherently unstable. They are sufficiently competitive that actors are tempted to violate the rules by which honor or wealth is attained. When enough actors behave this way, those who continue to obey the rules are at a serious handicap. There is a strong incentive for all but the most ethically committed actors to defect. Cheating in schools and doping in sports offer good illustrations. Students and athletes who would not otherwise cheat or use drugs come to recognize that they will be at a serious disadvantage if they do not. This dilemma is most acute in *thumos*-based worlds because of the relational nature of honor and standing that can make it a zero-sum game. However, cheating in schools and doping in sports indicate that it is also widespread when people seek material or other rewards. The problem calls for enforcement but is best alleviated in the longer-term by the proliferation of multiple pathways to honor and standing, which allow more people to achieve these goals. Competition may nevertheless be intense in some of these pathways, especially high-status ones.

Competition in appetite-based worlds need not be zero-sum because the total wealth of a society can be increased. Actors nevertheless can frame the acquisition of wealth as a winner-take-all competition even when cooperation would result in larger payoffs.[29] Here too, lack of self-restraint in the form of defection encourages others to follow suit. So too does conspicuous consumption, which is the principal means by which actors in appetite-based worlds claim status. In Georgian England, the Duke of Chandos kept 93 household servants at his country estate and a 27-piece orchestra, led by a *Kapellmeister* imported from Germany. According to Roy Porter, this "veritable orgy of conspicuous consumption" was partly for pleasure, partly for publicity but "perhaps above all, to consolidate personal stature within the world of politics."[30] In the eighteenth century, both Rousseau and Smith noted that material goods were increasingly desired not as an end in themselves but as a means of claiming standing.[31] Presumably, Donald Trump emblazons his name on every hotel and golf club he owns, and rents it out to others for much the same reason.

Conspicuous consumption of this kind can be an effective means of claiming status.[32] It often comes at a high price. The classic example is the potlatch, a practice of indigenous peoples in the northwest coast of British Columbia. The Chinook word means "to give away." It took the form of a feast, held by a rich clan, on the occasion of births, weddings, deaths, and other important events. Large numbers of guests were invited and offered gifts and entertainment. The host would challenge a visiting chieftain to compete with him in giving away or destroying goods, with their respective status being determined by how much was given away or destroyed.[33]

English feasts were not as self-destructive, but election to parliament, another form of status claiming, often was. In the Georgian and early Victorian Britain, contested elections involved hiring agents and bribing voters directly or indirectly through feasts and charitable donations.[34] In international relations, imperialism could be described as a kind of potlatch in which none of the players felt they could afford not to compete.[35] During the Cold War, Soviet and American competition in the space race, arms race, and for influence in the developing world was another version. These competitions were extremely costly. They benefitted recipients of "gifts" (e.g. some businesses and investors, the defense industry and so-called client states) at the expense of the superpowers and helped to destroy the Soviet Union.

Rules for achieving honor or wealth can be violated by actors at any level of their hierarchies. The most serious problem is defection by those at the top. It reduces the incentive others have for playing by the rules and can set in motion a vicious cycle that significantly weakens the order in question. Here too, I follow Thucydides and Aristotle in arguing that the principal cause of the breakdown of orders is the unrestricted pursuit by actors of parochial goals, whether they are individuals, factions or political units. Such behavior leads others to worry about their ability to satisfy their spirit or appetites, and perhaps fear for their well-being or survival. Fearful actors are likely to take precautions that run the gamut from bolting their doors at night to acquiring allies and more and better arms.

Such behavior is invariably paralleled by shifts in threat assessment. Actors who were initially regarded as friends, colleagues or allies, and evoked images rich in nuance and detail, give way to stereotypes of competitors, and then perhaps to adversaries and enemies. These transitions undermine trust and encourage worst-case analyses of others' motives, goals and behavior.[36] Mutually reinforcing changes in behavior and framing generally start gradually but can accelerate rapidly and bring about a phase transition. When this happens, actors enter fear-based worlds. In these worlds people seek tactical rather than strategic solutions. They are ad hoc, short-term, fragile, and more selfish. Such behavior has the potential to escalate tensions between adversaries.

The first recorded suggestion we have of elite abuse is from the Akkadian epic Gilgamesh – hence, his appearance on the cover design. Considered a real figure by historians, he is thought to have ruled Uruk sometime between 2800 and 2500 BCE. He was feared and hated by the populace for his practice of raping girls on the eve of nuptials. The first part of epic tells us how Enkidu was created by the gods to stop Gilgamesh from oppressing his people. The word "tyrant" is Lydian in origin, and applied to rulers who had no respect for law and custom and appropriated treasure and women belonging to others. Thucydides, Plato, and Aristotle attribute the lack of self-restraint on the part of high-status actors to psychological imbalance.[37]

Plato describes oligarchic people and regimes as ruled by spirit, and democratic people and regimes by appetite. The difficulty of appeasing spirit or appetite, or of effectively discriminating among competing appetites, leads both kinds of people and regimes down the road to tyranny.[38] Tyranny is initially attractive because a tyrant is unconstrained by laws. In reality Plato suggests, tyrants are true slaves because they are ruled by their passions and not in any way their own masters.[39] Thucydides uses the same trope in his account of the Peloponnesian War. First in Corcyra and Corinth, and then in Athens and Sparta, reason loses control to spirit or appetite.[40]

Building on these classical Greek understandings, we can formulate some propositions about why and how psychological balance and imbalance result in order and disorder. My starting point is with the different principles of justice and hierarchies associated with *thumos*- and interest-based worlds. *Thumos*-based worlds, I noted, are justified with reference to the principle of fairness and give rise to clientelist hierarchies. Every rank in these hierarchies, bottom rungs aside, has responsibilities toward actors beneath them and the right to look immediately above for support. To compensate for the boons actors receive from those of higher rank, they must honor and to some degree serve them. The rule packages associated with different statuses require different kinds of self-restraint. As one ascends toward the apex of the hierarchy, the more extensive the requirements for self-restraint become. Honor is not only a function of rank, but of how well higher status actors perform their roles. Clientelist hierarchies are designed to restrain selfishness and its consequences by embedding powerful and affluent actors in a social order that requires them to exercise self-restraint and protect and support those who are less advantaged. When clientelist orders are robust, they benefit the spirit of those with high status and the security and material needs of those beneath them.

In appetite-based worlds, hierarchies arise from the different degrees of success actors have in accumulating and displaying wealth. Such display is especially pronounced in kleptocratic regimes. Angola is a case in point. Its oligarchs leave 500 Euro tips at expensive Lisbon restaurants and govern over some of the world's poorest and unhealthiest people. The 2013 Angolan national budget increased significantly, but school funding was cut by a third. Money is extracted from oil export, not directly from the masses, but their labor is exploited. The regime relies on Western and Chinese contractors to run just about everything in the country, and they in turn put no pressure on the government to reform.[41]

Appetite-based hierarchies generally have no rule packages, and those at the top have no responsibilities to those beneath them. Responsibilities only develop if honor enters the picture. In nineteenth-century America, I noted in the last chapter, upper-class charitable giving became the norm and an important means of achieving standing within the elite.[42] This practice has declined, in part because it is less expected from the affluent. Rich givers attract publicity, but the wealthy overall give 1.3 percent of their income to charity, while the poorest donate 3.2 percent.[43] Society in appetite worlds is most robust when the gap between the wealthy and those less well-off is not extreme. This judgment is, of course, subjective and will vary from society to society and epoch to epoch. In appetite-based worlds, where equality has become the dominant principle of justice, the gap narrows, which is why, I contend, that its recent widening in the West has serious implications for order. It puts the burden on discourses to reconcile this gap, as liberals attempt to do.

Lack of restraint, especially by high-status actors, subverts the principles of justice associated with their hierarchies. Unconstrained spirit, which intensifies the competition for honor, can give rise to acute and disruptive conflict *within* the dominant elite. It has wider consequences for the society because it not infrequently leads to violence and reduces, if not altogether negates, the material and security benefits clientelist hierarchies are expected to provide for non-elite members of society. Unconstrained appetite also undermines an elite's legitimacy and arouses resentment and envy on the part of other actors. It encourages others to emulate elite self-indulgence and disregard the norms restraining the pursuit of wealth at the expense of the less fortunate. In the modern world, both kinds of imbalance are endemic.

Until the modern era, leadership struggles often had little direct consequences for the majority of the population. They were only likely to threaten the civil peace when ambitious men looked for support outside the elite. They attempted to overcome opposition to them within the elite by mobilizing support among the armed forces or the citizenry. This process destroyed the Roman republic. Opposing *nobiles* appealed to their respective armies and Rome was engulfed by a civil war from which Julius Caesar emerged as dictator after the defeat of Pompey. A new struggle for power erupted after Caesar's assassination in 44 BCE, and his nephew Octavian triumphed after his army defeated that of Anthony in 31 BCE. He took the name of Augustus and the title of *Princeps Civitatis* [First Citizen of the State]. He was subsequently considered Rome's first emperor.

Domestic conflicts of this kind can become internationalized. Thucydides describes the Archidamian War as the product of a chain reaction of escalation, beginning with the appeal of Epidamnus to their counterparts in Corcyra for support against the oligarchs, now in power at home.[44] The Russian, Spanish, Chinese and Syrian civil wars offer modern examples of this phenomenon, although none of them escalated to a general war among the great powers. This process of escalation is invariably triggered by lack of elite constraint, and its principal mechanism is the threat felt by others. It provides an incentive for them to act in kind.

Societies that emphasize honor are vulnerable to other kinds of imbalance. For much of history, such societies have given the highest honors to warriors and deflected competition outwards in the form of warfare against others. Skill in battle and defense of the homeland in turn provide a justification for a warrior elite's claim to honor, standing and political authority.[45] World War I and American military intervention in the post-Cold War world can be explained in part as expressions of this phenomenon.[46] Aggressive foreign policies risk defeat and collapse of orders by virtue of occupation or rebellion. They also encourage higher domestic rates of violence by veterans.[47]

Elite standing and authority is threatened when changes in the conduct of warfare require the skills of lower status groups. In Athens, the growing importance of the navy, staffed by less wealthy citizens aroused class conflict and paved the way for wider democratization of the society.[48] In the late nineteenth century, aristocratic cavalry officers resisted the implications of technology – artillery, barbed wire, and machine guns – and were all but eliminated in the opening phases of World War I. Their demise in Germany opened the way for the advancement of middle-class officers.[49] If external threats recede, warrior classes have an interest in generating new conflicts to sustain their authority and to avoid destructive, inward deflection of competition and aggression. Warrior societies accordingly have incentives to wage war frequently, but to limit and regulate these conflicts so they do not disrupt society or demand extraordinary resources.

For Thucydides, Plato and Aristotle, elite imbalance results in the same behavioral pathology: high-status actors violate the principles on which their elite status is based. They fail to exercise the prudence and self-restraint [*sophrosunē*] of their predecessors. Thucydides' account of Athenian politics during the Peloponnesian War indicates a second means by which intra-elite competition stimulates wider imbalance in societies. Members of the elite, intent on advancing their political standing, mobilize support among non-elite actors. Warring French aristocratic factions sought wider support in the late eighteenth century, providing an opportunity for public opinion to assert itself. The newly revived *parlements* demanded more authority and set in motion what would become a revolution.[50] E. E. Schattschneider describes a similar, if more benign, process in American politics: individuals or groups who lose a political struggle in one arena seek to expand the struggle into new arenas of contestation if they expect it to improve their chances of success.[51] Once extended beyond elite circles, conflict can be more acute and leaders less able to compromise given their need to maintain constituency support.

For Thucydides and Aristotle, the defining moment of civic breakdown is when actors or factions capture the institutions of state for partisan purposes. Assemblies and courts no longer serve to regulate and constrain competition for wealth and honor, but intensify it by enabling one faction to advance its standing or enrich itself at the expense of others. Those in power may use these institutions to expel, punish or kill opponents. When a cycle of aggrandizement, violence, and retribution begins it becomes difficult to stop. Herodotus describes the no holds barred contest for power between Cleisthenes and fellow aristocrat Isagoras. Their forces were evenly matched so they mobilized additional

support – Isagoras turned to Sparta, and Cleisthenes mobilized the
dēmos – and embroiled their polis in a nasty external and internal war.[52]
Thucydides provides a chilling account of how runaway civic tensions
escalated into an utterly destructive civil war [stasis] in Corcyra.[53]
Aristotle offers Rhodes, Thebes, Megara, and Syracuse as his examples.
He observes that when conflict becomes sufficiently acute, a leader,
faction or state can feel the need to act preemptively; they prepare to
strike out before they are victimized.[54]

There is an important cognitive-linguistic component to this process.
Thucydides describes a feedback loop between words [logoi] and deeds
[erga]. As language is stretched, words not only lose their meaning, but
take on new ones that justify, even encourage, behavior at odds with traditional nomos. His thoughtful analysis of the relationship between words
and deeds might be utilized to track empirically the transition to and
from fear-based worlds. Thucydides and Plato believe that intellectuals
accelerate the process of decay by undermining the values that encourage
public service, sacrifice, and self-restraint. Intellectuals problematize
values and practices that were previously accepted as natural. Politicians
skilled in the art of rhetoric are another source of corruption.

In Corcyra, Thucydides observes, they used "fair phrases to arrive
at guilty ends."[55] They twisted and deconstructed the language, giving
words meanings that were often the opposite of their traditional ones,
and use them to justify behavior at odds with conventional practices
and values. By the late fifth century, the code of "ancient simplicity"
[euēthes], so admired by Thucydides and Plato, had not merely declined,
Thucydides tells us, but had been "laughed down and disappeared."[56]
Victor Klemperer offers a more contemporary example. The Nazis, he
reports, regularly inverted the meanings of ordinary words with the goal
of turning vices into virtues. They thoroughly and effectively turned
the ungrounded hatred and fear of minority groups into a valued and
accepted emotion.[57]

In these circumstances, Thucydides observed that false rumors spread
rapidly, conveying exaggerated notions of threat, and encouraging preemption. Rossalyn Warren documents how rumors of this kind fueled
the genocide in Burundi.[58] The same phenomenon took place in the run
up to the Anglo-American intervention in Iraq, although in this instance
it originated almost entirely with the government.[59] Fake news has since
proliferated in western democracies, helped by the Internet, and generally sponsored by groups and countries with retrograde agendas.

Aristotle warns that elite corruption stimulates the appetites of poorer
people, making them want a greater share of the wealth and more supportive politicians who promise it to them. Livy and Machiavelli would

later advance a similar argument. Machiavelli attributes the failure of republican and other regimes to corruption. Following Polybius, he believes that all governments decayed. In Rome, corruption was due to decline of religion and accumulation of excessive power and wealth in the hands of a few individuals. He agrees with Livy that these changes upset the long-standing balance between patricians and plebians.[60]

Such a process appears to be well under way in the United States where elite greed is increasingly open and extreme and marked by ever-increasing gaps between the pay of employees and CEOs and increases in all forms of tax evasion by the wealthy. It was also evident in Republican efforts to repeal the Affordable Care Act (Obamacare); it would have deprived up to 30 million people of healthcare to pay for tax reductions for the wealthiest Americans.[61] This dynamic is not limited to affluent societies; Mao Zedong made a parallel argument about revolutionary bureaucracies and how quickly they become corrupted.[62]

One of the ways top-down orders prolong their existence in this situation is through attempts at "renormalization." People are encouraged to adjust their expectations in response to corruption and other transgressions. Consider Hollywood's response to political corruption. The 1939 Academy Award-winning film, "Mr. Smith Goes to Washington," portrays an honest outsider shaming Senators into voting for money to buy land for a national boy's camp. As my students can attest, the film strikes contemporary audiences as naïve with a plot bordering on the laughable. In "All the President's Men," first screened in 1976, two brave reporters, supported by their editor at the *Washington Post*, unravel and publicize the unconstitutional actions of the Nixon administration. It cannot be dismissed as naïve because it is based on historical fact, but forty years on it appears to describe a world that the public knows no longer exists: one in which agency and an independent press are willing and able to expose conspiracy at the highest levels of government and topple an administration by doing so. Today, extra-constitutional behavior, lying to the public, and pliant media are increasingly seen as the norm in the United States, and often provide the context for adventure, romance, or comedy films. The television show, *House of Cards*, which premiered in 2013, is a case in point. It portrays a Congress whose members ruthlessly seek and exercise power.

For Lenin and some academic students of revolution, civic unrest and revolution is most likely to occur when a sharp economic downturn follows a period of sustained economic growth.[63] The Greeks are also sensitive to what we call class conflict, but believe it will be most acute when discourses that reconcile diverse classes through a widely shared and overarching commitment to the community lose their authority.

In this situation, the wealthy and highborn become rapacious and the *dēmos* correspondingly less accepting of subordinate economic and political status. Thucydides and Plato understand that learning to live with affluence is just as difficult and disruptive as adjusting to poverty. Plato describes both extremes as destabilizing because wealth makes for luxury and idleness, and poverty for mean-mindedness and bad work.[64] Their observations suggest the proposition that neither wealth nor poverty per se produce instability and revolution; they are the result of loss of empathy and self-restraint. Hegel makes a similar argument.[65]

For purposes of analysis I have distinguished *thumos-* from appetite-based orders. In reality, all orders, especially modern ones, incorporate, channel, and derive legitimacy from both drives. The construction and deconstruction of orders accordingly has multiple and interacting pathways. Their intersections and consequences vary across orders, and much more case research is necessary to identify particular patterns and synergies. As a general rule, it seems evident that any pathway to disorder is likely to have across-the-board negative consequences.

To summarize, I follow Aristotle in arguing that the principal cause of the breakdown of orders is the unrestricted pursuit by individuals, factions or states of their parochial goals. Such behavior undermines the principles of justice that legitimize hierarchies and the unequal distribution of wealth and status. It makes other actors more resentful of the elite and its privileges. It also makes them more concerned about their ability to gain status or wealth, and in extreme circumstances fearful for their security. Appetite- and *thumos*-based orders are equally vulnerable to elite abuse but unravel in different ways until they segue into fear-based worlds.

Civic breakdown is the result of imbalance. When reason loses control to appetite, elite over-indulgence arouses envy, resentment, and emulation by the rest of the population. Elite imbalance in the direction of the spirit encourages subversion of institutions for parochial ends and counter-responses, even preemption, by those who feel threatened. Elite imbalance in the direction of the appetite leads to violation of *nomos*, which is aggravated by a process of elite appeals for support to other actors on the basis of mutual self-aggrandizement. In extreme circumstances, the competition in outbidding not only threatens other members of the elite, it exacerbates relations between the elite and the *dēmos* and encourages preemption by threatened actors. External forces enter into the picture when they create, or contribute to imbalance by exposure to different societies with different practices and levels of affluence, or by removing the basis, or changing the character, of outwardly directed elite competition for honor and standing.

These forms of imbalance can occur at the individual, domestic, regional, and international levels. More often than not, they are preceded and accompanied by changes in discourses that attempt to delegitimize existing norms and legitimize behavior at odds with them. Imbalance at any level threatens order at adjacent levels. My understanding of order and disorder offers a critical perspective on current practices and neo-liberal and realist discourses of wealth and power maximization. These theories value appetite and look favorably upon, even encourage, the pursuit of unlimited material gain. The only self-restraint considered worthwhile is tactical. Greek conceptions of balance, by contrast, emphasize deeper reasons for self-restraint, including the recognition that it makes it possible for others to achieve their goals. By doing so it provides more people with incentives to sustain the community that enables satisfaction of appetite and spirit alike.

Adherence to *nomos* by elites is an important source of order in its own right and by virtue of the example it sets for others. However, in some conditions it can have the opposite effect. If robust hierarchies support order, elite maintenance of those hierarchies can be a source of disorder when they restrict entry or upward mobility and arouse the resentment of those excluded. As Machiavelli maintained, order requires constant adjustment and rebalancing in response to change. Honor and standing are, by definition, relational, so hierarchies must have many more actors at their base than apex. They achieve their standing by limiting membership, especially to higher ranks. However, hierarchies that are too exclusive lose standing, as do those that do not admit or allow advancement of actors who excel in the activities or accomplishments on which they are based. Successful hierarchies are to some degree exclusive but also to some degree open. Local circumstances must determine just how much of either is appropriate.

Hierarchies are also threatened when there is a change in the relative importance of *thumos* and appetite and their respective principles of justice. Such shifts undermine the legitimacy of some hierarchies and strengthen that of others. In the modern era, the shift from *thumos* to appetite, and fairness to equality, sharply reduced the standing of the aristocracy and hierarchy of birth while greatly increasing that based on wealth. Hierarchies that recognize shifts in principles of justice and change their practices in response (e.g. all-male, white, Protestant clubs admitting minorities and women) are more likely to endure. There is every reason to believe that short- and longer-term changes are at least in part related, but in complex ways.

All orders embed tensions, even contradictions, in their values and practices. Homer's *Iliad* exposes those of warrior-based honor societies.

It shows how violation *and* upholding of one of the most important values and practices was the fundamental cause of the Trojan War. *Xenia*, best translated as "guest friendship," required ancient Greeks to offer shelter and food to travelers. Travelers in turn were not to abuse the hospitality of their hosts. Many neighboring cultures had their own versions of *xenia* and Immanuel Kant later described it as the most universal of all human customs.[66] The Trojan Paris is guest of the Greek Menelaus and runs off with his wife Helen and various portable treasures. The young couple seeks refuge in Troy, and Paris' father, King Priam, feels compelled to honor Helen's request for sanctuary. The abduction fills Menelaus with thoughts of revenge against Paris – and the need to reclaim Helen to retain standing among his peers. Violation of *xenia* by Paris, and Priam's honoring of it, put Greeks and Trojans on a collision course.

The modern world offers numerous examples of this phenomenon. Consider the practice of taking in refugees, a form of *xenia*, and one now given sanction in international law. It can cause domestic conflict because modern people are far less welcoming than the mythical Trojans, and some "guests" less willing to honor their part of the bargain. They may work against the regimes or military occupations they fled, creating tensions between this state and their new one, or against their hosts, creating serious internal tensions. In Britain, which accepted only a small number of refugees, it nevertheless fueled exclusionary nationalism and provided the support for Brexit. At the time of writing, the refugee crisis has made a shambles of Schengen and threatens the European project.[67] The conceptual parallel with *xenia* in Homer is striking, as adherence – or violation – of a value central to liberal democracy can threaten it.

Value conflicts are more likely to become acute when societies become sufficiently developed to differentiate public from private spheres. Conflicts between these spheres often revolve initially around the proper manner of seeking retribution. Aeschylus' *Oresteia*, first performed in Athens in 458 BCE, dramatizes a destructive cycle of revenge within a family that is only halted when it is taken out of private hands and addressed by law courts. Shakespeare's *Romeo and Juliet*, published in 1597, offers evidence that the problem is not so easily resolved. The prince of Verona – to whom Shakespeare, one assumes intentionally, gives the name "Escalus" – decrees the death penalty for violent feuding that sets in motion a chain of events that lead to the deaths of Romeo and Juliet. State building in early modern Europe was characterized by efforts to suppress private violence and secure a monopoly for the state, which Max Weber would later make its defining characteristic.[68]

Disputes over the boundaries between civic and public realms, and private and public domains, continue to this day, as these realms and relative responsibilities shift in response to changes in values and technology, among other factors. Current controversies concern the degree to which states should regulate sexual practices and marriage, and their rights to monitor the activities of citizens by photographic and electronic means. These conflicts can become intense, but do not threaten order unless one faction captures the institutions of government and uses them to impose its will on its opponents and to punish them for non-compliance.

The most serious underlying source of civic tension is the growing discrepancy between a society's hierarchies and principles of justice. In the introduction, I offered the example of the increasing stratification of western societies in an age where equality is ever more the dominant value. A similar situation prevails in international society. The tension between hierarchies and principles of justice is not so much a trigger of conflict as it is a deep underlying cause, just as their correspondence is an underlying cause of stability. Challenges to the existing order do not follow automatically, but are highly context dependent. So are the forms these challenges take.

Tensions also arise when changes in the division of labor and values give rise to new classes who seek admission into the status hierarchy. If denied, they are likely to develop counter hierarchies and discourses to justify them. Conflicts between these elites and their respective hierarchies can become acute when the dominant elite feels threatened and refuses to recognize the competing hierarchy as legitimate or attempts to co-opt its leading members. The rise of the commercial classes in eighteenth- and nineteenth-century Europe led its representatives to propagate discourses that devalued honor and vaunted the political, economic, and social benefits to society of appetite.[69] In Britain, where co-option was greatest, the challenge to the political order was minimal. Moving east across the continent, challenges became increasingly severe in response to social exclusion and political marginalization.[70]

There is never a linear relationship between exclusion and protest. In Germany and Austria-Hungary, where the commercial and professional classes were denied real political power and declined in relative status in the course of the century, many sought to ape rather than oppose the aristocracy and the military. In their search for self-esteem, they emphasized their professional titles and many became avid supporters of imperialism and nationalism. Karl Marx lamented that the German bourgeoisie failed to develop an appropriate class consciousness.[71] Max Weber, who was an outspoken imperialist and nationalist, offered an equally jaundiced view of the *Mittelstand* at the end of the century.[72] Left critiques of Germany in the twentieth century continued to stress the country's arrested liberalism and pre-industrial traditions.[73]

The Central European example suggests that hierarchy can be sustained, and opposition to it muted, by effective balancing of appetite against *thumos*, or vice versa. Individuals and classes allowed, even encouraged, to amass wealth may become reconciled to being denied elite status. Conversely, populations rewarded with status can be reconciled to their relative lack of affluence. Imperialism served this latter function in Britain and Germany, and was consciously used for this by Benjamin Disraeli.[74] So too did the policy of divide and rule in Northern Ireland where, following partition in 1921, the Protestant elite encouraged ethnic-religious division and reserved the best jobs and, later, housing estates for Protestants. In the shipyards, Protestant workers were reconciled to low pay and low status but received higher pay and had higher esteem than their Catholic counterparts, largely denied employment in skilled positions. By this means, Protestant workers were effectively discouraged from unionizing.[75]

Finally, there is the problem of the values on which hierarchies and orders rest. When they are upheld, order is robust, but too great a commitment to their values is a source of conflict. Principles of justice support diverse customs and practices, not all of which are easily reconciled. This problem becomes most acute when important actors have unyielding commitments to different and clashing principles of justice. Sophocles' *Antigone*, written in about 441 BCE, pits Antigone, with her commitment to family and religion, against her uncle Creon, ruler of Thebes, and his equal commitment to civil order. Neither party will compromise and their ensuing conflict leads to the deaths of Antigone and Creon's son Haemon and brings the city back to the brink of civil war – precisely what Creon was desperate to avoid. This play can also be read as a conflict between top-down and bottom-up orders and their clashing values and practices.

Efforts to order principles of justice hierarchically generate conflict because people have different beliefs about their respective importance. Some degree of ranking is nevertheless necessary to provide order and predictability to society but rigid ranking and, even worse, enforcement guarantee conflict. Well-ordered and stable societies require lots of slack and willingness to overlook or tolerate inconsistencies between and across principles and practices. For these reasons, efforts to shore up order often have the opposite effect. There is no rational justification for these orders, only a pragmatic one. Robust orders require a sophisticated recognition by elites and as many other actors as possible that *nomos* must be upheld, but within reason. Practices ultimately rest on justice, but justice must be tempered by understandings that rules are never universally applicable, and must be applied with restraint and tolerance for differences. Robust order is above all a state of mind.

How Are Orders Reconstituted?

One of the enduring problems of politics is the reconstitution of order in the aftermath of its breakdown. In *A Cultural Theory of International Relations*, I describe three levels of change. The most superficial and frequent is the breakdown of order due to reason's loss of control to spirit or appetite. It makes other actors worry about their ability to satisfy these needs, or physically protect their loved ones, and brings about a phase transition to a fear-based system. Stasis is like a lobster pot in that is easy to enter and very difficult to leave. All top-down orders ultimately decline, but only a few have approached conditions resembling Hobbes' state of nature. This is because bottom-up orders generally continue to exist and may assume at least some of the former responsibilities of top-down orders.

The process of restoration will depend in the first instance on how order dissolved. It will be different for civil wars that end in negotiated settlements versus those that end in victory. Orders also dissolve because of corrupt, ineffective governments. They can break down in more subtle ways, leaving a shell of civil order but hollowing out civil society and requiring people to rely on private or informal arrangements for basic services.

Top-down orders are often reconstituted by force. Powerful agents succeed in asserting authority over a territory and its people. This process benefits from the deep desire of people for order. This is most evident in conditions of near anarchy, where many people cope by pretending that some degree of order still exists. At the height of the violence in Srebrenica in Kosovo driving schools stayed open and flourished although the offices that issued licenses had closed.[76] Other examples could be cited from accounts of shipwrecked people and urban ghettos.[77] People may be willing to accept with relief something far less than perfect in their eyes when they perceive it as a significant improvement over present conditions.

Threats of punishment have the ability to compel, at least in the short term. Order is nevertheless difficult to maintain on this basis as even people who initially welcome the iron fist will turn against it unless they are rewarded, not merely intimidated. The latter is almost impossible in the long term; among the most successful examples may be the Mongol use of terror to subdue and extract tribute from the Russians for several hundred years.[78] In modern times, this task verges on the impossible. The Nazis were willing to use any and all means to suppress opposition, but almost everywhere aroused resistance movements.[79]

Newly restored political orders often rely heavily on fear. They engage in mass arrests, detention without trial, and sometimes random punishment and terror. To survive, such regimes must ultimately create some basis of popular support and voluntary compliance. Even successful coercion generally relies on some degree of compliance. To have any hope of being accepted by the population, it must be on a micro- not macro scale, and target specific individuals and groups. This requires intelligence about violators, or would-be violators, and widespread understanding about what is and what is not allowed. Some percentage of citizens must supply intelligence to the new top-down order for this to happen. Ultimately, effective enforcement depends upon a high degree of voluntary compliance. In democratic societies, it has been estimated that effective enforcement requires at least 90 percent voluntary compliance.[80] The near impossibility of enforcing Prohibition in the United States and, more recently, of preventing the sale and use of marijuana, were due to the failure of anti-alcohol and anti-drug laws to win anything close to full support from the populace.

Reconstitution of top-down order occasionally comes about through truces or settlements between or among the warring parties. Athens is the first political unit to have attempted to restore democracy by means of a reconciliation pact; its citizens agreed that no one would be prosecuted for the crimes committed during the tyranny and opposition to it that followed defeat in the Peloponnesian War. Reconciliation was remarkably successful as democracy endured down to the Battle of Chaeronea in 338 BC and de facto conquest by Macedon.[81] The 1598 Edict of Nantes stipulated that "memory be extinguished and put to rest."[82] It might have worked had Louis XIV not revoked it and made war against Protestants. Somewhat more effective were the 1648 treaties ending the Thirty Years War; the Treaties of Westphalia required signatories to accept "perpetual oblivion and amnesty."[83] Thomas Hobbes called forgetting the basis of a just state, and amnesia the cornerstone of the social contract.[84] English Civil War adversaries agreed to forget, and the 1660 Acts of Oblivion pardoned men who fought against Charles II in 1690, as did a later act to forgive those who bore arms against William III.[85] Recent history offers us more examples of attempts at reconstruction by this means.[86]

Perhaps the most efficacious route to restore order is the recoupling of top-down and bottom-up orders. New governments can augment and build on the services and local solidarity provided by bottom-up orders. If successful, they can gradually take over some or all of the add-on services provided by bottom-up orders in the aftermath of a top-down collapse. Bottom-up orders in turn can function as conveyer belts and intermediaries for new top-down orders. Cooperation across levels has the potential to strengthen both orders. For top-down orders, it involves some degree of power sharing, recognition of local autonomy, and acceptance and support for practices already in place.[87] It imposes limits, not only on governmental authority, but on the kinds of initiatives governments can pursue. New governments can improve their authority and legitimacy by cultivating supporters and allies at the local level, relying less on coercion, and increasing their chances of survival and legitimacy.

The top-down and bottom-up binary is undoubtedly simplistic when applied to fluid, violent, or post-violent conflicts. Stathis Kalyvas notes that there are often multiple participants in such conflicts with varying degrees of control over territories.[88] In a comparative study of armed groups and governance, Kasfir, Frerks, and Terpstra make a compelling case for multi-levels of governance.[89] They may include competing and overlapping kinds of would-be top-down governance, external actors, and other layers of governance, some of the bottom-up, and others in between. This multiplicity greatly complicates conflict resolution and governance.

Coupling of top-down to bottom-up orders allows more effective enforcement of norms and rules through shaming, which Durkheim envisaged as the most effective form of social control.[90] It works best in small, tightly knit groups and societies – in effect, bottom-up orders. The BaMbuti of the Ituri Forest in Zaire exclude offenders from social gatherings and in extreme cases expel them from their camp. Individuals cannot survive alone in the forest so friends sneak out to feed them. After some interval, the presumably chastened offender returns to the camp and is treated as if nothing has happened.[91]

Shaming and punishment are reinforcing in robust orders, but also have a downside. Nietzsche insisted that the "herd imposes conformity by the threat of ostracism. Even the strongest person … fears a cold look or a sneer on the face of those among whom he has been brought up."[92] Counter-cultures often emerge in these circumstances and develop their own norms. They have the potential to become their own bottom-up orders if they stress group cohesion and put pressures on "members" to engage in what others consider anti-social acts and suffer social ostracism.[93]

In effect, there is often something of a recursive relationship between top-down and bottom-up orders, and among bottom-up orders. Bottom-up orders may provide the basis for top-down orders, as they did in colonial America. Or they may facilitate the emergence of new top-down orders in the aftermath of their breakdown. Top-down orders can benefit from robust bottom-up orders, which can provide support and help them build legitimacy. They in turn can create the security and infrastructure on which some kind of bottom-up orders depend. Counter-cultures generally overlap considerably with the cultures from which they distance themselves and interact in ways that can change the character of the dominant culture. They are a major catalyst of the evolution of bottom-up orders, just as they in turn – in democratic societies – influence the values and practices of top-down orders.

Building on a questionable reading of Hobbes, present-day realists and liberals offer a parsimonious but less convincing account of order at the international level. They attribute it to a hegemon. The definition of hegemony is a source of great debate among liberals and realists but it is generally equated with the ability of a dominant power to shape the rules of the system, create incentives for others to cooperate and punish defectors.[94]

In reality, American hegemony was short-lived, largely limited to the Americas, and a feature of the country's extraordinary economic primacy at mid-century in a world devastated by history's costliest and most destructive war. At the time, many people welcomed American military and economic power as a source of political stability and economic reconstruction. The rapid comeback of Western Europe and Japan, and later the economic development of the Pacific Rim, were greatly assisted by American aid, loans, and markets. Success made hegemony superfluous. Charles Kindleberger, the father of the concept, thought it had run its course by 1963, and was certainly history by the 1970s.[95] American leaders and academics nevertheless convinced themselves that their hegemony was alive and benign. Following the Cold War and the collapse of the Soviet Union, then Secretary of State Madeleine Albright proclaimed that the United States was "the indispensable nation."[96] President Obama said something similar prior to his reelection in 2012.[97] President Trump campaigned to "Make America Great Again," on the grounds that it had lost its foremost rank on the watch of his predecessors.

Charles Kindleberger maintained that hegemons have three responsibilities: shaping the policy agenda of global institutions and coalitions, economic management, and enforcement of global initiatives.[98] Today these functions are performed by multiple states, sometimes in collaboration with non-state actors. Western Europeans have made consistent efforts to extend their normative influence by promoting agendas in environmental and human rights initiatives, but also security issues and corporate regulation. Asian states, most notably China, have increasingly assumed a custodial role in economic relations. Global enforcement is also shared, and on those occasions where the United States has acted unilaterally or without United Nations support, it has arguably threatened rather than enhanced regional and global security.[99]

Hegemony is not a realistic goal, and would resemble tyranny if it could be achieved. It is an ideological claim by American leaders and academics advanced to justify American exceptionalism and privileges. It is not only unnecessary for global order but also detrimental to it. In international affairs, it is bottom-up order that counts, not top-down. International society is defined and sustained by formal and informal arrangements among actors. It is not as robust as domestic orders because actors share fewer values and interact at more social remove. It is robust enough to keep anarchy at bay for most of the time in most parts of the world. Where it is most robust – in Western Europe – it has generated a weak top-down order. International relations may offer the most graphic example of the importance of bottom-up orders, and scholars who theorize imaginary order are blind to the substance of international order and its causes.

Order is foundational to domestic, regional, and international politics. They cannot exist in conditions of anarchy but only in societies that establish roles, norms and practices, constitute actors and enable them to formulate and pursue interests. Anarchy is an ideal type, and rarely if ever a description of the world. Hobbes, I believe, intended his state of nature as a thought experiment; without the roles and norms of society people had only their appetites and instrumental reason and were a danger to themselves and everyone around them. This is no binary of anarchy and order, but rather a continuum along which all societies, domestic and international, are arrayed.[100]

Empirical Perspectives

The robustness of society largely determines the character of its politics, and most importantly, the extent to which violence is acceptable and the conditions under which this is so. In robust societies, political cleavages can be acute, conflicts intense and their outcomes very much influenced by power, but resorts to violence are frowned upon and rare because there is a deeply ingrained respect for other actors and social and political norms. An order of this kind – what Aristotle referred to as a *koinônia* – is an ideal type, and real orders rarely approximate it. But many have significantly reduced violence and made it peripheral to the resolution of conflicting interests. This is also true at the international level, where Karl Deutsch observed the emergence of what he called "pluralistic security communities."[101] Since this concept saw the light of day in 1957, security communities have proliferated and come to include most of the developed world.[102]

One of the most interesting questions of politics – and one relevant to domestic, regional, and international levels of aggregation – is how either bottom-up or top-down orders reach the level of robustness where violence is no longer a constant, or even serious, threat. There is more than one road to robustness and more than one kind of robust political order. Liberals proclaim that the only rational and effective response to modernity is a capitalist, democratic order. Chinese authorities, among others, reject this claim and are attempting to develop and maintain an alternate, authoritarian model. If liberal, democratic countries emphasize civil society – and, with it, bottom-up social, economic, and political orders – China and other authoritarian regimes favor top-down orders and feel threatened by civil society.

Chapter 7 investigates both questions. Through a case study of Georgian Britain, it analyzes how a threatened authoritarian regime intent on imposing and maintaining top-down order evolved into a robust democratic one. This exercise provides a framework for assessing China's future, the likelihood that it might evolve into something more liberal and western, sustain an authoritarian order in the long-term, or face a serious political challenge and disorder if it fails to do either. As we will see below, most western analysts put their money on the last outcome as the most likely.

Eighteenth-century Britain – and England, particularly – was ruled by a tightly integrated elite that maintained itself by limiting intra-elite conflict, creating conditions favorable to rapid economic growth, and successfully controlling frequent violent protest by the less privileged. Bread and food riots were common, and highwaymen were romanticized as a form of rebellion. "Yet," Roy Porter writes, "this political fabric – endlessly abused, spat upon, pulled, torn, tattered and patched – was never ripped to pieces."[103] There can be little doubt that the Whig-dominated political order would have been destroyed by the Jacobite rebellions of 1715 and 1745, the Gordon Riots of 1780, or the radicalism of the 1790s had its social fabric been less robust. Even at the height of radicalism, the voice of opposition was couched in the language of reform and used reasoned arguments – in pamphlets, speeches, and petitions – to advance their causes. Piecemeal violence – a weekly occurrence – never erupted into revolution because these outbreaks were largely defensive and limited, and with specific goals: restoration of bread prices, wage rates and other traditional arrangements.[104]

Power in Georgian England was maintained through two levels of corruption: election to parliament, and the formation of governing coalitions. Whigs and Tories cut deals, divided constituencies or maintained rotten boroughs, gerrymandered and bought votes when in competition. The development of sophisticated political techniques of management, and sharing of spoils, kept the upper classes relatively united. In 1761, only 18 out of 201 borough constituencies, most with fewer than 500 voters actually went to the polls. Robert Walpole and the Duke of Newcastle had built a system based on the assumption that local grandees needed access to political power and favors, hence could be bought.[105]

J. H. Plumb writes that "Place was power; patronage was power" and patronage "scarcely bothered to wear a fig leaf."[106] Georgian ministerial politics consisted of milking society at large. This was achieved through control of elections through rigged and rotten boroughs, cajoled voters, and bribes. These practices "brought cynicism into the open, which defused tensions amongst the elite by concentrating attention on the division of spoils."[107] Judicious distribution of patronage, pensions, and private member bills, combined with the cultivation of client interests and family alliances, were all used by governments to build and maintain coalitions. Opposition was akin to shadow boxing because nobody who was close to power, or had a chance of getting there, wanted to kill the goose that laid the golden egg.[108]

There are striking parallels between eighteenth-century England and contemporary China. Institutions are equally powerful and corrupt. Deals and pay-offs keep politicians and bureaucrats content and discourage them from attempting to go outside the elite and mobilize support among the masses.[109] There are upwards of 20,000 protests each year, many of them violent. They are invariably a response to abusive behavior by local officials or capitalists, but have little effect as they lack leadership, are focused on specific grievances, are successfully suppressed, and with rare exceptions are not publicized.[110] Protests with leadership and broader political goals are feared and arouse fierce opposition, as the Umbrella Movement did in Hong Kong.[111]

Georgian Britain and post-Maoist China achieved these ends in similar ways. Both also benefitted from urban development and economic growth, and from poor rural communications that kept villages and protests relatively isolated. Many adventurous young men, who might have provided the backbone of rural resistance, migrated to cities. Many of them improved their situation and developed loyalty to the regime. Both regimes also benefitted from foreign threats – "Papists" and "Imperialists" – whose dangers they exaggerated.

Robustness has a vertical as well as horizontal dimension. The former refers to the seeming stability of an order at any given moment, and the latter to its stability over time. In the ancient world, some orders remained extremely stable with minimal change. The Old Kingdom of Egypt (2686–2181 BCE) is a case in point. All stable orders in the modern era reveal considerable flexibility. In Victorian Britain, Catholic emancipation in 1829; the reform acts of 1832 and 1867; legal, educational, poor law, and prison reforms; and a variety of other measures, including a sharp reduction of death penalty offenses, slowly but significantly democratized the country, made justice more even-handed, and offered more opportunity for economic advancement to the lower classes. New problems arose, largely the product of population growth and industrialization, but outside of Ireland threats to the order subsided.[112]

Post-Maoist China has also evolved faster and more dramatically than Victorian Britain. In Britain, this led to increasing elite confidence in stability. Only die-hard, anti-Catholic, pro-protectionist, and anti-reform law Tories worried that socialism would take over, at the ballot box or by violence. They were a sufficient minority that Trollope felt free to parody them in his novels.[113] In China, debate is constrained, but there is ongoing controversy among foreign "China hands" about the regime's stability and longer-term prospects.[114]

David Shambaugh, who offers one of the more pessimistic accounts, argues that China's stability is seriously threatened by its administrative, centralized, extractive, and dictatorial communist party-state. No regime of this kind has managed successfully to cope with industrialization and its consequences. China's party and government must become more responsive, inclusive, compromising, tolerant, transparent, and genuinely decentralized. The party-state was attempting to adapt and become more inclusive and tolerant from 1998 to 2008, but since 2009 has abandoned this path. Even had it continued, it is not clear that the regime could "ride the tigers" of simultaneous economic, social, and political reform. Its current ossification, which Shambaugh characterizes as "Hard Authoritarianism," is, he believes, doomed to failure. By cracking down instead of loosening up, the Xi Jinping regime is bringing the country continued relative economic stagnation, increased social tensions, and political decline possibly leading to the collapse of the Chinese Communist regime.[115]

Eric Li offers perhaps the most upbeat account. He acknowledges that China's growth has declined for structural reasons over straight quarters. Its program of rapid industrialization, labor-intensive manufacturing, large-scale government investments in infrastructure, and export growth appears to have run its course. He nevertheless remains confident of the party's adaptability, meritocracy, and legitimacy in the eyes of the Chinese people. In the next decade, he insists, the country's leaders will consolidate the one-party model and, in the process, challenge the West's conventional wisdom about the inevitable march of industrialized states toward electoral democracy.

The party's expected success rests in the first instance on its adaptability. It has not shied away from political reform. In the 1980s and 1990s it established term and age limits for most political positions. It is no longer possible for those few at the top to consolidate long-term power. Upward mobility within the party has also increased. The most successful workers are promoted to the *fu chu* and *chu* levels, at which point a typical assignment is to manage districts with populations in the millions or companies with hundreds of millions of dollars in revenues. A small number of very talented officials move up several more ranks, and eventually may make it to the party's Central Committee. The entire process could take two to three decades, and most of those who make it to the top have had managerial experience in just about every sector of Chinese society.

Westerners assume that multiparty elections are the only source of political legitimacy. In the most recent iteration of the argument, Eric Li notes that the party has only maintained its hold on power because it has delivered economic growth.[116] Performance legitimacy, he insists, is only one source of the party's support. More significant is Chinese nationalism and moral legitimacy. The party's role in saving and modernizing China is a more durable source of its legitimacy than the country's economic performance. It explains why, even in the worst political times – the Great Leap Forward and Cultural Revolution – the party was able to retain the support of the population long enough for it to correct its mistakes. In present circumstances, it can count on their support for decades to come.

As for political repression, Eric Li argues that the party increasingly practices what he calls "smart containment." It is intended to give people the widest possible range of personal liberties. "The Chinese people are freer today than at any other period in recent memory; most of them can live where they want and work as they choose, go into business without hindrance, travel within and out of the country, and openly criticize the government online without retaliation." Officials attempt to constrain a small number of individuals who want to topple the one-party system. The more serious problem is corruption. Family members of party leaders use their political influence to enrich themselves. The party has adopted a three-pronged strategy to tackle corruption, which, if successful, will further enhance its legitimacy.[117]

Victor Shih, Christopher Adolph, and Mingxing Liu find no evidence that Chinese officials with good economic track records are more likely to be promoted over those who performed poorly.[118] Yashang Huang argues that advancement is largely by means of patronage, what Wu Si, a prominent Chinese historian, calls the "hidden rule" of the promotion system. China has undeniably made huge economic and social gains in recent decades but the regime has not been successful in reducing the gap between rich and poor, curbing graft, or containing environmental damage. Its long-term legitimacy depends on success in these domains, and all the more so when surveys indicate that 72.3 percent of Chinese polled said they believed that democracy is "desirable for our country now" and 67 percent believed that democracy is "suitable for our country now."[119]

Minxin Pei is more pessimistic still in light of economic contraction and external assertiveness by what he describes as "a repressive inward-looking regime." Autocratic regimes destroy themselves through their economic modernization programs. They foster wealth, but also a shift in power away from the regime and toward the society. In China this is already evident, and will continue even if economic development continues at a slower pace. Diverse groups already possess the capabilities necessary to organize resistance and present an existential threat to the regime's survival.

Pei contends that the anti-corruption drive, and accompanying austerity measures to reduce elite privileges, has destroyed the elite's sense of security and removed many of its incentives to tow the party line. Echoing Aristotle, he argues that there is constant high-stakes jockeying for top positions in autocracies. With elite disillusionment, struggles for power are more likely to spread, as contenders search for support at lower levels of the party and bureaucracy. Government will become accordingly more politicized and less effective, and as a result alienation, passivity, and even resistance on the part of tens of millions of local officials and party members will increase. This does not bode well for regime survival.[120] We will return to the question of China's regime and its survival in Chapter 7.

Notes

1 Plutarch, *Life of Aristides*, p. 24.
2 Galtung, "Structural Theory of Aggression."
3 Beaumarchais, *Marriage of Figaro*; Bourdieu, *Outline of a Theory of Practice*.
4 Weber, *Political Writings*, p. 311; Fiske, "Interpersonal Stratification: Status, Power, and Subordination."
5 Lebow, *Politics and Ethics of Identity*, ch. 2.
6 John Leland, "Why America Sees the Silver Lining," *New York Times*, Week in Review, June 13 2004, p. 1.
7 Wilson, *Holy Roman Empire*, pp. 42–43.
8 Ibid., p. 240.
9 Alberto Nardelli, Jennifer Rankin and George Arnett, "Vladimir Putin's approval rating at record levels," *Guardian*, July 23 2015, www.theguardian.com/world/datablog/2015/jul/23/vladimir-putins-approval-rating-at-record-levels (accessed September 6 2017); Seria Rusli, "Overwhelming majority of Russians support Putin's handling of world affairs, study shows," *Telegraph*, June 22 2017, www.telegraph.co.uk/news/2017/06/22/overwhelming-majority-russians-support-putins-handling-world/ (accessed September 6 2017).

10 Gallup News, Presidential Approval Ratings – Donald Trump, 13–19 November 2017, http://news.gallup.com/poll/203198/presidential-approval-ratings-donald-trump.aspx (accessed November 23 2017).

11 On ethnic conflict, Lake and Rothshild, *International Spread of Ethnic Conflict*; McAdam, McCarthy, and Zald, *Comparative Perspectives on Social Movements*; McAdam, Tarrow, and Tilly, *Dynamics of Contention*; Tilly, *Identities, Boundaries and Social Ties*; Kaufman, *Nationalist Passions*.

12 Guicciardini, *Ricordi*, no. 53.

13 Ibid., book 1, ch. 2.

14 Machiavelli, *Discourses*, book 1, ch. 3.

15 Clausewitz, *On War*, ch. 26.

16 Kindleberger, *Manias, Panics and Crashes*; Keohane, *After Hegemony*.

17 Reich and Lebow, *Good-Bye Hegemony!*

18 Lebow, *Why Nations Fight*, ch. 2 for elaboration and literature.

19 Ibid., ch. 4; Kaufman, Little, and Wohlforth, *Balance of Power*.

20 Schroeder, "Transformation of Political Thinking" and *Transformation of European Politics*; Lebow, *Between Peace and War*, chs. 5–6 and *Cultural Theory of International Relations*, chs. 7–9; Steiner, *Triumph of the Dark*.

21 Talleyrand-Périgord, *Correspondence of Charles Maurice de Talleyrand-Périgord and King Louis XVIII*, p. 289; Tocqueville, *Democracy in America*, I.2.9 and II.2.1, pp. 301 and 482.

22 Some scholars argue the reverse: Keal, *European Conquest and the Rights of Indigenous Peoples*; Pagden, *Lord of All the World*.

23 Amanda Marcott, "Clinton's First Speech Is All About Feminism," *Slate*, April 24 2015, www.slate.com/blogs/xx_factor/2015/04/24/hillary_clinton_s_first_campaign_speech_it_s_all_about_feminism.html (accessed January 20 2017).

24 Claire Cain Miller, "Republican Men Say It's a Better Time to be a Woman Than a Man," *New York Times*, January 17 2017, www.nytimes.com/2017/01/17/upshot/republican-men-say-its-a-better-time-to-be-a-woman-than-a-man.html?module=WatchingPortal&region=c-column-middle-span-region&pgType=Homepage&action=click&mediaId=thumb_square&state=standard&contentPlacement=3&version=internal&contentCollection=www.nytimes.com&contentId=https%3A%2F%2Fwww.nytimes.com%2F2017%2F01%2F17%2Fupshot%2Frepublican-men-say-its-a-better-time-to-be-a-woman-than-a-man.html&eventName=Watching-article-click&_r=0 (accessed January 18 2017).

25 John F. Kennedy, "Inaugural Address, January 20 1961," John F. Kennedy Presidential Library and Museum, www.jfklibrary.org/Asset-Viewer/BqXIEM9F4024ntFl7SVAjA.aspx (accessed January 20 2017).

26 Zelditch, "Process of Legitimation"; Zelditch and Walker, "Normative Regulation of Power"; Johnson, Dowd, and Ridgeway, "Legitimacy as a Social Process"; Tyler, "Psychological Perspectives on Legitimacy and Legitimation."

27 Ian Urbina, "Stowaways and Crimes Aboard a Scofflaw Ship," "A Renegade Trawler, Hunted for 10,000 Miles by Vigilantes," "Murder at Sea: Captured on Video, But Killers Go Free," and "Sea Slaves The Human Misery That Feeds Pets and Livestock," *New York Times*, and July 17, 20, and 28 2015, p. 1.

28 Zelditch, "Process of Legitimation"; Zelditch and Walker, "Normative Regulation of Power"; Johnson, Dowd, and Ridgeway, "Legitimacy as a Social Process"; Tyler, "Psychological Perspectives on Legitimacy and Legitimation."

29 Akerloff and Shiller, *Phishing for Fools*, for examples.

30 Porter, *English Society in the Eighteenth Century*, p. 60.

31 Rousseau, *Discourse on the Origin and Foundations of Inequality*, pp. 147–60; Smith, *Theory of Moral Sentiments*, I.iii.2; Lebow, *Cultural Theory of International Relations*, pp. 314–23, for discussion and the blending of *thumos* and appetite in the modern world.

32 Veblen, *Theory of the Leisure Class*, p. 75.

33 Johansen, *Empire of the Columbia*, pp. 7–8; Harkin, "Potlatch in Anthropology."

34 Plumb, *Origins of Political Stability in England*, pp. 45–46, 72–73, 87–92; Trollope, *Duke's Children* and *Prime Minister* for fictional accounts.

35 Lebow, *Cultural Theory of International Relations*, ch. 7.

36 Lebow and Stein, *We All Lost the Cold War*, chs. 3, 5–6, 8–9.

37 Aristotle, *Politics*, 1302b34–1303a-21, adds demographic balance among classes as a cause of disorder.

38 Ibid.; Plato, *Republic*, 439d1–2, 553d4–7.

39 Plato, *Republic*, 571c8–9. 579d9–10.

40 Lebow, *Tragic Vision of Politics*, ch. 3.

41 Soares de Oliveira, *Magnificent and Beggar Land*.

42 Zunz, *Philanthropy in America*, chs. 1–4.

43 Ken Stern, "Why the Rich Don't Give to Charity," *Atlantic*, April 2013, www.theatlantic.com/magazine/archive/2013/04/why-the-rich-dont-give/309254/ (accessed December 25 2016).

44 Thucydides, *Peloponnesian War*, book I, pp. 24–55.

45 Weber, *Economy and Society*, II, pp. 904–9; Schumpeter, *Imperialism and Social Classes*.

46 Schumpeter, *Imperialism and Social Classes*; Lebow, *Cultural Theory of International Relations*, ch. 9.

47 David J. Morris, "War is Hell, and the Hell Rubs Off," *Slate* April 17 2004, www.slate.com/articles/health_and_science/medical_examiner/2014/04/ptsd_and_violence_by_veterans_increased_murder_rates_related_to_war_experience.html; (accessed January 17 2017); Sonya Norman, Eric B. Elbogen, and Paul B. Schnuur, "Research Findings on PTSD and Violence," US Department of Veteran Affairs, National Center for PTSD, no date, argued that violence is more likely when PTSD is combined with other problems like alcoholism, www.ptsd.va.gov/professional/co-occurring/research_on_ptsd_and_violence.asp (accessed January 17 2017).

48 Aristotle, *Politics*, 1297b16ff. 1305a18; Raaflaub, "Equalities and Inequalities in Athenian Democracy."

49 McElwee, *Art of War*, pp. 198, 314–15; Luvaas, *Military Legacy of the Civil War*, Hironaka, *Tokens of Power*, pp. 93–99.

50 Blanning, *Culture of Power*, pp. 414–15.

51 Schattschneider, *Semisovereign People*.

52 Herodotus, *Histories*, 8.3.

53 Thucydides, 3.69–85.

54 Aristotle, *Politics*, 1302b22–34.
55 Thucydides, 3.82.
56 Ibid., 3.83.
57 Klemperer, *Language of the Third Reich*.
58 Rossalyn Warren, "Fake news fueled civil war in Burundi: Now it's being used again," *Guardian*, February 28 2017, www.theguardian.com/world/2017/feb/28/burundi-fake-news-fuelled-civil-war-used-again-resident-nkurunziza (accessed February 28 2017).
59 Joby Warrick and Walter Pincus, "Bush Inflated Threat From Iraq's Banned Weapons, Report Says," *Washington Post*, June 6 2008, summarizing the Senate Intelligence Committee report, www.washingtonpost.com/wp-dyn/content/article/2008/06/05/AR2008060501523.html (accessed July 9 2017). Schuessler, *Deceit on the Road to War*, for a broader treatment of this phenomenon.
60 Machiavelli, *Discourses on Livy*, book 1, chs. 2–4.
61 Robert Pear, Thomas Kaplan, and Emily Kaplan, "Health Care Debate: Obamacare Repeal Fails as McCain Casts Decisive No Vote," *New York Times*, July 28 2017, www.nytimes.com/2017/07/27/us/politics/senate-health-care-vote.html?_r=0 (accessed July 28 2017).
62 Young, "Mao Zedong and the Class Struggle in Socialist Society."
63 Lenin, *State and Revolution*.
64 Plato, *Republic*, 421e4–422a3.
65 Hegel, *Philosophy of Right*, paras. 195, 239, 244, 253, 266, 271–72, argues that the polarization of wealth between the rich and poor, brought about by the love of luxury and extravagance of the business (*gewerbetriebenden*) classes, encouraged a sense of inward resentment and rebellion against the rich, the society and the government.
66 Kant, "Conjectures on the Beginning of Human History."
67 Ian Traynor, "Is the Schengen dream of Europe without borders becoming a thing of the past?," *Guardian*, January 5 2016, www.theguardian.com/world/2016/jan/05/is-the-schengen-dream-of-europe-without-borders-becoming-a-thing-of-the-past (accessed February 21 2016); Christianne Schlötzer, "Greichenland raus aus Schengen? Was für eine dumme Idee," *Süddeutsche Zeitung*, February 7 2016, www.sueddeutsche.de/politik/fluechtlinge-griechenland-raus-aus-schengen-was-fuer-eine-dumme-idee-1.2850656 (accessed February 21 2016).
68 Jordan, *Louis IX and the Challenge of the Crusade*; Kaeuper, *War, Justice, and Public Order*, pp. 211–35; Weber, "Politics as a Vocation," p. 78, and *Economy and Society*, I, p. 54.
69 Hirschman, *Passions and the Interests*; Hont and Ignatieff, *Wealth and Virtue*; Lebow, *Cultural Theory of International Relations*, ch. 6.
70 Lebow, *Cultural Theory of International Relations*, ch. 7, for a discussion.
71 Marx, "The Bourgeoisie and the Counter-Revolution."
72 Weber, "Die *Handelshochschulen*," *Berliner Tageblatt*, no. 548, October 27 1911, quoted in Mommsen, *Max Weber and German Politics*, p. 95; Weber, *Economy and Society*, vol. II, pp. 920–21.
73 Rosenberg, *Imperial Germany*; Veblen, *Imperial Germany and the Industrial Revolution*; Gerschenkron, *Economic Backwardness in Historical Perspective*,

and *Bread and Democracy in Germany*; Dahrendorf, *Society and Democracy in Germany*. For a critical review, Eley, "British Model and the German Road: Rethinking the Course of German History Before 1914."

74 Feuchtwanger, *Disraeli, Democracy and the Tory Party*; Smith, *Disraelian Conservatism and Social Reform*; Semmel, *Imperialism and Social Reform*.

75 Lebow, "Divided Ireland."

76 Private communication from Karsten Friis, Oslo, January 11 2017.

77 On the latter, Whyte, *Street Corner Society*.

78 Halpern, *Russia and the Golden Horde*.

79 Fritzsche, *Iron Wind*.

80 Karl Deutsch Lecture, Yale University, New Haven, CT, October 1963.

81 Euben, *Athens After the Peloponnesian War*; Loraux, *Divided*, pp. 40–41; Wolpert, *Remembering Defeat*, pp. 29–30, 118; Cartledge, *Democracy*, pp. 105–22.

82 Cottret, *L'Édit de Nantes*, p. 363.

83 Fisch, *Krieg und Frieden im Friedensvertrag*; Ricoeur, *Memory, History, Forgetting*, pp. 454–55.

84 Hobbes, *Leviathan*, ch. 15, 7th law of nature, and *Dialogue Between a Philosopher and a Student on the Common Laws of England*; De Scudéry, *Curia Politiae*, p. 98.

85 Wolin, *Presence of the Past*, p. 142.

86 Ricoeur, *Memory, History, Forgetting*; Todorov, *Hope and Memory*; Weinrich, *Lethe*.

87 Kasfir, "Rebel Governance."

88 Kalyvas, *Logic of Violence in Civil War*, pp. 210–20.

89 Kasfir, Frerks, and Terpstra, "Introduction: Armed Groups and Multi-layered Governance."

90 Durkheim, *The Division of Labor in Society*, pp. 400–1.

91 Turnbull, *Forest People*, pp. 114–20.

92 Nietzsche, *Gay Science*, p. 50.

93 Whyte, *Street Corner Society*.

94 Doyle, *Empires*, p. 40; Mastanduno, "Hegemonic Order"; Kaufman, Little, and Wohlforth, *Balance of Power in World History*, p. 7; Ikenberry and Kupchan, "Socialization and Hegemonic Power."

95 Kindleberger, "Dominance and Leadership in the International Economy" and *Manias, Panics and Crashes*, p. 202.

96 Michael Dobbs and John M. Goshko, "Albright's Personal Odyssey Shaped Foreign Policy Beliefs," *Washington Post*, December 6 1996, p. A25.

97 Barack Obama in the third presidential debate, "America remains the one indispensable nation. And the world needs a strong America." Transcript and Audio: Third Presidential Debate," October 22 2012, www.npr.org/2012/10/22/163436694/transcript-3rd-obama-romney-presidential-debate (accessed March 29 2014).

98 Kindleberger, "Dominance and Leadership in the International Economy."

99 Reich and Lebow, *Good-Bye Hegemony!*

100 Lebow, *National Identifications and International Relations*, ch. 1.

101 Deutsch, et al., *Political Community and the North Atlantic Area*.

102 Adler and Barnett, *Security Communities*, on their expansion in the late twentieth century.

103 Porter, *English Society in the Eighteenth Century*, p. 105.
104 Ibid., p. 104.
105 Ibid., pp. 104–20.
106 Plumb, *England in the Eighteenth Century*, p. 120.
107 Porter, *English Society in the Eighteenth Century*, pp. 110–11.
108 Ibid., p. 112.
109 Pearson, *Political Consequences of Economic Reform*.
110 China Law Blog, "China Rural Protests Decline: It's The Economy Stupid," February 1 2007. Citing the Beijing *People's Daily*, which reported 23,000 such incidents in 2006. www.chinalawblog.com/2007/02/china_rural_ protests_decline_i.html (accessed March 30 2018); Ariana Eunjung Cha, "As China's Jobless Numbers Mount, Protests Grow Bolder," *Washington Post*, January 13 2009. www.washingtonpost.com/wp-dyn/content/article/ 2009/01/12/AR2009011203014.html (accessed March 30 2018); Michael Wines, "A Village Revolt Could be a Harbinger for China," *New York Times*, December 26 2011, p. 1; Perry, *Challenging the Mandate of Heaven*.
111 2014 Hong Kong Protests, Wikipedia, https://en.wikipedia.org/wiki/2014_ Hong_Kong_protests (accessed December 25 2016); Cheng, Emergence of Radical Politics in Hong Kong"; Ortman, "Umbrella Movement";
112 Woodward, *Age of Reform*; Hinton, *Mad, Bad, and Dangerous People?* for evolving takes on reform, change, and stability.
113 Trollope, *Eustace Diamonds*, p. 71; *Barchester Towers*, pp. 163–66; and *Duke's Children*, pp. 351–54.
114 Li, "Life of the Party"; Huang, "Democratize or Die"; Pei, "Beginning of the End" and *China's Trapped Transition*; Shambaugh, "Contemplating China's Future" and *China's Future*.
115 Shambaugh, "Contemplating China's Future" and *China's Future*.
116 Li, "Life of the Party."
117 Ibid.
118 Shih, Adolph, and Liu, "Getting Ahead in the Communist Party."
119 Huang, "Democratize or Die."
120 Pei, "Beginning of the End" and *China's Trapped Transition*.

5   The United States: Self-Interest

"Greed is good."
Gordon Gecko[1]

Americans have been consistently smug about their political system, capitalist economy, social cohesion, and way of life. They have not for the most part questioned the stability of their political and economic institutions since the Great Depression of the 1930s. Their survival, in contrast to the collapse of so many European democracies, and subsequent robust performance in the postwar era, reaffirmed the view of many Americans that Providence has blessed them. They were fulfilling their prophecy as "the city on the hill," a phrase from the Sermon on the Mount used by Puritan preacher Jonathan Edwards in 1630 to describe the Massachusetts Bay Colony on the eve of its founding.[2] President Kennedy would refer to Edward's sermon in his first post-election speech, as Ronald Reagan did on the eve of his presidency.[3]

Today, such rhetoric has a hollow ring. Americans are increasingly critical of their political and economic order. Fringe groups aside, it is the first time since the Great Depression that mainstream commentators have voiced concern for its survival. In the 1930s, many questioned the utility of capitalism or its ability to survive without extensive government intervention, and a smaller number wondered if an archaic, federal, electoral system built on the principle of checks and balances was relevant to an era when "strongmen" seemed essential. Capitalism is once again the villain for many, and for more or less the same reasons as before.[4] There is equal disillusionment with American institutions, especially the Congress and Electoral College. The House of Representatives has been extensively gerrymandered, and the Electoral College is unrepresentative of the popular vote. Even with these advantages, President Trump could not impose his ban on immigrants from selected Muslim countries or gain congressional support for doing away with the Affordable Care Act [Obamacare]. He attributed his failure to the constitutional checks and balances built into US governance. "It's a very rough system," he said, referring to checks and balances. "It's an archaic system ... It's really a bad thing for the country."[5]

The decline of comity in the Congress has been notable, and has given way to a destructive "winner-takes-all" approach to politics.[6] This is not an institutional problem but a reflection of a broader value shift in American society. Friendships and compromise across the aisles flourish when people share common values and practices, respect one another, value the institution of which they are part, and want it to function effectively and responsibly. Absent friendship and compromise, hostility can become acute, as it has between Republicans and Democrats, and arguably as much so within the Republican Party.[7] Comity and cooperation sharply decline, at the expense of the national interest. Republicans have been willing to impeach a president who was certainly not guilty of "high crimes and misdemeanors"; hold the federal budget hostage to partisan demands; and refuse to hold hearings on an Obama supreme court nominee.

Many pundits assert that America is in the midst of a "culture war," a profound ideological struggle between liberal and conservative, blue and red state, urban and rural, pro-government and pro-market, pro-choice and pro-life, secular and religious.[8] They point to the front-line battles being fought by political advocacy organizations, religious and community groups, student clubs, news agencies, activist non-profits, and engaged citizens all across the country to contend that entrenched and deeply opposed citizen armies are engaged in a titanic struggle for the soul of America. Some consider the culture war the primary cause of congressional dysfunction while others see it as more a consequence of the ferocious battles being waged by America's political elites.[9] It is reasonable to assume that they are mutually reinforcing. Consider the struggle over transgender bathroom rights. Bowing to pressure from the religious right, Donald Trump, early on in his administration, rescinded President Obama's directive that transgender students should be allowed to use the bathroom of their choice. Subsequently, he revoked Obama's "Deferred Action for Childhood Arrivals," that shields some 800,000 young undocumented immigrants from deportation.[10] Some Republican legislators considered these initiatives distractions from "bread-and-butter" economic issues, but their concerns were ignored by the president.[11] Trump's appointments to high office of committed anti-birth control, anti-abortion, and climate change deniers intensified the culture war.

Plato and Aristotle believed that personal and political orders require reason to control and then educate appetite and *thumos*. When reason loses control to appetite among high-status actors they fail to exercise the prudence and self-restraint (*sôphrosunê*) of their predecessors. Corruption among political and business elites, special interest legislation that benefits corporations and the rich at the expense of the poor give evidence of this phenomenon.

Thucydides and Plato argue that intellectuals accelerate the process of civic decay by undermining the values that encourage public service, sacrifice, and self-restraint. They produce discourses that problematize values and practices that were previously accepted as natural. Neoliberalism, Ronald Reagan's legitimization of greed, the radical right and the Tea Party's attack on government and taxes, and Donald Trump's verbal assaults on the constitution, the media and facts can all be read in this light. Within a month of Trump's inauguration, spin had given way to outright lies in the confirmation hearings of a clear majority of Trump's cabinet appointments. The father of "birtherism" who claimed that "I won the popular vote," had the "largest" inaugural crowd ever, "Obama had my wires tapped," climate change is "nonexistent" and "mythical," any "collusion story is a total hoax," and the FBI's investigation into the firing of the FBI director James Comey is a "taxpayer funded charade." Paul Krugman rightly observed that Trump could not get away with such blatant mistruths without the support of many enablers: Republican officials, some of the media, and a large bloc of voters.[12]

Elite over-indulgence arouses envy, resentment, and emulation among the population. Conspicuous consumption has trickle-down consequences and encourages people to emulate the lifestyles of the wealthy and to compete with one another in the process. In the United States this is evident in, among other things, the more elaborate nature and greater costs of birthday and graduation parties, weddings and greater expenditures on other forms of display. It results in the rise of credit card and other forms of debt, a corresponding decline in savings, and younger age groups seeking status on the basis of material possessions.

Elite imbalance also leads to violation of political *nomos*. It takes several forms. Elites appeal for support from other actors on the basis of mutual self-aggrandizement. Tea Party rhetoric and a spate of statements by prominent public figures that "greed is good" provide a rationalization for this behavior. The Trump administration has responded by filling cabinet positions with bankers and businesspeople intent on lowering taxes for the rich and rolling back as far as possible governmental constraints on banking, business, coal, and oil. As this book goes to press, Trump's appointment to the Federal Communications Commission is revoking Internet neutrality in the interest of the Telecoms.[13]

The next step is "outbidding" among elites. This is already evident in the Republican Party, where the principal hurdle to election is the primary and where right-wing extremists wield influence out of all proportion to their numbers and compel would-be officials to respond to their demands or go down in defeat. Their demands include rewriting the "rules of the game," to lock in any temporary political advantage and pursue policies that reward themselves and punish their adversaries in ways that violate traditional norms of give-and-take and compromise.

External forces often aggravate this competition and resulting fears. The events of 9/11 were exploited by the Bush administration to justify the invasions of Afghanistan and Iraq. The "war on terror" continues to exaggerate external threats to the United States, and possibly helps make them in part self-fulfilling, but it has not connected with domestic politics in a way that intensifies elite competition and the kinds of fears that lead to extreme behavior.

The final step in breakdown is intensification of conflict to the point that it encourages preemption by threatened actors. Extra-legal behavior leads to violence and counter-violence, of that observed in the last days of the Weimar Republic, or as I write, in several South American countries – most notably, Venezuela – where leaders have tried to prolong their rule by changing constitutions in circumstances where disillusioned voters would turn them out of office.[14] This has not happened in the United States, and I am not predicting that it will. Nevertheless, many reasonable people are worried about the survival of its democratic order.

There are many reasons for these disturbing developments, some superficial and others more fundamental. In this and the next chapter I explore what I consider to be two of the most important underlying causes. These are two related value shifts, one in the way self-interest is understood, and the other in principles of justice. This chapter focuses on the first shift and its implications for how people define their goals, frame interpersonal relationships, and relate to their communities.

Following Alexis de Tocqueville, I conceive of self-interest as a continuum. One end is anchored by what Tocqueville called "self-interest well understood." It is characterized by a commitment to the local community, and to a lesser extent the nation, in the recognition that one's own interests are best defined and advanced through cooperative relationships with others. Individual material success and self-esteem depend on communal well-being and recognition. Tocqueville was impressed by the extent to which Americans framed self-interest this way and were accordingly willing to work together to help others and carry out common projects.[15] At the other end of the continuum is what he called "individualism," best described in today's language as "privatism." It is self-interest, narrowly defined, in which people consider their own interest, or that of their families, in isolation from others. People who think and act this way have traditionally been described as selfish. Postwar America, I contend, has witnessed a shift away from communal to individual interests, from self-interest well understood to privatism, with more people willing to advance their interest at the expense of the community. This has serious political implications because self-interest well understood is essential to democratic culture and its survival.

As Tocqueville understood, the two value shifts are related. Privatism is a product of equality and democracy. In democratic societies, "devotion toward one man becomes rarer: the bond of human affections is extended and loosened." Individuals increasingly develop the habit "of always considering themselves in isolation, and they willingly fancy that their whole destiny is in their hands."[16] As people withdraw into their private lives, political skills and interests decline, making the population politically passive and vulnerable to exploitation by those who cater to their most immediate pleasure. Tocqueville struggles to find a name for this despotism because it is like nothing that has preceded it. He expects it to be more extensive but milder than traditional forms of tyranny, and "degrades men without tormenting them."[17] This "tyranny of the majority," as he calls it, is simultaneously a triumph of democracy and its parody. Its distinctive characteristic, Sheldon Wolin observes, "is not regimentation but privatization, not Brezhnev drabness but glitter and lavish consumption."[18]

Evidence

I use multiple streams of data to track these the value shifts. To study the decline of self-interest well understood and correspondingly the rise of narrow self-interest, I rely on machine-coded content analyses and qualitative analyses of presidential speeches, popular sitcoms, and songs over a period of sixty years. This data provided the core evidence for a second, parallel book *Self-Interest from Tocqueville to Trump*, also published in 2018. It documents the shift in the formulation of self-interest and explores its implications for democracy. This chapter offers a summary of its data and my findings with regard to presidential speeches and popular music.

To study the shift from fairness to equality – the subject of the next chapter – I once again turn to presidential speeches, but also to the campaign speeches of Donald Trump and Hillary Clinton in the 2016 presidential election. I also rely on qualitative analyses of popular sitcoms from the last two decades. I chose two television shows – *Duck Dynasty* and *Modern Family* – because of their popularity and appeal to different audiences. The former, often described as a reality show rather than a sitcom, attracts the highest percentage of Trump voters of any sitcom, and the latter is the most popular sitcom watched by the most Clinton voters. My analysis of these sitcoms allows me to make some inferences not only about these two principles of justice but about their relative appeal to different demographics.

To explore further the political implications of the principles of equality and fairness I turn to experiments. There is a large literature on the relative appeal of these principles and the kinds of trade-offs people make between them, in the United States and internationally. There are a few experiments and surveys discriminating between Republicans and Democrats, and their findings run parallel to the inference I draw from the sitcoms. Roger Giner-Sorolla, Laura Niemmi, and I conducted our own experiment with a sample of Trump and Clinton voters.

The presidential addresses from Roosevelt to Bush were coded by students in my 2006 undergraduate seminar in American Politics at Dartmouth College. I coded subsequent addresses of Presidents George H. W. Bush, Barack Obama, and Donald Trump. Sitcoms from *I Love Lucy* to *Sex and the City* were coded jointly with my Dartmouth students, as were popular songs. I coded the two sitcoms used to study fairness and equality, with the help of Prof Carol Bohmer, Maryyum Mehmood, and Timothy James Potenza, the last two at the time PhD students at King's College London. Roger Giner-Sorolla, who took the lead in conducting our experiment, is Professor of Psychology at the University of Kent.

The three discourses I use to study the first shift reveal a similar pattern: a decline in self-interest well understood, becoming apparent in the second half of the 1960s and more pronounced in subsequent decades. Presidents increasingly appeal to individuals rather than the community as a whole, and do so on the basis of material self-interest. Sitcoms move away from functional and hierarchical families in which father knows best, or at least means well, to groups of friends held together by their hostility and distrust of the wider world. In the early postwar period, the top of the charts is consistently populated by love songs in which young men and women seek fulfillment by expanding their identities to that of couple and family. By the 2000s, popular music describes, and sometimes celebrates, young people seeking instant gratification of sexual appetites, and treating it as a semi-commercial transaction or the imposition of their will on reluctant others.

Presidential Speeches

Presidential speeches are intended to influence people – the wider public as well as the Congress – so their authors exercise great care in the language they use, the values to which they appeal and the policies they advocate. Successful politicians and their speechwriters have a finely honed skill at putting their fingers on the public pulse; this is, after all, a precondition of political success. For all these reasons, presidential inaugural and State of the Union speeches are excellent barometers of public attitudes, values, and expectations. They are also powerful vehicles for molding public opinion and mobilizing the country in support of desired ends.[19] President Obama's second inaugural address in 2009 had an all-time high television audience of 38 million.[20] President Trump caused a huge political stir by insisting, contrary to fact, that his inauguration had a larger audience than any of its predecessors.[21] His efforts, and those of his press secretary, to sustain their discredited claim offer further evidence of the importance presidents attach to inaugural addresses.

My sample of presidential speeches includes all seventy-six inaugural and state of the union addresses delivered by US presidents since 1945.[22] Dylan Matthews, a student in my 2008 Dartmouth seminar on self-interest, did the coding for presidential speeches from Truman to George H. W. Bush. I coded the speeches for Presidents Obama and Trump. The analysis of the Trump to Bush speeches relies in part on a software package developed by Dartmouth Professor of Mathematical Social Sciences Joel Levine.[23] Called Data Without Variables, it compares the frequency of word usage in multiple documents. The program takes multiple text documents and locates each text on a field as a function of their use of words and the frequency. It then rearranges the words in relationship to each of their texts. The more frequently a word appears in any text, the closer it is displayed to that text in the non-Euclidean landscape of the field.[24]

Word lists require considerable editing before they can be used. All articles, prepositions, conjunctions, and standard phrases like "thank you," "ladies and gentlemen" must be deleted. We made a second cut of the remaining nouns and verbs to excise those that did not appear germane to self-interest. We then combined words of similar meaning (e.g. American, Americans, America, country, nation; protection, security, safeguarding). Some words have inherent meaning and their relative frequency within speeches will tell us something about self-interest. Other words only take on meaning in context, so their use within a speech must be examined to see what purpose they serve. Having identified important words by both methods, we then selected a set of relevant key words and used their frequency to relocate the speeches on our grid.[25]

The speeches reveal a general progression within the cluster of inaugural addresses from self-interest well understood to privatism. Presidents from the 1940s through the 1960s – Truman, Eisenhower, Kennedy,

Nixon, and Johnson – are grouped fairly close together despite their party differences. Decade in office, not party affiliation, offers the best account for their location. The only significant outlier is Jimmy Carter. This distribution provides some support for my supposition that presidential speeches are carefully attuned to public attitudes and values. To the extent that presidents aim to maximize their support, they choose language calculated to appeal to the center of the electorate. As the public changes in attitudes and values, we would expect to see a similar shift in presidential language.

One of the most striking features is the frequency of second person pronouns. It begins with Ronald Reagan who makes repeated references to the individual citizens. These speeches mark the first time a State of the Union address is directed specifically at the television audience. Viewers are conceptualized as autonomous, egoistic actors and appeals to them are almost entirely on the basis of self-interest.[26] From Reagan on, presidents invoke individuals in a negative sense far more than did their predecessors. They speak of deviant individuals, the threat they pose, and what must be done to protect against them. This is evident in their use of the word "criminal," which, like second person pronouns, is found near the center of the cluster. In his 1989 State of the Union address, George W. Bush proclaimed: "I mean to get tough on the drug criminals."[27] He conjures up "a drug dealer" against whom he issues a direct threat. He continues and extends Reagan's framing of the State of the Union address as a conversation between the president and an autonomous, egoistic individual. There are no references to a common American identity, desire for safety or shared interests, only references to individual interests.

This trend toward privatism is almost as evident in the speeches of Bill Clinton. His frequent use of the word "paycheck" reveals how much more individualistic his rhetoric is than that of the previous Democratic president, Jimmy Carter.[28] He makes no reference to the general economy or common prosperity, only to individual families. With Bush and Clinton, references to the common good or wider community – that permeate the speeches of Truman, Eisenhower, and Kennedy – have all but disappeared.

The same pattern is evident in a comparative qualitative analysis of presidential speeches on a single topic. I have chosen energy conservation because every president since Harry Truman has given at least one major speech on the subject. They indicate a gradual shift in how presidents understand their audience, the basis of their appeals, and the nature and timeline of the benefits energy conservation can be expected to bring. This evolution is the form of step changes in three discrete historical periods (1945–63, 1969–81 and 1989 to the present). At least one Democratic and Republican president is represented in each period.

Between 1945 and 1963, presidents couch their appeals to the national community and ask everyone to do their part. The frame of reference and rhetoric are something of a holdover from World War II and presumably motivated by the expectation that they would prove effective in inspiring a degree of self-sacrifice and collective behavior. The second period of national concern over energy began in the late 1960s and increased dramatically after the 1973 OPEC oil embargo and the rapid price rise in petroleum products it triggered. Presidents Richard Nixon, Gerald Ford, and Jimmy Carter address themselves to Americans individually rather than to the nation at large. They appear to have little expectation that people will make sacrifices voluntarily on behalf of the community or that the community can be aroused to generate the kind of social pressure that had been so helpful in the past. After 1989, energy conservation again becomes an important national concern. Oil reached a new high in 2008, well over $100 a barrel. Once again presidents of both parties appeal directly to the material well-being of individual citizens. There is no talk of communal gain, only of the short-term financial benefits businesses and individuals could reap from conservation. Republican presidents favor voluntary compliance, while Democrats are more likely to support legislation. Democrat and Republican presidents alike prefer tax incentives to taxes and penalties. Presidents of both parties are adamant that they will not require sacrifices of the American people or businesses.

President Obama addresses energy in his 2009 inaugural address. However, he notes the problem only in passing and his focus is not on cost but the environment. He promises support for programs that "will harness the sun and the winds and the soil to fuel our cars and run our factories."[29] There are no references to energy in his second inaugural. It is always possible that this shift reflects an improved economy, where less sacrifice is required by individuals. However, concern for saving energy, while largely economic in earlier decades, is driven more by the environment in recent ones. This is evident in the first Obama inaugural. To the extent that people believe – more Democrats do than Republicans – that climate change constitutes an existential threat, there is all the more reason to describe the fight against it in communal terms. It is accordingly all the more striking that so much of the pro-environmental presidential and other political rhetoric is nevertheless framed in selfish terms. People are repeatedly told of the need to protect *their* grandchildren.

Quantitative comparisons between Obama and Trump speeches are complicated by the fact that Obama gave two inaugural speeches and eight State of the Union addresses. To date, Trump has made one inaugural and one State of the Union address. Obama's speeches are slightly longer and make use of a larger vocabulary. He also gave more speeches so his overall word total is roughly five times higher. What is most important for my purposes is the relative frequency of word use for each candidate. This allows comparison without having to weight the word totals to compensate for their differing word totals. Figure 5.1 shows the resulting word list.

The word counts of the two presidents are similar in many ways. The most frequent references of both presidents are to "America," "Americans," the "country," and "nation." I scored these collectively under the rubric "America." There is a big drop for both leaders between "America" and the next frequently used words, and here is where differences become apparent. Obama's next most common words are "education," "jobs," "together," "right," and "economy." They reflect his concern, and more generally that of the Democratic Party, for ordinary people, their economic future, and security. Obama then speaks of "rights" and "justice," and somewhat less about "giving, "caring," and "health. "Rights" and "justice," when examined in context, refer to applications of the principle of equality – the subject of Chapter 6. "Giving" and "caring" emphasize the importance of community and the responsibility of all Americans – and the government – to come to the aid of the needy, oppressed, and stigmatized. They reflect self-interest well understood.

For Trump, "America" is followed by "jobs" and "workers" and then "great," the last in keeping with his campaign slogan to "Make America Great Again." Next comes "protect," used in the context of protecting Americans from immigrants, terrorists, and foreign dumping of cheap goods injurious to American businesses. Afterwards come many of the same words used by Obama, although as we shall see there are important differences in their valence and application. Trump often uses them to construct a series of "us" and "others," with some of the "others" being immigrants and the American political establishment.

The qualitative analysis is more revealing. Obama invokes traditional American values as the key to addressing new challenges. In doing so, he emphasizes self-interest well understood, as these values put a premium on contribution and sacrifice for the community – now extended from the nation to the world:

Our challenges may be new, the instruments with which we meet them may be new, but those values upon which our success depends, honesty and hard work, courage and fair play, tolerance and curiosity, loyalty and patriotism – these things are old.

WORD	COUNT
OBAMA	
AMERICAN	905
JOBS/ECONOMY/WORKERS	450
EDUCATION	281
TOGETHER	196
WORLD	140
RIGHT	133
JUST	126
FAMILIES	112
TAX	110
WANT	105
CONGRESS	100
ENERGY	98
CHANGE	90
GOVERNMENT	88
SECURITY	87
FUTURE	86
GIVING	85
CARING	81
HEALTH	70
GENERATIONS	64
COMPANIES	62
TRUMP	
AMERICAN	189
JOBS, WORK, WORKERS	43
GREAT	25
PROTECT	23
WORLD	23
FAMILIES	22
UNITED	19
RIGHTS	16
CITIZENS	15
JUST	15

Figure 5.1 Word Distribution: Presidents Obama and Trump

These things are true. They have been the quiet force of progress throughout our history.

What is demanded then is a return to these truths. What is required of us now is a new era of responsibility – a recognition, on the part of every American, that we have duties to ourselves, our nation and the world, duties that we do not grudgingly accept but rather seize gladly, firm in the knowledge that there is nothing so satisfying to the spirit, so defining of our character than giving our all to a difficult task.[30]

Both Obama inaugurals stress the diversity of America, and how this constitutes "a strength, not a weakness." It has allowed the country to overcome the kinds of suspicions and fears that encourage hatred. "As the world grows smaller, our common humanity shall reveal itself; and that America must play its role in ushering in a new era of peace." He extends the olive branch to Islam, telling the Muslim world: "we seek a new way forward, based on mutual interest and mutual respect." In effect, he is extending the circle of community whose well-being is key to that of individual Americans.

Trump's inaugural offers a sharp contrast in its emphasis on division and privatism. He opens by throwing down the gauntlet with the claim that politicians have exploited the people:

For too long, a small group in our nation's Capital has reaped the rewards of government while the people have borne the cost. Washington flourished – but the people did not share in its wealth. Politicians prospered – but the jobs left, and the factories closed.

The establishment protected itself, but not the citizens of our country. Their victories have not been your victories; their triumphs have not been your triumphs; and while they celebrated in our nation's capital, there was little to celebrate for struggling families all across our land.[31]

Trump insists that "January 20th, 2017, will be remembered as the day the people became the rulers of this nation again. The forgotten men and women of our country will be forgotten no longer." His appeal is to privatism, what Americans can expect to get from their country and government. This includes good schools, safe neighborhoods, and good jobs. "These are the just and reasonable demands of a righteous public."[32]

If politicians are portrayed as villains, so too are foreigners:

For many decades, we've enriched foreign industry at the expense of American industry; subsidized the armies of other countries while allowing for the very sad depletion of our military; we've defended other nations' borders while refusing to defend our own; and spent trillions of dollars overseas while America's infrastructure has fallen into disrepair and decay.

We've made other countries rich while the wealth, strength, and confidence of our country has disappeared over the horizon.

One by one, the factories shuttered and left our shores, with not even a thought about the millions upon millions of American workers left behind. The wealth of our middle class has been ripped from their homes and then redistributed across the entire world.

But that is the past. And now we are looking only to the future. We assembled here today are issuing a new decree to be heard in every city, in every foreign capital, and in every hall of power.[33]

Trump goes on to present a picture of America that must advance its individual interests in competition with others and certainly not as part of any international community: "We must protect our borders from the ravages of other countries making our products, stealing our companies, and destroying our jobs." From this day forward, "it's going to be America First." Americans in turn must follow "two simple rules: Buy American and hire American."[34] If Obama attempted to expand the definition of community, Trump is narrowing it and encouraging Americans to strengthen the binary between "us" and "them."

Trump's inaugural breaks new ground in the populist binaries his inaugural address sets up between politicians and people, and between Americans and foreigners. It depicts a hierarchical world, with America rightfully at the top, but unfairly deprived of the advantages of this position by crafty foreign businesses and government. Wily and out-of-control politicians have abetted this process and must be restrained. Past presidents attempted to speak to all Americans and to minimize the partisan nature of politics and the antagonisms it arouses. Trump speaks only to his supporters – less than half of the voters – and stokes these differences and antagonisms. It is perhaps the most dramatic evidence of his narrow framing of self-interest.

Rock to Rap

Music is even more responsive to changing values than presidential speeches or sitcoms. The rhetoric of presidential speeches is constrained by all the expectations that surround high public office, while sitcoms are a commercial medium, dominated by profit. Music moguls are generally more cautious than adventurous, and anxious to avoid offending political authority, sponsors or any significant segment of their audience. Music is also commercial, but is a more pluralistic form of entertainment. For most of the period under study there were only three major television networks, and even today there are only a handful of additional cable networks that produce their own shows. There were always many record companies and independently owned radio stations to play their releases. Over the course of the postwar era, recording companies proliferated while the growth of radio allowed stations to aim increasingly for niche markets. Both developments made music more responsive to an increasingly affluent youth culture. As youth sets most social trends, popular music, like the Internet, is usually ahead of the curve as far as media go in reflecting changes in social patterns and behavior in American society.

My students and I analyzed the lyrics of popular songs over most of the postwar era. Using *Billboard's* Top Song Lists for each decade, we sampled seventy of the top 100 songs from each decade. Seventy songs seemed a sufficient sample, and we chose them in order of their ranking.[35] Singers and narrators vary across songs, and we included only those who speak in the first person or about another person with whom they had some kind of relationship. When we excluded a song for this reason we went to the next ranked song on the top 100 list, and continued until we had seventy songs that met our criteria. For purposes of evaluation, we used a five-point scale, with five denoting behavior we consider strongly consistent with self-interest well understood. A score of 1 goes to behavior that exhibits the highest degrees of narrow self-interest or privatism.

We explore four dimensions of self-interest: identity, goals, behavior, and time perspective. To generate scores, we asked the following questions about the lyrics of each song: To what extent do the main character(s) identify solely with themselves or with others as well? Are their goals and activities pursued to the benefit or at the expense of others? Do they act as individuals or in collaboration with others? Is the goal or gratification they seek instant or deferred? All songs were coded on all four dimensions and were also given a mean value based on the four scores.[36]

The coding was done by eight students who initially met as a group in seminar. With copies of the lyrics in hand, we listened together to a few songs the lead coders considered emblematic – or problematic – for their coding. Students coded these songs independently, and we then shared codings and discussed our differences. After working through these sample codings, sharing reasons for them, and reaching consensus, when possible, on coding procedures and outcomes, students began to code other songs independently. Their codings were generally similar, differing by no more than one interval in 80 percent of the songs, and no more than two in the remainder. In 70 percent of the songs, there was agreement at the outset among at least six of eight coders. Through discussion, we ultimately reached a consensus in 90 percent of the songs and used compromise codings for the remainder.

Popular music revealed increasing privatism over time. Many of the songs are about romance, and love is generally not considered a selfish emotion, although this too changed.[37] Such songs nevertheless received individual, or more selfish, ratings to the extent that their lyrics speak of only the narrator's satisfaction, and more so if it is at the expense of their "partner." When an individual's love for a partner displaces purely individual concerns, identity is considered collective. An example is

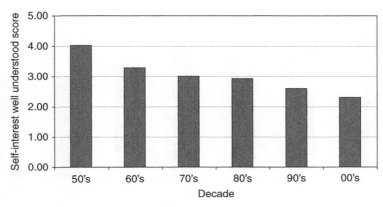

Figure 5.2 Identity as Group or Individual

"Endless Love," a 1980s song, in which Diana Ross and Lionel Ritchie proclaim: "My love, There's only you in my life. The only thing that's bright."

Figure 5.2 indicates that the 1950s are the highpoint of collective identification. There is a steady drop to the current decade with an overall decline on the order of almost 37 percent. Characters in songs have come to think of themselves as increasingly detached from their society.

Our second dimension goal refers to the envisaged beneficiaries of the behavior in question. Is it expected to benefit the individual, a couple or group, or the wider community? The lowest scores go to behavior that is expected to benefit or gratify the individual at the expense of others. The highest scores are for altruistic behavior. Here too, as Figure 5.3 illustrates, we observe a decline over six decades, in this case of 28 percent.

In our third dimension, behavior, we are interested in the extent to which the main characters in songs act alone or in concert with others. Individual behavior can be benign, and collective behavior malign, but it is on the whole a reasonable measure of social integration. Our codings took into account the nature of the collective activity in question, and excluded any with anti-social goals (e.g. drug dealing, bank robbery). Much, although certainly not all, isolated individual behavior is indicative of alienation from society. By alienation, I mean what sociologist Robert Nisbet called a "state of mind that can find a social order remote, incomprehensible or fraudulent; beyond real hope or desire; inviting apathy, boredom, or even hostility."[38]

Figure 5.3 indicates that once again the 1950s had the highest score. The decline over almost six decades was 22 percent and generally linear.

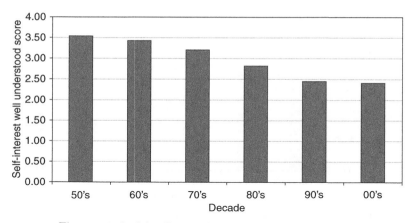

Figure 5.3 Activity Centered on Group or Individual

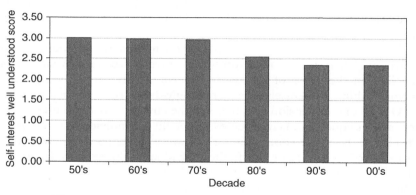

Figure 5.4 Time Perspective

The final dimension was time perspective. Self-interest well understood often leads people to defer immediate gratification in pursuit of longer-term goals. Privatism, which more often finds expression in efforts to satisfy appetites, lends itself to more immediate gratification than longer-term goals, especially those that require collective action. Songs that emphasized short-term costs for longer-term rewards received the highest coding, while the lowest went to behavior aimed at achieving immediate returns. Figure 5.4 indicates the highest scores in the 1950s and 1960s, with a 30 percent decline from this high to the present decade. This pattern is consistent with the scores for the other three dimensions.

When we combine these dimensions for an overall evaluation of self-interest, the result, shown in Figure 5.5, indicates a regular decline over

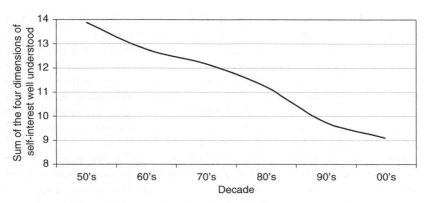

Figure 5.5 Aggregate Self-Interest

the six decades of the study. Our qualitative analysis reveals how this has occurred. We identified and analyzed three major substantive themes of popular music: romantic relationships, materialism, and attitudes toward the law and prevailing social norms. All three themes have significant implications for understandings of self-interest.

By the 1990s we encounter songs that regard the impoverishment of others to advance one's own wealth as acceptable behavior. In "I'll Be Missing You," Puff Daddy reminisces about his murdered friend Christopher Wallace, a.k.a. Notorious B.I.G. Puff Daddy talks about the joy they shared buying new cars, clothes, shoes, and stealing from others. In "This Is How We Do It," rhythm and blues singer Montell Jordan recognizes spending for drugs, alcohol, and flashy cars as something of a norm. He gloats about how money buys him sexual favors. In "Can't Nobody Hold Me Down," Mase and Puff Daddy ridicule others who do not own expensive cars and jewelry and access to the women they want. At the same time, they mock those who have aspirations for higher social status. In "No Scrubs," TLC disclose that you need money to receive their love. They deride the unclean, lazy, and impoverished – all of whom are lumped together as "scrubs" – and chastize poor men for even making sexual advances.

Self-interest well understood requires people to restrain their appetites and respect reasonable legal and social constraints. Self-restraint is related to trust because people are more likely to follow norms – like not cheating on exams or taxes – when they believe that others will behave similarly. The more they distrust others and fear being made chumps, the less likely they are to exercise self-restraint. As we have seen, postwar sitcoms and popular music alike track increasing self-indulgence. They also indicate declining respect for legal and social norms.

The 1950s was the era of rock 'n' roll, considered at the time to be music of rebellion.[39] In retrospect, its agenda appears relatively juvenile and tame. "Rock Around the Clock," which arguably ushered in the genre, questions the norms of early curfews as kids party and dance through the night. In "Wake Up Little Susie," another signature hit, the Everly Brothers are concerned that they have remained out with a girl too late in the evening and that her parents will be furious and her reputation will suffer. Elvis Presley's "Jail House Rock" is about a party the warden throws at the county jail. The prison band begins to wail and the jailbirds start to dance. In the fifth verse, the warden coerces a loner to join the party by singing: "Hey, buddy, don't you be no square. If you can't find a partner use a wooden chair." For better and worse, songs of the era largely reinforce social norms and stress conformity.

As early as the middle 1960s, popular music begins to show contempt for social norms and the legal establishment. This is most evident in the frequent and favorable references to drugs. "Puff the Magic Dragon," a 1963 hit by Peter, Paul, and Mary, was a heavily coded account of a drug high that resonated strongly with young people. Songs such as "Get Back," "Aint Seen Nothing Yet," and "Seasons in the Sun" contain more open and positive references to drugs. Another important contrast with the 1950s is the rise and idolization of pessimistic outsiders, known as "Lone Rangers." Songs like "Rhinestone Cowboy," "SHAFT," and "I Can't Get No Satisfaction" celebrate people who reject conventional values and norms and seek satisfaction elsewhere.

By the 1990s, songs openly celebrate "bad boys" who break laws and commit crimes. "Mo Money Mo Problems," a 1997 posthumous release of Notorious B.I.G., and featuring guest vocals by Mase and Sean "Puff Daddy" Combs, topped the *Billboards* hits for ten consecutive weeks. It explicitly addressed marijuana and drug sales. Christopher Wallace, the Notorious B.I.G., was a crack dealer turned rapper who was involved in an East Coast-West Coast hip-hop feud and was killed by an unknown assailant. "Gangsta's Paradise," "Here Comes the Hotstepper," and "California Love" make theft and murder important themes in their own right.

The first two decades of the current century show the sharpest decline in our coding categories and, accordingly, the greatest shift away from self-interest well understood to privatism. Songs become increasingly focused on individual short-term sexual gratification, often accompanied by alcohol or other drugs. "Blurred Lines" by T. I. and Pharrell is representative. It is also degrading to women, who are described as "animals" moved by their sexual needs, who need liberating by men who repeatedly tell them, "I know you want it."

This and other songs by men about their women project their sexual desires on to their sexual partners, who rarely are given a voice or acknowledged to have preferences of their own. They are often not shown in the video and invariably objectified, as in Ed Sheeran's "Shape of You," in which he sings of his love, not of his partner, but of her body.

Lyrics are correspondingly more explicit. Eminem's "Cold Wind Blows" are particularly crude, and possibly deliberately so, to gain attention. He opens with "Fuck your worms," tells his woman that, "I want my duck sicked, mommy," and he will laugh when, "I call you a slut, it's funny."

Women also have a voice, and some, like Beyoncé and Rihanna, are at the top of the charts. In the current decade Rihanna has had 41 weeks as the leading artist, with second place Bruno Mars at 31 weeks.[40] Rihanna became one of the few black women to reach the top of the male-dominated pop music business. "S&M," released in January 2011, mimics her male counterparts by focusing on her sexual desire and bragging about her skills at being "bad." She appears to confess her taste for S&M, singing that "Sticks and stones may break my bones, But chains and whips excite me." She pleads with her lover to "make my body say ah ah ah, I like it-like it."

"S&M" reached number 2 on *Billboard*'s "Hot 100" chart, which encouraged a remix starring Britney Spears. "S&M" had worldwide appeal, making number one in Australia, Canada, Hungary, Israel, and Poland, and among the top five in France, Germany, Ireland, Spain, and the UK.[41] Rihanna told *Spin* magazine that the lyrics were metaphorical. Critics for the most part said the obvious about that song: that it embraced violence as a fetish.[42] The video suggests that Rhianna is aping, or mocking, men who seek sex for their own satisfaction and see it as an aggressive, if not violent act against others. Rihanna insisted the song was about confidence in one's identity.[43]

Feminists took umbrage at "S&M" and Rihanna's video, "Bitch Better Have My Money" (BBHMM).[44] The seven-minute long film is about extracting revenge on an accountant who has defrauded the singer. Assisted by two friends, she kidnaps his wife, a stereotype of a rich woman with flashy dogs and jewels. They strip her, hang her upside down, hit her over the head with a bottle and almost drown her in a pool. When the accountant refuses to return the money he stole, Rihanna ties him to a chair, threatens to dismember him with her collection of knives, and leaves him dripping blood over a trunk of money. In a reprise of "Thelma and Louise," Rihanna and her helpers ride away in a 1960s blue convertible.

The song has been described as Rihanna's revenge on Peter Gounis, against whom she filed a lawsuit in 2012, claiming he gave her "unsound" financial advice that led to a loss of $9m in 2009 alone. She won a multi-million pound settlement. Predictably, BBHMM ignited a furious debate. A headline on Refinery29 declared the video "Not Safe For Work or Feminists," while Twitter users accused Rihanna of glorifying violence against women, and condemned the "kidnapped female" trope. *Rolling Stone* was attacked for praising the video and crediting the two minor male roles while not even giving a name to the actress who plays the main role.

It is interesting, perhaps significant, that misogyny in popular lyrics has become more pronounced as women have gained more rights under law and in practice. It might be considered in part a reaction against this change and a reassertion of male supremacy. Several of my students observed that the seeming dehumanization of women is the greatest in songs sung by Black men, who are at the bottom of the socio-economic hierarchy, and perhaps most threatened by such a change.

We must exercise caution in drawing inferences about behavior from the lyrics of popular music. The idealized love of the 1950s reflected the practice of the 1950s only in part. It was an ideal, but one that influenced people and shaped their expectations of romance, love, and marriage. It also supported the double standard that permitted premarital sexual experience for men but not for women. This encouraged men to create a binary of women with whom they sought sex and those from whom they sought love. The top songs of the 1950s, and most from the first half of the 1960s, are about the latter group of women and full of praise for them. Songs undoubtedly had some influence on beliefs and behavior. However, they did not prevent a sea change in sexual attitudes and practices and the general loosening of social constraints that began in the 1960s.

Together with the emergence of a youth culture, wide experimentation with marijuana and other drugs, readily available and inexpensive methods of birth control, and the civil rights and anti-war movements, rock 'n' roll helped to produce and legitimate the so-called revolution of the late 1960s. But this was an unintended consequence, and not a direct function in any way of the lyrics. In retrospect, the transformation of the 1960s was a classic example of a non-linear confluence; multiple developments with largely independent chains of causation combined to produce a transformation. The postwar economic boom made rock 'n' roll possible and both developments, along with access to automobiles and burgeoning college enrollments, generated a distinctive youth culture. The birth control pill, the civil rights movement and the Vietnam War, all of which arrived hard on the heels of rock 'n' roll, made that culture increasingly distinct and defiant.[45]

The music of the later 1960s and 1970s helped to negotiate this change. What about the music of the 2000s and 2010s? Causal inferences are hard to make in the social world under almost any circumstances, and particularly difficult in this instance. Popularity does not necessarily translate into assimilation and practice of the values conveyed by the lyrics – and perhaps more importantly now, the message of the videos. Images supplement, occasionally compete with, and are at least as important as lyrics. Some listeners read lyrics and images metaphorically, as a rebellion about society and its conventions. Some associate the lyrics with an oppressed minority who admit to deriving a frisson of excitement from listening to them. A few students I interviewed admitted they listened because everyone else did and they would be at a social disadvantage not being conversant with the music.[46]

We may confront an interesting conundrum: the lyrics and visual images of the present decade are far more radical a departure from existing social conventions than were the lyrics or images (e.g. a gyrating Elvis, musicians, and singers clad in counter-culture garb) of the 1960s, yet may have less of a behavioral impact. If this is so, I theorize it has much to do with the way in which rock 'n' roll was one causal chain in a confluence that had non-linear effects in contrast to today's popular music. The reverse may be true here. That is, there may be other factors at work that minimize its behavioral consequences. Most important, perhaps, is the frame of reference young people bring to the music. They no longer recognize it as either providing cues about appropriate social behavior and personal goals, or as defining and pioneering a social rebellion to which they are attracted.

When describing popular music, we must also be careful about defining our audiences. Popular songs of the 1940s and early 1950s were national in reach and appeal. For the most part they cut across class, religious, political, and racial divides. This began to change in the mid 1950s, where rock 'n' roll was very much a youth phenomenon.[47] It was also very white, despite its African-American roots. Motown Record Corp, founded in 1959, achieved considerable crossover success in the 1960s and helped to break this barrier, but whites and Blacks continued to form distinct markets until late in the century. In the twenty-first century the fragmentation of the popular music market is more political than racial. Christian rock and evangelical pop emerged in the 1970s, and became increasingly important as a genre. It conveys on the whole conservative religious and social values.[48]

Conclusion

Our three discourses reveal a strikingly similar pattern: a decline in self-interest well understood, becoming apparent in the second half of the 1960s and continuing unabated to the present decade. Presidents increasingly appeal to individuals rather than the community as a whole, and do so on the basis of their economic self-interest. Sitcoms move away from their focus on functional and hierarchical families to groups of friends held together by their hostility and distrust of the outside world. In the early postwar period the top of the charts is consistently populated by love songs in which young men and women seek fulfillment by expanding their identities to that of couple and family. By the 2000s popular music describes, and sometimes celebrates, young people seeking instant gratification of their sexual appetites, and treating it as a semi-commercial transaction or an act of domination in which they impose their will on others.

The shift in discourse parallels and follows on the general loosening of social constraints that began in the 1960s. Together with the emergence of a youth culture, wide experimentation with marijuana and other drugs, readily available and inexpensive methods of birth control, and the civil rights and anti-war movements, it helped to produce and legitimate the so-called revolution of the late 1960s.

I follow constructivists in arguing that conventions create the intersubjective understandings on which all action depends. The language that sustains these norms, conventions, and practices, invariably describes a world that is never fully represented in practice. The democratic ideology of America posits equality among all citizens in their rights, and their freedom, within reason, to pursue life, liberty, and happiness. The reality is very different. Presidential speeches, popular music and also sitcoms of the 1950s and 1960s present a highly idealized portrait of the American people and their families, and how both act in terms of self-interest well understood.[49] These discourses might be described as goals toward which the country and its people should aspire.

Beginning in the 1960s, many traditional American norms were challenged in theory and practice. In response, language became more problematic and contentious. Those defending traditional norms circled their linguistic wagons; they invoked conventional understandings of words and norms to condemn and constrain challenges. Political, religious, and social conservatives did this in their unsuccessful struggle against rock 'n' roll in the late 1950s. Those challenging long-established norms justified their behavior with reference to other well-entrenched norms, expanding or stretching their meaning or the domains in which they applied to cover the practices in question. The greater freedom from parental and school authorities demanded by the youth culture was routinely justified in terms of self-reliance and the broader principles of democracy. In the 1960s, the civil rights movement and sexual revolution challenged more serious norms. The language of liberation and self-expression was invoked and extended to justify behavior very much at odds with traditional norms. After much resistance, these new understandings became widely accepted and provided justification and incentives for further challenges to traditional norms. Equality, as opposed to subjugation, of women is a prime example of such a beneficial change.

These changes were made possible, as Tocqueville understood, by the reinforcing feedback loop between words and deeds. At the same time, and by the same means, understandings of self-interest changed in other ways to undermine long-standing norms. In the 1950s, where I begin my analysis, there was some degree of fit between words and deeds. Presidents could reasonably appeal to citizens on the basis of the longer-term national interest, and sitcoms and popular music could attract audiences by portraying close-knit, hierarchical families and young people were moved by the ideal of ever-lasting romantic love. These values were still taken seriously, if not always honored in practice. As noted, these discourses represented a highly idealized depiction of American life, but one many, if not most, Americans accepted as valid.

Representations of self-interest began to change markedly in the late 1960s. Presidents increasingly address the American people as self-interested individuals and appealed to them on the basis of their short-term economic interests. Popular music was more responsive to public opinion, and especially the youth culture, its principal market. Its transformation began in the 1950s, but became more marked in the 1960s and later decades. Song lyrics became dominated by short-term individual interest, and the satisfaction of sexual appetite freed from moral and legal restraints.

With these changes in discourse, we enter a second stage of evolution marked by hypocrisy. Its advent varies across media, but everywhere it enters the picture and over time becomes increasingly evident in language and behavior. Hypocrisy has always been pronounced in politics, but it is absent or understated in presidential speeches in the 1950s. It becomes more pronounced in the 1960s and 1970s, in the speeches of Presidents Johnson and Nixon on the war in Indochina, and of Nixon and Reagan on civil rights. Nixon, for instance, deftly presented himself as a friend of the civil rights movement, but did "not see any significant area where additional legislation could be passed that would be helpful in opening doors that are legally closed."[50] The most striking – and most transparent examples – may be Nixon's attempts to defend himself and his administration during the Watergate scandal. In April 1973, Nixon declared that he was "appalled at this senseless, illegal action" and was "shocked to learn that employees of the Re-Election Committee were apparently among those guilty."[51] Real life reprises art. Louis, the Vichy Préfect in *Casablanca*, standing outside Rick's Café with his winnings in his hand, is "shocked" to discover that gambling goes on inside. Many of those who watched Nixon's speech would have made the connection.

The seventeenth-century French author François La Rochefoucauld suggested that, "Hypocrisy is the homage which vice pays to virtue." Presidential speeches and popular music validate his observation. Their hypocrisy shows that older norms are still valued, even considered proper, but no longer judged as accurate predictors of behavior.

In a third and final stage, new discourses emerge to justify behavior at odds with traditional values but which by now has more or less become routine. New discourses normalize this behavior. In presidential speeches, this is apparent in the reformulation of interest in the 1980s and 1990s. In contrast to their predecessors, Presidents Reagan, Bush, and Clinton largely reframe the national interest as the sum of individual interests – usually economic interests – of voters or their families.

In the 1987 movie, *Wall Street*, the ruthless and rapacious tycoon Gordon Gecko proclaims: "Greed is good." In the cinematic world of the 1930s and 1940s, only a character unambiguously identified as a villain could make such a statement. Gecko's observation was understood by movie audiences in the 1980s to reflect actual prac-tice, although practice that was still shocking to acknowledge openly as he did.

The Great Communicator was never as blunt as Gordon Gecko, but Reagan speeches are full of applause for untrammeled capitalism and the profit motive that serves as its driving force. In his first inaugural address on January 20 1981, Reagan told the nation: "Government is not a solution to our problem, government is the problem." Thus began a grand experiment: release the American economy from the "shackles" of government regulation. Individual enterprise and initiative, the free market and unrestricted competition were expected to usher in a new era of personal liberty and unrivaled prosperity. The result, according to Reagan's critics, was an extraordinary giveaway of public wealth to the rich in the form of tax breaks, sweetheart contracts, and governmental subsidies. The poor and the middle class paid the price, directly through tax dollars and indirectly through the unprecedented public debt that the administration ran up over the course of eight years in office. Ronald Reagan added $1.86 trillion to the national debt, a 186 percent increase from the $998 billion debt at the end of Carter's last budget.[52]

These policies were even more pronounced during the presidency of George W. Bush. On the one hand, his favor for the wealthy was perhaps

clearest in the undeniably regressive 2001 tax cut and the 2005 bankruptcy bill, written by the credit card companies themselves. Publicly
committed to a balanced budget, Bush added $1.55 trillion, a 54 percent
increase from the $2.8 trillion debt at the end of Reagan's last budget,
Fiscal Year 1989.[53] His apathy toward the less well-off was nowhere
clearer than in the Administration's lethargic and half-hearted response
to Hurricanes Katrina and Rita.

The Reagan revolution was justified with reference to shaky economic
theories. Supply-side economics and the so-called Laffer Curve, both
of which were dismissed out of hand by serious economists. They were
mobilized to justify lower taxes on high incomes and corporate profits on
the grounds that this was in the interests of the poor and unemployed.
The "trickle-down" benefits of more disposable income for the rich would
create jobs and more wealth for everyone else. "Reaganomics" might be
considered a masterful display of economic hypocrisy. We suspect that
it was well received by so many people only because of an underlying
shift in values. Many voters reacted positively to Reagan's redefinition of
government as an institution whose purpose was to abet striving for the
dollar, protect accumulated wealth from any form of confiscation, and
especially any form of redistribution to help the less fortunate.

The change in discourse was equally evident in the academic community where the discipline of economics became increasingly powerful. Its
central premise of *homo economicus* – the entirely self-interested rational
actor – enabled parsimonious theories that their advocates claimed had
predictive values. Their approach was adopted by other social sciences
hoping to gain similar status by putting themselves on a more "scientific"
footing. They also took from economics the definition of rationality as
complete and transitive preferences and behavior designed to maximize
these preferences in an efficient way. Political scientists substituted power
for wealth. These imaginary accounts of how people behaved quickly
morphed into normative arguments about how they should act. In effect,
an academic discourse developed to justify a highly questionable and
unrealistic approach to economics and political science generated an
ideology that justified self-serving policies of corporate managers and the
upper middle class. Efficiency replaced social justice as the benchmark
of policy, consolidating and legitimating the shift in values that had been
under way throughout the postwar era.

Donald Trump and his administration, I suggested in the introduction,
have taken norm violation to a new level. Trump groped women, encouraged
violence against peaceful protestors, insulted other candidates, sitting
officials, and the former president, refused to release his taxes, mixed
high office and business, and perhaps had questionable, if not illegal,

contact with Russians. As I write, the president is said to be considering pardoning himself if he is convicted of any crime.[54]

Notes

1 Character in the 1987 film, *Wall Street*.
2 John Winthrop, "A Model of Christian Charity," Collection of Massachusetts Historical Society, http://history.hanover.edu/texts/winthmod.html (accessed February 22 2017).
3 Address of President-Elect John F. Kennedy Delivered to a Joint Convention of the General Court of the Commonwealth of Massachusetts, January 9 1961, https://en.wikipedia.org/wiki/City_upon_a_Hill (accessed February 22 2017); Ronald Reagan, "Election Eve Address: 'A Vision for America,'" November 3 1980, The American Presidency Project, www.presidency.ucsb.edu/ws/?pid=85199 (accessed February 22 2017).
4 For example, Streeck, *How Will Capitalism End?*; Foster and Magdoff, *Great Financial Crisis*; Akerloff and Shiller, *Phishing for Phools*.
5 Julian Borger, "Trump blames constitution for chaos of first hundred days," *Guardian*, April 30, www.theguardian.com/us-news/2017/apr/29/trump-blames-constitution-for-first-100-days-chaos-presidency#img-1 (accessed May 1 2017).
6 Uslaner, *Decline of Comity in Congress*, and "Comity in Context."
7 Webster and Abramovitz, "Ideological Foundations of Affective Polarization in the U.S. Electorate."
8 Hunter, *Culture Wars*; Hartman, *War for the Soul of America*; Chapman, *Culture Wars*; D'Antonio, Tuch, and Baker, *Religion, Politics, and Polarization*; MacLean, *Democracy in Chains*.
9 Fiorina, *Culture War*, for the argument that it is a myth.
10 Michael D. Shear and Julie Hirschfield Davis, "Trump Moves to End DACA and Calls on Congress to Act," *New York Times*, September 5 2017, www.nytimes.com/2017/09/05/us/politics/trump-daca-dreamers-immigration (accessed September 5 2017).
11 Jeremy W. Peters, Jo Becker, and Julie Hirschfeld Davis, "Trump Rescinds Rules on Bathrooms for Transgender Students," *New York Times*, February 22 2017, www.nytimes.com/2017/02/22/us/politics/devos-sessions-transgender-students-rights.html?_r=0 (accessed February 23 2017); Liam Stack, "Transgender Students Turn to Courts as Government Support Erodes," *New York Times*, July 14 2017, www.nytimes.com/2017/07/14/us/transgender-students-trump.html (accessed July 15 2017).
12 Paul Krugman, "Goodbye Spin, Hello Raw Dishonesty," *New York Times*, March 3 2017, www.nytimes.com/2017/03/03/opinion/goodbye-spin-hello-raw-dishonesty.html?action=click&pgtype=Homepage&clickSource=story-heading&module=opinion-c-col-right-region&region=opinion-c-col-right-region&WT.nav=opinion-c-col-right-region&_r=0 (accessed March 3 2017).
13 Cecelia Kang, "F.C.C. Plans Net Neutrality Repeal in a Victory for Telecoms," *New York Times*, November 21 2017, www.nytimes.com/2017/11/21/technology (accessed November 26 2017).

14 Nick Miroff, "Protests sweeping South America show rising anti-government anger," *Telegraph*, April 15 2017, www.washingtonpost.com/world/the_ americas/protests (accessed May 6 2017); Reuters, "Hugo Chávez statue torn down as death toll rises in Venezuela protests," *Guardian*, May 6 2017, www.theguardian.com/world/2017/may/06/hugo-chavez-statue-torn-down-as-death-toll-rises-in-venezuela-protests (accessed May 6 2017).

15 Tocqueville, *Democracy in America*, II.2.5, p. 489; Lebow, *Self-Interest from Tocqueville to Trump*, ch. 2.

16 Tocqueville, *Democracy in America*, II.4.6, p. 663.

17 Ibid., II.4.6., p. 662.

18 Wolin, *Tocqueville Between Two Worlds*, p. 569.

19 This analysis and coding was conducted by Dartmouth student, at the time, Dylan Matthews.

20 Nikita Vladimirov, "Trump inaugural TV ratings lower than Obama, Reagan: Report," *The Hill*, January 21, http://thehill.com/blogs/blog-briefing-room/news/315507-trump-inaugural-ratings-are-lower-than-obamas-and-reagans (accessed April 4 2017).

21 Matt Ford, "Trump Press Secretary Falsely Claims: 'Largest Audience Ever to Witness and Inauguration, Period," *Atlantic*, January 21 2017, www.theatlantic.com/politics/archive/2017/01/inauguration-crowd-size/514058/ (accessed April 4 2017).

22 *The American Presidency Project*, Santa Barbara: University of California – Santa Barbara, 1790–2008, www.presidency.ucsb.edu/

23 Joel Levine, Aaron Klein and James Mathews, "Data Without Variables." *Journal of Mathematical Sociology*, 23, no. 3 (2001), pp. 225–73.

24 To generate the field, one adds the squares of changes in the X and Y positions of the two points (the speech and the word), multiplies by 1.5, and then takes the square root to determine the degree of association.

25 This procedure was carried out by Dylan Matthews and Jennifer Ross.

26 Ronald Reagan, "Address Before a Joint Session of the Congress on the State of the Union," January 25 1984, www.presidency.ucsb.edu/ws/index.php?pid=40205; "Address Before a Joint Session of the Congress on the State of the Union," January 27 1987. www.presidency.ucsb.edu/ws/index.php?pid=34430 (accessed January 12 2017)

27 George H. W. Bush, "Address on Administration Goals Before a Joint Session of the Congress," The American Presidency Project. Santa Barbara, CA: University of California, Santa Barbara, 1989. www.presidency.ucsb.edu/ws/index.php?pid=16660 (accessed April 10 2017).

28 Bill Clinton, "Address Before a Joint Session of the Congress on the State of the Union." The American Presidency Project. Santa Barbara, CA: University of California, Santa Barbara, 1999, www.presidency.ucsb.edu/ws/index.php?pid=57577 (accessed April 12 2007).

29 Barack Obama, Inaugural Address, January 4 2009, The American Presidency Project, State of the Union Addresses and Messages, www.presidency.ucsb.edu/sou.php (accessed April 14 2017).

30 Ibid.

31 Ibid., Donald Trump, Inaugural Address, January 20 2009, The American Presidency Project, State of the Union Addresses and Messages, www.presidency.ucsb.edu/sou.php (accessed April 14 2017).

32 Ibid.
33 Ibid.
34 Ibid.
35 Appendix A for the list of songs.
36 The coding and initial was conducted by Kyle Uberhaupt and Eric Shuster.
37 David Brooks, "What Romantic Regime Are You In?" *New York Times*, March 8 2017, www.nytimes.com/2017/03/07/opinion/what-romantic-regime-are-you-in.html?action=click&pgtype=Homepage&clickSource=story-heading&module=opinion-c-col-right-region&region=opinion-c-col-right-region&WT.nav=opinion-c-col-right-region&_r=0 (accessed March 8 2017).
38 Nisbet, *Quest for Community*, preface.
39 Altschuler, *All Shook Up*, chs. 2–5.
40 "List of *Billboard* 100 chart achievement by decade," *Wikipedia*, April 10 2017, https://en.wikipedia.org/wiki/List_of_Billboard_Hot_100_chart_achievements_by_decade#Songs_by_total_weeks_at_number_one (accessed April 18 2017).
41 Wikipedia, "Rihanna," April 13 2017, https://en.wikipedia.org/wiki/Rihanna (accessed April 16 2017).
42 Jake Conway, "Review: S&M," "*Q Magazine at Yale*, April 21 2011; Chris Ryan, "Song You Need To Know: Rihanna, 'S&M,'" *MTV*, November 8 2010; Sal Cinquemani, "Rihanna: Loud | Music Review," *Slant*, November 12 2010; Thomas Conner, "'Loud' a well-deserved party for Rihanna," *Chicago Sun-Times* (Chicago), November 19 2010; Leah Greenblatt, "Loud," *Entertainment Weekly*, November 10 2010, http://theweek.com/articles/489027/rihanna-loud (accessed April 19 2017).
43 Kevin O'Donnell, "Preview: Rihanna Discusses 'Bad Ass' New Album," *Spin*, October 19 2010, www.spin.com/2010/10/preview-rihanna-discusses-bad-ass-new-album/ (accessed April 17 2017).
44 Tracy McVeigh and Edward Helmore, "Feminists fall out over 'violent, misogynistic' Rihanna video," *Guardian*, July 24 2015, www.theguardian.com/music (accessed April 16 2017).
45 Lebow, *Forbidden Fruit*, ch. 1.
46 Informal interviews with thirty students at King's College London (October 2016) and Dartmouth College, Hanover, NH (June 2016).
47 Salisbury, *All Shook Up Generation*, p. 136; Frith, *Sound Effects*; Altschuler, *All Shook Up*, ch. 4.
48 Gerald Clarke, "New Lyrics for the Devil's Music," *Time*, March 11 1985, p. 60; Romanowski, "Evangelicals and Popular Music."
49 Lebow, *Self-Interest from Tocqueville to Trump*, chs. 5–6 for sitcoms and comics.
50 Cited in Walter Mears, Associated Press, "How Nixon Will Handle America's Problems," *University of Michigan Daily*, November 13 1968, p. 3.
51 Watergate.Info, "Nixon's First Watergate Speech," April 30 1973, www.watergate.info/nixon/73-04-30watergate-speech.shtml (accessed April 22 2017).

52 Kimberly Amadeo, "U.S. Debt by President: Dollar and Percent," *The Balance*, February 21 2007, www.thebalance.com/us-debt-by-president-by-dollar-and-percent-3306296 (accessed April 7 2017).
53 Ibid.
54 Peter Baker, "Trump Says He Has 'Complete Power' to Pardon," *New York Times*, July 22 2017, www.nytimes.com/2017/07/22/us/politics/donald-trump-jeff-sessions.html?hp&action=click&pgtype=Homepage&clickSource=story-heading&module=first-column-region&region=top-news&WT.nav=top-news&_r=0 (accessed July 22 2017).

6   The United States: Fairness vs. Equality

In this chapter I explore the second value shift: from fairness to equality. As noted in Chapter 3, each principle of justice has two generic formulations. Fairness can mean giving the most to those who contribute the most, or to those who need it the most. Equality can mean equal distribution of rewards, or equal opportunity to compete for them. I contend that there has been a general shift in the western world from a preference for fairness to that of equality and an extension of the domains into which it is thought to apply. These changes have been accompanied by novel understandings of both principles. There is no consensus about the relative importance of these principles, their respective formulations, or the domains to which they apply. These differences are major sources of political controversy.

Fairness as a principle of distribution remains deeply entrenched, and I will explore this further in the next section of this chapter. The second understanding of fairness – giving more to those who need it – has grown in importance. It finds expression in such things as welfare and job training, handicap seating and parking, special education, senior discounts, and foreign aid. Not surprisingly, many, if not all, of these policies and programs are highly controversial. They represent an extension of the principle of fairness, and one at odds, and generally in competition with, the more traditional understanding. For both reasons they arouse opposition. This helps to explain why those who are against welfare are also likely to oppose racial preferences in university admissions and foreign aid.

Equality in the distribution of rewards is a time-honored practice. It finds its widest acceptance in small groups, especially families, where sharing is often a general rule. Experiments indicate that people are more likely to make distributions on the basis of equality when doing it for groups to which they belong, and to individuals as opposed to populations.[1] Equality loses traction as we move up the level of social aggregation and to people unknown to us personally. We feel the least sympathy and responsibility for people of other cultures and nations, and this may be one of the reasons why the principle of equality is a latecomer to international relations.[2]

Within the United States, the principle of equality has been widely extended in the postwar era. Legal and social restrictions against Catholics, Jews, African-Americans, women, and homosexuals have largely disappeared, although prejudice remains. Equality has been applied in other ways. Earlier in the century, it was the moral force behind constitutional amendments mandating direct election of senators and voting rights for women. In more recent decades it has promoted, among other measures, a lowered voting age, state laws or court decisions that make the drinking age the same for men and women, mandate the same level of expenditure per capita student in schools in rich and poor communities, and try to provide equal access to legal counsel for the poor through public defender programs.

Not all of these efforts have been successful in leveling the playing field, but all of them are controversial. They violate traditional norms and practices, often involve public expenditure, and are at odds with the first understanding of the principle of fairness. Public expenditure to help others has long been a rallying point for conservative groups and their justification for limiting government in the name of "liberty."[3] Some efforts at establishing equality have been more fiercely resisted than others; school integration is perhaps the most prominent example. Others have met sufficient opposition to have been watered down or revoked, as happened to racial preferences in university admissions, and the 1965 Voting Rights Act that attempted to secure full voting rights for minorities. Congress had voted on five occasions to extend the provisions of the Act, but a conservative Supreme Court voided it by a 5–4 majority in 2013 on the grounds that it was no longer necessary.

Fairness and equality are rooted in different philosophical traditions. Fairness was invoked by ancient Greek and Roman aristocrats to justify hierarchy and was adopted by Christianity. In the Middle Ages, Neo-Platonists theorized the *scala naturae,* or "Great Chain of Being," a hierarchy with God at the apex that progressed downward through angels, demons, stars, the moon, kings, princes, nobles, commoners, wild beasts, domesticated animals, trees, other plants, precious stones, precious metals, to other minerals. Like fractals, the same order was replicated within countries and families, where the king, prince, husband or father had near-absolute authority over other members of his "family."[4] Many religious Americans adhere to this view of the world, or some variant, as God-given. They accept hierarchies as natural, and extend them to economic and civic life and to foreign affairs. Their common belief in fairness and hierarchies helps to explain why the Republican Party and

Donald Trump are supported by otherwise strange bedfellows, i.e. white evangelical Christians; non-church attending, less educated white men, affluent, college-educated free-marketeers.

Equality has roots in the Greek concept of *isonomia*. In the ancient world, it was associated with democracy, a political system sharply opposed to aristocratic oligarchy and tyranny. In the modern era, it was one of the watchwords of the French Revolution, which asserted the equality of all "men." It finds political expression in socialism but also in many liberal understandings of capitalism.[5] Both forms of economic organization value individual and achieved over ascribed status. They differ in the form of equality they advocate: socialism mandates equal distribution of rewards, and liberalism equal opportunity to compete for them.

The previous chapter tracked the shift in the conceptualization of self-interest in the postwar era. The shift from fairness to equality has been a longer process, recognizable at least since the Renaissance but more pronounced since the late eighteenth century. It is also an uneven shift, as different principles and formulations of them appeal to different people. For both these reasons, I eschew historical tracing of narratives in favor of the analysis of contemporary discourses representing different takes on these principles of justice. Toward this end I compare the campaign speeches of Hillary Clinton and Donald Trump in the 2016 presidential election and two popular sitcoms of the last decade. The sitcoms – *Duck Dynasty* and *Modern Family* – appealed to two very different demographics: the former to rural, southern and mid-Western Trump voters, and the latter to urban, coastal, Clinton voters. I also review the experimental literature on fairness and equality to understand where Americans think they apply and how they make trade-offs between them. I report on an experiment of my own, conducted with Roger Giner-Sorolla and Laura Niemmi.

Campaign Speeches

Belief in hierarchy is more common among conservatives and religious Americans, and support for equality among their liberal and secular counterparts.[6] There is nevertheless some crossover as some religious groups like the Friends eschew hierarchy, and very secular groups like communists embrace it. Hierarchy is more appealing to political conservatives than to liberals. Conservatives from Edmund Burke to the *National Review* describe it as natural and beneficial, and decry its absence as a threat to political and social order. I posit that political orientations are in part determined by beliefs about the relative importance of these two principles of justice and the kinds of hierarchies they generate and justify. Political orientations also reinforce these beliefs.

For conservatives, the important kind of hierarchy is based on the understanding of fairness that rewards those who contribute the most to the common good of the unit. For traditional conservatives, this meant government by the propertied elite. Their view of order was represented in the constitution by the creation of a bicameral legislature, with the upper house composed of men of property and political experience elected by state legislatures, a president elected by an electoral college, and federal judiciary appointed by the president and approved by the Senate.[7] Only the House of Representatives reflected the principle of equality and the Framers accordingly expected it to be populist in politics and in need of constraint by the propertied elite that would comprise the Senate.

For many contemporary Republicans, hierarchy has different connotations. It is traditional, but only in the sense that it has existed for much of the twentieth century. It privileged white Protestant men, providing them more economic opportunity, status, and access to political and military office. People of color and women were "kept in their place" and all but denied access to the business elite, professions, political office, or any other position of status. Many Republican voters regard such a hierarchy as more legitimate than what has replaced it; they felt more comfortable in such a world, had better prospects, and higher status. Since the 1990s, the Party and its voters have increasingly become the Party of so-called "family values," which is a widely understood signifier for a return to a world dominated by white Protestant men.[8] Many Republicans also see minorities and immigrants as hostile to them, their values, and their vision of America. A 2014 Pew survey indicates that 35 percent of Republicans identify ethnic and religious hatred – with themselves the targets – as the greatest threat America confronts.[9]

A 2017 study indicates that five distinct demographics account for Trump's majority in the 2016 election.[10] First comes staunch *Fiscal Conservatives* (31 percent) who also embrace traditional morality. They want taxes slashed for the wealthy, business regulations repealed, and oppose government-provided healthcare. They take conventional conservative positions on the environment and cultural issues like same-sex marriage, and oppose Muslim immigration. Staunch Conservatives tend to be slightly older, more male than female, and upper middle class, but with only moderate levels of education. They are the most likely group to own guns and belong to the National Rifle Association. They are the most politically interested and aware segment of Trump voters and more likely than others to have correct knowledge of relevant political facts.

Second are *Free Marketeers* (25 percent). They favor small government, balanced budgets, free trade, and hold moderate to liberal positions on immigration and race. They are most likely to come from the West, be politically well-informed, male, middle-aged, and are the most educated and highly paid group of voters. They are more liberal than other Trump voters on social issues, having positive feelings toward immigrants and not by any means unanimous in their support of Trump's efforts to ban Muslim travel to the United States. They voted primarily against Clinton rather than for Trump. They were and remain skeptical of Trump.[11]

American Preservationists (20 percent) make up the third demographic. They believe the economic and political systems are rigged, oppose immigration, and think of Americans as white and Christian – like themselves. They have minimal formal education, the lowest incomes of the Trump voters, are most likely to be on Medicaid, have a permanent disability that prevents them from working, and to smoke cigarettes. They believe that anti-white discrimination is as pervasive as other forms of discrimination, and do not on the whole regard minorities favorably. Despite being the most likely group to say that religion is "very important" to them, they are the least likely to attend church regularly. They watch more television than other Trump voters and are also the least well-informed. Almost half of preservationists had positive views of Hillary Clinton in 2012, but not in 2016. They helped to propel Trump to victory in the early Republican primaries.[12]

American preservationists are closer to Democrats on domestic economic issues. They bear an animus toward Wall Street, feel powerless against moneyed interests and the politically connected, and tend to distrust other people. They nevertheless agree with liberals about the environment, believing that global warming is a serious threat and human activity is primarily to blame.[13]

Anti-Elites (19 percent) are the fourth demographic. They are middle-class, with moderate levels of education, and slightly younger than other Trump supporters. They are the least likely group to own guns, attend church, or be politically informed. They tend to favor government intervention in the economy, but also believe that the economic and political systems are rigged. They take more moderate positions on immigration, race, and American identity than American Preservationists. They are the most likely group of Trump voters to favor political compromise. Anti-Elites have relatively cooler feelings toward Donald Trump than American Preservationists; nearly half had a favorable opinion of Clinton in 2012. They moved away from Clinton *en masse* in November 2016. They were the least likely group to vote in the Republican primary, but of those who did they disproportionately favored moderate John Kasich.[14]

The Disengaged (5 percent) constitute our final category. They are younger, more female, and less religiously affiliated than other Trump voters. They know little about politics, feel detached from institutions and elites, and are very skeptical of immigration. They do not identify strongly as Republicans and do not reveal many strong preferences on surveys. They voted for Trump primarily because they are concerned about immigration and support a ban on Muslim travel and immigration.[15]

If only economic interests dictated votes, the last three demographics would not be part of Trump's electoral coalition. They were brought together by social issues, dislike of immigration – excluding Free Marketeers – and, above all, by their intense dislike of Clinton; at least 90 percent of each demographic has an unfavorable opinion of her. It is apparent that none of the demographics are drawn to the principle of equality. At best, it gets tepid support from Free Marketeers, who reveal little to no animus toward non-whites and non-Christians. Fairness is central to all demographics, although defined differently by them. Fiscal conservatives and Free Marketeers believe in the traditional definition of fairness – those who contribute the most should receive the most – and anchor their political demands in it. American preservationists also emphasize the principle of fairness, but define the most deserving as "Americans," by which they mean white Christians born in the country. Anti-elites and the Disengaged give no evidence of being particularly involved with either principle of justice.

Although there are important differences between Clinton and Trump voters, there are more significant differences between them. Trump won white voters with the same margin as Mitt Romney. Non-whites and Hispanics went for Clinton, but not as many turned out as four years earlier. Women supported Clinton over Trump by 52 to 42 percent. There was an equally wide gap between voters with college degrees and those without. College graduates backed Clinton by a 9-point margin; the widest gap revealed in exit polls since 1980. Young people preferred Clinton over Trump by an 18 percent margin. Voters 65 and older went for Trump by an 8 percent margin. However, Clinton received a lower share of the vote among 18–29-year-old voters than Obama did in 2012 or 2008.[16]

Wealthier, more urban, younger voters, women, ethnic and sexual minorities, and immigrants – the groups from whom Clinton drew her support – are the Americans most drawn to and supportive of the principle of equality. Women, minorities, and immigrants benefit directly from policies based on equality. The college educated are better off than the rest of the population, but those who vote for the Democrats do so knowing that it is often not to their economic advantage – at least in the short term. They favor government intervention in the economy, some degree of wealth redistribution, and are willing to pay higher taxes for ideological reasons. Some may also act on the basis of self-interest well understood, reasoning that a more equal America will ultimately be a more cohesive and prosperous America.

My analysis of 2016 presidential campaign speeches offers support for my hypothesis that Republican and Democratic voters respond to different appeals, and that these appeals rest on, or are justified by appeals to, different principles of justice. Similar to the word counts of Obama and Trump inaugurals and State of the Union addresses, the table below provides word counts from Trump and Clinton campaign speeches. I used a sample of these campaign speeches, but made sure to include their opening speeches declaring their candidacy and their initial speeches after the election results were announced. I sampled fifteen speeches of each candidate, choosing longer rather than shorter speeches, and spreading them out across the length of the campaign. More than half are between their respective nomination and the election. A careful reading of the speeches does not indicate any significant shift in emphasis from beginning to end.

As with the Obama and Trump data, I removed words that were neutral or not germane to the political messages of the speeches. I also combined words that conveyed the same or very similar meanings. For example, "fair," "fairly," and "fairness" were grouped under "fairness," and "women," "women's," "ladies," under "women," and "child" and "children" under "children."[17] Figure 6.1 includes all the words, or combined word counts, that appear at least 160 times in each candidate's speeches.

Clinton gave marginally longer addresses than Trump did, making her word counts slightly higher; eight of her words have totals over 100, whereas Trump has only five. Trump speeches are more repetitive, making his use of "greatest" the most frequently used word of either candidate. There are some differences that are striking, but not germane to my analysis of fairness and equality. Trump's third most common substantive word is "she," which is always a reference to his opponent. Clinton, by contrast, referred only infrequently to Trump, and almost always by name. Direct comparisons of words can be misleading as the candidates often use them in different ways or give them a different valence. This is true of such frequently used words as "children," "immigrants," "refugees," "others," "benefits," and "fair." This is more proof, if it was needed, as to why qualitative analysis must complement its quantitative counterpart; the former can put words in context where they take on their meanings.

Clinton makes frequent direct and indirect appeals to the principle of equality. She also seeks out and attracts audiences who respond favorably

CLINTON		TRUMP	
WOMEN	268	GREATEST	311
JUSTICE	257	JUSTICE	252
FAMILY	246	SHE (i.e. Hillary)	202
RIGHTS	209	NEED	100
NEED	182	CHILDREN	80
CHILDREN	140	IMMIGRANTS	71
GREATEST	138	COMMUNITIES	65
EVERYONE	134	FAMILY	62
COMMUNITIES	84	EVERYONE	60
HOPE	62	REFUGEES	40
OPPORTUNITY	54	ORDER	33
RESPECT	50	POVERTY	33
SHARE	38	PROUD	33
PROUD	32	CHOICE	32
FAIR	30	RESPECT	30
BLACK	25	HONOR	27
FREE	25	GROWTH	26
STANDING	25	RICH	25
CHOICE	22	WOMEN	25
FEAR	21	SHARE	22
FAR	20	DEFEND	21
LATINO	20	FAIR	21
POVERTY	20	WEALTH	21
IMMIGRANTS	19	FREE	20
BENEFITS	18	TOUGH	19
EQUAL	18	TRUTH	19
FREEDOM	18	FAR	18
GRANDCHILDREN	17	SANCTUARY	18
PRIVILEGE	17	SOCIETY	17
SOCIAL	17	HISPANIC	16

Figure 6.1 Campaign Speech Word Frequency

to this leitmotif. "Women" is her most frequently used word on the edited list, followed by "justice," "family," "rights," "need," and "children." "Everyone," "communities," "hope," and "opportunity," also rank high. She uses "justice" to refer to equality and equal opportunity – both formulations of the principle of equality – and words like "poverty" and "privilege" to refer to the consequences of inequality.

Trump speaks the language of fairness. His frequent invocation of "great" and "greatest" – combined on the word list – is followed by "justice," with the latter used in the sense of fairness defined as rewards going to those who deserve them the most. He is astute enough not to spell out in any detail who is the most deserving in the United States,

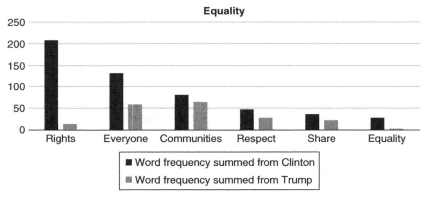

Figure 6.2 Frequency of Equality Related Words

but, as I describe in the qualitative analysis that follows, he implies that this is the white working class. He leaves no doubt about this in the case of international relations, where it is the United States. His largely negative references to immigrants, and refugees, can be read as coded ways of suggesting this, and so too his positive references to "proud," "respect," "honor," "defend," "free," and "tough." Unlike his opponent, "order" ranks high on his list, and it is framed in terms of hierarchy.

Both candidates use "respect" with some frequency – 50 for Clinton and 30 for Trump. Their different uses of the word is revealing. For Clinton, it most often refers to the respect owed to women, African-Americans, other minorities, immigrants, and those with different sexual or gender preferences. For Trump, it is the white working and middle class, and the United States.

The bar graphs in Figures 6.2 and 6.3 group words around the concepts of equality and fairness. The words listed were selected by the procedure I previously described. There is admittedly an element of subjectivity in the selection of relevant nouns, verbs, and adjectives. Some words are clearly associated with fairness or equality, and some less obviously so. My selection went hand in hand with my qualitative analysis. I dropped or added words as they appeared germane to my reading of the candidates' speeches.

The dark grey represents Clinton and the light grey Trump. Clinton scores higher than Trump in every word that can reasonably be interpreted to suggest equality. The chart is more revealing than suggested at first glance because all of these words have multiple meanings. In the case of "rights" – the word on the graph with the biggest gap between the candidates – it is used in different ways by them. For Clinton, it is the

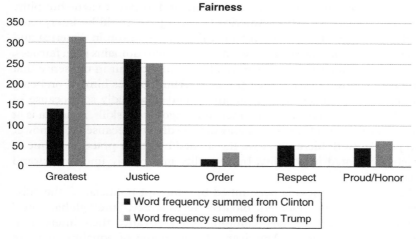

Figure 6.3 Frequency of Fairness Related Words

rights of women, African-Americans, ethnic minorities, immigrants, the poor. For Trump, respect is primarily due to the white working and middle class and the United States. This difference is also notable, as noted, with the word "respect." It applies equally to "share," which Trump uses to berate America's allies for not assuming their share of the defense burden. Trump uses the word equality only once (see Figure 6.2).

When we turn to fairness, Trump receives the higher score. The biggest difference is in their use of the word "greatest." For Trump, "great" and greatest" – coded as one word – almost always applies to America. It is the greatest nation in the world and should be recognized by others as such. American leaders should recognize their power and not buckle in to the demands or free-riding of others. By making America great, Trump also refers to restoring manufacturing, and keeping out undesirable aliens, and thus creating more jobs for the white working class. "Proud" and "honor" are almost equally used by the candidates, but differently. Trump uses these words to emphasize the greatness of America and, implicitly, to appeal to and build the self-esteem of his overwhelmingly white working- and middle-class audiences. For Clinton, they most often have to do with groups who have been stigmatized, and who deserve equality, not only of treatment, but also of respect (see Figure 6.3).

The qualitative analysis allows me to expand the scope of my inquiry. If Clinton praised stigmatized groups, Trump found a receptive audience by belittling women and the handicapped, opposing immigrants, and making attacks on the political establishment. His rather vague but pithy campaign slogan to "Make America Great Again" could be interpreted by them to recreate a world in which they were on top in America and America on top in the world. The emphasis in both domains is on fairness, not equality. Hierarchies are natural, but should be fair in the sense that the people on top deserve their position. Trump prides himself on being toward the top of the wealth hierarchy, and deservedly so, because of his self-proclaimed business acumen and negotiating skills. America is at the top of the world hierarchy, and deservedly so, because of its power and people. Both hierarchies are threatened by unfair practices, some of which are rooted in equality, but equality improperly understood and misapplied.

At home, unfairness is personified by "corrupt politicians," the "dishonest media," the "bloated, bloated bureaucracy," the "global elite," "Obamacare," and "Hillary Clinton." They advance their interests at the expense of ordinary Americans. In the name of equality, they are responsible for freeing criminals, opening the country's borders, and wasting your taxes. Immigrants draw Trump's special ire. They are "Trojan Horses" who hate America and its values or illegal immigrants who steal jobs from Americans, live off welfare, and commit crimes. In Phoenix, Arizona, in August 2016 he told a cheering crowd: "While there are many illegal immigrants in our country who are good people, many, many, this doesn't change the fact that most illegal immigrants are lower skilled workers with less education, who compete directly against vulnerable American workers, and that these illegal workers draw much more out from the system than they can ever possibly pay back."[18]

President Obama and Hillary Clinton are responsible for out-of-control immigration and other problems. "Countless Americans who have died in recent years would be alive today if not for the open border policies of this administration and the administration that causes this horrible, horrible thought process, called Hillary Clinton."[19] "How stupid are our leaders? How stupid are these politicians to allow this to happen? How stupid are they?"[20] Trump promises to clean house, stop unfair practices, "double our [economic growth] and have the strongest economy in the world." "Every single American will have the opportunity to realize his or her fullest potential. The forgotten men and women of our country will be forgotten no longer."[21] Proper hierarchy will be restored.

Trump makes the same claims about foreign policy. He will stop foreign currency manipulation, the dumping of cheap foreign goods in American markets, multilateral trade agreements that work to America's disadvantage, make allies pay their fair share of defense costs, and reassert American power. He promises "to deal fairly with everyone" but "to put

America's interests first." Fairness at home and abroad come together in two "simple" rules: "Buy American and hire American."[22] Fairness will replace equality as the governing principle of his administration to the advantage of America and all of its citizens. Trump opined: "We're like the big bully that keeps getting beat up. You ever see that? The big bully that keeps getting beat up."[23] Being a bully seems fine. But there is something inherently unfair about being the biggest and meanest dude around and being stepped on by others.

Democrats are more likely to invoke equality than fairness. Not surprisingly, Democrats and Republicans see some different things as core to the nation's identity. Judicial fairness, liberty, and freedom granted by the Constitution, the ability to achieve the American dream, and the country's government are seen as key to American identity in high numbers, regardless of party identification. But Democrats are more likely than Republicans to consider the nation's diversity and the ability of people to immigrate to the United States as important, while Republicans are more inclined to cite the importance of the use of English and sharing a culture, preferably based on Christian beliefs and European customs.[24]

Both Barack Obama inaugurals have a striking emphasis on equality – in education, employment, voting – for all Americans regardless of their ethnicity, gender, religion, or sexual preference. He is the first president to specifically identify "nonbelievers" among the diverse groups deserving equal treatment and respect. Obama justifies his demand for equality as the right of all Americans, but also appeals to the self-interest of those who do not face discrimination.[25] His 2009 Inaugural Address repeats the liberal mantra that, "The success of our economy has always depended not just on the size of our gross domestic product, but on the reach of our prosperity; on the ability to extend opportunity to every willing heart – not out of charity, but because it is the surest route to our common good."[26]

Hillary Clinton and the Democrats associated themselves with the principle of equality. In her campaign kick-off speech on Roosevelt Island in New York City, Clinton paid homage to Roosevelt, her husband, and Obama, and then made an explicit pitch for the support of African-Americans, Hispanics, women, and LGBTs.[27] The Clinton campaign emphasized wider access to healthcare and education, pursuit of justice for African-Americans, Latinos and Latinas, equal rights for the LGBT community, the accomplishments of women and minorities of all kinds. She spoke out against hate crimes and in favor of tolerance and respect for all. She equated fairness with equality, telling a Michigan voter: "I think that Americans are fair-minded, and we'll move forward on an agenda of equality."[28]

Clinton surrounded herself with liberal personalities from the entertainment world, many of them of minority background, and was closely associated with Wall Street and the political establishment. She spoke to audiences like the Human Rights Campaign, the Children's Defense Fund, and at venues like African-American picnics and *Saturday Night Live* that responded positively to her vision of a multi-ethnic, individualistic, outward-looking America in a globalizing world. In Selma, Alabama, she told her audience that she envisaged her mission as carrying forward the great American dream and mission of equality: "We've got to stay awake. We've got to stay awake, because we have a march to finish, a march toward one America, that should be all America was meant to be. That too many people before us have given of themselves time and again, to make real. How can we rest while poverty and inequality continue to rise? How can we sleep, while 46 million of our fellow Americans do not have health insurance?"[29] She made a similar pitch to the Veterans of Foreign Wars: "And we will continue our history in an unbroken line from those first soldiers who fought for our revolutionary ideal that all men are created equal to those young men and women who are fighting for us and our ideals right now."[30]

Clinton sought to build a winning coalition of African-Americans, Hispanics, other minorities, college-educated whites, women, and liberals.[31] She appealed to very different demographics than did Trump. Not surprisingly, the Pew Research Center found that Americans who expressed a preference for Clinton identified the gap between the rich and the poor as the greatest danger the country faces.[32] If Trump subordinated equality in terms of fairness, Clinton did the reverse. Campaigning in New Hampshire during its primary, she announced: "We also have to restore fairness to our economy. We have more inequality than we've had since the Great Depression. The rich are going so much richer, the middle class is running in place, and people are falling back into poverty.[33]

Sitcoms

I turn again to popular culture narratives to evaluate further my claims about equality and fairness. I focus on sitcoms, in contrast to songs, as they have greater content, are more continuous, and are more readily identified with particular demographics to which they appeal. I do not track any shift in the relative appeal of these principles of justice over the course of seven decades. Rather, I want to see how fairness and equality are currently represented, and the extent to which different formulations of them appeal to different demographics.

I accordingly adopt a horizontal versus vertical research strategy and examine narratives that have been popular in the last decade and known

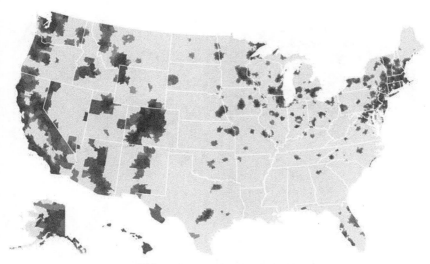

Light to dark signifies less to more popular

Figure 6.4 Television Programs Most Common in Urban Areas

to appeal to people of different political persuasions. A December 2016 *New York Times* study of television shows and their audiences reveals a sharp cultural divide along urban–rural lines. It is the same divide reflected in the 2016 presidential election; Clinton won in cities, college towns, Native American reservations, and areas with Black and Hispanic majorities. Trump won majorities in rural areas and smaller cities.[34]

New York Times reporters looked at how many active Facebook users there were in different ZIP codes who "liked" certain television programs. They found that the fifty most-liked shows clustered into three groups with distinct geographic distributions. They reveal a national culture divided into three regions: cities and their suburbs; rural areas; and an extended Black Belt. The last is an irregular-shaped swathe that extends from the Mississippi River through the Deep South and up the East coast to Washington, DC, but also includes cities and other places with large non-white populations (see Figure 6.4).

In urban areas, the most popular television programs are *Adventure Time, American Horror Story, Family Guy, Game of Thrones, It's Always Sunny in Philadelphia, Modern Family, MythBusters, Once Upon a Time, Orange Is the New Black, Saturday Night Live, So You Think You Can Dance, South Park, The Big Bang Theory, The Daily Show, The Simpsons, The Tonight Show,* and *Tosh.0* (see Figure 6.5).

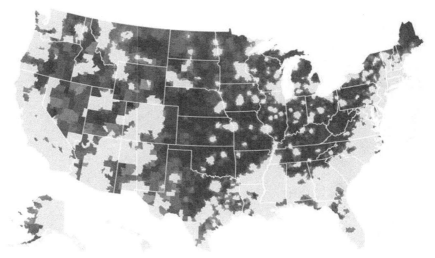

Light to dark signifies less to more popular

Figure 6.5 Television Programs Most Common in Rural Areas

In rural regions and small cities the most popular television programs are *16 and Pregnant*, *American Dad!*, *America's Funniest Home Videos*, *Bones*, *Cake Boss*, *Criminal Minds*, *Dancing With the Stars*, *Deadliest Catch*, *Duck Dynasty*, *Fast n' Loud*, *Grey's Anatomy*, *NCIS*, *Pawn Stars*, *Pretty Little Liars*, *Ridiculousness*, *Rob Dyrdek's Fantasy Factory*, *Supernatural Teen Mom*, *The Vampire Diaries*, *The Voice*, *The Walking Dead*, and *Wipeout*.

In what the *New York Times* describes as the "Black Belt," the most popular television programs are *106 & Park*, *Bad Girls Club*, *Empire*, *Keeping Up With the Kardashians*, *Law & Order: SVU*, *Love & Hip Hop*, *Real Housewives of Atlanta*, *Scandal*, *SpongeBob SquarePants*, *The First 48*, and *The Tom and Jerry Show*. There is really little to no overlap in the three regions (see Figure 6.6).

These geographic differences in appeal reflect the business of television as much as they do the fractured national culture. James Poniewozik, the chief television critic for the *New York Times*, reports that big network shows like *The Beverly Hillbillies* reflected a business model in which audience number was the most important consideration. Today, advertising money is driven less by volume and more by demographics. Networks make more money from sponsors, Poniewozik explains, by appealing to younger, more affluent, urban viewers.[35]

Duck Dynasty is a sitcom on A&E that premiered in March 2012 and quickly became the most popular program in rural America. It is one of

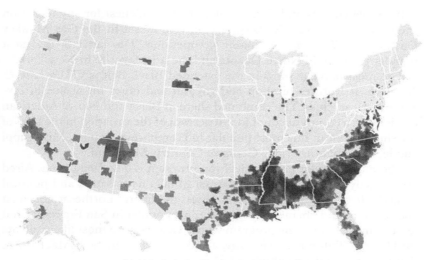

Light to dark signifies less to more popular

Figure 6.6 Television Programs Most Common in the Extended Black Belt

the two programs that I analyze. By late 2013 the show was averaging nine million viewers a week, making it the biggest reality series in cable television.

Duck Dynasty follows the over-the-top lives of the squirrel-eating, bible-thumping Robertson clan of West Monroe, Louisiana. It features men with long beards, homespun antics, and Christian values, disenfranchised by globalization and the information economy, but rewarded for their honest ingenuity. They have become wealthy from producing accessories for duck hunters, beginning with the Duck Commander wooden duck call whistle. The Robertson men are bearded and Christian, self-proclaimed Rednecks, and assert traditional male values in often self-defeating ways. The men are the central characters, but unlike traditional sitcoms from earlier decades it is generally the women who know best. The show broke several ratings records on cable television. The fourth-season premiere in 2016 drew 11.8 million viewers, making it the most-watched cable series in history.

Duck Dynasty is the most geographically divisive show in the *New York Times* data set. It is part of a wave of "redneck reality" shows like *Swamp People*, *Bayou Billionaires*, and *Moonshiners* that portray white, rural America as the last authentic place on earth, untarnished by the secularism, cynicism or the corruption of urban elites. Phil Robertson, the show's central figure, was a vocal supporter of Trump.[36] The correlation between its viewers and Trump voters was the highest for any television show. Next came *Fast N' Loud*, a reality show set in the Gas Monkey Garage, and *The Voice*, a singing competition. The latter is the most popular program in North Dakota and the least favorite in New York.[37]

The most popular show in the extended Black Belt is VH1's *Love & Hip Hop*. It features hip-hop and rhythm and blues musicians in several American cities. The combined share of Black and Native American residents in a county account for 90 percent of the variation in the level of the show's appeal. It is most popular in Humphreys County, Mississippi and least popular in Prince George's Country, Maryland.

The most popular liberal television program is *The Daily Show*. Aired on Comedy Central, it offers a format of talk, news satire, and political comedy. It has its most appeal in cities, the liberal northeast and west coast, and inland liberal pockets. It is most popular in San Francisco and least so in Alabama. The program whose viewers were most likely to vote for Hillary Clinton is *Family Guy*, a sitcom created by Seth MacFarlane that spoofs American culture.

The most popular liberal sitcom – and the one I accordingly code – is ABC's *Modern Family*. It premiered in 2009 and was hailed as edgy, fresh, funny, and clever. It ranks seventh in the *New York Times* survey. *Modern Family* won 21 Primetime Emmy Awards and 6 Writers Guild of America Awards. The show also received a GLSEN Respect Award for its portrayal of "positive images and storylines" that reflect a diverse America, including the depiction of a family headed by a gay couple. Barack Obama told British Labour leader Ed Miliband that it was his family's favorite TV show.[38]

Modern Family is a "mockumentary" about an extended and blended Los Angeles family. Jay Pritchett's family includes his much younger, Latina, second wife; his cerebral stepson; his two neurotic adult children, one of them gay, both partnered and with children. The show won many Emmy Awards over its eight-season run, including for outstanding comedy five seasons in a row. Its audience pattern is the prototypical example of a city show – most popular in liberal, urban clusters in Boston, San Francisco and Santa Barbara – and least popular in the more rural parts of Kentucky, Mississippi and Arkansas.

My coders and I sampled episodes from each season of the selected programs. We watched a total of 24 episodes of *Duck Dynasty* and 24 of *Modern Family*. We devised qualitative coding protocols to evaluate the extent to which fairness and equality appeared on a show and how they were presented and evaluated. We broke out each principle into its two formulations. Coding principles of justice is a challenging task. In contrast to more standard forms of content analysis there are no keywords that are readily associated with what we are trying to identify and track. Even the words "fairness" and "equality" are ambiguous in meaning because they can refer to different manifestations of these principles. They can also be used ironically, in jest, or merely as throwaway lines.

Context is all-important. References to equality or fairness are more likely to be behavioral than verbal. These principles and their meanings must be inferred from such cues as who gathers or consults with whom; who receives what rewards or punishments, and for what reasons; how individuals behave in groups, especially when making decisions, adjudicating disputes, or distributing benefits; and how others act toward the major characters in the program, or expect them to behave when with them. We accordingly began our study without firm protocols but rather with each researcher acting independently. We watched and coded three episodes of each sitcom, with the goal of observing how often we could detect fairness and equality in behavior or speech, its consequences for others, and the ways actors evaluated its application and consequences. We also paid attention to the dogs that did not bark: occasions where social norms or the past behavior of characters would suggest that fairness or equality would come into play. We were on the lookout for any overt discussion of either principle of justice. We compared our results and refined our protocols before proceeding to watch and code additional episodes of these sitcoms.

One of the recurrent themes in *Duck Dynasty* is the tension between fairness and equality. This is apparent from the very first episode. The elder brother, Willie, is CEO of a duck whistle company. Other family members and friends work for him. They feel a strong sense of equality and, accordingly, freedom to ignore Willie's commands and do what they want. Instead of fulfilling a large order to go to Finland they flood the loading dock to let previously caged ducks out to swim. Willie is furious and orders them back to work. This encounter suggests that equality and fairness are equally important values. The same episode reveals tension between Willie and his wife Cora. She is trying to make a DVD of recipes for which she has a contract. He leaves her in the lurch to return to headquarters to discipline his employees. Cora is treated as an equal, in large part because she is important to the business and behaves responsibly. The family is nevertheless extremely hierarchical with the grandfather Phil at the apex. Every episode closes with him at the head of the table saying grace before a meal.

Season one, episode two elaborates further on these themes. Willie is unhappy with his brothers and other employees because, "They're clowns who don't respect dedication." His brother Jase is nevertheless made acting CEO for the day as Willie must go out of town in pursuit of a large contract. Jase complains that "working for his brother is like dating his cousin." He rebels by making new rules for employees. The "Number one rule," he announces, is "there ain't no rules." He attempts to combine fairness and equality by mixing comradely fun and work. As a result, Jase and the crew fail to fulfill the order, and he "fesses up" to his brother. Willie forgives him and accepts him because, he explains, they are family. This is followed by a homily about working together as a family, and how playing and working hard are not so different. The tension between fairness and equality has been finessed, not addressed.

In almost every episode, *Duck Dynasty* emphasizes patriotism, "core values" and backwoods "survival" skills. Willie always wears a bandana with an American flag design. He and others makes fun of learning, "Hollyweird," and New York. His father Phil is a Vietnam War veteran, but never discusses the conflict or politics surrounding it. Rather, he tells tall tales about hunting that nobody believes. He and Willie push the Roberston children to play football instead of video games. They should get rid of their cell phones, clear the yard, know their way around guns and fishing rods, and learn to be "low tech men in a high-tech world." Grandpa Phil teaches the young how to eat squirrel meat and brains. He warns against make up as it "covers up the true woman." Your girlfriend, he advises, should be as good a cook as your mom, especially when it comes to squirrel dumplings. "If you shoot squirrel for your woman," he insists, "she'll never disappoint you in bed."

Being a Robertson requires knowing how to live off the land. Season three, episode one takes place as the duck hunting season is about to open and Willie's employees convince him that they should knock off early. They set off to rough it in the woods and make fun of Willie who sleeps in a camper. Phil returns home, eats his wife's homemade Jambalaya, and only agrees to bathe because he wants sex. The show takes the mickey out of redneck pretensions of masculinity, and foregrounds the power of their women. The other tension, as always, is between Willie and his staff. He has less of a need to demonstrate his masculinity because of his success in business. They in turn tease him, suggesting that his idea of roughing it is opening his garage door manually.

Women's traditions are offered as a counterpoint to their men's. They emphasize subordination of person to family interests, washing and being clean. They are under the thumb to their men but assert their power indirectly and by traditional means. Men attempt to prove their masculinity by establishing control over nature – a constant theme of the sitcom– and by manipulating symbols of manhood like beards, rifles, trucks, and hunting. They fail some of the time against nature – they miss the hunting on one episode because they sleep through it – and are regularly outwitted by their women, as they and other rednecks are by the wider economic powers beyond the confines of their rural world.

The stress on rugged privatism but also on togetherness as a family nicely parallels the mix of self-centered and altruistic behavior. Both are male tensions, but in repeated episodes – unlike real life – family and altruism consistently triumph, and to everyone's advantage. The sitcom has more difficulty in balancing fairness and equality. It superficially features fairness in the form of traditional male hierarchies implicitly backed by Christian beliefs. However, women, employees, and teenagers – all of whom appear to accept this understanding of fairness – struggle to assert their equality. A sophisticated viewer might conclude that the show operates at two levels. It features a tight-knit, appealing and economically successful redneck family with traditional values and backwoods interest to attract a rural, conservative and Christian audience. At the same time scriptwriters undercut, or at least problematize, many of its values and practices, sneaking in, so to speak, more modern values and practices.

Duck Dynasty became controversial more for what happened off camera than on. In December 2013, A&E suspended Phil Robertson from the show in response to remarks he made in an interview with Drew Magary of *GQ Magazine*. When asked what he thought sinful, Robertson replied: "Start with homosexual behavior and just morph out from there. Bestiality, sleeping around with this woman and that woman and those men."[39] The Robertson family supported Phil. The agreed that some of his comments were "coarse, but insisted that his beliefs are "grounded in the teachings of the Bible."[40] He received backing from social conservatives, religious groups, and some Republican politicians, including Sarah Palin, Bobby Jindal, and Mike Huckabee.[41] A&E reversed Robertson's suspension but also announced that it would launch a public service announcement across the channel's "entire portfolio" that would promote "tolerance and acceptance among all people."[42] However, after eleven seasons and a declining viewership, especially after the controversy, A& E terminated *Duck Dynasty* at the end of 2016.[43] In the opinion of one reviewer, it had "run out of gas."[44]

Embattled patriarch Phil Robertson endorsed Senator Ted Cruz of Texas for president in 2016. "I've looked at the candidates," Robertson said in a video. "Ted Cruz is my man. He fits the bill. He's godly, he loves us, he's the man for the job, and he will go duck hunting because today we're going." The video closes with the two men firing away at ducks.[45] In November 2016, at the invitation of Donald Trump, Willie Robertson, wearing his signature American flag bandana, appeared on the podium at the opening night of the Republican National Convention.[46]

In *Modern Family* fairness and equality are in more open conflict and the sitcom relies more on these conflicts for drama, humor, and continuity. In season 1, episode 3, Jay Pritchett makes a model-powered airplane and attempts to fly it through a loop held up by his son-in-law Phil. He misses the loop and hits Phil in the face with the plane, knocking him out. Jay is more concerned about the condition of the plane than about the condition of his son-in-law.

The straight male characters are more self-centered and egoistic. As a general rule, the women, like those of *Duck Dynasty*, are more thoughtful and considerate and temper their behavior for the general good. Season 1, episode 4 features a race between Phil and his wife Clare. She runs every day and is fit, and he is not. Phil nevertheless insists that he is the faster runner. He cajoles Clare into a race to prove his physical superiority and she lets him win. Clare slows down because she realizes the effects of losing on Phil's ego. He is utterly oblivious to what is happening. In contrast to Phil, Claire is better able to think and act in terms of the family.

In season 3, episode 3, Claire and Phil get into an argument after a supermarket accident. Claire insists it is Phil's fault because he backed their shopping cart into her while ogling an attractive woman. He denies it. The conflict escalates in the family with everyone ganging up on Claire for always needing to be right. At a dinner at which Cameron and Mitchell intend to announce they are adopting a second child, Claire makes everyone watch the surveillance video she has obtained from the store to prove her point. In the same episode, Claire's daughters argue over their choice of rooms. Self-interest runs amok.

In season 1, episode 6, Jay's new, young Columbian wife Gloria locks horns with Jay's adult daughter Claire. The conflict escalates to everyone's discomfort, and Claire's apology to Gloria fails to resolve it. Gloria tells Claire she will only be forgiven if she jumps in the pool with all her clothes on. She does this at a family party, and other family members follow until everyone is in the pool. The incident suggests equality and solidarity, but also how it was the product of narrow self-interest. As in most episodes, writers attempt to square fairness and equality, but can only do so momentarily and through contrived events that produce shared embarrassment.

As in *Duck Dynasty* there is intergenerational conflict. It pits fairness (parents run the family because they know best) against equality (kids should have autonomy), with the latter more often than not given only lip service. In season 1, episode 3, Claire's daughter Haley refuses to wear a dress to a family wedding, but her mother insists. Haley argues that it should be her choice, and assumes that she should be treated as an equal. The value conflict is never resolved, but the problem goes away when

Haley is taken to lunch by her grandmother-in-law Gloria who convinces her that she will look pretty in a dress. Haley conforms to a traditional stereotype of a girl's role and the desire for equality recedes. Despite the striking superficial differences between *Modern Family* and *Duck Dynasty*, they are not so different in their adherence to gender stereotypes.

Modern Family is more open in its endorsement of hypocrisy. In an early season episode Manny, Gloria's precocious pre-teen and son from her first marriage, has picked up and not returned a locket dropped by a girl at school. The principal calls to accuse Manny of stealing it. Gloria – cast as a stereotype of a sexy, emotional Latina – explodes on the telephone and lambasts the principal for succumbing to the stereotype of Colombians as dishonest. Manny did keep the locket because he likes the girl and regrets that her family is leaving town. Jay convinces Manny to fess up to his mother. He does and they go to school to see the principal but, when nobody is looking, Gloria sneaks the locket back into the girl's locker and has Manny deny stealing it. They make a pact not to tell Jay.

As in *Duck Dynasty*, there is constant competition among the characters. In *Modern Family*, it is less restrained – as in the race between Phil and Claire or the sibling rivalry among the children. They want their children to excel on the grounds that excellence matters for both self-esteem and external rewards. It is evident that they buy into the principle of fairness, with rewards being distributed on the basis of achievement. They worry about their younger son, who does not appear to excel at anything. Phil buys him a new baseball glove and tries to teach him in the hope of making him an outstanding player. He is awful. At the end of the show, they conclude, in something of a non-sequitur, that they have a great family.

Competition is sometimes used to contrast traditional and modern values. Manny excels at fencing but initially refuses to participate in the final school competition because his opponent is a girl and this would be against his "honor." His parents persuade him to participate on the grounds that girls and boys should be treated equally – in all situations – and it would be an offense not to compete against her. This is presented to viewers as the triumph of American over Latin values, but it is clear Manny learned these traditional values from his mother. She is now outspoken in favor of American ones.

If *Duck Dynasty* exudes backwoods verisimilitude, *Modern Family* is infused with trendiness. Cameron and Mitchell indulge in therapy speak. Everything they say appears to have somebody else in mind but is really self-centered. Along with the other couples in the sitcom, they routinely engage in blame shifting, another sign of self-interest. The children have not yet succumbed to this subterfuge and display their hostility honestly and openly. Lilly, the young daughter of Cameron and Mitchell, is aggressive toward other children, wants to kill a prospective brother, and clings to one of her parents. They try to address her problem by changing their behavior, but also by teaching her to be less direct.

Modern Family appears to be poles apart from *Duck Dynasty* in its acceptance of homosexuality. It features an openly gay couple who have gained acceptance from their extended family. For many viewers, the author included, Mitchell is one of the most attractive characters in the sitcom. The program nevertheless drew criticism from the LGBT community for its failure to portray any physical affection between Cameron and Mitchell. This concern spawned a Facebook campaign to demand that the couple be allowed to kiss on screen. In response, producers released a statement that a season 2 episode would address Mitchell's discomfort with public displays of affection. Executive producer Steve Levitan said that it was unfortunate that the issue had arisen, since the show's writers had always planned on such a scene "as part of the natural development of the show."[47] The episode "The Kiss" eventually aired with the kiss scene in the background, which drew praise from multiple critics. The sitcom also drew fire for its women characters, all of whom are housewives in an era where most women have jobs, if not careers.[48]

Experiments

My third stream of evidence is experiments and surveys. They allow one to ask a number of questions about principles of justice and their relative importance. For my purposes, the most important questions are:

1. The extent to which people consciously frame distributive decisions in terms of principles of justice.
2. Alternatively, are they more like many primates who merely appear to act unreflexively in terms of these principles?
3. If principles of justice are central to people's decisions, what principles do they use or choose, and under what circumstances?
4. How path dependent are their choices and how sensitive are they to self-interest, affiliation, education, class, nationality, and experimental priming?
5. Do people employ other decision rules having little or nothing to do with principles of justice?
6. If so, how often and under what conditions do they do this?

Friedrich Hayek is one of the few scholars to assert a strong position on question 1. He insists that social justice is a misguided concept and irrelevant to how people behave.[49] Many economists implicitly make this assumption. Psychologists, by contrast, accept the importance of principles of justice, but disagree about how people apply them to specific situations.

David Miller, a philosopher, suggests that people's decisions about distributing rewards are more cognitive than ethical.[50] Sidney Verba and his colleagues documented this in Sweden, Japan, and the United States, where people expressing distributional preferences take their cue from existing distributions.[51] In Sweden, where variation in incomes is relatively low, they make the smallest adjustments to reach an ideal; in Japan, where it is higher, they make greater adjustments; and in the United States, where it is the most pronounced, they make the greatest adjustments.[52] The same pattern prevails in the three countries with respect to preferred differentials between worker and executive pay.[53] Other studies show that Americans – and presumably other nationalities as well – consistently underestimate the extent of inequality in their society.[54] After being shown charts of the wealth distribution in the United States and Sweden, 92 percent of participants chose the Swedish model.[55]

Most research to date is focused on question 3: the use of fairness or equality as a seeming decision rule.[56] It evaluates choices by different kinds of people in different situations. Since the 1970s surveys and experiments have been carried out in diverse domains (e.g. business, pensions, healthcare), with individuals and small groups, and with people of different gender, age, class, and nationalities. They indicate that the triumph of the principle of equality is far from total. Americans opt for equality in making certain kinds of distributions but for fairness (generally called equity by experimenters) in making others.[57] Depending on what is at stake, they may go with a different principle. An everyday example is a group of friends paying the bill in restaurants. They generally opt for tab splitting, but not if there is big variation in what people have consumed. Choices are accordingly context dependent, and can to some degree be manipulated by experimenters.

Some researchers have directed their attention to children, presumably on the assumption of trying to find some innate, or at least, less socially conditioned response to distribution rules. Konow and his collaborators find that 3–4 year olds tend to opt for equality in distributing rewards, 5–6 year olds rectified inequality in their distributions, and 7–8 year olds rectified inequality but judged equal distributions less positively than fair ones.[58] Melis, Altrichter, and Tomasello find that children tend to share equally, but favor collaborating partners over free riders.[59] Assuming these differences are meaningful, we would have to do cross-cultural studies to determine the extent to which they reflect socialization versus some kind of genetic programming.

More persuasive are experiments that involve groups. Social identity theory posits that groups performing even meaningless tasks develop some degree of common identity.[60] Research indicates that temporary groups are more likely to make distributions on the basis of fairness and reward people on the basis of their contribution to group tasks. Groups that work together for longer periods and develop more robust identities put more emphasis on maintaining relationships and group solidarity. They are accordingly more likely to show a preference for equal distribution.[61]

Brickman and collaborators find that people may apply different allocation criteria when focusing on individuals as opposed to populations. With individuals, people are more likely to make distributions on the basis of fairness, but tend to favor equality when addressing groups, and more so with populations. They speculate that people rely on two different principles of justice in allocating resources: micro-justice and macro-justice. The former reflects faith in the market and the reward of merit, and the latter a desire for a normative commitment to greater equality.[62]

A number of other studies have people make society-wide rather than individual distributions. They tend to support Brickman's claim that moving to higher levels of social aggregation affects how people frame distributional questions. When asked if "the fairest way of distributing wealth and income would be to give everyone an equal share," about one-third of Americans concur. This percentage drops markedly when people are presented with a statement to the effect that "under a fair economic system people with more ability would earn higher salaries."[63]

Swift, Marshall, and Burgoyne asked people to decide if those working in different professions of different gender and marital statuses were over or under paid. Their findings support other studies that indicate that Americans consider fairness the most applicable principle to income distribution. However, they also think equality germane because they favor income distributions less unequal than they are in practice.[64] Occupation turns out to be the single most important variable, with participants favoring more rewards for those in high-status professions.[65] However, a 2016 Gallup poll found that 63 percent of Americans think that rich Americans pay too little in taxes, down from a high of 77 percent in the 1990s.[66] British distributional preferences are roughly similar, although reveal a greater commitment to equality.[67]

An alternate formulation of fairness is the distribution of rewards on the basis of need. Americans appear willing to take individual needs into account when making distributions.[68] The difficulty is how needs are determined – a problem recognized by many participants because they are more willing to reward people who describe their needs and when they have confidence in their revelations.[69] People appear attracted to both principles of justice because the same participants will use different decision rules in different domains. Reeskens and Oorschot report that most Europeans apply the equality principle to unemployment benefits, but differ among themselves about whether equality or fairness is most appropriate to pension schemes.[70] These preferences are not firm because they are easily affected by priming.[71] When Leventhal instructed people to raise efficiency or productivity they opted for the fairness rule of distribution, but when asked to promote harmony they were more likely to choose equality.[72]

Decision rules may also vary as a function of self-interest. Balafoutas et al. find the more people earn in an experiment the more they oppose redistribution on the basis of equality.[73] According to Reeskens and Oorschot, "haves" are more likely to opt for fairness in determining pensions in contrast to "have nots" who prefer equality.[74] However, in a comparative study of the United States, UK, and Germany, Swift, Marshall, Burgoyne, and Routh find that only in the United States is class a significant determinant of distributional preference.[75] McCloskey and Zaller nevertheless report that close to 75 percent of people at the bottom of the American economic ladder still favor the principle of fairness. They regularly endorse statements like, "People with more ability should earn higher salaries."[76]

Lerner and Clayton argue that the literature errs in attempting to reduce all decisions to self-interest. Many – if not most – studies simply assume that people are motivated by self-interest, and interpret their behavior accordingly.[77] More sophisticated studies recognize the importance of justice, but, in line with Schumpeter, treat it more as a rationalization than a motive in its own right. A seminal 1957 study by Morton Deutsch suggests that people adopt whatever principle of justice will advance their interests in a given situation.[78]

There is considerable research indicating that justice is a fundamental motive and sometimes takes priority over self-interest.[79] The "belief in a just world" hypothesis refers to the pervasive belief that good and bad outcomes are deserved. People believe that they get what they deserve, but not always because the world can be pernicious, constraining, and irrational. This belief in justice has considerable influence on how people behave.[80] Other research indicates that after believing they have been treated unjustly, people are more sensitive to justice and more motivated to behave in ways they think just.[81] They are also more willing to compensate victims and punish evil-doers.[82] Personal contract theory has as its central hypothesis that people who develop what is called a personal contract – a commitment to goals or procedures – are more likely to follow socially mandated rules of behavior and justice than attempt to maximize their perceived self-interest.[83] This also appears to be the case when people take the time and effort to think about likely reactions to their behavior.[84] In effect, there is a growing research agenda in psychology to study the influences of the justice motive on evaluative, emotional, and behavioral responses.[85]

There are also efforts to understand the relationship between political beliefs or preferences and the application of principles of justice. Mitchell, Tetlock, Newman, and Lerner asked participants to judge the fairness of different distributions of wealth in hypothetical societies. In the first study, the level of meritocracy in the hypothetical societies and the frame of reference from which participants judged alternative distributions of wealth interacted to influence fairness judgments. As meritocracy increased, all participants became more tolerant of economic inequality, particularly when they judged fairness from a redistribution frame of reference that made salient transfers among socioeconomic classes. Liberal participants placed a greater emphasis on equality than conservative participants did across all conditions. In the second study, reactions to income transfers depended on the efficiency of the transfers and the identity of the groups receiving the benefits, but conservatives placed a greater emphasis in their fairness judgments on tying benefits to workfare requirements, whereas liberals did not distinguish between unconditional welfare transfers and workfare transfers.[86]

There is a growing corpus of cross-cultural research. Several studies find a greater emphasis on equality than fairness in societies that are less hierarchical.[87] Other researchers claim to have found a greater preference for equality among Europeans than Americans, and among Asians than westerners. Mayser and von Wagenheim found only moderate differences between Germans and Americans in their responses to differential treatment of customers by companies. In both countries consumers understand that service providers treat customers based on profit considerations. American customers perceive this as less unfair than their German counterparts do.[88] Konow, Saijo and Akai find more differences within nationalities than between them. Third-party arbitrators who do not know disputing parties generally favor fairness. They move toward equality when anonymity is lifted and more so when they have a stake in the outcome.[89] Montoya, Huang, Lynch, and Cassondra conducted a comparative study in Canada, the United States and China. Asked whether they believed equality between individuals and groups was beneficial, the Chinese said "yes" for individuals, but "no" for groups. The Americans preferred fairness, and the Canadians were in between.[90]

These findings are consistent with my claims. I am arguing that equality has become the dominant principle of justice, initially in the West, and now elsewhere in the world. Tocqueville understood equality and privatism to be tightly bundled. Equality provides individuals with the political and social room to develop and advance themselves – or at least the illusion.[91] It does not necessarily do away with hierarchies or the principle of fairness. Ironically, the principle of equality can help to legitimate hierarchies to the extent that they are seen as "just," that is arising from conditions of equality. This is one of the goals of liberalism: to provide the kind of opportunities and rules that makes everyone equal at the starting line. The resulting hierarchies would be just because they are not the product of unfair advantages for some competitors. So paradoxically, in liberal theory a more equal society can be one in which fairness – defined here as giving the most rewards to those who contribute the most to society – is the appropriate rule of distribution.[92] Put another way, equality in practice enables and justifies fairness enabled by equality. In theory, and in the popular mind, in part, the principles of fairness and equality have become connected, making it difficult to separate them for analytical purposes.[93]

Research on equality and fairness is to some degree problematic for other reasons. In experiments and surveys, there may be inadvertent framing effects. When justice enters the picture, we risk getting "Sunday best" answers; participants may respond as they think researchers want them to, or in a manner they think consistent with their own beliefs about justice. Like all social psychological theories, the evidence for all these propositions is illustrative rather than demonstrative. It shows what might happen, not what will happen. Most research ignores the interactional process and consequences of exchange relationships. Rather, it somewhat artificially explores what appears to go on in the heads of isolated individuals. There is usually no communication, bargaining, or structuring of their relationship by those involved in exchanges or distributions. Many studies make arbitrary and questionable motivational assumptions. They assume, as noted, that people are selfish utility maximizers. They discount or entirely ignore as motives, not only justice, but other rewards, including those associated with maintaining good relationships. Many also make standard and questionable cognitive assumptions by treating individuals as fully rational in their information processing and decision making.[94]

More fundamentally, researchers are often not at all clear in what they mean by justice.[95] They have not carefully parsed either equality or fairness; most assume they have obvious meanings. As frequently noted, I contend that equity and equality can each take two forms. Equity can mean the most to those who contribute the most, or to those who need it the most. Equality can also mean an equal distribution of what is at stake, or equal opportunity to compete for it. All the studies use only the first meaning of these concepts. I have not encountered research that allows participants to define their own approaches or rules of distributive justice. Of equal concern, the principles of equality and fairness have wider applications than the distribution of monetary rewards, which is what almost all studies focus on.

I am interested in fairness and equality in the context of American society because I believe there are sharp differences within the population in preferences for these principles of justice and also of understandings of them. These differences find political expression and, I hypothesize, correlate with voting choices. A study of the 1984 presidential election by Rasinski offers support. He conducted three surveys and found strong correlations between evaluations of fairness and equality and preferences for candidates. Those endorsing the value of proportionality – what I describe as fairness – believed that Ronald Reagan would be a fairer president than Walter Mondale. These respondents also emphasized the procedural aspects of government when judging government fairness. Respondents endorsing the value of equality preferred Mondale. They emphasized the distributive, over procedural, aspects of government when judging government fairness.[96]

These questions have also been approached with survey data from the American National Election Studies. They indicate that more than 80 percent of the population supports equality of opportunity. However, division appears when it comes to means that might produce this end. When people are asked if, "We have gone too far in pushing equal rights in this country," conservatives on the whole agree and liberals do not.[97] These preferences correlate tightly with religious ones. Jews, Friends, Episcopalians, and secular people support government efforts to create greater equality through legislation and taxes. Evangelicals, Latter-Day Saints, and Catholics are on the whole opposed.[98] A similar division shows up with respect to moral and cultural issues. Between 65 and 87 percent of Evangelical Protestants, Catholics, and Latter-Day Saints believe that new lifestyles are destroying society.[99] These groups also oppose women's rights, gay rights, and abortion.[100]

These differences were reflected in the 2016 presidential election. Liberals, minorities, and the college-educated voted for Clinton, while Evangelical Protestants, Latter-Day Saints, and the non-college educated – especially the white working class – voted for Trump.[101] Trump voters favor fairness – rewards to those who deserve them – over equality, and Clinton voters preferred equality, defined as equal rights and opportunities. For many Trump voters, I hypothesize, fairness refers to the "traditional" principles that have governed distribution: a preference for white men of Protestant background. For most of the country's history Protestants considered themselves "to have a unique capability for self-government." Other races were assumed to lack this "supreme Anglo-Saxon virtue."[102]

A new study by Diane Mutz offers support for my interpretation of presidential campaign speeches and their relative appeal to voters.[103] Using survey data from a representative sample of 1200 voters, Mutz finds that Trump voters were less driven by anger about what has happened than of fears of what may come to pass. White, Christian, and male voters turned to Mr. Trump because they felt their status was at risk. "It's not a threat to their own economic well-being; it's a threat to their group's dominance in our country over all."

Her survey also assessed "social dominance orientation," a psychological measure of a person's belief in hierarchy as necessary and inherent to a society. People who exhibited a growing belief in such group dominance were also more likely to move toward Mr. Trump, reflecting their hope that the status quo be protected. "It used to be a pretty good deal to be a white, Christian male in America, but things have changed and I think they do feel threatened."[104]

Trump voters embrace other kinds of hierarchies, including the international one that has America at the top. They resonate to Trump's electoral catchphrase – "Make America Great Again" – because they believe their country has declined due to the rise of the principle of equality and, as Trump claims, allowing other states to take advantage of their country. The two hierarchies are related because America's greatness confers status on them and this builds self-esteem. Trump voters are also attracted to his strong anti-immigration stance because many of them believe that the growing population of non-whites undercuts their status and economic opportunities.

I suspect there are sharp differences among Clinton voters in how they envisage equality – equal distributions vs. opportunities. But most favor equality of opportunity regardless of gender, race, religion, or sexual identity and preference. Clinton voters are also more supportive of immigration. Hillary Clinton campaigned almost entirely on issues of equality, especially for women and minorities. Her appeals turned off many traditional Democratic voters, who were drawn to Trump because fairness was more important to them. Clinton's behavior – pandering to bankers for big fees – partially undercut her claims to support equality.

Roger Giner-Sorolla, Laura Niemmi and I conducted an experiment to evaluate the preferences of Americans for the distribution of rewards on the basis of equality vs. fairness.[105] We designed a game in which four players invest different amounts money and receive returns according to different principles of justice.

Fairness and equality each have two formulations, so we constructed four scenarios. Participants were asked to judge the appropriateness of the distribution of money in each scenario. In the first equality scenario, everyone in the game receives back the same sum of money from the pool regardless of how much they contributed. In the second equality, everyone receives back the amount they contributed. The first fairness scenario rewards players in proportion to what they contributed, so those who invested more make more money if there is a profit. In the second fairness scenario, those who contributed less get proportionately more on the assumption that they need it more.

Participants in the experiment overwhelmingly prefer the first fairness distribution, where people receive back in proportion to what they have contributed. When choosing between the two equality distributions, they prefer the first equality scenario of equal outcomes vs. equal returns. In each scenario, there is a "boss" who decides which of the four distribution rules to use. In a variant of the game, participants were asked to play "boss" and decide on the distribution in lieu of evaluating distributions made by control. Here, there was even stronger support for the equal outcome distribution. We did not ask people how they voted in the 2016 presidential election but had a series of questions to determine where they fit on the liberal–conservative spectrum. We also tried to ascertain what kind of liberal or conservative they were. We found that liberals were more attracted to conditions of equality than conservatives, and conservatives more attracted to the proportional framing of fairness. This preference was strongest among economic conservatives, as opposed to social and national ones.

Conclusion

At the outset of this chapter I raised the question of American political stability. Few people think democracy is on the verge of collapse, about to be replaced by dictatorship, or simply descend into chaos due to congressional gridlock. Many, however, regard the deep political chasm between conservative Republican and liberal Democratic voters as a matter of concern. More threatening still to some are the election and presidency of Donald Trump. They characterize him as demagogic in his appeal, demeaning of his opponents, playing fast and loose with facts, yet finding wide support among voters who, for diverse reasons, were hostile to the establishment. In the course of his campaign, Trump encouraged violence among supporters, pledged to prosecute Hillary Clinton, threatened legal action against unfriendly media, and suggested that he might not accept the election results. His presidency to date has been marked by scandals and escalating attacks on the media and, some allege, on the constitution. Well before Trump's inauguration, the mainstream media carried analyses by respectable scholars who worried that constitutional safeguards might be insufficient to save democracy from such an authoritarian challenge.[106] These concerns grew more pronounced after the first six months of his presidency.[107]

I share these concerns but am reasonably confident that, in at least the short term, constitutional safeguards will preserve democracy – even with Trump in the White House. The gist of my critique is different in that it is less focused on the individual authoritarian leader and more on the underlying conditions that make such a leader possible. I argue that the ongoing political and cultural wars in the United States are very much a product of the two value shifts I have described: from self-interest well understood to privatism, and from fairness to equality.

Self-interest well understood teaches people to think of themselves independently of the community that enables them to formulate interests intelligently and pursue them in a manner from which others gain as well. Privatism, by contrast, encourages greed, the pursuit of short-term interests at the expense of longer-term goals, and a take-no-prisoners attitude toward others. It is in part responsible for business practices that place profit over all other considerations, the decline in comity in the Congress, and the greater unilateralism of American foreign policy.

The shift to privatism is apparent in presidential speeches, sitcoms, and popular songs. Quantitative and qualitative analysis of these three narratives reveals a consistent movement away from self-interest well understood in the postwar era. I theorize that these narratives reflect national values and also to some degree help to shape them. The narratives suggest that the shift is a fairly uniform one, although there are undoubtedly many people, perhaps demographics, where it is less evident.

The second value shift, from fairness to equality, has been responsible for the growth of tolerance and, with it, greater legal protections for and social acceptance of minorities of all kinds and women. It also extends to the handicapped and sexual preferences, and most recently to gender variation. The shift is readily tracked in presidential addresses, campaign speeches, and sitcoms. It is less uniform than the shift to privatism, and therefore more controversial. Many people oppose the application of equality in a wide range of domains and make arguments – to the extent they do – based on the principle of fairness. As our experiments indicate, for some there is a clear connection between this principle and their policy preferences. For others, we suspect, the appeal to fairness provides a justification to oppose something they understand as not in their interest. This, of course, also holds true for those who invoke equality in defense of their preferences.

Either way, these opposing preferences are far less amenable to compromise than those understood only as matters of interest. There is compelling evidence that once people frame a question in terms of justice, they are more likely to dig in their heels, in part because they view compromise as unprincipled. Moralized attitudes, in effect, reorient behavior from maximizing gains to adhering to rules. They prompt voters to oppose compromises – even if this involves forsaking material gains – and to punish politicians who compromise.[108] Some politicians and opinion makers have in turn encouraged this framing as a means of advancing their careers and policy preferences.[109] Accordingly, questions of interest and principle have become increasingly connected or intertwined, extending the scope of issues on which compromise is no longer acceptable. This phenomenon exacerbates the culture war and makes it more political, and in turn contributes to the division of the country and electorate. Striking evidence is provided by the extreme hostility displayed by voters to presidents elected from the other party. After six years in office, three in ten wanted to impeach first Bush and then Obama. Trump provoked this opposition within a month of taking the oath of office.[110]

A root cause of the collapse of the Weimar Republic was legislative deadlock. Extremist parties on the right and left had sufficient votes to make a grand coalition of more moderate parties unworkable. President Hindenburg invoked emergency powers, provided for in the constitution, to appoint prime ministers. When the first two failed to overcome the deadlock, he turned to Hitler. By a combination of legal and illegal means, Hitler gained extraordinary powers and established the Nazi dictatorship.[111] I invoke the collapse of Weimar only to highlight the danger of *immobilisme* in democracies. A similar story can be told about Italy in the immediate post-World I era.[112] When presidents or prime ministers are hamstrung by legislatures, and legislatures in turn cannot govern, democracy cannot survive in the long term.

This impasse has not been reached in the United States, and may well be avoided. However, it is by no means impossible to construct a future in which gerrymandering, lower voter turnouts, and the decline of comity in both parties make the federal government all but unworkable. Popular support for the legislature is already at an all-time low, and people will grow increasingly restive in a situation of extended deadlock.[113] Perhaps for this reason, many people are already willing to support a leader who demands extraordinary powers, or abuses executive powers for the same end.[114] In May 2017 a Gallup Poll indicated that Trump had a strikingly high 84 percent approval rating among Republicans. Self-identified Republicans were willing to excuse or justify Trump campaign contacts with the Russians and the firing of FBI Director James Comey.[115] Perhaps for this reason, Republican leaders like Paul Ryan, Mitch McConnell, and other Republican leaders do not condemn these constitutional abuses but seek to justify them. Many politicians in Weimar behaved the same way for much the same reason.

Washington is not Weimar. The American constitution does not allow for emergency powers – although President Lincoln certainly exercised them during the Civil War. Most importantly, Trump is not Hitler.

There are still free elections despite Republican efforts at denying voters the right to cast their ballots and by state legislatures to gerrymander districts in a way that many votes do not matter. It is possible – even likely – that future congressional and presidential elections will make responsible government possible again at the Federal level. It is nevertheless disturbing that politics in America have reached the point where one must consider the alternatives.

Notes

1 Brickman, Folger, Goode, and Schul, "Microjustice and Macrojustice"; Lerner, "Justice Motive"; Shapiro, "Effect of Expectations of Future Interaction on Reward Allocation in Dyads"; Mikula, *Justice and Social Interaction*; Deutsch, *Distributive Justice*"; Törnblom and Jonsson, ""Distribution versus Retribution"; Griffith and Sell, "Effects of Competition on Allocators' Preferences for Contributive and Retributive Justice Rules."

2 Lebow, *National Identities and International Relations*, ch. 7.

3 MacLean, *Democracy in Chains*, for an excellent if controversial history of such efforts from the time of Calhoun to the present. For an overview of the controversy, Jonathan H. Adler, "Does 'Democracy in Chains' paint an accurate picture of James Buchanan? [with updates]," *Washington Post*, June 28 2017, www.washingtonpost.com/news/volokh-conspiracy/wp/2017/06/28/does-democracy (accessed July 15 2017); Henry Farrell and Steven Teles, "Even the intellectual left is drawn to conspiracy theories about the right. Resist them," *Vox*, July 14 2017, www.vox.com/the-big-idea/2017/7/14/15967788/democracy-shackles-james-buchanan-intellectual-history-maclean (accessed July 15 2017).

4 Lovejoy, *Great Chain of Being*, esp. ch. 6.

5 Hartz, *Liberal Tradition in America*; Diamond, *Spirit of Democracy*; Manent and Seigel, *An Intellectual History of Liberalism*.

6 Lipset, "Psychology of Voting"; Jost, Glaser, Kruglanski, and Sulloway, "Political Conservatism as Motivated Social Cognition"; Rathbun, "Hierarchy and Community at Home and Abroad"; Lebow, *Politics and Ethics of Identity*, chs. 2, and 6–7.

7 Hamilton, Madison, and Jay, *Federalist Papers*, nos. 48–51, 63–66, 80–85.

8 Survey research of Ron Lesthaeghe and Lisa Neidert, University of Michigan Population Studies Center, reported by Thomas B. Edsall, "Trump is the Enemy of Their Enemies," *New York Times*, May 5 2017, www.nytimes.com/2017/05/04/opinion/president-trump-is-the-enemy-of-their-enemies.html (accessed May 8 2017).

9 Jacob Poushter, "What is the greatest threat in the world? Depends on where you live," *Pew Research Center*, Spring 2014 world survey, www.pewresearch.org/fact-tank/2014/10/16/what-is-the-greatest-threat-to-the-world-depends-on-where-you-live/ (accessed May 6 2017).

10 Emily Ekins, "Five Kinds of Trump Voters: Who Are They and What They Believe," Voter Study Group, June 2017, www.voterstudygroup.org/reports/2016-elections/the-five-types-trump-voters (accessed August 5 2017). For a

roughly similar typology, Drew DeSilver, "A closer look at who identifies as Democrat and Republican," June 1 2014, www.pewresearch.org/fact-tank/ 2014/07/01/a-closer-look-at-who-identifies-as-democrat-and-republican (accessed August 5 2017).

11 Emily Ekins, "Five Kinds of Trump Voters."

12 Ibid.

13 Ibid.

14 Ibid.

15 Ibid.

16 Alec Tyson and Shiva Manium, "Behind Trump's victory: Divisions by race, gender, education," *Pew Research Center*, November 9 2016, www .pewresearch.org/fact-tank/2016/11/09/behind-trumps-victory-divisions-by-race-gender-education/ (accessed August 6 2017).

17 A difficult choice involved combining "gay" and "LGBT," as it made a comparison between Clinton and Trump, who used the word "gay," but not "LGBT." Another defensible choice, I believe, was combining "everyone" and "everybody," and both with "community."

18 Donald Trump, "Remarks on Immigration," Phoenix, Arizona, August 31 2017, American Presidency Project, www.presidency.ucsb.edu/2016_ election_speeches.php?candidate=45&campaign=2016TRUMP&doct ype=5000 (accessed May 13 2017).

19 Ibid.

20 Donald Trump, "Remarks Announcing His Candidacy," New York City, June 16 2016, American President Project.

21 Donald Trump, "Transcript: Donald Trump's Victory Speech," November 8 2016, New York City, *New York Times*, November 9 2016, www.nytimes.com/ 2016/11/10/us/politics/trump-speech-transcript.html?_r=0 (accessed May 12 2017).

22 Donald Trump, "Transcript: Donald Trump's Speech at Rally in Melbourne, Florida," February 2017, *VOX*, www.vox.com/2017/2/18/14659952/trump-transcript-rally-melbourne-florida (accessed May 16 2017).

23 Trump Speech, Phoenix, Arizona, September 1 2016, *New York Times*, www .nytimes.com/2016/09/02/us/politics/transcript-trump-immigration (accessed May 16 2017).

24 The Associated Press-NORC Center for Public Affairs Research, "The American Identity: Points of Pride, Conflicting Views, and a Distinct Culture," http://apnorc.org/projects/Pages/points-of-pride-conflicting-views-and-a-distinct-culture.aspx (accessed May 28 2017). The nationwide poll was conducted February 16–20 2017, using the AmeriSpeak Panel, the probability-based panel of NORC at Chicago University. Online and telephone interviews using landlines and cell phones were conducted with 1004 adults.

25 Ibid.; Barack Obama, Inaugural Address, January 21 2013, White House, Office of the Press Secretary, https://obamawhitehouse.archives.gov/ the-press-office/2013/01/21/inaugural-address-president-barack-obama (accessed April 23 2017).

26 Barack Obama, "Inaugural Address," January 20 2009.

27 Allen and Parnes, *Shattered*, pp. 16–18, on the thinking that went into the speech.

28 Hillary Clinton, "Remarks: Let the Conversation Begin Website," January 23 2016, American Presidency Project, www.presidency.ucsb.edu/2016_ election_speeches.php?candidate=70&campaign=2016CLINTON&doct ype=5000 (accessed May 14 2017).

29 Hillary Clinton, "Remarks on the 42nd Anniversary of Bloody Sunday in Selma, Alabama," March 4 2016.

30 Hillary Clinton, "Speech to the Veterans of Foreign Wars," August 20 2016.

31 Allen and Parnes, *Shattered*, p. 397.

32 Ibid.

33 Hillary Clinton, "Speech on College Affordability," Plymouth, New Hampshire, October 11 2016, American Presidency Project.

34 Joseph Katz, "'Duck Dynasty' vs. 'Modern Family': 50 Maps of the US Cultural Divide," *New York Times*, December 27 2016, www.nytimes.com/ interactive/2016/12/26/upshot/duck-dynasty-vs-modern-family-television (accessed March 5 2017).

35 Quoted in Ibid.

36 Fox News Insider, "Competing Endorsements for Trump and Cruz," January 25 2016, http://insider.foxnews.com/2016/01/25/willie-and-phil-robertson-duck-dynasty-explains-support-donald-trump-and-ted-cruz-hannity (accessed March 6 2017).

37 Katz, "'Duck Dynasty' vs. 'Modern Family.'"

38 Martin Chilton, "Barack Obama's 10 favorite TV shows," *Daily Telegraph*, July 22 2014, www.telegraph.co.uk/culture/tvandradio/10982412/Barack-Obamas-10-favourite-TV-shows.html (accessed May 11 2017).

39 Drew Magary, "What the Duck," *GQ*, December 17 2003, www.gq.com/story/ duck-dynasty-phil-robertson; Charles Blow, "'Duck Dynasty' and Quackery," *New York Times*, December 20 2016, www.nytimes.com/2013/12/21/opinion/ blow-duck-dynasty-and-quackery.html (both accessed March 6 2017).

40 Holly Yan and Dana Ford, "'Duck Dynasty' family stands behind family patriarch," CNN Entertainment, http://edition.cnn.com/2013/12/19/ showbiz/duck-dynasty-suspension/ (accessed May 9 2017).

41 Dana Davidsen, "Palin, Cruz, Jindal: 'Duck Dynasty' star suspended over intolerance of politically incorrect," *CNN Politics*, December 19 2013, http://politicalticker.blogs.cnn.com/2013/12/19/jindal-palin-duck-dynasty-star-suspended-over-intolerance-of-politically-correct/comment-page-11/ (accessed May 9 2017).

42 Stuart Oldham and Cynthia Littleton, "'Duck Dynasty': A&E Ends Phil Robertson Suspension; Aims to Turn Controversy into Teachable Moment," *Variety*, December 27 2013, http://variety.com/2013/tv/news/phil-robertson-to-return-to-duck-dynasty-in-2014-1201003922/ (accessed May 9 2017).

43 Katie Mettler, "After 11 seasons and declining viewership, 'Duck Dynasty' says goodbye," *Washington Post*, November 17 2016, www.washingtonpost .com/news/morning-mix/wp/2016/11/17/after-11-seasons-and-declining-viewership-duck-dynasty-says-goodbye/?utm_term=.eeb38993cbf0 (accessed April 12 2017).

44 Neil Genzingler, "'Duck Dynasty' Legacy: Real, Fake and Upfront About It," *New York Times*, November 17 2016, www.nytimes.com/2016/11/18/arts/ television (accessed March 6 2017).

45 Todd Starnes, "Exclusive: Duck commander Phil Robertson endorses Ted Cruz," *Fox News*, January 13 2016, www.foxnews.com/opinion/2016/ 01/13/exclusive-duck-commander-phil-robertson-endorses-ted-cruz.html (accessed May 9 2017).

46 Lisandra Villa, "Meet the *Duck Dynasty* Star Speaking at the Republican Convention," *Time*, July 18 2016, http://time.com/4410817/republican-convention-willie-robertson-duck-dynasty/ (accessed May 9 2017).

47 Elizabeth Guider, "*Modern Family* actors practicing gay kiss," *Hollywood Reporter*, August 28 2010, www.hollywoodreporter.com/news/modern-family-actors-practicing-gay-27186 (accessed May 11 2017).

48 Michelle Haimoff, "Not so Modern Family: Top sitcoms make for sexist, inaccurate television," *Christian Science Monitor*, January 27 2012, www .csmonitor.com/Commentary/Opinion/2012/0127/Not-so-Modern-Family-Top-sitcoms-make-for-sexist-inaccurate-television (accessed May 11 2017).

49 Hayek, *Mirage of Social Justice*.

50 Miller, *Principles of Social Justice*, p. 75.

51 Verba et al., *Elites and the Idea of Equality*, pp. 127–28, 133.

52 Ibid.

53 Ibid., pp. 139–40.

54 Norton and Airely, "Building a Better America."

55 Ibid.

56 Homans, *Social Behavior* and Deutsch, "Equity, Equality, and Need," for pioneering studies.

57 For discussion, Greenberg and Cohen, *Equality and Justice in Social Behavior*; Deutsch, *Distributive Justice*, evaluated the two principles and "winner takes all" under different conditions. Also, Lerner and Clayton, *Justice and Self-Interest*, pp. 40–58.

58 Konow, Saijo, and Akai, "Equity versus Equality."

59 Melis, Altrichter, and Tomasello, "Allocation of Resources to Collaborators and Free-Riders in 3-Year Olds."

60 Tajfel, Billing, Bundy, and Flament, "Social Categorization and Intergroup Behavior"; Tajfel and Turner, "Social Identity Theory of Intergroup Behavior"; Tajfel, *Human Groups and Social Categories*.

61 Lerner, "Justice Motive"; Shapiro, "Effect of Expectations of Future Interaction on Reward Allocation in Dyads"; Mikula, *Justice and Social Interaction*; Deutsch, *Distributive Justice*; Törnblom and Jonsson, "Distribution versus Retribution"; Griffith and Sell, "Effects of Competition on Allocators' Preferences for Contributive and Retributive Justice Rules."

62 Brickman, Folger, Goode, and Schul, "Microjustice and Macrojustice."

63 McCloskey and Zaller, *American Ethos*, pp. 154–56.

64 Swift, Marshall, and Burgoyne, "Which Road to Social Justice?"

65 Jasso and Rossi, "Distributive Justice and Earned Income"; Alves, "Modeling Distributive Justice Judgments"; Alves and Rossi, "Who Should Get What?"; Verba and Orren, *Equality in America*.

66 Frank Newport, "Americans Still Say Upper-Income Pay Too Little in Taxes," Gallup, April 15 2016, www.gallup.com/poll/190775/americans-say-upper-income-pay-little-taxes.aspx (accessed June 22 2017).

67 Kluegel and Smith, *Beliefs about Inequality*; Mack and Lansley, *Poor Britain*; Smith, "Inequality and Welfare."

68 Lamm and Schwinger, "Norms Concerning Distributive Justice" and Schwinger, "Need Principle of Distributive Justice."

69 Mikula and Schwinger, "Intermember Relations and Reward Allocation."

70 Reeskens and Oorschot, "Equity, Equality, or Need?"

71 Konow, Saijo, and Akai, "Equity versus Equality?"

72 Leventhal, "Fairness in Social Relationships."

73 Balafoutas, Koucher, Putterman, and Sutter, "Equality, Equity and Incentives."

74 Reeskens and Oorschot, "Equity, Equality, or Need?"

75 Swift, Marshall, Burgoyne, and Routh, "Which Road to Social Justice?"

76 McCloskey and Zaller, *American Ethos*, ch. 5.

77 Lerner and Clayton, *Justice and Self-Interest*, pp. 59–97.

78 Deutsch, "Equity, Equality, and Need." Also, Messick and Sentis, "Fairness Preference and Fairness Biases"; Lind and Tyler, *Social Psychology of Procedural Justice*; Brockner and Wiesenfeld, "Integrative Framework for Explaining Reactions to Decisions"; Tyler and Blader, "Group Engagement Model"; Epley and Caruso, "Egocentric Ethics"; Skitka, "Do the Means Always Justify the Ends or do the Ends Sometimes Justify the Means?" Deutsch, *Distributive Justice*, makes the case that conceptions and expectations of justice also influence determination of interests and behavior.

79 Lerner and Clayton, *Justice and Self-Interest* for discussion.

80 Lerner, *Belief in A Just World*; Montada and Lerner, *Responses to Victimization and Belief in a Just World*; Lipkus, Dalbert, and Siegler, "Importance of Distinguishing the Belief in a Just World for Self Versus Others"; Hafer and Begue, "Experimental Research on Just World Theory"; Lerner and Clayton, *Justice and Self-Interest*, pp. 26–32.

81 Hafer, "Do Innocent Victims Threaten the Belief in a Just World?"; Aguiar, Vala, Correia, and Pereira, "Justice in Our World and in that of Others?"

82 Simmons and Lerner, "Altruism as a Search for Justice"; Goldberg, Lerner, and Tetlock, "Rage and Reason"; Lerner, Goldberg, and Tetlock, "Sober Second Thoughts."

83 Long and Lerner, "Deserving, the 'Personal Contract' and Altruistic Behavior by Children"; Mischel, "Preference for Delayed Reinforcement and Social Responsibility"; Braband and Lerner, "'Little Time and Effort'"; Hafer, "Investment n Long Term Goals and the Commitment to Just Means Drive the Need to Believe in a Just World"; Callan, Shead, and Olson, "Foregoing the Labor for the Fruits."

84 Lerner and Lichtman, "Effects of Perceived Norms on Attitudes and Altruistic Behavior Toward a Dependent Other"; Bazerman, White, and Lerner, "Perceptions of Fairness in Interpersonal and Individual Choice Situations"; Miller, "Norm of Self-Interest."

85 Lerner, "Justice Motive."

86 Mitchell, Tetlock, Newman, and Lerner, "Experiments Behind the Veil."

87 Murphy-Berman and Berman, "Cross-Cultural Differences in Perceptions of Distributive Justice"; Fischer and Smith, "Reward Allocations and Culture."

88 Mayser and von Wagenheim, "Perceived Fairness of Differential Customer Treatment."

89 Konow, Saijo, and Akai, "Equity versus Equality."

90 Montoya, Huang, Lynch, and Cassondra, "Is Equality Perceived as a Solution to Societal Problems?"

242 The United States: Fairness vs. Equality

91 Lebow, *Politics and Ethics of Identity*, chs. 1 and 8.
92 Rawls, *Justice as Fairness*, makes this kind of argument.
93 See Chapter 2.
94 Törnblom, "Social Psychology of Distributive Justice"; Lerner and Clayton, *Justice and Self-Interest*, pp. 59–97; Deutsch, *Distributive Justice*, pp. 25–30.
95 Törnblom, "Social Psychology of Distributive Justice"; Deutsch, *Distributive Justice*, pp. 28–30.
96 Rasinski, "What is Fair – Or Is It?
97 Sears, Sidanious, and Bobo, *Radicalized Politics*, pp. 127.
98 Feldman and Zaller, "Economic Privatism in American Public Opinion"; Barker and Carman, "Spirit of Capitalism?"; Park and Riemer, "Revisiting the Social Sources of American Christianity"; Smith and Farris, "Socioeconomic Inequality in the American Religious System."
99 Wald and Calhoun-Brown, *Religious Politics in the United States*, p. 188.
100 Ibid., pp. 185–204.
101 K. K. Rebecca Lai, Alicia Parlapiano, Jeremy White, and Karen Yourish, "How Trump Won the Election According to Exit Polls," *New York Times*, November 8 2016, www.nytimes.com/interactive/2016/11/08/us/elections/exit-poll-analysis.html?_r=0; Alec Tyson and Shiva Maniam, "Behind Trump's victory: Divisions by race, gender, education," Pew Research Center, November 9 2016, www.pewresearch.org/fact-tank/2016/11/09/behind-trumps-victory-divisions-by-race-gender-education/ (accessed June 18 2017)
102 Higham, *Strangers in the Land*, p. 10.
103 Diane Mutz, "Status threat, not economic hardship, explains the 2016 presidential vote," *Proceedings of the National Academy of Sciences*, 23 April 2010, www.pnas.org/content/early/2018/04/18/1718155115 and "People Voted for Trump Because They Were Anxious, Not Poor" *Atlantic*, 23 April 2018, www.theatlantic.com/science/archive/2018/04/existential-anxiety-not-poverty-motivates-trump-support/558674/ (both accessed 27 March 2017).
104 Niraj Chokshi, "Trump Voters Driven by Fear of Losing Status, Not Economic Anxiety, Study Finds," *New York Times*, 24 April 2018, www.nytimes.com/2018/04/24/us/politics/trump-economic-anxiety.html?action=click&contentCollection=Canada&module=Trending&version=Full&region=Marginalia&pgtype=article (assessed 27 March 2018).
105 Giner-Sorolla, Lebow, and Niemmi, "Principles of Justice and Presidential Choice," January 2018, paper submitted for publication.
106 Steven Levitsky and Daniel Ziblatt, "Is Donald Trump a Threat to Democracy?," *New York Times*, December 16 2016, www.nytimes.com/2016/12/16/opinion/sunday/is-donald-trump-a-threat-to-democracy (accessed May 14 2017).
107 Brian Klaas, "The threat Donald Trump poses to democracy is not overblown," *Chicago Tribune*, May 3 2007, www.chicagotribune.com/news/opinion/commentary/ct-donald-trump-threatens-democracy-20170502-story.html (accessed May 16 2017); APF, "Rights report warns Donald Trump-style populism threatens democracy," *Daily Nation*, January 13 2017, www.nation.co.ke/news/world/Trump-style-populism-threatens-democracy--Report/1068-3515794-tufoi6z/ (accessed May 16 2017); Ian Johnston, "Donald Trump threatens 'the very future of democracy,'

top scientist warns," *Independent*, February 19 2017, www.independent
.co.uk/news/world/americas/noaa-donald-trump-compared-hitler-
mussolini-fascist-jane-lubchenco-aaas-usc-a7587981.html (accessed May
16 2017); Kenneth Roth, "We Cannot Afford to Sit Back While Trump
Threatens America's Democracy," *Huffington Post*, February 21 2017,
www.huffingtonpost.com/entry/trump-threat-democracy_us_58ac7d8ce4
b002e2bdc79292 (accessed May 16 2017).

108 Ryan, "No Compromise"; Bauer, Yong, and Krupnikov, "Who is Punished?"

109 Frank, *What's Wrong with Kansas*.

110 Thomas B. Edsall, "To Impeach or Not to Impeach?" *New York Times*,
May 25 2017, www.nytimes.com/2017/05/25/opinion/donald-trump-
impeachment.html?action=click&pgtype=Homepage&clickSource=st
ory-heading&module=opinion-c-col-left-region&region=opinion-c-col-left-
region&WT.nav=opinion-c-col-left-region&_r=0 (accessed May 25 2017).

111 Eyck, *History of the Weimar Republic*, vol. 2; Dorpalen, *Hindenburg and the Weimar
Republic*; Broszat, *Hitler and the Collapse of Weimar Germany*; Mommsen, *Rise
and Fall of Weimar Democracy*; Evans, *Coming of the Third Reich*.

112 Samuels, *Machiavelli's Children*, ch. 4.

113 Huffington Post, Pollster, "Congress Job Approval," May 11 2017, http://
elections.huffingtonpost.com/pollster/congress-job-approval (accessed May
16 2017), shows a 17 percent approval and 63.7 percent disapproval in
October 2016. By May 2017, their survey of eleven polls revealed a spread
with average of 15 percent approval and 79 percent disapproval, with the
remainder undecided.

114 Editorial Board, "The Republican's Guide to Presidential Behavior,"
New York Times, May 15 2007, www.nytimes.com/2017/05/13/opinion/
sunday/the-republicans-guide-to-presidential-behavior.html?action=cli
ck&pgtype=Homepage&clickSource=story-heading&module=opinion-
c-col-left-region&region=opinion-c-col-left-region&WT.nav=opinion-
c-col-left-region&_r=0 (accessed May 15 2017), notes the following
violations: President Trump has accused a former president, without evidence, of an impeachable offense; employs top aides with financial and other
connections to a hostile foreign power; blames the judiciary, in advance, for
any terror attacks; brands the media "the enemy of the American people";
demands personal loyalty from the FBI director; threatens the former FBI
director; accepts foreign payments to his businesses, in possible violation of
the Constitution; occupies the White House with the help of a hostile foreign power; intimidates congressional witnesses; allows White House staff
members to use their personal email for government business; neglects to
fill thousands of crucial federal government positions; falsely claims that
millions of people voted illegally; fails to fire high-ranking members of his
national security team for weeks, even after knowing they lied to the vice-
president and exposed themselves to blackmail.

115 Philip Bump, "The one little number that – so far – is all the protection
Donald Trump needs," *Washington Post*, May 12 2017, www.washingtonpost
.com/news/politics/wp/2017/05/12/the-one-little-number-that-so-far-is-
all-of-the-protection-donald-trump-needs/?utm_term=.7886a62b4416
(accessed May 16 2017).

7   Georgian Britain

The man of wealth and pride
Takes up a space that many poor supplied;
Space for his lake, his park's extended bounds,
Space for his horses, equipage, and hounds:
The robe that wraps his limbs in silken sloth
Has robbed the neighbouring fields of half their growth.

Oliver Goldsmith[1]

Many western scholars assume that liberal capitalist democracy is the only rational response to the modern world. Liberals believe that pressures from below for a political voice and greater affluence, and from above in the form of system-level incentives, will ultimately result in a world of stable, peaceful, free-market democracies. These scholars expect China's regime to collapse unless it transforms itself into something approaching the liberal model. Are these accurate readings of modernity and of China's future or are they ideologically driven and blind to the failings of liberal democracy and alternative pathways to political stability? Our chapter attempts to shed some light on the second question by means of a comparative case study.

Britain and the People's Republic of China may appear to be odd bedfellows. One was a relatively small, sparsely populated, pre-industrial, European kingdom with a powerful aristocracy, small army, and multi-ethnic and confessional population. The other is a twenty-first century, geographically vast, Asian, industrial, one-party state with a large army, and a relatively homogenous population constituting almost a third of the world's people. These differences are enough to make one wary of pairing them in any meaningful way. When comparisons are made between China and England they invariably stress the differences between them to show why, for example, the industrial revolution developed in the former and not the latter.[2]

There are many striking similarities between eighteenth-century Britain and contemporary China. They include remarkable economic growth, rise to great power status, one-party governance (de facto in

Georgian England), self-replicating elites who used their control over government and administrations to enrich themselves and their families, tight controls over judiciary and media to propagate official discourses and limit critical ones, violent suppression of demonstrations and transport or imprisonment of dissidents, and rural areas ruled by local officials largely independent of central control who provoked or struggled to control almost daily popular protests.

Both regimes came to power after civil wars, devoting considerable efforts – especially in their first few decades – to suppress dissidents and rebellious nationalities in outlying provinces. Due to the spread of market relations, and central authority in the case of China, disparate regions became more integrated and economically interdependent. However, both countries were a patchwork of distinctive regions and communities with distinct traditions and dialects. As the dominant ideologies of divine right and communism lost appeal, elites became more corrupt and made increasing use of nationalism, economic rewards, and fear of instability as props for their respective regimes.

Acquisitiveness and venality gained widespread acceptance throughout these societies and traditional values and norms declined. "Getting rich became glorious."[3] Leaders provided entrepreneurs with competitive advantages and protection. The upwardly mobile in turn became supporters of the regime. Desire for wealth spread through both societies, which in turn encouraged people lower down the economic ladder to make the same kinds of deals with the devil in the hope of prospering.

These similarities are revealing, but so are the differences, and it is the latter that point to divergent trajectories for the two countries. We nevertheless contend that the most important differences between the two countries are of degree, not of kind, making comparison possible and fruitful. Georgian Britain was never as authoritarian, repressive, administratively rigid as China, and never as single-minded in imposing Church of England doctrine as China was with its communist ideology. Both countries ultimately eased their initial ideological commitments, but in different ways. Here too, British leaders became more relaxed, requiring only outward obeisance of those who held political office. Greater self-confidence, tolerance, and political fluidity made it possible for Georgian Britain to evolve into a different kind of state, with institutions that made government and administration more responsive to the people. They also enabled the people to gain sufficient power to transform over time the goals and modus operandi of the institutions of state. This seems unlikely in China.

We do not engage in direct cross-case comparisons. But we do ask the same questions about each country. How did the Glorious Revolution and the People's Republic consolidate their rule and build legitimacy? To what degree can post-1688 Britain and present-day China be considered stable regimes despite their undemocratic governance and rapid economic and social transformation? What were or are the greatest threats to their legitimacy, and to what extent did leaders of both regimes recognize and cope with them? How did leaders and other relevant political actors perceive the strength and vulnerability of these regimes over time? Did these beliefs help to buttress or undermine the stability of their political systems? And in the case of Georgian England, what accounts for its evolution into a highly stable regime able to survive without any serious internal challenge after the revolution in France?

Our pairing of these cases is motivated by more than the surprising similarities we enumerate. Britain is *the* quintessential democratic success story. Without revolution, civil war, or foreign invasion, it made the transformation from a divine right monarchy and tiny political and economic elite to a burgeoning democracy that reformed its institutions and allowed a transfer of political power first to parliament and then to the "middling" and working classes. Are there lessons to be learned about change and political stability that might help us better frame our inquiry into China?

We begin with a discussion of what we mean by political stability, and then proceed to our case studies. The British case – the subject of this chapter – dates from the so-called Glorious Revolution of 1688, when the Protestant, Dutch, William of Orange replaced the Catholic James II on the throne. The Georgian era begins with the accession of George I in 1714 and extends through the reign of George IV, which ended in 1830. We discuss post-1688 Britain, but focus primarily on the Georgian era. Over time, it has been assessed very differently. Victorians looked back on it as soulless, cynical, and dissolute. Twentieth-century left-wing historians condemned its hierarchy, inequality, privilege, and confined life of the masses. Nostalgic Tories have come to see it as "the Augustan Age," an ordered epoch due to monarch, church, and aristocracy. There is ongoing controversy among historians about how long the *ancien régime* lasted, the extent to which it was supported by ordinary people, how rapidly it was transformed, and the reasons for that transformation.[4] We tread gingerly through these intellectual minefields relying on concepts and propositions developed in the earlier chapters to come up with our own answers.

We emphasize that contemporary China is different from Georgian England in several important respects: higher frequency of contention; pervasive censorship; elite corruption and division; and unwillingness to sanction the existence of opposition parties. Order is maintained through economic growth, ideological flexibility, the inclusion of potential rivals in the communist party, and the promotion of institutions of accountability. We outline conditions under which the current sources of order may no longer serve as a stabilizing force.

Political Stability

Chapter 2 defines stability in the first instance as legible, predictable behavior in accord with recognized and accepted norms. Behavior of this kind has the potential to build solidarity, which makes orders more efficient and resilient. The absence of norm-based, predictable behavior and solidarity are marks of disorder. It is often characterized by violence, and a breakdown of top-down authority. Put crudely, political stability might be defined in terms of regime survival, but as noted in Chapter 2 some of the most "stable" political systems – measured in terms of their longevity and absence of major violence – are those that have changed the most over the years. Longevity and stability are most often, and perhaps always in the modern era, the product of cumulative, largely peaceful change. Key to such change is the existence of rules about how change is brought about, and also the possibility to challenge and change these rules. Longevity can be a marker of stability, if change is achieved peacefully. So too is the distribution of means used to ensure order and regime compliance. The more stable the regime, the less its leaders must rely on violence and punishment to maintain authority.

Stability is an analytical concept, but it is also a state of mind. If enough actors believe their political system is stable – or fragile – their expectations are almost certain to have important behavioral implications. Beliefs of this kind can even be made self-fulfilling. We accordingly need to know what British people in the Georgian era and present-day China thought or think about their political systems, as it is these assessments that matter. Such judgments can be wrong and those who make them can subsequently be pleasantly or unpleasantly surprised. More interesting, negative assessments of stability can augment tensions, but under some conditions can contribute to stability. We observe both outcomes in Georgian England.

In the aftermath of the Glorious Revolution, many members of the political elite thought another civil war a real possibility. William and Mary were rejected as usurpers by sizeable English and Scottish minorities and a majority in Ireland; some of them looked to France for military support to restore James II to the throne. The relative tranquility that prevailed – Ireland aside – represented a sharp break with the murderous disorder and civil wars of the previous fifty years. There were tense moments. In 1715 up to 20,000 Scots rallied to a Jacobite uprising. In 1745 the French, at war with Britain, supported the Stuart pretender, and a Jacobite army marched on London. The rebels were defeated, but it might have ended differently. In 1789, the French Revolution erupted. In response to the terror and French encouragement of revolution throughout Europe, the British government suspended habeas corpus, arrested agitators and reformers, banned meetings and organized Volunteer regiments throughout the country. Two naval mutinies, neither of them revolutionary in intent, were the worst the government faced in England. Ireland aside, there was never a threat of revolution. Ever since, historians have devoted much effort to explain the *revolution manquée*.

In China, the first decade of communist rule was a turbulent one. The regime faced a series of domestic and foreign threats. The new regime struggled to establish control over the country's territory, and especially its periphery. The People's Liberation Army invaded and suppressed dissent in Tibet. It fought Kuomintang armies and bandit groups along their southern border, faced a defeated but hostile Kuomintang regime that found refuge on Taiwan, and met fierce opposition from landlords in their efforts to impose land reform throughout the country. Collectivization and the Laogai camp system were responsible for millions of deaths.[5]

The conventional wisdom about political stability for a very long time followed Edmund Burke's depiction of it as a slow, sedimentary growth, laid down over the centuries and the product of prudence, experience, and wisdom of a culture and its elite. David Hume wrote his *History of England* to demonstrate that stability was a new feature in a constitutional system that bore little relationship with what preceded it. Noting the rapid change from instability to stability between 1688 and 1725, J. H. Plumb argues that countries can move just as quickly into stable configurations as they do away from them.[6] Similar arguments are made about European stability after World War II.[7]

When positive phase transitions occur, there is almost certain to be a considerable time lag before people recognize the new state of affairs. Beliefs, as noted, have important behavioral consequences. Fear of civil war may make people more cooperative and compromising in the hope of forestalling a slide to disorder. Fear of instability seems to have had this effect in post-1688 England, and the aftermath of World War II, where it was a prime catalyst of the European project. By contrast, uncertainty about stability emboldened Jacobites in Scotland and anti-Communists in post-1949 China.

After about three decades, the new regimes in Britain and China came to be considered relatively stable by most political actors. It was more of an uphill struggle in China because domestic resistance was far more entrenched. It was encouraged by the Kuomintang from its refuge in Taiwan, just as Irish and Jacobite rebels were encouraged by France. Britain waged a far-flung war with France, and China with the United States and its allies on the Korean Peninsula. The Korean War was costly to China, but nothing in comparison to the self-inflicted damage of the so-called Great Leap Forward; the latter was responsible for the great famine and tens of millions of deaths.

James II was in many ways analogous to Chiang Kai-chek. The former king found refuge onshore, the latter offshore, and both, supported by foreign powers, espoused a rival ideology, encouraged defections, and promised to overthrow the new regimes and return to power. The Stuarts posed a longer-lasting threat: from 1688 to 1746, when Charles Edward Stuart, the Pretender, and his Scottish army were crushed at the Battle of Culloden.[8] William III and his Protestant Whig backers in parliament were more accommodating than their Chinese counterparts; they persecuted Catholics in England, brutally suppressed a Catholic uprising in Ireland, but extended the olive branch to Protestant dissenters and built bridges to agricultural and commercial elites.

Political stability is achieved in the first instance by overcoming or marginalizing domestic and foreign threats. This buys time for a new regime to attempt to achieve legitimacy by building and consolidating support beyond its initial supporters. Regimes can choose different strategies to this end, as Georgian England and China did. The choice of strategies gives rise to path dependency; it makes certain strategies feasible in later decades and all but precludes others. Problems of creating stability are accordingly closely connected to the problems of maintaining it, as the strategies employed to do the former help determine those available to address the latter. Of equal importance, they help shape the kinds of problems mature regimes face. This kind of path dependency is strongly marked in both England and China.

Regimes based on force do not endure. They must advance the material interests and self-esteem of their populations to build legitimacy and make compliance voluntary and then habitual. Habit provides an enormous cushion of support in parlous times and also makes it possible to identify and target dissidents. Georgian Britain – which now encompassed Scotland and Ireland as well as England – and Communist China succeeded in building legitimacy in most of the territory they controlled. Success also brought new challenges. It created important administrative and political capabilities, but limitations in repertoire and mindset that made it both easier and more difficult to cope with new challenges. Georgian Britain succeeded in surmounting the challenge of population growth, economic development, the emergence of new classes, new political ideas, and demands for reform. The verdict on China is open.

Single-Party Rule

The Glorious Revolution was a response to growing opposition to James II and the fear that a male heir would try to reimpose Catholicism in

England. Influential Whigs, with some Tory backers, invited James' Protestant daughter and her husband, William of Orange, to England to replace James. William landed with his army at Brixham in November 1688, James II fled to France, and in January 1689 the Convention Parliament proclaimed William and Mary co-rulers of England, Scotland, and Ireland. The House of Commons made William accept a Bill of Rights that affirmed habeas corpus, and its authority. The new rulers were widely welcomed, but opposed by many Catholics and those committed to the divine right of kings, who rejected parliament's authority to appoint a monarch.[9]

The first decades of the new order were turbulent. William confronted an Irish rebellion, whose suppression reduced local governance, imposed new limitations on Catholics, and left the majority of the population deeply resentful of British rule.[10] Scotland was forced into a union with Britain in 1707, resented by many Scots, especially highlanders.[11] In England, where there had been two generations of persecution and counter-persecution between Anglicans and Dissenters, conflict between them intensified once the Catholic threat receded.[12] Between 1689 and 1715 there were twelve bitterly contested parliamentary elections, more in number than in any comparable period before or since. In Queen Anne's reign (1702–14) the Tories introduced new penalties against Dissenters but also ended the increasingly unpopular war against France.[13] With the accession of George I in 1714, the Whigs returned to power, where they would stay until 1760.

Traditional Whig accounts dated the two-party system from the Exclusion crisis of 1679–81. In an influential 1929 book, Lewis Namier all but demolished this claim, and also questioned the utility of using parties for purposes of political analysis.[14] In recent decades there has been renewed interest in parties.[15] Summarizing the emerging consensus, Boyd Hilton writes: "In retrospect it looks like single party rule" for much of the eighteenth century, "but at many points the government seemed likely to fall."[16] A two-party system did not effectively emerge until 1760.[17]

The postwar debate about Georgian stability begins with J. H. Plumb's famous argument that it was a consequence of single-party Whig governance.[18] Other scholars accept that Whig supremacy in the Hanoverian era was a "spectacle of parliamentary tranquility" compared to what preceded it.[19] Plumb attributes Whig success to a reaction against the excesses of Queen Anne, Hanoverian preference for Whigs over Tories and, above all, to the skillful management of parliament and crown by Robert Walpole between 1721 and 1742.[20]

The Whig Junto of the 1720s maintained absolute majorities in the Commons and Lords, established authority over the court and administration, purged Tories of their civil and military offices, and constructed a strong Protestant identity that bridged confessional differences. Also important, Plumb maintains, was the relative shift in power from crown to parliament. Parliament met more regularly and passed the Triennial Act of 1694 to protect itself against William's growing high-handedness. The Hanoverian monarchs were equally jealous of their prerogatives, but the movement toward what would become a constitutional monarchy accelerated in the course of the eighteenth century.

Whig rule under Walpole and his successors was oligarchical. The Whigs marginalized the Tories by publicizing the Jacobite sympathies of some of their stalwarts. Walpole spent considerable sums on anti-Tory propaganda and created a network of spies and informers.[21] He further increased Whig majorities by gerrymandering, graft, and other kinds of chicanery. The Whig party was so effective in its control of the House of Commons that elections were often uncontested.[22] In 1761, only 18 of 201 borough constituencies went to the polls.[23] The Commons was filled with "placemen," MPs who owed their seats and, in return, their votes, to Whig administrations. By 1780, there were as many as 180 "placemen."

Oligarchy was somewhat softened in its effects by the diversity of the Whig coalition and the resulting difficulty of balancing urban against rural interests, agricultural against commercial, and Anglicans against Dissenters.[24] The Whigs won support of landed and other proper-tied classes because they supported their property and privileges and provided favorable conditions for their enrichment. They improved communications through turnpikes, and after 1750 canals, making it easier for produce and other goods to reach markets. These improvements were sanctioned by parliament, usually through private member bills, and financed by incorporated companies. They cut the trip from Manchester to London from four-and-a-half days to 28 hours and from Liverpool to London from six to two days.[25] In previous centuries local power had resisted the centralizing efforts of the monarchy. But practical men in London and the provinces welcomed the many improvements parliament was able to authorize.[26]

If the government relied on the countryside for votes, it turned to the City of London for money. The Whigs pursued a costly interventionist policy on the continent against France, so were in constant need of loans. They engineered a financial reformation that included creation of the Bank of England. As many of the most important figures in the City were Dissenters, the Whigs removed the obligation to attend Anglican services and licensed their chapels. Dissent prospered and was protected by William III and the Hanoverians.[27]

A powerful parliament was able to establish effective control over a wider range of offices, appointments, and pensions and the patronage this allowed. Whig politicians used their new power to reward themselves and their kinsmen, but also to build support in the Commons and the country. They engaged in "old corruption" in which governmental offices were structured as sinecures. They created many highly remunerative positions that involved no work, or where others did it for a pittance, and so-called reversions, where the office became hereditary and was regarded as transferable property. Edward Gibbon was made Lord of Trade, for which he received £800 a year with no requirement beyond consistent votes for Lord North's ministry.[28] Many of these offices were profitable beyond their immediate remuneration because they brought control over other offices and contracts that could be sold. John Huggins paid £5,000 for the wardenship of the Fleet jail and had to bilk the government and prisoners to recoup his investment and turn a profit.[29]

The highest government officials took pecuniary advantage of their offices. Walpole used admiralty barges to transport smuggled French wine up the Thames.[30] Smugglers working for him or other officials shot at excise officers with near impunity. It became increasingly difficult to distinguish crime from politics. The corruption of high officials was public knowledge and a regular theme of cartoons, songs and theater, as in John Gay's *The Beggar's Opera*. Periodically, the government would arrest and try some official for corruption to give the appearance of being on the side of reform. The elite not only used access to parliament to enrich itself but increasingly flaunted its wealth in competitive shows of conspicuous consumption. It found expression in estates, gardens, entertainment, and purchases of fine art and furnishings.[31] There was nothing new about greed and showing off one's wealth, but it was no longer treated as sinful. "Acquisitiveness and opportunism found a new respectability."[32]

In Chapter 4 I theorize that elite corruption is one pathway to disorder. It arouses envy and emulation, as it did in Georgian England, leading to an erosion of values and practices that sustain key norms. This was apparent in the pervasiveness of corruption, which spread throughout the government, and from government to business. It did not, however, threaten the political order. Rather, it helped to smooth over differences and reconcile important actors to the government and political system. Even some Tories came over to the Whigs to reap the rewards. Corruption might be said to have molded "a consensus" among affluent and aspirant, creating a bond of values, expectations, and rewards, and making the latter more supportive of the former. It was also a social solvent that bridged the otherwise sharp divide between aristocrats and commoners. It provided the ruling classes with a carrot, but also with a stick in the form of exclusion from the largesse enabled by corruption.[33]

The system worked, but was inherently unstable because of the costs of corruption to society. It led to overpriced contracts that were often not honored, gross inefficiency due to incompetence, negligence, a surfeit of offices with overlapping responsibilities, and blatant wastage of a significant percentage of public income that was funneled into private hands.

Elite Cohesion

All sizeable societies are hierarchical. Georgian England was more hierarchical than most. England, and Britain more generally, was run, and largely owned, by a surprising small elite. At the apex were some 5,000 families of the nobility and gentry.[34] Nobility, or aristocracy, in contemporary usage referred to a group of people, constituted by heredity, seen as superior to others and who regarded themselves as the natural ruling class. The gentry were people of wealth, manners, and breeding, who came beneath them and above the yeomanry.

There was no unified middle class, but what were called the "middling orders." These freeholders, farmers, and tenants constituted up to 30 percent of the population in some rural districts. They also included men in the professions and commerce, of whom there were an increasing number in towns and cities. Some merchants, and later manufacturers, accumulated sufficient wealth to purchase landed estates and live the life of gentlemen. The shopkeepers and tradesmen beneath them were still of higher status than artisans and those engaged in handicrafts.[35]

The social order was finely graded, and more so within that across groupings. The pecking order was well known and upheld through dress, practices, salutations, and order of precedence. In 1806, Patrick Colquhoun, a Scottish merchant and statistician, published an elaborate twenty-nine-step table of social structure and the incomes of each gradation.[36] Upward mobility was possible into the middling orders and from them into the gentry. It was achieved by making money, self-fashioning, and marrying in. Anyone could claim to be a gentleman if he could afford the right clothes and other material accouterments, spoke with good grammar and diction, and learned proper manners. Jane Austen novels offer insights into this form of social mobility and the resistance it sometimes encountered.[37]

In response to the growing wealth of middling and lower classes, the aristocracy and gentry began to fence off their properties and entertainments. They began, for example, to charge admission to cricket matches. English society was nevertheless more open than France or most German states, but the aristocracy remained closed.[38] The peerage remained remarkably stable in the eighteenth century. It increased only slightly, from 173 members in 1700 to 181 in 1760. Most of the new peers were related by blood to existing ones.[39] Unlike their continental counterparts, peers had no special legal privileges, but they were entitled to a seat in the House of Lords. The nobility and gentry did benefit from their wealth in other ways; in comparison to the rest of the population they were healthier, taller, more fertile, reached sexual maturity at an earlier age, and lived longer.[40]

Peers dominated the government. Almost 60 percent of them held office during the century. Commoners did not predominate in cabinets until the mid-nineteenth century.[41] The nobility monopolized the diplomatic service, higher officer ranks, and the equivalent in the civil administration.[42] Peers also had an important voice in the selection of the House of Commons. Frank O'Gorman estimates that they exercised some degree of influence in a quarter to half of all seats between 1700 and 1800.[43] In 1715, 224 of 558 MPs were sons of MPs. By 1754, the figure was 294. In the same year 400 MPs were related to one another. Most members of the House of Commons were Anglican and aristocratic or noble in background. They were increasingly educated in public schools and Oxbridge. In 1761, only about 15 percent of 558 MPs came from non-elite backgrounds. By 1812, this had risen to 26 percent, excluding Irish MPs.[44] The electorate also constituted an elite. In 1700, it amounted to about 4 percent of the population, and less than 20 percent of the adult male population. These percentages would decline during the century because of population growth.[45]

Parliamentary seats were famously weighted in favor of rural boroughs in the southeast of England. Their total electorate was only 85,000, but the 15,000 voters of the region controlled half the seats in the Commons. Cornwall had twenty-one boroughs and Lancashire only six. The Septennial Bill of 1716 extended parliaments to seven years, encouraging candidates to spend more to win office. Even so, electioneering became a hobby only the rich could afford. The costs of contested elections rose proportionately given the expected monetary rewards of winning a seat.[46] Many elections went uncontested as they were in the pockets of large landlords, or because a candidate pulled out when canvassing indicated that he would lose. In Oxfordshire, the Tories spent £40,000 in 1754 to unseat the Whig incumbent.[47] Even in so-called rotten boroughs, electors could make their voice heard. Earl Fitzwilliam lost his seat in Malton in 1806 because he had not treated his tenants well during the near famine of 1799–1800.[48] Parliament, universities, and the administration were closed to all but Anglicans, but this began to change in the course of the century. Dissenters took control of dozens of seats where the corporation or freemen were the majority of the electorate.[49] Only a small cohort of merchants made in into the Commons and never constituted more than 15 percent of the total. There was no secret ballot until 1872.

The pyramid was, if anything, narrower by the end of the century. Peers were still few in number, and a significantly smaller percentage of the population due to significant growth. The 5.2 million people of England in 1700 had become 10.5 million people of Britain – England, Scotland, and Ireland – by the end of the century. The gap between the rich and the others increased in the countryside throughout the century. Great estates, almost all owned by the nobility, prospered at the expense of smaller estates of the gentry because they were better able to cope with falling agricultural prices. Their owners used low-interest mortgages to expand and improve. The survival of this hierarchy *and* the development of political stability in an era of dramatic change is a remarkable achievement. Single-party control of Parliament and co-option through corruption at best provides only a partial explanation.

Administration and Economic Growth

Despite rampant corruption, numerous sinecures and useless offices, and many arcane practices, Britain had the most efficient administration in Europe by the end of the eighteenth century. It did much to reconcile people in all orders to the government and political system. The nobility, gentry, and commercial classes benefitted from the economic growth it enabled. Unlike France, England solved its food problem; there were no famines and it briefly became an exporter of grain. The lower classes had a steadier supply of food, although there were noticeable shortages following bad harvests, as in 1693–95 and 1708–10.

Administration expanded greatly after 1720. Under Walpole, the government budget was £5 million per annum. It was £10 million by 1748, £20 million by 1760, and £130 million in 1800.[50] There was a land tax, but governments increasingly relied on indirect and unprogressive sales taxes. They laid a heavier burden on the poor. The government also collected more money through excise duties on the country's rapidly expanding trade. By 1718 there were already 561 full-time customs officers, and 1,000 part-time, and this was just in London.

Reform gathered momentum in the second half of the century. The administration gave up Roman numerals and Tudor script, and the Exchequer the use of willow wands and Latin. The Treasury became dominant in domestic affairs, imposed a hierarchy, and the Secretaryship did something similar in foreign affairs.[51] Various Acts reduced the number of superfluous offices, but not all were abolished. Weights and measures were standardized, as was spelling, and mile signposts erected.

By the time William Pitt the Younger served as prime minister (from 1783 to 1801, and again from 1804 to 1806), Britain had become a "fiscal-military" state.[52] Between the Glorious Revolution and defeat of Napoleon, tax revenue increased ten-fold, and total revenue extracted per capita increased almost five times.[53] At home, the government raised more revenue more efficiently, making Britain one of the most heavily taxed states. Abroad, it oversaw an expanding colonial empire.[54] The administration was still in many ways ramshackle; its failures were readily apparent in leaky and ineffective warships, poor provisioning of soldiers, and other failures that contributed to the loss of the American colonies. People at all levels of society preferred it this way, as they regarded a truly efficient and intrusive government as unacceptable. By default, not by design, the administration developed in ways that made it useful but not feared.

Revenue collection and economic growth went hand-in-hand. In the course of the eighteenth century, domestic consumption increased six-and-a-half fold, and cotton production by a factor of thirty-two. In 1700 Londoners consumed 800,000 tons of coal. By 1790, this had risen to 2.5 million tons. Pig iron output increased 35 times, and sales abroad of iron products rose two-fold. Britain's iron output was equal to the rest of Europe and the United States combined.[55] In the first half of the century this growth was based almost entirely on expansion and improvements in commerce, finance, and agriculture; manufacturing only began to have a significant impact after 1770. Growth benefitted from the absence of internal customs duties and trade barriers, in contrast to France and the German states. The number of acres under cultivation increased by 50 percent in the first half of the century. In 1700, 45 percent of the population was engaged in agriculture. By 1800, it had dropped to 36 percent, although it increased in absolute numbers.[56]

The economy also benefitted from foreign and colonial trade and production in the form of slaves and sugar.[57] Between 1714 and 1760, shipping in tonnage increased 30 percent, the value of exports by 80 percent, re-exports by 50 percent.[58] Between 1675 and 1730, the national demand for goods and services increased at a faster rate than the population.[59] Population growth meant that by 1800, 60 percent of the population was less than 24 years of age.[60] An increasing percentage of the population lived in cities; 16 percent versus 9 percent for the rest of Europe in 1800. London was the largest city in Europe.[61] Its phenomenal growth, and that of other cities like Bristol, Birmingham, and Liverpool, encouraged the construction of canals, roads, and turnpikes. Coal could be brought to urban areas, and later to factories. Commerce, infrastructure development, and manufacturing were facilitated by, and stimulated the development of, long-distance credit, bills of exchange, banks, and currency.

The "Middling" Orders

The concept of class had not yet emerged in the first half of the eighteenth century, and what we call the middle class or bourgeoisie was referred to as "the middling orders."[62] Nor is there any evidence of class consciousness among the middle stratum of society.[63] Historians have imposed class in retrospect, and offer two- and three-class models of it in eighteenth-century English society. The three-class model differs from the two in considering the middling orders as a distinct class.[64] More germane to our purposes is the difference among historians about the extent to which relations between the middling classes on the one hand and the landed gentry and nobility on the other were hostile or cooperative. Those who argue for the two-class order tend to see relations between gentry and workers as brutal and exploitative. Those who espouse the three-class order regard the clientelist system as to some degree effective and supportive of solidarity.[65]

The nobility and gentry had no interest in entering into finance, commerce, industry or the professions, but were willing to invest in them. The middling classes were accordingly the prime movers and beneficiaries of commercial expansion, urbanization, and the beginnings of industrialization, as were ambitious and successful members of the "lower orders." Aristocrats and manufacturers often cooperated locally, and worked together on the national scene through lobbies, trade associations, and chambers of commerce.[66] In rapidly expanding Liverpool, the corporation resembled a private company, and rich families like the Rathbones made substantial contributions to fund schools, hospitals, utilities, gardens, and libraries.[67] In elections, members of the middle class served as agents, canvassers, and publicity agents.[68] Cooperation of this kind across classes often generated mutual respect.

Many successful businessmen were Dissenters. Quakers in particular were overrepresented in banking (Barclays and Lloyds), and manufacturing (Wilkinson, Fry, and Cadbury). Parliament was largely deaf to pleas for reform from the rising commercial and manufacturing elite, but they had more success on the local level. Businessmen were well represented on statutory bodies, especially those responsible for turnpikes, canals, and urban improvements.[69] By 1800, the middling classes owned 20 to 25 percent of the land. They sent their children to elite public schools and universities. This was part of a broader effort by the middling classes to acquire education and culture as means of gaining status.[70]

The middling classes were strong supporters of the existing order, only in part because they benefitted from it. They had been successfully socialized into believing it was just, necessary, and even natural. They acted against the government when they believed it threatened the constitution, as they did in the 1730s when Walpole was in power. They rallied even more strongly behind the government in the face of foreign and domestic threats – from the American colonists in the 1770s, the French after 1789, and the lower orders in the 1790s. As the middling orders became more prominent in economic and civic life they became more critical of landed elite. They were on the whole dismissive of its profligacy and propagated a counter-discourse stressing hard work, frugality, and civic responsibility.

Status is just as important as wealth for most people, and here too the middling classes made important gains that reconciled them to the order. In England, and Britain more generally, the nobility and aristocracy were neither dismissive nor hostile to the commercial classes, willing to cooperate with them in business and charity, and even in politics. The middling orders did not feel looked down upon or excluded in quite the same way their French, Prussian, or Austrian counterparts did. They did, however, found their own clubs and associations and published their own newspapers and periodicals. In London, other cities and, increasingly, in towns as well, they socialized with and married one another, although they occasionally also married into the gentry. They were, on the whole, contented with their life and position in society.

The Lower Orders

In 1689, the overwhelming majority of people lived in the countryside. The vast majority were small farmers, tenants, drovers, artisans, and laborers of all kinds. They ran the gamut from comfortable to indigent. Perhaps 10 percent of households did not earn enough to survive and were dependent on relief and charity. Their numbers increased in years of bad harvests.[71] Men and women with jobs had some disposable income and could indulge in minor luxuries like tobacco and tea, both of which spread down the social ladder. In 1688, the average family was buying £10 of British-made goods a year. By 1811, this sum had risen to £40.[72] The Poor Law provided outdoor relief for the indigent, but was increasingly challenged by those who thought it encouraged idleness.[73]

During the eighteenth century, the percentage of people living in towns of 5,000 people or more rose from 13 to 25 percent.[74] The so-called lower orders lived very different lives in towns and cities than they did in the countryside. Different means were used to reconcile them to the political order, and restrain them when they rebelled. The countryside was visibly hierarchical. Traditional hierarchies are clientelist: those at the top receive respect, honor, and obedience from those beneath them, and they in turn are expected to provide practical assistance to those who require it. Every step of the social ladder comes with rule packages, and they are thicker and more elaborate the higher one ascends. As noted in earlier chapters, such hierarchies, when they function well, reward and restrain those at the top and protect those at the bottom.

For much of the eighteenth century, such a hierarchical order prevailed in the English countryside. Many farmers had no leases and depended on the generosity of landlords in bad times and their wisdom of not expelling improving tenants in good times.[75] Squires had close interactions with tenants, sponsored feasts to celebrate important events in their families, and many helped out any tenants in dire straits. Paternalism led to greater honesty and hard work by employees. The commercial classes also benefitted because belief in property as an expression of the natural order led the nobility and gentry to defend their property rights.[76]

The hierarchy derived its legitimacy from the Christian concept of the "Great Chain of Being." It assigned everyone a proper place, from God on top, to animals on the bottom. Like fractals, the same order was replicated in countries and families, where the king, prince, husband or father had near-absolute authority over other members of the family. The Anglican Church propagated the Great Chain of Being through catechisms, sermons, and the printed word. So too would many dissenting sects, especially the Methodists.[77] The virtue of obedience was widely accepted. Inequality was regarded as fair, inevitable, and beneficial, as anarchy was the only alternative most people could envisage.[78] Church attendance dropped throughout the century but faith in God remained high, if not nearly universal. Samuel Johnson insisted, perhaps correctly, that "there were very few infidels."[79] Faith helped to sustain the hierarchy, as did xenophobia. Patriotism and hatred of foreigners were deeply entrenched and easily mobilized. Rural and urban crowds would readily cheer for the king.[80] Christian beliefs and sermons also affected the behavior of landowners. Sitting up front in specially reserved and fitted pews, under the nose of the priest, and visible to the lesser orders, they were under pressure from both directions to live up to their responsibilities. Most were charitable and willing to reduce or forego rents in hard times, although there were many examples of indifference and even cruelty.[81]

Respect was engendered through display and ritual. Large houses, with well-tended gardens, servants who bowed and scraped, owners dressed to the nines with fancy carriages and livery, encouraged respect for authority. Hierarchy and subordination permeated dress, social encounters, the law courts, churches, and public events. These rituals not only advertised hierarchy but also enforced it by including the middling classes, and often the lower orders, and assigning them subordinate roles. "Through such processes," Frank O'Gorman writes, "most people evinced a deference that did much to ensure a general acceptance of inequality and thus a legitimation of the power of the political and social elite in Hanoverian society."[82] Festivals like Christmas, Guy Fawkes Day, the birthday of William III, in which the different orders came together, demonstrated hierarchy but also helped to bridge it. Social mixing was easier and more likely to occur in a small society where everyone knew everyone else. Like church services, rituals and processions reminded the aristocracy and gentry of their responsibilities and socialized them into accepting them as necessary and beneficial to the preservation of their status.[83]

The clientelist hierarchy was on the wane in the last quarter of the eighteenth century. Landowners spent more time hunting, at the racetrack, at the spas, seaside, and in London during "the season." Their sense of paternal responsibility correspondingly declined. By 1758, only one-third of those appointed as Commissioners of the Peace in Kent actually took up their positions.[84] Nostalgia for the past set in. It is evident in Oliver Goldsmith's 1770 poem, "The Deserted Village," a lament for a society in which people knew and accepted their place.[85]

Even at its height, clientelist hierarchy did not prevent protests and violence. Riots were something of a way of life in city and countryside. Many involved no more than a dozen people but others brought out hundreds. Labor shortages and rising wages in the first half of the century dampened agricultural and working-class resentment. Growth industries needy of workers encouraged a new appreciation of labor's bargaining power, which led to different kinds of conflict. They were still desperately poor people, and for them, "a riot was a clarion call to their instinct to survive, for in the burning and looting there was many a windfall."[86]

Most rioters, however, were skilled workers and artisans, not the unemployed, vagrants, or criminals. Riots were calls for redress by traditional means. Those involved often resorted to parodies, parades, songs, and caricatures rather than violence.[87] While disturbances were local and focused on specific grievances, rioters nevertheless framed their demands in terms of broader principles of justice. Banners and placards proclaimed such things as "No General Warrants," "Restore Ancient Liberties," and "Old Prices."[88]

The food riot was the most common disturbance. It was directed against high prices, and hoarders. There were also protests against new taxes, enclosures, toll roads, and conscription.[89] Rioters were relatively restrained in their behavior as they sought redress of particular grievances. They sometimes destroyed property, but rarely attacked anyone because most participants were employed workers, anxious to keep their jobs, but desperate because of what they considered was the failure of landlords, employers, shopkeepers, or authorities to honor or defend their traditional rights.[90] The few riots that seriously threatened order, notably the Sacheverell riots of 1710 and the Gordon Riots of 1780, took place in cities.

Walpole relied on reforms, but in contrast to many European countries there was no secret police, censorship, torture, or religious orders to use for spying and enforcement. Proposals for professional police forces were consistently voted down because electors and their representatives were more fearful of a police state and its cost.[91] The Riot Act of 1715 was cumbersome and useless for dealing with local, as opposed to national disturbances. There was nevertheless considerable elite uncertainty that prompted parliament to increase the number of capital offenses. They rose from 50 in 1689 to 200 in 1800, but judges and juries were increasingly loath to impose the death penalty.[92] The Anglican Church was of little help in retraining the lower orders, who had little regard for it and largely stayed away from its services. The Church was all but absent in the most rapidly growing towns, where disorder was most pronounced.

The official on the spot was often the Justice of the Peace, usually a squire or clergyman, who had immediate supervision of rural parishes. He could issue warrants, administered the poor law, and tried minor offenses like vagrancy and poaching. In corporate towns, the dominant alderman performed this role. Justices wielded considerable authority, and more so when they met in Quarter Sessions where they adjudicated more serious offenses.[93] Justices of the Peace had to rely on habit, respect for authority, and the paternal authority of landowners. Justices of the Peace and the officials above them were loath to request government forces for fear of alienating locals, escalating conflict, and undermining their authority by giving greater power to the central government. They had to make do with little, and relied on negotiation and concession more than repression.[94] On occasion, the army was called out to quell disturbances, and most often succeeded through a show of force. It marched in a manner intended to awe spectators. Rioters in turn often organized spontaneously to mimic the army with their own parades. Both sides then backed off. In many instances, Justices of the Peace, or other local agents, did something to address and alleviate the local grievance that had led to the riot.[95]

Dissent and Opposition

We define dissent as well-intended policy differences and criticism intended to improve government, the economy, and social life. Opposition is motivated by rejection of a regime and its leaders with the goal of radical change. Dissent can become opposition, so the two categories should be regarded as totally distinct.

Dissent in Georgian England took a variety of forms. The minority that constituted the electorate could vote an MP or a government out of office, as happened to the Whigs in 1760 and the short-lived Tory government three years later. Intellectuals could air their grievances through newspapers, books, and on the stage. Intellectuals and religious leaders could organize reform movements. As noted, the less well-off could riot.

The end of licensing in 1695 opened the door to widespread and inexpensive publications. By 1720, there were 70 printers in London and 30 in the provinces. Newspapers had ever-larger circulation: 50,000 a week by 1760s with much wider readership as they circulated in cafes, reading rooms, and clubs.[96] Twenty years later, 500,000 newspapers were sold every morning in London.[97] Newspaper writing changed with increased circulation; ornate writing with many references that would resonate with only the educated was increasingly replaced by straightforward, simple prose that drew on a reduced vocabulary.[98] Beginning in the 1770s, the press began to cover parliamentary debates, something that was previously illegal. To the extent that there was censorship it was mostly self-imposed. The public discourse was enriched by a range of prominent writers, among them Addison, Defoe, Fielding, Goldsmith, Johnson, Steele, and Swift. Many books were hostile to the government, but books were expensive and often published through subscriptions.[99]

Reformers, many of them evangelicals or Quakers, had diverse foci, but almost all agreed on the need to trim and control a corrupt and bloated administration. A more radical minority aimed at the franchise. They wanted it extended, by lowering or dropping property requirements, and parliament redistricted to eliminate rotten boroughs and make it more reflective of the population.[100] The reform movement took on momentum following the loss of the American colonies, widely understood to be the product of political misjudgment and administrative incompetence. In the 1780s, Rockingham Whigs sought to make the administration more efficient. The Establishment Act of 1782 abolished 130 "inefficient offices." William Pitt, who came to office two years later, created a commission, with some fanfare, to rationalize administration. Their efforts brought little meaningful change and convinced reformers like William Cobbett that parliament itself would have to be reformed.[101]

The saga of John Wilkes revealed the arbitrary nature of the Whig oligarchy, but also its limits. Wilkes was the son of a wealthy newly rich distiller. He got hold of a pre-delivery copy of the King's 1763 speech, which he denounced in his journal, *North Britain*. George II was enraged, and had Wilkes arrested on a general warrant. His house was ransacked and his papers were confiscated. The government claimed to act in "a state of necessity," but Charles Pratt, First Lord Camden, Chief Justice of Common Pleas, ruled in favor of the defendant, arguing that as a member of the House of Commons he possessed parliamentary immunity. This was the first significant opposition from the bench to a long string of encroachments against Common Law.[102]

The government now deprived Wilkes of his parliamentary privilege and immunity; he was condemned by both houses of parliament, wounded in a duel, and forced to flee to France. He courageously returned and was reelected to the Commons in 1768. The government now went after him because he was an outspoken supporter of the American colonists. George III demanded that he be expelled once again from the Commons. His supporters were killed and the culprits cleared in mock trials. Londoners took to the streets in large numbers in support of Wilkes and goaded the government into taking steps that made it looks very mean and foolish.[103]

Many of Wilkes' supporters were anti-oligarchical and asserted that those in power should be responsible to the people. It was the first mass demonstration in Georgian England associated with this democratic principle. Pamphlets in support of Wilkes were very Lockean in tone and argument. Previous London riots had been focused on single issues. Rioters put a stop to the Excise in 1733–34 and Jewish naturalization in 1753. Drury Lane was wrecked by mobs in 1743, 1750, 1755, 1763, 1770, and 1776. There were riots against Dissenters, but more against Catholics. The anti-Papist Gordon Riots of June 1780 were the most destructive in London's history; they morphed from a peaceful demonstration into six days of violence and looting. The propertied classes were terrified by the Gordon Riots. So were erstwhile reformers like John Wilkes, who supported military intervention. Close to 300 people were shot, another 200 wounded, and 450 people imprisoned[104]

The shameless hounding of Wilkes and the loss of American colonies generated support for reform. Christopher Wyvill, an English cleric and landowner, led a movement to give more seats to rural areas, but also to cut patronage and administrative costs. The more radical Chartists and other groups organized in preparation for the 1781 election. But the 1780 Gordon Riots stopped reform in its tracks because of the fear of change it aroused within the government and the propertied classes.

Even so, the complacent oligarchy of Walpole and the Pelhams came to an end. The political elite recognized the growing challenge posed by population growth and shifts from countryside to cities, rapid economic growth, the growing wealth and local power of the middling orders, and the more politically active and better-organized urban poor. William Pitt the Younger, who entered office in 1783 and would lead Britain in its wars against revolutionary France, struggled to make administration more efficient and keep revolutionary sentiment at bay.[105]

The French Revolution put the government under greater pressure still and, not surprisingly, promoted overreactions to the perceived domestic threat. Pitt resorted to extreme measures. In 1790 and 1794, the government suspended habeas corpus. It suppressed Corresponding Societies and introduced laws against combination: the Traitorous Correspondence Act of 1793; the Treason and Sedition Acts of 1795; the Unlawful Oaths Acts of 1797; and the Combination Acts 1799–1800. Nascent trade unions were also suppressed, and their members protested with placards that read: "Peace and Large Bread, or a King without a head."[106]

Historians disagree about how close Britain came to revolution. The country was stressed economically as well as politically after 1789 because the cost of living rose due to poor harvests and population growth. There was widespread rioting in 1795–96, 1799–1801, and 1811–13. The crisis was overcome in the first instance because Britain retained the upper hand in its long struggle with France. Had the French been able to land a sizeable force in Ireland and make headway with local support, the outcome might well have been different. In England, the perceived threat of French invasion prevented the radicals from mobilizing any significant percentage of the population. King George remained more popular than Thomas Paine.[107] Even so, to paraphrase the Duke of Wellington's judgment of Waterloo, it was "a damned close run thing."

Political Change

Let us return to our two-stage framework of the creation and consolidation of new regimes. Consolidation was made possible by the raw power of the new regime. William and the English army were able to put down rebellion in Ireland and compel an Act of Union with Scotland. Domestic conflict was acute between Tories and Whigs, which largely reflected pro-James II versus pro-William sympathies. But English Catholics and Protestant divine righters never rallied behind subsequent Scottish revolts and the short-lived 1745 attempt by the Pretender and his Scottish supporters to march on London.

William and his supporters sought to legitimize their rule as necessary to preserve the fruits of the revolution: Protestant succession and the rights of parliament and the people enshrined in the Bill of Rights. Whigs used their authority to defend property, expand the rights of parliament, and expand religious freedoms for Dissenters. Under Walpole they created a broad enough coalition, greased by corruption, and kept in power with strong majorities by playing fast and loose with the electoral system. Englishmen came to believe in the stability of the system, which in turn helped to make this expectation self-fulfilling.

Whig success enabled Edmund Burke later in the century to pass off the fiction that 1688 was a restoration of traditional English liberties. This discourse was facilitated by deliberate Whig efforts to avoid defining the political settlement they had reached with the monarchy. Everybody could interpret it as they saw fit. As most political actors had strong incentives to go along with Whig oligarchy, they emphasized what they considered positive about the Glorious Revolution. Pro-William Tories accepted the fiction that James had abdicated and the reality that the Bill of Rights preserved Protestantism and the Anglican establishment. Protestant Dissenters valued the religious freedom it provided them. English Catholics welcomed its protection of property and the government's relaxed attitude to loyal Catholic nobility and gentry. Ulster Protestants were grateful to William for establishing their authority over their Catholic neighbors. Radical Whigs claimed it as a victory over tyranny.[108] Moderate Whigs invented the fiction, exposed by Hume, but successfully publicized by Burke, that there had been no revolution; Whigs and their supporters had merely removed a monarch to uphold the "ancient" constitution.[109]

In the course of the century, the Whig Oligarchy benefitted from economic growth; rural paternalism that maintained order and provided some relief, along with the Poor Law, to those in distress; a political elite that gradually closed ranks; and a decline in the Jacobite threat that led to a relaxation of authoritarian rule, a freer press and more tolerance of dissent. There was more upwards – and downwards – mobility than elsewhere in Europe. Money and manners opened doors. Profits, not tradition, ruled social exchange. Enterprising people from the lower and middle orders could seize economic opportunity without interference. In retrospect, the Jacobite threat was useful because it made it possible for the regime to mobilize support against a foreign enemy and deflect hostility against France that might otherwise have been directed against it.

There are deeper causes of stability, institutional and ideational. David Hume expressed a commonly held belief that France was more stable than Britain because rule was vested in a single individual able to maintain order and follow a consistent policy line. In reality, one of the most important sources of British stability was the shift from personal to institutional rule. In the Tudor and Stuart eras, authority was vested in the court and its personalities, as in France. Monarchs who were psychologically disturbed put personal preferences above those of the state, and abused their authority. For these reasons Henry VIII and Charles II brought their reigns to the brink of chaos.

In Georgian England individuals were less important because of the shift in authority from crown to parliament. Within parliament, individuals like Walpole were extremely important but authority was more diffuse and more effectively institutionalized. This allowed a more stable political system to develop and consolidate. Consider the counterfactual of how much more damage George III, a vindictive and deeply disturbed individual, could have done if not checked and constrained by parliament. Our own era gives more evidence of the political importance of a shift from personal to institutional rule; the Soviet Union and China benefitted greatly when Stalin and Mao gave way to leaders more beholden to their peers in the communist party.

Hume was on firmer ground in attributing the English civil war to religious fervor and the intolerance and unwillingness to compromise that it encouraged. The Protestants would not suffer royal imposition of Catholicism, and Charles I did not understand the need to reach a modus vivendi with his opponents. Both sides invoked history to justify extremist positions; the Protestants appealed to supposed ancient liberties, and the monarch to the divine right of kings.[110] Passions subsided considerably after the Glorious Revolution, but political cleavages in Britain still coincided with religious ones, making politics, in Hume's view, highly charged and unstable. But this gradually changed, in part due to astute Whig leadership, but also because of major shifts in values and practices.

The political and economic interests of the different orders, of town and country, and north and south, were all but impossible to harmonize. But everyone shared an interest in property and status. The latter found new foci in the eighteenth century. There was a new and celebratory focus on the land in literature, painting, architecture, landscape, and gardening. There was also a renewed interest in manners. Joseph Addison, Richard Steele, and Anthony Ashley Cooper, the Third Earl of Shaftesbury, made a strong and successful case for "politeness," defined by Lord Shaftesbury as "dexterous management of our words and actions" that makes others "have a better opinion of us and of themselves."[111] Through their writings, and especially the short-lived but influential *Spectator*, Addison and Steele propagated the view that personal satisfaction was possible from civil and social activities, including conversation and family life. Entertaining and hunting at country estates and social intercourse at city clubs, along with increased social interactions among the landed elite, regardless of their birth, helped to produce something of a common identity that transcended and muted traditional cleavages.

Materialism also muted religious and class antagonisms. All levels of the aristocracy invested in commercial enterprises.[112] The Duke of Chandos engaged in mining, major urban development in Bath, pearl fishing off Anglesey, and invested in Covent Garden and American mining and building companies.[113] The rise in materialism encouraged, perhaps compelled, the Anglican Church to soften its message as spiritual goals gave way to secular ones. A widely circulated sermon by John Tillotson, Dean of Canterbury, insisted that God's commandments were in the interests of Christians because they contributed to business success. Evil, sin, redemption, and sermons invoking fire and brimstone, became the preserve of evangelical sects, to which many of the rural and urban poor now turned.[114] Among the landed elite, political economy all but supplanted moral economy. They were dedicated to "procuring jobs for family, friends, and self," and their behavior was accordingly increasingly pragmatic and devoid of ideological commitments.[115]

Greater elite satisfaction and unity avoided one of the pathways to disorder theorized in Chapter 4. Intra-elite conflict did not intensify to the point where losers looked to the lower orders for support, thereby expanding the domain in which conflicts were fought and resolved. In the past, this had been a major cause of two civil wars. Elite restraint in the Georgian era might be attributed to learning, but it was also a product of cooption (discussed below) that made it likely that even losers in elite struggles – Catholic aristocracy and nobility – would still receive sufficient rewards to deter defection.

The elite succumbed to the other pathway to disorder: using its influence to gain wealth and then displaying it visibly. It got away with it because clientelism was still in place and rich landowners still felt a compulsion to alleviate the plight of those dependent on them. Of equal importance, this display of wealth occurred before equality became the dominant value in western society. Its effects were probably also softened by economic growth and high employment.

Eric Hobsbawm and George Rudé claim to expose a contradiction in Georgian England. Its rulers wanted to be "both capitalist and traditionalist and hierarchical." They "advocated an economy which implied mutually antagonistic classes, but did not want it to disrupt a society of 'ordered ranks.'"[116] Fellow Marxist Roy Porter goes a step further and argues that by embracing capitalism the elite may have been "digging their own graves."[117] Capitalism certainly created a new, wealthy class with different values that in due course would demand and obtain its share of political power. It was a class, moreover, that criticized the landed gentry for its profligate lifestyle. But the aristocracy and gentry built bridges to the new capitalists and they in turn sought more to integrate rather than to supplant them. The business class, from bottom to top, valued hierarchy just as strongly as the landed elite and had a common interest in controlling the lower orders. This was evident in their horror at the Gordon Riots and agitation during the French revolutionary era.

In practice, the old elite's dual commitment to hierarchy and wealth was a major source of regime strength and social cohesion. Chapter 2 suggests that one of the principal sources of conflict and instability is the emergence of a new hierarchy in competition with an older, dominant one for power and status. Dominant hierarchies can frame new ones as threats and attempt to repress them, as Marxist theory stipulates they will.[118] Alternatively, they can try to coopt them, which is a much better option when it has a chance of success, which it often does.[119]

A Cultural Theory of International Relations argues that in the nineteenth and early twentieth century there was considerable variation in the response of aristocracies to the rising commercial classes. A cooption gradient ran from west to east, from most to least willing. In Britain, they co-invested, shared political power, and began to intermarry. In effect, an accommodation was worked out, with both hierarchies adopting some of the values and practices of the other. This helps to explain why the British aristocracy has maintained its social standing and wealth down to the present day, and why Britain remained the most stable major power in Europe.

The "long eighteenth century" thesis sees Georgian England as an extension of the *ancien régime* and stresses its similarity with its continental counterparts.[120] Until the 1830s, England was governed by a monarchy that rested on divine right, the Church of England, and a hereditary, land-based aristocracy. The regime is said to have ended abruptly, between 1828 and 1832, with Catholic Emancipation and the First Reform Act. Later came the Repeal of the Corn Laws in 1846 and disestablishment of the Church in Ireland.[121] The Victorian era was indeed different in politics and social values, but I see more an evolution than any sharp break. Catholic Emancipation and the Reform Acts were a continuation of Georgian practices, based on the belief that opposition could best be managed, if not overcome, by a judicious combination of cooption and compromise. Their sponsors thought they would preserve the existing order more than change it. Historians see them as short-sighted in this regard. But maybe it is the historians who are blind.

Notes

1 Oliver Goldsmith, "The Deserted Village," 1770, lines 275–300, *The Poetry Foundation*, www.poetryfoundation.org/poems-and-poets/poems/detail/44292 (accessed February 7 2017).

2 Jones, *European Miracle*; Landes, *Wealth and Poverty of Nations*; Pomeranz, *Great Divergence*.

3 Quote from Coase and Wang, *How China Became Capitalist*, p. 10. On Britain, Porter, *English Society in the Eighteenth Century*, pp. 3–4.

4 Porter, *English Society in the Eighteenth Century*, pp. 1–4; O'Gorman, *Long Eighteenth Century*, pp. 168–72, for brief overviews.

5 Dikötter, *Mao's Great Famine* Wu, *Laogai*.

6 Plumb, *Origins of Political Stability*, pp. xi–xii, 29–30.

7 Judt, *Postwar Europe*, pp. 241–77; Maier, "Two postwar eras and the conditions for stability in twentieth-century Western Europe."

8 Lenman, *Jacobite Risings in Britain*; Monod, *Jacobitism and the English People*; Szechi, "Jacobite Movement."

9 Pincus, *First Modern Revolution*; Cruikshanks, *By Force or Default*; Israel, *Anglo-Dutch Moment*.

10 McGrath, *Making of the Eighteenth-Century Irish Constitution*; McFarland, *Ireland and Scotland in the Age of Revolution*; McNally, "Ireland"; Powell, "Ireland."

11 McFarland, *Ireland and Scotland in the Age of Revolution*; Murdoch, "Scotland and the Union."

12 Catholicism also receded. In 1720, there were 115,000 Catholics, and only 69,000 by 1780. Porter, *English Society in the Eighteenth Century*, p. 179.

13 O'Gorman, *Long Eighteenth Century*, pp. 43–61; Boyd, *Mad, Bad, and Dangerous People?*, pp. 39–109; Gregg, *Queen Anne*.

14 Namier, *Structure of Politics at the Accession of George II*.

15 Dickinson, *Liberty and Property*; O'Gorman, *Whig Party and the French Revolution* and *Emergence of the British Two-Party System*; O'Gorman, *Voters, Patrons, and Parties*; Hill, "Parliament, Parties, and Elections"; Colley, *In Defiance of Oligarchy*.

16 Hilton, *Mad, Bad, and Dangerous People?*, pp. 197–203.

17 O'Gorman, *Voters, Patrons, and Parties, Emergence of the British Two-Party System* and *Long Eighteenth Century*, pp. 49–56, 75–101; Lee, "Parliament, Parties, Elections."

18 Plumb, *Origins of Political Stability*.

19 Hill, "Parliament, Parties, and Elections."

20 Black, *Robert Walpole and the Nature of Politics in Early Eighteenth Century Britain*; Colley, *In Defiance of Oligarchy*; Dickinson, *Walpole and the Whig Supremacy*.

21 Porter, *English Society in the Eighteenth Century*, p. 110.

22 Ibid., p. 112.

23 Ibid., p. 109.

24 Black, *Robert Walpole and the Nature of Politics in Early Eighteenth-Century Britain*; Dickinson, *Walpole and the Whig Supremacy*; O'Gorman, *Long Eighteenth Century*, pp. 80–94; Lee, "Parliament, Parties and Elections."

25 Porter, *English Society in the Eighteenth Century*, p. 271.

26 Plumb, *Origins of Political Stability*, p. 21.

27 Ibid., pp. 22–26; Porter, *English Society in the Eighteenth Century*, pp. 71–82; O'Gorman, *Long Eighteenth Century*, pp. 172–79; Haydon, "Religious Minorities in England."

28 Porter, *English Society in the Eighteenth Century*, p. 112.

29 Ertman, *Birth of the Leviathan*; Brewer and Hellmuth, *Rethinking Leviathan*; Hartling, *Waning of "Old Corruption."*

30 Porter, *English Society in the Eighteenth Century*, pp. 99–100.

31 Felus, *Secret Life of the Georgian Garden.*

32 Ibid., pp. 3–4.

33 Plumb, *Origins of Political Stability*, pp. 83–86.

34 O'Gorman, *Long Eighteenth Century*, p. 21.

35 Porter, *English Society in the Eighteenth Century*, pp. 71–82; O'Gorman, *Long Eighteenth Century*, p. 22.

36 Colquhoun, *Treatise on Indigence*, p. 23; Lindert and Williamson, "Revising England's Social Tables."

37 Especially *Sense and Sensibility*, *Pride and Prejudice*, *Mansfield Park*, and *Emma*.

38 Porter, *English Society in the Eighteenth Century*, pp. 50–63.

39 Cannon, *Aristocratic Century*, ch. 4; Wilson, "Landed Elite."

40 Porter, *English Society in the Eighteenth Century*, p. 16.

41 Cannon, *Aristocratic Century*; Beckett, *Aristocracy in England*; Wilson, "Landed Elite."

42 Holmes, *Augustan England*, for a description of the growth and character of the professions.

43 O'Gorman, *Long Eighteenth Century*, p. 115.

44 Lee, "Parliament, Parties, Elections."

45 Ibid.

46 Plumb, *England in the Eighteenth Century*, p. 39.

47 Porter, *English Society in the Eighteenth Century*, p. 108.

48 Lee, "Parliament, Parties, Elections."

49 O'Gorman, *Long Eighteenth Century*, p. 116.

50 Holmes, *Augustan England*, pp. 239–61.

51 Plumb, *Origins of Political Stability* pp. 100–10.

52 Holmes, *Augustan England*, pp. 262–87; O'Brien, *Power with Profit*; Harding, *Waning of "Old Corruption."*

53 Hellmuth, "British State."

54 Brewer, *Sinews of Power*; Hilton, *Mad, Bad, and Dangerous People?*, pp. 119–24; O'Brien, "Finance and Taxation."

55 Hilton, *Mad, Bad, and Dangerous People?*, pp. 2–23; Porter, *English Society in the Eighteenth Century*, p. 187.

56 Mingay, "Progress of Agriculture, 1750–1850"; Price, "Changing Rural Landscape"; Mingay, *Agrarian History of England and Wales*, vol. VI; Rackham, *History of the Countryside*, p. 190.

57 Inikori, *Africans and the Industrial Revolution in England*, pp. 405–86; Pomeranz, *Great Divergence*, pp. 274–97, 313–15.

58 O'Gorman, *Long Eighteenth Century*, p. 118.

59 Eversley, "Home Market and Economic Growth in England."

60 Berg, *Age of Manufactures*; Daunton, *Progress and Poverty.*

61 Borsay, "Urban Life and Culture."

62 Briggs, "Language of Class in Early Nineteenth-Century England"; Hilton, *Mad, Bad, and Dangerous People?* pp. 124–33; Rogers, "Middling Orders."

63 O'Gorman, *Long Eighteenth Century*, p. 121.

64 Briggs, "Language of Class in Early Nineteenth-Century England." On the three class model, Langford, *Polite and Commercial People*; Money, *Experience and Identity.*

65 For the confrontational perspective, Thompson, *Whigs and Hunters*; Hay, Linebaugh, and Thompson, *Albion's Fatal Tree*. For reciprocity, Cannon, *Aristocratic Century*. Speck, *Stability and Strife*; Christie, *Stress and Stability in Late Eighteenth-Century Britain*; Clark, *English Society.*

66 Langton, "Industrial Revolution and the Regional Geography of England."

67 Porter, *English Society in the Eighteenth Century*, p. 200.

68 Dickinson, "Popular Politics and Radical Ideas"; Clark, *British Clubs and Societies*; Barker, *Newspapers. Politics and Public Opinion in Late Eighteenth-Century England.*

69 Erle, *Making of the English Middle Class*; Barry and Brooks, *Middling Sort of People*; Rogers, "Middling Orders."

70 Henry, "Making of Elite Culture."

71 Lees, *Solidarities of Strangers*; Malcolmson, *Life and Labour in England*; Rule, "Labouring Poor."

72 Porter, *English Society in the Eighteenth Century*, p. 144; O'Gorman, *Long Eighteenth Century*, p. 119.

73 Plumb, *England in the Eighteenth Century*, p 145; Porter, *English Society in the Eighteenth Century*, pp. 123–34.

74 Dickinson, "Popular Politics and Radical Ideas."

75 Mingay, "Agriculture and Rural Life" and *Agricultural Revolution.*

76 Porter, *English Society in the Eighteenth Century*, pp. 64–65; O'Gorman, *Long Eighteenth Century*, p. 121.

77 Porter, *English Society in the Eighteenth Century*, pp. 176–78; Ditchfield, "Methodism and the Evangelical Revival."

78 Porter, *English Society in the Eighteenth Century*, p. 16; O'Gorman, *Long Eighteenth Century*, p. 21.

79 Cited in Porter, *English Society in the Eighteenth Century*, p. 168.

80 Ibid., p. 300.

81 O'Gorman, *Long Eighteenth Century*, p. 114–15.

82 Ibid., p. 114; Porter, *English Society in the Eighteenth Century*, pp. 83–97, 139–42.

83 O'Gorman, *Long Eighteenth Century*, p. 115.

84 Landau, *Justices of the Peace*, p. 141.

85 Goldsmith, "Deserted Village."

86 Plumb, *England in the Eighteenth Century*, p. 16.

87 Porter, *English Society in the Eighteenth Century*, pp. 102–3; O'Gorman, *Long Eighteenth Century*, pp. 129, 239; Stevenson, *Popular Disturbances in England*, pp. 69–114.

88 Porter, *English Society in the Eighteenth Century*, p. 102.
89 Griffin, *Protest, Politics and Work in Rural England*, pp. 65–117; Archer, *Social Unrest and Popular Protest in England*, pp. 8–41.
90 Dickinson, "Popular Politics and Radical Ideas"; Porter, *English Society in the Eighteenth Century*, pp. 108–9; Archer, *Social Unrest and Popular Protest in England*, pp. 42–74; Griffin, *Protest, Politics and Work in Rural England*, pp. 42–81; Stevenson, *Popular Disturbances in England*, pp. 45–68.
91 Porter, *English Society in the Eighteenth Century*, p. 119.
92 Ibid., pp. 83–97, 138–44; Eastwood, "Local Government and Society."
93 Plumb, *England in the Eighteenth Century*, pp. 35, 145; Porter, *English Society in the Eighteenth Century*, pp. 123–25.
94 Porter, *English Society in the Eighteenth Century*, pp. 100–3; Hilton, *Mad, Bad, and Dangerous People?*, pp. 31–38.
95 Porter, *English Society in the Eighteenth Century*, p. 105; Archer, *Social Unrest and Popular Protest in England*, pp. 75–88; Myerly, *British Military Spectacle*, pp. 120–38; Fox, *Making Life Possible*.
96 Porter, *English Society in the Eighteenth Century*, pp. 234–36; O'Gorman, *Long Eighteenth Century*, p. 137; Harris, "Print Culture."
97 Harris, "Print Culture"; Hilton, *Mad, Bad, and Dangerous People?*, p. 25; St. Clair, *Reading Nation and the Romantic Period*, pp. 103–21; Raven, *Judging New Wealth*, pp. 32–35; Harris, *Politics and the Rise of the Press*; Barker, *Newspapers, Politics, and Public Opinion in Late Eighteenth-Century England*.
98 Plumb, *England in the Eighteenth Century*, p. 32.
99 Porter, *English Society in the Eighteenth Century*, pp. 234–38.
100 Ibid., pp. 294–98.
101 O'Gorman, *Long Eighteenth Century*, pp. 231–40; Hilton, *Mad, Bad, and Dangerous People?*, pp. 119–24; Macleod, "Crisis of the French Revolution."
102 Plumb, *England in the Eighteenth Century*, pp. 120–23; Stevenson, *Popular Disturbances in England*, pp. 81–93.
103 Plumb, *England in the Eighteenth Century*, pp. 120–23; Stevenson, *Popular Disturbances in England*, pp. 81–93.
104 Porter, *English Society in the Eighteenth Century*, p. 100; Stevenson, *Popular Disturbances in England*, pp. 94–113; Archer, *Social Unrest and Popular Protest in England*, p. 57; O'Gorman, *Long Eighteenth Century*, pp. 232–37.
105 Ehrman, *Younger Pitt*, for the most authoritative account.
106 Porter, *English Society in the Eighteenth Century*, pp. 348–52; O'Gorman, *Whig Party and the French Revolution*; Morris, *British Monarchy and the French Revolution*; Macleod, "Crisis of the French Revolution."
107 Porter, *English Society in the Eighteenth Century*, p. 350; Christie, *Stress and Stability in Late Eighteenth-Century Britain*; Cookson, *British Armed Nation*; Dickinson, *British Radicalism and the French Revolution*; Philip, *French Revolution and British Popular Politics*; Macleod, "Crisis of the French Revolution"; Morris, *British Monarchy and the French Revolution*; Spence, *Birth of Romantic Nationalism*.
108 O'Gorman, *Long Eighteenth Century*, p. 107.
109 Burke, *Reflections on the Revolution in France*; Hume, *History of England*, vol. 2.

110 Hume, *History of England*, vol. 2; Haakonssen, "Introduction."

111 A. Boyer, *The English Theophrastus* (1702), p. 106, quoted in Klein, "The Third Earl of Shaftesbury and the Progress of Politeness."

112 Jones, *Agriculture and the Industrial Revolution*, pp. 67–84.

113 Porter, *English Society in the Eighteenth Century*, p. 58.

114 Plumb, *England in the Eighteenth Century*, p. 41.

115 Ibid., pp. 130–58; Porter, *English Society in the Eighteenth Century*, p. 4; Hilton, *Mad, Bad, and Dangerous People?*, p. 32.

116 Hobsbawm and Rudé, *Captain Swing*, p. 47.

117 Porter, *English Society in the Eighteenth Century*, p. 343.

118 Lebow, *Cultural Theory of International Relations*, ch. 7.

119 The same holds true for dominant power vis-à-vis rising ones. Like Marxism, power transition theory predicts war, but the history of modern international society indicates that the first option is cooption and that it is almost invariably successful. Lebow and Valentino, "Lost in Transition"; Lebow, *Why Nations Fight?*

120 Hilton, *Mad, Bad, and Dangerous People?*, pp. 24–31 for this debate.

121 Clark, *English Society*; Price, *British Society*. Boyd, *Mad, Bad, and Dangerous People?*, p.30, argues that the invocation of *ancien régime* ideology was a reaction to the American and French revolutions and progressive, liberal ideologies. The "real change in sensibility" was signaled by the reaction to the 1780 Gordon Riots.

8   China

Martin K. Dimitrov and Richard Ned Lebow

The previous chapter described the striking similarities between Georgian Britain and contemporary China. It analyzed how Georgian England maintained order as a single-party state. It emphasized elite cohesion, efficient administration, and economic growth, managing the middling orders and lower orders, and allowing for some dissent and opposition. This chapter turns to China, another single-party state that has experienced remarkable economic growth. Analysis of China nevertheless highlights differences between the two countries, albeit more of degree than of kind. It suggests that high-growth single-party systems can rely on very different institutional mechanisms to maintain order over the long term, and that each strategy entails risks.

Economic Growth

One area in which Georgian England and China exhibit substantial similarity is their record of successful economic growth. Despite a recent slowdown, China has experienced four decades of robust growth since the initiation of reforms in 1978. During the 1978–2016 period, average annual GDP growth has been 9.6 percent.[1] During the same period, per capita GDP (in constant 2010 US dollars) increased 22.4-fold, from $308 to $6,894.[2] China also achieved impressive reductions in poverty (measured as people living on $1.25 or less a day, in 2005 dollars at purchasing power parity) from 84 percent of the population in 1981 to 6 percent in 2011.[3] During the reform period, China has successfully transformed itself from an underdeveloped country into the second largest economy in the world, as measured by the absolute size of its GDP. Recently, China earned another distinction: after decades of absorbing large amounts of foreign direct investment (FDI), in 2016 the country's outward direct investment (ODI) was greater than the inbound FDI.[4] This spectacular economic success is one of the main pillars of regime stability.

An important difference with Georgian England is that growth in China occurred in the absence of strong administrative capacity, secure property rights, and consolidated rule of law.[5] This goes against standard arguments that assume institutions are a precondition for growth. To address this inconsistency, Ang has advanced a theory of co-evolution, positing that institutions were being built as markets were developing.[6] Unquestionably, certain bureaucracies have been strengthened over the past decade and a regulatory state has begun to emerge in some issue areas.[7] There also are indications of the rise of a limited form of commercial rule of law.[8] At the same time, China is plagued by rampant corruption and by a largely inefficient bureaucracy.[9] One open question is how much longer the relatively weak currently existing institutions may be able to underpin economic growth.

Single-Party Rule

Another consequential difference between China and Georgian England concerns the extent to which their respective systems of single-party rule expressly prohibited the existence of opposition parties. It is important to emphasize that although the Whigs established de facto single-party rule in England, the Tories were not banned. This stands in sharp contrast to the Chinese case, where the Chinese Communist Party (CCP) nominally allows another eight parties to exist, but all of these parties are loyal allies of the CCP and have no potential to act as a political opposition.

The Tiananmen Square protests and the fall of the Berlin Wall impressed upon the Chinese leadership the fragility of communist regimes. Although the CCP had never sanctioned the existence of competing political parties prior to 1989, its resolve to maintain single-party rule only strengthened as it witnessed the collapse of communist systems in Europe.

Archival materials from Eastern Europe and the Soviet Union demonstrate that China followed with keen interest the events in the Eastern Bloc in the 1980s and early 1990s.[10] The demise of the Soviet Union in particular was met with alarm. In January 1992, the Chinese ambassador in Moscow asked academician Titarenko whether the collapse of the Soviet Union was the planned outcome of Gorbachev's policies or rather reflected mistakes made during *perestroika*.[11] This query is indicative of the pervasive uncertainty about the future of communism that was spreading to China following the transformative events of 1989–91.

It is also confirmed by contemporaneous Chinese internal publications evaluating the reasons for the collapse of communism in Eastern Europe and in the Soviet Union.[12] These documents reveal a generally unsympathetic attitude toward Gorbachev, whose political and economic policies are portrayed as misguided.[13] Economically, Gorbachev was criticized for his blind embrace of capitalism and uncritical acceptance of the "Harvard plan."[14] Politically, he was berated for his failure to resist "peaceful evolution" (*heping yanbian*), a strategy of western countries to subvert socialism from within through economic, cultural, and political means such as trade, promotion of western lifestyles, and pressure on the communist world to protect human rights.[15] Even today, Gorbachev is repudiated for advocating "humane, democratic socialism," which China understands as a source of disintegration of the system because of its promotion of competitive multi-party elections and human rights.[16] The clear implication for China is that it should not pursue a Gorbachev-style political reform. This point has been emphasized by Xi Jinping in a number of internal speeches that have been delivered since he became General Secretary of the CCP in 2012.

On a practical level, the fundamental reassessment of the existing ideological justifications of the regime that was necessary after the collapse of communism in Europe initially led to a retrenchment that lasted from 1989 until Deng Xiaoping's Southern Tour in 1992. Following the Southern Tour, China abandoned traditional Marxist-Leninist commitments to building communism through revolutionary class struggle and started to describe itself as being "along the road of Chinese-style socialism."[17] Ideology continues to be important, as demonstrated by the extraordinary energy that each of the three leaders since Deng Xiaoping has invested into branding a concept that is associated with him: the Three Represents (Jiang Zemin); scientific development (Hu Jintao); and the China Dream and the core socialist values (Xi Jinping). Because these slogans cannot form a comprehensive belief system (either alone or in combination), China can be characterized as experiencing a slow process of de-ideologization since the death of Mao and especially since 1989.

Despite abandoning Marxism-Leninism, to this day China remains a single-party state where opposition parties are banned. The leadership has retained its commitment to maintaining the CCP as a vanguard party and has banned all attempts to establish independent political entities. Efforts to change the status quo can be traced back to Wei Jingsheng's call for a "fifth modernization" (democracy) in the late 1970s, which resulted in his imprisonment. Independent political parties were formed in the 1990s (the China Democracy Party) and the 2000s (the New Democracy Party of China), but in both cases their leaders were arrested.

Apart from the 1989 Tiananmen events, the most significant challenge for the regime to date has been the Charter 08 movement. Drafted in 2008, Charter 08 called for a set of revolutionary changes that included freedom of association (and specifically demanded an end to single-party rule), the implementation of competitive elections for all public officials, constitutional amendments, and guarantees for the freedoms

of assembly, expression, and religion.[18] The response of the authorities was swift: Charter 08's author Liu Xiaobo was sentenced to eleven
years of imprisonment on charges of inciting subversion of state power.
Remarkably, in stark contrast to the impact of Charter 77, which paved
the way for eventual democratization in Czechoslovakia, Charter 08
had no afterlife either domestically or internationally. Liu Xiaobo was
awarded the Nobel Peace prize in 2010 but spent the rest of his life in
prison, being released on medical parole only weeks before his death
from liver cancer on July 13 2017. None of the other 303 original signatories of Charter 08 took an active political stance. The international
response to the imprisonment of Liu Xiaobo and the harassment of some
of the other signatories of the charter was similarly muted. The lack of
a significant domestic or international reaction to the quashing of the
Charter 08 movement represents a tacit endorsement of China's model
of single-party rule.

Single-party rule is also maintained by restricting electoral choice. In
China, there are two types of elections: grassroots elections for village
and urban neighborhood chiefs, and legislative elections for township
and county congresses.[19] These elections feature very restricted electoral
choice, with the final slate of candidates being approved by the communist
party, which makes it exceedingly difficult for independent candidates to
run and to be elected. The restrictions on electoral choice are extreme
even by the standards of communist regimes. Contrast China with the
case of Vietnam, where the deputies to the National Assembly are elected
through direct elections.[20] Because candidates are vetted through a process known as "the three consultations," these elections offer very limited
choice. Although in principle candidates may self-nominate, only 15 self-
nominated candidates were able to pass the process of vetting by the
party and the Fatherland Front in the 2011 legislative elections. And
self-nominated candidates faced an uphill election battle: only 4 of the
15 were elected to the National Assembly.[21] In the 2016 elections, 2 of
the 11 self-nominated candidates were elected.[22]

Thus, even in Vietnam, which has arguably made the most progress
among any remaining communist regime in terms of political reform, the
communist party has successfully used candidate vetting to prevent high-
profile independents from forming an opposition party. Nevertheless, in
contrast to China, national-level elections exist and feature some choice,
even involving the possibility of electing self-nominated independent
candidates. For this reason, Chinese media have been commenting nega-
tively on political reform in Vietnam.[23]

Thus far, the Chinese regime has also successfully limited the liber-
alizing influence of several factors that the general comparative politics

literature has argued might be conducive to regime change and democratization over the long term: increased affluence, urbanization, growing levels of literacy and education, and a larger middle class. Although it has many proponents – ranging from Seymour Martin Lipset to Samuel Huntington – the idea that increasing wealth will result in democracy in China has been most prominently espoused by Henry Rowen, who argued that China would become democratic by 2015.[24] This prediction has not, alas, been borne out.

China has also defied those who believe that urbanization fosters political liberalization.[25] Similarly, although Chinese students were a pro-democratic force in the 1980s – as were university students elsewhere in Europe and Asia – there are no indications today that they have any inclination to challenge the regime.[26] Free markets and foreign direct investment, though for a while seen as the panacea that would usher in democracy, have strengthened the regime by fragmenting the previously unified working class (thus making it more difficult for workers to mount coordinated protests).[27] They have also generated economic growth, which has formed the basis of "performance legitimacy" that is widely believed to be the wellspring of regime stability today.[28]

Finally, numerous studies have concluded that, in contrast to Barrington Moore's famous dictum "no bourgeois, no democracy," despite its rapidly expanding size, the cohort of private entrepreneurs is unlikely to serve as a vehicle of democratization in China.[29] The reason is that capitalists are satisfied with the political status quo (the CCP nurtured entrepreneurs even before it officially allowed them to join the party in 2002) and thus show low support for a multi-party system.[30] These findings about entrepreneurs are consonant with research on the political attitudes of ordinary citizens, which shows that the general public also associates a multi-party system with chaos and thus favors the status quo.[31] Survey evidence indicates that the central government benefits from a high level of trust, which translates into support for the single-party system.[32]

In other political settings, civil society groups ranging from churches and independent trade unions to historical societies (*Memorial*) and environmental NGOs have acted as vehicles of democratization.[33] In China, however, civil society groups with a political agenda are expressly forbidden, lest they challenge the monopoly of the party on power. This holds for religious groups: followers of Tibetan Buddhism, practitioners of Islam in Xinjiang, and those attending services at underground Christian churches, quasi-religious entities (Falun Gong), independent trade unions, and NGOs focusing on human rights. Despite such restrictions, the number of NGOs has grown exponentially since the 1980s.[34] Yet these

NGOs are only allowed to operate if they provide social services that the state cannot or will not provide; if they remain local rather than aim to establish a nationwide network; and if they refrain from voicing democratic claims.[35] In general, successful churches and NGOs have displayed a cooperative attitude with the state.[36] Although some scholars classify them as civil society, Chinese churches and NGOs are not equivalent to the civil society groups that emerged in Eastern Europe prior to and during *perestroika* and challenged the legitimacy of the existing political model.[37] They work with the state, rather than against it.

In sum, nearly seven decades after the establishment of the communist regime, the CCP remains firmly committed to the maintenance of the single-party system. Following the 1989 Tiananmen Square protests, the party has enjoyed three decades of rule during which the most serious organized challenge that confronted it was the Falun Gong movement in 1999. At present, no social group or movement seems capable of mounting a credible threat to the continued dominance of the CCP and moving China toward a more liberal political order.

Censorship

Another area in which Georgian England and contemporary China exhibit significant differences is their degree of censorship.[38] Censorship is pervasive in contemporary China and applies to all media from books and periodicals to broadcast media and the Internet. For books, the primary method of preventing publication is by refusing to issue a publication permit; books that have been published without permission are targeted during the regular anti-pornography and anti-counterfeiting campaigns (*saohuang dafei xingdong*).[39] For print media, low-tech physical removal of offending content is still practiced, especially for foreign newspapers and magazines, which may be sold with the offending article excised. This is not a practical method for Chinese publications, which have significantly larger print runs and therefore necessitate more sophisticated pre-publication censorship and more severe post-publication sanctions that may involve the removal of transgressive editors-in-chief – like *Caijing*'s Hu Shuli – and the temporary or permanent closure of the outlets (*Strategy and Management; Freezing Point*). For broadcast media, all Chinese radio and TV stations are controlled by the state. Foreign broadcasts are either jammed (Radio Free Asia and Voice of America) or are transmitted with a 12-second delay (CNN), which allows the censors to interrupt the show if offensive content is being screened.[40] Finally, when it comes to the Internet and social media, a complex system of website blocking, keyword filtering, and content removal – especially for *weibo* and WeChat posts – helps ensure that offending material will not be available to Internet users.[41]

The pervasiveness of censorship reflects in part the evolution of technology, which has given China access to an array of censorship tools that was unimaginable even a few decades ago, let alone in the eighteenth century. Yet we should be mindful that the simple existence of censorship technology does not mean that it will be used. Pervasive censorship requires a conscious decision on the part of the state to devote significant resources to this activity. One explanation for China's zeal may be that it is a communist regime. As is well known, during the Cold War the Eastern Bloc prioritized censorship.[42] However, the pervasiveness and sophistication of censorship in contemporary China goes beyond that observed in the extinct and the still extant communist regimes. For example, although they have access to the relevant technology, Cuba and Vietnam do not block Gmail, Youtube, Facebook, and Twitter as China does. This suggests that China assigns a greater importance to censorship than other autocracies. A closer look at the content subject to censorship reveals why this activity is understood to play a strategic role in regime preservation.

What political logic guides decisions about censorship? It is widely accepted that reporting topics are classified into three categories: those that cannot be covered (e.g. Tiananmen, Falun Gong, Taiwanese independence, Tibetan independence, the personal lives of top leaders); those whose coverage is encouraged (e.g. economic and social development, sports and cultural achievements, ethnic harmony); and those that fall in a gray zone, where coverage may sometimes be permitted.[43] Most recent research has focused on understanding the gray zone, especially with regard to Internet censorship, where the boundaries of what is permissible change often.

Based on research on social media posts from 2011, King, Pan, and Roberts argue that posts with a collective action potential are more likely to be deleted from websites than posts criticizing government policies.[44] Based on research with WeChat posts during the anti-rumor campaign in 2015, Ng and Pan report that criticism of government policies like housing demolition and stability maintenance is censored along with political terms like the death of the party (*wangdang*), freedom of the press, and freedom of speech.[45] Despite their different findings with regard to criticism of government policies, the two pieces reach similar conclusions about the type of content that is subject to censorship: namely, posts that can lead to destabilization, either by facilitating collective action or by spreading harmful rumors. This is consistent with the insight from the Chinese-language scholarly literature that online public opinion is managed with the paramount goal of maintaining social stability.[46] These functions of censorship explain why the Chinese regime assigns such extensive resources to it.

Repression

China has maintained levels of repression that are high. A direct comparison with Georgian England might not be instructive here, considering that the norms of the acceptability of different types of punishment have changed over time.[47] Perhaps more relevant are comparisons with communist regimes, both those that existed prior to 1989 and especially those that survive to this day. Such comparisons do not reflect well on China: as of 1989, it was more repressive than the communist regimes in the Eastern Bloc; today, it is more repressive than Cuba and Vietnam, though not North Korea.

As in all communist regimes, repression in China was very high during the stage of initial regime establishment and consolidation.[48] For example, according to statistics published in an internal circulation (*neibu*) compendium, no fewer than 1.8 million bandits (*tufei*) were exterminated (*jiaomie*) during the first eleven months of 1950.[49] There were numerous additional spikes in regime-initiated violence in the 1950s and 1960s. Although the general perception is that violence declined after the death of Mao, we need to point out that in contrast to Eastern Europe, where the labor camps were definitively closed down by the early 1960s, the shelter and investigation, re-education through labor (*laojiao*), and the gulag-like reform through labor (*laogai*) systems were all operating at a high volume throughout the 1980s in China.[50] Moreover, China was still practicing capital punishment against those accused of counterrevolutionary crimes in the 1980s and rates of execution increased following the death of Mao.[51] Contrast this with the GDR, which carried out its last execution in 1981 – curiously, of Werner Teske, a Stasi officer who attempted to defect – and where a grand total of 166 judicial executions were carried out in the four decades of communist rule (1949–89).[52]

In the years since 1989, both the frequency and severity of repression have declined in China. Counterrevolutionary crimes were stricken down from the Criminal Law in 1997. Officially, the shelter and investigation, *laogai*, and *laojiao* systems were all abolished in the 2000s and 2010s, though reports indicate that other types of extrajudicial detention mechanisms survive.[53] Political persecution today targets dissidents, human rights activists, and ethnic minorities. Nevertheless, China is significantly less repressive than North Korea, where the labor camps still operate and may house as many as 200,000 political prisoners.[54]

At the same time, China is considerably more repressive than a communist regime like contemporary Cuba, where the most important recent uptick in repression occurred during the Black Spring in 2003, when the government arrested and sentenced to lengthy imprisonment 75 human rights activists.[55] Following an international outcry and domestic pressure by groups like *Damas de Blanco* – formed by the wives of the incarcerated activists – all of those imprisoned in 2003 were released by 2011. This led Amnesty International to briefly declare that there were no prisoners of conscience in Cuba.[56] Although Amnesty International has since identified several dozen political prisoners, the overall level of repression on the island today is very low. The regime practices short-term detentions (*detenciones a corto plazo*) rather than imprisonment. Furthermore, political dissidents like Yoani Sánchez and groups like *Damas de Blanco* are allowed to operate. These important changes indicate that single-party rule in Cuba is not incompatible with increased tolerance for limited political dissent. China's adoption of a model featuring a higher level of repression is suggestive of high levels of anxiety among regime insiders about the regime-destabilizing potential of dissent that is left unchecked.

Protests

China has experienced at least a million protests since 1989, a level of dissent that is significantly higher than in Georgian England.[57] It is remarkable that the regime has held steady, considering that protests in autocracies are rare events that can lead to political instability. To illustrate this point, we need look no further than regimes in communist Europe, in the successor states of the Soviet Union, and in the Middle East that experienced long periods of relative quiescence but then collapsed as a result of a small number of protests during the Velvet Revolutions, the Color Revolutions, and Arab Spring. China appears anomalous against this background.

What explains China's paradoxical stability? The extensive literature on protests in China has not engaged with this question. In recent co-authored work, one of the authors of this chapter – Dimitrov – has turned to this puzzle by putting the Chinese case in a comparative perspective.[58] Dimitrov and Zhang argue that the literature has not confronted the question of why protests have not led to political destabilization because it has not – with the exception of Perry – addressed all types of protests in China in their totality.[59] Instead, existing research has advanced separate arguments about nationalistic protests, political dissent, and protests about socioeconomic rights.[60]

Dimitrov and Zhang's examination of the complete range of contentious activity in China leads to three central arguments regarding how the government can maintain social stability in the face of protests. First, they demonstrate that because they are potentially most destabilizing – even if they are also the rarest – political protests are managed most harshly. In such cases, repression through brute force is used. Second, because dissent in the capital is most likely to be destabilizing – regardless of whether it is political, nationalistic, or socioeconomic – the government makes a concerted effort to prevent the occurrence of protests in Beijing. If such contentious events take place, they will be managed more harshly than protests occurring outside the capital city. Third, they argue that socioeconomic protests outside the capital are least likely to be destabilizing and will therefore receive a less brutal response. Nevertheless, the government's reaction will be firm: police presence will be the modal response. Force is more likely to be used in rural protests – where local officials are less accountable and the grievances, such as land grabs are more divisive, and in large-scale disruptive protests.

Dimitrov and Zhang base their claims about contentious activity on a unique new source: a protest dataset that they created by hand coding over 65,000 instances of protests that took place between November 2013 and June 2016 throughout China. The dataset is the most extensive source of data on contention in China that has been generated thus far. It yields information about the geographic location of the protests; the issues about which citizens protest; the tactics used by protesters; the response of the government; and the outcomes of the protests. The dataset also sheds light on the difference between urban and rural protests in China. Although it is not possible to construct an exhaustive catalog of all protest events in China – the data are classified and have never been made available to researchers – the Dimitrov and Zhang dataset allows us to make more systematic claims about the nature of contentious activity in China than has been possible on the basis of previously available datasets, which have contained a considerably smaller number of protests.

On a broader comparative level, Dimitrov and Zhang argue that protests in China differ from those in other autocracies in three important ways. First is the nature of the protests, with those about overtly political issues being relatively rare; most protests in China are small-scale non-violent instances of "rightful resistance" involving socioeconomic demands.[61] In other autocracies these types of grievances would be resolved through petitions, but the inadequacies of the petitions system in China have led citizens to opt for protests.[62] Second, the location of protests is different, with contention in the capital deliberately kept at a very low level. And third, the government shows exceptional resolve when dealing with protests, both those that are overtly political (when violent force is used) and those that focus on socioeconomic rights (when the police are typically present, though violent force is rarely used). These features of contentious politics in China, which stand in sharp contrast to the characteristics of protests in other autocracies, explain why frequent dissent has not so far led to political instability in post-Tiananmen China.

Dimitrov and Zhang's research suggests that thus far discontent has been successfully managed – in part because, as in Georgian England, protesters call for redress using traditional means. However, further protest activity could lead to instability under three conditions. One is an increase in the incidence of political protest. Another is a higher frequency of protests in the capital. A third is further growth in the number of socioeconomic protests, especially should this occur under conditions of declining economic growth, which would mean that there would be more limited funds for buying off protesters and that more repressive measures would have to be used. The most destabilizing scenario would involve all three conditions being fulfilled at the same time.[63]

Equality vs. Fairness

China has moved very rapidly from a regime emphasizing equality to one based on fairness, as illustrated by the rise of the GINI coefficient from 0.25 in the early 1980s to 0.465 in 2016.[64] This change has had disruptive consequences for stability, expressed mainly in the form of socioeconomic protests, which raise demands about equality. What made the value shift possible? The short answer is the dismantling of the socialist social contract, which was initially attempted in the lead up to the 1989 Tiananmen protests, but was only implemented in the later 1990s.[65]

The initial two decades of economic reforms in China – 1978 to 1998 – are characterized as a period of reform without losers.[66] The main reason for this outcome is that urban residents were spared a reduction of the generous, but expensive, cradle-to-grave welfare benefits that they enjoyed under the centrally planned economy. A series of laws promulgated in 1986–88 aimed to reform the system. In 1986 an attempt was made to transition from enterprise-based retirement provision to a social pooling scheme (*shehui tongchou*).[67] The Four Provisional Decrees on the Reform of the Labor System in 1986 stipulated that all newly hired SOE employees had to sign a labor contract, which could be terminated, thus allowing SOEs to sever the lifetime employment relationship. In addition, a Law on Enterprise Bankruptcy was enacted in 1986 and the 1988 Law on Industrial Enterprises Owned by the Whole People stipulated that state-owned enterprises could be abolished through dissolution or bankruptcy. The rise of the Tiananmen protests in 1989 postponed the implementation of these welfare-reducing reforms by almost a decade: the central government supplied SOEs with sufficient funds to maintain and even expand their pre-1989 workforce, so the number of individuals employed by state-owned units (*guoyou danwei*) grew from 103 million in 1989 to 112 million in 1994.[68] Necessary reform could only be undertaken once the memory of Tiananmen had become more distant.

Prior to the late 1990s, the most important policy change that affected urban residents was the abolition of rationing in 1993, which had involved direct food subsidies. The dismantling of the socialist social contract for urban workers only began in 1997 when the Fifteenth Congress of the Chinese Communist Party inaugurated the policy of "grasping the large and letting go of the small" (*zhuada fangxiao*). The Congress authorized the dismantling of smaller SOEs, which were to be privatized and to have their workforce drastically reduced. Learning from Eastern Europe, where enterprise restructuring resulted in the massive rise of unemployment, China implemented SOE reform gradually. Workers were initially classified as "laid off" (*xiagang*) rather than unemployed. For three years these laid-off workers maintained a relationship with their work unit, drew a salary, received benefits, and engaged in retraining. It was only after the three-year period was over that workers still seeking employment were to be reclassified as unemployed.[69]

Another policy that was meant to ease the transition to a post-socialist social contract was that workers were allowed to purchase at below-market rates the subsidized housing provided to them by their work units. The late 1990s also inaugurated the *dibao* (minimum-living guarantee), which supplied means-tested financial assistance for those who were worst affected by the transition.[70] Recent research indicates that *dibao* is distributed on the basis of political considerations (threat of collective action) rather than demonstrated need, which doubtless limits its effectiveness in terms of alleviating inequality.[71]

The 2000s and early 2010s saw important steps toward the expansion and standardization of benefits provision. The New Rural Cooperative Medical System (*xinxing nongcun hezuo yiliao zhidu*) was introduced in 2002 as a way to reduce illness-related poverty among rural *hukou* holders.[72] The Labor Contract Law passed in 2008 stipulated that all employees were entitled to a labor contract. To the extent that it was properly enforced, this law made it harder for employers to fire workers without cause, to maintain forced labor conditions, to delay the payment of wages, and to avoid making benefits contributions. The 2010 Social Security Law mandated that employees and employers make contributions to five different types of social insurance: pensions, medical insurance, work-related injury insurance, unemployment insurance, and maternity insurance. Although the law is a step in the right direction, several serious problems remain: great inter- and intra-provincial variation in the extent of coverage of various social insurance schemes; nontransferability of benefits and entitlements from one location to another; and incomplete implementation and coverage, especially for migrant workers in the cities, for urban residents without fixed employment, and for residents of rural areas.[73]

The biggest issue is the existence of a two-track social benefits system: progressive (for urban residents) and regressive (for rural residents).[74] The situation is especially problematic for rural migrants who have worked in the cities for a long period of time but still possess a rural *hukou*, which only entitles them to rural pensions that are inadequate for survival in urban areas.[75] There is a forty-fold gap between the highest urban pension (for civil servants) and the lowest pension accorded to rural residents under the New Rural Social Pension Insurance Scheme.[76] Internal government publications reveal that the leadership is concerned about the potential regime-destabilizing effects of levels of inequality that approach those in Latin America.[77] Given the overall argument of this book about the sources of order, this concern seems fully justified.

Divided and Corrupt Elites

Another contrast to Georgian England is elite unity. In China, elites are divided along factional lines, with clear negative implications for the prospects for regime stability. A further hurdle to elite unity is widespread resentment of the current anti-corruption campaign among leading political cadres. Jointly, these sources of elite division work against maintaining the stability of the current system.

The Maoist period was characterized by violent disagreements that sometimes resulted in the physical elimination, imprisonment, or purging of members of the elite. Disunity was last on public display during the 1989 Tiananmen protests, when some members of the elite favored a compromise, while others opted for violent suppression of the protesters. On the face of it, there has been remarkable elite unity in China since 1989: elites have followed a retirement norm and decisions have been reached on the basis of consensus.

Two caveats are in order. The first is that the retirement norm is informal with regard to the top leader, as indicated by the great degree of uncertainty whether (and when) Jiang Zemin might relinquish his position as Chairman of the Central Military Commission during the

2002–4 leadership transition. The orderly transition from Hu Jintao to Xi Jinping in 2012–13 does not guarantee that Xi Jinping will step down from his posts in 2022–23. Second, the absence of overt leadership discord does not mean that such divisions are not present. Though difficult to identify, factions exist and introduce a source of instability in elite politics. A Politburo meeting on December 29 2014 specifically prohibited the formation of gangs, cliques, and factions in the party.[78] The timing of the meeting – in the wake of the Bo Xilai, Ling Jihua, Xu Caihou, and Zhou Yongkang scandals – and the subsequent identification in the press of a Bo-Zhou clique, are suggestive of the depth of elite discord that is created by factions in contemporary China.[79]

A second source of instability is the pervasiveness of corruption in China. Recent western investigative reporting has revealed that the family members of several former and current Politburo members are multimillionaires.[80] Considering the exceeding difficulty of accumulating vast fortunes without engaging in collusive practices, these same Politburo members lack public credibility when they champion anti-corruption activities. The example of Bo Xilai, who pursued a violent crackdown on corruption in Chongqing, but was thoroughly corrupt himself, is apposite here.[81] The length and the scope of the anti-corruption campaign waged by Xi Jinping raise several concerns. One is that taking into account the pervasiveness of corruption, officials are targeted not because they are corrupt but because they belong to a faction that is currently weak.[82] Related to this, the long-term effect of the anti-corruption struggle would be to further erode the loyalty of members of the elite who would fear that their assets are threatened with expropriation. In a crisis, such members of the elite may be willing to employ various wealth-defense strategies, including efforts to sideline the incumbent leader.[83] In sum, the anti-corruption campaign waged by Xi Jinping seems more akin to a divisive purge rather than to a mechanism for creating elite unity.[84]

The anti-corruption campaign may also have the unintended consequence of paralyzing the bureaucracy since mid- and low-level officials will fear that taking too much initiative in their work may cross the ever-elusive line between being bold and being corrupt. To some extent, this has happened in Xi's five-year rule. Because he purged so many top officials so ruthlessly, this has instilled fear among lower levels of the bureaucracy for doing too much in the current climate. Since China's social and economic reform depends on bold initiatives and undertakings from mid-level officials in particular, this has also adversely affected China's reform program.[85]

One of the central arguments of this book is that the appetite of elites needs to be kept in check, partly in order to build elite unity and partly so that popular resentment can be minimized. There are abundant indications that the party is increasingly less successful at curbing elite appetites. This trend has clear negative implications for the prospects for maintaining order.

Prospects for Maintaining Order

With the exception of robust economic growth, this section has emphasized differences between the single-party systems of Georgian England and contemporary China. This suggests that order can be maintained in different ways. China has used economically-derived performance legitimacy to justify maintaining the current politically restrictive system. Can this system persist?

As noted in Chapter 4, political scientists are currently divided in their assessments about the future of China. Optimists see a persistence of the current system, whereas those who express guarded or strong pessimism anticipate regime change, which may or may not involve a transition to democracy. The optimists mainly focus on the fact that the Chinese case does not conform to the expectations generated by modernization theory about the long-term causes of political change in autocracies: income, education, urbanization, free markets, private entrepreneurs, and civil society do not challenge the monopoly of the CCP on power.[86] This line of analysis is bolstered by the repeated survey findings that the CCP enjoys high levels of popular support.[87] Instead of pointing to the inherently unreliable nature of survey research about regime support in autocracies, pessimists focus on the ossification of the party, on the obstacles to institutional innovation and elite unity created by the pervasiveness of crony capitalism, on economic problems, on social tensions, and on external pressures.[88]

The verdict is open on the China experiment. The debate suggests that to survive the Chinese party and government must continue to deliver economically, become more open to new talent, less corrupt, more responsive to the needs of urban and rural dwellers alike, and more open with regard to dissent. None of these conditions noted above are impossible to fulfill, and the biggest barrier to them may be the mindset of the communist party. Elimination of corruption is not difficult when it is a marginal activity. In China, it is absolutely central to business and administration, making it exceedingly difficult to root out. In January 2017, the Swiss Watch Industry reported that its sales were down by 10 percent, which they attributed to Xi Jinping's crackdown on bribery and money laundering. For the same reason sales of luxury watches in Hong Kong were down 22–25 percent over a four-year period.[89]

The Chinese government's suppression of a range of diverse opinion, some of it entirely non-political, as in the case of the 1999 nationwide crackdown on *Falun Gong*, suggests that the party's authoritarian nature is deep-rooted and its members feel threatened by any action that is unauthorized and a surprise to them. They are also likely to overreact, as they clearly did in response to the Umbrella Movement in Hong Kong. The visceral and ingrained intolerance of dissent encourages party and government to respond in ways that invite further dissent, as it has with both *Falun Gong* and Hong Kong demonstrators, making suppression more likely and necessary. This kind of vicious spiral is sharply at odds with Li's strategy of "smart containment."

This phenomenon is by no means unique to China, but common to most authoritarian regimes. It suggests that they have little chance of escaping the dilemma hinted at by Shambaugh and Pi: authoritarian rule fosters economic development and civil society but is threatened by the latter and resorts to repression that limits growth and fosters deeper resentment. Regimes then have the choice of further repression and stagnation, or opening up, as Gorbachev's Soviet Union did, and setting in motion the kind of political activity and movements that destroys them.[90]

Chapter 4 suggests that elites abuse their privileges to the degree they are unconstrained by enforceable laws or internalized norms. Both restraints are notoriously difficult to achieve in authoritarian regimes. In many, there is no pretense, and high-ranking officials are free to indulge their appetites in the most shameless ways. Corruption of this kind filters down until it pervades the society. Pre-revolutionary France is a quintessential example. According to Daniel Roche, one of the more distinguished historians of the period, Turgot's dismissal as a reforming minister of finance in 1776 marked the triumph of absolutism and "the impossibility of overcoming entrenched privilege." It made revolution that much more likely.[91]

In communist countries, ideology is expected to have a restraining effect, but as Mao Zedong recognized, bureaucrats quickly lose their revolutionary fervor and work to no particular purpose beyond self-aggrandizement.[92] They can only be kept in line by shake-ups from above, as the Cultural Revolution sought to do. By contrast, Xi Jinping's drive against corruption is more for public show than substance. Corruption is so entrenched in the party and government that it has become the grease that lubricates the engines of both, if not the fuel. Effective efforts to address it would threaten both institutions, and would require public participation in the form of intelligence and pressure. The cure is more threatening to party leaders than the disease.

A corrupt, unresponsive, authoritarian, and self-aggrandizing bureaucracy alienates people and makes them deeply resentful. Many people, perhaps the majority, may nevertheless remain loyal, as Lei Xuchuan suggests, because of nationalism, economic gains, and respect for the party. They may also support the government because they fear upheaval, and due to simple habit. Nevertheless, the regime remains vulnerable. Some combination of economic decline, alienated intellectuals willing to provide leadership, a division within the armed forces, or between them and the government, and some catalyst in the form, say, of an accident, natural or ecological disaster that revealed gross governmental incompetence, could spark widespread protests. In East Germany, the regime's decision to allow holidaymakers in Hungary to leave the country via East Berlin created an unforeseen chain of events that brought home to the hitherto cowed population just how widespread opposition was. This realization emboldened people and led to protests that quickly escalated and toppled the regime.[93] Such a tipping phenomenon could happen in China. But as in East Germany, it would require a government uncertain about how to respond or unable to mobilize the army, as it did to quell the 1989 protests in Tiananmen Square.

Forecasting China's future is fraught with uncertainty, especially for those who see collapse in their crystal balls. Our ability to prognosticate about low-probability high-impact events like collapse is limited by the complexity of the social world and the importance of confluence, accidents, and stochastic elements in the chain of events that might bring such an event about. For these reasons, among others, past predictions of the collapse of China have not come to pass, and their arguments have been called into question by the ongoing survival of the regime.[94]

It may be more useful to develop theoretical insights into why the Chinese regime has survived thus far. We could then ask how changes in the conditions promoting survival might increase the likelihood of failure. As one of the authors of this chapter has argued elsewhere, the survival of the CCP for nearly three decades after the collapse of communism in Europe is a result of ongoing successful adaptations in four areas: economic reform, ideological reinvention, inclusion of potential rivals, and creating and maintaining systems of accountability.[95] Dimitrov's prior assessment of CCP's prospects to maintain power did, however, indicate that future adaptation in each of these areas had to take into account significant existing problems, which have been exacerbated in recent years.[96] To these four adaptations, we have to add the problem of aging, which we will discuss first.

Aging of the CCP: Communist autocracies are the most durable type of non-democratic regime, outlasting both noncommunist single-party regimes and non-democratic monarchies. As of 2000, the average life-span of noncommunist single-party regimes was 28.51 years and that of non-democratic monarchies was 34.75 years. In contrast, communist single-party regimes had an average lifespan of 46.2 years as of 2000.[97] As of 2017, the five remaining communist regimes have an average life-span of 60 years. This is an impressive record. Nonetheless, even the most resilient single-party regimes rarely last longer than 70 years. The main reason for this is the ossification of the apparatus of governance, which makes it harder to implement change. In China, for example, the most recent reforms that were instituted within the party were the retirement norm (introduced in the 1980s and refined in the 1990s and 2000s), and inner-party democracy (first articulated during the period of guerilla warfare in the 1930s and subsequently revived in 2002). The retirement norm ensures cadre turnover and inner-party democracy introduces limited electoral principles in the appointment of party cadres to certain posts. Therefore, to the extent that they continued to be followed – there is no guarantee that they will be – both of these reforms will limit ossi-fication. Still, they may turn out to be insufficient to prevent the demise of the party.

In 2017, the CCP will complete 68 years in power and will match the most conservative estimate of the longevity of the Communist Party of the Soviet Union (1922–90). In 2023, the year when Xi Jinping is due to step down, the CCP will match the most generous estimate of Soviet communist rule (1917–91). The likelihood that the CCP will surpass the lifespan of the CPSU will depend in large measure on its ability to avoid ossification.

Economic Slowdown: Strong economic performance is essential for regime resilience, as demonstrated by the extraordinary attention paid by the Chinese leadership to the inclusion of growth targets in the five-year plans – most recently the 13th Five-Year Plan for the 2016–20 period – as well as the fulfillment of annual GDP growth quotas. Expectations of growth mean that an economic slowdown may have serious political consequences. The effects could be indirect, but nonetheless real. In the case of China, a slowdown in growth may lead to higher unemployment, thus increasing the likelihood of labor unrest. We can already observe this trend in Guangdong, the province that has the highest strike activity according to the China Strike Map and the Dimitrov-Zhang protest dataset.[98] A slowdown may also increase popular discontent by putting downward pressures on wages. As such a wage reduction would occur under worsening conditions of inequality, we might expect the rise of collective action. Without access to funds that can be used to placate protesters, a more repressive response would be required, thus further increasing the potential for instability.

Because of its essential contribution to maintaining social stability, the promotion of economic growth is a top priority for the leadership. It is not clear, however, what the appropriate level of growth should be (currently, it appears to be about 7 percent per year), and what the sources of growth would be – foreign investment, government spending, or consumer spending. A more serious problem is how local governments will overcome their insolvency – each of the traditional methods of land grabs and accumulating debt carries significant negative side effects, thus raising the importance of a central government fiscal bailout of insolvent local governments.[99] These issues would need to be resolved expeditiously as the top leadership keeps fine-tuning the growth formula.

Incomplete Inclusion: Prominent scholars have argued that although communist regimes initially govern through mobilization, they eventually move to the stage of governance through inclusion.[100] A threat to resilience is presented by the emergence of groups that are not subject to inclusion and that successfully organize against the regime. In a classic move of rival incorporation, China has successfully included private entrepreneurs into the party. Academics also do not seem to pose a threat to stability. However, the regime has been unsuccessful in incorporating ethnic minorities, especially Uyghurs and Tibetans.[101] Recent evidence of this failure is that 150 Tibetans have self-immolated since 2009.[102] In addition, Xinjiang has been rocked by violent clashes between Han Chinese and Uyghurs almost every year since 2008. In the wake of Uyghur minority unrest in June 2013, the Xinjiang police department issued a public notice offering awards of 50,000–100,000 *yuan* (about $8,300–$16,600), along with guarantees of anonymity and protection, to informants from any ethnic groups (*ge minzu qunzhong*) who provide tips that can be used to solve cases of violent terrorism.[103] Ongoing ethnic unrest in Xinjiang well past 2013 testifies to the failure of such policies.

The response of the central government has been to step up repression. One technique for doing that has been the implementation of the so-called "grid-management system" (*wanggehua guanli*),[104] which employs sophisticated monitoring technology that enables the police and paramilitary forces in Tibet and Xinjiang to respond to social unrest extremely efficiently. The second has been increased prosecution of political crimes: with slightly more than 1 percent of the population of China, the Xinjiang Uyghur Autonomous Region has accounted for roughly half of the individuals prosecuted for crimes of endangering state security (*weihai guojia anquan zui*) in the 2000s and 2010s.[105]

Both techniques seem to be counterproductive in the long term, as they do not increase the loyalty of minority members and only exacerbate the already existing ethnic tensions. We should note that on its own the incomplete inclusion of social groups does not present an immediate threat. But regime stability is undermined when these groups coalesce and find broad social support, as revealed by the examples of Solidarity in Poland, ethnic minority mobilization in Bulgaria in 1984–89, and Falun Gong in China. For this reason, communist autocracies vigilantly monitor the success of inclusion policies, and when they appear to be failing do not hesitate to use repression against any groups that might be successful in mounting an organized challenge to the regime.

Insufficient Accountability: Communist regimes create multiple institutions of accountability, ranging from elections and investigative reporting to citizen complaints and microblogging. When these institutions operate effectively, they can help create "tacit minimal consensus" for the regime.[106] In contrast, malfunctioning institutions of accountability can increase the level of popular discontent and thus lead to regime instability. From the regime's perspective, two questions present themselves with regard to such institutions of accountability. First, what are the signs of crisis? And second, what is the appropriate regime response when a malfunction is detected? Although answering these questions is not easy, having answers to them is essential if the regime wants to keep popular discontent within a manageable level. With regard to the former, different accountability channels present different indicators of crisis. To take citizen complaints as an example, declining use of this formal channel (demonstrated by a falling rate of complaints), when coupled with an increasing rate of escalation of grievances outside the formal channel (revealed by engaging in protests), is a signal of crisis.

What should the regime do when crisis is detected? One response would be to ignore the problem. Another would be to engage in repression. A third would be to attempt to reform the shortcomings of the institution. With regard to citizen complaints, one needed reform is increased responsiveness that will encourage citizens to use this channel more frequently. This is precisely what occurred in Cuba when *Granma* started a rubric on citizen complaints in 2007, thus signaling leadership attention to this issue and providing a highly visible cue to citizens that the channel exists and that they are encouraged to use it.[107]

One of the most powerful examples of the effects of malfunctioning institutions of accountability on regime resilience is provided by East Germany, where widespread falsification of election results served as one of the triggers for anti-regime mobilization in 1989.[108] These historical precedents highlight the importance of monitoring all channels of accountability and of acting quickly to resolve problems detected in their operation. The Internet makes this task especially challenging, as illustrated by the case of China, where the government is interested in accountability – and therefore allows online criticism – but the goal of promoting accountability conflicts with the goal of maintaining stability, so we observe the censoring of blogs that are conducive to the emergence of protests.[109] Continuous efforts to provide a degree of accountability that is sufficient to keep public discontent at manageable levels are essential for maintaining stability.

Ideological Stasis: Ideological erosion played a significant role in alienating citizens from the regimes in Eastern Europe. We have evidence that the Chinese leadership is acutely aware of the importance of maintaining a solid ideological foundation for the single-party system. Internal Chinese government documents from the 1990s reveal the consensus view that ideological crisis was one of the main reasons for the Soviet collapse.[110] This was reiterated by President Xi Jinping during a speech in December 2012, when he said: "Why did the Soviet Union disintegrate? Why did the Soviet Communist Party collapse? An important reason was that their ideals and beliefs had been shaken. In the end, 'the ruler's flag over the city tower' changed overnight. It's a profound lesson for us! To dismiss the history of the Soviet Union and the Soviet Communist Party, to dismiss Lenin and Stalin, and to dismiss everything else is to engage in historic nihilism, and it confuses our thoughts and undermines the Party's organizations at all levels."[111]

Now that the utopian goals of building communism have been definitively abandoned and the redistributive commitments of the state have been reduced, China has made a sustained effort to promote nationalism, which serves as the main ideological justification for its rule. Chinese nationalism seems unlikely to wane in the future. Economic success, especially during the global economic crisis, was a source of national pride. In addition, the growing territorial assertiveness of China serves to fuel offensive nationalism. A possible challenge to the ideological foundations of the Chinese regime might be presented if nationalism escalates beyond pure rhetoric and thus places pressures on the party to deliver on its nationalist claims or risk losing credibility with the masses. One question that arises is whether this ideological foundation is sufficient. The core socialist values (prosperity, democracy, civility, harmony, freedom, equality, justice, the rule of law, patriotism, dedication, integrity, and friendship), which were promulgated at the 2012 Party Congress, are too abstract to be meaningful. The China Dream seems more specific, with its promise of prosperity and strength, but it does depend on ongoing economic growth and of the willingness of other countries to continue to acquiesce to China's growing territorial assertiveness. Should this cease to be the case, then Xi Jinping's ideological innovation of the China Dream will ring hollow, which will serve to alienate citizens from the regime.

Conclusion

Chapter 7 sought to explain the stability of Georgian Britain and its subsequent transformation into a parliamentary system with a more independent judiciary, free press, and religious toleration. This explanation is in no way structural, although political, economic, and other conditions imposed the limits in terms of which policy and meaningful political behavior could be formulated. These conditions in no way dictated policy or behavior, and they were understood quite differently by different actors. We accordingly focus on actors and their choices, and the goals, beliefs and expectations behind them.

The second section of this chapter advanced a more structural explanation for the resilience of the Chinese regime. By extension, changes in the conditions that facilitate resilience will make regime collapse more likely. An economic slowdown, a failure of inclusion, malfunctioning institutions of accountability, and ideological stasis are the main structural changes that can weaken the single-party system and make its collapse more likely. However, collapse will not occur simply because the structural foundations of resilience are weakened; certain contingent leadership choices have to be made as well. Simply put, elite resolve to rule has to weaken. In this regard, the argument presented in this chapter is consistent with the Georgian case study and rest of the book that emphasizes the importance of actor beliefs and behavior for maintaining order. It explains these choices and behavior with reference to actor goals, beliefs, and assessments.

Our two-country comparison has been revealing in other ways. The similarities between Georgian Britain and China derive in their first instance from their rapid economic growth and industrialization – or at least the beginnings of this process in England and Scotland. They stem secondarily from their de facto one-party regimes manned by people fearful for their survival and jealous of their privileges. Georgian leadership relaxed their surveillance, controls, and repression once they began to feel more secure, although returned to repressive measures in the aftermath of the French Revolution. China's leadership is presumably much more secure than that of its predecessors in the 1950s and 1960s, but has not allowed independent voices, let alone dissent.

We believe that the most significant differences between these countries affecting their political development were of degree than of kind. Our narrative offered evidence to this effect. A quintessential example concerns repression of religion. *Falun Gong* is a Chinese spiritual practice, drawing on Buddhist and Taoist traditions that involve meditation and exercises and preaches values of truthfulness and compassion. Up to the mid-1990s, it enjoyed considerable support from Chinese officialdom. It then came to be regarded as a threat due to its size, ability to attract a devoted following, and independence from state control. In 1999, it was condemned as an "evil cult," outlawed and many of its followers were arrested. Human rights organizations estimate that more than 2,000 *Falun Gong* practitioners have died as a result of abuse in custody.[112]

In Georgian Britain Catholics constituted a real threat to the Protestant Establishment because many believed in the divine right of kings, opposed the Glorious Revolution, and some supported the Scottish Pretender to the throne. However, English Catholics and Protestant divine righters never rallied behind subsequent Scottish revolts and the short-lived 1745 attempt by the Pretender and his Scottish supporters to march on London. Over time, sensible Whig governments eased their persecution of Catholics, although they were still prohibited from holding office. Catholic aristocrats were reintegrated socially, and Catholic entrepreneurs benefitted from the same advantages as their Protestant counterparts. The Whig ascendancy transformed an opposition group into a prop of the order.

The Georgian regime became more inclusive over time, in sharp contrast to its Chinese counterpart. It also maintained a high degree of elite unity, another key feature that sets it apart from China. There were divisions within the elite over political, economic, social, and religious questions, but they never led to serious ruptures, those between particularly excitable individuals aside. This cohesion cannot effectively be explained by class unity, although its importance is not to be dismissed. It had more to do with the existence of institutions that functioned to adjudicate disputes, most notably parliament and the courts. They were regarded as legitimate by most of the elite and only rarely used to punish political opponents or rivals in ways that threatened their livelihood, status, or, most importantly, their freedom.

Finally, we cannot stress enough the negative role models that were dominant for the two elites. For the Georgians, it was the French Revolution, and for the Chinese, Gorbachev's reforms and the resulting collapse of the Soviet Union. The former made Georgians more amenable to loosening the reins of power and making the political system more open and inclusive. The latter had the reverse effect on the Chinese. Timing was probably also important. The French Revolution came well after the Georgian order was established and the regime already in the process of becoming less authoritarian. The Gorbachev reforms arrived just as the Chinese were experimenting with economic reforms and feeling more vulnerable as a result.

What do we gain by our comparison? In some ways, China and Georgian England are quite different. China is a high-growth regime that has maintained order despite elite division and frequent protests that largely reflect a transition from equality to fairness that was executed too quickly. Moreover, in contrast to England, the Chinese system of single-party rule features a lack of toleration for dissent and opposition and pervasive censorship. Some may think that we cannot learn much by comparing systems that are so different. Yet this would not be the lesson drawn by the Chinese Communist Party, which is actively examining both historical and contemporary models of political evolution from single-party rule.[113] What Georgian England indicates is that single-party systems can both last a long time and gradually transform themselves into democracies without experiencing revolutionary turmoil. As the CCP thinks about the future, this might be a path it would like to follow. What it may lack, however, is precisely what Georgian England (and Taiwan under the KMT) had – toleration for dissent and opposition.

We also learn something of conceptual value. Approaching the analysis of another polity with beliefs, concepts, and expectations learned from one's own is very natural. It can also be misleading, as evidenced by the application of American economic and political development models to the rest of the world. For much of the postwar era, political science – and international relations and comparative politics especially – were mired in parochialism. Earlier in the book, hegemonic stability theory, modernization theory, democratization theory, and the Washington Consensus were offered as examples.

We have tried our best to escape from this kind of intellectual straitjacket by searching elsewhere for our concepts and comparisons. In China, we have based our analysis and forecasts in the first instance on an analysis of what has been responsible for the regime's stability up to this point. This approach requires us to leave aside dominant liberal expectations and develop concepts appropriate to the question. We also utilize a counterintuitive comparison with Georgian Britain. It offered a template for analyzing China, given their many remarkable similarities. Its peaceful evolution to parliamentary government in the Victorian era was a remarkable accomplishment and begs explanation. Our search for answers was productive of a second set of questions we used to analyze China.

Notes

1 World Development Indicators Online, http://databank.worldbank.org/data/reports.aspx?source=world-development-indicators (accessed July 20 2017).
2 Ibid.
3 Kroeber, *China's Economy*, 34.

4 China received 785 billion yuan of FDI and accounted for 1.12 trillion yuan of ODI (www.reuters.com/article/us-china-economy-investment-idUSKBN14F07R (accessed July 20 2017).

5 On administrative capacity, see Wang and Hu, *Political Economy of Uneven Development*; Wedeman, *From Mao to Market*. On property rights, see Oi, *Rural China Takes Off*; Oi and Walder, *Property Rights and Economic Reform in China*. On the rule of law, see Lubman, *Bird in a Cage*.

6 Ang, *How China Escaped the Poverty Trap*.

7 Yang, *Remaking the Chinese Leviathan*; Hsueh, *China's Regulatory State*; Dimitrov, "Evolution and Adaptation of Business-Government Relations in Zouping."

8 Dimitrov, *Piracy and the State*, esp. pp. 280–83; Wang, *Tying the Autocrat's Hand*; Dimitrov, "Structural Preconditions for the Rise of the Rule of Law in China."

9 On corruption, see Wedeman, *Double Paradox*; Pei, *China's Crony Capitalism*. On administrative capacity, see Chung, *Centrifugal Empire*.

10 For Soviet materials on China, see *Gosudarstvennyi arkhiv Rossiiskoi Federatsii* (State Archive of the Russian Federation (GARF)) f. 9654 op. 7 d. 286, l. 28–33; GARF f. 9654 op. 10 d. 266; GARF f. 10063 op. 2 d. 182; GARF f. 10026 op. 1 d. 2290 l. 36–38 (Martin Dimitrov would like to thank Peter Ruggenthaler for making these materials available) and Fond 89 per. 21 d. 25 (1990). For Bulgarian materials on China, see: "Memorandum Regarding the July 27, 1989 Meeting between Foreign Minister Mladenov and the Chinese Ambassador Li Fenglin" (secret), Central State Archive in Sofia (TsDA) f. 1B op. 101 a. e. 2156. For German materials on China, Sarotte, "China's Fear of Contagion." For Soviet materials on North Korea, GARF f. 9654 op. 10 d. 266 l. 160–162; GARF f. 10063 op. 2 d. 126; GARF f. 10026 op. 4 d. 2803, l. 1–3; GARF f. 10026 op. 1 d. 2290 l. 32–33 (Martin Dimitrov would like to thank Peter Ruggenthaler for making these materials available).

11 GARF f. 10026 op. 1 d. 2290 l. 76.

12 Yang Hua, *Dong'ou jubian jishi* (Record of the Eastern European Collapse); Ma Shaohua, *Dong'ou 1989–1993* (Eastern Europe 1989–1993).

13 See, for example, coverage in *Cankao xiaoxi* (Reference News), no. 11880 (August 20 1991); no. 11991 (August 21 1991); no. 11882 (August 22 1991); no. 11883 (August 23 1991); no. 11884 (August 24 1991); no. 11885 (August 25 1991); and no. 11886 (August 26 1991).

14 *People's Daily* Editorial Office, *Neibu canyue*, no. 40 (1991).

15 Ibid.

16 Zhou Xincheng, "Sulian yanbian guocheng zhong de yishi xingtai yu zhishifenzi."

17 Preamble of the Constitution of the People's Republic of China (2004).

18 Congressional-Executive Commission on China, "Charter 08 (Chinese and English Text)," December 10 2008, www.cecc.gov/resources/legal-provisions/charter-08-chinese-and-english-text (accessed July 17 2017).

19 Li, "Direct Township Elections"; O'Brien and Han, "Path to Democracy?"; Read, *Roots of the State*.

20 Abrami, Malesky, and Zheng, "Vietnam Through Chinese Eyes."

21 Lü Yusheng, *Yuenan guoqing baogao 2012* (2012 Annual Report on Vietnam's National Situation).

22 Inter-Parliamentary Union, *Vietnam Quoc-Hoi (National Assembly)*, www .ipu.org/parline-e/reports/2349_E.htm (accessed July 19 2017).

23 Abrami, Maleski, and Zheng, 237–238.

24 Lipset, *Political Man*; Huntington, *Third Wave*; Rowen, "Short March."

25 Wallace, *Cities and Stability*.

26 Yan, "Engineering Stability"; Perry, "Higher Education and Authoritarian Resilience."

27 For the original idea, see Fukuyama, "End of History?" For a reassessment, see Gallagher, "'Reform and Openness'" and *Contagious Capitalism*.

28 Zhu, "'Performance Legitimacy' and China's Political Adaptation Strategy."

29 Moore, Jr., *Social Origins of Dictatorship and Democracy*; Dickson, *Red Capitalists in China*; Tsai, *Capitalism Without Democracy* and "Cause or Consequence?"; Dickson, *Wealth into Power*.

30 Chen and Dickson, *Allies of the State*.

31 Chen, *Popular Political Support in Urban China*; Dickson, *Autocrat's Dilemma*.

32 Tang, *Populist Authoritarianism*.

33 Neubert, *Geschichte der Opposition in der DDR 1949–1989*; Ekiert, *State Against Society*; Kenney, *Carnival of Revolution*; Tullius, "Environmental Groups as Catalysts for Political Liberalization in Authoritarian Societies"; Láng-Pickvance, *Democracy and Environmental Movements in Eastern Europe*; Jancar-Webster, "Environmental Movement and Social Change in the Transition Countries"; Chang, "Environmental Protests and Dispute Resolution Mechanisms in Taiwan's Democratic Transition."

34 Saich, "Negotiating the State"; Dickson, *Dictator's Dilemma*, p. 125.

35 Spires, "Contingent Symbiosis and Civil Society in an Authoritarian State"; Hsu, *State of Exchange*.

36 Koesel, *Religion and Authoritarianism*; Teets, *Civil Society under Authoritarianism*.

37 For an argument that Chinese NGOs are civil society, see Teets, "Let Many Civil Societies Bloom." For a discussion of civil society in Eastern Europe, see Bernhard, "Civil Society and Democratic Transition in East Central Europe."

38 For an extended treatment of censorship in China, see Dimitrov, "Political Logic of Media Control in China."

39 Dimitrov, *Piracy and the State*, esp. pp. 227–30.

40 CNN, "Some International News Media Signals, Websites Blocked in China," December 10 2010, www.cnn.com/2010/WORLD/asiapcf/12/09/ china.media.blocked/ (accessed July 15 2017).

41 Freedom House, *Freedom on the Net 2016*.

42 Puddington, *Broadcasting Freedom*; Johnson and Parta, *Cold War Broadcasting*.

43 Wang, *Transformation of Investigative Journalism in China*; Stern and O'Brien, "Politics at the Boundary."

44 King, Pan, and Roberts, "How Censorship in China Allows Government Criticism but Silences Collective Expression."

45 Ng and Pan, "Online Rumors as Targets and Tools of Chinese Censors."

46 Gao Hongling, *Wangluo yuqing yu shehui wending* (Internet Public Opinion and Social Stability); Jiang Shenghong, *Wangluo yaoyan yingdui yu yuqing yindao* (Internet Rumor Response and Public Opinion Guidance); Yu Guoming, *Zhongguo shehui yuqing niandu baogao 2013* (Annual Report on Public Opinion in China 2013).

47 Farriss, "Respect for Human Rights Has Improved Over Time."

48 Dimitrov, "Understanding Communist Collapse and Resilience."

49 *Jianguo yilai gong'an gongzuo dashi yaolan* (Important Events in Public Security Work Since the Founding of the PRC), p. 19.

50 Wu, *Laogai*.

51 Scobell, "Death Penalty in Post-Mao China."

52 Only some of these executions were for political crimes. See Marxen and Werle, *Strafjustiz und DDR-Unrecht* vol. 5, pt. 2.

53 For example, "black jails" serve as illegal detention centers for petitioners.

54 Hawk, *Hidden Gulag*, p. 27.

55 Dimitrov, "Regime Survival in Cuba in Comparative Perspective," *Panoramas* (December 9 2014), www.panoramas.pitt.edu/news-and-politics/regime-survival-cuba-comparative-perspective (accessed 18 July 2017).

56 Associated Press, "Cuba grants amnesty to thousands of prisoners," *Guardian*, December 24 2011, www.theguardian.com/world/2011/dec/24/cuba-grants-amnesty-thousands-prisoners (accessed July 19 2017).

57 This is almost certainly a significant undercount. Protest data have been released for 15 of the 29 years of the 1989–2017 period: 1993–2000, 2002–6, 2008, and 2010 (see Wedeman, "Enemies of the State: Mass Incidents and Subversion"; Sun Liping, "Shehui shixu shi dangxia de yanjun tiaozhan"). For these 15 years, the total number of protests is 821,100. We should bear in mind that protest did occur in the other 14 years of this period, for which no total counts of protests have been made available.

58 Dimitrov and Zhang, "Patterns of Protest Activity in China."

59 Perry, *Challenging the Mandate of Heaven*, esp. pp. ix–xxxii.

60 On nationalistic protests, see Weiss, *Powerful Patriots*. On political protests, see Zhao, *Power of Tiananmen*; Hastings, "Charting the Course of Uyghur Unrest"; Tong, *Revenge of the Forbidden City*. On socioeconomic protests, see Bernstein and Lü, *Taxation without Representation in Contemporary Rural China*; Mertha, *China's Water Warriors*; Obrien, *Popular Protest in China*; Cai, *Collective Resistance in China*; Chen, *Social Protest and Contentious Authoritarianism in China* (New York: Cambridge University Press, 2012); Tong and Lei, *Social Protest in Contemporary China*; Heurlin, *Responsive Authoritarianism in China*.

61 On rightful resistance, O'Brien and Li, *Rightful Resistance in Rural China*.

62 On the link between unsuccessful petitions and protests, Dimitrov, "Internal Assessments of the Quality of Governance in China."

63 Dimitrov and Zhang, "Patterns of Protest Activity in China."

64 *CIA World Fact Book* (2017), www.cia.gov/library/publications/the-world-factbook/ (accessed July 14 2017).

65 Cook and Dimitrov, "Socialist Social Contract Revisited."

66 Naughton, *Chinese Economy*.

67 Zou Dongtao, *Zhongguo gaige kaifang 30 nian, 1978–2008*, p. 638.

68 National Bureau of Statistics, *Zhongguo tongji nianjian 2010*, p. 118.

69 Tang and Yang, "Chinese Urban Caste System in Transition."

70 Solinger and Hu, "Welfare, Wealth, and Poverty in Urban China."

71 Chen, Pan, and Xu, "Sources of Authoritarian Responsiveness."

72 Klotbuecher, Laessig, Qin, and Weigelin-Schwiedrzik, "What is New in the 'New Rural Co-operative Medical System.'"

73 Frazier, *Socialist Insecurity*; Huang, "Four Worlds of Welfare."

74 Gao, "Redistributive Nature of the Chinese Social Benefit System."

75 The *hukou* system is currently undergoing major reform that will improve access to urban welfare for at least some migrants.

76 Frazier and Li, "Urbanization and Social Policy."

77 *Lingdao canyue*, Nr. 3/2012 (January 25 2012), 36–41.

78 Alice L. Miller, "The Trouble with Factions," *China Leadership Monitor*, no. 46 (Winter 2015), www.hoover.org/sites/default/files/research/docs/clm46am-2.pdf (accessed July 19 2017).

79 *China Daily*, January 15 2015, http://usa.chinadaily.com.cn/china/2015-01/15/content_19322690.htm (accessed July 19 2017).

80 On this coverage, Barbara Demick, "The *Times*, Bloomberg News, and the Richest Man in China," *The New Yorker*, March 5 2015, www.newyorker.com/news/news-desk/how-not-to-get-kicked-out-of-china (accessed July 19 2017).

81 Garnaut, *Rise and Fall of the House of Bo*.

82 Zhu and Zhang, "Weapons of the Powerful."

83 On wealth defense in general, see Markus and Charnysh, "The Flexible Few: Oligarchs and Wealth Defense in Developing Democracies."

84 For another perspective, see Keliher and Wu, "Corruption, Anticorruption, and the Transformation of Political Culture in Contemporary China," who argue that the anti-corruption campaign can be seen as aimed at changing China's political culture; Feng Zhang, "Beijing's anti-corruption drive: what's at stake?" September 24 2015, http://fengzhangmc.com/beijings-anti-corruption-drive-whats-at-stake/ (accessed September 12 2017).

85 Feng Zhang to authors, email, September 10 2017.

86 See the discussion above on single-party rule.

87 Chen, *Popular Political Support in Urban China*; Tang, *Populist Authoritarianism*; Dickson, *Dictator's Dilemma*.

88 For a perceptive interpretation of the finding of high levels of trust, Li, "Reassessing Trust in the Central Government: Evidence from Five National Surveys." For an argument that political weariness cannot be detected in surveys administered in China, Lei and Lu, "Revisiting Political Weariness in China's Public Opinion Surveys." For pressures, internal and external, Fewsmith, *Logic and Limits of Political Reform in China*; Pei, *China's Crony Capitalism*; Shambaugh, *China's Future*.

89 Rupert Neate, "Hard times for luxury watches as sales drop 10%," *Guardian*, January 27 2017, www.theguardian.com/business/2017/jan/26/swiss-watch-sales-fall-10-per-cent-china-corruption-crackdown (accessed January 27 2017).

90 On the end of communism in the West and the Soviet Union, Lévesque, *Enigma of 1989*; Brown, *Rise and Fall of Communism*; Sebestyen, *Revolution 1989*; Plokhy, *Last Empire*.

91 Roche, *France in the Enlightenment*, p. 475.

92 Joint Publications Research Service, *Selected Works of Mao Tse-tung*, "Twenty Manifestations of Bureaucracy," February 1970, www.marxists.org/reference/archive/mao/selected-works/volume-9/mswv9_85.htm (accessed December 30 2017).

93 Lebow and Stein, "End of the Cold War as a Non-Linear Confluence"; Sarotte, *Collapse*.

94 Rowen, "Short March"; Chang, *Coming Collapse of China*; Gilley, *China's Democratic Future*.

95 Dimitrov, *Why Communism Did Not Collapse*, esp. pp. 3–39.

96 Ibid., pp. 303–12.

97 Calculations based on a dataset including 39 noncommunist single-party regimes (based partially on Smith, "Life of the Party"), 20 non-democratic monarchies, and 15 communist regimes.

98 China Labor Bulletin, *China Strike Map*, http://maps.clb.org.hk/strikes/zh-cn (accessed July 19 2017); Dimitrov and Zhang, "Patterns of Protest Activity in China."

99 On land grabs, see Takeuchi, *Tax Reform in Rural China*, esp. ch. 4; Heurlin, *Responsive Authoritarianism in China*. On local debt, Kroeber, *China's Economy*, pp. 111–27.

100 Jowitt, *New World Disorder*; Geddes, "Stages of Development in Authoritarian Regimes."

101 For statistics on the number of Uyghurs and Tibetans in the Party, see Communist Party of China, *Zhongguo gongchangdang dangnei tongji ziliao huibian*, pp. 12–21.

102 International Campaign for Tibet, "Self-Immolations by Tibetans," July 14 2017, www.savetibet.org/resources/fact-sheets/self-immolations-by-tibetans/ (accessed July 19 2017).

103 *Jiefang ribao*, July 3 2013, p. 3.

104 On this system generally, see Stratfor, "China: Where Big Brother Meets Big Data" (April 18 2016), https://worldview.stratfor.com/article/china-where-big-brother-meets-big-data (accessed July 19 2017).

105 Hastings, "Charting the Course of Uyghur Unrest." For prosecution statistics, see *Zhongguo tongji nianjian* (China Statistical Yearbook) and www.duihuaresearch.org/search/label/ESS (accessed July 19 2017).

106 Lindenberger, "Tacit Minimal Consensus."

107 Dimitrov, "Functions of Letters to the Editor in Reform-Era Cuba."

108 Kloth, *Vom "Zettelfalten" bis zum freien Wählen*.

109 King, Pan, and Roberts, "How Censorship in China Allows Government Criticism but Silences Collective Expression," and "How the Chinese Government Fabricates Social Media Posts for Strategic Distraction"; Dimitrov, "Political Logic of Media Control in China."

110 *People's Daily* Editorial Office, *Neibu canyue jingxuan* (Internal Reference Selections, pp. 489–534.

111 "Leaked Speech Shows Xi Jinping's Opposition to Reform," January 27 2013, http://chinadigitaltimes.net/2013/01/leaked-speech-shows-xi-jinpings-opposition-to-reform (accessed January 28 2013).
112 Jacobs, "China Still Presses Crusade Against Falun Gong," *New York Times*, April 27 2009, www.nytimes.com/2009/04/28/world/asia/28china .html (accessed April 30 2017).
113 Shambaugh, *China's Communist Party*.

9   Order Revisited

Shakespeare is the happy hunting ground
of all minds that have lost their balance.
James Joyce[1]

This chapter and the next revisit principal themes of the book drawing on evidence from the case studies of Chapters 5–8 and other historical evidence to revisit my understanding of order and the conditions, mechanisms, strategies, and judgments that affect the likelihood of orders surviving the kinds of challenges they face in the twenty-first century.

The opening section of this chapter returns to the definition of order. I elaborate and examine some of the tensions inherent in it. My definition has more internal tensions than a simpler, parsimonious one, but, I maintain, is more useful. Rather than papering over, or trying to resolve, these tensions in favor of one side or the other, I believe we should keep them alive, even foreground them. They provide a framework for a more dialectical and comprehensive analysis, and one based on forthright recognition that my definition – indeed, any formulation – is, of necessity, subjective. We are drawn to study order and to define it in particular ways because of the present-day problems that drive our research. As they change, so too will our interest in and framings of the order.

I consistently argue against the tendency to explain political behavior with reference to material capabilities and so-called structural conditions. What matters most, I contend, are actors' goals and subjective understandings of the contexts in which they pursue them. This is no different when it comes to the survival of political orders. We must identify and analyze conditions and pressures we think important, but also the beliefs of leaders and other relevant actors about the viability of their orders, the nature of the threats they face, the likelihood that they can be addressed successfully, and by what means. Important too are the negative and positive role models that shape actor aspirations and fears about their societies and their status within them.

Actor beliefs – like those of analysts – are highly subjective, often ill-informed, and frequently motivated, or influenced by, political agendas or needs. The vulnerability or robustness of a society is as much a state of mind as it is a political reality. Collective states of mind often constitute that reality. To some degree, fears of disorder or expectations of robustness can be made self-fulfilling. So too can these fears or expectations prompt policies – or inaction – that produce results the opposite of those intended. The second section of the chapter accordingly explores leader estimates of robustness and some of their consequences.

I next turn to deviance. I am particularly interested in free-riding and exploitation as they are endemic to most societies but vary in frequency and character. I posit a negative relationship between free-riding and exploitation on the one hand and the perceived robustness of orders on the other. In developed, democratic countries, both activities should decline, because they are increasingly regarded as deviant, and those who engage in them the objects of shaming or punishment. The perception of what constitutes free-riding and exploitation should also change as the principle of equality becomes increasingly dominant in western societies. A rise in either free-riding or exploitation, and more tellingly the emergence of discourses that justify them, are signs of decline and disorder. Drawing on the empirical findings of Chapter 5, I suggest that these discourses have become more evident in the United States and free-riding and exploitation more acceptable. These changes do not bode well for political stability.

I then address deviance, but from the perspective of those in power. I theorize a curve of tolerance. Leaders of new regimes, and supporters, are likely to be relatively intolerant of deviance and political dissent – I treat dissent as one form of deviance. So are leaders and supporters of declining regimes, although this will depend on their perceived ability to suppress and punish deviance. Leaders and supporters of established regimes that possess some degree of robustness are likely to be more tolerant. Leader assessments of robustness are accordingly a reasonable predictor of responses to dissent. Dissent also tells us something about robustness. It should be the greatest when orders are perceived to be robust or weak and declining, but dissent will differ in character in each of these circumstances.

Top-Down and Bottom-Down Orders

At the outset of this book, I defined order as legible, predictable behavior in accord with recognized norms. I claimed that robust orders require a high degree of solidarity among their members. Solidarity is the product of social interaction and cooperation, which in turn requires appropriate norms and predictable patterns of behavior. In Chapter 4 I argued that declining orders reveal a breakdown of solidarity, often attributable in the short term to elite violation of rule packages and the sharper contradictions they create in perceptions between existing practices and the principles of justice on which orders rest. Elite violation of rule packages can lead to expanding and more acute conflict in a society but also encourages others to violate norms that sustain solidarity. In the longer term, I attribute decline in solidarity and, in part, elite violations of rule packages, to loss of traction of principles of justice and shifts in the relative appeal of competing principles and their different formulations.

In Chapter 3 I stress that all but the smallest of orders (e.g. hunter-gatherers, *kibbutzim*) are to varying degrees hierarchical. One of the fundamental paradoxes of top-down orders, and societies more generally, is that there is always a minority who receives more of whatever is valued and a majority that receives less. The paradox is made more acute by the fact that in so many orders – western and non-western alike – those who receive less are often the strongest supporters of their orders. I suggest multiple reasons for this curious phenomenon, among them the fewer life choices available to the disadvantaged. It makes them more concerned with preserving the few they have; more risk averse, and often more fearful of change. Because they are less educated, and perhaps less confident or arrogant, they are also more likely to internalize the discourses elites propagate to justify the existing order and their privileges. When those who are disadvantaged – by far the majority in any order – do become disenchanted, they may become more risk prone, and more willing to support change. Orders rapidly lose their legitimacy in this circumstance and are likely to confront a crisis.

Top-down and bottom-up orders draw strength from their ability to satisfy fundamental human needs. These include physical and material security, self-esteem, and social contact. We might refine our definition of order and describe it as a hierarchical arrangement, supported by most of its members, that fosters security, self-esteem, and social contact, encourages solidarity, and results in legible, predictable behavior. To some degree, people understand the relationship between order and human fulfilment. Many are motivated to overvalue the benefits they receive and undervalue those they lack. This bias helps to rationalize acceptance, even support, of the status quo. It may also help to explain why those at the bottom of the hierarchy are often so hostile to those who criticize their orders.

The principles of justice that enable and sustain orders find expression in discourses and practices. Discourses define justice and its associated norms and practices. They also attempt to justify discrepancies between the behavior required by these principles and how people act. I documented how in the United States popular discourses have, over time, undermined some of these practices for ordinary people, while elite discourses – most notably, neoliberalism – have done so for many in the elite. These popular discourses might be regarded as counter-discourses as they undermined existing practices supportive of order. The irony here is that these counter-discourses were sponsored by the elite in the case of neo-liberalism, and to some extent propagated by them in the case of popular discourses. We tend to conceive of counter-discourses as products of those opposed to the status quo, and this is often correct. The American experience suggests that counter-discourses may be produced by those who support the existing order and hope to profit from it. This was certainly true of presidential speeches, television sitcoms, and popular music. It is not only capitalism, but successful orders of all kinds, which generate immanent critiques.

I distinguish top-down from bottom-up orders, and government from society. Governments are always top-down, and most institutions of civil society are bottom-up. But we should be careful not to consider this distinction as any kind of hard and fast binary. The more local top-down institutions become, the more they are likely to incorporate features of both kinds of order. Schools and hospitals are cases in point. The same mixture in reverse characterizes many largely bottom-up institutions of civil society. I have developed the distinction in this book between two kinds of order and made it central to my analysis. Given the purposes of the book I have not provided an extensive analysis of the relations between the two kinds of orders beyond noting some of their different features and the kinds of tensions to which they give rise. This is the subject of a book in its own right.

Society precedes government, and often outlives it, and regimes not imposed by force only come into power by to some degree instantiating societies' values. Societies can constrain government in the sense of providing incentives for it to conform to valued norms and practices. Governments can over time transform society. Strong governments like France and so-called totalitarian regimes like the Soviet Union, China, and North Korea have successfully fostered top-down social transformations. Such success is always Janus-faced. It creates greater expectations among populations about what government can and will do for them, creating more alienation when and if they fail to deliver. This phenomenon was pronounced in the Soviet Union and most communist countries in Eastern Europe. It is a serious risk in contemporary China.

The society-state difference is important to keep in mind when analyzing the origins of states and their decline. As noted, societies precede states and generally survive them. Chaos is the opposite of order; it is characterized by the absence of rule-based behavior, functioning institutions, lawlessness, and often unpredictability. True chaos would require the collapse of both top-down and bottom-up orders and this rarely happens. When it does, some kind of bottom-up order quickly forms, often initially, of a rapacious, gang-based kind. As noted in Chapter 1, order and predictability do not necessarily co-vary. Hobbes' state of nature is lawless and violent but all too predictable. So too are Brazilian favelas and the streets of Mogadishu.

One of the most important political facts of the last 100 years is how long-lived societies are in comparison to states, and how much more so compared to regimes, many of which have a short life. Societies too can decline, but it is usually a much slower process. My analysis of decline focuses largely on political orders – states and their regimes. But I implicate societies in this process because social change can be, and often is, the principal underlying cause of regime or state decline. Chapters 5 and 6 analyze value shifts in American society that have important implications for the political system, its legitimacy, and perhaps its survival.

We need to know more about the interaction of top-down and bottom-up orders. To what extent do they share values and practices, have numerous channels of communication, and show their respect and tolerance for one another? When these conditions are met, *ceteris paribus*, the more effective and robust any kind of superordinate order is likely to be. Shared values, good channels of communication, and mutual respect and tolerance facilitate – and are undoubtedly, in part, a product of – reasonably defined domains in which the two orders operate.

Also important are the liminal spaces between both kinds of order. How and to what degree are they recognized? How are their differences handled? Liminality has been described as a principal site of disorder, but disorder here may enhance order elsewhere by letting off steam or by allowing for experimentation that ultimately benefits both kinds of order. In the anthropology literature, liminality occurs in the middle stage of rituals, when participants no longer hold their pre-ritual status but do not yet hold the status they will attain when the ritual is complete. During a ritual's liminal stage, participants "stand at the threshold" between their previous way of structuring their identity, time, or community, and a new way, which the ritual establishes. More recently, anthropologists have used the concept to describe social and political change. Elsewhere, I have argued that role playing has the potential to make people feel they have entered a liminal space from which it is difficult, sometimes impossible, to return.[2] It offers a strong incentive for self-fashioning, through it can become a vehicle of social and political change.

Liminality has a downside when those who experience it find it difficult afterwards to reintegrate into their societies. Rupert Emerson argued
that this sense of alienation and not belonging was particularly acute
among western-educated members of native elites. They had rejected
many traditional values and practices, but were not accepted as equal
by colonizers and so turned to nationalism to create a larger community
in which they could belong.[3] Robert Wohl attributes much of the social
and political chaos following World War I to the same phenomenon.[4] As
these examples indicate, liminality has diverse and context-dependent
consequences for orders.

The frontispiece of Chapter 1 is a quote about order from Shakespeare's
Troilus and Cressida. This chapter begins with a line from James Joyce
warning us to be wary of those who turn to the bard for guidance. Joyce's
remark is assuredly tongue-in-cheek, and not unlike Plato's dissing of
Homer. Joyce was deeply affected by Shakespeare, just as Plato was by
Homer. Joyce was also influenced by Homer; he named his great novel
Ulysses and critics find many parallels in its structure and imagery with
the *Odyssey*, and some with *Troilus and Cressida*.

To complete this circle, we must consider the influence of Homer on
Shakespeare.[5] It is Homer's character Ulysses who gives the famous order
speech in *Troilus and Cressida*. For the Greeks, Ulysses was a trickster,
a wily character who frequently violated important norms, but almost
invariably for responsible ends. Having him say that society will fall apart
if people disobey its norms is nothing less than farcical, and a clear indication that Shakespeare was not defending the traditional ideology of
natural order as much as calling it into question.

Literary critics have been divided in their readings of Ulysses' speech.
Some see it as an embodiment of noble ideas of order and degree, while
others view it more cynically. They note that the speech enacts the loss
of order and control through excessive use of accumulation, climax,
and neologisms. Most contemporary critics support the more cynical
reading. They are nevertheless wary of interpreting Ulysses' speech as a
reflection of Shakespeare's views, and, more generally, avoid treating any
character as representative of the playwright's beliefs.

Shakespeare is, I believe, setting up a series of deliberate tensions. They
arise from the contrast between what is said and how it is said; who says it
and what we know about their character and behavior; the ideology seemingly espoused by the play and the action of its major characters; the palp-
able, visible, and predictable order seemingly represented by the heavens,
and the murky, poorly understood motives of characters and the unpredictable outcomes of their behavior; the use of tragedy and comedy, their
jarring contrasts, and, at times, the difficulty of knowing which of these

genres, if either, is being represented; differences between ancient times and the present; and finally, between a play and life.

These tensions encourage us to recognize that life is more complex than our conceptions of it acknowledge; that people's behavior is often motivated by multiple motives that they do not fully acknowledge or grasp; that the consequences of behavior are often unknowable in advance but people must act as if they are predictable, and the political order is something we require but do not really understand. We act to uphold or benefit from it and may unwittingly do the reverse. Shakespeare is telling us – and I follow him in this book – that political order cannot adequately be represented by a single, coherent, and consistent formulation. Such formulations blind us to tensions and contradictions and the behavior and uncertainty to which they give rise. Knowledge requires us to go beyond them, not to resolve the tensions, as that is rarely possible in practice, and often ill advisable in theory, but to foreground them and make them central to our definitions and analysis. What may appear intellectually sloppy and inelegant may have the virtue of being philosophically profound and conceptually useful.

Max Weber shared this understanding of politics and the concepts we bring to its study. One of the most striking and important features of his epistemology and substantive observations about politics is their unresolvable tensions – made that much more acute by modernity.[6] If Kant's thought cast a long shadow over the nineteenth century, Weber's did over the twentieth. He deeply influenced important and quite different thinkers like Joseph Schumpeter, Talcott Parsons, Carl Schmitt, Hans Morgenthau, Max Horkheimer, and Theodor Adorno. Schmitt, Horkheimer, and Adorno attempted to resolve these tensions, albeit in diametrically opposed directions. Morgenthau, to his credit, sought to keep them alive.[7] With respect to order, I think we need to follow his example.

As I unpacked my definition of order in this book, its tensions became increasingly evident. Order and disorder are not binaries, but closer to being co-constitutive. Disorder is inherent in order. Any kind of reasonably robust order must contain enough disorder to give agents some freedom from constraint and allow, or accept, at least tacitly, violations of its norms. This might be called productive disorder, because it allows, even encourages, challenges that may prove vehicles for its evolution. The cycle of challenge and response is a process critical to order.

Like order itself, my definition of it evolved in the course of the study. I struggled initially to resolve its internal contradictions and external difficulties but gradually came to appreciate and even revel in them. My definition embodies components (i.e. predictability, solidarity, hierarchy) that sometimes work at cross-purposes. More of one component may mean less of another – or not – depending, of course, on the circumstances. External tensions arise from efforts to apply the definition to historical worlds. Our categories never quite fit protean reality, or they do in ways that differ across societies. The several components of my definition may also have different interaction effects. Both sets of tension tell us important things about the nature of the order and politics, more so, I believe, than simple, seemingly consistent definitions that attempt to ignore or finesse these tensions.

Order and Deviance

In the postwar era, the stability of democratic orders has largely been taken for granted, at least until recently. This belief is beneficial because it encourages compliance with norms, which in turn strengthens them and may make compliance habitual. Belief in robustness nevertheless has a downside. It encourages free-riding and exploitation. The former rests on the assumption that others will do what is necessary to make things work, whether it be voting or paying taxes. The latter takes advantage of the trust, good will, and belief in the prevalence of norms-based behavior. Bernie Madoff's pyramid scheme succeeded for all these reasons – plus the greed of his victims.[8]

Exploitation preys on weakness and fear. In 2016, the US Internal Revenue Service and Federal Bureau of Investigation warned Americans of a telephone scam in which callers claim to be IRS agents about to send the police to arrest the person on the line unless they immediately transfer money to pay allegedly due back taxes. The elderly and uneducated are particularly vulnerable to this kind of extortion.[9] During the 1973 Middle East War, Henry Kissinger successfully exploited mutual superpower fears of escalation and nuclear war. He reasoned, correctly, that the Soviets feared superpower escalation as much as the Americans did. He could accordingly attempt to detach Egypt from the Soviet orbit and make it dependent on the United States instead. He confessed that he would never have challenged the Soviet Union this way in a world without nuclear weapons.[10]

Free-riding and exploitation occur at every level of social aggregation. What constitutes free-riding and exploitation is a matter of subjective judgment, and these judgments in turn are often highly politicized. The French government has historically been responsive to the farm lobby and negotiated the Common Agricultural Policy (CAP) with other EU member states. Farmers insist that subsidies are essential to French agriculture and that it in turn is necessary to maintain the countryside and

French values. Critics contend that it artificially inflates prices; impedes imports from poorer developing countries; sustains uneconomic agricultural operations; and degrades the environment. They condemn it as a form of free-loading and exploitation.[11] The same phenomenon occurs in international society. For decades, US officials complained about the alleged failure of their European allies to pay their "fair share" of the common defense burden. Europeans rebutted the charge or ignored the complaint, and independent American analysts often weighed in their support.[12] In the eyes of their allies and many economists, Americans are guilty of free-riding because of their extraordinary foreign debt.[13]

Deviance is a pejorative label for behavior at odds with social norms, rules or laws.[14] It is a rhetorical weapon of those who support the status quo and want to stigmatize and marginalize actors who reject values and practices from which they benefit. Émile Durkheim describes deviance as a necessary feature of social organization. It defines moral boundaries, teaches people the difference between right and wrong, and creates solidarity by bringing people together to collectively confront challenges to their norms, values, and practices.[15]

Deviance pushes social boundaries, which has the potential to change these norms, values, and practices – even understandings of the concept itself. Deviance is thus a double-edged sword. It can isolate those who violate norms and minimize sympathy and support for them. It can also enhance their solidarity; give them and their practices much-desired publicity; and attract followers and make groups labeled as deviant the cutting edge of social, political, religious and economic change – for better and worse. Throughout history, many social practices and political movements initially labeled as deviant ultimately became the establishment, as did love-based marriage, premarital sex, Christianity, democracy, and socialism. Changes of this kind can reverse the understanding of what is deviant.

Deviance offers insight into the robustness of orders. Tax avoidance has been the norm in most societies and people who succeeded in escaping the taxman often gained respect and status. In 1731, Jean-Jacques Rousseau, then a young man, walked from Paris to Lyon and found shelter one evening in the simple dwelling of a peasant. He was served a meal of barley bread and milk, but when their conversation convinced the peasant that Rousseau was not an agent of the government, he opened a trap door to a basement, descended and returned with a white loaf, haunch of ham, and a bottle of good wine. Rousseau cursed France, not the farmer, for a government of such rapacity that people could only avoid ruin by feigning poverty.[16]

Today, in developed countries – and increasingly in developing countries – tax evasion is frowned upon. There is, of course, variation in its frequency and how it is regarded by populations. In northern Europe tax evasion is more difficult, those who engage in it are considered deviants, and governments impose stiff penalties. In southern Europe, tax evasion is easier and more controversial. In Greece, it has been called the national sport, and is estimated to reach 6 to 9 percent of GDP.[17] Since the economic crisis of 2008 many now consider it deviant, and there are pressures from the EU and IMF to reign it in. In a recent 2014 poll 85.5 percent of Greeks agreed that tax evasion was "theft," but 35.1 percent said they would cheat if they could because "everybody else does it."[18] Even tax avoidance, which is legal, has aroused considerable ire as witnessed by the public reaction to the *Süddeutsche Zeitung*'s release to newspapers around the world of the so-called "Paradise Papers" documenting the use of tax havens by the rich.[19]

In the United States, tax evaders have long been regarded as deviants. In my home state of New Hampshire, Edward Brown and his wife, Elaine, gained national news media attention in 2007 for denying the US government's right to levy a federal income tax and subsequently for refusing to surrender to federal government agents after having been convicted of tax crimes. They were joined at their rural residence by anti-tax supporters from around the country and a long, armed stand-off with federal law enforcement authorities ensued. It ended with their arrest and subsequent imprisonment in October 2007.[20]

Tax avoidance, as opposed to tax evasion, has long been a much-admired art in the United States and the principal commitment of tax accountants. Republican presidents have reduced the number of Internal Revenue Service (IRS) agents, making it less likely that rich people who fail to report unsalaried income will get caught. More people cheat and brag about it to their peers. Most people still consider tax cheats to be deviants, but this consensus may be on the wane. In the 2016 presidential election, Trump broke with convention and refused to release any income tax returns.[21] Some of his supporters cited his failure to pay any federal taxes as a sign of his "genius" and qualification for the presidency.[22] An increase in tax evasion and a decline in its stigmatization are indications of a less robust order.

Tax evasion is a form of free-riding. It is also exploitation because others must pay more taxes to cover governmental expenditures. I noted at the outset of this discussion that robust orders enable free-riding and certain kinds of exploitation. In the absence of order, free-riding is not possible, but exploitation is, and is almost certain to be pronounced. Hobbes describes it as the principal form of social interaction in his state of nature. I posit that an increase in free-riding is a sign of order, as it is impossible in its absence. Free-riding should nevertheless decline as order becomes more legitimate and, hence, robust. We can see this today in many developing countries, like India, where efforts are under way to promote uniform and enforceable tax systems.[23] To the extent that free-riding can be measured – and this is a difficult task – I would expect a rise followed by a decline. Any subsequent increase in free-riding would be an indication of a decline in an order's robustness. In this situation, it would be likely to be manifest in multiple domains, attract public attention, and perhaps prompt a debate about why it is happening, the extent to which it should be regarded as deviant, and perpetrators punished or shamed.

Free-riding and exploitation are related, but in a complex way. Exploitation is rife in the absence of order, but this may also be observed in ordered societies. Rousseau and his peasant host were not alone in regarding the French government and its agents as oppressors. The *ancien régime* extracted taxes to pay for the profligate lifestyles of the aristocracy and the wars they and the king fought. Taxes were collected indirectly by tax farmers, who bought the right to collect taxes from the king. They attempted to extract as much as they could to make as large a profit as possible. Exploitation encourages resistance – passive or active – depending in part on the perceived degree of exploitation, relative power of exploiters and exploited, and the ability of the latter to organize effectively.

Resistance may also depend on whether the exploiters are local or national. Local exploiters are easier to resist when government or outside forces can be mobilized against them. In the old American West, sheriffs were dispatched – often at the request of local citizens – to newly settled towns with this end in mind. Similar problems exist today at sea.[24] Beginning on wagon trains in their travels west, settlers formed their own laws and enforced them vigilante style.[25] Sometime these bottom-up orders were ineffective against better-armed gangs. In the 1960 American film, *The Magnificent Seven*, Mexican villagers, who have no hope of support from a weak and corrupt national government, hire American gunfighters to protect them against bandits. More often, governments are in cahoots with exploiters, as the US government was for decades with corporations resisting unionization or local southern governments enforcing Jim Crow.[26]

In present-day China, the evolution of free-riding can be demonstrated by the issue of intellectual property rights (IPR). Traditionally, the Chinese understanding has been that IPR is a legal regime that protects the copyrights, trademarks, and patents of foreigners.[27] As a result, in the 1980s and 1990s there was excessive piracy and counterfeiting, which are two forms of IPR free-riding.[28] However, as China began to produce indigenous IPR, free-riding clashed with domestic commercial interests. As a result, an important shift toward stronger protection of indigenous IPR through the specialized IPR courts could already be detected in the 2000s.[29] This trend became more pronounced in the 2010s, when China emerged as the top filer of patent applications in the world.[30] The case of IPR demonstrates that norms about free-riding can change as underlying perceptions of the national interest evolve.

In orders that are perceived as legitimate, free-riding and exploitation will be frowned upon, and those responsible for them labeled as deviants. This obviously varies as a function of the activity. In most western countries, voting is not mandatory, and many citizens stay home on polling day. In the United States, in primary elections over 80 percent of the voters may do so, and most without being subjected to any stigmatization.[31] At the other end of the spectrum, efforts to take advantage of needy people can provoke national rage. The Republican Party's failed attempt in 2017 to replace the Affordable Care Act (Obamacare) with a healthcare plan of their own – and if that was impossible, just to do away with the existing one – is a telling example. The initial Senate version would have introduced sharp cuts in Medicare and deprived 22 million Americans of medical insurance. It met such strong resistance among voters that moderate Republican senators and governors opposed it.[32] The bill was described by many as a blatant effort of exploitation: it would have deprived the poor and elderly of medical care to pay for tax cuts for the very rich.[33]

Perceptions of free-riding and exploitation depend very much on what principles of justice are used as the frame of reference. Fairness, defined as giving the most to those who contribute the most, prompts different assessments than equality, defined as giving the same rewards to everyone. In our medical care example, cutting taxes for the rich is justified with reference to a neo-liberal conception of fairness and general hostility to government. Republicans who want to "starve the beast" hate government intervention and the spending that enables it – unless it is for the military – in large part because government programs, in their view, are a form of income redistribution.[34] For those committed to equality, tax cuts and the GOP healthcare bill are blatantly unjust. So too is tax avoidance – even if perfectly legal – because it takes advantage of a tax code written to reward the rich and punish the poor. Chapter 5 documented the change in self-interest that underlies and justifies this kind of behavior.

To some degree principles of justice are self-serving. The surveys and experiments discussed in Chapter 6 make it apparent that on the whole wealthy people are attracted to fairness and the less well-off to equality. However, there is considerable cross-over. Most working-class Americans believe that pay should be based on the contribution people make to society, and many well-off people vote Democrat because they believe government should come to the aid of the less fortunate. There is widespread support for both principles of justice, but no agreement as to the domains in which they should apply or to how they should be implemented in practice. I will return to this problem.

In summary, the prevalence and nature of free-riding and exploitation tell us something important about the degree of robustness of social orders. In developed, democratic countries, both free-riding and exploit-ation should decline and become increasingly regarded as deviant and the subject of shaming or punishment. A rise in either, and more telling, the emergence of discourses that justify them, are signs of disorder. The perception of what constitutes free-riding and exploitation should also change as the principle of equality becomes increasingly dominant in western societies. This shift is an uneven one across domains where these principles apply, and also challenged by counter-discourses based on the principle of fairness. Neoliberalism and libertarianism are the two dom-inant discourses based on fairness, and they have the most appeal in the United States. Critics could argue that they reflect and justify the kind of individualism Tocqueville identified as the principal threat to democracy. But the same argument is made by critics of equality discourses who contend that they are used to justify economic and other privileges for the disadvantaged at the expense of other members of society.

Beliefs, Deviance, and Policy

Those social scientists interested in change routinely invoke system pressures at either the domestic or international level to explain it.[35] Some draw analogies to biology and the ways in which natural selection can promote convergence.[36] They ignore the well-established finding that evolution can promote convergence or divergence depending on the circumstances.[37] They generally attribute convergence in institutions and practices to material incentives and pressures (e.g. the industrial revolu-tion, nuclear weapons, globalization). For mechanisms of change, they turn to selection or rational adaptation. Democratization theory is a case in point, as are the expectations that globalization and education will inevitably lead to a world largely populated by democratic regimes. Juan Linz rightly derides these beliefs as a form of "white Marxism."[38]

In addition to their often crude determinism, structural theories invoke multiple mechanisms (i.e. evolution, adaptation, imitation) and often fail to identify them properly or distinguish between or among them.[39] They assume that the constraints and opportunities of the environment that they identify are "objective," and accordingly understood – or should be – the same way by political actors. However, so-called system pressures are invariably the products of theories, and in the imagination of scholars not features of the real world. Political elites rarely share similar understandings of the constraints and opportunities they face, the policies they adopt often have little to do with the constraints and opportunities they do perceive, and may have entirely unintended consequences. Change, like order, is more often an emergent property than the product of design.

Even when system-level pressures are real they do not necessarily promote convergence. Here too, evolutionary biology offers a cautionary tale. There are frequently different functional ways of adapting to an environment.[40] Mammals have responded to predators by developing the ability to sprint, protective camouflage, and the ability to fight back. Thus, the impala has long legs, the tortoise a shell, and the cape buffalo horns. The same is true for predators; cheetahs developed flexible spines and long legs that propel them at their prey at upwards of 70 miles per hour, while slower hyenas run for great distances and exhaust their prey.[41] These evolutionary responses were not random but depended on initial conditions. François Jacob, Nobel laureate in biology, compares nature to an engineer. It does not search for the best theoretical solution, but the most practical given material and other constraints. It is a tinkerer, that uses what is available to refashion living things to make them more likely to survive and reproduce.[42]

This principle also applies in politics. Even under strong system pressures, political orders – like impalas, tortoises, and buffalo – may respond in diverse ways. David Lebow provides a nice example in a comparative analysis of American and German legal systems. Similar theoretical developments in the Progressive and Weimar eras promoted similar kinds of change, but it had almost diametrically opposed effects in the two countries.[43]

Adaptation – here a conscious strategy, not an evolutionary one – can take different forms and encourage divergence as well as convergence, or convergence with important differences. These outcomes will depend on existing political forms and practices, resources available for restructuring, and the decisions of leaders. Bricolage is already in the conceptual tool box of comparative politics. In his book on Italian and Japanese political development, Richard Samuels argues that revolutionary leaders may create new institutions, but equally important, and perhaps more successful in the longer term, are those who change the trajectory of their states through bricolage. They redeploy or recombine heterogeneous "fragments" of institutions and practices to facilitate their goals or adapt to changing circumstances. Just as they were constrained by the past, they may "lock in" their preferences or institutions in a way that constrains their successors in how they respond to future domestic or foreign pressures and challenges.[44]

Our British and Chinese case studies offer strong evidence for these suppositions. Georgian leaders supported trade and manufacturing without an inkling of their likely consequences for the economic, political, and social life of the country. Most did so for reasons of immediate personal economic or political gain, not in response to any perceived domestic or foreign pressures. They give no evidence of ever considering the longer-term implications or of imagining the industrial revolution, let alone its consequences. Chinese leaders consciously encouraged industrialization as a necessary means of making the country stronger and its people better off. As a latecomer to industrial development, they better understood what they were setting in motion. Nonetheless, the reforms initiated in 1978 were conducted without a clear blueprint. Leaders embraced the spirit of experimentation, which meant that some reforms could fail and that others would succeed.[45] Importantly, as the reforms were initiated before the collapse of communism in Europe, there was no sense prior to 1989 that they would contribute to the longevity of the regime; this was a positive unexpected consequence. The reform process also resulted in manifold negative unintended consequences of all kinds, the most severe of which are environmental degradation and corruption.[46]

Georgian Britain and China differ in their use of bricolage. The Chinese communists came to power in the aftermath of a long civil war. They did away with as much of the old order as was possible, and attempted not only to remake society, but the Chinese people as well. Like any other government they had to make do with materials at hand, but undertook an extraordinary mobilization of people and resources to restructure society. The Georgians did nothing of the kind. They preferred compromise to coercion whenever possible, sought to buy off opposition rather than repress it, believed in minimum intervention in society, and resorted to extensive bricolage to "muddle through." Their goals were correspondingly short-term in contrast to the longer-term vision of their Chinese counterparts. In recent decades, Chinese leaders have become more "normal" in their governance in the sense of focusing more on shorter-term goals and using less disruptive means to achieve them. But fundamental differences remain between the two orders, with serious implications for how their respective leaders sought to preserve their power and regimes.

Throughout the Georgian era, and up through the 1830s, England was governed by a monarchy that rested on divine right and was supported by the Church of England, and a hereditary, land-based aristocracy. Elite privileges were diminished by Catholic Emancipation in 1828 and the First Reform Act of 1832. In 1846, the Corn Laws were repealed, depriving landlords of high prices for grain and providing cheaper bread to the masses. In 1869, parliament disestablished the Church in Ireland.[47] The sponsors of all these measures thought – incorrectly – that they were preserving the existing order, not changing it. Their critics were closer to the mark, but they too failed to predict how the country would evolve politically. Most thought – incorrectly – that the changes in question would lead ineluctably and quickly to socialism.[48]

The Representation of the People Act of 1867, known as the Second Reform Act, offers a particularly cogent example because its consequences were different from those expected even in the short term. It doubled the number of enfranchised working-class men in England and Wales. A year later, all male heads of household were enfranchised as a result of the end of compounding of rents. Introduced by the Conservative Party in the expectation of increasing its number of seats in the Commons, the Representation of the People Act was a principal cause of their defeat in the 1868 general election. To the surprise of almost everyone, the redistribution of seats increased the dominance of the upper classes in the House of Commons; only they and rich merchants could afford the dramatically increased campaigning costs of contested seats. The abolition of certain rotten boroughs, moreover, removed some of the middle-class international merchants who had previously attained seats.[49]

Almost every other significant change in British politics or policy carries its own tale of motives independent of system pressures, or responses to system pressures poorly understood, and with consequences often the opposite of those intended. Recent examples include key decisions by two Conservative Prime Ministers. David Cameron greatly exaggerated the threat posed by UKIP, a new party dedicated to taking Britain of the European Union (EU). Hoping to outflank UKIP and keep his own anti-European backbenchers in line, he called for a nationwide referendum on the EU. To his horror, ambitious politicians like Boris Johnson deserted him to headline the well-funded campaign for "Brexit." Jeremy Corbyn, no friend of the EU, made sure the Labour Party did not conduct any active, coherent campaign on its behalf. Brexit won a narrow electoral majority, Cameron had to resign his position, and the new Tory leader, Theresa May, chose to pursue a "hard Brexit" and to call a snap election for June 2017 to strengthen her hand within the Party and vis-à-vis the EU. The Tories lost their majority, were forced into a tactical alliance with a minority, extremist Northern Irish party, and Theresa May became a lame duck prime minister.[50] These events put the United Kingdom in an unenviable economic and political situation, and one moreover that made it difficult to negotiate seriously with the EU because almost any terms to which May agreed were certain to alienate a significant faction within her party.

In the Chinese case, neither the Great Leap Forward nor the Cultural Revolution, which are the two most disastrous policies of the Maoist period, could be explained by system pressures, either internal or external. On some level, the Great Leap Forward was driven by the desire to jumpstart industrialization and by the need to outperform the Soviet Union, but the scale and speed of this process did not reflect external pressures. Instead, they were determined by Mao Zedong's personal preferences for policymaking and policy implementation. Similarly, the Cultural Revolution reflected Mao's views of the importance of reviving the spirit of the revolution, rather than some objective systemic pressure to reinvigorate the party. Both of these events had cataclysmic unintended and unexpected consequences – the deaths of tens of millions of citizens during the Great Leap Forward and violence whose length and scope far exceeded what Mao had expected during the Cultural Revolution.

The preceding discussion and historical examples suggest that top-down orders – and here again, I speak of political regimes – must jump through at least four major hoops to survive. Their leaders must recognize that changing domestic and foreign circumstances require some kind of extraordinary response, as opposed to business as usual. They must respond to these pressures in appropriate ways. To endure in the long term regimes must satisfy to some degree popular demands for security, well-being, and status. Regime survival also depends on the timing and execution of their initiatives.

Only the first of these conditions is directly related to so-called systemic constraints or opportunities. The others hinge on more idiosyncratic features of context that include political culture, leader beliefs, skills, and authority, and the momentary configuration of domestic and foreign circumstances. As we have seen, these factors are absolutely critical to the outcomes of initiatives. Political culture also shapes policymaking, but as we have seen actors of similar background in the same elite can hold diametrically opposed views of the constraints and opportunities their regimes face, the kinds of responses they think appropriate, the risks they associate with them, and the need to act versus temporizing. Elites are also prone to misjudge pressures and risks alike, and in both directions. For all these reasons, systemic and rationalist models of politics are at best starting points for narratives that engage context, agency, confluence, and unintended consequences.

Let me return to timing, as it is critical in the Britain and China cases. In England, Scotland, and Wales, London's initiatives were ahead of the curve. Electoral and other reforms were introduced in a timely way, alleviating more pressures from below as they invited. These reforms also made it possible to address subsequent pressures by legislative means, reconciling the rising middle classes, and later, the working classes, to the political system. In Ireland, the reverse was the case; Catholic emancipation, disestablishment of the Protestant Church, and Home Rule in 1914 were all late in coming. Each was regarded in Ireland as a concession extracted only because British leaders feared the possibly violent consequences of denying them. Rather than reconciling Irish Catholics to British rule, they increased the appeal of nationalism and support for independence.[51] There are important lessons here for other leaders, including those of China.

Change may be motivated by leaders with visions – or nightmares – and they may be instrumentally rational or not. Regardless, the consequences are difficult, and at times impossible, to predict, because they are so often unintended. Sometimes, this is the result of their failure to take into account relevant dimensions of a problem. More often it is a feature of open-endedness and complexity. Political outcomes are the product of interactions among multiple actors with multiple goals and perspectives. For this reason, the world moves forward in ways that not only are unpredictable but also do not lend themselves to ex post facto explanation with reference to so-called system imperatives and the responses of rational actors to them.

To this point I have analyzed toleration of deviance and dissent in terms of regimes. Toleration of dissent also varies across historical epochs. Recognition of its value, and of the right of people to lead their own lives, is very much a modern and western belief. However, different kinds of deviance were tolerated over the course of history. For the most part, rulers had little interest in what ordinary people did as long as they were obedient, paid their taxes, and performed military service and other duties. Elites generally had more leeway to lead their own lives, although this too varied across cultures and epochs. I nevertheless want to offer a generalization that has to do with modernity and tolerance and provides a nice segue to the next section of this chapter.

Modernity has its roots in the Renaissance and its changing perspective on time. It was increasingly seen as open-ended – thanks in part to clocks and other mechanical devices that made its measurement possible – and linear rather than cyclical, and a resource to be exploited. Recognition that history was not endless repetition, as most of the

Ancients had believed, but forward moving, encouraged a belief not only in change, but in the possibility of progress. Renaissance humanists like Bacon and Erasmus were alert to this possibility. It gradually led to rejection of the belief that the ancient world had been the high point of human civilization, and their own age one of barbarism. Receptivity to positive change encouraged interest in news about current events, and in the arts and emerging sciences. Both were regarded as vehicles of change, and the former of self-fashioning as well.[52]

Optimism, embrace of change, questioning of long-standing conventional wisdom, and rejection of Aristotle and the Church as the source of this wisdom were naturally seen as threatening by many. They produced a backlash. Many rulers and the Catholic Church became increasingly committed to orthodoxy and intolerant of new ideas and practices. They condemned them as deviance, and became more committed to ancient wisdom – especially Aristotle's views about science – and less tolerant of the arts. Republican enthusiasm for humanism declined, except in the Venetian Republic, distinct in so many ways from the rest of Europe.[53] In the words of Johann Huizinga, they sought order with a renewed vengeance, and through "a system of conventional forms" to combat the alleged "passion and ferocity" that threatened to "make havoc" of life.[54] Across Europe, free thinking was reigned in and punished, more control was exercised over the arts in defense of the social and political order, and intellectuals retreated from the more radical positions of early humanism and became more conformist.[55]

Renaissance deviance and the backlash against it is a dramatic and well-documented instance of a general pattern. Authorities are most likely to label free-thinking as deviance and attempt to restrain or repress it when they believe their order is at risk. In the course of the book, I have cited other examples of this phenomenon, including Britain and Austria-Hungary in the aftermath of the French Revolution. We could add the repression initiated by Brezhnev following the Politburo's removal of Khrushchev in 1964. As noted, perceptions of decline or fragility are not in any way objective judgments. Xi's crackdown in China may be more a response to imagined than real threats, and repression may make such threats more rather than less likely.

Brezhnev's crackdown was motivated by his belief, widely shared in the Politburo, that any loosening of cultural controls would inescapably lead to more vocal political dissent, and even rebellion. Gorbachev's policies of *glasnost* and *perestroika* had just this effect, confirming Brezhnev's fears in the eyes of conservatives. However, the Soviet Union of 1964 was not the Soviet Union of 1985. Meaningful reform and easing of cultural and intellectual restraints might have prolonged the life of the country and its regime.[56] Perhaps the most interesting case is Austria-Hungary in the early twentieth century. In retrospect, it is apparent that the Empire was living on borrowed time, but that was not at all the feeling at the time – nationalists and some intellectuals aside, who were hoping for its collapse. Complacency was the order of the day, captured so effectively in novels like Joseph Roth's *Radetzky March* and Robert Musil's *The Man Without Qualities*.

A large part of censorship in the late Renaissance was self-imposed. Intellectuals themselves felt insecure and began to search for order in science, religion, social relations, and politics.[57] This phenomenon was also evident following the horrors of World War I and its immediate aftermath. The Vienna School sought to order and regularize truth claims in science. The Bauhaus sought order and simplicity in architecture, leading the rebellion against the decoration, free forms, and whimsy associated with *Jugendstil*. The twelve-tone technique did something similar in music. It decreed that all twelve notes of the chromatic scale be sounded as often as one another in a piece of music without emphasis on any one note. It achieved this through the use of tone rows, rigid orderings of the twelve pitch classes. In Eastern and Southern Europe, existing or newly created postwar democracies were replaced by right-wing authoritarian regimes, which everywhere stressed traditional values, order, and uniformity.

Insecurity and censorship can come from both sides of the political spectrum. In the United States of 2017, right- and left-wing groups attempted to suppress deviance and dissent. Neither can achieve this through the instruments of the state, but attempt to do so through institutions they influence or control. Right-wingers have resorted to violence against their opponents, attacking churches and liberal protest meetings.[58] Left-wingers have used protest, even violence, to prevent speakers they oppose from having a rostrum or audience on many university campuses.[59] It is hardly surprising that these efforts have intensified in an environment characterized by acute cultural and political wars in which those on the right fear for their way of life and those on the left for their civil liberties and democracy.

Two interesting research questions arise. The first has to do with the conditions associated with leadership perceptions of decline and threat. As they bear only a passing relationship to the judgments analysts might make at the time – and more importantly, in retrospect – we need to look to other determinants, political, ideological, and psychological. There is a parallel here to perceptions of the balance of power, where understandings often diverge dramatically within the same leadership group, and ex post facto assessments made by historians. The eve of World War I offers a dramatic example, as there was no consensus within or across great power elites as to which country was a rising power and which was a declining one.[60] During the Cold War, American officials had equally dramatic differences concerning Soviet power and whether it was increasing or decreasing vis-à-vis the United States.[61] The same is presumably true regarding perceptions of regime vulnerability, as it demonstrably was in Georgian Britain.

The second is the degree to which these reflect a broader cultural zeitgeist, not just parochial perceptions of particular political elites. Seventeenth-century political leaders and intellectuals considered their culture in decline, in part a response to the religious wars, but also due to confusion and uncertainty about the nature of truth and where to find it. This pessimism undoubtedly influenced judgments of individual leaders about the relative fragility of their respective political units. The late Victorian era offers a sharp contrast. Political, business, and banking leaders were upbeat and optimistic about the future. Most believed that war was increasingly unlikely.[62] Leaders were accordingly less concerned with deviance and the perceived need to maintain order.

Notes

1 Joyce, *Ulysses*, ch. 9, Scylla and Charybdis.
2 Lebow, *Politics and Ethics of Identity*, ch. 8.
3 Emerson, *From Empire to Nation.*
4 Wohl, *Generation of 1914.*
5 Homer's influence on Shakespeare divides literary scholars. Some critics do not believe that Shakespeare knew Homer in the original Greek, while others suggest that his reworking of the Trojan War points to some engagement with the Greek text. It is, however, generally accepted that Shakespeare utilized George Chapman's English translation of the *Iliad* – seven books of which were in print by 1598 – and especially in his presentation of Ulysses' speech on order.
6 Lebow, "Max Weber and International Relations," and "Weber's Search for Knowledge"; Jackson, "Production of Facts"; Guzzini, "Max Weber's Power": Steffek, "International Organizations and Bureaucratic Modernity"; Hobson, "Decolonizing Weber."
7 Lebow and Lebow, "Weber's Tragic Legacy."
8 Henriques, *Madoff and the Death of Trust.*
9 IRS, Tax Scams/Consumer Alerts, "IRS-Impersonation Telephone Scams," March 8 2017, www.irs.gov/uac/tax (accessed March 11 2017).
10 Lebow and Stein, *We All Lost the Cold War*, ch. 10.
11 Keeler, "Agricultural Power in the European Community"; "Europe's Farm Follies," *Economist*, December 8 2005, www.economist.com/node/5278374; Andrew Critchlow, "Only French farmers will save us from the madness of Europe," *Daily Telegraph*, September 11 2015, www.telegraph.co.uk/finance/commodities/11858718/Only-French-farmers-will-save-us-from-the-madness-of-Europe.html (accessed July 3 2017).

12 Simon de Galbert, "Are European Countries Really 'Free riders'?" *Atlantic*, March 24 2016, www.theatlantic.com/international/archive/2016/03/obama-doctrine-europe-free-riders/475245/ (accessed March 11 2017); Richard Sokolsky and Gordon Adams, "Penny Wise, Pound Foolish: Trump's Misguided Views of European Defense Spending," *Carnegie Endowment for World Peace*, March 7 2017, http://carnegieendowment.org/2017/03/07/penny-wise-pound-foolish-trump-s-misguided-views-of-european-defense-spending-pub-68202 (accessed March 11 2017).

13 Schwartz, *Subprime Nation*; Reich and Lebow, *Good-Bye Hegemony!*

14 Durkheim, *Suicide*; Meltzer, Petras and Reynolds, *Symbolic Interactionism*; Merton, *Social Theory and Social Structure*.

15 Durkheim, *Rules of Sociological Method*, pp. 85–107.

16 Rousseau, *Confessions*, pp. 163–64.

17 Thodoros Georgakopoulos, "Tax Evasion in Greece: A Study," *DiaNeosis*, June 2016, www.dianeosis.org/en/2016/06/tax (accessed July 8 2017).

18 Ibid., "Greek Taxation: A National Sport No More," *Economist*, November 6 2012, www.economist.com/news/europe/21565657-greek-tax (accessed July 1 2017).

19 Nicholas Richter, "Das Paradies der Reichen," *Süddeutsche Zeitung*, November 6 2017, www.sueddeutsche.de/wirtschaft/paradise-papers-das-paradies-der-reichen-1.3735767; Nick Hopkins, "Why we are shining a light on the world of tax havens again," *Guardian*, November 5 2017, www.theguardian.com/news/2017/nov/05/why-shining-light-world-tax-havens-again-paradise-papers (accessed November 14 2017); Rowena Mason, "Tackle tax avoidance in budget, Labour urges Philip Hammond," Guardian, November 14 2017, www.theguardian.com/news/2017/nov/14/tackle-tax-avoidance-in-budget-labour-urges-philip-hammond (accessed November 14 2017).

20 "Edward and Elaine Brown," Wikipedia, May 3 2017, https://en.wikipedia.org/wiki/Edward_and_Elaine_Brown (accessed June 29 2017).

21 David Barstow, Susanne Craig Russ Buettner, and Megan Twohey, "Donald Trump Records Show He Could Have Avoided Taxes for Nearly Two Decades, New York Times Found," *New York Times*, October 1 2016, www.nytimes.com/2016/10/02/us/politics/donald-trump-taxes.html (accessed October 9 2015); "Latest Election Polls 2016," *New York Times*, October 9 2016, www.nytimes.com/interactive/2016/us/elections/polls.html (accessed October 9 2016).

22 "US election 2016: Trump 'a genius' if he paid no taxes – allies," BBC News, October 2 2016, www.bbc.com/news/election-us-2016-37533263 (accessed June 29 2017).

23 Reuters, "India Launches New Economic Era With Sales Tax Reform," *New York Times*, June 30 2017, www.nytimes.com/reuters/2017/06/30/business/30reuters-india-tax (accessed July 1 2017).

24 Ian Urbina, "Stowaways and Crimes Aboard a Scofflaw Ship," "A Renegade Trawler: Hunted for 10,000 Miles by Vigilantes," "Murder at Sea: Captured on Video, But Killers Go Free," and "Sea Slaves: The Human Misery That Feeds Pets and Livestock," *New York Times*, 17, 17, 20, and July 28 2015, p. 1.

25 Settlers often made their own law, keeping violence to low levels, in contrast to how Hollywood and television portray the "Wild West." DiLorenzo, "Culture of Violence in the American West."

26 Katznelson, *Fear Itself*, on how Franklin Roosevelt brought southerners into his governing coalition on the basis of their shared economic goals, and to do so had to accept their denial of civil rights to African-Americans.

27 William Alford, *To Steal a Book Is an Elegant Offense*.

28 Mertha, *Politics of Piracy*.

29 Dimitrov, *Piracy and the State*.

30 Dimitrov, "Structural Preconditions for the Rise of the Rule of Law in China."

31 United States Elections Project, "Voter Turnout, National Turnout Rates, 1787–2012," September 6 2012, www.electproject.org/home/voter-turnout/voter-turnout-data (accessed July 1 2017).

32 Thomas Kaplan and Robert Pear, "Vote Delayed as G.O.P. Struggles to Marshal Support for Health Care Bill," *New York Times*, June 27 2017, www.nytimes.com/2017/06/27/us/politics/republicans-struggle-to-marshal-votes-for-health-care-bill.html; Thomas Kaplan and Robert Pear, "Senate Health Bill in Peril as C.B.O. Predicts 22 Million More Uninsured," *New York Times*, June 26 2017, www.nytimes.com/2017/06/26/us/politics/senate-health-care-bill-republican.html (accessed July 2 2017).

33 Paul Krugman, "Understanding Republic Cruelty," *New York Times*, June 30 2017, www.nytimes.com/2017/06/30/opinion/understanding-republican-cruelty.html; Ben Cohen, "Paul Krugman Sums Up Senate Health Care Bill in One Devastating Chart," *Banter*, June 27 2017, https://thedailybanter.com/2017/06/krugman-sums-up-senate-health-care-bill/ (accessed July 2 2017); Tami Luhby, "Senate health care bill gives $250,000 gift to the mega-rich," CNN Money, June 26 2017, http://money.cnn.com/2017/06/26/news/economy/senate-health-care-bill-rich/index.htm (accessed July 2 2017).

34 Buchanan, *Deficit and American Democracy*.

35 Linz, *Breakdown of Democratic Regimes*, pp. 3–4, for a similar complaint.

36 Lebow, "Darwin and International Relations," for a critical review of this literature.

37 Losos, *Improbable Destinies*, for a good discussion of the convergence-divergence debate and the conditions that appear to be associated with both.

38 Linz, *Breakdown of Democratic Regimes*, p. 37.

39 Lebow, "Darwin and International Relations."

40 For the debate on divergence and convergence, see Gould, *Wonderful Life*; Morris, and Gould, "Showdown on the Burgess Shale"; Morris, *Life's Solution* and *Runes of Evolution*; McGhee, *Convergent Evolution*; Losos, *Improbable Destinies*.

41 Losos, *Improbable Destinies*, pp. 92–93.

42 Jacob, "Evolution and Tinkering."

43 Lebow, "Leviathans Unbound."

44 Samuels, Machiavelli's Children."

45 Tsai, "Cause of Consequence? Private Sector Development and Regime Resilience in China."

46 On the environment, see Economy, *River Runs Black*. On corruption, Pei, *China's Crony Capitalism*.

47 Clark, *English Society*; Price, *British Society*. Boyd, *Mad, Bad, and Dangerous People?*, p. 30.

48 Trollope, *Phineas Finn* and *Duke's Children*, for a fictional representation of this controversy.

49 Woodward, *Age of Reform*, pp. 187–91.

50 Shipman, *Fall Out*; Ross and McTague, *Betting the House*; Ashcroft, *Lost Majority*.

51 Beckett, *Making of Modern Ireland*, pp. 284–434.

52 Greenblatt, *Renaissance Self-Fashioning*; Aston, *Crisis in Europe*; Burke, *European Renaissance*; Bouwsma, *Waning of the Renaissance*, pp. 52–56, 165–78; Lebow, *Politics and Ethics of Identity*, ch. 2.

53 McKay, *Impact of Humanism on Western Europe*; Bouwsma, *Waning of the Renaissance*, pp. 179–97, 215–58.

54 Huizinga, cited in Bouswma, *Waning of the Renaissance*, p. 246.

55 Welch, *Art and Authority in Italy*; Bouswma, *Waning of the Renaissance*, pp. 246–58.

56 Lebow, "Understanding the End of the Cold War as a Non-Linear Confluence."

57 This is a principal theme of Bouwsma, *Waning of the Renaissance*.

58 Frances Robles, "Two Men Arrested in Connection with Charlottesville Violence," *New York Times*, August 26 2017, www.nytimes.com/2017/08/26/us/charlottesville-arrests.html (accessed September 15 2017).

59 On Berkeley, see "The Free Speech-Hate Speech Trade-Off," *New York Times*, September 13 2007, www.nytimes.com/2017/09/13/opinion/berkeley-dean-erwin-chemerinsky.html?_r=0 (accessed September 15 2017); Bari Weiss, "A Political Conservative Goes to Berkeley," *New York Times*, September 12 2017, www.nytimes.com/2017/09/12/opinion/conservative-berkeley-ben-shapiro.html (accessed September 15 2017); Jacey Fortin, "Richard Dawkins Event Canceled Over Past Comments About Islam," *New York Times*, July 24 2017, www.nytimes.com/2017/07/24/us/richard-dawkins-speech-canceled-berkeley.html (accessed September 15 2017).

60 Lebow and Stein, *When Does Deterrence Succeed and How Do We Know?*

61 Lebow and Sein, *We All Lost the Cold War*, ch. 14.

62 Afflerbach, "Topos of Improbable War Before 1914"; Lebow, *Forbidden Fruit*, ch. 3.

10   The Crises of Modernity

House warm in winter, city free of vice,
Tree that outstood the equinoctial gales:
Dry at the heart, they crashed
On a windless day.
                            Malcolm Cowley[1]

In this final chapter I step back from my data to take a longer-range perspective on political orders and the problems late modernity poses for them. Modernity is associated with intellectual, material, social, and cultural changes that transformed western societies, and later the rest of the world.[2] These changes generated a series of political shocks that destabilized monarchies in the eighteenth and nineteenth centuries, democracies in the early twentieth and seemingly robust and powerful authoritarian regimes later in the century. They were the underlying causes of successive waves of revolutions, two World Wars, decolonization, and a spate of violent conflicts within and between the successor states to empires. They are currently the cause of political instability in western democracies and may constitute an even greater threat to China's authoritarian regime.

The political shocks of modernity have many causes. In this volume, I highlight and analyze one of them: the growing appeal of the principle of equality. All successful orders rest on principles of justice, although none come close to realizing them in practice. Orders are seriously threatened when discourses fail to justify these discrepancies to citizens. They are also at risk when there is a shift in the principles of justice, or their formulation, at odds with those offered by elites as justifications for their authority. My argument is in no way intended to excuse political leaders, bankers, and businesspeople, whose bad judgment and greed have been important immediate causes of crisis. It is meant to help explain why this kind of behavior – greed especially – is increasingly prevalent, and its political consequences more significant than in the past.

I conclude with epistemological reflections that draw on Max Weber's approach to knowledge. He believed that the starting point of ethical social science was for researchers to make explicit their substantive and epistemological assumptions. Beliefs and related assumptions about politics and how it should be studied are invariably parochial. They are a function of one's place in society and culture, and that culture's place in history. Weber maintained that these beliefs largely determine what we choose to study, how we approach the subject, what we consider evidence, how we evaluate, and therefore the conclusions we reach. There is no effective way of separating facts from values. Weber struggled – largely unsuccessfully – to come to terms with his political assumptions and how they affected his research agenda and findings. I have made mine as explicit as possible, but recognize that my research questions, approach to them, and findings reflect my life experiences, the broader zeitgeist, and the moment in history when I research and write. I consider some of these limitations, the consequences, and ways of reducing them.

Crises of Modernity

For many social scientists, modernity is a product of material changes. These changes are held to be responsible for the territorial state, division of labor, increased wealth, education, and personal choice, and longevity. More nuanced explanations of these developments do not deny the influence of material developments, but give at least co-equal billing to ideas, culture, and politics.[3] For philosophers, modernity is a more complicated phenomenon, as are its causes. I follow Kant and Hegel in emphasizing the importance of the heightened sense of self as a distinguishing feature of modernity. In two recent books, I develop an account of modernity that builds on their insights but also identifies some of the pathways that made economic, political, and philosophical developments mutually reinforcing in their consequences.

The Politics and Ethics of Identity argues that the goal of the autonomous self is inseparable from the development of richer mental lives that focus people's attention on their feelings, needs, and goals. Introspection of this kind is at least partially dependent on discourses that legitimize it and make the self, rather than the cosmos, the principal source of reference and development. Role proliferation also encouraged introspection by making it economically and socially rewarding for people to present diverse faces to others, some of which were at odds with how they conceived of themselves. Interiority and reflexivity – the constituents of internal autonomy – are intellectual developments that were well under way before the economic changes we associate with modernity. Role proliferation is largely a function of the division of labor and the diverse hierarchies and economies of scale to which it gives rise. Autonomy and role proliferation are mutually supportive in that autonomy presupposes life choices and role proliferation provides them.[4]

The autonomous self and role proliferation provide reinforcing sources of alienation. Once we step back from our social selves to reflect upon them, we become to some degree detached psychologically from our surroundings. Detachment prompts alienation if we conclude that the roles we perform compel us to communicate different, perhaps contradictory, even "false" selves to diverse audiences. Alienation of this kind made identity a primary concern in the modern era. As I noted in the introductory chapter, it gave rise to the four generic strategies to overcome alienation that I described in the introduction.

Constructing Cause in International Relations advances a novel approach to causation based on the premise that almost everything transformative in international relations is singular in nature and it and just about everything else important is highly context dependent. I illustrate my approach to causation in a case study of the rise of the territorial state. I attribute it in the first instance to changes in visual frames of reference that made it both imaginable and desirable. Visual frames have important causal implications because we think in images, not only in words. The ways in which we organize and present images enable and constrain our thoughts and practices just as language does.

The Renaissance visual revolution was characterized by linear perspective, but also by a concern to represent people as distinct individuals. There was a greater commitment to what we call realism and to life in this world in contrast to the next. The principal mechanism linking developments in the arts to political conceptions was maps, which underwent a radical transformation in design and purpose. To make my case, I compare this visual revolution with the more recent one that began in the nineteenth century. In the Renaissance revolution, there were numerous connections between developments in art on the one hand and mathematics and science on the other.

I argue that the Renaissance visual revolution was part and parcel of another transformation: the emergence of the autonomous individual. It started as a philosophical project and later found expression in the arts and political and social thinking and practices. The autonomous individual began to emerge in the High Middle Ages, became more pronounced in the Renaissance and continued into the modern era. It is on-going, as almost every generation of writers down to the present, and more recently, social scientists, have noted a continuing trend toward individual autonomy.[5]

In this volume, I extend my exploration of modernity to another of its key features: principles of justice and their shifting appeal and consequences. The demand for equality is not only a distinguishing feature of modernity but is intimately connected with the emergence of the self. Once people began to conceive of themselves as quasi-autonomous individuals – something more and even independent of the sum of the roles they performed in society – they faced fundamental choices about who they were. As noted in Chapter 1, this redefinition of the self is liberating but anxiety-provoking, and some people sought to escape anxiety in anti-modern identity projects that seek to limit or do away with the autonomous self. A majority of westerners welcomed to some degree the possibility of self-fashioning and responded favorably to the liberal and Romantic identity projects. The four generic identity strategies I identify require novel social and political conditions for fulfillment. They extended or reconfigured the principles of equality and fairness toward this end.

The two anti-modern strategies adopted the traditional meaning of equality: uniform distribution of rewards. Some Protestant sects and Marxists were committed to the abolition of private property. Like many breakaway religious factions, Puritans extended the principle of equality to other domains; they favored simple and uniform dress and prohibited makeup and jewelry, further minimizing differences among people. The most radical sects did away with marriage and shared women among their members, removing another source of differentiation and competition. Some Marxists advocated "free love," a secular equivalent, and one intended to equalize the status of men and women.

Anti-modern strategies also endorsed fairness, which they mobilized to justify their hierarchies. Puritans elected elders and governors, whose office was justified on the basis of the soundness of their religious views and personal propriety. Most breakaway sects, like the Massachusetts Bay Colony Puritans, were rigidly authoritarian and intolerant of dissent. Marx and Lenin's concept of "vanguardism" was the socialist equivalent; the most class-conscious and politically advanced sections of the proletariat would lead larger sections of the working class to revolutionary politics. Under Lenin, the Bolsheviks assumed this role and rivaled Puritans in their commitment to ideological purity and coercion to enforce their authority.

There are unresolvable tensions between anti-modernist formulations of equality and fairness. Dissenting sects opposed the hierarchy of existing Protestant churches and their insistence that doctrine be determined and enforced by those at the top. Central to most dissenting sects, including the Puritans, was the belief that people should read and interpret the bible in their own way. Once in a position of authority, they nevertheless created more extreme hierarchies than the established religions they opposed. For religions that preach equality, sharp differences in wealth emerged in the twentieth century between ministers and their congregations. Many television evangelicals became extremely wealthy on the basis of contributions from their flocks. The same hierarchy developed among communists in countries where they came to power. Party officials had more money, access to shops selling foreign goods, and their children had more opportunities for higher education. The gap between high-ranking party officials and the population in China and North Korea is among the greatest in the world.

Evangelicals and Marxists sought to overcome these contradictions by sleights of hand. Some evangelical sects adopted the time-honored Christian solution to the problem: people should accept hierarchy, inequality, and suffering in the present life, and be rewarded in the after-life. Leninists adopted a secular variant: with socialism, the state would fade away, people would be equal in every respect and their lives happy and fulfilled. In the late twentieth century, some evangelicals began to emphasize fairness over equality. Others insisted that Jesus would make believers rich, and that contributions to their church would buy prayers toward this end.

Nikita Khrushchev adopted a similar strategy in the 1960s; he increas-ingly justified socialism as a system that deserved loyalty because it would outperform capitalism and make its citizens richer and happier. The failure of Leninist regimes to resolve these contradictions or deliver on their promises was a key cause of their demise. Evangelical sects have fared better, especially Dispensationalists, who preach the imminent return of Jesus and the heavenly reward of believers and eternal damnation of non-believers. Their vision of heaven and hell represent the ultimate expres-sion of hierarchy based on fairness, but of a theological kind.[6]

The two modern identity projects also mobilized the principles of equality and fairness in ways to advance their respective goals. For liberals, equality was defined in terms of the legal status of persons. Everyone was to be equal before the law and have freedom to act any way they liked so long as it did not interfere with the same rights of others. Government was to be restricted in powers and functions to prevent tyranny and ensure individual freedom. Liberals did not oppose hier-archy in principle, but were highly critical of those based on ascribed as opposed to achieved status.

Liberals belatedly came to recognize that legal equality was a neces-sary but insufficient condition to bringing about the kind of just society they envisaged. Many people possessed other kinds of advantages that privileged them enormously in life (e.g. high birth, wealth, better access to education, well-paying and high-status jobs). Liberals proposed a new meaning of equality: equal opportunity to compete for rewards. This was a response to the obstacles that stood in the way of equality in practice, but can also be viewed as an attempt to reconcile the principles of equality and fairness. In theory, it might be possible to bring about social equality at the starting line, but there would still be differences among people in their physical and mental capacities and in their dispositions. More fundamentally, the liberal solution assumes that everyone wants to compete, or can properly be socialized into doing so. This is not only highly questionable but violates the fundamental liberal premise of freedom of choice.

Romantics also valued the equality of people, but in contrast to liberals considered society a barrier, not an enabler of this goal. Rousseau and his successors believed that people must take themselves outside of society and commune with nature or look inwards to discover their true nature and begin the process of self-fashioning. Romantics rejected hierarchies of all kinds as they regarded them as a principal way for society to discipline and enslave people. This was also true for those at the apex of hierarchies, perhaps more so, because their rule packages were the thickest. Romantics rejected the liberal view that society could be a neutral enforcer of rules that enabled freedom. It was the source of physical and psychological tyranny. Romanticism does not confront a problem in attempting to reconcile equality and fairness since it rejects all hierarchies. Its rejection of hierarchy may be one of the reasons for the limited appeal of anarchy, the political expression of Romanticism.

The problem of reconciling equality and fairness is a central feature of utopias. Many utopias are anarchist and reject outright fairness and any hierarchy it would produce. An example is William Morris's *News From Nowhere*. It depicts a society without government, money, or the kinds of professions that encourage hierarchy.[7] Alternatively, utopias introduce the second definition of fairness: giving more to those who need it the most. Marx does this in his pithy 1875 dictum about the two principles that would govern communism: "From each according to his abilities, to each according to his needs."[8]

Most utopias try to balance the two principles of justice because they recognize the need for some kind of authority in any large society. From Plato to Rawls, their authors create "guardians" who are informed, as Plato's are, by a superior understanding of justice, or of science, as they are for Bacon, Huxley, and Skinner.[9] Either way, fairness and equality are in theory reconciled because their elites govern in the interests of the people. This is, of course, the traditional understanding of fairness. Utopias claim to be different because their elites, in contrast to historical ones, their authors insist, really have the best interests of the society in mind. They do not use authority to satisfy their appetites and *thumos* at the expense of those less wealthy and powerful.[10]

Utopias share another quality: they create worlds without politics or the possibility of change. With Plato a notable exception, their authors invariably believe that they have done away with conflict by creating worlds that fulfill all human needs. This vision of social engineering is based on the premise that human needs can be reconciled and satisfied. This is a dangerous illusion and efforts to put any such worlds into place, in all or in part, intensify rather than resolve conflicts.

Dystopias debunk this claim and make the case that the societies envisaged by utopias would be more authoritarian, rigid, and dehumanizing than most historical societies. Evgeny Zamyatin's *We*, Aldous Huxley's *Brave New World*, George Orwell's *1984*, and William Golding's *Lord of the Flies* are classic representatives of this genre. Ortega y Gasset and Karl Popper accuse utopian thinking of laying the intellectual foundations for totalitarianism.[11]

In the real world, political orders struggle to balance fairness and equality. They have made a wide range of accommodations. Among developed democracies, the Scandinavians are generally seen as anchoring the equality end of the spectrum and the United States the fairness side. Accommodations between fairness and equality in any democracy are intensely political in their nature and application. They are generally, if not always, controversial, logically indefensible, and evolve over time to the degree that the societies in question are democratic.

There is strong experimental support for the proposition that people understand and value both principles of justice. They are willing to consider trade-offs between them, and often make them themselves. Their choice of fairness or equality, how they apply it, and to what populations, is context dependent and to varying degrees subject to manipulation. Temporary groups are more likely to reward people on the basis of their contribution to group tasks. Groups that work together for longer periods and develop more robust identities put more emphasis on maintaining relationships and group solidarity and are accordingly more likely to favor equal distributions.[12] People tend to use different allocation criteria when focusing on individuals as opposed to populations. With the former, they are more likely to opt for fairness, but equality with the latter.[13] The smaller the group, the more tightly integrated it is, the more likely its members are to favor equality in dealing with one another.

With regard to income distribution, Americans are very sensitive to how the question is posed. About one-third agree with the statement that "the fairest way of distributing wealth and income would be to give everyone an equal share." This percentage drops markedly when people are primed with the statement that "under a fair economic system people with more ability would earn higher salaries."[14] Studies indicate that on the whole Americans consider fairness the most applicable principle to income distribution. However, they want income distributions less unequal than they are in practice.[15] American also favor taking individual needs into account when making distributions.[16] Studies show that their willingness to do so hinges on credible demonstration of need.[17]

Decision rules also to some degree reflect self-interest. The more people earn the less they support redistribution of income or pensions on the basis of equality.[18] However, a whopping 75 percent of people at the bottom of the American economic ladder still appear to believe in the principle of fairness. They regularly endorse statements like, "People with more ability should earn higher salaries."[19] When asked to judge the fairness of wealth distributions in hypothetical societies, Americans were more willing to accept inequality the more it appeared to be based on merit. Under all conditions, liberals place more emphasis on equality than conservatives.[20]

These and other studies described in Chapter 6 indicate that justice is important for people. It helps them to frame decisions about distributions and procedures for reaching them. Studies further suggest that people gravitate toward principles of fairness and their application that they believe will increase their wealth and status. The arrow of influence points in two directions, and we know little about the circumstances in which people's decisions are motivated by their understanding of justice versus those in which their perceived interest motivates their choice of principles of justice.

Roger Giner-Sorolla, Laura Niemi and I conducted an experiment to evaluate the preferences of Americans for the distribution of rewards on the basis of equality vs. fairness. We designed a game in which four players invest different amounts of money and receive returns according to different principles of justice.[21]

Fairness and equality each have two formulations, so we constructed four scenarios. Participants were asked to judge the appropriateness of the distribution of money in each scenario. In the first equality scenario, everyone in the game receives back the same sum of money from the pool regardless of how much they contributed. In the second equality, everyone receives back the amount they contributed. The first fairness scenario rewards players in proportion to what they contributed, so those who invested more make more money if there is a profit. In the second fairness scenario, those who contributed less get proportionately more on the assumption that they need it more.

Participants in the experiment overwhelmingly prefer the first fairness distribution, where people receive back in proportion to what they have contributed. When choosing between the two equality distributions, they prefer the first equality scenario of equal outcomes vs. equal returns. In each scenario, there is a "boss" who decides which of the four distribution rules to use. In a variant of the game, participants were asked to play "boss" and decide on the distribution in lieu of evaluating distributions made by control. Here there was even stronger support for the equal outcome distribution.

We did not ask people how they voted in the 2016 presidential election but had a series of questions to determine where they fit on the liberal–conservative spectrum. We also tried to ascertain what kind of liberal or conservative they were. We found that liberals were more attracted to conditions of equality than conservatives, and conservatives more attracted to the proportional framing of fairness. This preference was strongest among economic conservatives, as opposed to social and national ones.

Justice and Order

Conflicts between fairness and equality are inevitable and ultimately unresolvable because they are expressions of two distinct and often competing human drives: appetite and *thumos*. In *A Cultural Theory of International Relations*, I argue that each drive, and that of reason too, gives rise to a different approach to cooperation and conflict and risk taking as well as generating hierarchies based on different principles of justice. I also document *longue durée* alternations in the relative importance of appetite and *thumos* and the evolution of the ways in which they find expression – summarized in Chapter 3. These progressions are the product of material and ideational changes, and cannot be explained with reference to either alone. In the contemporary West, equality is the dominant principle of justice, but fairness is also widely supported. As we have seen, liberals place more emphasis on equality, and conservatives on fairness, but both rely on these two principles.

The conflict between fairness and equality would be less acute if these principles were applied in different domains, but they are not. They compete in most domains of political, economic, and social life. In the United States, I suggest that this value conflict is a principal underlying cause of an escalating culture war. This phenomenon is not unique to the United States but evident almost everywhere in Europe when the principle of equality challenged that of fairness. It has historical roots in Europe. In Germany, as in the United States, the Protestant population had long considered itself the natural leaders of the country's political and cultural life. Many Protestants opposed the Weimar Republic because it rested on the principle of equality, which threatened to under-mine their leading role and reduce their status and political influence. Indeed, Weimar quickly became the project of socialists, Catholics, and liberals, and confirmed their worst fears by doing away with the mon-archy and Protestantism as the state religion. Protestant resentment was one of the wells of support that Hitler fed upon.[22]

Fairness and equality can be mutually supportive. Women's suffrage was resisted in Britain and the United States in the decade before 1914. After World War I, women were allowed to vote in national elections in both countries. The shift in public opinion that enabled legislation in Britain and a constitutional amendment in the United States, was largely due to the belief that women had "earned" the right to vote by virtue of their contributions to the war effort. Fairness paved the way for equality. This phenomenon was also evident in the aftermath of World War II, where it was responsible for the G.I. Bill and arguably helped break down legal and de facto discrimination against Jews and African-Americans.

Pleas for equality accordingly benefit on occasion from the principle of fairness. Pleas for special privileges based on fairness run counter to equality and are hard to square with them in today's world. However, given the strength of the principle of equality, they must often be couched in terms of them. American corporations justify their demands for lower tax rates on the grounds that it would make them equal to what corporations are taxed in most other developed countries. They further allege that the resulting economic benefits will "trickle down" and benefit ordinary people.[23] India, Brazil, Nigeria, and South Africa all aspire to permanent seats on the UN Security Council. They are asking for special privileges but couching their claims in the language of equality because they recognize its dominance.[24]

Invocations of one principle of justice to advance claims for another are relatively commonplace. This can reduce or intensify political con-flict, depending on the context. Conflicts are likely to arise when people extend a principle of justice into a domain where others believe it is inappropriate. Conflict will become acute if there are sharp divisions about the relative importance of fairness and equality in the society. The American case is particularly interesting in this respect because of the presence, or confluence, of five aggravating conditions of conflict.

The first is a shift in the relative appeal of different principles of justice. Tocqueville noted that the United States was the first country in which equality became the dominant principle of justice. So much so that even people who were not committed to it nevertheless felt the need to act as if they were.[25] Fairness has, however, reasserted itself and has become the dominant principle of distribution. It permeates the domains of business, sports, even non-profit organizations, where the differential in salaries between the highest and lowest paid has increased multiple-fold in recent decades. This shift in values is equally evident in popular narratives like sitcoms and songs, as Chapter 5 demonstrated.

The second condition is the absence of any consensus within society about the relative importance of the two principles or the domains in which they should apply. Both principles frequently compete, making political, economic, and social conflicts more acute. When people form decisions and outcomes in terms of principles of justice they become less amenable to compromises than they are with conflicts considered mere matters of interest. Polarization is further aggravated when politicians on both sides of the divide adopt extreme positions in the hope of winning votes. They sometimes feel compelled to do this for fear of being outflanked by rivals. We can observe this phenomenon in such issues as school funding, affirmative action, and healthcare.

The third condition pertains to the distribution of preferences. The more random they are among a population, the more disagreement and conflict is likely to be diffused. In the United States, they are associated with specific demographics that are already divided on other issues. Differences about fairness and equality coincide with these other cleavages and intensify the urban–rural, north–south, coastal–inland, political, cultural, religious, and economic divides. Cultural and political wars merge, making them less distinguishable from one another and more intense.[26]

The fourth condition is the use of principles of justice to legitimize narrow self-interest. Cases in point are the neo-liberal discourse advocated by many Republicans, and the economic theories associated with it – including the demonstrably false claim that reducing taxes for the rich helps to generate more jobs for the unemployed. These discourses are thinly veiled justifications for laws that allow the rich to get richer at the expense of everyone else, as most of the intellectuals and officials advocating them are well aware. These discourses have lost much of their legitimacy in recent years, and are now regarded by many as pure hypocrisy. The rhetoric of the Trump and Sanders campaigns appealed to people who thought the rich were largely undeserving and selfish, and presumably helped further to delegitimize these discourses.

Fairness also appeals to many have-nots, but they apply it in a different way than do neo-liberals. Many white, non-educated workers accept fairness as giving the most rewards to those who contribute the most to the general welfare. But they believe that they deserve more than they currently receive, and many resent the relative rise in status and wealth of women, minorities, and African-Americans. They conceive of themselves as the backbone of America, and the upholders of belief in God, the Protestant religion and family values that made the country great. They resent their loss of relative status and wealth, and want to return to a world in which the old hierarchy is restored, and with it their more favorable position. Not surprisingly, they voted for Trump over Clinton by a wide margin.[27]

The principle of equality is most attractive to liberals, immigrants, minorities, and coastal businesspeople. It offers a contrasting image of America and narrative of what makes it a great country. It emphasizes openness to immigrants; new ideas and practices; access to education, employment, and other rewards on the basis of merit; and toleration of political, religious differences, and now, those of race, gender, and sexual identity and preference.[28]

These different preferences for fairness or equality are embedded in the television programs Americans watch. Chapter 6 analyzed two recent sitcoms: *Duck Dynasty* and *Modern Family*. The former is the sitcom most popular with Trump voters and the latter with Clinton voters. *Duck Dynasty* encodes the values and interpretation of fairness associated with white, religious, conservative voters. It portrays a lovable, self-identified Redneck, Louisiana family that displays so-called traditional values, with the head of the family saying grace at the meal that ends every show. It differs from everyday life in that the family is extraordinarily successful financially, but in large part because of its traditional values. *Modern Family* offers a liberal contrast, and not surprisingly is particularly popular in San Francisco. It features an extended and blended Los Angeles family that includes a man married to a much younger, divorced and Latina immigrant wife; a cerebral stepson; two neurotic adult children; and a gay couple who adopt a baby girl. It foregrounds liberal values, showing how they have the potential to produce tolerance, cooperation, and happiness.

Chapter 6's analysis of the campaign speeches of Republican and Democrat candidates in the 2016 election is equally revealing. Donald Trump, whose lifestyle and personal values reflect narrow self-interest, pursued in the crudest way – financially and sexually – appealed to traditional Republican voters for economic reasons, but also to white, Protestant Middle America because of his rejection of the Washington establishment and seeming commitment to traditional understandings of fairness. Hillary Clinton mooted many more practical measures in her campaign that might have improved the economic position of those who have paid the price of globalization, but she was closely associated with free trade, Wall Street, and the coastal liberal elite. Her campaign speeches, and the people she surrounded herself with on the podium, emphasized the value of equality. For both reasons, many traditional

Democrats voted for Trump. Bernie Sanders, who lost the Democratic nomination to Clinton, invoked both equality and fairness, and repeatedly emphasized how, in his view, the corporate and banking elite was corrupt and receiving rewards far beyond any contribution they made to society. He appealed to liberals, but also to many traditional Democrats.

The fifth condition is the general failure of reason and emotions to restrain *thumos* and appetite. People increasingly frame self-interest in narrow, selfish ways. They reveal a strong preference for their inner circle with little to no regard for those outside of it, and pursue short-term interests at the expense of the wider community. Chapter 5 demonstrates how this shift from interest well understood to individualism is well under way in the United States and can be tracked through the analysis of presidential speeches, sitcoms, and songs. The rise of individualism makes the tensions between these principles more obvious, more caustic in debate, and accordingly less amenable to compromise among their respective adherents. It not only encourages intense politicization of differences, but also makes the outcomes of political struggles appear more momentous in their consequences.

In these circumstances, self-interest narrowly construed has the potential to take these struggles to the next stage – open violation of the norms that hitherto governed and restrained political conflicts. This has happened in the United States where it is evident in blatant gerrymandering; the decline of comity in legislatures; holding the federal budget hostage to narrow partisan demands; and using maneuvers previously considered unacceptable to advance partisan interests (e.g. refusing to consider judicial nominations made by the other party, and use of the so-called "nuclear option" to shut off debate).[29] Each party laments the decline in comity but blames it on the other and views their opposition to the other side's candidates as "payback."[30]

What are the broader implications of the conflict over principles of justice and their application for political order? In *A Cultural Theory of International Relations*, I turned to Homer's *Iliad* for an analysis of the irreconcilable tensions of honor-based warrior societies where fairness is the only principle of distributive justice. The *Iliad* graphically demonstrates that the very values and practices that sustain such societies also have the potential to destroy them, as it almost does in the conflicts between Greeks and Trojans and Achilles and Agamemnon. I then document these tensions and their consequences in the historical, honor-based, warrior societies of classical Greece, Macedon, and the Roman Republic.[31]

Appetite-based orders display different tensions. Like their honor-based counterparts, the more successful they become, the more pronounced their contradictions. Marx – a close reader of Homer – was among the first to make this kind of observation, in this instance about capitalism. It would inevitably give rise to its antithesis, and this would lead to socialism via revolution.[32] Also inspired by Homer, I create an ideal-type appetite world in *A Cultural Theory of International Relations*. In Chapter 4 of this volume, I identify "Homeric" pathways of decline. They are, in effect, patterns of behavior made possible for the order's success that expose and intensify its contradictions. As modern societies encourage both appetite and honor, I construct distinct pathways for each. Both pathways are triggered by elite excess but set in motion different processes and activate different mechanisms. They ultimately converge at preemption if breakdown goes far enough. Although these pathways are separate, they can interact with the effect of intensifying the progression toward disorder along both pathways.

Modern society, with its emphasis on both appetite and honor, complicates any assessment of order. It contributes to order by opening more pathways to success and self-esteem, as does the proliferation of ways in which honor can be achieved. Excellence in almost any activity achieves the respect of others, and especially those who also engage in or follow it. Multiple status hierarchies also reduce conflict because they are for the most part non-zero sum. Winning renown as a chef, chess master, or corporate raider does not in any way undercut or reduce the status of others who gain fame in the silver screen, political arena, or sports field. Multiple hierarchies also make it easier to accept unpleasant, even threatening, developments in other domains, because people have the option of withdrawing into their own worlds or bubbles where they make their livings and/or gain status.

Multiple hierarchies are also a cause of conflict, as they were in the *Iliad*. The conflict between Achilles and Agamemnon is at its core one between competing hierarchies. Achilles is at the apex of the hierarchy of achieved status, and Agamemnon, as a *wanax* or king, of the ascribed status. In warrior-based honor societies, the king, or leader, is expected to be the best warrior. When these roles diverge, serious trouble arises. Modern societies face numerous variants of this problem, some of which I described in Chapter 4. Robust orders find ways of adjudicating or finessing these conflicts, or of harnessing them for productive ends. The US constitution created a federal system and a federal government with three branches (legislature, executive, judiciary). The state and national governments, but also the three branches of government, have separate but overlapping powers. Attempts by government at any level, or any branch of government, to expand its power must, of necessity, be at the expense of others and will accordingly arouse their opposition. Checks and balances were expected to preserve the liberties of the people.[33]

Fairness and equality are associated with different principles of justice, so emphasis on both by any society produces another source of conflict. Disagreements are almost certain to arise about the relative importance of these principles, the domains in which they are appropriate, and discrepancies between these claims and current practices. These conflicts become more likely and more acute when actors feel less constrained by social norms. This in turn encourages the kind of irresponsible elite behavior I identify as the first step toward disorder in both appetite and honor worlds.

Elite abuse is rife in the United States and China. In both countries, government has exacerbated the problem. In the United States, where tax codes demonstrably favor the rich, there has been a reduction in the number of officials who monitor tax returns, banking, and environmental regulations have been repealed or not enforced. There have been across-the-board cutbacks in welfare and social programs to pay for tax cuts for the wealthy. In China, the close connection between government and business has enabled officials to enrich themselves and their families, forestall for the most part legal action against them, and suppress and punish those who complain or attempt to expose these and other abuses. The two political systems and cultures see themselves as very different but share more in common than is generally recognized. Both face a crisis of legitimacy and, ultimately, the possibility of serious disorder.

For America, and democracies more generally, a fundamental question is to what extent does appetite sustain or undermine order? Liberals sing the political praises of appetite, a position developed in opposition to the long-standing belief, going back to the ancient Greeks, that appetite was destructive. Plato argued that appetite unconstrained by reasons could never be satisfied as people motivated by desire for wealth, sex, food, and drink, always wanted more. They were slave-like and to be pitied.[34] Honor was held in high esteem, because it put a premium on restraint and sacrifice for the greater good, and its pursuit was thought to be a prop of political and social order. Beginning with Cervantes, honor, and by extension, the aristocracy, came under attack. It was now held responsible for war and conflict. In the late eighteenth century Mandeville and Smith upgraded appetite, arguing that the individual pursuit of wealth benefitted the society as a whole.[35] Their nineteenth-century successors, like Bright, Cobden, and Mill, maintained that societies motivated by material gain would be peaceful, an argument that finds resonance today in the Democratic Peace research program.[36]

Many approaches to democratic politics frame it around appetite. They describe it as articulation and aggregation of demands, demands that are largely economic.[37] Modern economic theory assumes that above all else people seek material gains and that any other motive can be given a monetary value. During the postwar era and immediately afterwards, some democratic theorists went so far as to claim the end of ideology due to the triumph of liberal, capitalist democracy.[38] Recent events in Europe and America have revealed the absurdity of such predictions, but many political scientists still subscribe to the assumption underlying these arguments: that politics is – and should be – about the distribution of material rewards. They understand these kinds of struggles as manageable by governments and their successful adjudication of them as beneficial, even necessary, for the survival and robustness of democratic orders. A social science that focuses almost entirely on material interests cannot offer useful insights into the ills of democracy because it is part of the problem.

From the vantage point of the twenty-first century, World Wars I and II appear to be two stages of a larger European struggle for dominance.[39] With hindsight, historians have come to regard both wars as manifestations of epochal material and ideational changes that transformed Europe and the world. They undermined respect for traditional religion and authority, gave rise to new classes, urbanization, the ideologies of liberalism, nationalism, Social Darwinism, and socialism, promoted a shift in the relative importance of the principles of equality and fairness, and produced the nation-state as a political reality or aspiration of peoples increasingly identified and organized along so-called national lines. World War I is increasingly regarded as the product of the dislocations, fears, tensions, domestic, and foreign rivalries created or exacerbated by these changes.[40] This is not to say that it was inevitable, that agency was not absolutely critical to its outbreak, or that those responsible for the decisions that led to war should not be held accountable.[41]

Agency was equally responsible for World War II, as war was a deliberate choice by the leaders of the axis powers. These dictatorships were nevertheless made possible by the collapse of the Russian, Austro-Hungarian, and German empires at the end of World War I; a Bolshevik dictatorship in Russia; reinforcing political and economic crises that undermined weak democratic orders elsewhere in Europe and Japan; an incomplete and flawed peace settlement that spawned as many national grievances as its resolved; and the relative isolation of the United States. The Second World War was an outgrowth of the first. On a superficial level, it was a continuation of Germany's quest for dominance. More fundamentally, it was another catastrophic manifestation of modernity and the political pressures it generated that either were not, or could not, be addressed or resolved by peaceful means.

Politicians and scholars alike have taken great satisfaction in the achievements of the post-World War world. American, European, and

Japanese leaders learned important lessons from the past and were able to construct a stable global political and economic order. Economic development was impressive, particularly in Europe and the Pacific Rim.[42] Problems remained in the Middle East and South Asia, and nationalism resurfaced with a vengeance in the post-Cold War world. But the political crisis of modernity seemed to have been surmounted, enough so that 1945 appeared to represent a sharp break with the past. The current international political crisis suggests that this optimism may be misplaced, or at least overstated.

China is now a great power whose political and economic influence is felt worldwide. It is also a growing military power, and not averse to flexing its muscles in pursuit of questionable interests like its Nine-Dots-Line in the South China Sea.[43] Its government is stable, but faces long-term demographic, environmental, political, and economic threats. It is by no means evident that its leaders and regime have the insight, skill, and flexibility to cope with these ultimately reinforcing crises. They have put their eggs in two baskets: nationalism and economic growth. As the latter stalls they are likely to fall back more on the former, which has the potential to deprive them of their freedom of action in international confrontations. They may be forced to choose between commitment to a risky foreign policy initiative or political defeat at home. As my studies of deterrence failure and the origins of war indicate, this is a certain recipe for motivated bias and policy disaster.[44]

The political crisis is not limited to regions of the world that have never democratized and developed and are in thrall to kleptocratic leaders and authoritarian regimes. It affects what until now were regarded as core areas of stability: the United States and Western Europe. Right-wing authoritarians have come to power in Hungary and Poland, and threatened to in Austria, the Netherlands, and France. The economies of Southern Europe are in shambles, and this too has sparked support for right-wing, even neo-Nazi political parties. The European Union (EU) has been regarded as a primary source of European stability, but the United Kingdom is in the process of leaving it, and it has declining support in just about every other member country. President Trump is dismissive of it and President Putin of Russia is doing what he can to undermine it. Europe without the EU, even with just a weaker EU, will be a more insecure Europe.

There are many reasons for Europe's political crisis, some of them the same as those at the root of the American crisis. In the United States, I argued, a fundamental, underlying cause of conflict is the double shift in values. These shifts are a product of modernity, and are associated with the rise and success of the commercial classes and their propagation of discourses intended to advance their claims to status and authority and undermine those of the aristocracy. The behavioral manifestations of the two shifts have been enabled, if not encouraged, by changes in popular discourses, the prevalence of the rich and glitterati as role models, the increasingly blatant display of wealth, and the envy and hostility it inspires. These are all products of late modernity, and perhaps inescapable ones.

There is accordingly at least one more wave of turbulence that modernity has generated and is now breaking over us. Its causes are plain, as are its immediate consequences. It confronts us with the prospect that democratic and authoritarian regimes, as currently constituted, are subject to serious destabilization. Nor is it evident that leaders and elites in leading countries will show more skill and moral courage in confronting them than their predecessors did in the decades before 1914 and 1939.

There is no solution to the dilemmas of democracy or those of modernity. We must learn to live with them, develop a nuanced view of their benefits and evils, and with them, a search for ways to improve on their benefits and moderate their evils. We must be wary of intellectual and political projects that promise to do more, and think too about ways in which we can inculcate and encourage self-interest well understood, even if such behavior may be more costly in the short term in a society increasingly dominated by individualism.

One example of the novel threat created by the most recent wave of modernity concerns freedom of speech. Long a liberal ideal, it is once again under threat, but in a very different way than it was under fascism or communism. Until the late 1980s, US television was dominated by a small number of networks and their many affiliates. Cable networks and transmissions via satellite greatly increased the number of stations, and in 2016 there were more than fifty broadcasting networks.[45] This proliferation, and even more so the Internet, has encouraged stations and sites that target specific audiences. As widely noted in the western press, it allows and encourages people to limit their exposure to contrary values and opinions. The Internet also encourages what is now called "post-truth," the Oxford Dictionary's word of the year for 2016. People pass off opinions and lies online as facts, and to great effect. Studies of US public opinion reveal that a significant percentage of people across the political spectrum believe in demonstrable nonsense (e.g. President Obama was born in Kenya).[46] Segregated channels of information increase certainty of belief, decrease tolerance for other opinions, and encourage "take no prisoners" style of politics in which articulation of political viewpoints becomes more important than aggregation of interests. This was certainly evident in the 2016 presidential election and its aftermath.

Democracy and freedom of speech are inseparable; each has long been regarded as the precondition for the other. The Internet and social media permit much wider access to information and opinion than was previously possible. In theory, they have the potential to strengthen democracy. In practice, it is not so evident. Newspapers, radio, and television in western democracies, while never unbiased, provided some useful filters when it came to separating fact from fiction. Admittedly, they also exercised censorship by keeping from the public subjects considered too delicate, inappropriate, or controversial. Today, more than half of Internet users are still more trusting of TV and radio news than they are of what they find in on-line searches. Nevertheless, 44 percent of Germans, 52 percent of Americans, and 57 percent of Poles say they believe what they read on-line.

In the early years of the Internet, there was tremendous excitement about the prospect of having a world of information just a click away from anyone, anywhere, anytime. Until quite recently hope was widespread that this inherently democratic technology would lead to better-informed citizens more easily participating in public debate and discourse. Today, many observers are concerned that search algorithms and social media are undermining the quality of online information people retrieve. They worry that bad information, propaganda, and downright lies may be weakening democracy in the digital age. The Internet undeniably allows opinions and allegations of all kinds to spread and find large audiences. It encourages the formation of distinct communities – "filter bubbles" of like-minded people – that get news and opinion from preferred sites, enter virtual echo chambers of reinforcing opinions, and limit discussion and interaction with people with different opinions. Some research suggests that this fear is exaggerated and Internet users are more discerning and discriminating than generally supposed.

Still, the implications for democracy are not that promising. John Stuart Mill naively contended that facts and sound beliefs would triumph over falsehoods and unsound beliefs in the marketplace of ideas. The reverse may be closer to the truth given the ease with which the far-right groups can game algorithms to create a false world in which Hitler is a hero, Jews are evil, and hated by everyone in the world. The Internet spreads every imaginable kind of falsehood, false scientific claim (e.g. serious scientists doubt evolution, vaccinations are bad for your children) and patently false conspiracies (e.g. the CIA invented and spread AIDS in Africa, Jews were warned beforehand about the 9/11 attack on the World Trade Center, Hillary Clinton is a sex trafficker).

Social media affect democracy in a variety of other ways. They may be putting the right to a fair trial at risk, according to a public consultation launched by the British government's chief legal adviser. The initiative follows recommendations by the senior appeal court judge, Sir Brian Leveson, following legal challenges over what could be published about the trial of two schoolgirls who were eventually convicted of murdering Angela Wrightson in Hartlepool in 2014. The first trial of the teenagers, who were 13 and 14 at the time of the killing, was abandoned by the crown court judge amid a torrent of social media comments and abuse that threatened to prejudice the hearing.[47]

Authoritarian regimes do not face this problem as they repress freedom of speech. The Soviet Union, China, and North Korea enforced severe censorship, attempting to allow their citizens access to only official "facts" and perspectives. Martin Dimitrov found the People's Republic of China historically more repressive than the Soviet Union and currently more repressive than remaining communist regimes.[48] As this book goes to press, two of China's main online databases for scholarly articles removed dozens of articles that questioned the Communist party's commitment to the rule of law. Cambridge University Press, the world's oldest publisher, was asked by Chinese censors to block access to hundreds of academic articles by some of the world's leading Sinologists. LexisNexis, which runs a database of historical news cuttings from the world's main media companies, withdrew some of its products from the China market in March after authorities asked it to remove some stories about China.[49]

Most western analysts are convinced that such efforts ultimately fail, as people find ways around censorship; mimeographed samizdat in the pre-computer age, and loopholes in Internet censorship in the present era. In addition, efforts at enforcement undermine the legitimacy of regimes that attempt it. In East Germany and the Soviet Union, censorship aroused anger and contributed to the demise of both regimes and countries. It may be that neither openness nor repression achieves their intended goals. Each creates different kinds of problems for the governments and political orders that rely on them.

Some countries have tried a third way. Social Democratic governments in New Zealand and Sweden feared the effects of television on their populations. New Zealand did not introduce television until 1960, and did not permit privately owned stations until 1988. Sweden began televising in 1954 and did not allow commercial channels until the 1980s. The Swedish penal code criminalizes defamation, and editors of newspapers are legally responsible for their content. In a famous essay, Herbert Marcuse argued that acceptance of diverse political viewpoints in the media is actually partisan and a form of intolerance.[50] He called for tolerance of the Left, subversion, and revolutionary violence, combined with intolerance of the Right, existing institutions of civil society, and opposition to socialism. His critics, among them Alasdair MacIntyre and Maurice Cranston, condemn his position as just as partisan and intolerant as those he opposes.[51] Efforts to find some halfway position are both logically indefensible and unstable in practice.

Information is accordingly a double-edged sword that cuts against the grain of democratic and authoritarian regimes. Liberals long considered it a powerful tool in their arsenal against communist and other authoritarian regimes. The United States Information Agency, Radio Free Europe, and various other public and private organizations sought to exploit this perceived advantage during the Cold War by broadcasting news and commentary into so-called "Iron Curtain" countries. Post-Cold War analyses indicate that these broadcasts had significant effects, although not necessarily those intended by those funding or responsible for them. The 2016 US presidential election revealed the potential for authoritarian regimes to influence public opinion and elections in democratic regimes. Information technology and access have the potential to be destabilizing across regime types.

It is, of course, too early to predict the consequences of the information revolution for politics, and for regime survival in particular. If I had to place a bet it would be with the ability of democratic regimes to weather this transformation more successfully than their authoritarian counterparts. There is a significant potential for data protection but, judging on the basis of past performance, it is not very likely that democratic electors will become more sophisticated and less immune to efforts at manipulation – regardless of their source. Authoritarian regimes might be more successful with light forms of censorship, but are by their very nature ham-fisted. Their leaders do not believe in or see the benefits of openness and feel threatened, as do Chinese leaders, by people and organizations who do not oppose them, but whom they do not control. As there are no legal or other restrictions on their efforts at censorship, they are tempted to extend further government control over information. The most compelling may be protecting themselves, friends, and family members from exposure for crimes, corruption, and scandal. This is also the form of censorship most likely to arouse opposition.

Order and Social Science

I want to conclude with some reflections on research and its inescapably normative content. Max Weber is often misread as a defender of the fact–value distinction that lies at the core of social science's claims to objectivity. A more accurate reading of his works indicates that he found it impossible to separate facts from values, and came to regard rationality, the fundamental tool of social science, as subjective in its formulation and application.

Weber conceived of rationality as an ideal type: something that was not often encountered in practice but provided a template for analysis.[52] He would have analysts ask ex post facto what would have constituted a rational response given an actor's goals. They need only turn to psychological and other explanations to the extent that the actor's behavior departed from their rational counterfactual. Weber nevertheless recognized the subjective nature of this approach to explanation because it hinges on what we think would have been rational behavior.[53] This in turn depends on what motives we think are in play, what ends actors sought, and what course of action had the best chance of producing them. None of these assessments are necessarily obvious or can reasonably be ascertained by research.[54] We ultimately rely on our judgments, which, like those of the actors we analyze, are subjective and may or may not be rational.

Weber tried to separate instrumental from substantive rationality, and to deal as far as possible with facts, not values. He nevertheless recognized the impossibility of doing either in practice. We cannot avoid introducing substantive rationality because we need to know if an end is attainable to judge efforts to achieve it instrumentally rational. Such judgments underlie – indeed, are the very foundation – of any analyses of American democracy or Chinese authoritarianism. They influence, if not determine, the types of political systems we consider rational, and the kinds of theories and propositions we devise or select to study them and other systems. They in turn provide the templates for judging the instrumental and substantive rationality of actor behavior.

For Weber, social science was inherently subjective as findings were determined by the starting perspectives of researchers, no matter how rigorously they conducted their inquiries. Different perspectives would lead to different, equally defensive, conclusions. Findings were useful if they helped us address real-world problems.[55] Warrants for knowledge were not based on logical consistency or supporting empirical evidence, but on utility.

The subjective nature of social science makes it essential for researchers to recognize their own priors and to make them as explicit as possible to themselves and their readers. Weber tried to do this and inadvertently demonstrated just how difficult it is to do. His research was shaped in unacknowledged ways by his Kantian and Hegelian intellectual foundations and his German nationalism. He believed in the higher moral status of the state and adopted a Darwinist view of international relations and beliefs, along with an intense German nationalism that significantly guided the research questions he asked and many of the answers he found.[56]

If Weber tried and failed to come to recognize his priors and the extent to which his view of politics was historically and culturally specific, what does it say about the rest of us? We are undoubtedly as blind to the parochial nature of our beliefs and expectations as he was, and with equally empowering and limiting consequences for our research. Awareness of the problem does not make its solution any easier.

I have struggled with this dilemma from the moment I conceived of this book project. My focus on order initially arose in the 1990s, at the end of the Cold War, and was a response to the pressing need to restructure international society, but also to the increasingly unilateral foreign policies of the United States that made this goal increasingly impossible. *The Tragic Vision of Politics* and *A Cultural Theory of International Relations* were driven by my normative concerns. I have tried to make them more explicit in this book and to show the links between them and my research questions. By the time I began this last volume of my trilogy in 2012, the problem of order had become more acute. The Middle East was the site of foreign invasion, civil wars, intense sectarian conflict, and corrupt governments lacking legitimacy. In Asia, a newly assertive China was advancing claims to oil-rich islands and surrounding waters at the expense of many other Pacific Rim states. North Korea was pushing ahead with its missile and nuclear weapons programs. In the West, the backlash against globalization and social change gave new life to nativism and nationalism in the United States, United Kingdom, and continental Europe that threatened the survival of the EU, if not democratic order itself. These events encouraged my focus on decline and associated pathways.

My choice of case studies was also dictated by events, although on the basis of a longer-term perspective. I wondered about the prospects for the survival of western democracies and of China's authoritarian regime. Liberals assume that democracy and capitalism are the only rational responses to the modern world. Their claim seems reasonable if we accept the assumptions on which it is based: (1) that people are driven by appetite and want the political order that maximizes their chances of material gain; (2) that capitalism – some would assert, laissez-faire capitalism – is the economic system most advantageous to this end; and (3) most people are rational enough to understand the connection and act accordingly. It is by no means self-evident that these assumptions are warranted. We know that people are driven by other goals, and often sacrifice wealth to them. Opponents of globalization challenge the second assumption, and point to the growing inequality and decline in mobility in advanced capitalist states as evidence. Rationality may be the most problematic assumption.

When these assumptions underlie an analysis of China they lead to the conclusion that its authoritarian regime flies in the face of history and that its collapse is inevitable. This "White Marxism" is no more helpful in understanding China than "Red Marxism" was in understanding the capitalist West. It is important to address the futures of democracy and authoritarianism with an open mind, and not assume that one system is a more rational response to modernity than the other, and more troubling still, to analyze the assumed atavistic one with concepts developed to study the other. We have tried to avoid doing this by using Georgian Britain as our template for analyzing China. The two societies shared much in common, and the former evolved into a democracy and the most stable regime in nineteenth-century Europe. Georgian Britain may not offer the perfect perspective on China, but it is a different one than is ordinarily used and accordingly generates a different set of expectations and questions. At the very least, a new perspective is a good way of distancing ourselves from and problematizing the dominant perspective.

Liberal expectations reflect liberal ideology but also draw support from the seeming triumph of liberal, capitalist democracies in the twentieth century. Elsewhere I have used counterfactual arguments to show just how contingent this outcome was. Had Germany won World War I, which was a very near thing, authoritarian-corporatist regimes in Germany, Japan, and probably Russia too, would have given liberal democracies a run for their money.[57] Our beliefs and expectations – and by extension, our theories – are very much shaped by history, and we routinely exaggerate their likelihood, if not their inevitability.

Counterfactual thought experiments are the best tool for probing contingency and beliefs based on the so-called lessons of history. I have consistently used them toward this end and sought to query not only the assumptions of liberals and realists, but my own. These experiments have helped to shift my beliefs and expectations about politics and international relations. I have also sought to escape my moment in history by turning to the ancient Greeks for insights and concepts that have wider, if not some degree of universal applicability. This still does not provide me with a privileged perspective, and the passage of time will undoubtedly reveal the ways in which the questions I asked and the beliefs and expectations promoted them and concepts used to answer them were parochial products of their time and life experience and limited and inappropriate. The most universal error, Michel de Montaigne maintained, is generalization on the basis of one's own experience. "It seems to each man that the ruling pattern of nature is in him; to this he refers all other forms as to a touchstone. The ways that do not square with his are counterfeit and artificial. What brutish stupidity!"[58]

Notes

1 Malcolm Cowley, "The End of the World," *The New Yorker*, November 22 1941. Reprinted in Finder and Harvey, *New York Book of the 40s*, pp. 567–68.
2 Yack, *Fetishism of Modernities*, for a discussion of the various meanings of modernity.
3 For the debate over the territorial state, see North and Thomas, *Rise of the Western World*, for a strong economic claim. For critiques and political and cultural explanations, see Ruggie, "Territoriality and Beyond"; Spruyt, *Sovereign State and Its Competitors*; Nexon, *Struggle for Power in Early Modern Europe*; Lebow, *Constructing Cause in International Relations*, ch. 4. Herz, "Rise and Demise of the Territorial State"; Tilly, *Formation of National States in Western Europe*; Mann, *Sources of Social Power*. vol. I; Parker, *Military Revolution*; Ertman, *Birth of the Leviathan*.
4 Durkheim, *Division of Labor in Society.*
5 Lebow, *Politics and Ethics of Identity*, ch. 7.
6 Ibid.
7 Morris, *News From Nowhere.*
8 Marx, *Critique of the Gotha Program*, p. 27.
9 Plato, *Republic*; Rawls, *Theory of Justice*; Bacon, *New Atlantis*; Huxley, *Island*; Skinner, *Walden II.*
10 Lebow, *Politics and Ethics of Identity*, ch. 2.
11 Ortega y Gassett, *Goya*; Popper, *Open Society and Its Enemies.*
12 Lerner, "Justice Motive"; Shapiro, "Effect of Expectations of Future Interaction on Reward Allocation in Dyads"; Mikula, *Justice and Social Interaction*; Deutsch, *Distributive Justice*"; Törnblom and Jonsson, ""Distribution versus Retribution"; Griffith and Sell, "Effects of Competition on Allocators' Preferences for Contributive and Retributive Justice Rules."
13 Brickman, Folger, Goode, and Schul, "Microjustice and Macrojustice."
14 McCloskey and Zaller, *American Ethos*, ch. 5.
15 Swift, Marshall, and Burgoyne, "Which Road to Social Justice?"
16 Lamm and Schwinger, "Norms Concerning Distributive Justice," and Schwinger, "Need Principle of Distributive Justice."
17 Mikula and Schwinger, "Intermember Relations and Reward Allocation."
18 Balafoutas, Koucher, Putterman, and Sutter, "Equality, Equity and Incentives"; Reeskens and Oorschot, "Equity, Equality, or Need?"
19 McCloskey and Zaller, *American Ethos*, ch. 5.
20 Mitchell, Tetlock, Newman, and Lerner, "Experiments Behind the Veil."
21 As yet unpublisher paper.
22 Flasch, *Die geistige Mobilmachung*; Ohnezeit, *Zwischen "Schärfster Opposition und dem "Willen zur Macht"*; Tanner, "Protestant Revolt Against Modernity."

23 Jim Tankersley, Thomas Kaplan, and Alan Rappeport, "Republican Plan Delivers Permanent Corporate Tax Cut," *New York Times*, November 2 2017, www.nytimes.com/2017/11/02/us/politics/tax (accessed November 16 2017); Kelsey Snell, "Republicans defend tax plan as a middle-class tax cut." *Washington Post*, October 1 2017, www.washingtonpost.com/powerpost/republicans-defend-tax-plan-as-a-middle-class-tax-cut/2017/10/01/061e6ccc-a6c7-11e7-850e-2bdd1236be5d_story.html?utm_term=.a956cc709c75 (accessed November 16 2017).

24 Lebow, *National Identifications and International Relations*, p. 192–93.

25 Tocqueville, *Democracy in America*, 2.II.ii.

26 Robert P. Jones, "The Collapse of American Identity," *New York Times*, May 2 2017, www.nytimes.com/2017/05/02/opinion/the-collapse-of-american-identity (accessed May 3 2017); Associated Press-NORC Center for Public Affairs Research, "The American Identity: Points of Pride, Conflicting Views, and a Distinct Culture," study conducted February 6–10 2017, http://apnorc.org/projects/Pages/HTML%20Reports/points-of-pride-conflicting-views-and-a-distinct-culture.aspx (accessed May 3 2017).

27 By 53 percent to 41 percent, more men supported Trump than Clinton (the 12-point margin is identical to the margin by which women supported Clinton). The advantage for Trump among men is larger than the 7-point advantage Romney had in 2012 and much different than in 2008, when men preferred Obama over McCain by a single point. Trump's performance among men is similar to that of George W. Bush in the 2004 and 2000 elections, where he won men by 11 points in each election. Alec Tyson and Shiva Maniam, "Behind Trump's victory: Divisions by race, gender, education," *Pew Research Center*, November 9 2016, www.pewresearch.org/fact-tank/2016/11/09/behind-trumps-victory-divisions-by-race-gender-education/ (accessed July 4 2017).

28 Associated Press-NORC Center for Public Affairs Research, "American Identity."

29 Emily Bazelon, "The New Front in the Gerrymandering Wars: Democracy vs. Math," *New York Times*, August 29 2017, www.nytimes.com/2017/08/29/magazine/the-new-front-in-the-gerrymandering-wars-democracy (accessed August 31 2017); Chen, "Effect of Electoral Geography on Competitive Elections and Partisan Gerrymandering," for a study that argues that geography more than gerrymandering is responsible for the bias toward Republicans in elections to congress.

30 Matt Flegenheimer, "The Roots of the Battle Over Neil Gorsuch: 'They Started It,'" *New York Times*, March 31 2017, www.nytimes.com/2017/03/31/us/politics/supreme-court-neil-gorsuch-senate.html?hp&action=click&pgtype=Homepage&clickSource=story-heading&module=first-column-region&region=top-news&WT.nav=top-news (accessed April 1 2017).

31 Lebow, *Cultural Theory of International Relations*, chs. 4–5.

32 I admire Marx for his immanent critique but reject his teleology. The future is opaque and not determined by any scientific law, unless it be entropy, and its consequences are a long way off. There was nothing inevitable about the Trojan War, the rise of capitalism or its demise. Such developments are

non-linear outcomes of multiple chains of causation, many of them influenced by human choices.

33 Madison, *Federalist Papers*, no. 47.

34 Plato, *Republic*, 441d12–442b4, c6–8, 443c9–444a3, 472b7–d2, 580c1–4, 588c7–d5.

35 Hirschman, *Passions and the Interests*; Hont, *Jealousy of Trade*.

36 Lebow, *Why Nations Fight*, chs. 4 and 7, for elaboration and critique.

37 Among the most famous is Lasswell, *Politics: Who Gets What, When, How*. Unlike many other students of American politics, Lasswell acknowledges multiple human motives and how their attainment can be an end in itself or a means toward achieving other ends.

38 Bell, *End of Ideology*; Fukuyama, *End of History and the Last Man*.

39 There are parallels here to the Hundred Years War and Peloponnesian War, both of which comprised multiple wars in the case of the former and two in the case of the latter (Archidamian and Peloponnesian). Only in retrospect were they subsumed into a single, larger conflict.

40 Lebow, "World War I."

41 Lebow, *Forbidden Fruit*, ch. 3, and *Archduke Franz Ferdinand Lives!*; Stevenson, *Anticipating Total War*.

42 Ikenberry, *After Victory*; Friedman, *Lexus and the Olive Tree*; Fukuyama, *End of History and the Last Man*.

43 Zhang and Lebow, *Rethinking Sino-American Relations*, ch. 3, for references and discussion.

44 Lebow, *Between Peace and War*; Jervis, Lebow, and Stein, *Psychology of Deterrence*; Lebow and Stein, *We All Lost the Cold War*; Lebow, *Avoiding War, Making Peace*.

45 "List of over-the-air television networks," Wikipedia, December 30 2016, https://en.wikipedia.org/wiki/List_of_United_States_over-the-air_television_networks (accessed January 2 2017).

46 You Gov, US, "Belief in conspiracies largely depends on political identity," December 27 2016, www.washingtonpost.com/news/rampage/wp/2016/12/28/americans-especially-but-not-exclusively-trump-voters-believe-crazy-wrong-things/?utm_term=.416354d2e07c (accessed December 30 2016); Catherine Rampell, *Washington Post*, December 28 2016, www.washingtonpost.com/news/rampage/wp/2016/12/28/americans-especially-but-not-exclusively-trump-voters-believe-crazy-wrong-things/?utm_term=.416354d2e07c (accessed December 30 2016).

47 Owen Bowcott, "Attorney general begins inquiry about social media impact on UK trials," *Guardian*, September 15 2017, www.theguardian.com/politics/2017/sep/15/attorney-general-begins-inquiry-impact-social-media-trials (accessed September 15 2017).

48 Dimitrov and Zhang, "Patterns of Protest Activity in China."

49 Ben Bland, "China rewrites history with new censorship drive," *Financial Times*, September 5 2007, www.ft.com/content/4ffac53e-8ee4-11e7-9084-d0c17942ba93 (accessed September 5 2017).

50 Marcuse, *Repressive Tolerance*.

51 MacIntyre, Marcuse; Cranston, "Marcuse."

52 Weber, "Die 'Objektivität' sozialwissenschaftlicher und sozialpolitischer Erkenntnis" ['Objective' Social Science and Social-Political Knowledge) and "Kritische Studien auf dem Gebiet der kulturwissenschaftlichen Logik" [Critical Studies on the Role of the Logic of Cultural Science].
53 Lebow, "Weber and Knowledge."
54 Lebow, *Forbidden Fruit*, pp. 32–34, on the problems of fathoming motives in evidence-rich research environments.
55 Weber, "Die 'Objektivität' sozialwissenschaftlicher und sozialpolitischer Erkenntnis" and "Kritische Studien auf dem Gebiet der kulturwissenschaftlichen Logik"; Lebow, "Weber and Knowledge."
56 Lebow, "Max Weber and International Relations."
57 Lebow, *Forbidden Fruit*, chs. 1–3, and *Archduke Franz Ferdinand Lives!*
58 Cited in Bouwsma, *Waning of the Renaissance*, p. 41.

Bibliography

Abrami, Regina Edmund Malesky and Yu Zheng, "Vietnam Through Chinese Eyes: Divergent Accountability in Single-Party Regimes," in Martin K. Dimitrov, ed., *Why Communism Did Not Collapse: Understanding Authoritarian Regime Resilience in Asia and Europe* (New York: Cambridge University Press, 2013), pp. 237–75.

Abramowitz, Alan, "Partisan Polarization and the Rise of the Tea Party Movement," paper presented at the American Political Science Association annual meeting, Seattle, WA, September 2011. http://papers.ssrn.com/sol3/papers.cfm?abstract_id=1903153 (accessed January 17 2014).

Abramowitz, Alan and Steven Webster, "All Politics is National: The Rise of Negative Partisanship and the Nationalization of U.S. House and Senate Elections in the 21st Century," prepared for presentation at the Annual Meeting of the Midwest Political Science Association, Chicago, Illinois, April 16–19 2015.

Acemoglu, Daron and James Robinson, *Why Nations Fail: The Origins of Power, Prosperity, and Poverty* (New York: Crown Business, 2012).

Adler, Emanuel and Michael Barnett, eds., *Security Communities* (Cambridge: Cambridge University Press, 1998).

Adorno, Theodor, "On the Social Situation of Music," in Theodor W. Adorno, *Essays on Music*, ed. Richard Leppert, trans. Susan H. Gillespie (Berkeley and Los Angeles, CA: University of California Press, 2002), pp. 391–436.

Adorno, Theodore and Max Horkheimer, *Dialectic of Enlightenment* (New York: Herder and Herder, 1972).

Aeschylus, *The Oresteia*, trans. A. Shapiro and P. Burian (Oxford: Oxford University Press, 2003).

Afflerbach, Holger, *Falkenhayn: Politisches Handeln und Denken i Kaiserreich* (Munich: Oldenbourg, 1994).

"Topos of Improbable War Before 1914," in Holger Afflerbach and David Stevenson, eds., *An Improbable War: The Outbreak of World War I and European Political Culture Before 1914* (New York: Berghahn Books, 2007), pp. 161–82.

Aguiar, P., J. Vala, I. Correia, and C. Pereira, "Justice in Our World and in that of Others: Belief in a Just World and Reactions to Victims," *Social Justice Research* 21 (2008), pp. 50–68.

Akerlof, George A. and Robert J. Shiller, *Phishing for Phools* (Princeton, NJ: Princeton University Press, 2015).

Alexander, R. D., *The Biology of Moral Systems* (New York: De Gruyter, 1987).

Alford, William, *To Steal a Book Is an Elegant Offense: Intellectual Property Law in Chinese Civilization* (Stanford, CA : Stanford University Press, 1995).

Allen, Jonathan and Amie Parnes, *Shattered: Inside Hillary Clinton's Doomed Campaign* (New York: Crown, 2017).

Almond, Gabriel and Sidney Verba, *The Civic Culture* (Princeton, NJ: Princeton University Press, 1963).

Althusser, Louis, "Ideology and Ideological State Apparatuses [Notes Towards and Investigation]," in Althusser, ed., *Lenin and Philosophy, and Other Essays*, trans. Ben Brewster (New York: Monthly Review Press, 1971).

Altschuler, Glenn C., *All Shook Up: How Rock 'n' Roll Changed America* (New York: Oxford University Press, 2003).

Alves, W. M., "Modeling Distributive Justice Judgments," in Peter H. Rossi and Steven L. Nock, eds., *Measuring Social Judgments* (Beverley Hills, CA: Sage, 1982), pp. 205–34.

Alves, W. M. and P. H. Rossi, "Who Should Get What? Fairness Judgments of the Distribution of Earnings," *American Journal of Sociology* 84, no. 3 (1978), pp. 541–64.

Andersen, RonNell Jones and Lisa Grow Sun, "Enemy Construction and the Press," Brigham Young University Law Research Paper No. 17–23, August 29 2017, https://papers.ssrn.com/sol3/papers.cfm?abstract_id=2929708 (accessed March 4 2018).

Anderson, Benedict R., *Imagined Communities: Reflections on the Origin and Spread of Nationalism* (London: Verso, 1983).

Ang, Yuen Yuen, *How China Escaped the Poverty Trap* (Ithaca, NY: Cornell University Press, 2016).

Archer, John E., *Social Unrest and Popular Protest in England, 1780–1840* (Cambridge: Cambridge University Press, 2000).

Archer, Richard, *As if an Enemy's Country: The British Occupation of Boston and the Origins of Revolution* (New York: Oxford University Press, 2010).

Arias, Enrique Desmond and Corinne Davis Rodrigues, "The Myth of Personal Security: Criminal Gangs, Dispute Resolution, and Identity in Rio de Janeiro's Favelas," *Latin American Politics and Society* 48, no. 4 (2006), pp. 53–81.

Aristotle, *De Anima, Eudaemonian Ethics, Nicomachean Ethics, Poetics, Politics, and Rhetoric in The Complete Works of Aristotle*, Jonathan Barnes, ed. (Princeton, NJ: Princeton University Press, 1984), 2 vols.

Armey, Dick, *Give Us Liberty: A Tea Party Manifesto* (New York: HarperCollins, 2010).

Armstrong, Kenneth A., *Brexit Time: Leaving the EU – Why, How and When?* (Cambridge: Cambridge University Press, 2017).

Armstrong, Nancy, *How Novels Think: The Limits of Individualism from 1719–1900* (New York: Columbia University Press, 2005).

Arnold, Magda, *Emotion and Personality*, vol. 1 (New York: Columbia University Press, 1960).

Ashcroft, Michael, *The Lost Majority* (London: Biteback, 2016).

Asimov, Isaac, *Foundation* (New York: Street & Smith Publications, 1951).

Asma, Stephen, "Darwin's Causal Pluralism," *Biology and Philosophy* 11, no. 1 (1996), pp. 1–20.

Aspinwall, L. G. and A. McNamara, "Taking Positive Change Seriously: Toward a Positive Psychology of Cancer Survivorship and Resilience," *Cancer* 104 (11, Supplement) (2005), pp. 2549–56.

Aspinwall, L. G. and S. E. Taylor, "A Stitch in Time: Self-Regulation and Proactive Coping," *Psychological Bulletin* 121 (1997), pp. 417–36.

Assmann, Jan, *The Mind of Egypt. History and Meaning in the Time of the Pharaohs*, trans. Andrew Jenkins (New York: Metropolitan Books, 2002).

Aston, Trevor, ed., *Crisis in Europe, 1540–1600* (London: Routledge & Kegan Paul, 1965).

Atkinson, Anthony, *Inequality: What Can Be Done?* (Cambridge, MA: Harvard University Press, 2015).

Audoin-Rouzeau, Stéphan, "Combat and Tactics," in Jay Winter, ed., *The Cambridge History of the First World War*, vol. II: The State (Cambridge: Cambridge University Press, 2014), pp. 151–73.

Augustine, *The City of God*, trans. R. W. Dyson (Cambridge: Cambridge University Press, 1988).

Austen, Jane, *The Complete Novels of Jane Austen* (New York: Race Point, 2012).

Autessere, Séverine, *Peaceland* (Cambridge: Cambridge University Press, 2014).

Avant, Deborah D., Martha Finnemore, and Susan K. Sell, "Who Governs the Globe?" in Deborah D. Avant, Martha Finnemore, and Susan K. Sell, eds., *Who Governs the Globe?* (Cambridge: Cambridge University Press, 2010), pp. 1–34.

Axelrod, Robert M., "Building New Political Actors," *The Complexity of Cooperation: Agent-Based Models of Competition and Collaboration* (Princeton, NJ: Princeton University Press, 1997), pp. 121–44.

The Evolution of Cooperation (New York: Basic Books, 1984).

Axelrod, Robert M. and W. D. Hamilton, "The Evolution of Cooperation," *Science* 211, no. 4489 (1981), pp. 1390–96.

Axelrod, Robert M. and D. Dion, "The Further Evolution of Cooperation," *Science* 242 (1998), pp. 1385–90.

Axelrod, Robert M. and Robert O. Keohane, "Achieving Cooperation Under Anarchy: Strategies and Institutions," *World Politics* 38, no. 1 (1985), pp. 226–54.

Ayers, Edward L., *Vengeance and Justice: Crime and Punishment in the 19th Century American South* (New York: Oxford University Press, 1984).

Babst, Dean, "Elective Governments – A Force for Peace," *The Wisconsin Sociologist* 3, no. 1 (1964), pp. 9–14.

Bacon, Francis, *New Atlantis and The Great Instauration*, rev. ed., ed. Jerry Weinberger (Arlington Heights, IL: H. Davidson, 1989).

The New Organon, ed. F. Anderson (New York: Macmillan, 1960).

Badie, Bertrand, *Les Temps des Humiliès: Pathologie des Relations Internationales* (Paris: Odile Jacob, 2014).

Bafumi, Joseph and Michael Herron, "Prejudice, Black Threat, and the Racist Voter in the 2008 Election," *Journal of Political Marketing* 8, no. 4 (2009), pp. 334–48.

Bailey, William C. and Ruth D. Peterson, "Murder, Capital Punishment, and Deterrence: A Review of the Evidence and an Examination of Police Killings," *Journal of Social Issues* 50 (Summer 1994), pp. 53–75.

Bain, William, "*The Anarchical Society* as Christian Political Theology," in Hidemi Suganami, Madeline Carr, and Adam Humphreys, eds., *The Anarchical Society at 40: Contemporary Challenges and Prospects* (Oxford: Oxford University Press, forthcoming).

Bak, Per and K. Chen, "Self-Organized Criticality," *Scientific American* 264 (January 1991), pp. 46–53.

Baker, Keith Michael, "Public Opinion as Political Invention," in *Inventing the French Revolution* (Cambridge: Cambridge University Press, 1990), pp. 167–99.

Balafoutas, Loukas, Martin G. Koucher, Louis Putterman, and Matthias Sutter, "Equality, Equity and Incentives: An Experiment," *European Economic Review* 60 (2013), pp. 32–51.

Baldwin, Peter, "The Return of the Coercive State: Behavioral Control in Multicultural Society," in Paul, T. V., G. John Ikenberry, and John A. Hall, *The Nation-State in Question* (Princeton, NJ: Princeton University Press, 2003), pp. 106–38.

Balot, Ryan, "Civic Trust in Thucydides," in Christian R. Thauer and Christian Wendt, eds., *Thucydides and Political Order: Concepts of Order and the History of the Peloponnesian War* (London: Palgrave Macmillan, 2017), pp. 151–74.

Baltzell, E. Digby, *Philadelphia Gentlemen: The Making of a National Upper Class* (Glencoe, IL: Free Press, 1958).

   The Protestant Establishment: Aristocracy and Caste in America (New York: Random House, 1964).

Barbieri, William, Jr., *Constitutive Justice* (London: Palgrave Macmillan, 2015).

Bargh, J. A., "The Automaticity of Everyday Life," in R. S. Wyer, ed., *The Automaticity of Everyday Life: Advances in Social Cognition*, Book 10 (Mahwah, NJ: Lawrence Erlbaum, 1997), pp. 1–62.

Barkawi, Tarak, *Soldiers of Empire: Indian and British Armies in World War II* (Cambridge: Cambridge University Press, 2017).

Barker, David and Christopher Jan Carman, "The Spirit of Capitalism? Religious Doctrine, Values, and Economic Attitude Constructs," *Political Behavior* 22 (2000), pp. 1–27.

Barker, Hannah, *Newspapers, Politics, and Public Opinion in Late Eighteenth Century England* (Oxford: Oxford University Press, 1998).

Barker-Benfield, G. J., "Origins of Anglo-American Sensibility," in L. J. Friedman and M. D. McGarvie, *Charity, Philanthropy, and Civility in American History*, pp. 71–90.

Barrett, L. F. "Are Emotions Natural Kinds?" *Perspectives on Psychological Science* 1 (2006), pp. 28–58.

Barrie, James M., *Peter Pan* (New York: Henry Holt, 1987 [1904]).

Barry, Brian, *Theories of Justice*, vol. I (Berkeley and Los Angeles, CA: University of California Press, 1989).

Barry, Jonathan and Christopher Brooks, eds., *The Middling Sort of People: Culture, Society and Politics in England, 1500–1800* (Basingstoke: Palgrave Macmillan, 1994).

Bartelson, Jens, *A Genealogy of Sovereignty* (Cambridge: Cambridge University Press, 1995).

"Towards a Genealogy of 'Society' in International Relations," *Review of International Studies* 41, no. 4 (2015), pp. 675–92.

War in International Thought (Cambridge: Cambridge University Press, 2018).

Barzini, Luigi, *The Italians* (London: Hamish Hamilton, 1964).

Bates, Robert H., "Probing the Sources of Political Order," in S. N. Kalyvas, I. Shapiro, and T. Masoud, *Order, Conflict, and Violence*, pp. 17–42.

Baudelaire, Charles, *The Painter of Modern Life and Other Essays*, trans. Jonathan Mayne (London: Phaidon, 1964).

Bauer, Nichole M., Laurel Harbridge Yong, and Yanna Krupnikov, "Who is Punished? Conditions Affecting Voter Evaluations of Legislators Who Do Not Compromise," *Political Behavior* 39, no. 2 (2017), DOI: 10.1007/s11109-016-9356-6

Bazerman, M. H, S. B. White, and M. J. Lerner, "Perceptions of Fairness in Interpersonal and Individual Choice Situations," *Current Research in Psychological Science* 4 (1995), pp. 39–42.

Beals, Derek, *Joseph II. vol. I: In the Shadow of Maria Theresa, 1741–1780* (Cambridge: Cambridge University Press, 1987).

Beard, Mary, *SPQR: A History of Ancient Rome* (London: Profile Books, 2014).

Beaumarchais, Pierre Augustin Caron de, *The Figaro Plays*, trans. John Wells (Indianapolis, IN: Hackett, 2010).

Beccaria, Cesare, *On Crimes and Punishments*, trans. H. Paolucci (New York: Macmillan, 1948 [1764]).

Becker, Gary, *The Economic Approach to Human Behavior* (Chicago, IL: University of Chicago Press, 1976).

Becker, Marcus C., "Organizational Routines: A Review of the Literature," *Industrial and Corporate Change* 13, no. 4 (2004), pp. 643–78.

Beckett, J. C., *The Making of Modern Ireland 1603–1923* (New York: Knopf, 1966).

Beckett, J. V., *The Aristocracy in England, 1600–1914* (Oxford: Oxford University Press, 1986).

Beetham, David, *The Legitimation of Power*, 2nd ed. (London: Palgrave Macmillan, 2013).

Behr, Hartmuth, *Politics of Difference: Epistemologies of Peace* (London: Routledge, 2014).

Bell, Daniel, *The End of Ideology* (Glencoe, IL: Free Press, 1960).

Bell, Duncan, "Beware of False Prophets: Biology, Human Nature and the Future of International Relations Theory," *International Affairs* 82, no. 3 (2006), pp. 493–510.

Bellair, Paul, "Social Interaction and Community Crime: Examining the Importance of Community Networks," *Criminology* 35 (1997), pp. 677–703.

Beller, Steven, *Francis Joseph* (London: Longman, 1996).

Bem, Daryl J., "Self-Perception: An Alternative Interpretation of Cognitive Dissonance Phenomena," *Psychological Review* 74 (1967), pp. 183–200.

"Self-Perception Theory," in L. Berkowitz, ed., *Advances in Experimental Social Psychology* (New York: Academic Press, 1972), vol. 6, pp. 1–62.

Benhabib, Seyla, *Claims of Culture: Equality and Diversity in the Global Era* (Princeton, NJ: Princeton University Press, 2002).

Benjamin, Roger and Raymond Duvall, "The Capitalist State in Context," in Roger Benjamin, ed., *The Democratic State* (Lawrence, KS: University of Kansas Press, 1985), pp. 19–57.

Benoit, Kenneth, "Democracies Really Are More Pacific (in General): Reexamining Regime Type and War Involvement," *The Journal of Conflict Resolution* 40, no. 4. (December 1996), pp. 636–57.

Bentham, Jeremy, *An Introduction to the Principles of Morals and Legislation*, J. H. Burns and H. L. A. Hart, eds. (Oxford: Oxford University Press, 1996).

Rights, Representation, and Reform: Nonsense Upon Stilts and Other Writings on the French Revolution, ed. Philip Schofield, Catherine Pease-Watkin, and Cyprian Blamires (Oxford: Oxford University Press, 2002).

Berend, Ivan T., *Decades of Crisis: Central and Eastern Europe before World War II* (Berkeley and Los Angeles, CA: University of California Press, 1998).

Berenskoetter, Felix, "Friends, There Are No Friends? An Intimate Reframing of the International," *Millennium* 35, no. 2 (2007), pp. 647–76.

Beresin, Anna R., *Recess Battles: Playing, Fighting, and Storytelling* (Jackson, MO: University of Mississippi Press, 2010).

Berg, Maxine, *The Age of Manufactures, 1700–1820: Industry, Innovation and Work in Britain*, 2nd ed. (London: Fontana, 1994).

Berlin, Isaiah, "Political Ideas in the Twentieth Century," (1949) in Berlin, *Liberty*, pp. 55–93.

"The Birth of Greek Individualism" (1998), in Berlin, *Liberty*, pp. 287–321.

"The Counter-Enlightenment," in Isaiah Berlin, ed., *Against the Current: Essays in the History of Ideas* (London: Pimlico, 1979), pp. 1–24.

Liberty, ed. Henry Hardy (Oxford: Oxford University Press, 2002).

Bernhard, Michael, "Civil Society and Democratic Transition in East Central Europe," *Political Science Quarterly* 108, no. 2 (1993), pp. 307–26.

Bernstein, Richard J., *The Abuse of Evil: The Corruption of Politics and Religion since 9/11* (Cambridge: Polity, 2005).

Bernstein, Thomas P. and Xiaobo Lü, *Taxation without Representation in Contemporary Rural China* (New York: Cambridge University Press, 2003).

Berridge, K. C, "Measuring Hedonic Impact in Animals and Infants: Microstructure of Affective Taste Reactivity Patterns," *Neuroscience and Biobehavioral Reviews* 24 (2000), pp. 173–98.

"Unfelt Affect and Irrational Desire," in A. S. R. Manstead and A. H. Fischer, eds., *Feelings and Emotions: The Amsterdam Symposium* (Cambridge: Cambridge University Press, 2004), pp. 243–62.

Bertrand, Marianne and Adiar Morse, "Trickle Down Consumption," National Bureau of Economic Research, Working Paper 1883, March 2013.

Bew, John, *Citizen Clem: A Biography of Atlee* (London: Riverrun, 2016).

Biersteker, Thomas J., "The 'Triumph' of Neoclassical Economics in the Developing World: Policy Convergence and Bases of Governance in the International Economic Order," in James N. Rosenau and Ernst-Otto Czempiel, eds., *Governance Without Government: Order and Change in World Politics* (Cambridge: Cambridge University Press, 1993), pp. 102–31.

Biesanz, Mavis Hiltunen, Richard Biesenz, and Karen Zubris Biesanz, *The Ticos: Culture and Social Change in Costa Rica* (Boulder, CO: Lynne Rienner, 1999).

Biesele, Megan and Robert K. Hitchcock, *The Ju/'hoan San of Nyae Nyae and Namibian Independence* (New York: Berghahn, 2011).

Bird, Graham, "The IMF and Developing Countries," *International Organization*, 50, no. 3 (Summer 1996), pp. 477–511.

Birmingham, Stephen, *"Our Crowd": The Great Jewish Families of New York* (New York: Harper & Row, 1967).

Black, Jeremy, *Robert Walpole and the Nature of Politics in Early Eighteenth Century Britain* (London: Palgrave Macmillan, 1990).

Blackburn, Simon, "Human Nature and Science: A Cautionary Essay," in F. De Waal, P. S. Churchland, T. Pievani, and S. Parmigiani, *Evolved Morality*, pp. 93–108.

Blackscheider, Paula R., *Spectacular Politics: Threatened Power and Mass Culture in Early Modern England* (Baltimore, MD: Johns Hopkins University Press, 1993).

Blanning, T. C. W., *Joseph II and Enlightened Despotism* (New York: Harper & Row, 1970).

Blanning, Tim, *The Culture of Power and the Power of Culture* (Oxford: Oxford University Press, 2002).

Frederick the Great: King of Prussia (London: Allen Lane, 2015).

The Romantic Revolution (London: Weidenfeld & Nicolson, 2010).

Bloom, Irene, "Confucius and the Analects," in William Theodore de Bary and Irene Bloom, eds., *Sources of Chinese Tradition, vol. I: From Earliest Times to 1600* (New York: Columbia University Press, 1999), pp. 41–43.

"Selections from the Analects," in W. T. De Bary and I. Bloom, *Sources of Chinese Tradition*, I, pp. 44–46.

Bodin, Jean, *Les six livres de la République* (Paris: Fayard, 1986).

Boehm, Christopher, *Hierarchy in the Forest: The Evolution of Egalitarian Behavior* (Cambridge, MA: Harvard University Press, 1999).

"The Moral Consequences of Social Selection," in F. De Waal, P. S. Churchland, T. Pievani, and S. Parmigiani, *Evolved Morality*, pp. 31–48.

Moral Origins: The Evolution of Virtue, Altruism, and Shame (New York: Basic Books, 2012).

Bohmer, Carol and Amy Shuman, *Political Asylum Deceptions: The Culture of Suspicion* (London: Palgrave Macmillan, 2018).

Bohmer, Richard M. J., *Designing Care: Aligning the Nature and Management of Health Care* (Cambridge, MA: Harvard Business Press, 2009).

Boin, Arjen, Magnus Ekengren, and Mark Rhinard, *The European Union as Crisis Manager: Patterns and Prospects* (Cambridge: Cambridge University Press, 2013).

Boix, Carles, "Civil Wars and Guerrilla Warfare in the Contemporary World: Toward a Joint Theory of Motivation," in S. N. Kalyvas, I. Shapiro, and T. Masoud, *Order, Conflict, and Violence*, pp. 197–218.

Political Order and Inequality: Their Foundations and Their Consequences for Human Welfare (Cambridge: Cambridge University Press, 2015).

Bokina, John, *Opera and Politics: From Monteverdi to Henze* (New Haven, CT: Yale University Press, 1997).

Borsay, Peter, *The English Urban Renaissance: Culture and Society in the Provincial Town, 1660–1770* (Oxford: Oxford University Press, 1982).

"Urban Life and Culture," in H.T. Dickinson, *Companion to Eighteenth Century Britain*, pp. 196–208.

Boulton, D'Arcy Dacre Jonathan, *The Knights of the Crown: The Monarchical Orders of Knighthood in Later Medieval Europe, 1325–1520* (New York: St. Martin's Press, 1986).

Bourdieu, Pierre, *Outline of a Theory of Practice* (Cambridge: Cambridge University Press, 2003).

Bouwsma, William J., *The Waning of the Renaissance: 1550–1640* (New Haven, CT: Yale University Press, 2000).

Bowler, Kate *Blessed: A History of the American Prosperity Gospel* (New York: Oxford University Press, 2013).

Bowles, Samuel and Herbert Gintis, *Democracy and Capitalism: Property, Community, and the Contradictions of Modern Social Thought* (New York: Basic Books, 1986).

  Schooling in Captialist America: Education Reform and the Contradictions of Economic Life (New York: Basic Books, 1976).

Bozeman, Adda B., *The Future of Law in a Multicultural World* (Princeton, NJ: Princeton University Press, 1971).

Braband, J. and M. J. Lerner, "'A Little Time and Effort' ... Who Deserves What from Whom?" *Personality and Social Psychology Bulletin* 29 (2003), pp. 747–58.

Bradsher, Henry S., *Afghanistan and the Soviet Union* (Durham, NC: Duke University Press, 1983).

Brass, Clinton T., "Shutdown of the Federal Government: Causes, Processes, and Effects," *Congressional Research Service*, February 8 2011.

Braumoeller, Bear F., *The Great Powers and the International System: Systemic Theory in Empirical Perspective* (Cambridge: Cambridge University Press, 2012).

Brewer, John, *The Sinews of Power: War, Money and the English State, 1788–1783* (Cambridge, MA: Harvard University Press, 1990).

Brewer, John and Anne Bermingham, eds., *The Consumption of Culture, 1600–1800: Image, Object, Text* (London: Routledge, 1985).

Brewer John and Roy Porter, *Consumption and the World of Goods* (London: Routledge, 1993).

Brewer, John and Eckhart Hellmuth, *Rethinking Leviathan: The Eighteenth-Century State in Britain and Germany* (Oxford: Oxford University Press, 1999).

Brewer, Marilynn B., "Ingroup Bias in the Minimal Group Situation: A Cognitive Motivational Analysis, *Psychological Bulletin* 86 (1979), pp. 307–24.

  "Ingroup Identification and Intergroup Conflict: When Does Ingroup Love Become Outgroup Hate?" in R. Ashmore, L. Jussim, and D. Wilder, eds., *Social Identity, Intergroup Conflict, and Conflict Reduction* (New York: Oxford University Press, 1991), pp. 17–41.

  "The Psychology of Prejudice: Ingroup Love or Outgroup Hate?" *Journal of Social Issues* 55, no. 3 (1999), pp. 429–44.

Bricker, Jesse, Arthur Kennickell, Kevin Moore, and John Sabelhaus, "Changes in U.S. Family Finances from 2007 to 2010: Evidence from the Survey of Consumer Finances," *Federal Reserve Bulletin* 98, no. 2 (February 2012), pp. 1–80.

Brickman, Philip, Robert Folger, Erica Goode, and Yaacov Schul, "Microjustice and Macrojustice," in J. Melvin and S. Lerner, eds., *The Justice Motive in Social Behavior* (New York: Plenum, 1981), pp. 173–202.

Briggs, Asa, "The Language of Class in Early Nineteenth-Century England," in Asa Briggs and John Saville, eds., *Essays in Labour History* (London: St. Martin's Press, 1967), pp. 43–73.

Broad, Robin, ed., *Global Backlash: Citizen Initiatives for a Just World Economy* (Blue Ridge, PA: Roman & Littlefield, 2002).

Brockner, J. and B. M. Wiesenfeld, "An Integrative Framework for Explaining Reactions to Decisions: Interactive Effects of Outcomes and Procedures," *Psychological Bulletin* 130 (1996), pp. 189–208.

Broszat, Martin, *Hitler and the Collapse of Weimar Germany*, trans. V. R. Berghahn (New York: Berg, 1987).

Brown, Archie, "Gorbachev and the End of the Cold War," in R. Herrmann and R. Lebow, *Ending the Cold War*, pp. 31–57.

The Rise and Fall of Communism (New York: Vintage, 2010).

Brown, Candy Gunther, *Global Pentecostal and Charismatic Healing* (New York: Oxford University Press, 2011).

Bryan, Dominic. *Orange Parades: The Politics of Ritual, Tradition and Control* (London: Pluto Press, 2000).

Buch, Esteban, *Beethoven's Ninth: A Political History*, trans. Richard Miller (Chicago, IL: University of Chicago Press, 2003).

Buchanan, Allen, "Assessing the Communitarian Critique of Liberalism," *Ethics* 99, no. 4 (1989), pp. 852–82.

Buchanan, James M. and Gordon Tullock, *The Calculus of Consent: Logical Foundations of Constitutional Democracy* (Ann Arbor, IL: University of Michigan Press, 1962).

Buchanan, James M., *The Deficit and American Democracy* (Memphis, TN: P. K. Steidman Foundation, 1984).

Buck, C. "Biological Affects: A Typology," *Psychological Review* 106 (1999), pp. 301–36.

Bukovansky, Mlada, Ian Clark, Robyn Eckersley, Richard Price, Christian Reus-Smit, and Nicholas J. Wheeler, *Special Responsibilities: Global Problems and American Power* (Cambridge: Cambridge University Press, 2012).

Bull, Hedley, "Order vs. Justice in International Society," *Political Studies* 19, no 3, (1971), pp. 269–83.

The Anarchical Society: A Study of Order in World Politics (New York: Columbia University Press, 1977).

Bull, Hedley and Adam Watson, eds., *The Expansion of International Society* (Oxford: Oxford University Press, 1984).

Bull, Stephen, *German Assault Troops of the First World War: Stosstrupptaktik – The First Stormtroopers* (Staplehurst, UK: Spellmount, 2007).

Burke, Edmund, *Burke's Speech on Conciliation with America* (New York: Harper & Bros., 1945).

Burke, Peter, *European Renaissance: Centres and Peripheries* (Oxford: Blackwell, 1998).

Burke, Edmund, *Reflections on the Revolution in France* (Stanford, CA: Stanford University Press, 2001).

Burney, Charles, *A General History of Music* (London: Becket, Robson, and Robinson, 1776).

Burrow, J. W., *The Crisis of Reason: European Thought, 1848–1914* (New Haven, CT: Yale University Press, 2000).

Bursik, Robert J., "Social Disorganization and Theories of Crime and Delinquency: Problems and Prospects," *Criminology* 26 (1988), pp. 519–52.

Buzan, Barry, *From International to World Society? English School Theory and the Social Structure of Globalization* (Cambridge: Cambridge University Press, 2004).

Buzan, Barry and George Lawson, *The Global Transformation: History, Modernity ad the Making of International Relations* (Cambridge: Cambridge University Press, 2015).

Caesar, Julius, *Thee Conquest of Gaul*, trans. S. A. Handford (Harmondsworth, UK: Penguin, 1951).

Cai, Yongshun, *Collective Resistance in China: Why Popular Protests Succeed or Fail* (Stanford, CA: Stanford University Press, 2010).

Callan, M. J., N. W. Shead, and J. M. Olson, "Foregoing the Labor for the Fruits: The Effect of Just World Threat on the Desire for Immediate Monetary Rewards," *Journal of Experimental Social Psychology* 45 (2009), pp. 246–49.

Campbell, David, *National Deconstruction: Violence, Identity, and Justice in Bosnia* (Minneapolis, MN: University of Minnesota Press, 1998).

Campbell, T. D., "Humanity Before Justice," *British Journal of Political Science* 4 (1974), pp. 1–16.

Cannadine, David, *Aspects of Aristocracy: Grandeur and Decline in Modern Britain* (New Haven, CT: Yale University Press, 1994).

Cannon, John, *Aristocratic Century: The Peerage of Eighteenth-Century England* (Cambridge: Cambridge University Press, 1984).

Carnevale, P. J. D. and A. M. Isen, "The Influence of Positive Affect and Visual Access on the Discovery of Integrative Solutions in Bilateral Negotiation," *Organizational Behavior and Human Decision Processes* 37 (1986), pp. 1–13.

Cartledge, Paul, *Democracy: A Life* (Oxford: Oxford University Press, 2016).

Cash, Arthur H., *John Wilkes: The Scandalous Father of Civil Liberty* (New Haven, CT: Yale University Press, 2006).

Cederman, Lars-Erik, "Articulating the Geo-Cultural Logic of Nationalist Insurgency," in S. N. Kalyvas, I. Shapiro, and T. Masoud, *Order, Conflict, and Violence*, pp. 242–70.

Cha, Victor, *North Korea: The Impossible State* (London: Bodley Head, 2012).

Chanda, Nayan, "When Asia Was One," *Global Asia* 1, no. 1 (2006), pp. 58–68.

Chandler, David, "Back to the Future? The Limits of Neo-Wilsonian Ideals of Exporting Democracy," *Review of International Studies* 32, no. 3 (2006), pp. 475–94.

Chang, Gordon G., *The Coming Collapse of China* (New York: Random House, 2001).

Chang, Ying-lei Charles, "Environmental Protests and Dispute Resolution Mechanisms in Taiwan's Democratic Transition," LLM Thesis, Harvard Law School, 2006.

Chapman, Roger, *Culture Wars: An Encyclopedia of Issues, Viewpoints, and Voices* (Armonk, NY: M. E. Sharpe, 2010).

Chen, Jidong, Jennifer Pan, and Yuqing Xu, "Sources of Authoritarian Responsiveness: A Field Experiment in China," *American Journal of Political Science* 60, no. 2 (2016), pp. 383–400.

Chen, Jie, *Popular Political Support in Urban China* (Washington, DC: Woodrow Wilson Center Press, 2004).

Chen, Jie and Bruce Dickson, *Allies of the State: China's Private Entrepreneurs and Democratic Change* (Cambridge, MA: Harvard University Press, 2010).

Chen, Jowei, "The Effect of Electoral Geography on Competitive Elections and Partisan Gerrymandering," unpublished paper, November 12 2012.

Chen, Xi, *Social Protest and Contentious Authoritarianism in China* (New York: Cambridge University Press, 2012).

Cheng, J.Y-S, "The Emergence of Radical Politics in Hong Kong: Causes and Impact," *China Review* 14, no. 1 (2014), pp. 199–232.

Chesterman, Simon, *You, the People: The UN, Transitional Administration, and Statebuilding* (Oxford: Oxford University Press, 2004).

Christie, Ian R., *Stress and Stability in Late Eighteenth-Century Britain. The British Avoidance of Revolution* (Oxford: Oxford University Press, 1984).

Chung, Jae Ho, *Centrifugal Empire: Central-Local Relations in China* (New York: Columbia University Press, 2016).

Cicero, *On Duties*, trans. Margaret Atkins (Cambridge: Cambridge University Press, 1991).

Ciompi, L. and Jaak Panksepp, "Energetic Effects of Emotions on Cognitions: Complementary Psychobiological and Psychosocial Findings," in R. Ellis and N. Newton, eds., *Consciousness and Emotions* (Amsterdam: Benjamins, 2004), I, pp. 23–55.

Clark, Christopher, *Sleepwalkers: How Europe Went to War in 1914* (London: Alan Lane, 2012).

Clark, Ian, *Legitimacy in International Society* (Oxford: Oxford University Press, 2005).

Clark., J. C. D., *English Society 1688–1832: Ideology, Social Structure and Political Practice During the Ancien Regime* (Cambridge: Cambridge University Press, 1985).

  Revolution and Rebellion: State and Society in England in the Seventeenth and Eighteenth Centuries (Cambridge: Cambridge University Press, 1986).

Clark, Peter, *British Clubs and Societies, 1580–1800: The Origins of the Associational World* (Oxford: Oxford University Press, 2000).

Clarke, Arthur C., *The City and the Stars* (New York: New American Library, 1987).

Clements, John P., "The Three Mile Island Unit 2: Case Study Overview," United States Nuclear Regulatory Commission, September 4 2015.

Clore, Gerald and Andrew Ortony, "Appraisal Theories: How Cognition Shapes Affect into Emotion," in M. Lewis, J. M. Haviland-Jones, and L. F. Barrett, *Handbook of Emotions*, pp. 628–42.

Clunan, Anne L., *The Social Construction of Russia's Resurgence: Aspirations, Identity and Security Interests* (Baltimore, MD: Johns Hopkins University Press, 2009).

Coase, Ronald and Nin Wang, *How China Became Capitalist* (London: Palgrave Macmillan, 2012).

Cochrane, Feargal, *Northern Ireland: The Reluctant Peace* (New Haven, CT: Yale University Press, 2013).

Cohen, G. A. "Equality of What? On Welfare, Goods, and Capabilities," *Recherches Économiques de Louvain/Louvain Economic Review* 56, nos. 3–4 (1990), pp. 357–82.

Cohen, Warren I., "China's Rise in Historical Perspective," in Guoli Liu and Quansheng Zhao, eds., *Managing the Chinese Challenge: Global Perspectives* (London: Routledge, 2008), pp. 23–40.

Cohn, Bernard S., "Representing Authority in Victorian India," in Eric Hobsbawm and Terence Ranger, eds., *The Invention of Tradition* (Cambridge: Cambridge University Press, 1992), pp. 165–201.

Coleman, James, *Foundations of Social Theory* (Cambridge, MA: Harvard University Press, 1990),

Colley, Linda, *Britons: Forging the Nation, 1707–1837* (New Haven, CT: Yale University Press, 2009).

  In Defiance of Oligarchy: The Tory Party 1714–1760 (Cambridge: Cambridge University Press, 1982).

Colquhoun, Patrick, *A Treatise on Indigence* (London: Hatchard, 1806).

Colquitt, Jason A., Greenberg, Jerald, and C. P. Zapata-Phelan, "What is Organizational Justice? A Historical Overview," in Jerald Greenberg and Jason A. Colquitt, *Handbook of Organizational Justice*, pp. 3–56.

Colquitt, Jason A., Jerald Greenberg, and Brent A. Scott, "Organizational Justice: Where Do We Stand?" in Jerald Greenberg and Jason A. Colquitt, eds., *Handbook of Organizational Justice* (Mahwah, NJ: Lawrence Erlbaum Associates, 2005), pp. 589–619.

Commission on the Review of the National Policy Toward Gambling, *Gambling in America* (Washington, DC: Government Printing Office, 1976).

Communist Party of China, Organization Department, *Zhongguo gongchangdang dangnei tongji ziliao huibian, 1921–2000* (Collection of Internal Party Statistics of the Chinese Communist Party, 1921–2000) (Beijing: Dangjian duwu chubanshe, 2011).

Comte, Auguste, *Cours de la philosophie positive* (Paris: Bacheler, 1830–42), 6 vols.

Connolly, William, *The Ethos of Pluralization* (Minneapolis, MN: University of Minnesota Press, 1995).

Converse, Philip E., "The Nature of Belief Systems in Mass Publics," in David Apter, eds., *Ideology and Discontent* (Glencoe, IL: Free Press, 1964), pp. 206–61.

Cook, Linda J. and Martin K. Dimitrov, "The Socialist Social Contract Revisited: Evidence from Communist and State Capitalist Economies," *Europe-Asia Studies*, 69, no. 1 (2017), pp. 8–26.

Cookson, J. E., *The British Armed Nation, 1793–1815* (Oxford: Oxford University Press, 1997).

Cooper, Alice, "When Just Causes Conflict with Acceptable Means: The German Peace Movement and Military Intervention in Bosnia," *German Politics and Society* 15, no. 3 (1997), p. 99–118.

Corbridge, Stuart, "Cartographies of Loathing and Desire: The Bharatiya Janata Party, the Bomb, and the Political Spaces of Hindu Nationalism," in Yale H. Ferguson and R. J. Barry Jones, eds., *Political Space: Frontiers of Change and Governance in a Globalizing World* (Albany, NY: State University of New York Press), pp. 151–69.

Cordesman, Anthony, "'Failed State Wars' in Syria and Iraq (III): Stability and Conflict in Syria," Center for Strategic and International Studies, Washington, DC, March 2016.

Cosmides, Leda and John Tooby, "Cognitive Adaptations for Social Change," in Jerome H. Bakow, Leda Cosmides, and John Tooby, eds., *The Adapted Mind: Evolutionary Psychology and the Generation of Culture* (Oxford and New York: Oxford University Press, 1992), pp. 163–228.

Cottret, Bernard, *L'Édit de Nantes: pour un finir avec des guèrres de religion* (Paris: Perrin, 1997).

Cover, Robert M., "The Supreme Court, 1982 Term – Foreword: Nomos and Narrative," Faculty Scholarship Series Paper 2705 (1983), http://digitalcommons.law.yale.edu/fss_papers/2705 (last accessed March 29 2018).

"Violence and the Word," Faculty Scholarship Series Paper 2708 (1986), http://digitalcommons.law.yale.edu/fss_papers/2708 (last accessed March 29 2018).

Craiutu, Aurelian, *Faces of Moderation: The Art of Balance in an Age of Extremes* (Philadelphia, PA: University of Pennsylvania Press, 2017).

Cranston, Maurice, "Herbert Marcuse," *Encounter*, 32 (March 1969), pp. 38–50.

Crawshaw, J. R., R. Cropanzano, R., C. M. Bell, and T. Nadisic, "Organizational Justice: New Insights from Behavioural Ethics," *Human Relations* 66, no. 7 (2013), pp. 885–904.

Crick, Bernard, *The American Science of Politics: Its Origins and Conditions* (Berkeley, CA: University of California Press, 1959).

Crooks, Peter and Timothy H. Parsons, *Empire and Bureaucracies in World History* (Cambridge: Cambridge University Press, 2017).

Crosland, C. A. R., *The Future of Socialism* (London: Cape, 1956).

Crozier, Michael, Samuel Huntington, and Joji Watanuki, *Crisis of Democracy: Report on the Governability of Democracies to the Trilateral Commission* (New York: New York University Press, 1975).

Cruikshanks, Eveline, ed., *By Force or Default: The Revolution of 1688–1689* (Edinburgh: Donald, 1989).

Cull, Nicholas, *The Cold War and the United States Information Agency: American Propaganda and Public Policy, 1945–1989* (Cambridge: Cambridge University Press, 2008).

Currie, Eliott, *Crime and Punishment in America* (New York: Holt, 1998).

D'Antonio, William V., Steven A. Tuch, and Josiah R. Baker, *Religion, Politics, and Polarization: How Religiopolitical Conflict Is Changing Congress and American Democracy* (Lanham, MD: Rowman & Littlefield, 2013).

Dahl, Robert A., "The Concept of Power," *Behavioral Sciences* 2 (1957), pp. 201–15.

Democracy and its Critics (New Haven, CT: Yale University Press, 1989).

"A Democratic Dilemma: System Effectiveness Versus Citizen Participation," *Political Science Quarterly* 109, no. 1 (1994), pp. 23–34.

Dilemmas of Pluralist Democracies: Autonomy vs. Control (New Haven, CT: Yale University Press, 1982).

"Power," in David L. Sills, ed., *International Encyclopedia of the Social Sciences* 12 (New York: Free Press, 1968), pp. 405–15.

Polyarchy: Participation and Opposition (New Haven, CT: Yale University Press, 1971).

A Preface to Democratic Theory (Chicago, IL: University of Chicago Press, 1956).

Dahrendorf, Ralf, *Society and Democracy in Germany* (New York: Doubleday, 1967).

Dakin, Douglas, *Turgot and the Ancien Régime in France* (London: Methuen, 1939).

Dallek, Robert, *Nixon and Kissinger: Partners in Power* (New York: Harper Collins, 2007).

Damasio, Antonio R., *Descartes' Error* (New York: Putnam, 1994).

The Feeling of What Happens (New York: Harcourt, Brace, 1999).

Darwin, Charles, *The Descent of Man* (London: Penguin, 2004 [1979]).

Darwin, Charles *The Expression of the Emotions in Man and Animals* (New York: Philosophical Library, 1955).

Daunton, Martin, *Progress and Poverty: An Economic and Social History of Britain, 1700–1850* (Oxford: Oxford University Press, 1995).

Davidson, Donald, "Actions, Reasons, and Causes," *Journal of Philosophy* 60, no. 23 (1963), pp. 685–700.

Dawes, Robyn, *House of Cards: Psychology and Psychotherapy Built on Myth* (New York: The Free Press, 1994).

Dawes, Robyn, David Faust and Paul E. Meehl, "Clinical Versus Actuarial Judgment," *Science* 243, no. 16 (1989), pp. 68–74.

Dawkins, Richard, *The Selfish Gene* (Oxford: Oxford University Press, 1976).

DeCelles, K. A. and M. I. Norton, "Physical and Situational Inequality on Airplanes Predicts Air Rage," *Proceedings of the National Academy of Sciences* 113 (2006), pp. 5588–91.

De Scudéry, Georges, *Curia Politiae: or, The Apologies of Severall Princes: Justifying to the World their Most Eminent Actions* (London: 1654).

de Sousa, R., *The Rationality of Emotion* (Cambridge, MA: MIT Press, 1987).

de Waal, Frans B. M., *Bonobo: The Forgotten Ape* (Berkeley, CA: University of California Press, 1997).

"Morality Evolved: Primate Social Instincts, Human Morality, and the Rise and Fall of "Veneer Theory,'" in de Waal et al., eds., *Primates and Philosophers: How Morality Evolved* (Princeton, NJ: Princeton University Press, 2006), pp. 1–82.

"Natural Normativity: The 'Is' and 'Ought' of Animal Behavior," in F. De Waal, P. S. Churchland, T. Pievani, and S. Parmigiani, eds., *Evolved Morality: The Biology and Philosophy of Human Conscience* (Leiden: Brill, 2014), pp. 185–204.

"The Tower of Morality," in de Waal et al., eds., *Primates and Philosophers: How Morality Evolved* (Princeton, NJ: Princeton University Press, 2006), pp. 161–82.

de Waal, Frans B. M., Patricia Smith Churchland, Telmo Pievani, and Stefano Parmigiani, *Evolved Morality: The Biology and Philosophy of Human Conscience* (Leiden: Brill, 2014).

de Waal, Frans B. M. and Peter L. Tyack, *Animal Social Complexity: Intelligence, Culture, and Individualized Societies* (Cambridge, MA: Harvard University Press, 2003).

de Waal, Frans B. M., Robert Wright, Christine M. Korsgaard, Philip Kitcher, and Peter Singer, *Primates and Philosophers: How Morality Evolved* (Princeton, NJ: Princeton University Press, 2006).

Deibert, Ronald J. "International Plug 'n Play? Citizen Activism, the Internet, and Global Public Policy," *International Studies Perspectives* 1, no. 3 (December 2000), pp. 255–72.

Delaney, Tim, *The March of Unreason: Science, Democracy, and the New Fundamentalism* (New York: Oxford University Press, 2005).

Dench, Emma, *Romulus' Asylum: Roman Identities from the Age of Alexander to the Age of Hadrian* (Oxford: Oxford University Press, 2005).

Derryberry, D., "Attentional Consequences of Outcome-Related Motivational States: Congruent, Incongruent, and Focusing Effects," *Motivation and Emotion* 17 (1993), pp. 65–89.

Deudney, Daniel and G. John Ikenberry, *Democratic Internationalism: An American Grand Strategy for a Post-Exceptionalist Era* (New York: Council on Foreign Relations, 2012).

Deutsch, Karl W., *Nationalism and Social Communication* (Cambridge: MIT Press, 1953).

The Nerves of Government (New York: Free Press, 1963).

Deutsch, Karl W. et al., *Political Community and the North Atlantic Area* (Princeton, NJ: Princeton University Press, 1957).

Deutsch, Morton, "Equity, Equality, and Need: What Determines Which Value Will Be Used as the Basis of Distributive Justice?" *Journal of Social Issues* 31 (1957), pp. 137–50.

Distributive Justice (New Haven, CT: Yale University Press, 1985).

"Equity, Equality, and Need: What Determines Which Value Will be Used as the Basis of Distributive Justice?" *Journal of Social Issues* 31 (1975), pp. 137–50.

Dewey, John, *Characters and Events: Popular Essays in Social and Political Philosophy*, vol. II (London: Allen & Unwin, 1929).

Human Nature and Conduct, vol. 14 of J. A. Boydston, ed., *The Middle Works, 1899–1924* (Carbondale, IL: Southern Illinois University Press, 1983 [1922]).

Diamond, Jared, *Collapse. How Societies Choose to Fail or Succeed* (New York: Penguin, 2011).

Diamond, Larry, "Is the Third Wave Over?" *Journal of Democracy* 7, no. 3 (July 1996), pp. 20–37.

The Spirit of Democracy (New York: Macmillan, 2008).

"Thinking About Hybrid Regimes," *Journal of Democracy* 13, no. 2 (April 2002), pp. 21–35.

Dicey, A. V., *Lectures on the Relation between Law and Public Opinion during the Nineteenth Century* (London: Macmillan, 1905).

Dickinson, H. T., *British Radicalism and the French Revolution, 1789–1815* (Oxford: Oxford University Press, 1985).

A Companion to Eighteenth-Century Britain (Oxford: Blackwell, 2002).

Liberty and Property: Political Ideology in Eighteenth-Century Britain (London: Methuen, 1977).

"Popular Politics and Radical Ideas," in H. T. Dickinson, *Companion to Eighteenth-Century Britain*, pp. 97–111.

Walpole and the Whig Supremacy (London: Hodder & Stoughton, 1973).

Dickson, Bruce J., *The Autocrat's Dilemma: The Chinese Communist Party's Strategy for Survival* (New York: Oxford University Press, 2016).

Red Capitalists in China: The Party, Private Entrepreneurs, and Prospects for Political Change (New York: Cambridge University Press, 2003).

Wealth into Power: The Communist Party's Embrace of China's Private Sector (New York: Cambridge University Press, 2008).

Diefendorf, Jeffry M., Axel Frohn, and Hermann-Josef Rupieper, *Ameican Policy and the Reconstruction of West Germany* (Cambridge: Cambridge University Press, 1993).

Dikötter, Frank, *Mao's Great Famine: The History of China's Most Devastating Catastrophe, 1958–1962* (London: Bloomsbury, 2010).

DiLorenzo, Thomas J., "The Culture of Violence in the American West: Myth versus Reality," *Independent Review* 15, no. 2 (2010), pp. 227–39.

Dimitrov, Martin K., "The Evolution and Adaptation of Business-Government Relations in Zouping," in Jean C. Oi and Steven M. Goldstein, eds., *Zouping Revisited: Adaptive Governance in a Chinese County* (Stanford, CA: Stanford University Press, 2018).

"The Functions of Letters to the Editor in Reform-Era Cuba," *Latin American Research Review*, 54, no. 1 (2019), pp. 3–39.

"Internal Assessments of the Quality of Governance in China," *Studies in Comparative International Development* 50, no. 1 (2015), pp. 50–72.

"The Political Logic of Media Control in China," *Problems of Post-Communism* 64, nos. 3–4 (2017), pp. 121–27.

Piracy and the State: The Politics of Intellectual Property Rights in China (New York: Cambridge University Press, 2009).

"Structural Preconditions for the Rise of the Rule of Law in China," *Journal of Chinese Governance* 1, no. 3 (2016), pp. 470–87.

"Understanding Communist Collapse and Resilience," in Martin K. Dimitrov, ed., *Why Communism Did Not Collapse: Understanding Authoritarian Regime Resilience in Asia and Europe*, pp. 3–39.

Dimitrov, Martin K. and Zhu Zhang, "Patterns of Protest Activity in China," paper presented at the Annual Meeting of the American Political Science Association, San Francisco, August 31–September 3 2017.

Di Palma, Giuseppe, *To Craft Democracies: An Essay on Democratic Transition* (Berkeley, CA: University of California Press, 1990).

Ditchfield, G. M., "Methodism and the Evangelical Revival," in H. T. Dickinson, *Companion to Eighteenth-Century Britain*, pp. 252–59.

Dobson, Richard B., *The Peasants Revolt of 1381* (Bath, UK: Pitman, 1970).

Doestoevsky, Fyodor, *Notes from the Underground*, trans. Constance Garnett (Harmondsworth, UK: Penguin, 1955).

Dolar, Mladen, "If Music Be the Food of Love," in Slavoj Žižek and Mladen Dolar, eds., *Opera's Second Death* (New York: Routledge, 2002), pp. 1–102.

Domínguez, Jorge I., "Latin America's Crisis of Representation," *Foreign Affairs* 76, no. 1 (January/February 1997), pp. 100–13.

Dornik, Wolfram, *Des Kaisers Falke: Wirken und Nach-Wirken von Franz Conrad von Hötzendorf* (Innsbruck: Studien Verlag, 2013).

Dorpalen, Andreas, *Hindenburg and the Weimar Republic* (Princeton, NJ: Princeton University Press, 1964).

Doyle, Michael W., *Empires* (Ithaca, NY: Cornell University Press, 1986).

Doyle, Michael, "Kant, Liberal Legacies, and Foreign Affairs, part 1," *Philosophy and Public Affairs* 12, no. 3 (1983), pp. 205–35.

"Kant, Liberal Legacies, and Foreign Affairs, part 2," *Philosophy and Public Affairs* 12, no. 4 (1983), pp. 323–53.

"Liberalism and World Politics," *American Political Science Review* 80 (1986), pp. 1151–69.

Ways of War and Peace: Realism, Liberalism, and Socialism (New York: Norton, 1997).

Doyle, William, *The Oxford History of the French Revolution*, 2nd ed. (Oxford: Oxford University Press, 2002).

Dryzek, John, *Deliberative Democracy and Beyond: Liberals, Critics, Conversations* (Oxford: Oxford University Press, 2000).

Discursive Democracy (Cambridge: Cambridge University Press, 1990).

Dunbar, Robin I. M. and Louise Barrett, *Oxford Handbook of Evolutionary Psychology* (New York: Oxford University Press, 2007).

Dunbar, Mark Van Vugt, Gilbert Roberts, and Charlie Hardy, "Competitive Altruism: A Theory of Reputation-Based Cooperation in Groups," in R. Dunbar and L. Barrett, *Oxford Handbook of Evolutionary Psychology*, pp. 532–40.

Dunn, John, "Trust and Political Agency," in Diego Gambetta, ed., *Trust: Making and Breaking Cooperate Relations* (Oxford: Blackwell, 1990), pp. 73–93.

Durkheim, Emile, *The Division of Labor in Society*, trans. W. D. Halls (New York: Macmillan, 1984).

The Elementary Forms of the Religious Life, trans. Carol Cosman (Oxford: Oxford University Press, 2001).

"The Field of Sociology," in Anthony Giddens, ed., *Emile Durkheim: Selected Writings* (Cambridge: Cambridge University Press, 1972), pp. 51–68.

Moral Education: A Study in the Theory and Application of the Sociology of Education, trans. Everett K. Wilson and Herman Schnurer (New York: Free Press, 1961).

Professional Ethics and Civic Morals (London: Routledge, 1992).

Suicide: A Study in Sociology, trans. George Spaulding and George Simpson (Glencoe, IL: Free Press, 1951).

Dusinberre, Edwin, *Beethoven for a Later Age: The Journey of a String Quartet* (London: Faber, 2015).

Dworkin, Ronald, "Liberal Community," *California Law Review* 77, no. 3 (1989), pp. 479–504.

"What is Equality? Part I; Equality of Welfare," and "What is Equality? Part II: "Equality of Resources," *Philosophy and Public Affairs* 10 (1981), pp. 185–246, 283–345.

Earle, Peter, *The Making of the English Middle Class: Business, Society and Family Life in London, 1660–1730* (Berkeley, CA: University of California Press, 1989).

Easterlin, Richard A., "Does Economic Growth Improve the Human Lot? Some Empirical Evidence," in Paul A. David and Melvin W. Reder, eds., *Nations and Households in Economic Growth: Essays in Honor of Moses Abramovitz* (New York: Academic Press, 1974), pp. 89–126.

"Will Raising the Incomes of All Increase the Happiness of All?" *Journal of Economic Behavior & Organization* 27, no.1 (1995), pp. 35–47.

Easton, David, "An Approach to the Analysis of Political Systems," *World Politics* 9 (1957), pp. 383–400.

The Political System: An Inquiry into the State of Political Science (New York: Knopf, 1953).

Eastwood, David, "Local Government and Society," in H. T. Dickinson, *Companion to Eighteenth-Century Britain*, pp. 40–54.

Ebenstein, William, ed., *Great Political Thinkers*, 4th ed. (New York: Holt, Rinehart & Winston, 1969).

Eberstadt, Nicholas, *The North Korean Economy: Between Crisis and Catastrophe* (New Brunswick, NJ: Transaction, 2009).

Eckstein, Harry, "On the Etiology of Internal Wars," *History and Theory* 4, no. 2 (1965), pp. 133–63.

Economy, Elizabeth, *The River Runs Black: The Environmental Challenge to China's Future* (Ithaca, NY: Cornell University Press, 2004).

Edelstein, David M., "Why Military Occupations Succeed or Fail," *International Security* 29, no. 1 (Summer 2004), pp. 49–91.

Edgeworth, F.Y, *Mathematical Psychics: An Essay on the Application of Mathematics to the Moral Sciences* (London: C. K. Paul, 1881).

Editorial Committee (anonymous), *Jianguo yilai gong'an gongzuo dashi yaolan* (Important Events in Public Security Work Since the Founding of the PRC) (Beijing: Qunzhong Chubanshe, 2003).

Edward, Keene, "International Hierarchy and the Origins of the Modern Practice of Intervention," *Review of International Studies* 29, no. 5 (2013), pp. 1077–90.

Edwards, Pamela, "Political Ideas from Locke to Paine," in H. T. Dickinson, *Companion to Eighteenth-Century Britain*, pp. 294–310.

Ehrlich, Isaac, "The Deterrent Effect of Capital Punishment: A Question of Life and Death," *American Economic Review* 65, no. 3 (1975), pp. 397–417.

Ehrman, John, *The Younger Pitt: The Consuming* (Stanford, CA: Stanford University Press, 1996).

Einhorn, Eric, *Modern Welfare States: Scandinavian Politics and Policy in the Global Age* (Boulder, CO: Praeger, 2003).

Ekiert, Grzegorz, *The State Against Society: Political Crises and Their Aftermath in East Central Europe* (Princeton, NJ: Princeton University Press, 1996).

Ekman, P., "An Argument for Basic Emotions," *Cognition and Emotion* 6 (1992), pp. 169–200.

Eley, Geoff, "The British Model and the German Road: Rethinking the Course of German History Before 1914," in David Blackbourn and Geoff Eley, eds., *The Peculiarities of German History: Bourgeois Society and Politics in Nineteenth-Century Germany* (Oxford: Oxford University Press, 1984), pp. 1–158.

Elshtain, Jean Bethke, *Public Man, Private Woman: Women in Social and Political Thought* (Princeton, NJ: Princeton University Press, 1981).

Elster, Jon, *The Cement of Society: A Study of Social Order* (Cambridge: Cambridge University Press, 1989).

"Marxism, Functionalism, and Game Theory," *Theory and Society* 11, no. 4 (1982), pp. 453–82.

Local Justice: How Institutions Allocate Scarce Goods and Necessary Burdens (Cambridge: Cambridge University Press, 1992).

"Norms of Revenge," *Ethics* 100 (1990), pp. 862–85.

Nuts and Bolts for the Social Sciences (Cambridge: Cambridge University Press, 1989).

"Strategic Uses of Argument," in Kenneth Arrow, Robert H. Mnookin, Lee Ross, Amos Tversky, and Robert Wilson, eds., *Barriers to Conflict Resolution* (New York: W. W. Norton, 1995), pp. 236–57.

Emerson, Rupert, *From Empire to Nation: The Rise to Self-Assertion of Asian and African Peoples* (Boston, MA: Beacon Press, 1960).

Epley, N. and E. M. Caruso, "Egocentric Ethics," *Social Justice Research* 17 (2004), pp. 171–88.

Ericson, David F. and Louisa Bertch Green, eds., *The Liberal Tradition in American Politics: Reassessing the Legacy of American Liberalism* (New York: Routledge, 1999).

Erikson, Erik H., *Childhood and Society* (New York: Norton, 1950).

"The Development of Ritualization," in Donald R. Cutler, ed., *The Religious Situation* (Boston, MA: Beacon, 1968), pp. 711–33.

Gandhi's Truth: On the Origins of Nonviolence (New York: Norton, 1969).

Young Man Luther: A Study in Psychoanalysis and History (New York: Norton, 1958).

Erikson, Kai, *Wayward Puritans: A Study in the Sociology of Deviance* (New York: Wiley, 1966).

Erle, Peter, *The Making of the English Middle Class: Business, Society and Family Life in London, 1600–1730* (Berkeley, CA: University of California Press, 1989).

Erskine, Andrew, *Troy Between Greece and Rome: Local Tradition and Imperial Power* (Oxford: Oxford University Press, 2005).

Erskine, Toni, "'Citizen of Nowhere' or the 'Point where Circles Intersect'? Impartialist and Embedded Cosmopolitanisms," *Review of International Studies* 28 (2002), pp. 457–78.

Erskine, Toni and Richard Ned Lebow, eds., *Tragedy and International Relations* (London: Palgrave, 2012).

Ertman, Thomas, *Birth of the Leviathan: Building States and Regimes in Medieval and Early Modern Europe* (Cambridge: Cambridge University Press, 1997).

Etzioni, Amitai, "The Epigenesis of Political Communities at the International Level," *American Journal of Sociology* 68, no. 4 (1963), pp. 407–21.

"The Evils of Self-Determination," *Foreign Policy*, no. 89 (Winter 1992–93), pp. 21–35.

"The Global Importance of Illiberal Moderates," *Cambridge Review of International Affairs* 19, no. 3 (September 2006), pp. 369–85.

"A Self-Restrained Approach to Nationbuilding by Foreign Powers," *International Affairs* (London) 80, no. 1 (2004), pp. 1–17.

Euben, J. Peter, *Athens After the Peloponnesian War* (Ithaca, NY: Cornell University Press, 1986).

"Democracy Ancient and Modern," *PS: Political Science and Politics* 26 (1993), pp. 478–80.

"Democracy and Political Theory: A Reading of Gorgias," in John R. Wallach, J. Peter Euben, and Josiah Ober, *Athenian Political Thought and the Reconstitution of American Democracy* (Ithaca, NY: Cornell University Press, 1994), pp. 198–226.

Evans, Richard J., *The Coming of the Third Reich* (London: Penguin, 2005).

Evans, St. B. T., "Dual-Processing Accounts of Reasoning, Judgment, and Social Cognition," *Annual Review of Psychology* 59 (2008), pp. 255–78.

Eversley, D. E. C., "The Home Market and Economic Growth in England, 1750–1780," in Eric L Jones and Gordon Edmund Mingay, eds., *Land, Labour and Population in the Industrial Revolution* (London: Arnold, 1967), pp. 206–59.

Eyck, Erich, *A History of the Weimar Republic*, trans. Harlan Hanson and Robert Waite, 2 vols. (Cambridge, MA: Harvard University Press, 1962–63).

Falk, A., E. Fehr, and U. Fischbacher, "On the Nature of Fair Behavior," Institute for Empirical Research in Economics, University of Zurich, Working Paper No. 17 (August 1999).

Falk, Richard A., *End of World Order* (New York: Holmes and Meier, 1983).

"Global Civil Society and the Democratic Process," in Barry Holden, ed., *Global Democracy: Key Debates* (London: Routledge, 2000), pp. 162–78.

Predatory Globalization: A Critique (Cambridge: Polity Press, 1999).

Falk, Richard A., Samuel S. Kim, and Saul H. Mendlovitz, *The United Nations and a Just World Order* (Boulder, CO: Westview Press, 1991).

Fallows, James, *Blind into Baghdad: America's War in Iraq* (New York: Vintage, 2006).

Farrell, Henry and Jack Knight, "Trust, Institutions and Institutional Change: Industrial Districts and the Social Capital Hypothesis," *Politics and Society* 31, no. 4 (2003) pp. 537–66.

Farriss, Christopher, "Respect for Human Rights Has Improved Over Time: Modeling the Changing Standards of Accountability," *American Political Science Review* 108, no. 2 (2014), pp. 297–318.

Feldman, Stanley and John Zaller, "Economic Individualism in American Public Opinion," *American Politics Quarterly* 11 (1992), pp. 3–29.

Felus, Kate, *The Secret Life of the Georgian Garden* (London: Tauris, 2016).

Feuchtwanger, E. J., *Disraeli, Democracy and the Tory Party* (Oxford: Oxford University Press, 1968).

Fewsmith, Joseph, *The Logic and Limits of Political Reform in China* (New York: Cambridge University Press, 2013).

Finder, Henry and Giles Harvey, eds., *The New York Book of the 40s: Story of A Decade* (London: William Heinemann, 2014).

Finkelstein, Norman H., *American Jewish History* (Philadelphia, PA: Jewish Publication Society, 2007).

Finley, Moses I., *Ancient Greeks: An Introduction to their Life and Thought* (New York: Viking, 1963).

The World of Odysseus (New York: Viking, 1978).

Finnemore, Martha and Stephen Toope, "Alternatives to 'Legalization': Richer Views of Law and Politics," *International Organization* 55, no. 3 (2001), pp. 743–58.

Fiorina, Morris P., with Samuel J. Abrams and Jeremy C. Pope, *Culture War? The Myth of a Polarized America* (Berkeley and Los Angeles, CA: University of California, 2004).

Fisch, Jörg, *Krieg und Frieden im Friedensvertrag* (Stuttgart: Klett-Cotta, 1979).

Fischer, Markus, *Well-Ordered License: On the Utility of Machiavelli's Thought* (Boulder, CO: Lexington Books, 2000).

Fischer, R. and P. Smith, "Reward Allocations and Culture: A Meta-Analysis," *Journal of Cross-Cultural Psychology* 34 (2003), pp. 251–68.

Fisher, Joseph C., *Killer Among Us* (Westport, CT: Praeger, 1997).

Fiske, Susan T., "Interpersonal Stratification: Status, Power, and Subordination," in Susan T. Fiske, Daniel T. Gilbert, and Gardner Lindzey, eds., *Handbook of Modern Psychology*, vol. 2 (New York: Wiley, 2010), pp. 941–82.

Flasch, Kurt, *Die geistige Mobilmachung: Die deutschen Intellektuellen und die Erste Weltkrieg* (Berlin: Alexander Fest Verlag, 2000).

Fleischacker, Samuel, *A Short History of Distributive Justice* (Cambridge, MA: Harvard University Press, 2004).

Fligstein, Neil, *Euro-Clash: The EU, European Identity, and the Future of Europe* (Oxford: Oxford University Press, 2008).

Foa, Roberto Stefan and Yascha Mounk, "The Danger of Deconsolidation: The Democratic Disconnect," *Journal of Democracy* 27, no. 3 (July 2016), pp. 2–17.

Foley, Elizabeth Price, *The Tea Party: Three Principles* (Cambridge: Cambridge University Press, 2012).

Foster, John Bellamy and Fred Magdoff, *The Great Financial Crisis: Causes and Consequences* (New York: Monthly Press, 2009).

Fox, Kenneth O., *Making Life Possible: A Study of Military Aid to the Civil Power in Regency England* (London: K. O. Fox, 1982).

Franck, Thomas M., *Fairness in International Law and Institutions* (Oxford: Oxford University Press, 1995).

   The Power of Legitimacy among Nations (New York: Oxford University Press, 1990).

Frank, Robert H., *Falling Behind: How Rising Inequality Harms the Middle Class* (Berkeley, CA: University of California Press, 2007).

   Passions Within Reason: The Strategic Role of Emotions (New York: Norton, 1988).

Frank, Thomas, *What's the Matter with Kansas: How Conservatives Won the Heart of America* (New York: Holt, 2005).

Frankfurt, Harry G., *On Inequality* (Princeton, NJ: Princeton University Press, 2015).

Franklin, John Hope, *The Militant South, 1800–1861* (Cambridge, MA: Harvard University Press, 1956).

Frazier, Mark W., *Socialist Insecurity: Pensions and the Politics of Uneven Development in China* (Ithaca, NY: Cornell University Press, 2010).

Frazier, Mark W. and Yimin Li, "Urbanization and Social Policy: Prospects for Social Citizenship in China," Paper presented at Emory University, November 7 2015.

Frederickson, B. L., "The Role of Positive Emotions in Positive Psychology: The Broaden-and-build Theory of Positive Emotions," *American Psychologist* 56 (2001), pp. 218–26.

Freedom House, *Freedom on the Net 2016: China* (New York: Freedom House, 2016).

Freud, Sigmund, *Civilization and its Discontents*, trans. Joan Riviere (Garden City, NY: Doubleday, 1958).

Freyberg-Inan, Annette and Daniel Jacobi, eds., *Human Nature and International Relations* (Cambridge: Cambridge University Press, 2016).

Friedman, Albert, "'When Adam Delved ...': Contexts of an Historical Proverb," in Larry D. Benson, *The Learned and the Lewd: Studies in Chaucer and Medieval Literature* (Cambridge, MA: Harvard University Press, 1974), pp. 213–30.

Friedman, Lawrence J. and Mark D. McGarvie, eds., *Charity, Philanthropy, and Civility in American History* (New York: Cambridge University Press, 2002).

Friedman, Thomas L., *The Lexus and the Olive Tree* (New York: Farrar, Straus and Giroux, 1999).

Frijda, Nico H., "The Psychologists' Point of View," in M. Lewis, J. M. Haviland-Jones, and L. F. Barrett, *Handbook of Emotions*, pp. 68–87.

Frith, Simon, *Sound Effects: Youth, Leisure, and the Politics of Rock and Roll* (New York: Pantheon, 1981).

Fritzsche, Peter, *An Iron Wind: Europe Under Hitler* (New York: Basic Books, 2016).

Fromm, Eric, *Escape From Freedom* (New York: Henry Holt, 1965 [1941]).

Frost, Mervyn, "Tragedy, Ethics, and International Relations," in T. Erskine and R. Lebow, *Tragedy and International Relations*, pp. 21–43.

Frost, Mervyn and Richard Ned Lebow, "Ethical Traps," as yet unpublished paper.

Fukuyama, Francis, "The End of History?" *The National Interest*, no. 16 (Summer 1989), pp. 3–18.

The End of History and the Last Man (New York: Free Press, 1992).

The Origins of Political Order: From Prehuman Times to the French Revolution (New York: Farrar, Straus and Giroux, 2011).

Galbraith, John Kenneth, *The Affluent Society* (Boston, MA: Houghton, Mifflin, 1958).

The Culture of Contentment (Boston, MA: Houghton Mifflin, 1992).

Galbraith, Peter W., *The End of Iraq: How American Incompetence Created a War Without End* (New York: Pocket Books, 2007).

Gallagher, Carolyn, *After the Peace: Royalist Paramilitaries in Post-Accord Northern Ireland* (Ithaca, NY: Cornell University Press, 2007).

Gallagher, Mary E., *Contagious Capitalism: Globalization and the Politics of Labor in China* (Princeton, NJ: Princeton University Press, 2005).

"'Reform and Openness': Why China's Economic Reforms Have Delayed Democracy," *World Politics* 54, no. 3 (2002), pp. 338–72.

Galston, William A., *Liberal Pluralism: The Implications of Value Pluralism for Political Theory and Practice* (Cambridge: Cambridge University Press, 2002).

Liberal Purposes: Goods, Virtue, and Diversity in a Liberal State (Cambridge: Cambridge University Press, 1991).

Galtung, Johan, "A Structural Theory of Aggression," *Journal of Peace Research* 1, no. 1 (1964), pp. 97–98.

Gao, Hongling, *Wangluo yuqing yu shehui wending (Internet Public Opinion and Social Stability)* (Beijing: Xinhua Chubanshe, 2011).

Gao, Qin, "Redistributive Nature of the Chinese Social Benefit System: Progressive or Regressive?" *China Quarterly*, no. 201 (2010), pp. 1–18.

Garnaut, John, *The Rise and Fall of the House of Bo: How a Murder Exposed the Cracks in China's Leadership* (London: Penguin, 2012).

Gaskill, Malcolm, *Between Two Worlds: How the English Became Americans* (Oxford: Oxford University Press, 2014).

Gat, Azar, "The Causes and Origins of 'Primitive Warfare': Reply to Ferguson," *Anthropological Quarterly* 73, no. 3 (2000), pp. 165–68.

"So Why Do People Fight? Evolutionary Theory and the Causes of War," *European Journal of International Relations* 15, no. 4 (2009), pp. 571–600.

Gaunt, Richard A. *From Pitt to Peel: Conservative Politics in the Age of Reform* (London: Tauris, 2012).

Gauthier, David, *Morals by Agreement* (Oxford: Oxford University Press, 1986).

Gazzaniga, Michael S., ed., *The Cognitive Neurosciences* (Cambridge: MIT Press, 2004).

Geddes, Barbara, "Stages of Development in Authoritarian Regimes," in Vladimir Tismaneanu, Marc Morjé Howard, and Rudra Sil, eds., *World Order After Leninism* (Seattle, WA: University of Washington Press, 2006), pp. 149–70.

Geis, Anna and Carmen Wunderlich, "The Good, the Bad, and the Ugly: Comparing the Notions of 'Rogue' and 'Evil' in International Politics," *International Politics* 51, no. 4 (2014), pp. 458–74.

Genovese, Eugene D., *The World the Slaveholders Made: Two Essays in Interpretation* (New York: Pantheon, 1969).

George, Alexander L. and Juliette George, *Woodrow Wilson and Colonel House: A Personality Study* (New York: Dover Publications, 1964).

Gerschenkron, Alexander, *Economic Backwardness in Historical Perspective: A Book of Essays* (Cambridge, MA: Harvard University Press, 1962).

Gerstein, D. R., R. A. Volberg, M.T. Toce, R. Harwood, E.M. Christiansen, J. Hoffmann, et al., *Gambling Impact and Behavior Study: Report to the National Gambling Impact Study Commission* (Chicago, IL: National Opinion Research Center, 1999).

Gibson, William, *The Church of England, 1688–1832: Unity and Accord* (London: Routledge, 2001).

Gill, Stephen, "Epistemology, Ontology and the 'Italian School,'" in Stephen Gill, ed., *Gramsci, Historical Materialism on International Relations* (Cambridge: Cambridge University Press, 1993), pp. 21–48.

"Global Hegemony and the Structural Power of Capital," in Gill, *Gramsci*, pp. 93–126.

Gramsci, Historical Materialism and International Relations (Cambridge: Cambridge University Press, 1993).

Gillespie, Michael Allen, *The Theological Origins of Modernity* (Chicago, IL: University of Chicago Press, 2008).

Gilley, Bruce, *China's Democratic Future: How It Will Happen and Where It Will Lead* (New York: Columbia University Press, 2004).

Gilligan, Carol, *In a Different Voice: Psychological Theory and Women's Development*, 2nd ed. (Cambridge, MA: Harvard University Press, 1993).

Giner-Sorolla, Roger, Richard Ned Lebow, and Laura Niemmi, "Principles of Justice and Presidential Choice," as yet unpublished paper, January 2018.

Glaser, Daniel, "Criminology and Public Policy," *American Sociologist* 6 (1971), pp. 30–37.

Gleick, James, *Chaos: Making a New Science* (New York: Viking, 1987).

Godfrey-Smith, Peter, *Other Minds: The Octopus and the Evolution of Intelligent Life* (London: William Collins, 2017).

Goldberg, J., M. J. Lerner, and P. A. Tetlock, "Rage and Reason: The Psychology of the Intuitive Prosecutor," *European Journal of Social Psychology* 29 (1999), pp. 781–95.

Goldhill, Simon, "The Great Dionysia and Civic Ideology," in John J. Winkler and Froma I. Zeitlin, eds., *Nothing to Do with Dionysos? Athenian Drama in Its Social Context* (Princeton, NJ: Princeton University Press, 1990), pp. 97–129.

Golding, William, *Lord of the Flies* (New York: Berkeley, 1959 [1954]).

Goldsmith, Jack L. and Tim Wu, *Who Controls the Internet? Illusions of a Borderless World* (Oxford: Oxford University Press, 2006).

Goldstein, Jeffrey, "Emergence as a Construct: History and Issues," *Emergence: Complexity and Organization* 1, no. 1 (2001), pp. 49–72.

Goldstein, Joshua L., *Winning the War on War: The Decline of Armed Conflict Worldwide* (New York: Dutton, 2011).

Goldstone, Jack A., *Revolutions in the Early Modern World* (Berkeley, CA: University of California Press, 1991).

Goldstone, Jack A., Ted Robert Gurr, and Farrokh Moshiri, eds., *Revolutions in the Late Twentieth Century* (Boulder, CO: Westview Press, 1991).

Goldthorpe, John, *Social Mobility and Class Structure in Modern Britain*, in collaboration with Catriona Llewellyn and Clive Payne (Oxford: Oxford University Press, 1987).

Goodliffe, Gabriel, *The Resurgence of the Radical Right in France from Boulangisme to the Front National* (New York: Cambridge University Press, 2012).

Goodwin, Brain, *How the Leopard Changed Its Spots: The Evolution of Complexity* (Princeton, NJ: Princeton University Press, 2001).

Goodwin, Robert, *Spain: The Centre of the World 1519–1682* (London: Bloomsbury Press, 2015).

Gorelik, G., T. K. Shackelford, and V. A. Weekes-Shackelford, "Resource, Acquisition, Violence, and Evolutionary Consciousness," in T. K. Shackelford and V. A. Weekes-Shackelford, eds., *Oxford Handbook of Evolutionary Perspectives on Violence, Homicide and War* (Oxford: Oxford University Press, 2012), pp. 506–23.

Gould, Stephen J., *It's a Wonderful Life: The Burgess Shale and the Nature of History* (New York: Norton, 1979).

Punctuated Equilibrium (Cambridge, MA: Harvard University Press, 2007).

Gourevitch, Peter, "The Second Image Reversed: The International Sources of Domestic Politics," *International Organization* 32, no. 4 (Autumn 1978), pp. 881–911.

Gramsci, *Letters from Prison*, 2 vols., trans. Raymond Rosenthal (New York: Columbia University Press, 1994).

Granovetter, Mark, "The Strength of Weak Ties," *American Journal of Sociology* 78, no. 6 (1973), pp. 360–80.

Gray, Jeffrey Alan, *The Psychology of Fear and Stress* (Cambridge: Cambridge University Press, 1987).

Greenberg, J. and J. A. Colquitt, *Handbook of Organizational Justice* (Mahwah, NJ: Lawrence Erlbaum Associates. 2005).

Greenberg, J. and R. L. Cohen, *Equality and Justice in Social Behavior* (New York: Academic Press, 1982).

Greenberg, Kenneth S., *Honor and Slavery* (Princeton, NJ: Princeton University Press, 1996).

Greenblatt, Stephen, *Renaissance Self-Fashioning: From More to Shakespeare* (Chicago, IL: University of Chicago Press, 1980).

Gregg, Edward, *Queen Anne* (New Haven, CT: Yale University Press, 2001).

Gregory, Jeremy, "The Church of England," in H. T. Dickinson, *Companion to Eighteenth-Century Britain*, pp. 225–40.

Griffin, Carl J., *Protest, Politics and Work in Rural England, 1700–1850* (London: Palgrave Macmillan, 2016).

Griffith, W. I. and J. Sell, "The Effects of Competition on Allocators' Preferences for Contributive and Retributive Justice Rules," *European Journal of Personality and Social Psychology* 18 (1988), pp. 443–55.

"The Effects of Competition on Allocators' Preferences for Contributive and Retributive Justice Rules," *European Journal of Personality and Social Psychology* 18 (1988), pp. 443–55.

Gross, Robert A., "Giving in America: From Charity to Philanthropy," in J. Friedman and M. D. McGarvie, *Charity, Philanthropy, and Civility in American History*, pp. 29–48.

Grossman, Joel B. and Mary H. Grossman, eds., *Law and Social Change in Modern America* (Pacific Palisades: Goodyear, 1971).

Guicciardini, Francesco, *Ricordi*, in *Maxims and Reflections*, trans. Mario Domandi (New York: Harper & Row, 1972).

Guihai, Guan, "The Influence of the Collapse of the Soviet Union on China's Political Choices," in Thomas P. Bernstein and Hua-yu Li, eds., *China Learns from the Soviet Union, 1949–Present* (Lanham, MD: Lexington Book, 2010), pp. 505–15.

Gutiérrez, Sanín, "Clausewitz Vindicated? Economics and Politics in the Columbia War," in S. N. Kalyvas, I. Shapiro, and T. Masoud, *Order, Conflict, and Violence*, pp. 219–41.

Gutmann, Amy, *Identity in Democracy* (Princeton, NJ: Princeton University Press, 2003).

Guttmann, Allen, *The Olympics: A History of the Modern Games* (Urbana, IL: University of Illinois Press, 1992).

Guzzini, Stefano, "Max Weber's Power," in R. Lebow, *Max Weber and International Relations*, pp. 97–118.

Guy, John, *Elizabeth: The Forgotten Years* (London: Viking, 2006).

Habermas, Jürgen, *Knowledge and Human Interests*, trans. Jeremy Shapiro (Boston, MA: Beacon Press, 1971).

Legitimation Crisis (Boston, MA: Beacon Press, 1975).

On the Logic of the Social Sciences (Cambridge, MA: MIT Press, 1994).

Moral Consciousness and Communicative Action, trans. Christian Lenhardt and Shierry Weber Nicholsen (Cambridge, MA: MIT Press, 1990).

The Structural Transformation of the Culture Sphere: An Inquiry into a Category of Bourgeois Society, trans. Thomas Burger (Cambridge: MIT Press, 1989).

Theory and Practice, trans. John Viertel (Boston, MA: Beacon, 1973).

The Theory of Communicative Action, trans. Thomas McCarthy (Boston, MA: Beacon Press, 1984–87).

Hafer, C. L., "Do Innocent Victims Threaten the Belief in a Just World? Evidence from a Modified Stroop Task," *Journal of Personality and Social Psychology* 79 (2000), pp. 165–73.

"Investment in Long Term Goals and the Commitment to Just Means Drive the Need to Believe in a Just World," *Personality and Social Psychology Bulletin* 26 (2000), pp. 1059–73.

Hafer, C. L. and L. Begue, "Experimental Research on Just World Theory: Problems, Developments, and Future Challenges," *Psychological Bulletin* 131 (2005), pp. 128–67.

Hafner, Katie and Matthew Lyons, *Where Wizards Stay Up Late: The Origins of the Internet* (New York: Simon & Schuster, 1996).

Hajnal, Peter I., *The G7/G8 System: Evolution, Role and Documentation* (Brookfield, VT: Ashgate, 1999).

Hale, T. and David Held, eds., *Handbook of Transnational Governance: New Institutions and Innovations* (Cambridge: Polity, 2011).

Hallinan, Joseph, *Going Up the River: Travels in a Prison Nation* (New York: Random House, 2001).

Halpern, Charles, *Russia and the Golden Horde* (Indianapolis, IN: University of Indiana Press, 1987).

Hamilton, Alexander, James Madison, and John Jay, *The Federalist Papers with Letters of "Brutus,"* ed. Terence Ball (Cambridge: Cambridge University Press, 2003).

The Federalist Papers (Baltimore, MD: Johns Hopkins University Press, 1981).

Hamilton, Richard F., *Marxism, Revisionism, and Leninism: Explication, Assessment and Commentary* (Westport, CT: Praeger, 2000).

Hamilton, W. D., "The Genetical Evolution of Social Behavior," *Journal of Theoretical Biology* 7 (1964), pp. 1–52.

Hampshire, Stuart, *Innocence and Experience* (London: Allen Lane, 1989).

Hanioğlu, M. Şükrü, *Preparation for a Revolution: The Young Turks, 1902–1908* (Oxford: Oxford University Press, 2001).

Harasim, L. M., ed., *Global Networks: Computers and International Communication* (Cambridge, MA: MIT Press, 1993).

Harcourt, Alexander H. and Frans De Waal, eds., *Coalitions in Humans and Other Animals* (Oxford: Oxford University Press, 1992).

Hardin, Russell, "Do We Want Trust in Government?" in Mark E. Warren, ed., *Democracy and Trust* (Cambridge: Cambridge University Press, 1999), pp. 22–41.

Trust and Trustworthiness (New York: Russell Sage, 2004).

Harding, Philip, *The Waning of "Old Corruption": The Politics of Economical Reform in Britain, 1779–1846* (Oxford: Oxford University Press, 1996).

Harford, Tim, *Messy: How to be Creative and Resilient in a Tidy-Minded World* (Boston, MA: Little, Brown, 2016).

Harkin, Michael E., "Potlatch in Anthropology," in Neil J. Smelser and Paul B. Baltes, eds., *International Encyclopedia of the Social and Behavioral Sciences* (New York: Elsevier, 2001), vol. 17, pp. 11885–89.

Harman, Oren, "A History of the Altruism-Morality Debate in Biology," in F. De Waal, P. S. Churchland, T. Pievani, and S. Parmigiani, *Evolved Morality*, pp. 11–30.

Harris, Bob, *Politics and the Rise of the Press, 1620–1800* (London: Routledge, 1996). "Print Culture," in H. T. Dickinson, *A Companion to Eighteenth-Century Britain*, pp. 283–92.

Harrison, Albert, *After Contact: The Human Response to Extraterrestrial Life* (New York: Plenum Press, 1997).

Hart, H. L. A., *The Concept of Law* (Oxford and New York: Oxford University Press, 1994 [1961]).

Hartling, Philip, *The Waning of "Old Corruption": The Politics of Economical Reform in Britain, 1779–1846* (Oxford: Oxford University Press, 1996).

Hartman, Andrew, *A War for the Soul of America: A History of the Culture Wars* (Chicago, IL: University of Chicago Press, 2015).

Hartz, Louis, *The Liberal Tradition in America* (New York: Houghton-Mifflin, 1955).

Harvey, David, *A Brief History of Neoliberalism* (Oxford: Oxford University Press, 2010).

Harwit, Martin, *An Exhibit Denied: Lobbying the History of Enola Gay* (New York: Springer-Vela, 1996).

Hasek, Jaroslav, *The Good Soldier Schweik*, trans. Paul Selver (New York: Unger, 1962).

Hastings, Justin, "Charting the Course of Uyghur Unrest," *China Quarterly*, no. 208 (2011), pp. 893–912.

Haun, Phil M., *Coercion, Survival, and War: Why Weak States Resist the United States*. (Stanford, CA: Stanford University Press, 2015).

Hausmann, Ricardo, "Will Volatility Kill Market Democracy?" *Foreign Policy*, no. 108 (Fall 1997), pp. 54–67.

Hawk, David, *The Hidden Gulag*, 2nd ed. (Washington, DC: Committee for Human Rights in North Korea, 2012).

Hay Douglas, Peter Linebaugh, and E. P. Thompson, eds., *Albion's Fatal Tree: Crime and Society in Eighteenth-Century England* (London: Allan Lane, 1975).

Hayden, Colin, "Religious Minorities in England," in H. T. Dickinson, *Companion to Eighteenth-Century Britain*, pp. 241–51.

Hayek, Friedrich A., *The Constitution of Liberty* (Chicago, IL: University of Chicago Press, 1960).
  Law, Legislation and Liberty, vol. I: Rules and Order (Chicago, IL: University of Chicago Press, 1973).
  Law, Legislation and Liberty, vol. II: The Mirage of Social Justice (London: Routledge & Kegan Paul, 1976).

Hechter, Michael and Nika Kabiri, "Attaining Social Order in Iraq," in S. N. Kalyvas, I. Shapiro, and T. Masoud, *Order, Conflict, and Violence*, pp. 43–74.

Hegel, Georg Wilhelm Friedrich, *Hegel's Philosophy of Right*, trans. T. M. Knox (Oxford: Oxford University Press, 1973).

Held, David and Charles Roger, eds., *Global Government at Risk* (Cambridge: Polity, 2013).

Hellmuth, Eckhart, "The British State," in H. T. Dickinson, *A Companion to Eighteenth-Century Britain* (2002), pp. 19–29.

Henrichs, J., Steven J. Heine, and Ara Norenzayan, "The Weirdest People in the World?" *Behavioral and Brain Sciences* 33 (2010), pp. 61–135.

Henriques, Diana B., *Bernie Madoff and the Death of Trust* (New York: St. Martin's Press, 2012).

Henry, Maura A., "The Making of Elite Culture," in H. T. Dickinson, *Companion to Eighteenth-Century Britain*, pp. 310–28.

Herbert Gintis, Samuel Bowles, Robert Boyd, and Ernst Fehr, "Explaining Altruistic Behaviour in Humans," in R. Dunbar and L. Barrett, *Oxford Handbook of Evolutionary Psychology*, pp. 605–19.

Herman, Arthur, *The Idea of Decline in Western History* (New York: Free Press, 1997).

Herodotus, *The Histories*, trans. George Rawlinson (New York: Knopf, 1997).

Herrmann, Richard K. and Richard Ned Lebow, "Hermann and Lebow, "Learning from the End of the Cold War," in R. Herrmann and R. Lebow, *Ending the Cold War*, pp. 219–38.

    eds., *Ending the Cold War: Interpretations, Causation and the Study of International Relations* (New York: Palgrave Macmillan, 2003).

Herwig, Holger H., "The Dynamics of Necessity: German Military Effectiveness during the First World War," in Allan R. Millett and Williamson Murray, eds., *Military Effectiveness, Vol. I: The First World War*, rev. ed. (Cambridge: Cambridge University Press, 2010), pp. 80–115.

Herz, John H., "The Rise and Demise of the Territorial State," *World Politics* 9, no. 4 (1957), pp. 473–93.

Hetherington, Marc J., "Resurgent Mass Partisanship: The Role of Elite Polarization," *American Political Science Review* 95, no. 3 (2001), pp. 619–31.

Heurlin, Christopher, *Responsive Authoritarianism in China: Land, Protests, and Policymaking* (New York: Cambridge University Press, 2016).

Hewson, Martin, "Did Global Governance Create Informational Governance?" in M. Hewson and T. J. Sinclair, *Approaches to Global Governance Theory*, pp. 97–115.

Hewson, Martin and Timothy J. Sinclair, eds., *Approaches to Global Governance Theory* (Albany, NY: State University of New York Press, 1999).

Higham, John, *Strangers in the Land: Pattern of American Nativism 1860–1925* (New York: Atheneum, 1973).

Hill, Brian, "Parliament, Parties, and Elections, 1688–1760," in H. T. Dickinson, *Companion to Eighteenth-Century Britain*, pp. 55–68.

Hilton, Boyd, *A Mad, Bad, and Dangerous People? England, 1783–1846* (Oxford: Oxford University Press, 2008).

Hironaka, Ann, *Tokens of Power: Rethinking War* (Cambridge: Cambridge University Press, 2017).

Hirschman, Albert O., *The Passions and the Interests: Political Arguments for Capitalism Before Its Triumph* (Princeton, NJ: Princeton University Press, 1977).

Hirschman, Nancy J., *The Subject of Liberty: Toward a Feminist Theory of Freedom* (Princeton, NJ: Princeton University Press, 2003).

Hirst, Paul Q., "The Global Economy – Myths and Realities," *International Affairs* 73, no. 3 (1997), pp. 409–25.

Hirst, Paul Q. and Graham Thompson, *Globalization in Question: The International Economy and the Possibilities of Governance* (Cambridge: Polity Press, 1996).

Hixson, Walter L., *Parting the Curtain: Propaganda, Culture, and the Cold War, 1945–61* (New York: St. Martin's Press, 1997).

Hjorth, Ronnie, *Equality in International Society: A Reappraisal* (London: Palgrave Macmillan, 2014).

Hobbes, Thomas, *Dialogue Between a Philosopher and a Student on the Common Laws of England* (Chicago, IL: University of Chicago Press, 1971 [1681]).

Leviathan, ed. Richard Tuck (Cambridge: Cambridge University Press, 1996).

Hobsbawm, Eric and George Rudé, *Captain Swing* (London: Verso, 2014).

Hobson, Jon M., "Decolonizing Weber: The Eurocentrism of Weber's IR and Historical Sociology," in R. Lebow, *Max Weber and International Relations*, pp. 143–72.

Hochschild, Jenifer, *Facing up to the American Dream: Race, Class, and the Soul of the Nation* (Princeton, NJ: Princeton University Press, 1995).

Hoffman, Martin L., "Empathy and Prosocial Behavior," in M. Lewis, J. M. Haviland-Jones, and L. Feldman Barrett, eds., *Handbook of Emotions*, pp. 441–55.

Hoffmann, Stanley, ed., *Conditions of World Order* (New York: Simon & Schuster, 1970).

Holland, John H., *Emergence: From Chaos to Order* (New York: Basic Books, 1998).

Holmes, Geoffrey, *Augustan England: Professions, State and Society, 1680–1730* (London: Allen & Unwin, 1982).

The Electorate and the National Will (London: Wilson, 1976).

Homans, George C., *Social Behavior: Its Elementary Forms*, rev. ed. (New York: Harcourt, Brace, Jovanovich, 1974 [1961]).

Homer, *Iliad*, trans. Robert Fagles (New York: Viking, 1990).

Odyssey, trans. Robert Fagles (New York: Viking, 1990).

Homer-Dixon, Thomas, *Environment, Scarcity, and Violence* (Princeton, NJ: Princeton University Press, 1999).

Honig, Bonnie, "'Declarations of Independence: Arendt and Derrida on the Problem of Founding a Republic," *American Political Science Review* 85, no. 1 (1991), pp. 97–113.

Democracy and the Foreigner (Princeton, NJ: Princeton University Press, 2001).

Political Theory and the Displacement of Politics (Ithaca, NY: Cornell University Press, 1993).

Hont, Istvan, *Jealousy of Trade: International Competition and the Nation-State in Historical Perspective* (Cambridge, MA: Harvard University Press, 2005).

Hont, Istvan and Michael Ignatieff, eds., *Wealth and Virtue: The Shaping of Political Economy in the Scottish Enlightenment* (Cambridge: Cambridge University Press, 1983).

Horkheimer, Max and Theodor W. Adorno, *Dialectic of Enlightenment* (Stanford, CA: Stanford University Press, 2002).

Horowitz, Donald, *Ethnic Groups in Conflict* (Berkeley, CA: University of California Press, 1985).

Horrocks, Roger and Nick Perry, *Television in New Zealand: Programming the Nation* (Auckland: Oxford University Press, 2004).

Horvath, Agnes, Bjørn Thomassen, and Harald Wydra, "Introduction: Liminality and Cultures of Change," *International Political Anthropology* 2, no. 1 (2009), pp. 3–4.

Hoyt, P. D., "The 'Rogue State' Image in American Foreign Policy," *Global Society* 14, no. 2 (2000), pp. 475–93.

Hsu, Jennifer Y. J., *State of Exchange: Migrant NGOs and the Chinese Government* (Vancouver: University of British Columbia Press, 2017).

Hsueh, Roselyn, *China's Regulatory State: A New Strategy for Globalization* (Ithaca, NY: Cornell University Press, 2011).

Huang, Xian, "Four Worlds of Welfare: Understanding Subnational Variation in Chinese Social Health Insurance," *China Quarterly*, no. 222 (2015), pp. 449–74.

Huang, Yasheng, "Democratize or Die: Why China's Communists Face Reform or Revolution," *Foreign Affairs* 92, no. 1 (2013), pp. 47–54.

Huch, Ricarda, *The Last Summer*, trans. Jaime Bulloch (London: Peirene, 2017).

Hughes, Lindsey, *Peter the Great: A Biography* (New Haven, CT: Yale University Press, 2002).

Hull, Isabel V., *Absolute Destruction: Military Culture and the Practices of War in Imperial Germany* (Ithaca, NY: Cornell University Press, 2005).

Hume, David, *Enquiries Concerning Human Understanding and Concerning the Principles of Morals*, ed. P. H. Nidditch (Oxford: Oxford University Press, 1975).
   History of England, (Indianapolis, IN: Liberty Fund, 1985), vol. II.
   "Hume, 'Of the Liberty of the Press,'" in Knud Haakonssen, ed., *Hume, Political Essays* (Cambridge: Cambridge University Press, 1994), pp. 1–3.
   A Treatise of Human Nature, ed. P. H. Nidditch, 2nd ed. revised (Oxford: Oxford University Press, 1978).

Hunt, Lynn, "The French Revolution in Global Context," in David Armitage and Sanjay Subrahmanyam, eds., *The Age of Revolutions in a Global Context, c. 1760–1840* (Basingstoke: Palgrave Macmillan, 2010), pp. 20–36.

Hunter, James Davison, *Culture Wars: The Struggle to Define America* (New York: Basic Books, 1992).

Huntington, Samuel P., *The Third Wave: Democratization in the Late Twentieth Century* (Norman, OK: University of Oklahoma Press, 1991).
   Who Are We? The Challenges to America's National Identity (New York: Simon & Schuster, 2004).

Hurka, Thomas, *Drawing Moral: Essays in Ethical Theory* (Oxford: Oxford University Press, 2011).

Hurrelmann, A., Schneider, S. and Jens Steffek, "Conclusion: Legitimacy – Making Sense of an Essentially Contested Concept," in Achim Hurrelmann, Stefan Schneider, and Jens Steffek, eds., *Legitimacy in an Age of Global Politics* (London: Palgrave Macmillan, 2007), pp. 29–237.

Huxley, Aldous, *Brave New World* (New York: Modern Library, 1956 [1932]).
   Island (New York: Harper & Row, 1962).

Ikenberry, H. John, *After Victory: Institutions, Strategic Restraint and the Rebuilding of Order After Major Wars* (Princeton, NJ: Princeton University Press, 2001).

Ikenberry, John G. and Charles A. Kupchan, "Socialization and Hegemonic Power," *International Organization* 44, no. 3 (1990), pp. 283–315.

Inayatullah, Naeem and David L. Blaney, *International Relations and the Problem of Difference* (New York: Routledge, 2004).

Inglehardt, Ronald, *Culture Shift in Advanced Industrial Society* (Princeton, NJ: Princeton University Press, 1999).

Inglehart, Ronald, *The Silent Revolution: Changing Values and Political Styles among Western Publics* (Princeton, NJ: Princeton University Press, 1977).

"Trust, Well-Being and Democracy," in Mark Warren, ed., *Democracy and Trust* (New York: Cambridge University Press, 1999), pp. 88–120.

Inglehart, Ronald and Hans D. Klingemann, "Party Identification, Ideological Preference and the Left-Right Dimension among Western Mass Publics," in Ian Budge, Ivor Crewe, and Dennis Farlie, eds., *Party Identification and Beyond: Representations of Voting and Party Competition* (London: John Wiley & Sons, 1976), pp. 243–76.

Inglehart, Ronald and Scott Flanagan, "Value Change in Industrial Societies," *American Political Science Review* 81, no. 1 (1987), pp. 289–31.

Inikori, Joseph E., *Africans and the Industrial Revolution in England: A Study in International Trade and Economic Development* (Cambridge: Cambridge University Press, 2002).

Inwood, Stephen, *A History of London* (London: Macmillan, 1998).

Isaac, Jeffrey C., *Democracy in Dark Times* (Ithaca, NY: Cornell University Press, 1998).

Isen, A. M. "Some Ways in Which Positive Affect Influences Decision Making and Problem Solving," in M. Lewis, J. M. Haviland-Jones, and L. Feldman Barrett, eds., *Handbook of Emotions*, pp. 549–73.

Isen, A. M., T. Shalker, M. S. Clark, and L Karp, "Affect, Accessibility of Material and Behavior: A Cognitive Loop?" *Journal of Personality and Social Psychology* 36 (1978), pp. 1–12.

Israel, Jonathan I., ed., *The Anglo-Dutch Moment: Essays on the Glorious Revolution and its World Impact* (Cambridge: Cambridge University Press, 1991).

Revolutionary Ideas: An Intellectual History of the French Revolution (Princeton, NJ: Princeton University Press, 2014).

Iyengar, Shanto and Masha Krupenkin, "The Strengthening of Partisan Affect," *Political Psychology* 39, Issue Supplement (2018), pp. 201–18.

Izard, C. E., *Human Emotions* (New York: Plenum, 1977).

Jackson, Patrick Thaddeus, "Production of Facts: Ideal-Typification and the Preservation of Politics," in R. Lebow, *Max Weber and International Relations*, pp. 79–96.

Jackson, Robert, *Classical and Modern Thought in International Relations: From Anarchy to Cosmopolis* (Basingstoke: Palgrave Macmillan, 2005).

Jacob, François, "Evolution and Tinkering," *Science* 196 (1977), pp. 1161–66.

Jaffee, S. N., *Thucydides and the Outbreak of War* (Oxford: Oxford University Press, 2017).

Jalal, Ayesha, *Democracy and Authoritarianism in South Asia: A Comparative and Historical Perspective* (Cambridge: Cambridge University Press, 1995).

The Struggle for Pakistan: A Muslim Homeland and Global Politics (Cambridge, MA: Harvard University Press, 2014).

Jancar-Webster, Barbara, "Environmental Movement and Social Change in the Transition Countries," *Environmental Politics* 7, no. 1 (1998), pp. 69–90.

Janowitz, Morris, "Sociological Theory and Social Control," *American Journal of Sociology* 81 (1975), pp. 82–108.

Jarausch, Konrad H., *After Hitler: Civilizing the Germans, 1945–95* (Oxford: Oxford University Press, 2006).

Jarrett, Mark, *The Congress of Vienna and Its Legacy: War and Great Power Diplomacy after Napoleon* (London: IB Tauris, 2013).

Jasso, G. and P. H. Rossi, "Distributive Justice and Earned Income," *American Sociological Review* 42, no. 4 (1977), pp. 639–51.

Jeffrey, Renee, *Evil and International Relations Human Suffering in an Age of Terror* (Houndsmills: Palgrave Macmillan, 2008).

Jeffries, Stuart, *Grand Hotel Abyss: The Lives of the Frankfurt School* (London: Verso, 2016).

Jencks, C., "The Social Basis of Unselfishness," in H. J. Gans, N. Glazer, J. Gusfield, and C. Jencks, eds., *On the Making of Americans: Essays in Honor of David Riesman* (Philadelphia, PA: University of Pennsylvania Press, 1979), pp. 63–86.

Jervis, Robert, *Perception and Misperception in International Relations* (Princeton, NJ: Princeton University Press, 1976).

Jervis, Robert, Richard Ned Lebow, and Janice Gross Stein, *Psychology and Deterrence* (Baltimore, MD: Johns Hopkins University Press, 1984).

Jiang, Shenghong, *Wangluo yaoyan yingdui yu yuqing yindao (Internet Rumor Response and Public Opinion Guidance)* (Beijing: Shehui Kexue Wenxian Chubanshe, 2013).

Johansen, Dorothy O., *Empire of the Columbia: A History of the Pacific Northwest*, 2nd ed. (New York: Harper & Row, 1967).

Johnson, A. Ross and R. Eugene Parta, eds., *Cold War Broadcasting: Impact on the Soviet Union and Eastern Europe* (New York: Central European University Press, 2010).

Johnson, Catherine, Timothy Dowd, and Cecelia Ridgeway, "Legitimacy as a Social Process," *Annual Review of Sociology* 32 (2006), pp. 53–78.

Johnson, James H., *Listening in Paris: A Cultural History* (Berkeley and Los Angeles, CA: University of California Press, 1995).

Jones, Adam, *Genocide: A Comprehensive Introduction*, 2nd ed. (London: Routledge, 2010).

Jones, Barry, *Political Space: New Frontiers of Change and Governance in a Globalizing World* (Albany, NY: State University of New York Press, 2002), pp. 151–69.

Jones, Colin, *The Great Nation: France from Louis XV to Napoleon, 1715–99* (New York: Columbia University Press, 2002).

Jones, E. I., *Agriculture and the Industrial Revolution* (Oxford: Oxford University Press, 1974).

Jones, Eric, *The European Miracle: Environments, Economies and Geopolitics in the History of Europe and Asia* (Cambridge: Cambridge University Press, 1981).

Jones, Mark, *Founding Weimar: Violence and the German Revolution of 1918–1919* (Cambridge: Cambridge University Press, 2016).

Jones, Susan Stedman, *Durkheim Reconsidered* (Cambridge: Polity, 2001).

Jordan, William, *Louis IX and the Challenge of the Crusade* (Princeton, NJ: Princeton University Press, 1979).

Jost, John T., Jack Glaser, Arie W. Kruglanski, and Frank J. Sulloway, "Political Conservatism as Motivated Social Cognition," *Psychological Bulletin* 129 (2003), pp. 339–75.

Jowitt, Kenneth, *New World Disorder: The Leninist Extinction* (Berkeley and Los Angeles, CA: University of California Press, 1992).

Joyce, James, *Ulysses* (New York: Oxford University Press, 2011).

Judt, Tony, *Postwar: A History of Europe Since 1945* (London: Vintage, 2010).

Jung, Courtney, Ellen Lust-Okar, and Ian Shapiro, "Problems and Prospects for Democratic Settlements South Africa as a Model for the Middle East and Northern Ireland?" in S. N. Kalyvas, I. Shapiro, and T. Masoud, *Order, Conflict, and Violence*, pp. 139–96.

Justice, Steven, *Writing and Rebellion: England in 1381* (Berkeley, CA: University of California Press, 1994).

Kaeuper, Richard W., *War, Justice and Public Order: England and France in the Later Middle Ages* (Oxford: Oxford University Press, 1988).

Kafka, Franz, *The Castle*, trans. Mark Harman (New York: Schocken Books, 1998).

Kalyvas, Andreas and Ira Katznelson, "Adam Ferguson Returns: Liberalism Through a Glass, Darkly," *Political Theory* 26, no. 2 (1998), pp. 173–97.

Kalyvas, Stathis N., *The Logic of Violence in Civil War* (New York: Cambridge University Press, 2006).

Kalyvas, Stathis N., Ian Shapiro, and Tarek Masoud, "Introduction," in S. N. Kalyvas, I. Shapiro, and T. Masoud, *Order, Conflict, and Violence*, pp. 1–16.

eds., *Order, Conflict, and Violence* (Cambridge: Cambridge University Press, 2008).

Kang, David, *China Rising: Peace, Power and Order in East Asia* (New York: Columbia University Press, 2010).

East Asia Before the West: Five Centuries of Trade and Tribute (New York: Columbia University Press, 2012).

"Hierarchy and Legitimacy in International Systems: The Tribute System in Early Modern East Asia," *Security Studies* 19, no. 4 (2010), pp. 591–622.

Kant, Immanuel, "An Answer to the Question: What is Enlightenment?" in H. Reiss, *Kant's Political Writings*, pp. 54–60.

Anthropology from a Pragmatic Point of View, ed. Robert Louden (Cambridge: Cambridge University Press, 2006).

"Conjectures on the Beginning of Human History," in H. Reiss, *Kant's Political Writings*, pp. 221–34.

"Idea for a Universal History with a Cosmopolitan Purpose," in H. Reiss, *Kant's Political Writings*, pp. 41–53.

Kant's Political Writings, 2nd ed., ed. Hans Reiss, trans. H. B. Nisbet (Cambridge: Cambridge University Press, 1991).

"Perpetual Peace," in H. Reiss, *Kant's Political Writings*, pp. 41–53.

Karnow, Stanley, *Vietnam: A History*, 2nd ed. (New York: Penguin, 1997).

Kasarda, John and Morris Janowitz, "Community Attachment in Mass Society," *American Sociological Review* 39 (1974), pp. 328–39.

Kasfir, Nelson, "Rebel Governance – Constructing a Field of Inquiry: Definitions, Scope, Patterns, Orders, Causes," in Arana Arjona, Nelson Kasfir, and Zachariah Mampilly, *Rebel Governance in War* (Cambridge: Cambrige University Press, 2015), pp. 11–46.

Kasfir, Nelson, Georg Frerks, and Niels Terpstra, "Introduction: Armed Groups and Multi-layered Governance," as yet unpublished paper, September 2017.

Katznelson, Ira, *Fear Itself: The New Deal and the Origins of Our Time* (New York: Liveright, 2013).

Kaufman, Stuart J., *Nationalist Passions* (Ithaca, NY: Cornell University Press, 2015).

Kavka, Gregory, "Nuclear Weapons and World Government," *Monist* 70, no. 3 (1987), pp. 298–315.

Keal, Paul, *European Conquest and the Rights of Indigenous Peoples: The Moral Backwardness of International Society* (Cambridge: Cambridge University Press, 2003).

Kearney, A. T., "Globalization's Last Hurrah? *Foreign Policy*, no. 128 (January/February 2002), pp. 38–51.

Keating, Michael, "Class, Sector, and Nation: Support for Minority Nationalism Among Peak Interest Groups in Four Western European Countries," *Territory, Politics, Governance* 2, no. 3 (2014), pp. 322–37.

"Must Minority Nationalism Be Tribal? A Study of Quebec, Catalonia and Scotland," in Kenneth Christie, *Ethnic Conflict, Tribal Politics: A Global Perspective* (Richmond, UK: Curzon Press, 1999).

Keating, Michael and Liesbet Hooghe, *By-Passing the Nation State? Regions and the EU Policy Process* (London: Routledge, 2006).

Kebschull, Harvey G., "Operation 'Just Missed': Lessons from Failed Coup Attempts," *Armed Forces and Society* 20 (Summer 1994), pp. 565–79.

Keck, Margaret and Kathryn Sikkink, *Activists Beyond Borders: Advocacy Networks in International Politics* (Ithaca, NY: Cornell University Press, 1998).

Keeler, John T. S., "Agricultural Power in the European Community: Explaining the Fate of CAP and GATT Negotiations," *Comparative Politics* 28, no. 2 (1996), pp. 127–49.

Keeley, Lawrence, H., *War Before Civilization* (New York: Oxford University Press, 1966).

Kehr, Eckart, *Der Primat der Innenpolitik* (Berlin: Walter de Gruyter, 1965).

Keliher, Macabe and Hsinchao Wu, "Corruption, Anticorruption, and the Transformation of Political Culture in Contemporary China," *Journal of Asian Studies* 75, no.1 (2016), pp. 5–18.

Kelley, Judith G., *Scorecard Diplomacy* (Cambridge: Cambridge University Press, 2017).

Kelly, Robert E., "A 'Confucian Long Peace' in pre-Western East Asia?" *European Journal of International Relations* 18, no. 3 (2012), 407–30.

Kempadoo, Kamala and Jo Dezema, *Global Sex Workers: Rights, Resistance, and Redefinition* (New York: Routledge, 1998).

Kenney, Padraic, *A Carnival of Revolution: Central Europe 1989* (Princeton, NJ: Princeton University Press, 2003).

Keohane, Robert O., *After Hegemony* (Princeton, NJ: Princeton University Press, 1984).

"Governance in a Partially Globalized World: Presidential Address," *American Political Science Review* 95, no. 1 (2001), pp. 1–12.

International Institutions and State Power: Essays in International Relations Theory (Boulder, CO: Westview Press, 1989).

Keohane, Robert O. and Lisa Martin "The Promise of Institutionalist Theory," *International Security* 20, no. 1 (Summer 1995), pp. 39–52.

Kidd, Colin, "Integration, Patriotism and Nationalism," in H. T. Dickinson, *Companion to Eighteenth-Century Britain*, pp. 369–80.

Kindleberger, Charles P., "Dominance and Leadership in the International Economy: Exploitation, Public Goods, and Free Rides," *International Studies Quarterly* 25, no. 2 (1981), pp. 242–54.

Manias, Panics and Crashes: A History of Financial Crises (New York: Basic Books, 1978).

King, Gary, Jennifer Pan, and Margaret E. Roberts, "How Censorship in China Allows Government Criticism but Silences Collective Expression," *American Political Science Review* 10, no. 2 (2013), pp. 326–43.

"How the Chinese Government Fabricates Social Media Posts for Strategic Distraction, not Engaged Argument," *American Political Science Review*, 111, no. 3 (2017), pp. 484–501.

King, Martin Luther Jr., "Letter from Birmingham City Jail," in James Melvin Washington, ed., *A Testament of Hope: The Essential Writings and Speeches of Martin Luther King, Jr.* (New York: Harper Collins, 1990), pp. 289–302.

Kinninmont, Jane, "Unrest in the Arab World: Why the 2011 Uprisings Still Matter," *International Affairs* 91, no. 5 (2015), pp. 1141–49.

Kissinger, Henry, *World Order: Reflections on the Character of Nations and the Course of History* (London: Allen Lane, 2014).

Kitcher, Philip, "Ethics and Evolution: How to Get There from Here," in de Waal et al., *Primates and Philosophers*, pp. 120–39.

Kitschelt, Herbert, and Staf Hellemans, "The Left-Right Semantics and The New Politics Cleavage, *Comparative Political Studies* 23 (1989), pp. 210–38.

Klein, Lawrence, *Shaftesbury and the Culture of Politeness: Moral Discourse and Cultural Politics in Early Eighteenth-Century England* (Cambridge: Cambridge University Press, 1994).

"The Third Earl of Shaftesbury and the Progress of Politeness," *Eighteenth-Century Studies* 18, no. 2 (1984–85), pp. 186–214.

Kleinman, Mark A. R., *Marijuana: Costs of Abuse, Costs of Control* (New York: Greenwood, 1989).

Klemperer, Victor, *Language of the Third Reich: LTI – Lingua Tertii Imperii* (New York: Continuum 2006 [1947]).

Klotbuecher, Sascha, Peter Laessig, Qin Jiangmei, and Susanne Weigelin-Schwiedrzik, "What is New in the 'New Rural Co-operative Medical

System'? An Assessment of One Kazak County of the Xinjiang Uyghur Autonomous Region," *China Quarterly*, no. 201 (2010), pp. 38–57.

Kloth, Hans Michael, *Vom "Zettelfalten"bis zum freien Wählen: Die Demokratisierung der DDR 1989/90 und die "Wahlfrage"* (Berlin: Ch. Links Verlag, 2000).

Kluegel, James R. and Eliot R. Smith, *Beliefs about Inequality: Americans'View of What Is and What Ought to Be* (New York: Aldine, 1986).

Knauft, Bruce B., "Violence and Sociality in Human Evolution," *Current Anthropology* 32 (1991), pp. 391–428.

Knoch, Daria, Alvaro Pascual-Leone, Kaspar Meyer, Valerie Treyer, and Ernst Fehr, "Diminishing Reciprocal Fairness by Disrupting the Right Prefrontal Cortex," *Science* 314, no. 5800 (2006), pp. 829–32.

Koesel, Karrie, *Religion and Authoritarianism: Cooperation, Conflict, and the Consequences* (New York: Cambridge University Press, 2014).

Kohn, Hans, *The Idea of Nationalism: A Study in its Origins and Background* (New York: Macmillan, 1944).

Kohn, Richard H., "History at Risk: The Case of the Enola Gay," in Edward T. Blumenthal and Tom Engelhard, eds., *History Wars: The Enola Gay and Other Battles for the American Past* (New York: Henry Holt, 1996), pp. 140–71.

Konow, James, Tatsuyoshi Saijo, and Kenju Akai, "Equity versus Equality," Munich Pesonal RePEc Archive, 2016, December 1 2016, https://mpra.ub.uni-muenchen.de/75376/

Konstan, David, *The Emotions of the Ancient Greeks: Studies in Aristotle and Classical Literature* (Toronto: University of Toronto Press, 2006).

Friendship in the Classical World (Cambridge: Cambridge University Press, 1997).

"Philia in Euripides' *Electra*," *Philologos* 129 (1985), pp. 176–85.

Pity Transformed (London: Duckworth, 2004).

Konstan, David and N. Keith Rutter, *Envy, Spite and Jealousy: The Rivalrous Emotions in Ancient Greece* (Edinburgh: Edinburgh University Press, 2003).

Kornhauser, Ruth, *Social Sources of Delinquency* (Chicago, IL: University of Chicago Press, 1978).

Korsgaard, Christine M., "Morality and the Distinctiveness of Human Action," in de Waal et al., *Primates and Philosophers*, pp. 98–129.

Koselleck, Reinhart, *Preussen zwischen Reform und Revolution: Allgemeines Landrecht, Verwaltung und Soziale Bewegung von 1791 bis 1848*, 3rd ed. (Stuttgart: Ernst Klett, 1981).

Koskenniemi, Martti, *The Gentle Civilizer of Nations: The Rise and Fall of International Law, 1870–1960* (Cambridge: Cambridge University Press, 2001).

Kotkin, Stephen, *Stalin, vol. II: Waiting for Hitler* (New York: Penguin Random House, 2017).

Kratochwil, Friedrich V., *International Order and Foreign Policy: A Theoretical Sketch of Post War International Politics* (Boulder, CO: Westview Press, 1978).

"Reflections on the 'Critical' in Critical Theory," *Review of International Studies* 33 (2007), pp. 25–46.

Rules, Norms, and Decisions: On the Conditions of Practical and Legal Reasoning in International Relations and Domestic Affairs (New York: Cambridge University Press, 1989).

Kroeber, Arthur R., *China's Economy: What Everyone Needs to Know* (New York: Oxford University Press, 2016).

Krugman, Paul, *The Great Unraveling: From Boom to Bust in Three Scandalous Years* (New York: Penguin, 2003).

Kuhn, Teresa, "Individual Transnationalism, Globalisation and Euroscepticism: An Empirical Test of Deutsch's Transactionalist Theory," *European Journal of Political Research* 50, no. 6 (2011), pp. 811–37.

Kutulas, Judy, "Who Rules the Roost? Sitcom Family Dynamics from the Cleavers to the Osbournes," in Mary Dalton and Laura Linder, eds., *The Sitcom Reader: America Viewed and Skewed* (Albany, NY: State University of New York Press, 2005), pp. 49–59.

Kwak, James, *Economism: Bad Economics and the Rise of Inequality* (New York: Pantheon, 2017).

Kymlicka, Will, *Contemporary Political Philosophy: An Introduction*, 2nd ed. (Oxford: Oxford University Press, 2002).

   Liberalism, Community and Culture (Oxford: Oxford University Press, 1989).

   Multicultural Citizenship (Oxford: Oxford University Press, 1995).

Ladurie, Le Roy, *The Ancien Régime: A History of France, 1610–1774*, trans. Mark Greengrass (Oxford: Blackwell, 1991).

Lake, David A., "Rightful Rules: Authority, Order, and the Foundations of Global Governance," *International Studies Quarterly* 54, no. 3 (2010), pp. 587–612.

Lake, David A. and Donald Rothchild, "Spreading Fear: The Genesis of Transnational Ethnic Conflict," in David A. Lake and Donald Rothchild, eds., *Ethnic Fears and Global Engagement: The International Spread and Management of Ethnic Conflict* (Princeton, NJ: Princeton University Press, 1996).

   "Containing Fear: The Origins and Management of Ethnic Conflict," *International Security* 21, no. 2 (1997), pp. 41–75.

Lake, David A. and Donald Rothshild, eds., *The International Spread of Ethnic Conflict: Fear, Diffusion and Escalation* (Princeton, NJ: Princeton University Press, 1998).

Lambie, J. A. and A. J. Marcel, "Consciousness and the Varieties of Emotion Experience: A Theoretical Framework," *Psychological Review* 109 (2002), pp. 219–59.

Lamm, Helmut and Thomas Schwinger, "Norms Concerning Distributive Justice: Are Needs Taken into Consideration in Allocation Decisions?" *Social Psychology Quarterly* 43 (1980), pp. 425–29.

Landau, Norma, *The Justices of the Peace, 1769–1760* (Berkeley, CA: University of California Press, 1984).

Landes, David S., *The Wealth and Poverty of Nations* (New York: Norton, 1998).

Láng-Pickvance, Katy, *Democracy and Environmental Movements in Eastern Europe: A Comparative Study of Hungary and Russia* (Boulder, CO: Westview Press, 1998).

Langford, Paul, *A Polite and Commercial People: England 1727–1783* (Oxford: Oxford University Press, 1989).

   Public Life and the Propertied Englishman, 1689–1798 (Oxford: Oxford University Press, 1991).

Langton, John, "The Industrial Revolution and the Regional Geography of England," *Transactions of the British Institute of Geographers* 9 (1984), pp. 145–67.

Lanni, Adriaan, "Transitional Justice in Ancient Athens: A Case Study," *University of Pennsylvania Journal of International Law* 32, no. 1 (2011), pp. 551–94.

Lasch, Christopher, *The Revolt of the Elites and the Betrayal of Democracy* (New York: Norton, 1996).

Lassman, Peter and Ronald Speirs, "Introduction" in *Weber*, pp. vii–xxv.

Lasswell, Harold, *Politics: Who Gets What, When, How* (New York: McGraw-Hill, 1936 and 1952).

Lattimore, Owen, "The Frontier in History," in Owen Lattimore, ed., *Studies in Frontier History: Collected Papers, 1928–1958* (Oxford: Oxford University Press, 1962), pp. 469–91.

Lazarus, R. S., *Emotion and Adaptation* (New York: Oxford University Press, 1991).

Leach, William, *Country of Exiles* (New York: Pantheon Books, 1999).

Leahy, Michael, *Covenant of Liberty: The Ideological Origins of the Tea Party Movement.* (New York: HarperCollins, 2012).

Lebow, David Bohmer, "Leviathans Unbound: Irrationalist Political Thought in Interwar United States and Germany," *Journal of Political Ideologies* (forthcoming).

Lebow, David Bohmer and Richard Ned Lebow, "Weber's Tragic Legacy," in R. Lebow, *Max Weber and International Relations*, pp. 172–99.

Lebow, Katherine, *Unfinished Utopia: Nowa Huta, Stalinism, and Polish Society, 1949–56* (Ithaca, NY: Cornell University Press, 2013).

Lebow, Richard Ned, *Archduke Franz Ferdinand Lives! A World Without World War I* (New York: Palgrave Macmillan, 2014).

Avoiding War, Making Peace (London: Palgrave Macmillan, 2017).

Between Peace and War: The Nature of International Crisis (Baltimore, MD: Johns Hopkins University Press, 1981).

Constructing Cause in International Relations (Cambridge: Cambridge University Press, 2014).

A Cultural Theory of International Relations (Cambridge: Cambridge University Press, 2003).

"Darwin and International Relations," *International Security*, 21, No. 2 (Autumn, 1996), pp. 41–75.

"David Hume," unpublished ms.

"Divided Ireland," in Gregory Henderson, Richard Ned Lebow and John G. Stoessinger, eds., *Divided Nations in a Divided* (New York: David McKay, 1974), pp. 197–266.

Forbidden Fruit: Counterfactuals and International Relations (Princeton, NJ: Princeton University Press, 2010).

"Generational Learning and Foreign Policy," *International Journal* 40 (Autumn 1985), pp. 556–85.

"Greeks, Neuroscience and International Relations," in Daniel Jacobi and Annette Freyberg-Inan, eds., *Human Beings in International Relations*, (Cambridge: Cambridge University Press, 2015), pp. 132–55.

"MaxWeber and Knowledge," in *Max Weber and International Relations*, pp. 40–78.
"Max Weber and International Relations," in *Max Weber and International Relations*, pp. 10–39.
ed., *Max Weber and International Relations* (Cambridge: Cambridge University Press, 2017).
National Identities and International Relations (Cambridge: Cambridge University Press, 2016).
Nuclear Crisis Management: A Dangerous Illusion (Ithaca, NY: Cornell University Press, 1987).
The Politics and Ethics of Identity: In Search of Ourselves (Cambridge: Cambridge University Press, 2012).
"Power, Persuasion and Justice," *Millennium* 33, no. 3 (2005), pp. 551–82.
Self-Interest in Business and Politics: From Tocqueville to Trump (London: Palgrave Macmillan, 2018).
"Thucydides and Order," in Christian R. Thauer and Christian Wendt, eds., *Thucydides and Political Order: Lessons of Governance and the History of the Peloponnesian War* (London: Palgrave Macmillan, 2017), pp. 21–54.
The Tragic Vision of Politics: Ethics, Interests and Orders (Cambridge: Cambridge University Press, 2008).
"Understanding the End of the Cold War as a Non-Linear Confluence," in R. Herrmann and R. Lebow, *Ending the Cold War*, pp. 189–217.
"World War I: Recent Historical Scholarship and IR Theory?" *International Relations*, 28 no. 2 (2014), pp. 245–50.
Why Nations Fight (Cambridge: Cambridge University Press, 2010).
"You Can't Keep a Bad Idea Down: Evolutionary Psychology and International Relations," *International Politics Reviews*, 1, no. 1 (2013), pp. 1–9.
Lebow, Richard Ned and Janice Gross Stein, "Beyond Deterrence," *Journal of Social Issues* 43 no. 4 (1987), pp. 5–71.
"Beyond Deterrence: Building Better Theory," *Journal of Social Issues* 43, no. 4 (1987), pp. 155–69.
"Conventional and Nuclear Deterrence: Are the Lessons Transferable?" *Journal of Social Issues* 43, no. 4 (1987), pp.171–91.
"The End of the Cold War as a Non-Linear Confluence," in Richard K. Herrmann and Richard Ned Lebow, eds., *Ending the Cold War: Interpretations, Causation, and the Study of International Relations* (New York: Palgrave MacMillan, 2004), pp. 189–218.
We All Lost the Cold War (Princeton, NJ: Princeton University Press, 1994).
When Does Deterrence Succeed and How Do We Know? co-authored with Janice Gross Stein (Ottawa: Canadian Institute for International Peace and Security, 1990).
Lebow, Richard Ned and Benjamin Valentino, "Lost in Transition: A Critique of Power Transition Theories," *International Relations*, 23, no. 3 (September 2009), pp. 389–410.
Le Carré, John, *A Small Town in Germany* (London: Heineman, 1968).
Le Doux, J. E., *The Emotional Brain* (New York: Simon & Schuster, 1996).
Lee, Namhee, *The Making of Mingjung: Democracy and the Politics of Representation in South Korea* (Ithaca, NY: Cornell University Press, 2007).

Lee, Richard B., *The Dobe Ju/'hoansi*, 3rd ed. (Toronto: Wandsworth, 2003).

Lee, Stephen M., "Parliament, Parties and Elections," in H. T. Dickinson, *Companion to Eighteenth-Century Britain*, pp. 70–80.

Lees, Lyn Hollen, *The Solidarities of Strangers: The English Poor Law and the People, 1700–1948* (Cambridge: Cambridge University Press, 1998).

Lei, Xuchuan and Jie Lu, "Revisiting Political Weariness in China's Public Opinion Surveys: Experimental Evidence on Responses to Politically-Sensitive Questions," *Journal of Contemporary China* 26, no. 104 (2017), pp. 231–32.

Lenin, V. I., *State and Revolution* (New York: International Publishers, 1932).

Lenman, Bruce, *The Jacobite Risings in Britain* (London: Methuen, 1980).

Lepore, Jill, *The Whites of Their Eyes: The Tea Party's Revolution and the Battle over American History* (Princeton, NJ: Princeton University Press, 2010).

Lerner, Melvin J., "The Justice Motive: 'Equity' and 'Parity' among Children," *Journal of Personality and Social Psychology* 29 (1974), pp. 339–50.

Lerner, Melvin J. and R. R. Lichtman, "Effects of Perceived Norms on Attitudes and Altruistic Behavior Toward a Dependent Other," *Journal of Personality and Social Psychology* 9 (1968), pp. 226–32.

Lerner, Melvin J., P. J. Goldberg, and Philip A. Tetlock, "Sober Second Thoughts: The Effects of Accountability, Anger, and Authoritarianism on Attributions of Responsibility," *Personality and Social Psychology Bulletin* 24 (1998), pp. 563–74.

Lerner, Melvin J. and Gerald Mikula, eds., *Entitlement and the Affection Bond: Justice in Close Relationships* (New York: Plenum, 2013).

Lesieur, Henry R., "Compulsive Gambling," *Society* 29, no. 4 (1992), pp. 43–50.

Leuchtenberg, William E., *Franklin Roosevelt and the New Deal: 1932–1940* (New York: Harper, 2009).

Leventhal, George S., "The Distribution of Rewards and Resources in Groups and Organizations," in Leonard Berkowitz and E. Walster, eds., *Advances in Experimental Psychology* 9 (New York: Academic Press, 1976), pp. 91–131.

"Fairness in Social Relationships," in J. W. Thibaut, J. T. Spence, and R. C. Carson, eds., *Contemporary Topics in Social Psychology* (Morristown, NJ: General Learning Press, 1976), pp. 211–40.

Lévesque, Jacques, *The Enigma of 1989: The USSR and the Liberation of Eastern Europe*, trans. Keith Martin (Berkeley, CA: University of California Press, 1997).

LeVine, R. A. and D. T. Campbell, *Ethnocentrism: Theories of Conflicts, Ethnic Attitudes and Group Behavior* (New York: Wiley, 1972).

Levinger, Matthew, *Enlightened Nationalism: The Transformation of Prussian Political Culture, 1806–1848* (New York: Oxford University Press, 2000).

Lewontin, Richard, *Biology as Ideology* (New York: Harper Collins, 1991).

Li, Eric, "Life of the Party: The Post-Democratic Future Begins in China," *Foreign Affairs* 92, no. 1 (2013), pp. 33–46.

Li, Lianjiang, "Direct Township Elections," in Elizabeth J. Perry and Merle Goldman, eds., *Grassroots Political Reform in Contemporary China* (Cambridge, MA: Harvard University Press, 2007), pp. 97–116.

"Reassessing Trust in the Central Government: Evidence from Five National Surveys," *China Quarterly*, no. 225 (2016), pp. 100–21.

Lieven, Dominic, *The Aristocracy in Europe, 1815–1914* (London: Palgrave Macmillan, 1992).

The End of Tsarist Russia: The March to World War I and Revolution (London: Penguin, 2016).

Lind, E. A. and T. R. Tyler, *The Social Psychology of Procedural Justice* (New York: Plenum, 1988).

Lind, E. A., R. Kanfer, and P. C. Earley, "Voice Control and Procedural Justice: Instrumental and Noninstrumental Concerns in Fairness Judgments," *Journal of Personality and Social Psychology* 59 (1990), pp. 952–59.

Lindenberger, Thomas, "Tacit Minimal Consensus: The Always Precarious East German Dictatorship," in Paul Corner, ed., *Popular Opinion in Totalitarian Regimes: Fascism, Nazism, Communism* (Oxford: Oxford University Press, 2009), pp. 208–22.

Lindert, P. H. and J. G. Williamson, "Revising England's Social Tables 1688–1812," *Explorations in Economic History* 19 (1982), pp. 399–408.

Lineweaver, Charles H., Paul C. W. Davies, and Michael Ruse, *Complexity and the Arrow of Time* (Cambridge: Cambridge University Press, 2013).

Linklater and Hidemi Suganami, *The English School of International Relations: A Contemporary Assessment* (Cambridge: Cambridge University Press, 2006).

Linton, Ralph, *The Study of Man: An Introduction* (New York: Appleton-Century-Crofts, 1936).

Linz, Juan, *The Breakdown of Democratic Regime: Crises, Breakdown, and Requilibration. An Introduction* (Baltimore, MD: Johns Hopkins University Press, 1978).

Totalitarian and Authoritarian Regimes (London: Lynne Rienner, 2000).

Linz, Juan J. and Alfred Stepan, *Problems of Democratic Transition and Consolidation: Southern Europe, South America, and Post-Communist Europe* (Baltimore, MD: Johns Hopkins University Press, 1996).

Lipkus, I. M., C. Dalbert, and I. C. Siegler, "The Importance of Distinguishing the Belief in a Just World for Self Versus Others: Implications for Psychological Well-Being," *Personality and Social Psychology Bulletin* 22 (1996), pp. 666–77.

Lipset, Seymour Martin, *Political Man: The Social Bases of Politics* (Garden City, NY: Doubleday, 1960).

"The Psychology of Voting: An Analysis of Political Behavior," in Gardner Lindzey, ed., *Handbook of Social Psychology*, vol. 2 (Reading, MA: Addison-Wesley, 1954), pp. 1124–75.

Lipson, Charles, *Reliable Partners: How Democracies Have Made a Separate Peace* (Princeton, NJ: Princeton University Press, 2003).

Loader, Brian D., *The Governance of Cyberspace: Politics, Technology, and Global Restructuring* (London: Routledge, 1997).

Locke, John, "Draft of a Representation Containing a Scheme of Methods for the Employment of the Poor," in David Wootton, ed., *Political Writings* (New York: Mentor, 1993), pp. 446–61.

Two Treatises of Government (New York: Cambridge University Press, 1988).

Logevall, Fredrik, *Embers of War: The Fall of an Empire and the Making of America's War in Vietnam* (New York: Random House, 2014).

Long, G. T. and M. J. Lerner, "Deserving, the 'Personal Contract' and Altruistic Behavior by Children," *Journal of Personality and Social Psychology* 29 (1974), pp. 551–56.

Loraux, Nicole, *The Divided City: On Memory and Forgetting in Ancient Athens* (London: Zone Books, 2001).

Losos, Jonathan, *Impossible Destinies: How Predictable is Evolution?* (London: Allen Lane, 2017).

Love, Maryann Cusimano, ed., *Beyond Sovereignty: Issues for a Global Agenda* (Belmont, CA: Wadsworth/Thomson, 2003).

Love, Richard A., "The Cyberthreat Continuum," in M. C. Love, *Beyond Sovereignty*," pp. 195–218.

Lovejoy, Arthur O., *The Great Chain of Being: A Study of the History of an Idea* (Cambridge, MA: Harvard University Press, 1936).

Lü, Yusheng, *Yuenan guoqing baogao 2012 (2012 Annual Report on Vietnam's National Situation)* (Beijing: Shehui kexue wenxuan chubanshe, 2012).

Lubman, Stanley B., *Bird in a Cage: Legal Reform in China after Mao* (Stanford, CA: Stanford University Press, 1999).

Ludi, Regula, "Past as Present, Myth, or History? Discourses of Time and the Great Fatherland War," in R. Lebow, W. Kansteiner and C. Fogu, *The Politics of Memory in Postwar Europe*, pp. 210–48.

Luhmann, Nicholas, *Essays on Self-Reference* (New York: Columbia University Press, 1990).

Luhtanen, Rita and Jennifer Crocker, "A Collective Self-Esteem Scale: Self-Evaluation of One's Social Identity," *Personality and Social Psychology Bulletin* 18, no. 3 (1992), pp. 302–18.

Lukács, Georg, *History and Class Consciousness*, trans. Rodney Livingstone (Cambridge: MIT Press, 1971).

Lukes, Steven, *Emile Durkheim: His Life and Work* (Stanford, CA: Stanford University Press, 1973).

Lutz, Donald, "Toward a Theory of Constitutional Amendment," *American Political Science Review* 88, no. 2 (1994), pp. 355–70.

Luvaas, Jay, *The Military Legacy of the Civil War: The European Inheritance* (Chicago, IL: University of Chicago Press, 1959),

Lynch, Dierdre S., *Economy of Character: Novels, Market Culture, and the Business of Inner Meaning* (Chicago, IL: University of Chicago Press, 1998).

Ma, Shaohua, *Dong'ou 1989–1993* (Eastern Europe 1989–1993) (Xi'an: Sha'anxi Renmin Jiaoyu Chubanshe, 1993).

McAdam, Doug, John D. McCarthy, and Mayer N. Zald, eds., *Comparative Perspectives on Social Movements* (Cambridge: Cambridge University Press, 1996).

McAdam, Doug, Sidney Tarrow, and Charles Tilly, *The Dynamics of Contention* (Cambridge: Cambridge University Press, 2001).

McClary, Susan, "The Blasphemy of Talking Politics during Bach Year," in Susan McClary and Richard Leppert, eds., *Music and Society: The Politics of Composition* (Cambridge: Cambridge University Press, 1987), pp. 21–41.

McCloskey, Deidre Nansen, *Bourgeois Inequality: How Ideas, Not Capital or Institutions, Enriched the World* (Chicago, IL: University of Chicago Press, 2016).

McCloskey, Hebert and John Zaller, *The American Ethos: Public Attitudes Toward Capitalism and Democracy* (Cambridge, MA: Harvard University Press, 1984).

McDermott, Rose, "The Feeling of Rationality: The Meaning of Neuroscientific Advances for Political Science," *Perspectives in Politics* 2 (December 2004), pp. 691–706.

ed., *Special Issue of Political Psychology on prospect theory, and Risk-Taking in International Politics*, 25 (April 2004), pp. 147–312.

McDonogh, Gary Wray, "A Night at the Opera: Imagery, Patronage and Conflict, 1840–1940," in McDonogh, ed. *Catalonia: Images of an Urban Society* (Gainesville, FL: Florida University Press, 1986), pp. 54–71.

Good Families of Barcelona: A Social History of Power in the Industrial Era (Princeton, NJ: Princeton University Press, 1986).

McElwee, *William, The Art of War: Waterloo to Mons* (Bloomington, IN: Indiana University Press, 1974).

McFarland, E. W., *Ireland and Scotland in the Age of Revolution: Planting the Green Bough* (Edinburgh: Edinburgh University Press, 1994).

MacFarquhar, Roderick and Michael Schoenhals, *Mao's Last Revolution* (Cambridge, MA: Harvard University Press, 2006).

McGhee, George R., *Convergent Evolution: Limited Forms Most Beautiful* (Cambridge, MA: MIT Press, 2011).

McGrath, Charles Iver, *The Making of the Eighteenth Century Irish Constitution: Government, Parliament, and the Revenue* (Dublin: Four Courts, 2000).

McIntyre, *Giordano Bruno* (London: Macmillan, 1903).

McKay, Angus and A. Goodman, ed., *Impact of Humanism on Western Europe During the Renaissance* (London: Routledge, 2017).

McKendrick, Neil, John Brewer, and J. H. Plumb, eds., *The Birth of a Consumer Society: The Commercialization of Eighteenth Century England* (Indianapolis, Ind.: University of Indiana Press, 1982).

McKinlay, Robert D. and Richard Little, *Global Problems and World Order* (Madison, WI: University of Wisconsin Press, 1986).

McNally, Paddy, "Ireland: The Making of the 'Protestant Ascendancy,' 1688–1815," in H. T. Dickinson, *Companion to Eighteenth Century Britain*, pp. 403–13.

McNeese, Tim, *The Robber Barons and the Sherman Antitrust Act: Reshaping American Business* (New York: Chelsea House, 2009).

Machiavelli, Niccolò, *The Prince and The Discourses,* Modern Library College Editions (New York: Random House, 1950).

Machiavelli, Niccolò, *Discourses on Livy*, trans. Julia C. Bondanella and Peter Bondanella (Oxford: Oxford University Press, 1997).

MacIntyre, Alasdair, *After Virtue*, 2nd ed. (Notre Dame: Notre Dame University Press, 1984).

Against the Self-Images of the Age: Essays on Ideology and Philosophy (London: Duckworth, 1971).

"How Moral Agents Become Ghosts or Why the History of Ethics Diverged from That of the Philosophy of Mind," *Synthese* 53 (1982), pp. 292–312.

Marcuse (London: Fontana, 1970).

Whose Justice? Which Rationality? (Notre Dame, IN: University of Notre Dame Press, 1988).

Mack, Joanna and Stuart Lansley, *Poor Britain* (London: Allen & Unwin, 1985).

Mackay, Christopher S., *Ancient Rome: A Military and Political History* (Cambridge: Cambridge University Press, 2004).

MacLean, Nancy, *Democracy in Chains: The Deep History of the Radical Rights Stealth Plan for America* (New York: Viking, 2017).

Macleod, Emma Vincent, "The Crisis of the French Revolution," in H. T. Dickinson, *Companion to Eighteenth-Century Britain*, pp. 112–24.

Maddox, Brenda, *Reading the Rocks: How Victorian Geologists Discovered the Secret of Life* (London: Bloomsbury, 2017).

Mahathir, Mohamad, *A New Deal for Asia* (Subang Jaya, Malaysia: Pelanduk Publications, 1999).

Maier, Charles S., "The Two Postwar Eras and the Conditions for Stability in Twentieth-Century Western Europe," *American Historical Review* 86, no. 2 (1981), pp. 327–52.

Maine, Henry S., *Ancient Law: Its Connection with the Early History of Society and its Relation to Modern Laws* (New York: Dorset Press, 1896).

Malcolmson, R.W., *Life and Labour in England: 1700–1800* (London: Hutchinson, 1981).

Manent, Pierre and Seigel, Jerrold, *An Intellectual History of Liberalism* (Princeton, NJ: Princeton University Press, 1996).

Mann, Michael, *The Dark Side of Democracy: Explaining Ethnic Cleansing* (Cambridge: Cambridge University Press, 2005).

 The Sources of Social Power. vol I: A History of Power from the Beginning to AD 1760 (Cambridge: Cambridge University Press, 1986).

Mansbridge, Jane J., "The Rise and Fall of Self-Interest in the Explanation of Political Life," in Jane J. Mansbridge, ed., *Beyond Self-Interest* (Chicago, IL: University of Chicago Press, 1990), pp. 3–24.

Marcus, George, W. Russell Neuman and Michael Mackuen, *Affective Intelligence and Political Judgment* (Chicago, IL: University of Chicago Press, 2000).

Marcuse, Herbert, "Repressive Tolerance," in Robert Paul Wolff, Barrington Moore, Jr., and Herbert Marcuse, *A Critique of Pure Tolerance* (Boston, MA: Beacon Press, 1965), pp. 95–137.

Markus, Stanislav and Volha Charnysh, "The Flexible Few: Oligarchs and Wealth Defense in Developing Democracies," *Comparative Political Studies*, 50, no. 12 (2017), pp. 1632–65.

Marmot, Michael, *The Health Gap: The Challenge of an Unequal World* (London: Bloomsbury, 2015).

Marquez, Xavier, "The Irrelevance of Legitimacy," *Political Studies* 64, no. 1 (2015), pp. 19–34.

Marsden, George, *Understanding Fundamentalism and Evangelicalism* (Grand Rapids, MI: William B. Erdmans, 1991).

Marx, Karl, "The Bourgeoisie and the Counter-Revolution, "*Neue Rheinische Zeitung*, 14 December 1848, in Karl Marx, ed., *The Revolutions of 1848* (Harmondsworth: Penguin, 1973), pp. 192–94.

 Critique of the Gotha Program (Rockville, MD: Wildside Press, 2008).

Marx, Karl and Friedrich Engels, *The German Ideology* (New York: Prometheus, 1998).

Marxen, Klaus and Gerhard Werle, *Strafjustiz und DDR-Unrecht*, vol. 5 pt. 2 (Berlin: De Gruyter, 2000).

Mastanduno, Michael, "Hegemonic Order, September 11, and the Consequences of the Bush Revolution," *International Relations of the Asia Pacific* 5 (2005), pp. 177–96.

Mastny, Vojtech, "The Soviet Non-Invasion of Poland in 1980/81 and the End of the Cold War," *Europe-Asia Studies* 51, no. 2 (1999), pp. 189–211.

Mayall, James, "Tragedy, Progress, and International Order," in T. Erskine and R. Lebow, *Tragedy and International Relations*, pp. 44–52.

Mayser, Sabine, and Florian von Wangenheim, "Perceived Fairness of Differential Customer Treatment: Consumers' Understanding of Distributive Justice Really Matters," *Journal of Service Research* 16, no. 1 (2013), pp. 99–113.

Mazower, Mark, *Governing the World: The History of an Idea* (New York: Penguin, 2012).

Mazrui, Ali, *Towards and Pax Africana: A Study of Ideology and Ambition* (London: Weidenfeld and Nicolson, 1967).

Melis, Alicia P., Kristin Altrichter, and Michael Tonmasello, "Allocation of Resources to Collaborators and Free-Riders in 3-Year Olds," *Journal of Experimental Child Psychology* 114, no. 2 (2013), pp. 364–70.

Menand, Louis, *The Metaphysical Club* (New York: Farrar, Strauss & Giroux, 2001).

Mendus, Susan, *Impartiality in Moral and Political Philosophy* (Oxford: Oxford University Press, 2002).

Mertha, Andrew C., *China's Water Warriors: Citizen Action and Policy Change* (Ithaca, NY: Cornell University Press, 2008).

The Politics of Piracy: Intellectual Property in Contemporary China (Ithaca, NY: Cornell University Press, 2005).

Merton, Robert K., *Social Theory and Social Structure* (Glencoe, IL: Free Press, 1957).

Messick, D. M. and K. Sentis, "Fairness Preference and Fairness Biases," in D. M. Messick and K. S. Cook, eds., *Equity Theory: Psychological and Sociological Perspectives* (New York: Praeger, 1983), pp. 61–94.

Metcalf, Thomas R., *Ideologies of the Raj* (Cambridge: Cambridge University Press, 1998).

Midlarsky, Manus, *The Killing Trap: Genocide in the Twentieth Century* (Cambridge: Cambridge University Press, 2005).

Migdal, Joel, *Strong Societies and Weak States* (Princeton, NJ: Princeton University Press, 1998).

Mikula, Gerold and Thomas Schwinger, "Intermember Relations and Reward Allocation: Theoretical Considerations of Affects," in Hermann Brandstätter, James H. Davis and Heinz Schuler, eds., *Dynamics of Group Decisions* (Beverley Hills, CA: Sage, 1978), pp. 229–50.

Mikula, Gerold, *Justice and Social Interaction* (New York: Springer, 1980).

"On the Role of Justice in Allocation Decisions," in G. Mikula, *Justice and Social Interaction*, pp. 127–66.

Mikula, Gerold, B. Petri, and N. K.Tanzer, "What People Regard as Unjust: Types and Structures of Everyday Injustices," *European Journal of Social Psychology* 20 (1989), pp. 133–49.

Mill, John Stuart, *On Liberty, Utilitarianism, and Other Essays*, 2nd ed. (Oxford: Oxford University Press, 2015).

Miller, Dale T., "The Norm of Self-Interest," *American Psychologist* 54 (1999), pp. 1053–60.

Miller, David, *Principles of Social Justice* (Cambridge, MA: Harvard University Press, 1999).

Mingay, Gordon Edmund, ed., *The Agrarian History of England and Wales*, vol. VI (Cambridge: Cambridge University, 1989).

Mingay, Gordon, "Agriculture and Rural Life," in H. T. Dickinson, *Companion to Eighteenth Century Britain*, pp. 141–57.

Mingay, Gordon Edmund, "The Progress of Agriculture, 1750–1850," in J. T. Mingay, *Agrarian History of England and Wales*, Part 10.

Minsky, Hyman "The Financial Instability Hypothesis," Jerome Levy Economic Institute, Bard College, Working Paper 74, May 1992.

Mischel, W. "Preference for Delayed Reinforcement and Social Responsibility," *Journal of Abnormal and Social Psychology* 62 (1961), pp. 1–7.

Mitchell, Gregory, Philip E. Tetlock, Daniel G. Newman, and Jennifer S. Lerner, "Experiments Behind the Veil: Structural Influences on Judgments of Social Justice," *Political Psychology* 24, no. 3 (2003), pp. 519–47.

Mitchell, Timothy, *Carbon Democracy. Political Power in the Age of Oil* (London, Verso, 2011).

Molloy, Seán, *Kant's International Relations: The Political Theology of Perpetual Peace* (Ann Arbor, MI: University of Michigan Press, 2017).

Mommsen, Hans, *The Rise and Fall of Weimar Democracy* (Durham, NC: University of North Carolina Press, 1998).

Mommsen, Theodore E., "Petrarch's Conception of the 'Dark Ages,'" *Speculum* 17 (April 1942), pp. 226–42.

Mommsen, Wolfgang J. *Max Weber and German Politics, 1890–1920*, trans. Michael S. Steinberg (Chicago, IL: University of Chicago Press, 1984 [1959]).

Money, John, *Experience and Identity: Birmingham and the West Midlands 1760–1800* (Manchester: Manchester University Press, 1977).

Monod, Paul K., *Jacobitism and the English People, 1688–1788* (Cambridge: Cambridge University Press, 1989).

Montada, L. and M. J. Lerner, *Responses to Victimization and Belief in a Just World* (New York: Plenum, 1988).

Montoya, R. Matthew, Mu-Quing Huang, Bridget P. Lynch, and Cassondra M. Faiella, "Is Equality Perceived as a Solution to Societal Problems?" *North American Journal of Psychology* 15, no 1 (2013), pp. 39–48.

Moore, Barrington Jr., *Social Origins of Dictatorship and Democracy: Lord and Peasant in the Making of the Modern World* (Boston, MA: Beacon Press, 1966).

Moors, A. and J. De Houwer, "Automaticity: A Theoretical and Conceptual Analysis," *Psychological Bulletin* 132 (2006), pp. 297–326.

Morgenthau, Hans J., *In Defense of the National Interest* (New York: Knopf, 1951). *Politics Among Nations* (New York: Knopf, 1948).

Morrill, Calvin, *The Executive Way: Conflict Management in Corporations* (Chicago, IL: University of Chicago Press, 1995).

Morris, A., and C. McClura Mueller, eds., *Frontiers in Social Movement Theory* (New Haven, CT: Yale University Press, 1992).

Morris, Conway, *Life's Solution: Inevitable Humans in a Lonely Universe* (Cambridge: Cambridge University Press, 2003).

"Life: The Final Frontier for Complexity," in C. Lineweaver, P. Davies and M. Ruse, *Complexity and the Arrow of Time*, pp. 136–61.

Runes of Evolution: How Life Became Self-Aware (West Conshocken, PA: Templeton Press, 2015).

Morris, Conway and Stephen Jay Gould, "Showdown on the Burgess Shale," *Natural History* 107, no. 10 (1998), pp. 48–55.

Morris, Marilyn, *The British Monarchy and the French Revolution* (New Haven, CT: Yale University Press, 1998).

Morris, William, *News from Nowhere* (Cambridge: Cambridge University Press, 1995 [1890]).

Mueller, John E, *Retreat from Doomsday: The Obsolescence of Major War* (New York: Basic Books, 1990).

Müller, Jan-Werner, *Contesting Democracy: Political Ideas in Twentieth-Century Europe* (New Haven, CT: Yale University Press, 2011).

What I Populism? (Philadelphia, PA: University of Pennsylvania Press, 2016).

Murakami, Haruki, *Absolutely Music: Conversations with Seiji Ozawa* (London: Haril Secker, 2016).

Murdoch, Alexander, "Scotland and the Union," in H. T. Dickinson, *Companion to Eighteenth Century Britain*, pp. 381–91.

Murphy-Berman, V. and J. J. Berman, "Cross-Cultural Differences in Perceptions of Distributive Justice: A Comparison of Hong Kong and Indonesia," *Journal of Cross-Cultural Psychology* 33 (2002), pp. 157–70.

Musil, Robert, *The Man Without Qualities*, trans. Sophie Wilkins (London: Picador, 1995).

Myerly, Scott Hughes, *British Military Spectacle: From the Napoleonic Wars through the Crimea* (Cambridge, MA: Harvard University Press, 1996).

Nader, Laura and Harry F. Todd Jr., eds., *The Disputing Process: Law in Ten Societies* (New York: Columbia University Press, 1978).

Nagel, Joane, *American Indian Ethnic Renewal: Red Power and the Resurgence of Culture* (New York: Oxford University Press, 1996).

Naím, Moisés, "Mexico's Larger Story," *Foreign Policy*, no. 99 (Summer 1995), pp. 112–130.

Naimark, Norman M., *The Russians in Germany: A History of the Soviet Zone of Occupation, 1945–49* (Cambridge, MA: Harvard University Press, 1995).

Naipaul, V. S., *Among the Believers: An Islamic Journey* (London: Andre Deutsch, 1981).

Namier, Lewis, *Structure of Politics at the Accession of George III*, 3rd ed. (London: Palgrave Macmillan, 1978).

Nathan, Andrew J. and Andrew Scobell, *China's Search for Security* (New York: Columbia University Press, 2012).

National Bureau of Economic Research, *"Finance at Center Stage: Some Lessons of the Euro Crisis,"* Centre for Economic Policy Research, CEPR Discussion Paper No. DP9415, April 2013.

National Bureau of Statistics, *Zhongguo tongji nianjian 2010* (China Statistical Yearbook 2010) (Beijing: China Statistics Press, 2010).

Naughton, Barry, *The Chinese Economy: Transitions and Growth* (Cambridge, MA: MIT Press, 2006).

Naumamm, Klaus, ed., *Nachkrieg in Deutschland* (Hamburg: Hamburger Edition, 2001).

Nelson, Richard R. and Sidney G. Winter, *An Evolutionary Theory of Economic Change* (Cambridge, MA: Harvard University Press, 1982).

Nelson, Stephen C. and Peter J. Katzenstein, "Uncertainty, Risk, and the Financial Crisis of 2008," *International Organization*, 56 (4): 693–723.

Neubert, Ehrhart, *Geschichte der Opposition in der DDR 1949–1989* (Berlin: Ch. Links, 1998).

Newbolt, Henry, *The Book of the Happy Warrior* (London: Longmans and Green, 1917).

Newhouse, John, "Europe's Rising Regionalism," *Foreign Affairs*, 76, no. 1 (1997), pp. 67–84.

Newman, Gerald, *The Rise of English Nationalism: A Cultural History* (New York: St. Martin's Press, 1987).

Nexon, Daniel, *The Struggle for Power in Early Modern Europe: Religious Conflict, Dynastic Empires, and International Change* (Princeton, NJ: Princeton University Press, 2009).

Ng, Jason Q. and Sienna Pan, "Online Rumors as Targets and Tools of Chinese Censors: Analyzing Censorship in WeChat's Public Accounts Platform," in Martin K. Dimitrov, ed., *China-Cuba: Trajectories of Post-Revolutionary Governance* (in preparation).

Nietzsche, Friedrich, *Human, All-Too-Human,* trans. R. Hollingdale (Cambridge: Cambridge University Press, 1986).

    The Birth of Tragedy, in *Basic Writings of Nietzsche*, trans. and ed. Walter Kaufmann (New York: Modern Library, 1962).

    The Gay Science, ed. Bernard Williams, trans. Josefine Nauckhoff and Adrian del Caro (Cambridge: Cambridge University Press, 2001).

    On the Genealogy of Morals, trans. Walter Kaufmann and R. J. Hollingdale (New York: Vintage, 1967).

    Thus Spake Zarathustra (New York: Dover, 1999 [1924]).

Nipperdey, Thomas, *Germany from Napoleon to Bismarck, 1800–1866*, trans. Daniel Nolan (Princeton, NJ: Princeton University Press, 1996).

Nisbet, Robert, *The Quest for Community* (New York: Oxford University Press, 1969 [1953]).

Nisbett, Richard E., *The Geography of Thought; How Asians and Westerners Think Differently* (New York: Free Press, 2003).

Nissen, Hans J., "The Emergence of Writing in the Ancient Near East," *Interdisciplinary Science Reviews* 10, no. 4 (1985), pp. 349–61.

    Early History of the Ancient Near East, 9000–2000 BC (Chicago, IL: University of Chicago Press, 1988).

Noreña, Carlos, "Nero's Imperial Administration," in Shadi Bartsch, Kirk Freudenburg, and Cedric Littlewood, eds., *Age of Nero* (Cambridge: Cambridge University Press, 2017), pp. 48–62.

North, Douglas C. and Barry R. Weingast, "Constitutions and Commitment: The Evolution of Institutions Governing Public Choice in Seventeenth Century England," *Journal of Economic History* 49 (1989), pp. 803–32.

North, Douglass C. and Robert Paul Thomas, *The Rise of the Western World: A New Economic History* (Cambridge: Cambridge University Press, 1973).

Norton, M. I. and D. Airely, "Building a Better America – One Wealth Quintile at a Time," *Perspectives on Psychological Science* 6 (2011), pp. 9–12.

Novick, Peter, *The Holocaust in American Life* (New York: Houghton-Mifflin, 1999).

Nowak, Martin M., Karen M. Page, and Karl Sigmund, "Fairness and Reason in the Ultimate Game," *Science* 289 (September 8 2000), pp. 1773–75.

Noyes, Dorothy, *Fire in the Placa: Catalan Festival Politics After Fascism* (Philadelphia, PA: University of Pennsylvania Press, 2003).

Nozick, Robert, *Anarchy, State, and Utopia* (New York: Basic Books, 1974).

Nussbaum, Martha, *Upheavals of Thought: The Intelligence of Emotions* (New York: Cambridge University Press, 2001).

O'Brien, Kevin J. and Lianjiang Li, *Rightful Resistance in Rural China* (New York: Cambridge University Press, 2006).

O'Brien, Kevin J. and Rongbin Han, "Path to Democracy? Assessing Village Elections in China," *Journal of Contemporary China* 18, no. 60 (2009), pp. 359–78.

O'Brien, Patrick, "Finance and Taxation," in H. T. Dickinson, *Companion to Eighteenth Century Britain*, pp. 30–39.

  Power with Profit: The State and the Economy, 1688–1815 (London: University of London, 1991).

O'Gorman, Frank, *The Emergence of the British Two-Party System, 1760–1832* (London: Edward Arnold, 1982).

  The Long Eighteenth Century: British Political and Social History, 1688–1832, 2nd ed. (London: Bloomsbury, 2016).

  Voters, Patrons, and Parties: The Unreformed Electorate of Hanoverian England, 1734–1832 (Oxford: Oxford University Press, 1989).

  The Whig Party and the French Revolution (London: Macmillan, 1967).

O'Reilly, Kelly, "Perceiving Rogue States: The Use of the 'Rogue State' Concept by U.S. Security Elites," *Foreign Policy Analysis* 3, no 4 (2007), pp. 295–315.

Oakeshott, Michael, "Contemporary British Politics," *Cambridge Journal* 1 (1948), pp. 474–90.

  Notebooks, 1922–1986, ed. Luke O'Sullivan (Exeter: Imprint Academic, 2007).

  Rationalism in Politics and Other Essays, 2nd ed., ed. Tim Fuller (Indianapolis, IN: Liberty Fund, 1991).

  Religion, Politics, and Moral Life, ed. Timothy Fuller (New Haven, CT: Yale University Press, 1993), p. 93.

Oakley, Francis, *The Crucial Centuries: The Medieval Experience* (London: Terra Nova, 1979).

  Natural Law, Laws of Nature, Natural Rights: Continuity and Discontinuity in the History of Ideas (New York: Continuum, 2005).

Oberdorfer, Don, *The Two Koreas: A Contemporary History*, 3rd ed. rev. (New York: Basic Books, 2013).

Obrien, Kevin J., ed., *Popular Protest in China* (Cambridge, MA: Harvard University Press, 2008).

Obstfeld, Maurice, "Finance at Center Stage: Some Lessons of the Euro Crisis," European Commission, *European Economy*, Economic Papers 493. April 2013.

Ofer, Avner, *The Challenge of Affluence: Self-Control and Well-Being in the USA and Britain since 1950* (Oxford: Oxford University Press, 2006).

Offe, Claus, *Europe Entrapped* (London: Polity, 2015).

   "How Can We Trust Our Fellow Citizens," in Mark E. Warren, ed., *Democracy and Trust* (Cambridge: Cambridge University Press, 1999), pp. 42–87.

   Industry and Inequality: The Achievement Principle in Work and Social Status (London: Arnold, 1976).

Ohnezeit, Maik, *Zwischen "Schärfster Opposition und dem "Willen zur Macht"; die Deutsch-National Volkspartei (DNVP) in die Weimarer Republik* (Düsseldorf: Droste, 2011).

Oi, Jean C., *Rural China Takes Off: Institutional Foundations of Economic Reform* (Berkeley and Los Angeles, CA: University of California Press, 1990).

Oi, Jean C. and Andrew G. Walder, eds., *Property Rights and Economic Reform in China* (Stanford, CA: Stanford University Press, 1999).

Onuf, Nicholas, "Recognition and the Constitution of Epochal Change, *European Journal of International Relations* 27, no. 2 (2013), pp. 121–40.

Ortega y Gasset, José, *Goya* (Madrid: Revista de Occidente, 1958).

Ortman, Stephen, "The Umbrella Movement and Hong Kong's Protracted Democratization Process," *Asian Affairs* 46, no. 1 (2015), pp. 32–50.

Ortony Andrew, Gerald Clore and A. Collins, *The Cognitive Structure of Emotion* (Cambridge: Cambridge University Press, 1988).

Orwell, George, *1984* (New York: Harcourt, Brace, 1949).

Ostrom, Elinor, Joana Berger, Christopher B. Field, Richard Norgaard, and David Policansky, "Revisiting the Commons: Local Lessons, Global Challenges, *Science* 284, April 9 1999, pp. 278–82.

Ostwald, Martin, *From Popular Sovereignty to Sovereignty of Law: Law, Society, and Politics in Fifth-Century Athens* (Berkeley, CA: University of California Press, 1986).

Otte, Thomas G., *July Crisis: The World's Descent into War, Summer 1914* (Cambridge: Cambridge University Press, 2014).

Ovid, *Heroides and Amores* (Cambridge, MA: Harvard University Press, 1914).

Ozouf, Mona, "Public Opinion at the End of the Old Regime," *Journal of Modern History* 60 (1998), pp. 1–21.

Pagden, Anthony, *Lord of All the World: Ideologies of Empire in Spain, Britain and France, c. 1500–c. 1800* (New Haven, CT: Yale University Press, 1995).

Panksepp, Jaak, "The Affective Brain and Core Consciousness: How Does Neural Activity Generate Emotional Feelings," in M. Lewis, J. M. Haviland-Jones, and L. Feldman Barrett, *Handbook of Emotion*, pp. 47–67.

   Affective Neuroscience: The Foundations of Human and Animal Emotions (New York: Oxford University Press, 1998).

Paris, Roland, "Saving Liberal Peacebuilding," *Review of International Studies* 36, no. 2, (2010), pp. 337–67.

Park, Jerry and Samuel Reimer, "Revisiting the Social Sources of American Christianity, 1972–1988," *Journal for the Scientific Study of Religion* 41 (2002), pp. 733–47.

Parker, Geoffrey *The Military Revolution: Military Innovation and the Rise of the West 1500–1800*, 3rd ed. (Cambridge: Cambridge University Press, 2000).

Payne, Keith, *The Broken Ladder: How Inequality Affects the Way We Think, Live, and Die* (New York: Viking, 2017).

Pearson, Margaret M., *The Political Consequences of Economic Reform* (Berkeley and Los Angeles, CA: University of California Press, 1997).

Peciña, S. K. and K. C. Berridge, "Hedonic Hot Spots in the Brain," *The Neuroscientist* 12 (2006), pp. 500–11.

Pei, Minxin, "The Beginning of the End," *Washington Quarterly* 39, no. 3 (2016), pp. 131–42.

    China's Crony Capitalism: The Dynamics of Regime Decay (Cambridge, MA: Harvard University Press, 2016).

    China's Trapped Transition: The Limits of Developmental Autocracy (Cambridge, MA: Harvard University Press, 2006).

Pelopidas, Benoit, "Nuclear Weapons Scholarship as a Case of Self-Censorship in Security Studies," *Journal of Global Security Studies* 1, no. 4 (2016), pp. 326–336.

Pengalese, Ben, "The Bastard Child of the Dictatorship: The *Comando Vermelho* and the Birth of 'Narco-Culture' in Rio de Janeiro," *Luso-Brazilian Review* 45, no. 1 (2008), pp. 118–45.

People's Daily Editorial Office, *Neibu canyue jingxuan* (Internal Reference Selections) (Beijing: Zhongyang Wenxian Chubanshe, 1998).

Perrow, Charles, *Normal Accidents: Living with High Risk Technologies* (New York: Basic Books, 1984).

Perry, Elizabeth J., *Challenging the Mandate of Heaven: Social Protest and State Power in China* (Armonk, NY: M. E. Sharpe, 2001).

    "Higher Education and Authoritarian Resilience: The Case of China, Past and Present," in Martin K. Dimitrov, ed., *Popular Authoritarianism: The Quest for Regime Durability* (in preparation).

Pflanze, Otto, *Bismarck and the Development of Germany*, 3 vols. (Princeton, NJ: Princeton University Press, 1963–90).

Phelps, Elizabeth A., "The Human Amygdala and Awareness: Interactions Between Emotion and Cognition" and Ralph Adolphs, "Processing of Emotional and Social Information by the Human Amygdala," in M. Gazzaniga, *Cognitive Neurosciences*, pp. 1005–16 and 1017–30.

Philip, Mark, *French Revolution and British Popular Politics* (Cambridge: Cambridge University Press, 1991).

Piketty, Thomas, *Capital in the Twenty-First Century*, trans. Arthur Goldhammer (Cambridge, MA: Harvard University Press, 2014).

    The Economics of Inequality (Cambridge, MA: Harvard University Press, 2015).

Pinker, Steven, *The First Modern Revolution* (New Haven, CT: Yale University Press, 2009).

The Better Angels of Our Nature: A History of Violence and Humanity (Harmondsworth: Penguin, 2012).

Pippin, Robert, *Modernism as a Philosophical Problem: On the Dissatisfactions of European High Culture* (Cambridge: Blackwell, 1991).

Plato, "Apology" and *The Republic*, in Edith Hamilton and Huntington Cairns, eds., *The Collected Dialogues* (Princeton, NJ: Princeton University Press, 1961).

Plokhy, Sergei, *The Last Empire: The Final Days of the Soviet Union* (London: Oneworld, 2015).

Plumb, John. H., *The Origins of Political Stability, England, 1675–1725* (Boston, MA: Houghton Mifflin, 1967).

England in the Eighteenth Century (London: Penguin, 1969).

Plutarch, "The Life of Aristides," in Plutarch, ed., *The Parallel Lives* (Cambridge: Loeb editions, 1914), II, pp. 211–99.

Pomeranz, Kenneth, *The Great Divergence: China, Europe, and the Making of the Modern World Economy* (Princeton, NJ: Princeton University Press, 2000).

Popper, Karl, *The Open Society and Its Enemies* (London: Routledge & Kegan Paul, 1957).

Porter, Roy, *English Society in the Eighteenth Century*, rev. ed. (London: Penguin Books, 1990).

Posner, Richard, *The Economics of Justice* (Cambridge, MA: Harvard University Press, 1983).

Powell, Martyn J., "Ireland: Radicalism, Rebellion and Union," in H. T. Dickinson, *Companion to Eighteenth Century Britain*, pp. 414–28.

Price, Hugh, "The Changing Rural Landscape, 1750–1850," in G. E. Mingay, *Agrarian History of England and Wales*, pp. 7–83.

Price, Richard, *British Society, 1660–1880: Dynamism, Containment and Change* (Cambridge: Cambridge University Press, 1999).

Puddington, Arch, *Broadcasting Freedom: The Cold War Triumph of Radio Free Europe and Radio Liberty* (Lexington, KY: University Press of Kentucky, 2000).

Pufendorf, Samuel von, *The Compleat History of Sweden from its Origin to This Time* (London: Wild, 1702).

Putnam, Robert D., *Bowling Alone: The Collapse and Revival of American Community* (New York: Simon & Schuster, 2000).

Rackham, Oliver, *The History of the Countryside* (London: J. M. Dent, 1986).

Rasinski, Kenneth A., "What's Fair is Fair – Or Is It? Value Differences Underlying Public Views about Social Justice," *Journal of Personality and Social Psychology* 53, no. 1 (1987), pp. 201–11.

Rathbun, Brian C., "Hierarchy and Community at Home and Abroad: Evidence of a Common Structure of Domestic and Foreign Policy Beliefs in American Elites," *Journal of Conflict Resolution* 51, no. 3 (2007), pp. 379–407.

Rauchensteiner, Manfred, *Der erste Weltkrieg und das Ende der Habsburger-Monarchie* (Vienna: Böhlau Verlag, 2013).

Raven, James, *Judging New Wealth: Popular Publishing and Responses to Commerce in England, 1750–1800* (Oxford: Oxford University Press, 1992).

Rawls, John, *Justice as Fairness*, ed. Erin Kelly (Cambridge, MA: Harvard University Press, 2001).

The Law of Peoples (Cambridge, MA: Harvard University Press, 1999).

A Theory of Justice, rev. ed. (Cambridge, MA: Harvard University Press, 1999).

Raz, Joseph, *The Authority of Law* (Oxford: Oxford University Press, 1979).

The Morality of Freedom (Oxford: Oxford University Press, 1986).

Read, Benjamin L., *Roots of the State: Neighborhood Organization and Social Networks in Beijing and Taipei* (Stanford, CA: Stanford University Press, 2012).

Reeskens, Tim and Wim van Oorschot, "Equity, Equality, or Need? A Study of Popular Preferences for Welfare Redistribution Principles Across 24 European Countries," *Journal of European Public Policy* 20 (2013), pp. 1174–95.

Reeves, Richard V., *Dream Hoarders: How the American Upper Middle Class Is Leaving Everyone Else in the Dust, Why That Is a Problem, and What to Do about It* (Washington, DC: Brookings, 2017).

Reich, Robert, *Saving Capitalism: For the Many, Not the Few* (New York: Knopf, 2015).

Reich, Simon and Richard Ned Lebow, *Good-Bye Hegemony! Power and Influence in the Global System* (Princeton, NJ: Princeton University Press, 2014).

Rengger, Nicholas J., *International Relations, Political Theory and the Problem of Order* (London: Routledge, 2000).

Richardson, Jeremy, ed., *Policy Making in the European Union* (London: Routledge, 1996).

Ricoeur, Paul, *Memory, History, Forgetting* (Chicago, IL: University of Chicago Press, 2004).

Riesbeck, David, *Aristotle on Political Community* (Cambridge: Cambridge University Press, 2016).

Roche, *France in the Enlightenment,* trans. Arthur Goldhammer (Cambridge, MA: Harvard University Press, 1992).

Roemer, John E., *Equality of Opportunity* (Cambridge, MA: Harvard University Press, 1998).

Theories of Distributive Justice (Cambridge, MA: Harvard University Press, 1996).

Rogan, Eugene, *The Fall of the Ottomans: The Great War in the Middle East* (New York: Basic Books, 2015).

Rogers, Nicholas, "The Middling Orders," in H. T. Dickinson, *Companion to Eighteenth Century Britain,* pp. 172–82.

Rogow, Arnold A., *James Forrestal: A Study of Personality, Politics, and Policy* (New York: Macmillan, 1963).

Romanowski, William D., "Evangelicals and Popular Music: The Contemporary Christian Music Industry," in Bruce David Forbes and Jeffrey H. Mahan, eds., *Religion and Popular Culture in America* (Berkeley and Los Angeles, CA: University of California Press, 2005), pp. 103–22.

Rose, Peter I., "Toward A More Perfect Union: The Contributions of Robin M. Williams, Jr.," *American Sociologist* 30 (1999), pp. 78–92.

Rosen, Stephen Peter, *War and Human Nature.* (Princeton, NJ: Princeton University Press, 2007).

Rosenau, James N., "Governance, Order, and Change in World Politics," in James N. Rosenau and Ernst-Otto Czempiel, E.-O., eds., *Governance Without Government: Order and Change in World Politics* (Cambridge: Cambridge University Press, 1992), pp. 1–29.

Rosenberg, Arthur, *Imperial Germany: The Birth of the German Republic, 1871–1918*, trans. Ian Morrow (Boston, MA: Beacon Press, 1964 [1928]).

Roseveare, Henry, *The Treasury, 1660–1870: The Foundations of Control* (London: Allen & Unwin, 1973).

Ross, Sharon Marie, "Talking Sex: Comparison Shopping through Female Conversation," in Mary Dalton and Laura Linder, eds., *The Sitcom Reader: America Viewed and Skewed* (Albany, NY: State University of New York Press, 2005), pp. 111–24.

Ross, Tim and Tom McTague, *Betting the House: The Inside Story of the 2017 Election* (London: Biteback, 2017).

Rotberg, Robert I., ed., *When States Fail: Causes and Consequences* (Princeton, NJ: Princeton University Press, 2004).

Roth, Jospeh, *The Radetzky March*, trans. Joachim Neugroschel (London: Penguin, 1995).

Rousseau, Jean-Jacques, *Confessions in Oeuvres Complètes*, eds., B. Gagnebin and M. Raymond (Paris: Gallimard,1959), vol. 1.

   Discourse on Science and the Arts (First Discourse) in Roger D. Masters and Judith R. Masters, trans., *First and Second Discourses* (New York: St. Martin's Press, 1969), pp. 1–76.

   Discourse on the Origin and Foundations of Inequality (Second Discourse), in Masters, *First and Second Discourses*, pp. 77–229.

   Du Contrat Social (Paris: Editions Garnier Frères, 1962).

   The Government of Poland, trans. Wilmore Kendall (Indianapolis, IN: Hackett, 1985).

Rowen, Henry S., "The Short March: China's Road to Democracy," *The National Interest*, no. 45 (Fall 1996), pp. 61–70.

Rowen, Ian and Jamie Rowen, "Taiwan's Truth and Reconciliation Committee: The Geopolitics of Transitional Justice in a Contested State," *International Journal of Transitional Justice* 11 (2017), pp. 1–21.

Rowlands, Mark, *Can Animals Be Moral?* (Oxford: Oxford University Press, 2012).

Royle, Edward, *Revolutionary Britannia? Reflections on the Threat of Revolution in Britain, 1789–1848* (Manchester: Manchester University Press, 2000).

Rozmin, Gilbert, "China's Concurrent Debate about the Gorbachev Era," in T. P. Bernstein and H.-Y. Li, *China Learns from the Soviet Union*, pp. 449–76.

Ruggie, John Gerard, "Territoriality and Beyond: Problematizing Modernity in International Relations," *International Organization* 47, no. 1 (Winter 1993), pp. 130–44.

Rule, John, "The Labouring Poor," in H. T. Dickinson, *Companion to Eighteenth Century Britain*, pp. 183–95.

   "Manufacturing and Commerce," in H. T. Dickinson, *Companion to Eighteenth Century Britain*, pp. 127–40.

Rupieper, Hermann-Josef, *Die Wuirzeln des westdeutschen Nachkriegsdemokratie: der amerikanische Beitrag 1945–1952* (Opladen: Westdeutscher Verlag, 1993).

Russell, J. A., "Core Affect and the Psychological Construction of Emotion," *Psychological Review* 110 (2003), pp. 145–73.

Rustow, Dankwart, "Transitions to Democracy," *Comparative Politics* 2, no. 3 (April 1970), pp. 337–63.

Ryan, Timothy J., "No Compromise: Political Consequences of Moralized Attitudes," *American Journal of Political Science* 61, no. 2. (2017), pp. 409–23.

Saich, Tony, "Negotiating the State: The Development of Social Organizations in China," *China Quarterly*, no. 161 (2000), pp. 121–41.

Salisbury, Harrison, *The All Shook Up Generation* (New York: Harper & Row, 1958).

Sampson, Robert J. and Per-Olof H. Wikström, "The Social Order of Violence in Chicago and Stockholm Neighborhoods: A Comparative Inquiry," in S. N. Kalyvas, I. Shapiro, and T. Masoud, *Order, Conflict, and Violence*, pp. 97–119.

Sampson, Robert J. and W. Byron Groves, "Community Structure and Crime: Testing Social Disorganization Theory," *American journal of Sociology* 94 (1989), pp. 774–802.

Samuels, Martin, *Command or Control? Command, Training and Tactics in the British and German Armies, 1888–1918* (London: Routledge, 1996).

Samuels, Richard J., *Machiavelli's Children: Leaders and Their Legacies in Italy and Japan* (Ithaca, NY: Cornell University Press, 2003).

Sandel, Michael J., *Liberalism and the Limits of Justice* (Cambridge: Cambridge University Press, 1982).

"America's Search for a New Public Philosophy," *Atlantic Monthly*, 227, no. 3 (March 1996).

Democracy's Discontent: America in Search of a Public Philosophy (Cambridge, MA: Harvard University Press, 1996).

Sapolsky, Robert M., "Stress and Cognition," in M. Gazzaniga, *Cognitive Neurosciences*, pp. 1031–42.

Sarotte, Mary Elise "China's Fear of Contagion: Tiananmen Square and the Power of the European Example," *International Security* 37, no. 2 (2012), pp. 156–82.

The Collapse: The Accidental Opening of the Berlin Wall (New York: Basic Books, 2014).

Saunders, Elizabeth N., "Setting Boundaries: Can International Society Exclude 'Rogue States?'" *International Studies Review* 8, no 1 (2006), pp. 23–53.

Saunders, Peter, *Unequal but Fair? A Study of Class Barriers in Britain* (London: Civitas, 2000).

Schattschneider, E. E., *The Semisovereign People: A Realist's View of Democracy in America* (New York: Holt, Rinehart, and Winston, 1960).

Schiedel, Walter, *The Great Leveler: Violence and the History of Inequality from the Stone Age to the Twenty-First Century* (Princeton, NJ: Princeton University Press, 2017).

Schiefflin, E. L., "Early Contact as Drama and Misrepresentation in the Southern Highlands of Papua New Guinea: Pacifications as the Structure of the Conjecture," *Comparative Studies in Society and History* 37 (1995), pp. 355–80.

Schiller, Friedrich, *Don Carlos: Infant von Spanien* (Berlin: Holzinger, 2016).

Schmitter, Philippe C. and Terry Lynn Karl, "What Democracy Is ... and is Not," *Journal of Democracy* 2 (1991), pp. 75–88.

Schneewind, J. B. "Good out of Evil: Kant and the Ideal of Unsocial Sociability," in Amelie Oksenberg Rorty and James Schmidt, eds., *Kant's Idea of Universal History with a Cosmopolitan Aim: A Critical Guide* (Cambridge: Cambridge University Press, 2009), pp. 94–111.

Scheidel, Walter, *The Great Leveler: Violance and the History of Inequality from the Stone Age to the Twenty-First Century* (Princeton, NJ: Princeton University Press, 2017).

Schneier, Bruce, *Secrets and Lies* (New York: Wiley, 2000).

Schneier, Edward, *Crafting Constitutional Democracies: The Politics of Institutional Design* (Lanham, MD: Rowman and Littlefeld, 2006).

Schopenhauer, Arthur, "The Wisdom of Life," in *Essays from Parenga and Parlipomena*, trans. T. Bailey Saunders (London: Allen & Unwin, 1951), pp. 70–92.

Schroeder, Paul, "The Transformation of Political Thinking, 1787–1848," in Robert Jervis, ed., *Coping with Complexity in the International System* (Boulder, CO: Westview Press, 1993), pp. 47–70.

Schroeder, Paul W., *The Transformation of European Politics, 1763–1848* (Oxford: Oxford University Press, 1994).

Schuessler, John M., *Deceit on the Road to War: Presidents, Politics, and American Democracy* (Ithaca, NY: Cornell University Press, 2015).

Schumpeter, Joseph A., *Capitalism, Socialism, and Democracy* (New York: Harper, 1942).

   Imperialism and Social Classes, trans. Heinz Norden (New York: Kelley, 1951).

Schwartz, Herman, *Subprime Nation: American Power, Global Capital, and the Housing Bubble* (Ithaca, NY: Cornell University Press, 2009).

Schweder, Richard A. Jonathan Haidt, Randall Horton and Craig Joseph, "The Cultural Psychology of the Emotions: Ancient and New," in M. Lewis and J. M. Haviland-Jones, eds., *Handbook of Emotions*, 2nd ed. (New York: Guildford Press, 2000), pp. 428–39.

Schwinger, Thomas, "Just Allocations of Goods: Decisions Among Three Principles," in G. Mikula, *Justice and Social Interaction*, pp. 95–125.

   "The Need Principle of Distributive Justice," in H. W. Bierhoff, R. L. Cohen, and J. Greenberg, eds., *Justice in Social Relations* (New York: Plenum, 1986), pp. 211–23.

Scobell, Andrew, *China's Use of Military Force: Beyond the Great Wall and the Long March* (New York: Columbia University Press, 2003).

   "The Death Penalty in Post-Mao China," *China Quarterly*, no. 123 (1990), pp. 503–20.

Scott, James C., *Against the Grain: A Deep History of the Earliest States* (New Haven, CT: Yale University Press, 2017).

Scott, Walter, *Heart of Midlothian* (Oxford: Oxford University Press, 2008).

Scriven, Michael, "Explanations, Predictions and Laws," *Minnesota Studies in the Philosophy of Science* 2 (1962), pp. 88–195.

Seaford, Richard, *Reciprocity and Ritual: Homer and Tragedy in the Developing City State* (Oxford: Oxford University Press, 1994).

Sears, David, Jim Sidanious, and Lawrrence Bobo, *Radicalized Politics: The Debate about Racism in America* (Chicago, IL: University of Chicago Press, 2000).

Sebestyen, Victor, *Revolution 1989: The Fall of the Soviet Empire* (London: W&N, 2010).

Sedgwick, William, *The House of Commons, 1715–54*, 2 vols. (London: Saunders, 1990).

Seigel, Jerrold, *Modernity and Bourgeois Life* (New York: Cambridge University Press, 2012).

Semmel, Bernard, *Imperialism and Social Reform* (Cambridge, MA: Harvard University Press, 1960).

Sen, Amartya, *Commodities and Capabilities* (Amsterdam: North Holland, 1985).

"Equality of What?" in Amartya Sen, ed., *Choice, Welfare, and Measurement* (Oxford: Blackwell, 1982), ch. 16.

Shadeen, Michael N. and Joshua L. Gold, "The Neurophysiology of Decision Making as a Window on Cognition," in M. Gazzaniga, *Cognitive Neurosciences*, pp. 1229–41.

Shaikh, Farzana, *Making Sense of Pakistan* (Oxford: Oxford University Press, 2012).

Shambaugh, David, *China's Communist Party: Atrophy and Adaptation* (Washington, DC: Woodrow Wilson Center Press, 2008).

China's Future (Cambridge: Cambridge University Press, 2016).

"Contemplating China's Future," *Washington Quarterly* 39, no. 3 (2016), pp. 121–30.

Shanks, Cheryl, Harold K. Jacobson, and Jeffrey H. Kaplan, "Inertia and Change in the Constellation of International Governmental Organizations, 1981–1991," *International Organization* 50 (Autumn 1996), pp. 593–628.

Shapiro, E. G. "The Effect of Expectations of Future Interaction on Reward Allocation in Dyads," *Journal of Personality and Social Psychology* 31 (1975), pp. 873–80.

Shapiro, Ian, *Moral Foundations of Politics* (New Haven, CT: Yale University Press, 2003).

The State of Democratic Theory (Princeton, NJ: Princeton University Press, 2003).

Sharpe, James A., "Crime and Punishment," in H. T. Dickinson, *Companion to Eighteenth Century Britain*, pp. 358–66.

Sherif, Muzafer and Carolyn W. Sherif, *Groups in Harmony and Tension: An Integration of Studies on Intergroup Relations* (New York: Harper, 1953).

Shibata, Masako, *Japan and Germany under the U.S. Occupation: A Comparative Analysis of Post-War Education Reform* (Boston, MA: Lexington Books, 2008).

Shih, Victor, Christopher Adolph, and Mingxing Liu, "Getting Ahead in the Communist Party: Explaining the Advancement of Central Committee Members in China," *American Political Science Review* 106, no. 1 (2012), pp. 166–87.

Shipman, *All Out War: The Full Story of How Brexit Sank Britain's Political Class* (London: William Collins, 2016).

Shipman, Tim, *Fall Out: A Year of Political Mayhem* (London: William Collins, 2017).

Shklar, Judith, "Let us not be Hypocritical," in J. N. Shklar, eds., *Ordinary Vices* (Cambridge, MA: Harvard University Press, 1984), pp. 45–86.

"Liberalism of Fear," in Nancy Rosenblum, ed., *Liberalism and the Moral Life* (Cambridge, MA: Harvard University Press, 1989), pp. 21–38.

Ordinary Vices (Cambridge, MA: Harvard University Press, 1984).

Simmel, Georg, *The Philosophy of Money*, 2nd ed., trans. Tom Bottomore and David Frisby (New York: Routledge, 2004).

Simmons, C. H. and M. J. Lerner, "Altruism as a Search for Justice," *Journal of Personality and Social Psychology* 9 (1968), pp. 216–25.

Simmons, P. J., "Learning to Live with NGOs," *Foreign Policy*, no. 112 (Fall 1998), pp. 82–95.

Simon, Walter M., *The Failure of the Prussian Reform Movement, 1807–1819* (Ithaca, NY: Cornell University Press, 1955).

Simpson, Gerry, *Great Powers and Outlaw States: Unequal Sovereigns in the International Legal Order* (Cambridge: Cambridge University Press, 2004).

Singer, Peter, *The Most Good You Can Do* (New Haven, CT: Yale University Press, 2015).

The President of Good and Evil: Questioning the Ethics of George W. Bush (New York: Dutton, 2004).

Singh, Naunihal, *Seizing Power: The Strategic Logic of Military Coups* (Baltimore, MD: Johns Hopkins University Press, 2014).

Skinner, B. F., *Walden Two* (New York: Macmillan, 1962).

Skitka, L. J., "Do the Means Always Justify the Ends or do the Ends Sometimes Justify the Means? A Value Protection Model of Justice," *Personality and Social Psychology Bulletin* 28 (2002), pp. 452–61.

Skocpol, Theda, *Protecting Soldiers and Mothers: The Political Origins of Social Policy in the United States* (Cambridge, MA: Harvard University Press, 1992).

State and Social Revolutions: A Comparative Analysis of France, Russia, and China (Cambridge: Cambridge University Press, 1979).

Skocpol, Theda and Vanessa Williamson, *The Tea Party and the Remaking of Republican Conservatism* (New York: Oxford 2013).

Smith, Adam, *An Inquiry into the Nature and Causes of Wealth of Nations*, ed. Edwin Canaan (Chicago, IL: University of Chicago Press, 1976).

Lectures on Jurisprudence, ed. R. L. Meek, et al (Oxford: Oxford University Press, 1978).

The Theory of Moral Sentiments (Cambridge: Cambridge University Press, 2002 [1759]).

The Wealth of Nations (New York: Modern Library, 1937).

Smith, Arthur L., *The War for the German Mind: Reeducating Hitler's Soldiers* (Providence, RI: Berghahn Books, 1996).

Smith, Benjamin, "Life of the Party: The Origins of Regime Breakdown and Persistence Under Single-Party Rule," *World Politics* 57, no.3 (2005), pp. 421–51.

Smith, Christian and Robert Farris, "Socioeconomic Inequality in the American Religious System: An Update and Assessment," *Journal for the Scientific Study of Religion* 44 (2005), pp. 95–104.

Smith, E. R. and Diane M. Mackie, "Intergroup Emotions," in M. Lewis, J. M. Haviland-Jones, and L. Feldman Barrett, *Handbook of Emotions*, pp. 428–39.

Smith, E. R. and S. Henry, "As In-Group Becomes Part of the Self: Response Time Evidence," *Personality and Social Psychology Bulletin* 22 (1996), pp. 635–42.

Smith, Paul, *Disraelian Conservatism and Social Reform* (London: Routledge & Kegan Paul, 1967).

Smith, Tom W., "Inequality and Welfare," in Roger Jowell, Sharon Witherspoon and Lindsay Brook, eds., *British Social Attitudes: Special International Report* (Aldershot: Gower, 1989), pp. 59–77.

Smith, William Beattie *From Violence to Power Sharing: The British State and the Northern Ireland Crisis, 1969–73* (Washington, DC: US Institute of Peace, 1973).

Snell, K. D. M., *Annals of the Labouring Poor: Social Change and Agrarian England, 1660–1900* (Cambridge: Cambridge University Press, 1985).

Snyder, Jack L., *The Ideology of the Offensive: Military Decision Making and the Disasters of 1914* (Ithaca, NY: Cornell University Press, 1984).

Soares de Oliveira, Ricardo, *Magnificent and Beggar Land: Angola Since the Civil War* (Oxford: Oxford University Press, 2014).

Solinger, Dorothy and Yiyang Hu, "Welfare, Wealth, and Poverty in Urban China: The *Dibao* and Its Differential Disbursement," *China Quarterly*, no. 211 (2012), pp. 741–64.

Solomon, R. C., *Not Passion's Slave* (New York: Oxford University Press, 2004).

Solzhenitsyn, Alexander, *Cancer Ward*, trans. Nicholas Bethell and David Beug (New York: Farrar, Strauss & Giroux, 1969).

Sombart, Werner, *Händler und Helden: Patriotische Besinningen* (Munich: Duncker & Graefe, 1915).

Sophocles, "Antigone," in D. Slavitt and P. Bovie, eds., *Sophocles*, vol. 2, trans. K. Cherry (Philadelphia, PA: University of Pennsylvania Press, 1999).

The Complete Greek Tragedies, vol. 2, trans. David Grene (Chicago, IL: University of Chicago Press, 1991).

Speck, W. A., *Stability and Strife: England, 1714–1760* (Cambridge, MA: Harvard University Press, 1977).

Spence, Peter, *The Birth of Romantic Nationalism: War, Popular Politics, and English Radical reformism, 1800–1815* (Aldershot: Ashgate, 1996).

Spencer, Herbert, *Principles of Sociology* (New York: Appleton, 1900), vol. 3.

Spero, Melford E., *Children of the Kibbutz* (Cambridge, MA: Harvard University Press, 1958).

Spires, Anthony J. "Contingent Symbiosis and Civil Society in an Authoritarian State: Understanding the Survival of China's Grassroots NGOs," *American Journal of Sociology* 117, no. 1 (2011), pp. 1–45.

Spruyt, Hendryk, *The Sovereign State and its Competitors: An Analysis of System Change* (Princeton, NJ: Princeton University Press, 1994).

Spufford, Frances, *Red Plenty: Inside the Fifties' Soviet Dream* (London: Faber & Faber, 2010).

St. Clair, William, *The Reading Nation and the Romantic Period* (Cambridge: Cambridge University Press).

Steffek, Jens, "International Organization and Bureaucratic Modernity," in R. Lebow, *Max Weber and Inernational Relations*, pp. 119–42.

Stein, Arthur A., *Why Nations Cooperate: Circumstance and Choice in International Relations* (Ithaca, NY: Cornell University Press, 1990).

Stein, Janice Gross, *The Cult of Efficiency* (Toronto: Anansi Press, 2001).

Stern, Rachel E. and Kevin J. O'Brien, "Politics at the Boundary: Mixed Signals and the Chinese State," *Modern China* 38, no. 2 (March 2012), pp. 174–98.

Stevenson, David, *Anticipating Total War, 1870–1914* (Cambridge: Cambridge University Press, 2006).

Stevenson, John, *Popular Disturbances in England, 1700–1832* (London: Routledge, 2013).

Stiglitz, Joseph E., *Globalization and its Discontents* (New York: W. W. Norton, 2002).

The Roaring Nineties (New York: Penguin, 2003).

Stone Sweet, Alec and Wayne Sandholz, *European Integration and Supranational Governance* (Oxford: Oxford University Press, 1998).

Straus, Scott, "Order in Disorder: A Micro-Comparative Study of Genocidal Dynamics in Rwanda," in S. N. Kalyvas, I. Shapiro, and T. Masoud, *Order, Conflict, and Violence*, pp. 301–20.

Strauss, Barry S., *Athens After the Peloponnesian War: Class, Faction, and Policy, 404–386 BC* (Ithaca, NY: Cornell University Press, 1986).

Strawson, Galen, "The Minimal Self," in S. Gallagher, *Oxford Handbook of The Self*, pp. 253–78.

Selves: An Essay in Revisionary Metaphysics (Oxford: Oxford University Press, 2009).

Streeck, Wolfgang, *How Will Capitalism End?* (London: Verso, 2016).

Stuart J. Kaufman, Richard Little, and William C. Wohlforth, *The Balance of Power in World History* (New York: Palgrave Macmillan, 2007).

Suchman, Mark, "Managing Legitimacy: Strategic and Institutional Approaches," *Academy of Management Review* 20 (1995), pp. 571–60.

Suzuki, Shogo, "Europe at the Periphery of the Japanese World Order," in Shogo Suzuki, Yongjin Zhang, and Joel Quirk, eds., *International Orders in the Early Modern World: Before the Rise of the West* (London: Routledge, 2014), pp. 76–93.

Svolik, Milan W., *The Politics of Authoritarian Rule* (New York: Cambridge University Press, 2012).

Swanbrow, Dianne, "Exceptional Upward Mobility in the U.S. is a Myth, International Studies Show, University of Michigan Institute for Social Research, September 5 2012, www.sampler.isr.umich.edu/2012/research/exceptional-upward-mobility-in-the-us-is-a-myth-international-studies-show/ (accessed March 29 2013).

Swift, Adam. G., Gordon Marshall, and Carole Burgoyne, "Which Road to Social Justice?" *Sociology Review* 2, no. 2 (1992), pp. 28–31.

Swift, Adam G., Gordon Marshall, Carole Burgoyne, and David Routh, "Distributive Justice: Does It Matter What People Think?" in Kluegel et al., *Social Justice and Political Change*, pp. 15–46.

Szakolczai, Arpad, "Liminality and Experience: Structuring Transitory Situations and Transformative Events," *International Political Anthropology* 2, no. 1 (2009), pp. 141–72.

Szechi, Daniel, "The Jacobite Movement," in H. T. Dickinson, *Companion to Eighteenth Century Britain*, pp. 81–96.

Sztompka, Piotr, "Trust and Emerging Democracy," *International Sociology* 11 (1996), pp. 37–62.

Tainter, Joseph, *The Collapse of Complex Societies*. Cambridge: Cambridge University Press, 1988).

Tajfel, Henri, *Human Groups and Social Categories* (Cambridge: Cambridge University Press, 1981).

Tajfel, Henri, M. Billing, R. Bundy, and C. Flament, "Social Categorization and Intergroup Behavior," *European Journal of Social Psychology* 1, no. 2 (1971), pp. 149–78.

Tajfel, Henry and John Turner, "The Social Identity Theory of Intergroup Behavior," in Stephen Worchel and William Austin, eds., *Psychology of Intergroup Relations* (Chicago, IL: Nelson-Hall, 1986), pp. 7–24.

Takeuchi, Hiroki, *Tax Reform in Rural China: Revenue, Resistance, and Authoritarian Rule* (New York: Cambridge University Press, 2014).

Talleyrand-Périgord, Maurice de, *The Correspondence of Charles Maurice de Talleyrand-Périgord and King Louis XVIII During the Congress of Vienna* (New York: Harper & Brothers, 1881).

Tang, Wenfang and Qing Yang, "The Chinese Urban Caste System in Transition," *China Quarterly*, no. 196 (2008), pp. 759–79.

Tang, Wenfang, *Populist Authoritarianism: Chinese Political Culture and Regime Sustainability* (New York: Oxford University Press, 2016).

Tanner, Klaus, "Protestant Revolt Against Modernity," in Rudy Koshar, ed., *The Weimar Moment: Liberalism, Political Theology, and Law* (New York: Lexington, 2012), pp. 3–16.

Taruskin, Richard, *Music in the Seventeenth and Eighteenth Centuries* (Oxford: Oxford University Press, 2010).

Taylor, Paul *The End of European Integration: Anti-Europeanism Examined* (London: Routledge, 2008), pp. 26–35.

Teasdale, J. D. and S. Fogarty, "Differential Effects of Induced Mood on Retrieval of Pleasant and Unpleasant Events from Episodic Memory," *Journal of Abnormal Psychology* 88 (1979), pp. 248–57.

Teets, Jessica C., "Let Many Civil Societies Bloom: The Rise of Consultative Authoritarianism in China," *China Quarterly*, no. 213 (2013), pp. 19–38.

  Civil Society under Authoritarianism: The China Model (New York: Cambridge University Press, 2014).

Tent, James F., *Mission on the Rhine: Reeducation and Denazification in American-Occupied Germany* (Chicago, IL: University of Chicago Press, 1982).

Teschke, Benno, *The Myth of 1648: Class, Geopolitics, and the Making of Modern International Relations* (London: Verso, 2003).

Thibaut, J. W. and L. Walker, *Procedural Justice: A Psychological Analysis* (Hillsdale, NJ: Erlbaum, 1975).

Thomas, Peter David Garner, *John Wilkes: A Friend of Liberty* (Oxford: Oxford University Press, 1996).

  The House of Commons in the Eighteenth Century (Oxford: Oxford University Press, 1971).

Thomassen, Bjørn, *The Uses and Meanings of Liminality, International Political Anthropology* 2, no 1 (2009), pp. 5–27.

Thompson, E. P., *Whigs and Hunters: The Origins of the Black Act* (London: Allen Lane, 1975).

Thucydides, *The Landmark Thucydides: A Comprehensive Guide to the Peloponnesian War*, ed. Robert B. Strassler (New York: Free Press, 1996).

Tilly, Charles, *The Formation of National States in Western Europe* (Princeton, NJ: Princeton University Press, 1975).

Identities, Boundaries and Social Ties (Boulder, CO: Paradigm, 2005).

Tirpitz, Alfred, *Deutsche Ohnmachtspolitik im Weltkriege* (Paderborn: Salzwasser Verlag, 2012 [1926]).

Tocqueville, Alexis de, *Democracy in America*, trans. and ed. Harvey C. Mansfield and Debra Winthrop (Chicago, IL: University of Chicago Press, 2000).

The Old Regime and the French Revolution, trans. Stuart Gilbert (Garden City, NY: Doubleday Anchor, 1955).

Todorov, Tzvetan, *Hope and Memory* (Princeton, NJ: Princeton University Press, 2003).

Tompkins, Sylvan S. *Affect, Imagery and Consciousness: Vol. 1. The Positive Affects* (New York: Springer, 1962).

Tong, James W., *Revenge of the Forbidden City: The Suppression of the Falungong in China, 1999–2005* (New York: Oxford University Press, 2009).

Tong, Yanqi and Xiaohua Lei, *Social Protest in Contemporary China, 2003–2010: Transitional Pains and Regime Legitimacy* (New York: Routledge, 2014).

Tönnies, Ferdinand, *Gemeinschaft und Gesellschaft: Abhandlung des Communismus und des Socialismus als empirischer Culturformen* (Leipzig: R. Reisland, 1887).

Tooby, John, "Conceptual Foundations of Evolutionary Psychology," in David M. Buss, *The Handbook of Evolutionary Psychology* (2005), pp. 5–67.

"The Evolutionary Psychology of the Emotions and their Relationship to Internal Regulatory Variables," in M. Lewis, J. M. Haviland-Jones, and L. Feldman Barrett, eds., *Handbook of Emotions, 3rd ed.* (New York: Guilford, 2010), pp. 114–37.

Tooby, John and Leda Cosmides, "The Past Explains the Present: Emotional Adaptations and the Structure of Ancestral Environment," *Ethology and Sociobiology* 11 (1990), pp. 375–424.

"Friendship and he Banker's Paradox: Other Pathways to the Evolution of Altruims," in W. G. Runciman, J. Maynard Smith, and R. I. M. Dunbar, eds., *Evolution of Social Behaviour Patterns in Primates and Man. Proceedings of the British Academy, 88,* (London: The British Academy, 1996), pp. 119–143.

Törnblom, K. Y., "The Social Psychology of Distributive Justice," in K. R. Scherer, ed., *Justice: Interdisciplinary Perspectives* (Cambridge: Cambridge University Press, 1992), pp. 177–284.

Törnblom, K. Y. and D. R. Jonsson, "Distribution versus Retribution: The Perceived Justice of the Contribution and Equality, Principles for Cooperative and Competitive Relationships," *Acta Sociologica* 30 (1987), pp. 25–52.

Trevelyan, George Macaulay, *The English Revolution, 1688–89* (Oxford: Oxford University Press, 1948).

Trinkunas, Harold A., "Crafting Civilian Control in Emerging Democracies: Argentina and Venezuela," *Journal of Interamerican Studies and World Affairs* 42, no. 3 (2000), pp. 77–109.

Trivers, R. L., "The Evolution of Reciprocal Altruism," *Quarterly Review of Biology* 46 (1971), pp. 35–57.

"Parent-Offspring Conflict," *American Zoologist* 14 (1974), pp. 249–64.

Trollope, Anthony, *Barchester Towers* (Oxford: Oxford University Press, 2014).

The Duke's Children (Oxford: Oxford University Press, 2011).

The Eustace Diamonds (London: Penguin, 2004).

Phineas Finn (Oxford: Oxford University Press, 2011).

The Prime Minister (London: Penguin, 1994).

Tsai, Kellee S., *Capitalism Without Democracy: The Private Sector in Contemporary China* (Ithaca, NY: Cornell University Press, 2007).

"Cause or Consequence? Private-Sector Development and Communist Resilience in China," in Martin K. Dimitrov, *Why Communism Did Not Collapse: Understanding Authoritarian Regime Resilience in Asia and Europe*, pp. 205–34.

Tucker, A. L. and A. C. Edmonson, "Why Hospitals Don't Learn from Their Failures: Organizational and Psychological Dynamics That Inhibit System Change," *California Management Review* 45 (2003), pp. 55–72.

Tucker, Robert C., *Stalin as a Revolutionary, 1879–1929* (New York: Norton, 1973).

Stalin in Power: The Revolution from Above, 1928–1941 (New York: Norton, 1990).

Tullius, John Darrin, "Environmental Groups as Catalysts for Political Liberalization in Authoritarian Societies: Bulgaria and Taiwan During the 1980s," PhD Dissertation, Department of Political Science, University of Oregon, 1997.

Turchin, Peter and Sergey Nefedov, *Secular Cycles* (Princeton: Princeton University Press, 2009).

Turnbull, Colin M., *The Forest People* (New York: Simon and Schuster, 1964).

Turner, Stephen T., *The Search for a Methodology of Social Science: Durkheim, Weber, and the Nineteenth-Century Problem of Cause, Probability, and Action* (Boston, MA: Reidel, 1986).

Turner, Victor Witter, *The Ritual Process: Structure and Anti-Structure* (Chicago, IL: Aldine, 1969).

Dramas, Fields, and Metaphors: Symbolic Action in Human Society (Ithaca, NY: Cornell University Press, 1974).

Liminal to Liminoid in Play, Flow, and Ritual: An Essay in Comparative Symbology, *Rice University Studies*, 60, no. 3 (1974), pp. 53–92.

Tyler, Tom R., "Psychological Models of the Justice Motive: Antecedents of Distributive and Procedural Justice," *Journal of Personality and Social Psychology* 67, no. 5 (1994), pp. 850–63.

"Psychological Perspectives on Legitimacy and Legitimation," *Annual Review of Psychology* 57 (January 2006), pp. 375–400.

Tyler, Tom. R. and S. L. Blader, "The Group Engagement Model: Procedural Justice, Social Identity, and Cooperative Behavior," *Personality and Social Psychology Review* 7 (2003), pp. 349–61.

Uslaner, Eric M., *The Decline of Comity in Congress* (Ann Arbor, MI: University of Michigan Press, 1997).

"Comity in Context: Confrontation in Historical Perspective," *British Journal of Political Science* 21, no. 1 (2009), pp. 45–77.

Valentino, Benjamin A. (2005), *Final Solutions: Mass Killing and Genocide in the Twentieth Century* (Ithaca, NY: Cornell University Press, 2005).

Van Dam, Nikolaos, *The Struggle for Power in Syria: Politics and Society under Asad and the Ba'ath Party* (London: IB Tauris, 2011).

Veblen, Thorstein, *The Theory of the Leisure Class: An Economic Study in the Evolution of Institutions* (New York: Modern Library, 1934).

Veitch, Colin, "'Play Up! Play Up! And Win the War!' Football, The Nation and the First World War 1914–15," *Journal of Contemporary History* 20 (1985), pp. 363–78.

Verba, Sidney and Gary R. Orren, *Equality in America: The View from the Top* (Cambridge, MA: Harvard University Press, 1985).

Verba, Sidney, Steven Kelman, Gary R. Orren, Ichiro Miyake, Johi Watanuki, Ikuo Kabashima, et al., *Elites and the Idea of Equality: A Comparison of Japan, Sweden, and the United States* (Cambridge, MA: Harvard University Press, 1987).

Vincent, R. J., *Human Rights and International Relations* (Cambridge: Cambridge University Press, 1986).

Virgil, *Aeneid*, trans. Robert Fagles (New York: Viking, 2006).

Viroli, Maurizio, *Niccolò's Smile: A Biography of Machiavelli* (New York: Hill & Wang, 2000).

Volkogonov, Dimitri A., *Stalin: Triumph and Tragedy*, trans. Harold Shukman (London: Weidenfeld & Nicholson, 1991).

Wade, Robert H., "Protecting Power: Western States in Global Organizations," in *Global Governance in Crisis: New Powers and the Restructuring of World Order*, David Held and Charles Rogers, eds., (Cambridge: Polity, 2013), pp. 77–110.

Wald, Kenneth D. and Allison Calhoun-Brown, *Religion and Politics in the United States*, 4th ed. (Lanham, MD: Rowman & Littlefield, 2003).

Wallace, Jeremy, *Cities and Stability: Urbanization, Redistribution, and Regime Survival in China* (New York: Oxford University Press, 2014).

Walsingham, Thomas, *Historia Anglicana*, ed. Henry Thomas Riley, vol. 2 (London: Longman, Green, 1864)

Walzer, Michael, "On the Role of Symbolism in Political Thought," *Political Science Quarterly* 82, no. 2 (1967), pp. 191–204.

Spheres of Justice: A Defense of Pluralism and Equality (New York: Basic Books, 1983).

"The Reform of the International System," in Øyvind Østerud, ed., *Studies of War and Peace* (Oslo: Norwegian University Press, 1986), pp. 227–40.

On Toleration (New Haven, CT: Yale University Press, 1997).

Wang, Haiyan, *The Transformation of Investigative Journalism in China: From Journalists to Activists* (Lanham, MD: Lexington Books, 2016).

Wang, Shaoguang and Angang Hu, *The Political Economy of Uneven Development* (Armonk, NY: M. E. Sharpe, 1999).

Wang, Yuhua, *Tying the Autocrat's Hand: The Rise of the Rule of Law in China* (New York: Cambridge University Press, 2015).

Warren, Mark E., "Democratic Theory and Trust," in M. E. Warren, *Democracy and Trust*, pp. 310–45.

ed., *Democracy and Trust* (Cambridge: Cambridge University Press, 1999).

Wawro, Geoffrey, *A Mad Catastrophe: The Outbreak of World War I and the Collapse of the Habsburg Empire* (New York: Basic Books, 2014).

Webber, Douglas, "How Likely is it that the European Union will *Dis*integrate?" *European Journal of International Relations* 20, no. 2 (2014), pp. 341–65.

Weber, Max, "Conceptual Exposition," in Guenther Roth and Claus Wittich, eds., *Economy and Society*, (Berkeley, CA: University of California Press, 1978), pp. 3–301.

Economy and Society, trans. Guenther Roth and Claus Wittich (Berkeley, CA: University of California Press, 1968).

"Kritische Studien auf dem Gebiet der kulturwissenschaftlichen Logik," in *Gesammelte Aufsätze zur Wissenschaftslehre*, pp. 276–80.

"Die 'Objectivität' sozialwissenschaftlicher und sozial politischer Erkenntnis," in Max Weber, *Gesammelte Aufsätze zur Wissenschaftslehre*, ed. Johannes Winckelmann, 3rd ed. (Tübingen: J. C. B. Mohr [Paul Siebeck], 1968), pp. 175–78.

Political Writings, ed. and trans. Peter Lassman and Ronald Speirs, (Cambridge: Cambridge University Press, 2000).

The Protestant Ethic and the Spirit of Capitalism, trans. Stephen Kalberg (Oxford: Oxford University Press, 2011).

"Science as a Vocation," in David Owen and Tracy Strong, ed., *The Vocation Lectures*, trans. Rodney Livingstone, (Indianapolis, IN: Hackett Books, 2004).

The Social Psychology of the World Religions (tr. and ed. H. Gerth and C. Wright Mills (London: Routledge, 1948), pp. 129–56, 267–301.

Webster, Charles, *The Congress of Vienna*, 2nd ed. (London: Bell, 1945).

Webster, Steven W. and Alan I. Abramovitz, "The Ideological Foundations of Affective Polarization in the US Electorate." *American Politics Research* (April 2017), http://journals.sagepub.com/doi/abs/10.1177/1532673X17703132

Wedeman, Andrew H., *From Mao to Market: Rent Seeking, Local Protectionism, and Marketization in China* (New York: Cambridge University Press, 2003).

Double Paradox: Rapid Growth and Rising Corruption in China (Ithaca, NY: Cornell University Press, 2012).

"Enemies of the State: Mass Incidents and Subversion," paper presented at the Annual Meeting of the American Political Science Association, Toronto, September 3–6, 2009.

Weinrich, Harald, *Lethe: The Art and Critique of Forgetting* (Ithaca, NY: Cornell University Press 2004 [1997]).

Weiss, Jessica C., *Powerful Patriots: Nationalist Protest in China's Foreign Relations* (New York: Oxford University Press, 2014).

Wetherell, Lorna, *Consumer Behavior and Material Culture in Britain, 1660–1760* (London: Routledge, 1988).

Wight, Martin, *Systems of States Systems of States* (Leicester: Leicester University Press, 1977).

Williams, Michael, "A Neo-Hobbesian Future?" in Ken Booth and Toni Erskine, eds., *International Relations Theory Today*, 2nd ed. (Cambridge: Polity, 2016), pp. 268–72.

Williamson, Samuel R. Jr., *Austria-Hungary and the Coming of the First World War* (London: Macmillan, 1990).

Wilson, David S., "Group-Level Evolutionary Processes," in R. Dunbar and L. Barrett, *Oxford Handbook of Evolutionary Psychology*, pp. 49–55.

Wilson, James Q., *Bureaucracy: What Government Agencies Do and Why They Do It*, 2nd ed. (New York: Basic Books, 1991).

Wilson, Peter H., *The Holy Roman Empire: A Thousand Years of Europe's History* (London: Allen Lane, 2016).

Wilson, Richard, "The Landed Elite," in H. T. Dickinson, *Companion to Eighteenth Century Britain*, pp. 158–71.

Wiseman, T. P., *Remus: A Roman Myth* (Cambridge: Cambridge University Press, 1995).

Wohl, Robert, *The Generation of 1914* (Cambridge, MA: Harvard University Pres, 1979).

Wolin, Sheldon, *The Presence of the Past* (Baltimore, MD: Johns Hopkins University Press, 1989).

Wolpert, Andrew, *Remembering Defeat: Civil War and Civic Memory in Ancient Athens* (Baltimore, MD: Johns Hopkins University Press, 2002).

Woodward, Llewleyn, *The Age of Reform, 1815–1870*, 2nd ed. (Oxford: Oxford University Press, 1962).

Woodward, Susan L., *The Ideology of Failed States: Why Intervention Fails* (New York: Cambridge University Press, 2017).

Worsthorne, Peregrine, *Tricks of Memory: An Autobiography* (London: Weidenfeld & Nicolson, 1993).

Wrangham, Richard W., W. C. McGrew, Frans B. M. de Waal, and Paul G. Heltne, eds., *Chimpanzee Cultures* (Cambridge, MA: Harvard University Press, 1994).

Wright, Robert, "The Uses of Anthropomorphism," in de Waal et al., *Primates and Philosophers*, pp. 83–97.

Wrigley, E. A., *Continuity, Chance, and Change: The Character of the Industrial Revolution in England* (Cambridge: Cambridge University Press, 1990).

  "A Simple Model of London's Importance in Changing English Society and Economy, 1650–1750," *Past and Present* 37 (1967), pp. 44–70.

Wu, Hongda Harry, *Laogai: The Chinese Gulag* (Boulder, CO: Westview Press, 1992).

Wyatt-Brown, Bertram, *Southern Honor: Ethics and Behavior in the Old South* (New York: Oxford University Press, 1956).

Yack, Bernard, *The Fetishism of Modernities: Epochal Self-Consciousness in Contemporary Social and Political Thought* (Notre Dame, IN: University of Notre Dame Press, 1997).

Yan, Xiaojun, "Engineering Stability: Authoritarian Political Control Over University Students in Post-Deng China," *China Quarterly*, no. 218 (2014), pp. 493–513.

Yang, Dali L., *Remaking the Chinese Leviathan: Market Transition and the Politics of Governance in China* (Stanford, CA: Stanford University Press, 2004).

Yang, Hua, *Dong'ou jubian jishi* (Record of the Eastern European Collapse) (Beijing: Shijie shishi chubanshe, 1990).

Young, Charles, "Aristotle on Justice," *Southern Journal of Philosophy* 27 (1989), pp. 233–49.

Young, H. P., *Equity* (Princeton, NJ: Princeton University Press, 1994).

Yu, Guoming, *Zhongguo shehui yuqing niandu baogao 2013* (Annual Report on Public Opinion in China 2013) (Beijing: Renmin Ribao Chubanshe, 2013).

Zahavi, Dan, "Unity of Consciousness and the Problem of Self," in Shaun Gallagher, ed., *The Oxford Handbook of The Self* (Oxford: Oxford University Press, 2011), pp. 316–38.

Zajonc, Robert B., "On the Primacy of Affect," *American Psychologist*, 39 (1984), pp. 117–23.

"Thinking and Feeling: Preferences Need no Inferences," *American Psychologist* 35 (1980), pp. 151–75.

Zamyatin, Evegnii Ivanovich, *We*, trans. Natasha Randall (New York: Modern Library, 2006 [1924]).

Zarakol, Ayse, *After Defeat: How the East Learned to Live with the West* (Cambridge: Cambridge University Press, 2011).

Zaslaw, Neal, *The Classical Era: From the 1740s to the End of the Eighteenth Century* (Upper Saddle River, NJ: Prentice-Hall, 1989).

Zaum, Dominik, "The Authority of International Administrations in International Society," *Review of International Studies* 32 no. 3 (2006), pp. 455–74.

Zelditch, M. and H. A. Walker, "Normative Regulation of Power," in Shane R. Thye and Edward J. Lawler, eds., *Advances in Group Processes*, 20 (Greenwich: JAI Press, 2000), pp. 217–50.

Zelditch, M., "Process of Legitimation: Recent Developments and New Directions," *Social Psychology Quarterly* 64, no.1 (2001), pp. 4–17.

Zhang, Feng, *Chinese Hegemony: Grand Strategy and International Relations in East Asian History* (Stanford, CA: Stanford University Press, 2015).

Zhang, Feng and Richard Ned Lebow, *Rethinking Sino-American Relations*, forthcoming.

Zhao, Dingxin, *The Power of Tiananmen: State-Society Relations and the 1989 Beijing Student Movement* (Chicago, IL: University of Chicago Press, 2001).

Zhou, Minglang, "The Fate of the Soviet Model of Multinational State-Building in the People's Republic of China," in Thomas P. Bernstein and Hua-yu Li, *China Learns from the Soviet Union, 1949–Present*, pp. 477–504.

Zhou, Xincheng, "Sulian yanbian guocheng zhong de yishi xingtai yu zhishifenzi" (Ideology and Intellectuals During the Evolution of the Soviet Union) in Li Shenming, ed., *Shijie shehui zhuyi genzong yanjiu baogao* (Follow-Up Report on World Socialism) (Beijing: Shehui kexue wenxian chubanshe, 2012), pp. 740–48.

Zhu, Jiangnan and Dong Zhang, "Weapons of the Powerful: Authoritarian Political Competition and Politicized Anticorruption in China," *Comparative Political Studies* 50, no. 9 (2017), pp. 1186–220.

Zhu, Yuchao, "'Performance Legitimacy' and China's Political Adaptation Strategy," *Journal of Chinese Political Science* 16, no. 2 (2011), pp. 123–40.

Zou, Dongtao, ed., *Zhongguo gaige kaifang 30 nian, 1978–2008* (Beijing: Shehui Kexue Wenxian Chubanshe, 2008).

Zucker, Lynne G., "Production of Trust: Institutional Sources of Economic Structure, 1840–1920," *Research in Organizational Behavior* 8 (1986), pp. 53–111.

Zuiderhoek, Arjan, *The Ancient City* (Cambridge: Cambridge University Press, 2017).

Zunz, Olivier, *Philanthropy in America, A History: Politics and Society in Twentieth-Century America* (Princeton, NJ: Princeton University Press, 2011).

Index